Correctional Facility Design and Detailing

Correctional Facility Design and Detailing

PETER CHARLES KRASNOW

Photographs by Bo Parker

McGraw-Hill

New York San Francisco Washington, D.C. Auckland Bogotá
Caracas Lisbon London Madrid Mexico City Milan
Montreal New Delhi San Juan Singapore
Sydney Tokyo Toronto

Library of Congress Cataloging-in-Publication Data

Krasnow, Peter Charles.
Correctional facility design & detailing / Peter Charles Krasnow.
p. cm.
Includes bibliographical references and index.
ISBN 0-07-036173-8
1. Prisons—United States—Design and construction. I. Title.
HV8827.K73 1997
365'.5—dc21 97-22721
CIP

McGraw-Hill

A Division of The ***McGraw-Hill*** *Companies*

1 2 3 4 5 6 7 8 9 0 KGP/KGP 9 0 1 0 9 8 7 6

ISBN 0-07-036173-8

The sponsoring editor for this book was Wendy Lochner, the editing supervisor was Christina M. Palaia, and the production supervisor was Sherri Souffrance. It was set in Century Schoolbook by North Market Street Graphics.

Printed and bound by Quebecor/Kingsport.

This book was printed on recycled, acid-free paper containing a minimum of 50% recycled de-inked fiber.

To Christine, my best friend and wife; to my parents, Zelma and Herbert; my children, Erica, Mark, and Christopher; and my sister Stephanie, for their love, continual emotional support, and belief in my ability to undertake and complete this project; to Paul for encouraging me to keep playing the guitar and Alan for sharing his knowledge of editing.

Finally, this book is dedicated in the memory of my cousin Lynn Luria-Sukenick for her art with words and her stories: "Danger Wall May Fall."

Contents

Preface

The idea behind this publication is offering professionals in the corrections and academic community a resource of correctional designs and details.

I thank McGraw-Hill for giving me the opportunity of creating a correctional facility design and details book. I have been directly involved with the planning, design, and detailing of correctional facilities for 22 years of my 32-year architectural career, and I still find it rewarding. It is satisfying producing buildings that serve to incarcerate persons who have committed crimes against society.

When I began to outline the number of details generally associated with the construction of this facility type, I estimated approximately 100. The issue for me was to determine how one would use this information to understand the subject matter and to correctly apply these details to the construction of a major facility. In fact, when a client retains the services of an architect for the entire process, from project inception through the planning, programming, and designing of a facility, this appears to be the appropriate format for the focus of this material. Presenting a logical sequence of events and issues as background information, prior to a review of details, seemed most useful.

This book has been prepared to provide material to readers for a comprehensive overview of current correctional facility planning, programming, operations, design, detailing, and technology.

Although many firms practicing architecture today continue to enter this specialized field of correctional design, a firm requires relevant knowledge and proven experience to create a successful project. Many have entered the field, recognizing a demand for the design and construction of justice facilities by state and county governmental agencies due to an increase in inmate population nationwide. A successful practicing *justice* architect requires years of correctional or justice facility experience to understand and, thereby, provide clients with quality designs, technical background, and the expertise required for this complex type. Other publications have provided information related to planning approaches, including illustrative drawings, photographs, and relationship diagrams. However, a publication is needed to provide a clearly organized overview of this building type that describes a generic program; operations/staffing guidelines and implications; building component design; facility designs; details; and security electronics/communications systems descriptions for actual application.

As a result of our country's recent focus on the Crime Bill, it is likely that we will see the design and construction of many more institutions in the coming years. Professionals responsible for building and/or renovating correctional facilities should find this reference publication helpful with design opportunities and information related to process, ideas, and technology.

Table of contents sections provide sequential understanding of issues in programming, design, and detailing. The written material is supported by a variety of architectural plan design solutions describing jails and prisons, from rural to urban site settings. Photographs and architectural plans also indicate campus to high-rise building design solutions. Each facility component is keyed to details that are important to the design, security, and technical requirements of a project.

Readers of this book should find the material organized and written for individuals involved with project capital budgets, planning, design, construction, and the operation of correctional facilities. The justice field continues to evolve with philosophical design and technological reexamination, revisions, and advances every few years. As directions change and technology develops greater sophistication, this book will also evolve with revised editions.

Anticipated users and decision makers include federal, state, and local agencies responsible for capital budgets and building programs; corrections administrators responsible for the operations of correctional facilities; practicing architects presently engaged in correctional design and others just entering the field; construction management organizations responsible for the construction of correctional facilities; architectural and law enforcement educational facilities; and school libraries with technical references.

ACKNOWLEDGMENTS

I am grateful to each person listed in the contributors section who worked closely with me to produce this book. Many of them are nationally recognized experts in corrections. Their skills and talents have provided insight, depth of knowledge, and a perspective in broadening the information covered in this book.

I wish to acknowledge the following few very special people who helped me:

Bill Hooper Jr. initiated the idea for a compendium of details book for corrections and provided me this opportunity and encouraged me with his support along the way.

Ruben Caro, with whom I have enjoyed a 10-year working and personal relationship, provided his technical expertise and leadership in the development of the details chapter.

Edgar Woh provided his technical and computer graphic skills in producing quality detail drawings and facility plans.

Buford Goff, with whom I have enjoyed a 13-year working relationship, has become a dear friend and provided me his technical expertise for the security electronics and communications chapters.

Bo Parker, a friend for 17 years and a great photographer, provided the beautiful architectural photographs of facility designs and details. *Every* picture is worth a thousand words.

McGraw-Hill's *Wendy Lochner, Robin Gardner, Roger Kasunic,* and *Maggie Webster-Shapiro,* and North Market Street Graphics' *Christina Palaia* for giving me the opportunity of publishing this book.

Introduction

An introduction to information required at the initiation of a project: a brief historical perspective on correctional facilities planning; justice process/justice system; planning and design process; transition planning; correctional planning standards; funding options for facility project costs; client requirements and expectations; impact of management philosophy on facility planning and design; architectural design considerations; and organization of material.

These first two sections provide the reader with an appropriate basis for facility planning, programming, design, and detailing. They also provide the background necessary for establishing a dialogue between the client, user, architect, and contractor that will surface issues that must be explored in order to create a functional and secure facility design and operation. The organization of the material in this document should help the reader understand how a facility is planned, programmed, designed, and detailed in sequence. This document may not include every detail or piece of information associated with correctional design, nor will it assure the reader of a facility free of liability.

A BRIEF HISTORICAL PERSPECTIVE ON CORRECTIONAL PLANNING

The beginning of correctional design, in the early part of the nineteenth century, viewed prisons as the means of punishing citizens who committed crimes. Jails had been in existence for centuries, created to hold offenders charged with crimes before trial and sentencing. In the United States, it was punishment to be locked up and denied basic freedom. The term *penitentiary* was derived from the notion that *time-out* or an attitude devoted to penitence or reform was sufficient punishment. The two types of facilities have carried forth into current society.

The initial architectural form or plan, known as the *telephone pole,* was a series of long perpendicular lines of cells extending from a central corridor. These wings were configured like spokes of a wheel (the Western Penitentiary, Pittsburgh, Pennsylvania, 1826, adopted from the Panopticon prison design by England's Jeremy Bentham, 1791) or aligned horizontally, often two, three, or four tiers high (the Auburn–Sing Sing model, New York, 1816–1825, flanking cell houses which set the model for the long cell block patterns that dominated correctional design). The cells were located back to back, sharing a centralized plumbing chase. The cell tiers looked out to an atrium space, with window walls at the exterior for natural light but which were inaccessible to inmates. These forms became the basis of most architectural solutions in designing jails and prisons. However, the first American jail that established the use of prisoner confinement with outside cell location with a central corridor was the Walnut Street Jail in Philadelphia, Pennsylvania, 1790.

In the early 1960s, federal and state courts made a number of significant rulings regarding prisoners' rights. Ensuing case law essentially developed a series of minimum standards for the physical environment of correctional facilities in areas such as housing, food service, exercise yards, and so forth.

In the early 1970s, a few of the earliest new generation management models emerged in the designs for the federal government known as Metropolitan Correctional Centers in New York City, Chicago, and San Diego, and a state prison in New Jersey known as Leesburg.

For the past 25 years, architects have struggled to interpret the goals of governmental agencies, numerous court rulings, and American Correctional Association Standards in creating design solutions. The sizes of housing units have varied from as few as 32 to those holding 128 inmates. With a series of differing forms, institutions have also grown in size from 300 to 400 inmates to some facilities supporting populations of 2000 or more. This publication describes and illustrates facility designs for jails and prisons of small size (200 beds) to large (2000 beds).

JUSTICE PROCESS/JUSTICE SYSTEM

The following charts identify the justice process from initial arrest to release, and four related justice departments: apprehension of criminals, investigation of crimes, detention for court-related activities, and holding facilities for convicted persons.

PLANNING AND DESIGN PROCESS

Beginning the process of planning a correctional facility can be overwhelming when considering the many tasks involved before a design phase can commence. What are the jurisdiction's needs? What population? What is the purpose of the facility—to meet what needs and deficits? The areas to focus on are as follows:

- ***A needs assessment.*** In the areas of investigation regarding a current facility's population and determining the mix of population types required for a new or renovated facility should yield some direction in the process of planning and programming.
- ***A feasibility study.*** Often included in the needs assessment phase but can be isolated for separate study. This study should include analysis of existing facility conditions to determine the potential for renovation or expansion of the existing facility. Addition to the existing facility should also be considered, combining the new

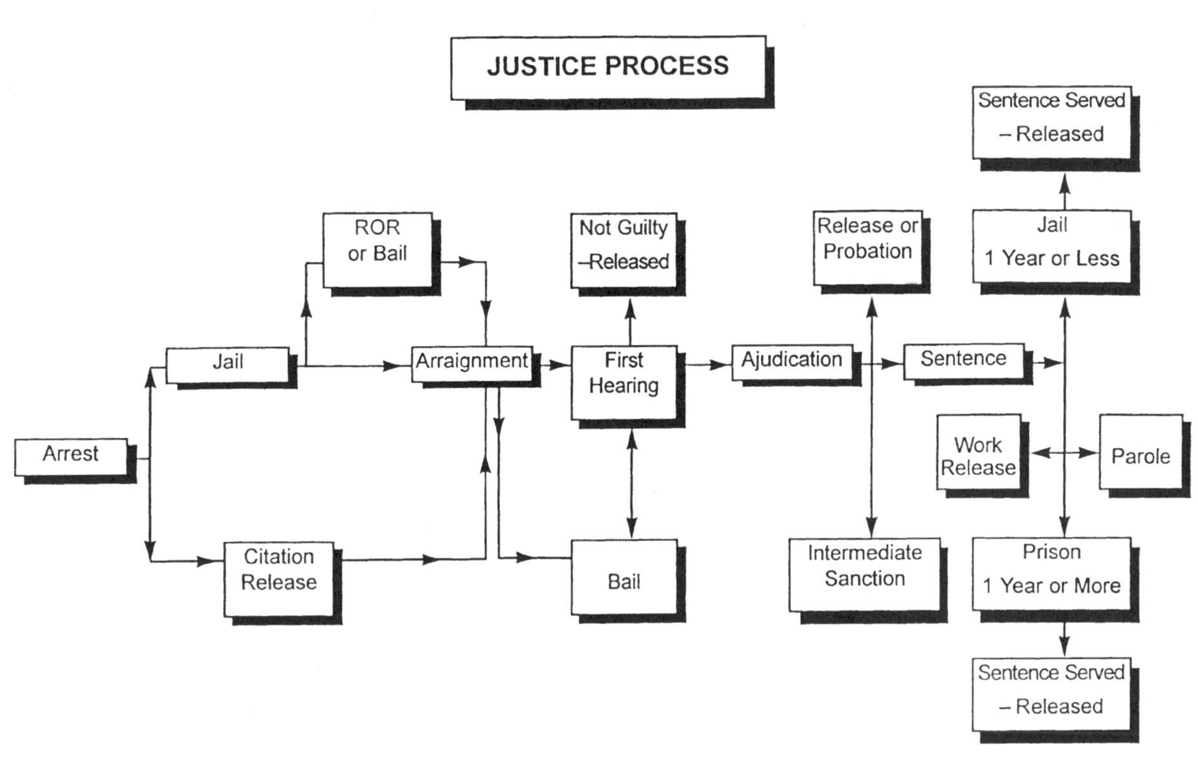
JUSTICE PROCESS
Arrest
Jail
Citation Release
ROR or Bail
Arraignment
First Hearing
Not Guilty –Released
Bail
Ajudication
Release or Probation
Intermediate Sanction
Sentence
Jail 1 Year or Less
Sentence Served – Released
Work Release
Parole
Prison 1 Year or More
Sentence Served – Released

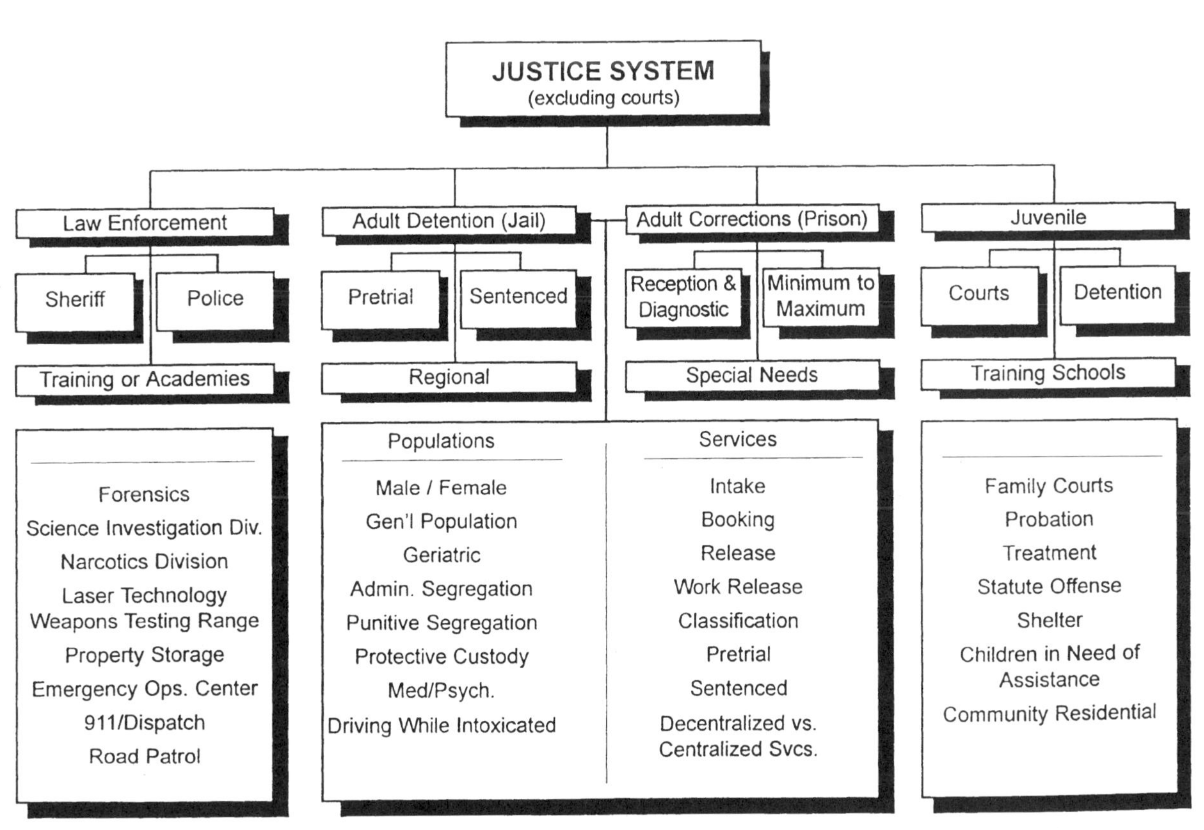
JUSTICE SYSTEM
(excluding courts)
Law Enforcement
Sheriff
Police
Training or Academies
Forensics
Science Investigation Div.
Narcotics Division
Laser Technology Weapons Testing Range
Property Storage
Emergency Ops. Center
911/Dispatch
Road Patrol
Adult Detention (Jail)
Pretrial
Sentenced
Regional
Adult Corrections (Prison)
Reception & Diagnostic
Minimum to Maximum
Special Needs
Populations
Male / Female
Gen'l Population
Geriatric
Admin. Segregation
Punitive Segregation
Protective Custody
Med/Psych.
Driving While Intoxicated
Services
Intake
Booking
Release
Work Release
Classification
Pretrial
Sentenced
Decentralized vs. Centralized Svcs.
Juvenile
Courts
Detention
Training Schools
Family Courts
Probation
Treatment
Statute Offense
Shelter
Children in Need of Assistance
Community Residential

with the old for potential operational efficiencies. If the existing facility is staff-intensive and cannot be efficiently planned for renovation, a new facility design may require abandonment of the existing site and search for a more favorable one.

- *A site selection study.* Is an exercise to explore possibilities and limitations that will determine the final location of a new or expanded facility. This study often takes place concurrently with the early planning, programming, and design phases (reference Chap. 2: Site Selection and Site Development). A site is sometimes identified early in the project process by the client; therefore, this stage can be disregarded, moving forward to the planning/programming phase.
- *A facility program.* To commence utilizing the information gathered from the needs assessment and feasibility study phases previously performed. The process begins with a discussion of facility mission; operational goals and objectives; operational and design philosophy; and others (reference Chap. 1: Planning and Design Principles; and Chap. 3: Program, Operations, and Design).

TRANSITION PLANNING

One of the more important activities for a client and its consultants is the development of a transition plan to which a client can commit. Often clients undertake their first new-facility building project and will hire qualified professional staff. At other times, they are building new, but utilize existing staff trained in their existing, older facility, perhaps with a different mode of operation from that proposed for the new one. In either case, the design team should focus attention on the critical importance of establishing client team representatives who will actually be responsible for the operation of the new facility. It is essential that a team of client representatives and planners, programmers, and architects assemble regularly from the first stages of the project process. A solid project team will ensure consistency of thought on all issues affecting operations and will provide continuity throughout the venture. The following is a brief overview of activities generally associated with transition planning, although each client, jurisdiction, and agency may have additional, special needs. Many of the activities can only take place after a design is defined and approved.

- ***An organizational structure of the team*** is critical in identifying a transition leader/coordinator and team members, establishing goals and objectives for transition in concert with facility's goals and objectives (reference Chap. 1: Facility Mission, Goals, and Objectives), and establishing a schedule for operational action with assigned personnel responsibilities, prior to occupancy.
- ***A schedule*** is critical for the transition team in meeting the team's goals for a smooth operational turnover of new facility. Weekly or biweekly meetings should be scheduled to review new agenda items and follow up on items from previous meetings. Update schedule on a monthly basis.
- ***A staffing plan*** is an essential part of the process in establishing the operational cost of the new facility. Planners must identify existing staff to be placed in the new facility and new positions required. Transition staff must plan training programs for staff, identifying each staff assignment and relative post position (reference Chap. 1: Staffing Principles).
- ***A start-up budget and first-year operation costs*** should be prepared identifying all costs not incorporated in the construction costs. Items should include operational manuals, staff uniforms, and furnishings, fixtures, and equipment (FF&E) for purchase (reference Chap. 1: Facility Operationals Costs).
- ***A policy and procedures manual*** will establish guidelines to form the basis for successful facility operations. Critical areas of operations, such as executive administration and management, admissions and release, and security control issues, among others, must be included.
- ***A functional training manual*** should be developed to provide hands-on staff training with knowledge of areas of operation such as inmate booking process, fingerprinting and photography, showering and clothing exchange, and many others.
- ***An operational training manual*** should be developed to provide staff with rules, regulations, and procedures for daily inmate-related activities, such as life safety and emergency situations, inmate counts, inmate searches, inmate transportation, and use of force.
- ***A moving plan for facility occupancy*** is required to provide staff and inmates a smooth transition into a new facility.
- ***A post-occupancy evaluation plan*** is a very useful activity in determining how well a new facility is operating, as supported by its architecture;

understanding through interviews, staff views of building performance, and staff and inmate morale; evaluating flexibility of building design from a current and future expansion perspective; and determining how the operational objectives and procedures are working with the physical plant.

CORRECTIONAL PLANNING STANDARDS

The most reliable source of information is found in the American Correctional Association's (ACA) publications related to detention and correctional facilities for adult males, females, and juveniles. State, county, and municipal standards are often provided, and they generally adhere to the ACA standards. Variations and comparison of these documents are important. Check local codes carefully, because local state building codes vary in different parts of the United States. The National Fire Protection Association (NFPA) code addresses the correctional environment specifically in terms of occupancy and fire protection areas. The code should also be compared to local building codes and ACA standards.

FUNDING OPTIONS FOR FACILITIES PROJECT COSTS

Municipal, county, state, and federal agencies offer a variety of methods of funding building programs. A project can be funded by the following:

- ***Legislative funding*** from a general fund for capital improvement.
- ***Capital outlay*** by a special tax, such as a sales tax.
- ***Insurance revenues*** with insurance yielding the lending of money for building projects.
- ***Bonds,*** for example, revenue bonds (or public sale of bonds) which may have legislative support for generating these revenues.
- ***Tax anticipation notes,*** from short-term notes anticipating increase in taxes based on population growth.
- ***Private funds*** from private lending institutions.
- ***Lease purchase*** by an agreement between an agency and a private developer to fund project construction through tax-exempt options, with an option for agency to own the facility after a designated number of years.
- ***Intergovernmental agreement programs*** with agreements between agencies, such as a county and the U.S. Marshal Services. This type of contract could provide federal funds to a county for the construction and annual rental of bed space for marshals and Immigration and Naturalization Services (INS) prisoners.

CLIENT REQUIREMENTS AND EXPECTATIONS

Clients expect justice expertise from their planner, architect, and engineering consultant. One should assume that the client's requirements will include project experience over a period of time and specialized expertise in the area of corrections. Multiple project experience is a standard by which an architect is often judged and is a requirement identified in most Requests for Proposals (RFPs) issued at the municipal, county, and state level. The federal government does not often request this requirement.

Clients will need to be assured that their programmatic and design goals are being met and that their consultant is not taking shortcuts and rehashing their previous designs or those of another consultant's. Presenting opportunities for design solutions to project-specific problems will enhance the architect's position and offer the client a choice in deciding on the appropriate direction for the project. The architecture should support operational goals and provide opportunities to the client for reducing staffing and yearly operational costs. Flexibility in attitude and design approach are also criteria by which the architect may be judged. The client will also expect a congenial working relationship and environment in which all its consultants respect each other's opinions and work together to deliver the project within the client's stated goals.

Meeting the client's budget and schedule are essentially the two key issues to be monitored from inception to occupancy during the design process. Constant monitoring of these two areas can become critical factors in meeting or exceeding the client's expectations.

IMPACT OF MANAGEMENT PHILOSOPHY ON FACILITY PLANNING AND DESIGN

The two most common styles of management—direct and indirect supervision—are still discussed at the beginning of each project and judged on their merits as applied to a specific client's requirements, ongoing operational philosophy, and/or preference.

- ***Direct supervision*** relates to the hands-on physical presence of an officer in managing the day-to-day inmate operations. This concept is applied most visibly in the design of the housing unit, where an officer is responsible for overseeing all inmate activities within the dayroom, generally from an open workstation with cell and other door controls but without physical barriers between him/her and the inmate population. This interaction and rapport between staff and inmates can minimize tensions and resolve problems and conflicts in a proactive manner often before they surface. In addition, as the officer moves freely within a housing unit, inmate territorial issues can be eliminated. Housing officers are supported by roving staff for relief during scheduled breaks and on an as-needed basis. The direct supervision concept generally begins at intake and carries through the entire facility supported by the facility's architectural design.
- ***Indirect supervision*** relates to an officer's use of visual observation and electronic control systems from within a control room which is protected with secure walls and glazing. The control officer is generally limited to observation of inmate behavior, minor infractions intervention, and to call for backup for additional staff response for major incidents. Communications with inmates is by intercom or public address system. Whether located within a housing unit or positioned between several housing units, the officer's responsibilities are to control access to rooms and housing activity areas and to monitor inmate behavior from this secure position. In some prison jurisdictions, the secure indirect supervision post is used to back up housing unit officers on the floor working with inmates.

A direct supervision operation has been proven to reduce violence and vandalism and to create a more normalized living environment. Although there are many advantages to direct supervision, it is not appropriate for, nor can it be applied to, all housing area designs. In particular, housing units that are subdivided into smaller groups, requiring an officer in each subunit, would be inefficient and expensive to operate under direct supervision. In addition, these units would also be inappropriate for housing inmates who are disruptive and violent.

DESIGN APPROACH: A CORRECTIONAL FACILITY DESIGN

- ***Is not a static condition*** since designs are constantly changing and improving in physical form, largely due to technological innovations and changes in operational philosophy.
- ***Is often driven by geography*** in responding to rural, suburban, or urban environments.
- ***Is often driven by clients*** who play a major role in the development of a facility's operational philosophy and physical layout. Local codes may also affect planning and operational decisions facing the architect and client.

Detention facilities/jails are for detainees being held for trial and individuals sentenced to short terms that are served locally. Since detainees are under the presumption of innocence until proven guilty, constitutional conditions of confinement mandate as normative an environment as possible. *Correctional facilities/prisons* are for individuals to serve sentences of one to two years or more and are similar in many respects to jails but differ in their overall operation. *Jails* generally incarcerate offenders for a few hours or a few days on admission, as well as pretrial detainees and inmates serving short sentences. *Prisons* generally house convicted felons with sentences of at least one to two years. The operational differences generally focus on the decentralization of services for inmates in jails and the centralization of similar services in prisons. In jails, many administrators prefer the limitation of movement of inmates, due to their unknown behavior and characteristics and the short turnaround time they are confined before trial and/or sentencing. In prisons, convicted felons are classified with greater scrutiny and are confined for longer periods of time. Therefore, controlled movement to services is less difficult and potentially therapeutic in support of a more normalized environment leading to a potential reduction in tension and anxiety.

A few of the general differences between jails and prisons can be described as follows:

Jails

- Living (housing) units are generally smaller to provide the usage of classifications that need to be separated from one another within the total capacity of the jail. They are often subdivided into multiple living units to separate men, women, juveniles, medical patients, psychiatric

Summary of Jail and Prison Differences

Component/area	Jails	Prisons
Living units	Smaller/subdivided by multiple custody classification	Larger/single custody levels with a separate special management unit
Dining	Decentralized to living unit(s)	Centralized in dining hall(s)
Recreation	Adjacent to living unit; generally no large outdoor areas; often a gym	Centralized in gymnasium(s) and outdoor recreation field(s)
Programs	Limited, due to short time inmates are held in facility	Education, vocational, and industry activities provided to encourage maximum inmate participation
Medical	Adjacent to living units; centralized medical treatment and infirmary	Treatment/infirmary centralized; triage adjacent to living units
Intake processing	Large number of inmates; intensive activity centralized; adjacent to classification housing unit	Scheduled admittance; less inmate movement/turnover
Visitation	Noncontact type located adjacent to living units to limit inmate movement	Centralized to encourage inmate movement and control activity and visitors' facility penetration
Vehicular sally port	Drive-through for volume of inmate delivery	Courtyard setting, separated from, but can share, service yard
Security perimeter	Building envelope usually serves as primary security perimeter	Perimeter is fenced, with detection system(s), and patrolled; often includes guard towers

patients, and known violent individuals and to provide administrative segregation and protective custody.

- Dining is generally located in the living unit to limit inmate movement and separate populations.
- Recreation is located adjacent to the living unit. Indoor activity space may also be provided.
- Limited outdoor recreation space is provided, generally without organized large group activities.
- Limited programs are provided due to the short time inmates are held (although this is changing in jails where sentenced inmates are also held).
- Medical screening is located adjacent to, or within, the living unit, with limited infirmary and centralized clinic space.
- Visitation is generally located closer and, sometimes, adjacent to the living unit.
- Intake processing areas and transfer areas are located adjacent to clothing/property storage.
- A drive-through vehicular sally port is preferred due to the unscheduled and constant volume of inmate delivery to and from the facility.
- Many jails utilize the building envelop (the exterior walls) as the prime security perimeter barrier, with inmate activities contained within the walls of the facility.
- Low-rise, mid-rise, and high-rise facilities are dictated by rural, suburban, urban, and/or restricted site conditions.

Prisons

- Living units are generally larger due to the classification of inmates related to behavior and status: minimum, medium, close custody, maximum, and segregation classification.
- Special living units represent approximately 10 percent of the total population and are generally subdivided into smaller groupings, similar to a jail plan.
- Education, vocational, and industry program spaces are generally provided to encourage maximum inmate participation. The current national average of use is approximately 10 percent of the general population. Current thinking, however, is striving toward a goal of 30 percent inmate participation.

- Large outdoor recreational fields for running, softball, and basketball activities are generally provided. Two or more areas are often provided where the inmate population exceeds 400–500.
- Low-rise facilities are generally preferred but require availability of a larger site, generally in more rural settings, although there are many examples of mid-rise and high-rise prison facilities.
- Most prisons on larger sites provide security perimeters with detection systems in conjunction with physical fence configurations.
- Perimeters are controlled, observed, and responded to by staff in either elevated towers or by vehicles traveling on roadways that run parallel to the fenced perimeter.

MATERIAL ORGANIZATION

This book provides the reader a source of information and material in the support of the planning, programming, designing, and detailing of correctional facilities. The order of the information presented is intended to form the basis of a logical progression through the siting, planning, and design principles generally acknowledged by professionals nationwide. It provides the reader with a logical application of architectural design principles and planning configurations, with examples of specific component layouts and facility design layouts. Plans are keyed to a compendium of appropriate details. Although this publication cannot guarantee that a facility design will be problem-free, with the use of the designs and details contained herewith, it can provide the basis for a logical application and understanding of the issues. Finally, supplemental information is provided for additional areas of critical concern: security perimeters, security electronics and communication, and acoustical design. This publication also provides a glossary of terminology used in the correctional field and a resource listing for additional and related information.

Many new products are consistently coming on the market that provide facility administrators with technological and physical improvements in support of their facility operations. Technology is the fastest changing element in support of operations. However, the information contained here is consistent with good operational practice and should apply to the most current electronic security and detention products available at any given time.

Summary List of Photographs

Summary List of Photographs*

***All photographs are by Bo Parker, unless indicated by *, which are either by the author or are anonymous.**

Summary List of Photographs* (*Continued*)

***All photographs are by Bo Parker, unless indicated by *, which are either by the author or are anonymous.**

Summary List of Photographs* (*Continued*)

***All photographs are by Bo Parker, unless indicated by *, which are either by the author or are anonymous.**

Summary List of Photographs* (*Continued*)

The cover, title sheet, and all chapter title page photographs are of the Eastern Kentucky Correctional Complex. See pages ix, xiii, 1, 11, 23, 117, 181, 321, 333, 345, 351, 363, and 367.

*All photographs are by Bo Parker, unless indicated by *, which are either by the author or are anonymous.

1 Planning and Design Principles

The dialogue required in establishing the basis of program identification and operational objectives. This section also provides a background perspective as a guide for knowledgeable programming, design, detailing, and construction of this facility type.

PROCESS

How one begins the planning, programming, and design process with a client is critical to the success of the project. One must create the dialogue required for establishing the basis for in-depth discussion of the subject. In the beginning, regularly scheduled meetings with specific agendas should focus the team on critical issues and discussions leading to consensus. Each topic should list key elements to be covered at each project phase to provide consistency in thought from an operational and design perspective: program, schematic design, design development, construction documents, and construction phases. Identifying program components and spaces, with emphasis on operational philosophy, should lead to a successful and specific design solution.

TOURS AND CONFERENCES

Designers should be interested in hearing how their clients are currently operating their facilities or, if none exists, how they envision the operation of new facilities. Many clients tour facilities throughout the country to expose themselves to different architectural solutions, operational philosophies, and currently available technology. Tours give the client a firsthand opportunity to speak directly with their corrections counterparts. If clients have not toured facilities similar in size, type, and complexity to which they have committed to build, programmers should encourage this activity as a fundamental tool in the initial planning process.

Equally important is a design team's participation in national correctional conferences, where specific workshops are available for interactive discussions. Important and relevant subjects, from direct supervision to security electronics, can provide an opportunity to gain knowledge that will help with decisions relevant to the specifics of a particular project. New products are displayed by manufacturers each year with improvements and features that continue to develop. The American Institute of Architects Committee on Architecture for Justice (AIA/CAJ) presents the most current design solutions for jails, prisons, and other justice-related facilities each year through exhibition displays and publications.

FACILITY MISSION, GOALS, AND OBJECTIVES

Before beginning any project, the architect should solicit and assist the client in the development of a facility mission statement. The team should identify the inmate population it intends to service: pretrial and/or sentenced inmates, juvenile, male and/or female, those with special needs, and those who require special management. One should determine under which or whose authority the facility will be operated: the state, local jurisdiction, or a group of officials representing several jurisdictions, as in regional jails.

A *mission statement* often provides the following content:

> The Mission of this facility is to provide a secure correctional environment that detains persons accused or convicted of illegal acts; to provide programs, services, and supervision in a safe, clean, humane environment; and to prepare incarcerated persons for reentry into society.

The *goals* and *objectives* will often include the following content and provide a secure facility that should

- Promote community safety
- Provide safe and humane treatment for inmates until their legal release, to affirm the dignities and rights of individuals
- Meet or exceed the minimum standards established by local, state, and national correctional standards (such as the ACA)
- Create an environment where visitors, staff, and inmates are free of physical and psychological abuse
- Meet or exceed constitutional requirements
- Foster healthy interaction among staff and inmates
- Offer inmates an appropriate level of mental health, medical, and dental care
- Offer inmates a range of programs for self-improvement and education to better themselves and prepare them for reentry into society
- Provide separation into manageable groups, where female and juveniles can be assured sight and sound separation from other populations
- Have the appropriate level of security based on the specific inmate population
- Expeditiously process all persons throughout the system and ensure prompt, lawful admission and discharge
- Be cost-effective and efficient to operate

PROGRAM

In many cases, a space program has been created prior to the selection of an architect and is given to the architect to begin the conceptual design phase. The first essential step before design begins is to test the program from an initial construction development and a future expansion perspective. Comparative analysis between a given program and projects of similar size can often provide an architect with the basis of determining the appropriate amount of space required for initial and future development. Planning and programming consultants are available to architects unfamiliar with the process and provide a valuable service. The program presented in Chap. 3: Program, Operation, and Design offers the reader a generic approach to providing components and spaces of a facility leading to design solutions. The program can be adapted, modified, and applied to most facility design goals and objectives. Consideration should be given to the difference between facilities designed for men, women, and juveniles and are also described in Chap. 3.

CRITICAL DESIGN DECISIONS

Design decisions to be made between the client and the architect at the initial stage require areas of design and operational discussion and consensus regarding the following:

- ***Direct versus indirect supervision*** preference in operating a facility (see the Glossary) can be an issue that is critical in developing a floor plan with all its implied relationships of officer control rooms, stations, and observation opportunities. The architecture can support a philosophy, but should follow the operational intent of the facility administrative executive staff. Often architectural plans can create the opportunity for conversion from one type of supervision to the other for future flexibility.
- ***Centralized versus decentralized*** programs and services will be based on client preference in operating the facility, either with a great deal of inmate movement from housing units to programs and services or with restricted inmate movement and programs and services provided where inmates are housed. These issues require discussion and resolution before the design process begins.
- ***Facility site location*** will often determine an appropriate design approach leading to an architectural solution. If a project site is adjacent to a residential community, it may require special security and aesthetic attention in providing a comfort level to neighboring residents. Attention to the physical appearance of a security perimeter may also be required to enhance a sense of acceptance. Restricted acreage can often lead a project toward a multi-rise solution. Each site adds specific criteria to the matrix and most likely will impact the architectural solution.

SECURITY CONCEPTS

Clients and architects generally agree to the principle of providing security for a facility utilizing a combination of elements: security perimeters, security zoning, building construction, operational security procedures, and electronic technology. Balancing these elements requires the awareness of the types of inmates incarcerated, types of area activities, and the number of staff provided to supervise inmates, activities, and areas in the most efficient manner. The client and architect should aim toward the appropriate level of security, utilizing the absolute minimum number of staff. The architectural design can often support this goal in creating effective and efficient solutions.

SECURITY PERIMETER SYSTEMS

Security perimeter systems are described in Chap. 6. They reflect a general cross section of technologies and/or systems available that can be considered for correctional and detention facilities. The intent of this section is to provide a summary of considerations relative to the selection of primary perimeter sensor types and configurations for the employment at correctional/detention facilities.

Generally, the design of a perimeter system will incorporate multiple technologies or system elements. Each segment of the perimeter must be evaluated to ensure that the selected system will perform to the desired expectations when implemented. Operational performance of a perimeter detection system is evaluated on the basis of the system's *probability of detection* and its associated *false alarm rate.*

SECURITY ELECTRONICS AND COMMUNICATIONS TECHNOLOGY

Security electronics and communications systems are described in Chap. 7. This section provides a brief description of systems that may be considered for integration into a correctional or detention facility. They provide support functions for the staff to enhance both the security of the facility and its operational effectiveness and efficiency. Systems should be reviewed in concept by the project architect and facility administrative/operations staff. During the design phase, these systems should be developed in detail, commensurate with the various stages of design.

SECURITY ZONES

Facilities are often divided into five zones to offer control in maintaining security. These areas require different security and are defined by purpose, level, and type. All movement within and outside of the facility can be monitored and controlled by direct staff observation, electronic surveillance, and the building construction. Each security zone creates its own control point(s) for monitoring and controlling vehicles, visitors, staff, and inmate movement in and out of any particular zone. Based on classification and/or policy, the admission or rejection or passage from one zone to another can be maintained. Inmates usually move within the facility by staff escort or assigned pass. Staff can move with or without a pass system based on the operational policy of the institution.

- ***Zone One: Building Perimeter.*** This is generally limited to the functions that are located outside of the secure perimeter, such as the public lobby, administrative offices, and employee services. Access is achieved with monitoring and control by direct staff observation and/or with electronic support.
- ***Zone Two: Security Perimeter.*** This is generally defined as the facility's building or security fences. This would include areas within the facility where inmates may be located, such as intake/release, program areas, inmate housing areas, and support areas where inmates are employed. Interior and exterior walls provide for security zoning. Access through these areas are generally via security valves with interlocking doors (sally ports). Master (central) Control monitors and controls these sally ports.
- ***Zone Three: Local (Unit) Control.*** This is generally often associated more with jails than prisons. This area supervises and controls movement in and out of the housing unit (jails) and/or buildings (prisons). Unit control is responsible for monitoring and/or controlling movement in the areas of inmates, staff, and other authorized persons' movement in this area. The unit control station has responsibility for monitoring functions such as visitation, medical, multipurpose rooms, and outdoor exercise areas often located at the housing unit.
- ***Zone Four: Housing Unit (Pod) Control.*** This is generally defined as the control officer who is responsible for all inmate activities within this unit. This station can directly supervise from an open desk area or indirectly supervise from within a secure control room. Either way, the officer is responsible for all movement in and out of the unit.
- ***Zone Five: Cells.*** This is generally defined as the individual cell enclosure within each housing unit. Access into and out of the cells is supervised and controlled by the living unit (pod) officer. Restrictions of access to cells is determined by inmates' classification and the facility's operational policy.

Reference Fig. 1.1.

SECURITY OPERATIONS/CONTROL STATIONS

The following responsibilities are generally accepted as the roles and the hierarchy of control stations.

Master (Central)

- Monitor facility access
- Control facility's security perimeter access
- Monitor overall facility security
- Control major area movement within the facility
- Coordinate facility's internal radio communications
- Coordinate emergency situations
- Monitor facility's smoke/fire detection systems
- Control emergency exiting, doors, gates, and so forth
- Monitor outside facility security

Local (Unit)

- Monitor and control of inmate and staff movement into and out of housing units
- Control exterior housing unit (pod) doors
- Coordinate inmate visitation (jail) with pod officer and direct visitors to same area
- Coordinate inmate and staff movement to services provided at the housing unit
- Monitor smoke/fire detection systems within the housing units; coordinate with Master
- Coordinate inmate counts between housing pods with Master

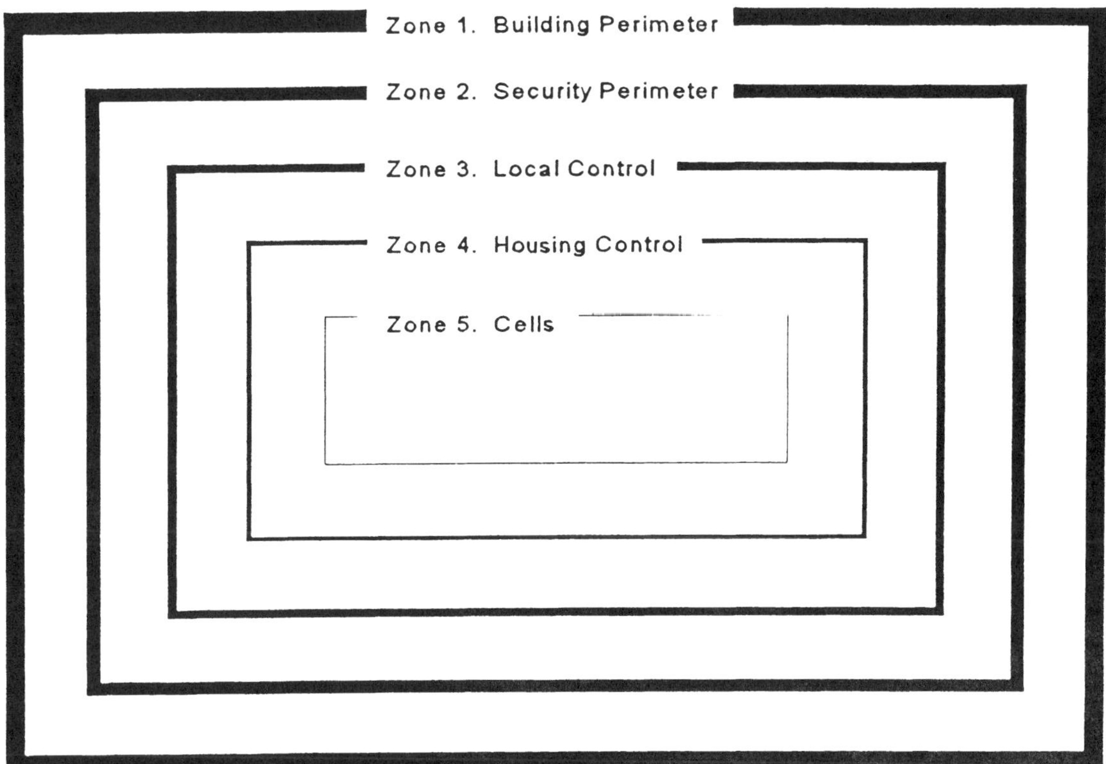

Figure 1.1 **Facility security zoning diagram.**

- Override security and locking systems/devices in housing units
- Provide backup for emergency situations for housing units; coordinate with Master

Housing (Pod)

- Control staff and inmate movement in and out of the living (pod) unit; coordinate with unit
- Supervise all inmate activity within the pod
- Control all cell doors in the pod
- Respond to requests from inmates within the pod
- Coordinate visitation with inmates within the pod
- Monitor smoke and fire detection systems in the pod
- Coordinate with and provide backup to unit control for emergency situations

Intake/Release

- Monitor and control vehicle access in and out of vehicular sally port (Master Control option)
- Control access to and from admissions and transfer/release from the vehicle sally port
- Control access from admissions/release areas into facility's main circulation corridor
- Provide backup for emergency situations in this area; coordinate with Master
- Monitor smoke/fire detection systems in this area; coordinate with Master

STAFFING PRINCIPLES

To manage a correctional facility effectively, staffing patterns must be established based on many factors, including, among others, operational objectives. The following are some of the factors affecting the creation of a staffing plan:

- ***24-hour operation*** is the basis by which a correctional facility is required to operate continuously, 7 days a week, 365 days a year. Therefore, many staffing positions must be operational on a 24-hour basis. Posts that are 24-hour positions must maintain staffing even when officers are on vacation, training assignments, or out on sick leave. The chart that follows these descriptions identifies the many conditions affecting one 24-hour staffing position and describes how one establishes relief factors in computing overall staffing needs.

- *Integration of staff and architecture* in a correctional facility is a primary goal. The facility operates like a small city in that it must provide all services required to maintain operations such as administration, law enforcement, food and laundry services, medical and mental health care, religious and social services, and appropriate utilities. Each component requires a different level of staff experience and a varied timetable. Integration of these staff positions requires a detailed plan for operational success.
- *The staffing plan* must provide the proper number of staff and the appropriate type of staff to coordinate normal activities, with emphasis on and consideration of security issues. Disruptions, contraband acquisition, covert organizations, extortion, and the potential for escapes are among the many issues confronting staff daily.
- *Basic requirements and responsibilities of staff positions* must be monitored by the courts and local governing agencies. The number of staff of a facility may vary and experience a need for an increase in staff, a reduction in numbers, an extension in hours, and so forth, over the course of any of the three operational periods.
- *High standards of performance* are expected for the staff. They are held to and must take responsibility for inherent danger to themselves, inmates, and the public, alike. Each facility administration, operational objective, and design presents different criteria in determining staff requirements. Shift patterns also differ within a facility and may not relate to standards of shift times. As an example, food service may operate in an early morning shift to have breakfast prepared and ready to serve to inmates. Each facility's design and components vary, and therefore a facility with a similar number of beds may have very different staffing needs. In order to understand staff requirements, it is important to describe the shift relief factors affecting a position or post.

The following work chart is a guide for determining a typical staffing position calculation.

1.	Number of days per year	365
2.	Number of regular days off for weekends (52 weeks × 2 days per week)	104
3.	Number of holidays off per year	12
4.	Number of vacation days per year	10
5.	Average number of sick days per year	4
6.	Number of in-service training days per year	5
7.	Average number of days off for military leave, litigation, and so forth	3
8.	Total number of days off per year (1., 2., 3., 4., 5., 6., and 7.)	138
9.	Total number of actual work days available per year (1. − 8.)	227
	Shift relief factor for five day per week positions ((1. − 2.) ÷ 9.)	1.15
	Shift relief factor for seven day per week positions (1. ÷ 9.)	1.61

Most control stations operate on a seven-day, 24-hour basis. Some that are less critical to inmate activities are not staffed weekends (central programs, as an example) and/or are not critical to security operation on a five-day-position basis. Relief factor will vary based on actual calculated information related to specific jurisdictions and their work regulations related to vacation, sick leave, training days, and so forth. The following chart can be used in creating a specific staffing plan based on the program, operational objectives, and architectural design.

This is based on decisions made as to size of facility, inmate population, inmate classification, and jurisdictional staffing standards.

Guide for Determining the Number of Required Staff

STAFFING SUMMARY				SHIFTS*				
	Component	**Position**	**Security Level**	**Day**	**Evening**	**Night**	**Relief Factor***	**Total**
example								
1.0	Public Lobby	Lobby Officer	Secure	1	1	0	1.7	3.4
		Lobby Officer	Secure	1	0	0	1.2	1.2
								4.6
2.0	**Visitation**							
3.0	**Hearings and investigations**							
4.0	**Executive administration**							
5.0	**Case management/inmate records**							
6.0	**Staff development services**							
7.0	**Intake/transfer/release**							
8.0	**Classification**							
9.0	**Communications**							
10.0	**Master Control**							
11.0	**Operations**							
12.0	**General inmate housing**							
13.0	**Special inmate housing**							
14.0	**Unit management**							
15.0	**Inmate/social services programs**							
16.0	**Educational/vocational programs**							
17.0	**Religious services**							
18.0	**Industry**							
19.0	**Recreation**							
20.0	**Health services**							
21.0	**Food service**							
22.0	**Commissary**							
23.0	**Laundry service**							
24.0	**Warehouse**							
25.0	**Engineering and plant maintenance**							
26.0	**Physical plant**							
27.0	**Transportation/perimeter access**							
					Total Corrections Personnel			

*Relief factor described in the section entitled Staffing Principles in this chapter, pages 5, 6.

FACILITY OPERATIONS COSTS

Projecting annual operating costs for a facility can be analyzed by understanding the variety of related services and direct costs required. In summary, the following list provides the client with a matrix of the typical types of components necessary in establishing an annual operating budget.

A. Personnel Security Positions	Salary	Benefits	No. of Positions	Total Salaries/Benefits
Administrator				
Assistant administrator				
Major				
Captain				
Lieutenant				
Sergeant				
Corporal				
Officers				
Food service manager				
Food service workers				
etc.				
B. Nonsecurity Positions	**Salary**	**Benefits**	**No. of Positions**	**Total Salaries/Benefits**
Admin. secretary				
Clerk/typist				
Business manager				
Personnel manager				
Accountant				
Purchasing agent				
Accounting clerk				
Receptionist				
Records clerks				
Program manager				
Teacher				
Librarian				
Medical administrator				
Nurse supervisor				
Medical secretary				
Physician				
Dentist				
Dental assistant				
Psychologist				
Mental health counselor				
Psychiatric social worker				
X-ray technician				
Medical records clerk				
Correctional health assistant				
Laundry worker				
Physical plant technician				
etc.				
C. Other Direct Costs				
Contractual services (professional health services; maintenance services; etc.)				
Materials and supplies (maintenance and repairs; office supplies; food and supplies; etc.)				
Communications (telephone; mail; equipment; etc.)				
Capital outlay (equipment and machines; furniture; computers; etc.)				
Insurance				
Travel expenses				
etc.				
D. Utility Costs				
Electricity				
Gas				
Water/sewer				
etc.				
Summary of Annual Operational Costs				
Personnel				
Other direct costs				
Utilities				
etc.				
E. Annual Operating Plan				

To project a facility's annual operating costs for a five-year period or greater, the following should be considered:

1. Current year dollars
2. Inflation per years of projection
3. A percentage for first year's operational start-up costs

BUILDING CONSTRUCTION, COST ESTIMATING, AND COST CONTAINMENT

The exterior wall construction is often the only physical barrier for facilities that are located in urban areas and are built close to or on a property line or street frontage. Therefore, wall materials need to be impenetrable. Interior wall construction is often utilized for security barriers between sensitive program components, such as housing, the pharmacy, and inmate records areas. Facilities should employ unit masonry construction for interiors. Security walls often divide larger areas or components from each other to prevent access through suspended ceilings to ductwork and/or mechanical rooms leading to the building's roof area and potential freedom. Construction types of walls, glazing, ceilings, and so forth are described in Chap. 5: Correctional Details.

Cost estimating and cost containment are critical to all phases of project development. They encompass all disciplines and are the essential tool utilized in producing projects within a project's goals and budget limitation. Utilizing a cost-estimating consultant or an architect's in-house data bank of information on similarly built justice projects is essential in establishing and maintaining an accurate cost of construction. With project funds generally fixed by clients, four other variables are available for adjustment: area of construction, detention equipment, security systems, and the quality of construction. Value engineering techniques generally focus on these areas, but also consider life-cycle cost evaluation. Often, items can be paid for within the first several years of operations and offer the facility a long-term perspective in reducing operational costs when compared with the initial expenditure.

Correctional Facilities Key Cost Considerations

- *Areas* contain a variety of security levels, durable materials, and finishes.
- *Security* of greatest concern generally have the greatest density of development; the highest ratio of perimeter to area, and the highest level of durability; therefore, the most costly.
- *Administrative and public areas* are generally of a more normative level of construction.
- *Program spaces* are of an intermediate level of construction.

Initial Cost Control Determining Factors

- *Space program* size and density of development for the variety of areas.
- *Levels of security* and types of systems to be employed.
- *General building components:* high-rise, single story; structural system; building geometry; exterior materials; and type of mechanical systems to be employed.
- *Site development costs* are of particular significance for nonurban projects.

Cost Control Methodology

- *Budget estimates* should be based on the cost of building systems, by general component breakdown, i.e., housing, administration, building services, program spaces, and so forth. Systems include foundations, superstructure, enclosures, interiors, mechanical, electrical, and security components.
- *Interim controls* should include budget estimate updates as decisions create changes in program, layout, systems, and so forth. This analysis can assist in preventing an increase in the probability of cost overruns by the time a particular phase is completed.
- *Phase estimates* are prepared to quantify cost estimates at completion of phases and specified milestones of design. Level of detail should increase as the design progresses. Estimates should be converted to a building system format for comparison with the approved budget. Areas of difference should be explained with corrective steps taken or budget adjusted.
- *VE/life cycle process at early phases* should include analysis of various systems and materials to determine impact on cost and construction duration. This evaluation process can aid in selecting materials and systems with highest cost per benefit ratio.
- *Constructability reviews* can assist in reducing cost by keeping the construction process efficient.

Potential Problem Areas

- *Building gross area* must be carefully monitored by the design team to make accurate judgments to maintain minimum required building areas including mechanical spaces at an early stage.

- ***Exterior walls*** directly affect the perimeter costs, which are generally high. Control of the level of security, wall construction, and amount and types of glazing have a major impact on cost.
- ***Internal security*** is relative to the cost of wall construction types appropriate to a building's classification; door hardware should be appropriate to the space and electronics security systems selection and is a major factor affecting cost.
- ***Equipment costs*** such as food service, laundry, and inmate industries are usually developed by specialty consultants and should be established at an early development phase.
- ***Site development*** costs are too often overlooked at an early stage. Large security perimeters are high-cost items to monitor and control, as may be the cost to obtain adequate primary utility systems (water, power, and sanitary sewage treatment).

There are many techniques available for estimating a project, including market trends, regional comparisons with your project, and establishing a cost model during the initial phase. This tool can facilitate the process and monitor the project during each phase of development. A *cost model* is defined as identifying the 17 sections of a project in a specification format for the design. The information associated with a correctional facility should be estimated with various area assignments such as gross square footage, cost per gross square foot, percentage of construction per discipline (historical data), and the total dollar amount.

Costs have not been entered in the following chart due to the wide variations between urban and rural projects. Many factors are impacted such as site development (generally of much greater significance in rural projects), systems dealing with the enclosure since urban and rural projects generally differ in height and footprint, and conveyance systems differ due to height variations.

The following simple chart summarizes the approach and is offered as a worksheet for cost modeling. Establish a budget for each area charted and assign each discipline leader a budgetary goal for his or her respective area for cost containment. Adjustments to areas can be made as long as other areas are balanced within the overall cost model. Know the implications of all design decisions. No other subject is as vitally important to the success of a project in the minds of clients, consultants, and the public/tax payers.

Facility Cost Model

Facility component	GSF	$/GSF	% of cost	Total
01 General conditions				
02 Site work				
03 Concrete				
04 Masonry				
05 Metals				
06 Wood and plastics				
07 Thermal and moisture				
08 Doors and windows				
09 Finishes				
10 Specialties				
11 Equipment				
12 Furnishings				
13 Special construction				
14 Conveying systems				
15 Mechanical				
16 Electrical				
17 Security electronics and communications				

2
Site Selection and Site Development

The criteria used in the selection of a site, including utilities, resources, access, and services perspective.

CRITERIA

A site can be selected prior to retaining planning, programming, and architectural design services from a consultant, or it can become the first step in the process of a project's development. A site's relationship between a facility and its off-site resources, such as the courts, police, other justice facilities, and medical services, can become an important factor in determining a new facility's location. The relationship between a facility and a given site will also require other services on-site or adjacent to a site, such as utilities, water, gas, electricity, and telephone lines. Landscaping, public transportation, parking, and the like are among other important issues for consideration in determining an appropriate location for a new institution.

Determining a Site Location

For a new facility, this site should provide the following:

- Access to community services and agencies (attorneys, crisis counselors, etc.) essential to the safe and secure and legal functioning of a correctional facility.
- Access to and from the courts.
- Access for local jurisdiction's law enforcement agencies.
- Access for relatives, spouses, and friends to visit those in custody.
- Access for staff employed by the facility.
- Availability of, and access for, emergency medical, hospital, fire services, and their vehicles.
- Availability of, and access for, support services, such as trash pickup, snow removal, and laundry services.
- Availability of, and access to, local utility companies providing power, water, telephone, and other utility services as required by the facility's needs.
- Land free of floodplains, wetlands, and earthquake fault lines.
- Proximity to, and provision of, existing roads and/or highways from the existing transportation network.
- Adequate soil load-bearing conditions to support the requirements of a facility's building(s).
- An opportunity for community acceptance of a facility in its neighborhood. This can become a major factor in determining an appropriate site location. Meetings with community leaders and the general public, early in the process, should provide information in answering questions and/or dispelling misconceptions, in creating the foundation for a successful project. Regularly scheduled meetings with the community, presenting the facility's project and design development, can enhance acceptance and prevent roadblocks to generally fast-track construction schedules. (See Figs. 2.1 and 2.2.)

Site and Facility Design Development

The site should provide the following:

- A site sufficient in size to support the needs of the initial facility construction and future expansion.
- Utility services to the facility, developed for initial and future building expansion.
- Topography as necessary for positive drainage of surface water; a logical grading of facility building(s); and direct vehicular and pedestrian access to all major entrances.
- Outdoor recreational needs of the facility's program for initial and future expansion.
- Circulation that does not produce conflicts between the public, staff, law enforcement, emergency, and service traffic onto the site and into the facility.
- Parking for staff, visitors, and law enforcement personnel, in numbers that serve their needs. It is often preferred to separate public and staff parking areas for the enhancement of staff security.
- A minimum number of entrances into the facility for staff, visitors, inmates (intake/transfer), and services.
- Screening of security entrances from public view.
- Screening of inmate outdoor activities and of windows from public view.
- Landscaping selected and installed on the basis of ease of maintenance and compatibility to climate and soil type, with maximum use of existing site foliage. Screening the entire facility from the community view is often considered an important goal for a successful project.
- Building forms and heights compatible with adjacent and neighborhood architecture. Becoming a good neighbor is often a criteria by which the project's success and community's acceptance is judged. (See Fig. 2.3.)
- Types of exterior lighting appropriate for the building(s), parking areas, service areas, and perimeter fencing to illuminate these areas for security without lighting up the neighborhood.

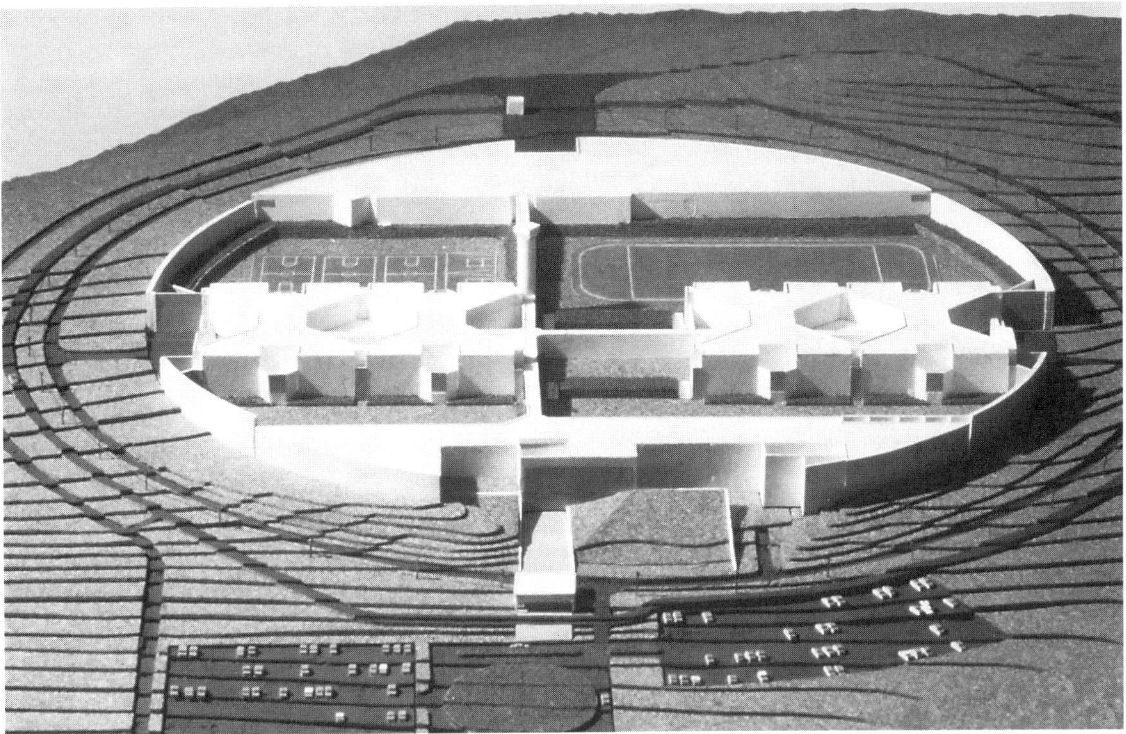

Figure 2.1 **Site study utilizing building mass model to determine entrance road, parking, buildings, security perimeter, and patrol road.**

Figure 2.2 **Facility buried into cliff on three sides with one story of administration building exposed toward neighborhood.**

Figure 2.3 **Architectural aesthetics in mass, detail, and color appropriate to neighborhood scale and context.**

Site location and facility design development can be summarized visually into three classifications: *rural setting, suburban setting,* and *urban setting.* Two examples of each site classification follows the summary of issues, identifying built and operating facilities' site design features.

Summary of Issues

Community access
Court access
Law enforcement access
Visitor access
Staff access
Fire/emergency access
Trash pickup
Freedom from flood plains and wetlands
Access to utilities
Roads/highway access
Adequate soil bearing
Community acceptance
Facility size initial/future expansion
Utilities support initial/future expansion
Topography for pedestrian/vehicular access
Outdoor recreation initial/future expansion
Public, staff, service, and emergency access
Public, staff, and law enforcement parking
Public, staff, inmate, and service entrances
Screened security entrances
Screened inmate activities
Landscaping
Contextual relationship
Exterior lighting

FIGURE 2.5 RURAL SETTING

Site Design Features:

1. Utilized main entrance road, from adjacent existing state penitentiary, for prison community.
2. Facility set back more than 1000 feet from main road—far from residential neighborhood.
3. Utilized existing topography to separate public and services, at different access levels.
4. Shared staff and visitors parking fields with adjacent diagnostic and evaluation center.
5. Facility control tower observes exterior courtyard accessible to all housing units.
6. Additional control towers observe perimeter and large outdoor recreation fields.

Figure 2.4 **Rural setting aerial photograph.**

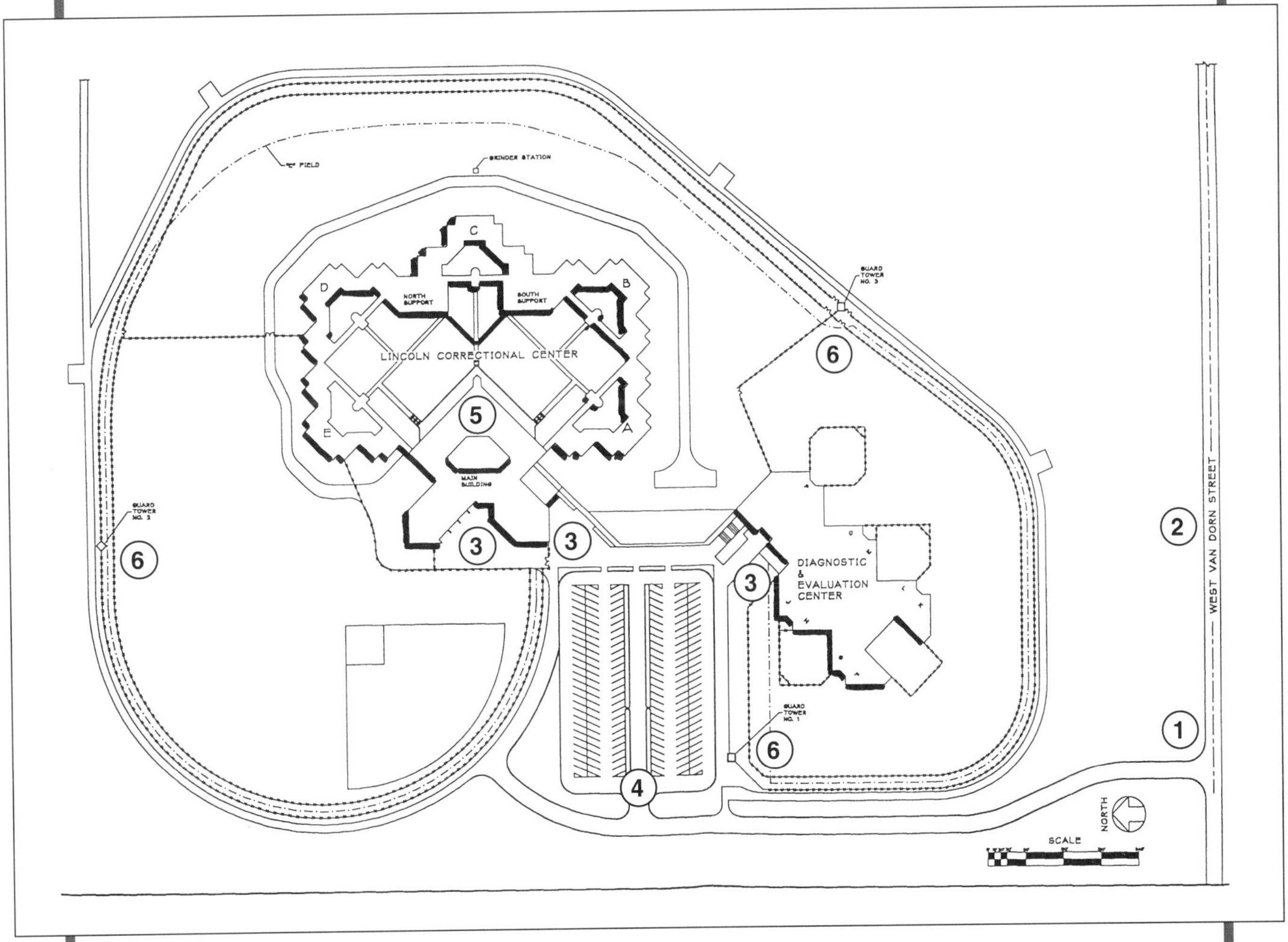

GRINDER STATION
C
D
B
NORTH SUPPORT
SOUTH SUPPORT
LINCOLN CORRECTIONAL CENTER
A
E
MAIN BUILDING
GUARD TOWER
DIAGNOSTIC & EVALUATION CENTER
WEST VAN DORN STREET
NORTH
SCALE
1 2 3 4 5 6

Figure 2.5

FIGURE 2.7 RURAL SETTING

Site Design Features:

1. Natural mountain range is used to physically and visually separate two different facilities.
2. Natural topography utilized to screen main facility grounds from lower-level public entrance.
3. Existing strip-mined site conditions used to level terrain for gentle grade access to all buildings.
4. Natural topography utilized to create amphitheater as center piece for passive activity program.
5. Screened inmate views of services and maintenance areas by buildings configuration.
6. Facility set back a great distance from main road, far from residential neighborhoods.

Figure 2.6 **Rural setting aerial photograph.**

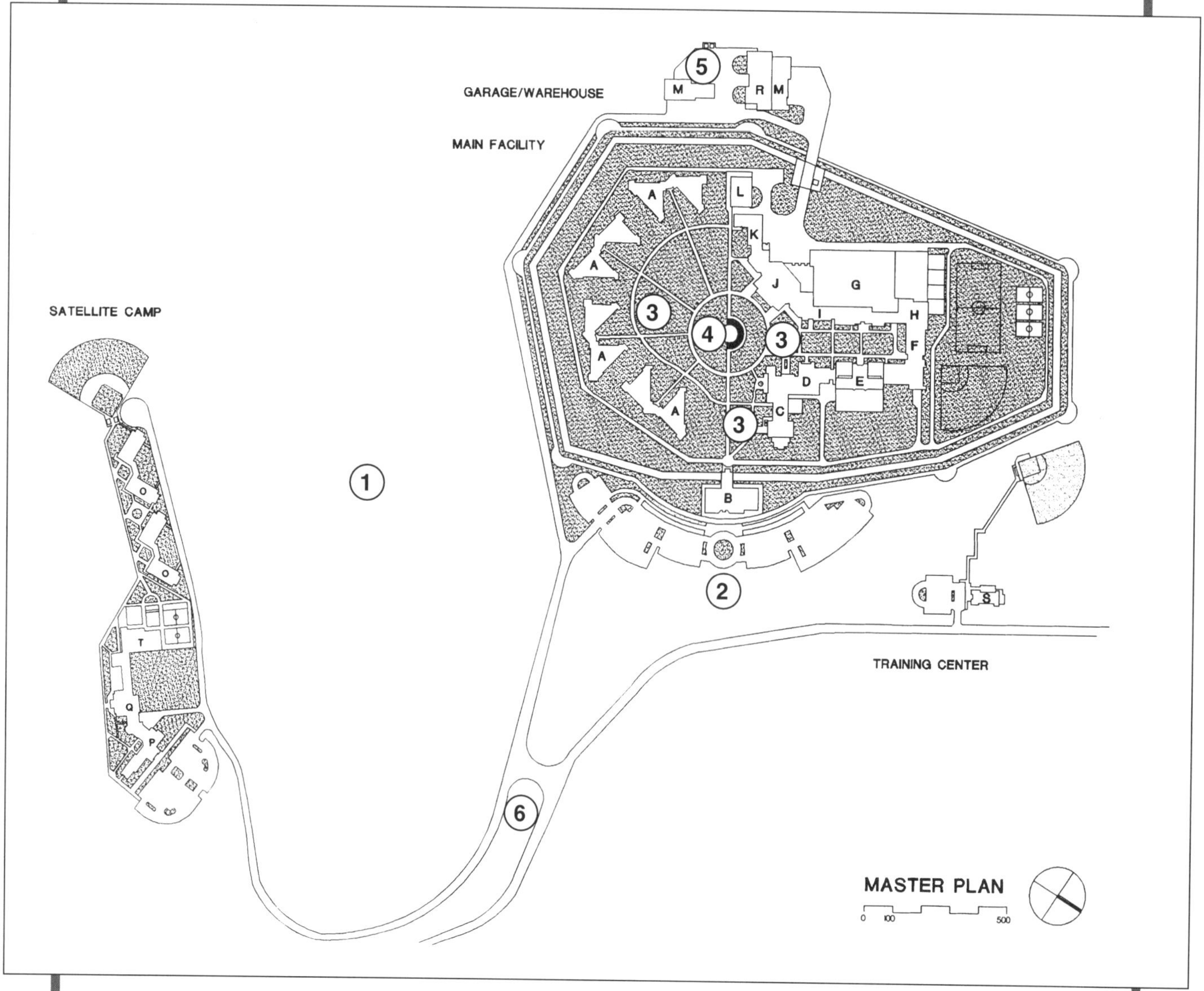

GARAGE/WAREHOUSE
MAIN FACILITY
SATELLITE CAMP
TRAINING CENTER
MASTER PLAN
0 100 500

Figure 2.7

FIGURE 2.9 SUBURBAN SETTING

Site Design Features:

1. Retained existing prison wall to screen facility from three street residential neighborhood exposures.
2. New building wall screened remaining street exposure along main entrance road and highway.
3. Large outdoor recreation fields internalized between buildings, screened from public view.
4. Utilized red brick masonry material for harmonious neighborhood context.
5. Building mass in plan and height, scaled down to residential neighborhood.
6. Existing exterior walls and new facility internally illuminated away from adjacent neighborhood.

Figure 2.8 **Suburban setting aerial photograph.**

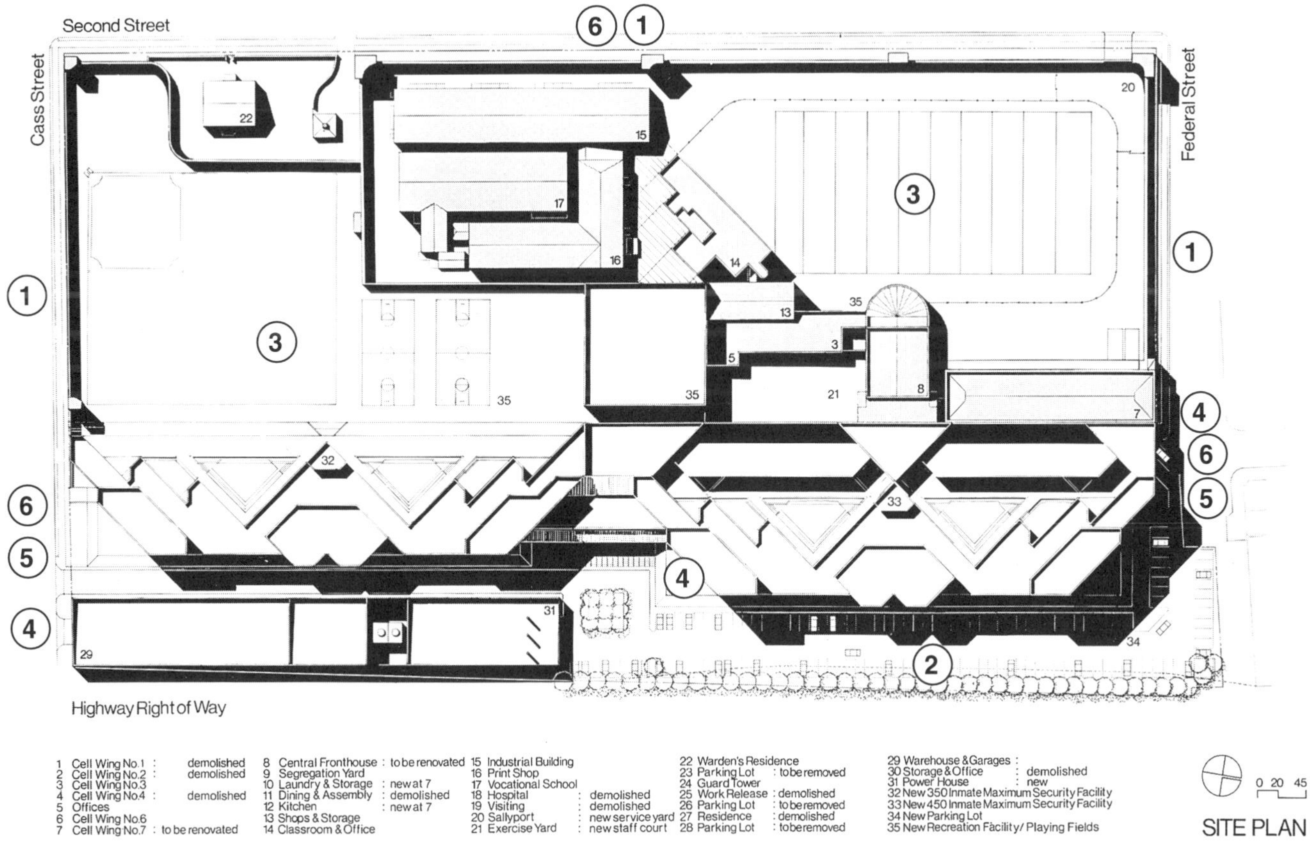

Second Street

Cass Street

Federal Street

Highway Right of Way

1 Cell Wing No.1 : demolished
2 Cell Wing No.2 : demolished
3 Cell Wing No.3
4 Cell Wing No.4 : demolished
5 Offices
6 Cell Wing No.6
7 Cell Wing No.7 : to be renovated
8 Central Fronthouse : to be renovated
9 Segregation Yard
10 Laundry & Storage : new at 7
11 Dining & Assembly : demolished
12 Kitchen : new at 7
13 Shops & Storage
14 Classroom & Office
15 Industrial Building
16 Print Shop
17 Vocational School
18 Hospital : demolished
19 Visiting : demolished
20 Sallyport : new service yard
21 Exercise Yard : new staff court
22 Warden's Residence
23 Parking Lot : to be removed
24 Guard Tower
25 Work Release : demolished
26 Parking Lot : to be removed
27 Residence : demolished
28 Parking Lot : to be removed
29 Warehouse & Garages :
30 Storage & Office : demolished
31 Power House : new
32 New 350 Inmate Maximum Security Facility
33 New 450 Inmate Maximum Security Facility
34 New Parking Lot
35 New Recreation Facility/ Playing Fields

0 20 45

SITE PLAN

Figure 2.9

FIGURE 2.11 SUBURBAN SETTING

Site Design Features:

1. Incorporated existing kitchen building into new facility plan, accent wall for public entrance.
2. Public entrance structure screens views of inmate housing exterior windows.
3. Inmate jalousie window design used for tropical climate winds for cooling.
4. Shallow depth support building plans also used natural breezes for cooling.
5. Site shape yielded two separate housing neighborhoods for inmate-specific populations.
6. New facility located adjacent to existing facility.

Figure 2.10 **Suburban setting aerial photograph.**

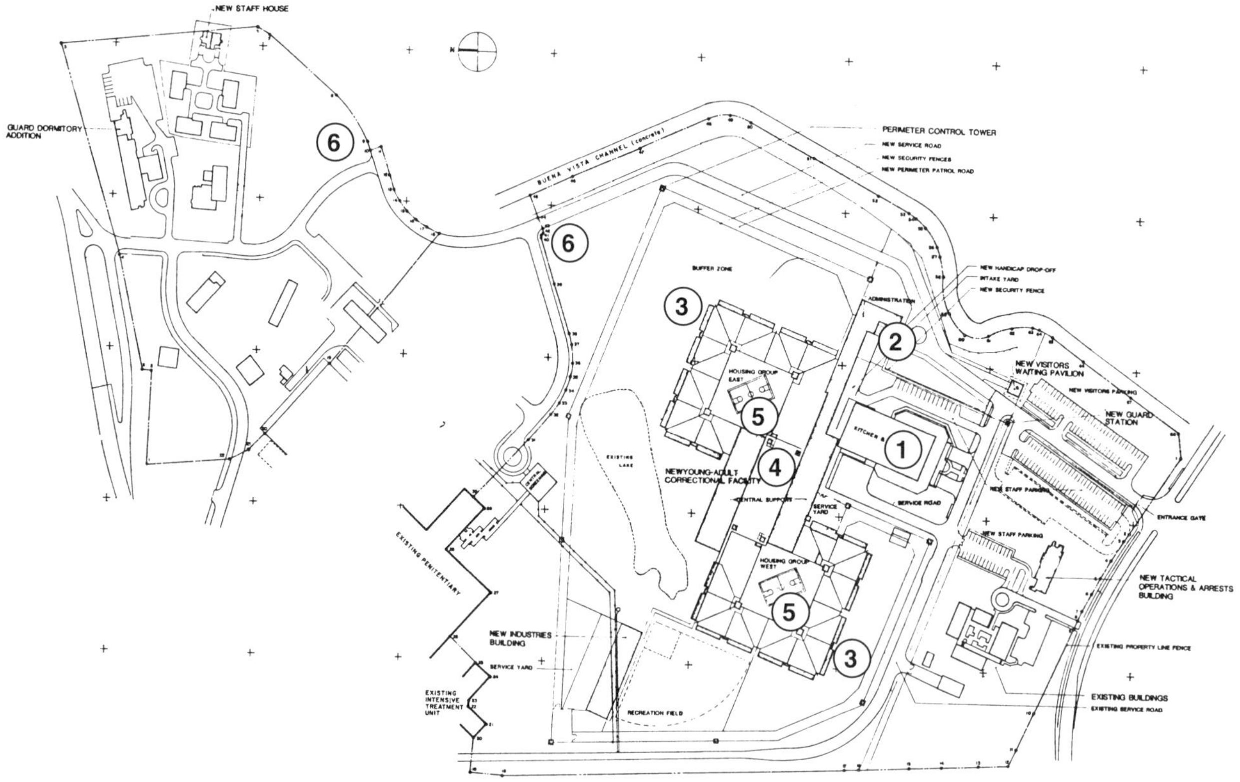

Figure 2.11

FIGURE 2.13 URBAN SETTING

Site Design Features:

1. Direct, physical connection to existing courthouse.
2. Excellent public mass transportation access to site.
3. Contextual relationship with new facility mass, height, and materials.
4. Public park and square created by building arrangement with access from through streets.
5. Security and service entrances screened from public view.
6. Planned future expansion, including basement-level connection, to location behind complex.

Figure 2.12 **Urban setting aerial photograph.**

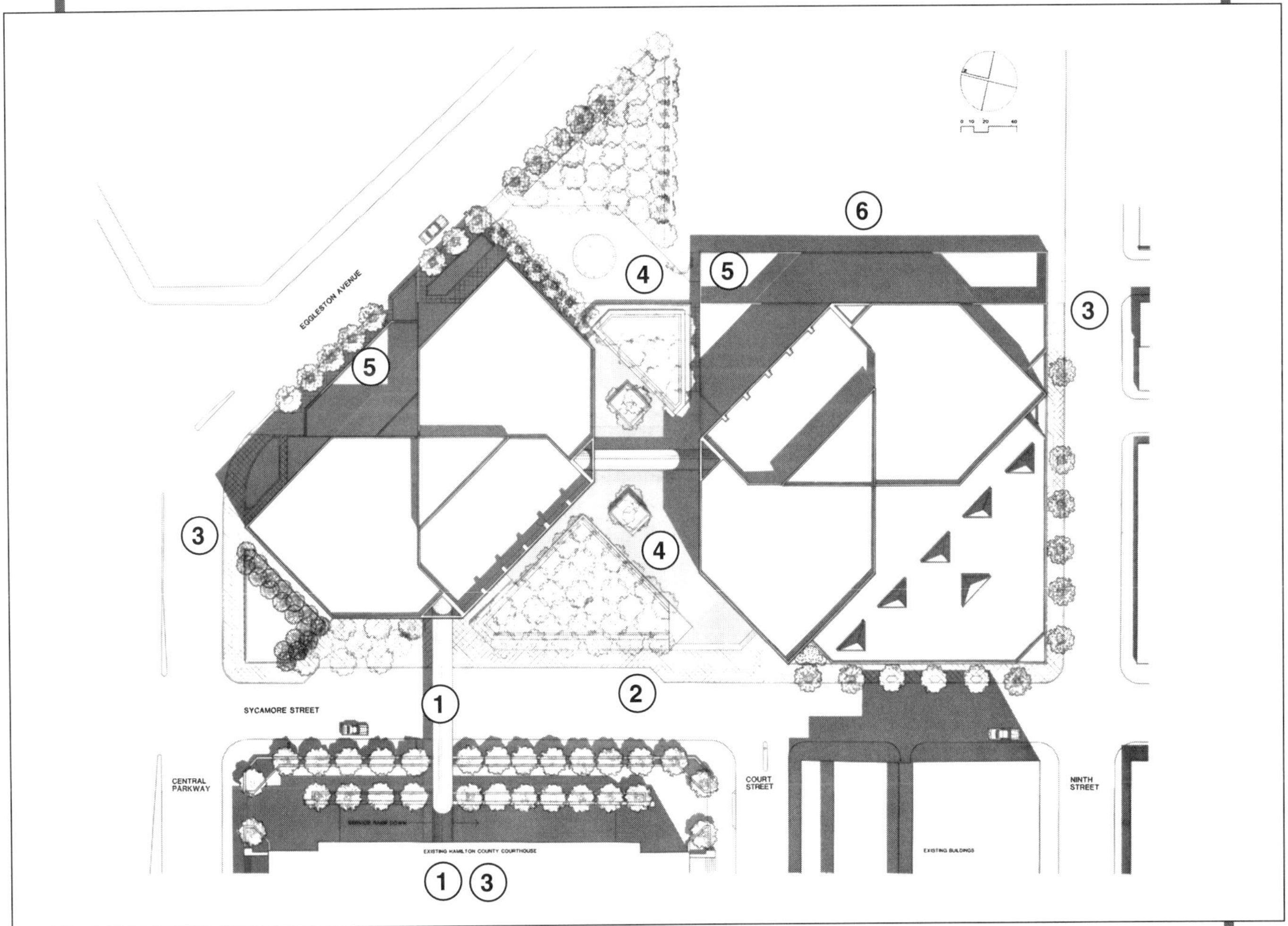

Figure 2.13

Figure 2.14 **Urban setting aerial photograph.**

FIGURE 2.15 URBAN SETTING

Site Design Features:

1. Facility screened and separated from public grade access by elevated interstate highway.
2. Public access road to park, along side of facility, improved, landscaped, and maintained.
3. Housing buildings location adjacent to existing facility planned for future expansion.
4. Support building location, mass, and height contextual to existing adjacent buildings.
5. Public parking minimized considering good mass transportation along main entrance road.
6. Security-sensitive intake, court transfer, and services areas screened from public view.

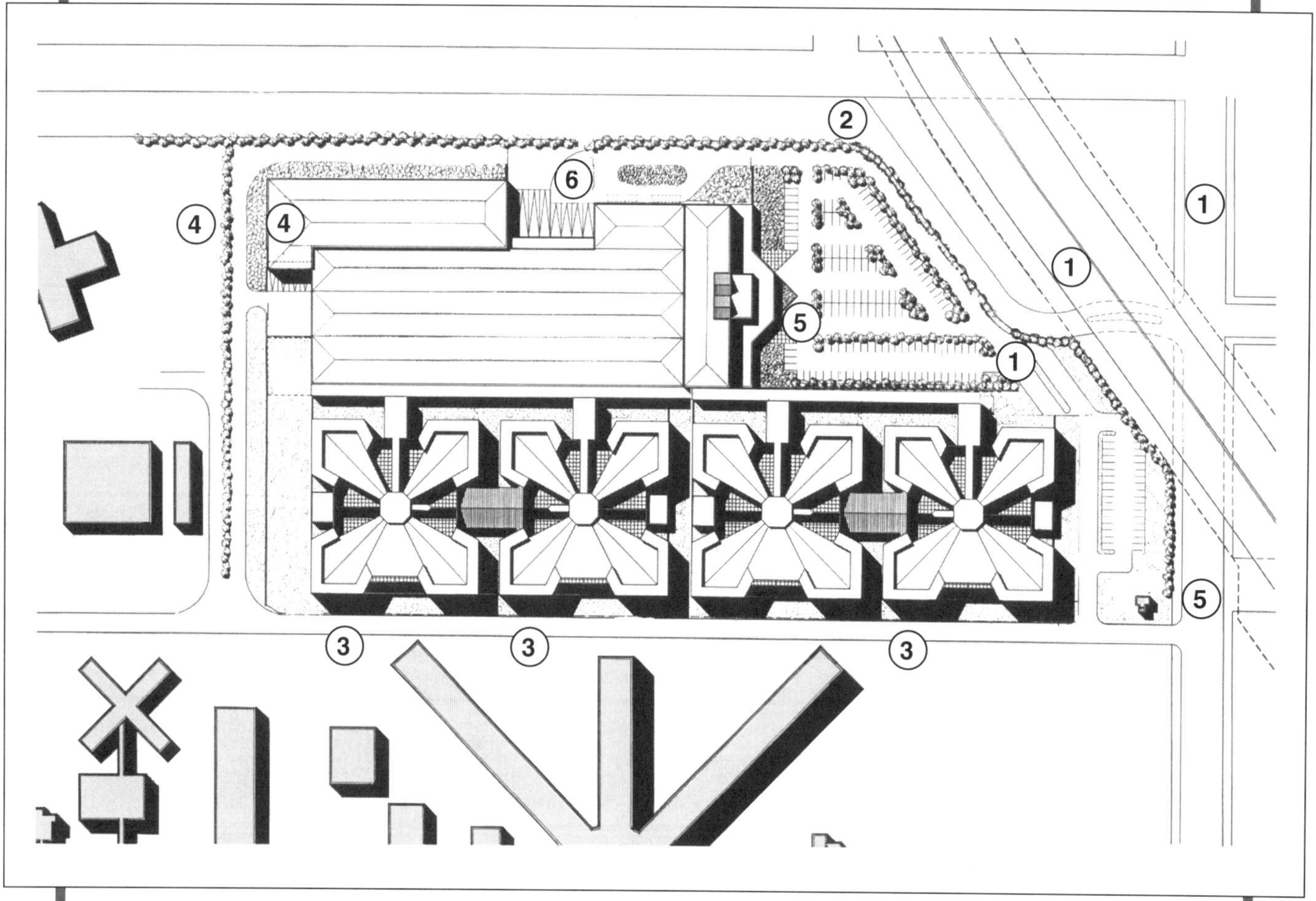

Figure 2.15

Summary	Facility reference	
FIGURE NUMBERS		
cells/staffing building area	facility name, location operational/type/housing design	client name, location design/architect of record
Rural		
2.4, 2.5	**Lincoln Correctional Center, Lincoln, NE**	**Dept. of Corrections**
324/170	1979, low-rise prison, connected campus-style environment,	Lincoln, NE
151,000 gsf	two 32-cell housing units for control and shared outdoor exercise	Gruzen/Kirkham Michael
2.6, 2.7	**Federal Correctional Institution, Manchester, KY**	**Federal Bureau of Prisons**
816/250	1992, low-rise prison, site adaptation of federal design model,	Washington, DC
554,663 gsf	two 64-bed housing units per building; 64-bed unit per control	DMJM/DMJM-GRW
Suburban		
2.8, 2.9	**Trenton State Prison, Trenton, NJ**	**Division Building Const.**
850/949	1983, high-rise prison, compact plan, connected buildings,	Trenton, NJ
359,518 gsf	three 48-cell housing units per floor (2059 beds, new and existing)	Gruzen/Gruzen-Grad
2.10, 2.11	**Young Adults Correctional Facility, Rio Piedras, PR**	**Commonwealth of PR**
504/376	1986, low-rise prison, three level housing tiers, campus-style plan,	San Juan, PR
187,860 gsf	two 48-cell housing units per control; two housing neighborhoods	Gruzen/G Z Mark
Urban		
2.12, 2.13	**Hamilton County Justice Center, Cincinnati, OH**	**County Commissioners**
848/326	1983, high-rise separated jail/prison/courts facility	Cincinnati, OH
512,000 gsf	four 48-cell housing units per floor (2-jail; 2-prison with controls)	Gruzen/Glaser Myers-Haupt
2.14, 2.15	**Curran Fromhold Reception and Detention Facility, Philadelphia, PA**	**Dept. of Public Properties**
2000/525	1995, mid-rise jail/reception and sentenced facility; connected bldgs,	Philadelphia, PA
750,000 gsf	four 64-bed housing units per unit management control	DMJM

3
Program, Operation, and Design

Program component descriptions required for a jail and/or prison facility. Each component includes program statement, prototypical spaces, operational objectives, operational procedures, staffing implications, and a design perspective. Material is supported with examples of architectural plans for each program component, illustrating small and large facilities. Plans are keyed to relative details, located in Chap. 5: Correctional Details.

INTRODUCTION

The following information provides the level of information required in planning and designing a correctional facility. The program is divided into components and subcomponents describing the general program intent, prototypical spaces required, operational objectives, operational procedures, staffing implications, and an architectural design perspective associated with most solutions. The program component list can be applied to the planning, design, and construction of most detention and correctional facilities. The square footage of each room or area is not indicated, since it is generally determined by the size of the facility, including the numbers of inmates, staff, and visitors it serves. Each space is generally determined by two sets of guidelines provided the architect, one entitled "Space Standards" and the other "Operational Standards."

During the planning and design phase of any facility, consideration should be given to the American Correctional Association's (ACA) "Standards for Adult Local Detention Facilities" (for jails), and the "Standards for Adult Correctional Facilities" (for prisons). Most of these standards pertain to the operations of a facility and require written policies and procedures governing each area of the facility. ACA accreditation requires that ACA operational requirements ". . . are frequently referred to by the executive, legislative, and judicial branches of local, state, and federal jurisdictions as the professional benchmark for judging the quality of a (facility) operation."

The operational objectives and procedures descriptions of each program component are offered to orient the reader as to how specific activities are envisioned, anticipated to take place, and transcribed into an architectural design. Each design should remain flexible to accommodate and adapt to different and changing management philosophies and operational approaches. The varying characteristics of inmate population by region can often have a direct impact on operations.

This section of the book offers a guideline to understanding the program intent and requirements, operational and staffing requirements, and design issues related to successful design solutions. Secure facilities represent complex operational environments since they must accommodate usual ongoing needs of staff and inmates day in and day out. As a means to facilitate understanding of user needs and operational relationships, the overall facility is typically broken down into functional components that represent areas/physical environments required to accomplish a related set of activities.

The organization of this section provides a discussion of each functional component which should assist in leading the project team to decisions during the initial design phase in terms of the following sequence of elements:

- Program statement
- Prototypical spaces
- Operational objectives
- Operational procedures
- Staffing implications
- Design considerations
- Architectural component floor plan(s)

In addition to these specific and important areas, each component will often include the following additional information for each room or area consideration and should be developed with dialogue between architectural team and client user group representative(s). The format used is sometimes referred to as *room data sheets.*

- Security issues
- Materials and finishes
- Furnishings
- Equipment
- Mechanical, electrical, and plumbing/fire protection issues

Specific information for these areas differ from project to project, based upon the type of facility (jail or prison), level of population classification, types of inmate incarcerated (male, female, and/or juvenile), and other factors related to client preferences. Generally, all inmate occupied space and area enclosures (walls, floors, and ceilings) should be constructed of secure materials such as concrete, masonry units (block and/or brick), and metals of gauges described in Chap 5: Correctional Details. The utilization of drywall construction is not recommended for any space contained within a correctional facility, unless specifically requested by a client. A correctional facility should consider long-term durability, ease of maintenance, and a minimum replacement of all of its materials and products. The text and diagrams described herewith are offered as guides that can lead to the development of a specific facility program with appropriate architectural design solutions.

Component identification		Facility type		Comments
	Component	Jail	Prison	
1.0	Public Lobby	+	+	
2.0	Visitation	+	+	
3.0	Hearings and Investigations	+	–	Smaller area for prisons
4.0	Executive Administration	+	+	May include sheriff's department in jails
5.0	Case Mgmt/Inmate Records	+	+	
6.0	Staff Development Services	+	+	
7.0	Intake/Transfer/Release	+	+	Small admissions/transfer area for prisons
8.0	Classification	+	–	Usually only for jails
9.0	Communications	+	+	Often combined with Master Control
10.0	Master Control	+	+	
11.0	Operations	+	+	
12.0	General Inmate Housing	+	+	Number, size, security level related to population
13.0	Special Inmate Housing	+	+	
14.0	Unit Management	+	+	Optional
15.0	Inmate/Social Services Programs	–	+	Community group volunteers
16.0	Educational/Vocational Programs	–	+	Programmed larger for prisons
17.0	Religious Services	+	+	
18.0	Industry	–	+	Programmed mostly for prisons
19.0	Recreation	+	+	Includes indoor and outdoor
20.0	Health Services	+	+	Includes dental, mental health, inpatient services
21.0	Food Service	+	+	Includes dining component
22.0	Commissary	+	+	
23.0	Laundry Service	+	+	
24.0	Warehouse	+	+	Separate vendors receiving for prisons
25.0	Engineering and Plant Maintenance	+	+	
26.0	Physical Plant	+	+	
27.0	Transport./Perimeter Access	+	+	

Juvenile and Female Facilities

There are specific differences in the program and design features of facilities for men versus women and adults versus juveniles. These differences are reflected in programs and physical design and can be identified and summarized with the following issues.

Juvenile Facilities. There are a number of issues to understand in the planning and design of a successful juvenile facility, which is different from an adult institution. There is a current trend toward building harder, more secure facilities for more violent juvenile offenders entering the criminal justice system. However, a focus remains on programs with goals of treatment and behavioral change development. Smaller numbers of juvenile groupings in housing units continue to support the treatment philosophy. Following are issues and/or conditions that juvenile facilities should provide:

- Sight and sound separation from an adult population (if facility types are combined)
- Continuing care, from incarceration to reentry into the community
- Smaller groupings in housing units
- Family conciliation programs
- Treatment programs, including child abuse and neglect orientation
- Psychological programs, including child advocacy and protective services
- Access to family courts and diversion programs
- Programs to build residents' self confidence, to effect behavioral change, and to expand learning skills and communications

- A building plan that reflects a normalized interior, with a variety of spaces, materials, and color
- A focus on academic, vocational education activities as part of the normal program day

Female Facilities. The are a number of issues and conditions related to the programming and design of facilities for female offenders. Many physical design features are also relevant to a male population; however, a number require different design solutions when planning for females. Programs are generally quite different from those found in male institutions, some of which include life skills, parenting, family relationships, art therapy, and culinary arts. The following is a summary of issues and/or conditions that female facilities should provide for:

- A population increase (200 percent since the 1980s), requiring the planning of facilities of significant size and program area
- Less violent inmates, although the numbers of women with violent histories are increasing
- A population majority of females who are single parents who require child care skills
- A population majority of females who were physically and/or sexually abused as children
- A population with serious mental health conditions
- Programs focused on self-esteem and confidence; parenting skills and values; communication skills; health and life care skills (hygiene); alcohol, drug, and partner abuse; interpersonal skills; and basic education
- An increasing number of pregnant females who require prenatal and postnatal medical care
- A flexibility to deal with a wider range of security classifications of inmates at each female facility, since there are fewer of them

CORRECTIONAL COMPONENT(S) EXAMPLES

1.0 PUBLIC LOBBY

Program Statement

This space serves as the reception point for visiting family members, friends, attorneys, clergy, and other groups (see Figs. 3.1 through 3.4). Law enforcement personnel, criminal justice system personnel, salespersons, and other general public enter the facility to meet with administration personnel in conducting business. It is the first checkpoint and processing area for public who are scheduled to visit with inmates. Some facilities

Figure 3.1 **Visitors' lobby, officer's processing desk, telephones, and metal detector with exit swing door.**

Figure 3.2 **Screened public waiting area with clerestory for natural light.**

separate public into two categories: those who are there for inmate visitation and others who may be scheduled to meet with administrative staff for official business. The latest trend indicates a benefit in speeding up the visiting process by separating traffic into two separate lobbies, the latter being utilized as a staff entrance.

The lobby area itself consists of space for seated waiting, public restrooms with diaper changing tables, public lockers for storage of all personal items to be left outside of security, and other support functions.

Prototypical Spaces

1.1 Weather vestibule (ADA accessible)
1.2 Information center
1.3 Facility lobby, public waiting area
1.4 Receiving officer's desk
1.5 Metal detector and x-ray machine
1.6 Public toilets
1.7 Janitor's closet
1.8 Public telephones
1.9 Public locker area
1.10 Public vending area (optional)
1.11 Weapons storage lockers (optional)
1.12 Public search room
1.13 Public sally port
1.14 Mail room (or located in staff lobby)

Operational Objectives

- Coordinate the processing of visitors in and out of facility in a orderly, safe, and controlled manner
- Maintain the security of the facility with the screening and processing of visitors prior to their admission into the facility's secure perimeter and visitation areas
- Prevent contraband from entering the secure facility
- Project a professional appearance and tone to all those entering the facility
- Maintain communications and contact with the Master (central) Control station

Operational Procedures

- Upon entering the public lobby, a visitor is required to register with a receiving officer, who will screen and admit persons into either the administrative office area for legitimate business with the staff or will admit visitors into the facility after the approval process, including metal detection and possible search.
- Master Control is generally located adjacent to the main lobby to maintain visual and electronic surveillance at all times and to assure that the

reception and processing procedures are maintained.

- Visitors to inmates engage in such activities as using vending machines while waiting, securing personal items in lockers, using public rest rooms and telephones, and, in some instances, leaving money for inmates at a station or window.
- Visitors to staff and administrators normally engage in such activities as registering and using phones and rest rooms, and armed law enforcement officers deposit their weapons in secure storage.
- A clear line should be established in the lobby that separates processed from unprocessed visitors; there should be means to direct official visitors and staff to bypass formal processing.
- A small search/holding room is needed in the event someone is suspected of trying to bring contraband into the facility.

Staffing Implications

The number of shifts of operations: One to Two
The number of days per week: Seven

Two officers for small facilities and potentially up to six for large facilities are generally assigned to the public lobby during its busiest period to handle the flow of processing visitors, attorneys, and other official visitors. One officer can manage the lobby during late afternoon and early evening shifts when process demand is greatly reduced, particularly if the central control room or other secure post has good visual supervision of the entry area.

Staff and official visitors use of the entry area is highest during weekdays, while visitor use is highest on weekends and holidays.

Design Considerations

1. Locate Master Control to observe the entrance vestibule, entire lobby area, the entrances to restrooms, search areas, and so forth.
2. Locate lobby officer to observe the entire lobby area and its functions. Position this station to maintain visual as well as voice communications with Master Control room.
3. Provide maximum amount of space in front of and on the sides of the lobby officer's desk to properly service visitors.
4. Locate lockers for visitors' personal property on a wall (or alcove) in complete view of officer's desk.
5. Locate public telephones on a wall in view of officer's desk (although some administrators prefer to minimize or eliminate certain visitor amenities to shorten their stay.
6. Provide a separate entrance and exit passage before entering the sally port. Enter through a metal detector and exit through a turnstile or door. These passages should be spaced some distance apart to facilitate processing and to separate traffic entering and leaving visitation.
7. Provide visitors with opportunity to deposit personal property in lockers before entering metal detector and to retrieve it when leaving the facility. Provide spatial separation between areas to facilitate traffic flow, both with observation by the lobby officer.
8. Provide visitors' waiting in two separate areas: one for preprocessing, the other after processing is complete and visitors have been cleared through metal detection and through the sally port.
9. Position Master Control to observe functions occurring in an adjacent staff lobby, if the program includes this component.
10. Provide an environment which reduces the anxiety of individuals. Visitors are often tense when entering a correctional facility. It is highly desirable to provide natural light into waiting areas to create a pleasant and nonthreatening environment; introducing color in materials and acoustical treatment to surfaces will assist in maintaining an ambiance and acoustically quiet environment.

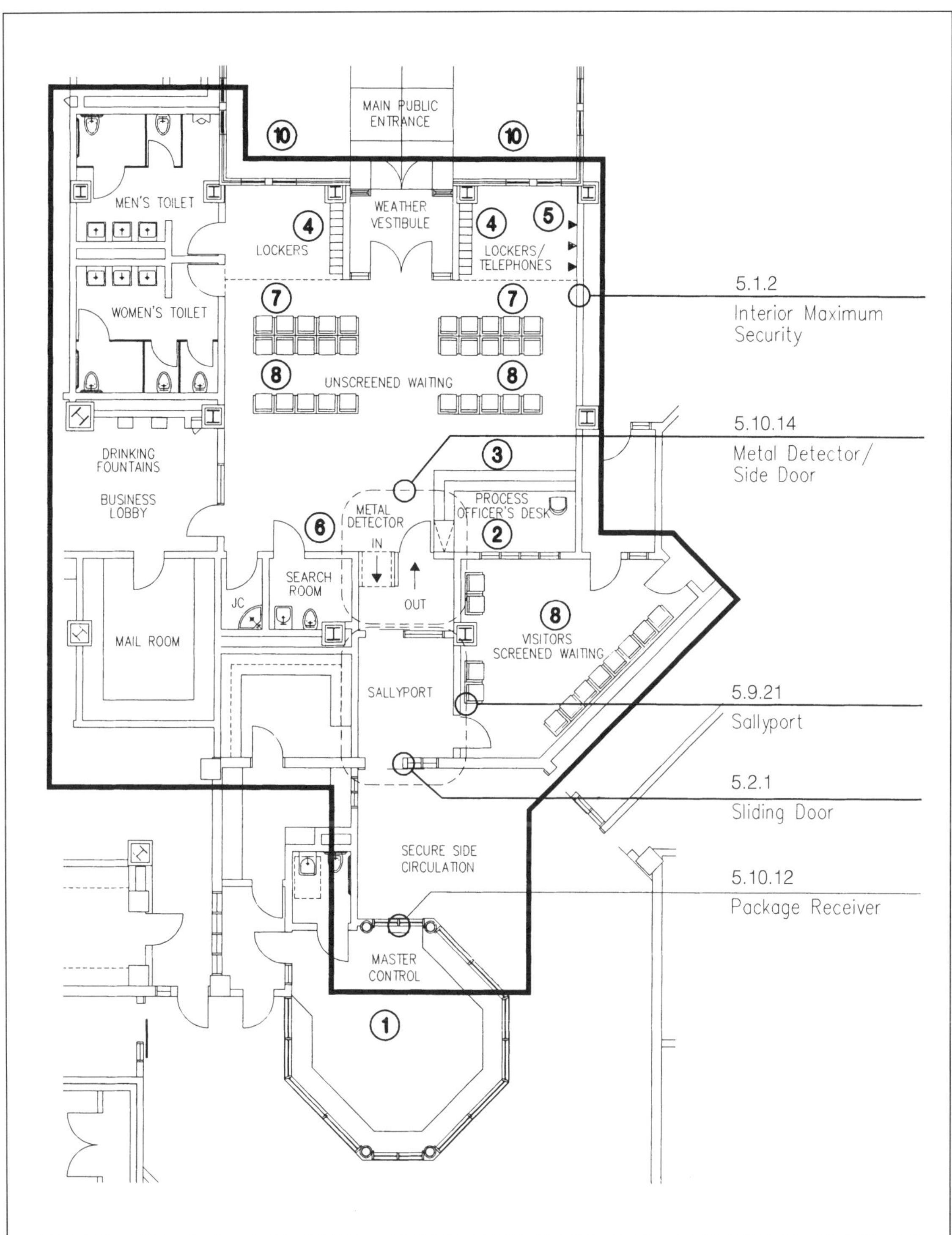

Figure 3.3 **Public lobby for a smaller facility.**

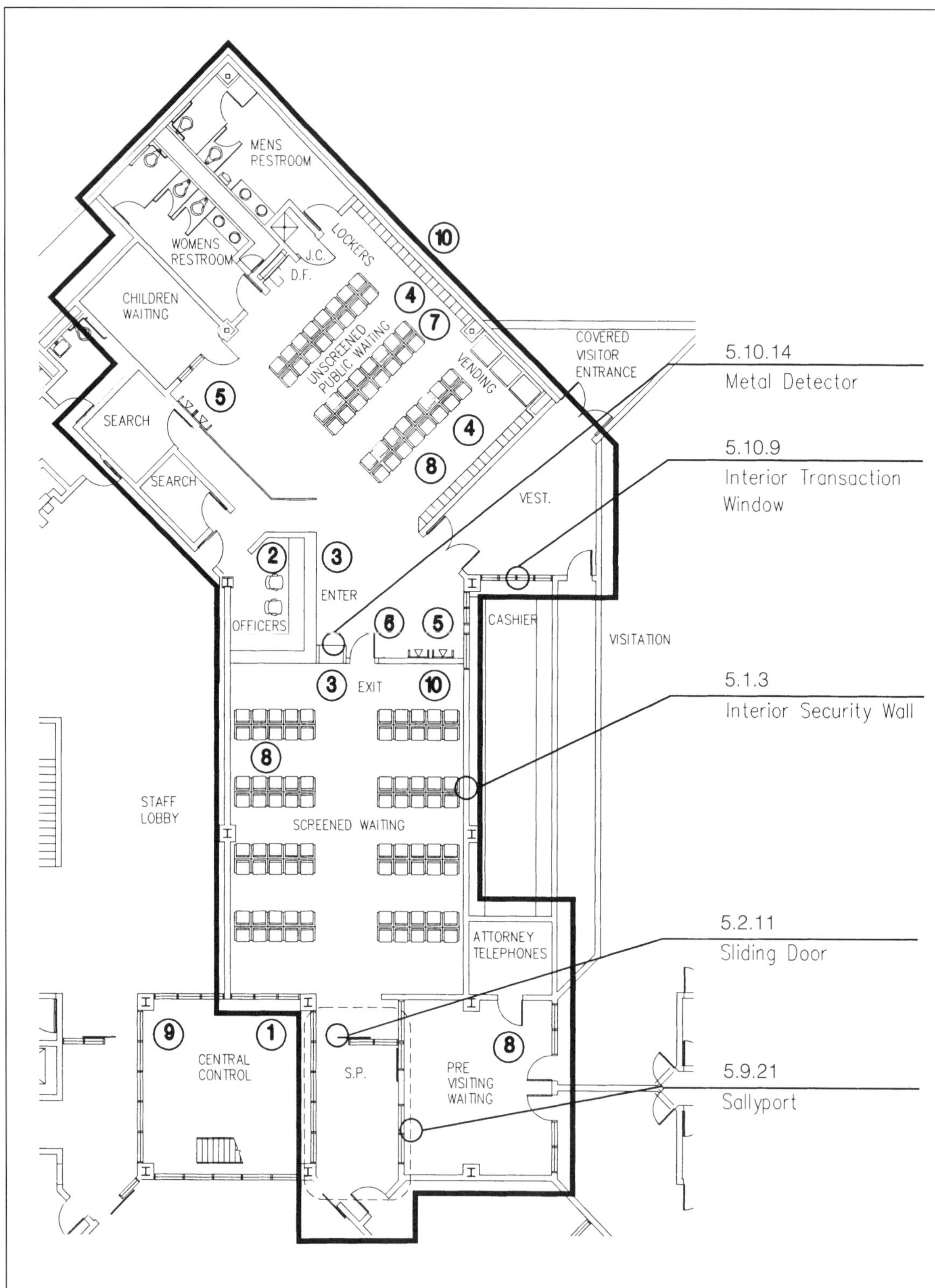

Figure 3.4 **Public lobby for a large facility.**

2.0 INMATE VISITATION

Program Statement

Frequent visits by family members and friends can help the inmate maintain family unity and ties to the community. A visitation program can assist the inmate in reducing negative psychological effects of incarceration and establishing a positive attitude for reentry into society. Strengthening inmate attitudes can improve the operations of the institution by reducing tension. Attorneys, law enforcement officers, and clergy visits also help in resolving problems.

Usually, the visitation area is located on the security boundary and within the secure side of the facility (see Figs. 3.5 through 3.8). It is generally close to the public lobby. In *prison* environments, inmates can travel considerable distance to the visitation room. In *jail* environments, the same can be true; however, some administrators prefer visitors to move to inmate housing areas via a separate corridor system for visiting, thereby minimizing inmate movement from housing. Visitors should be able to travel to the visiting area without entering any inmate contact area. Total separation of visitor and inmate access to the visitation area must be maintained at all times.

Contact (nonbarrier) and noncontact (barrier) visitation is provided in prisons and often in jails. Sometimes modified contact visitation is provided with physical barriers from desktop to floor. In some facilities, child care provisions are provided either in the public lobby or adjacent to the visitation room. Official visitation rooms for lawyers and religious persons are provided to maintain private conversations while providing total visibility from an officer's station. A room capable of one-way visibility into the contact visitation room has been provided in some facilities for staff to observe inmate behavior and activity. A room or section of a contact visitation room could be designed to provide interactive TV visits such as in jail settings where a TV arraignment opportunity between a judge and an inmate can improve operations by reducing transportation costs for daily inmate court appearance.

Some facilities prefer that inmates change into special uniforms before visitation to prevent the potential exchange of contraband between inmate and visitor. At other times, a separate area or corridor is provided for inmates entering and leaving the contact visitation room to maintain a security screening for contraband.

Prototypical Spaces

- 2.1 Sally port (from main lobby into corridor or visitation space directly)
- 2.2 Officer station(s)
- 2.3 Waiting or staging area for visitors
- 2.4 Visitor toilets (outside of visitation room, on the public side)
- 2.5 Vending (optional)
- 2.6 Contact visiting room/multipurpose room
- 2.7 Children waiting/play area
- 2.8 Noncontact visitation booths
- 2.9 Lawyer visitation rooms
- 2.10 Observation room (optional)
- 2.11 Inmate holding area
- 2.12 Inmate search room
- 2.13 Inmate toilet room(s)
- 2.14 Janitor's closet

Operational Objectives

- Promote inmate ties to family, friends, and the community
- Provide a secure environment for attorneys, clergy persons, and criminal justice personnel to meet with inmates
- Prevent contraband from entering the main facility from within the visitation area
- Provide both contact and noncontact visitation as appropriate for the inmate population

Operational Procedures

- Visitors deposit personal belongings and items not permitted inside in lockers off entry area.
- Persons with appointments with business administration personnel will be screened in the lobby by the lobby officer. After verification of their identity and determining their need to visit with appropriate administrative staff, the officer will remotely unlock the door and direct the person to an administrative waiting area. The lobby officer will contact appropriate administrative staff to announce the arrival of the visitor.
- After visitors have been screened in the public lobby (outside of security), they enter a sallyport, experiencing controlled movement from the non-secure, to the secure side of the facility.
- Once inside of security, visitors generally move on their own to the visitation area(s) and are usually observed from a control station.
- The visitation officer will open the door to the visitation room for visitors, and inmates will enter from different and separated entrances.

Figure 3.5 **Contact visitation room and special visiting rooms with clerestory for natural light.**

Figure 3.6 **Noncontact visitation booth with vision panels in doors at each end.**

- In contact visiting, an officer(s) will observe all inmate/visitor activity.
- In non-contact visitation booths, inmates and visitors will be monitored and supervised by an officer assigned to the area.
- At the conclusion of a visit, visitors will return to the public lobby, and inmates will proceed to a secure area for search and screening prior to returning to their respective housing units.

Staffing Implications

The number of shifts of operations: Two
The number of days per week: Varies from weekdays-only to all days

Generally, one officer is assigned to contact visitation and another to noncontact booths, attorney, clergy, and other individual visitation rooms. One officer is located near the public entry, the other adjacent to the inmate entry/exit/search area.

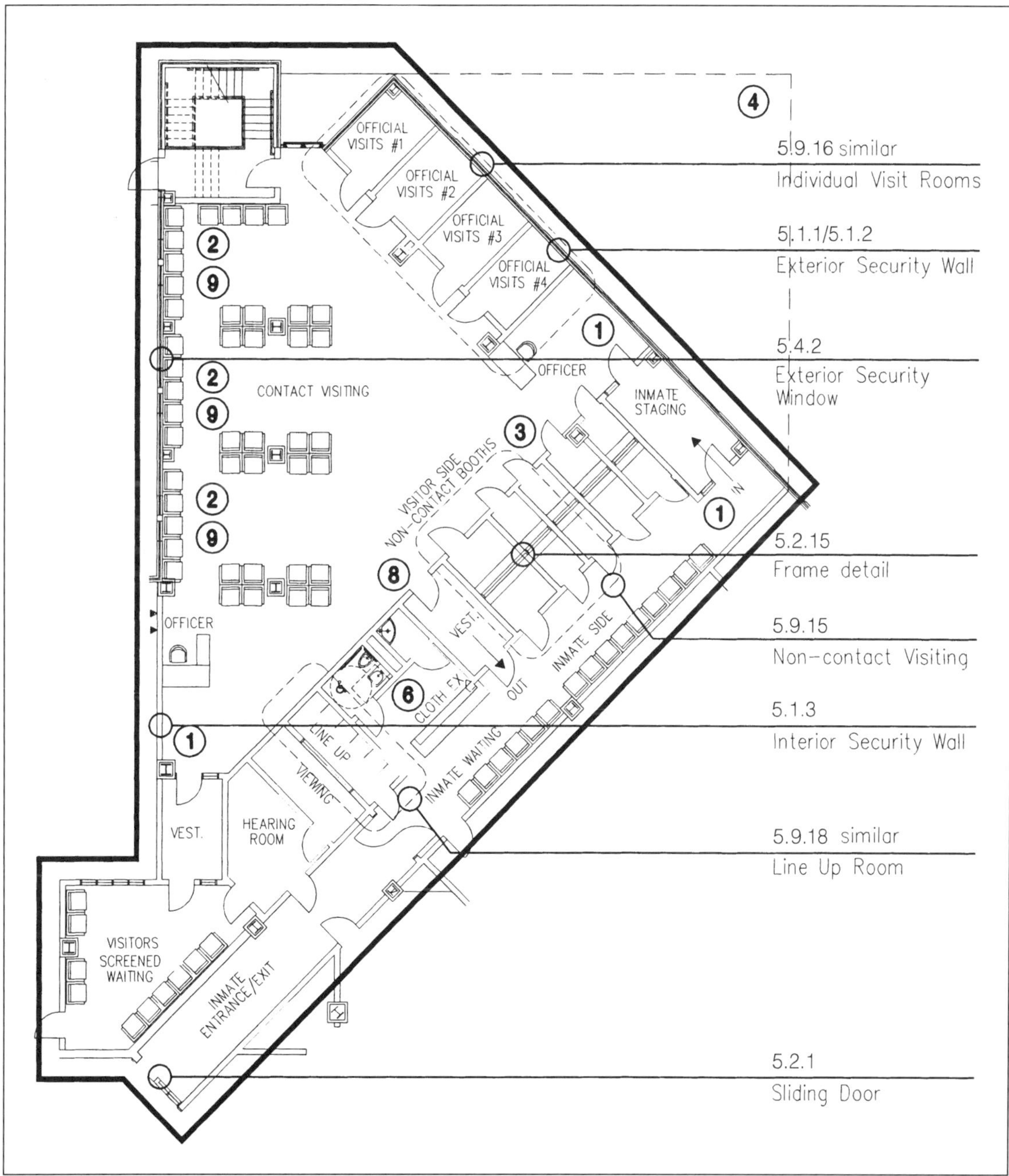

Figure 3.7 **Visitation plan for a small facility.**

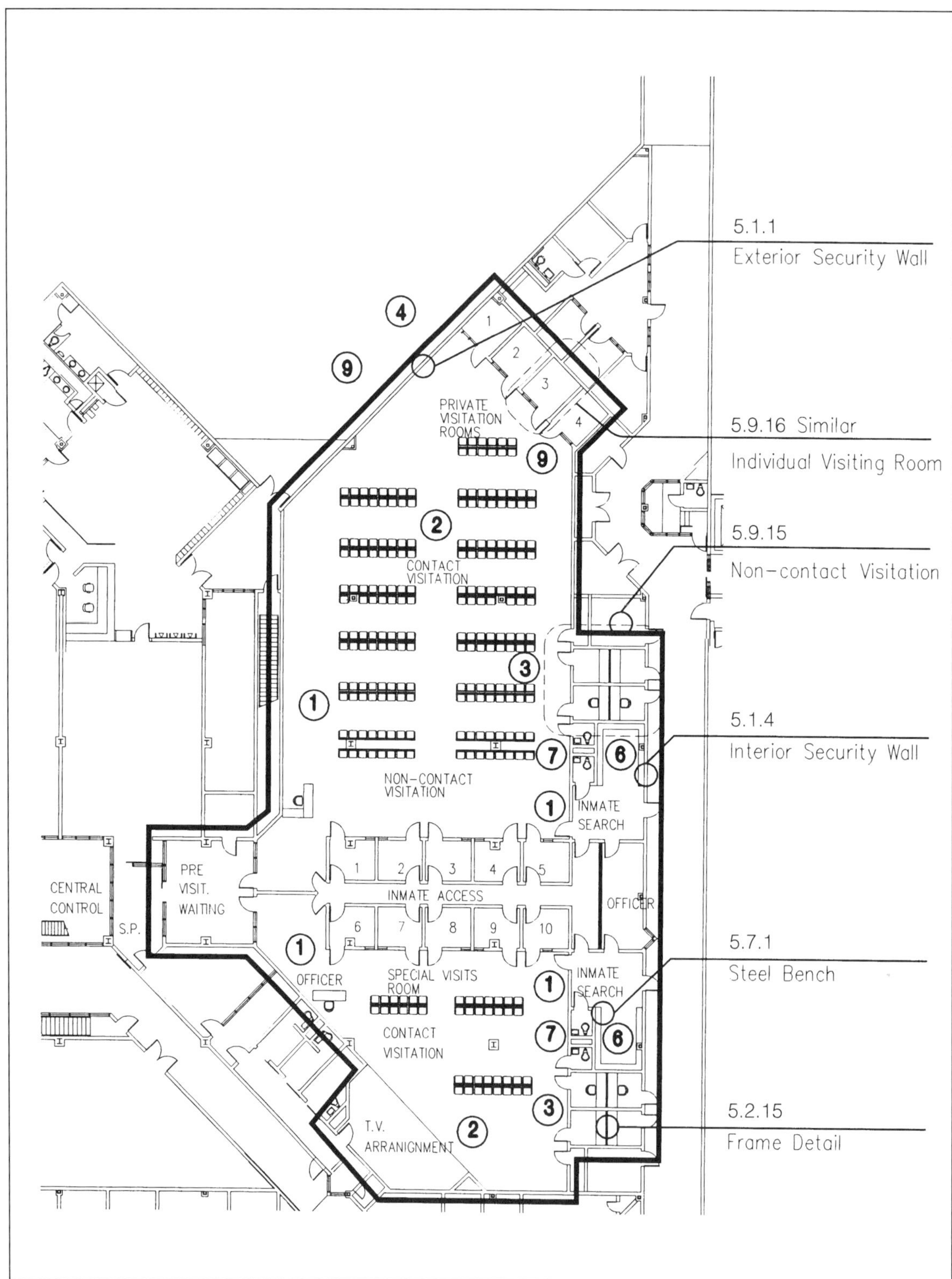

Figure 3.8 **Visitation plan for a large facility.**

Clear visual supervision of the area is essential to prevent inefficient staffing. The major determinant in visiting staffing is the frequency and duration of visits established by facility policy—which, in turn, establishes the number of visits to be accommodated at one time. Unless visits occur all day, every day, officers can usually be assigned other responsibilities at other times.

Design Considerations

1. Separate inmate and visitor entrances to maintain complete unobstructed observation from a visitation officer(s) area/desk.
2. Discuss main contact room open seating arrangements with project team to establish effective layout; this varies from client to client. Some administrators prefer side-by-side individual seats, barrier-free, to limit and discourage intimate contact and the potential of the passage of contraband. Others prefer a visiting arrangement across a wide table, minimizing physical contact.
3. Position noncontact visitation booths for officer observation, but limit public view from the main contact visiting room.
4. Plan for future expansion of the main contact visiting room, noncontact booths, and official visitation rooms.
5. Outdoor visitation for fair weather days can create normalized family visits (optional). Strategically locate this area to facilitate officer observation while maintaining security. Access is generally directly from the open contact visitation room.
6. Public and inmate toilets should be remote from one another, with inmate toilets in close proximity to an officer's station to prevent the passage of contraband.
7. A majority of visitors to male facilities are female; toilet fixture requirements should be adjusted accordingly.
8. Provide separate paths for entering and exiting the contact visitation room from inmate waiting areas. Provide each area with separate search, toilet(s), and waiting areas. A third separate area should be considered for noncontact visiting inmates to prevent altercations with contact visiting inmates.
9. Provide a normative environment through the use of materials, color, lighting, and acoustical treatment.

3.0 HEARINGS AND INVESTIGATIONS

Program Statement

This component is provided to enhance an orderly operation of the institution by ensuring that reasonable and necessary disciplinary standards of conduct are prescribed and enforced and by providing for a procedurally efficient and fair system of managing inmate proceedings for other criminal justice agencies.

Hearings provide for prompt, fair, safe, orderly, and efficient conduct of the releasing authority, disciplinary, court, and other fact-finding and decision-making proceedings. Flexibility in design must address the size, duration, purpose, and frequency of hearings.

Investigations provide for prompt, thorough, and professional investigation and reporting to facilitate discipline and criminal proceedings, the resolution of inmate claims, and provide needed data for administrative action and policy determination.

This component is often best located adjacent to the visitation area, sharing support functions such as public entry, inmate search, waiting, rest rooms, and security observation (see Figs. 3.9 through 3.11).

Prototypical Spaces

3.1 Public waiting room
3.2 Large hearing room
3.3 Small hearing room
3.4 Equipment room (interactive TV)
3.5 Chief investigator's office
3.6 Investigator's office
3.7 Hearing officer office (visiting attorney)
3.8 Evidence storage room
3.9 Clerical and file space
3.10 Staff toilets
3.11 Inmate holding area (cells optional)
3.12 Inmate toilets(s)
3.13 Inmate search room (optional)

Operational Objectives

- To facilitate other related criminal justice proceedings, thereby reducing transportation time and cost
- To provide a dedicated space for conducting disciplinary hearings
- To provide a dedicated space for facilitating release protocols
- To provide a fair, neutral, and appropriate setting in which to conduct judicial and facility due process hearings
- For judicial and parole board personnel, to minimize the depth they need to go into the facility in order to discharge their responsibilities

Operational Procedures

- Lawyers, parole officers, court officials, and others acting on behalf of criminal justice functions proceed to dedicated spaces for conducting criminal justice business.
- Inmates proceed through secure spaces to an area within the secure perimeter to participate in proceedings relevant to their criminal justice business.

Line-Up
Holding Cells

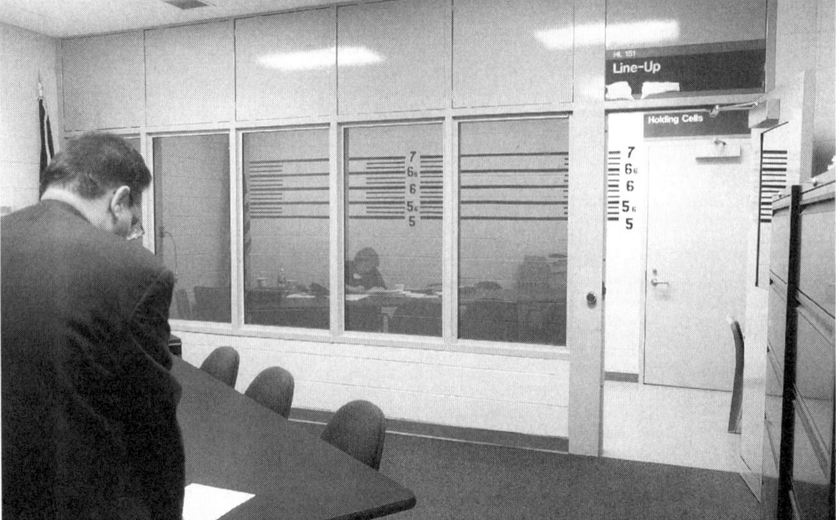

Figure 3.9 **Hearing room with one-way-vision glass wall into lineup room and inmate holding cell access.**

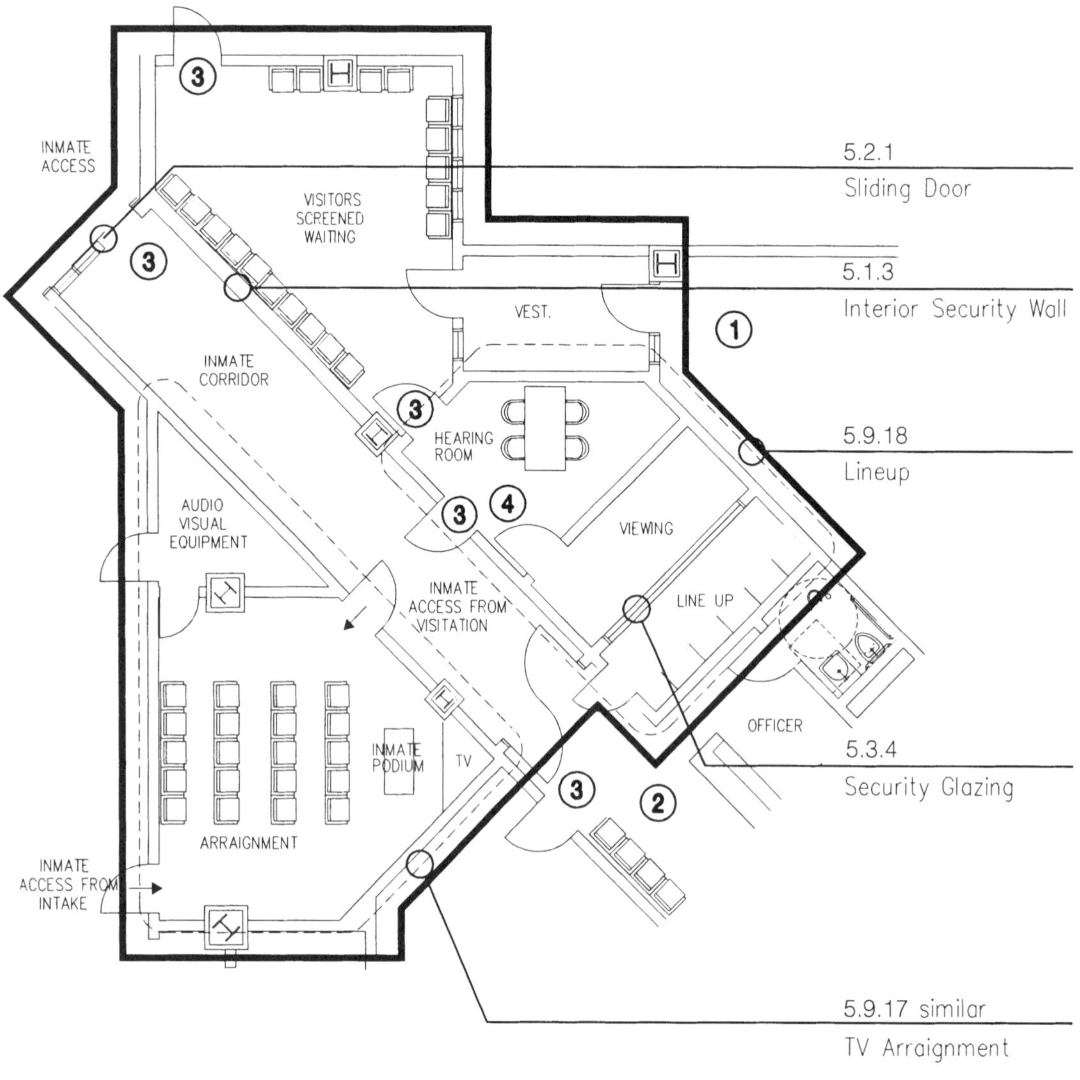
INMATE ACCESS
VISITORS SCREENED WAITING
VEST.
INMATE CORRIDOR
HEARING ROOM
AUDIO VISUAL EQUIPMENT
VIEWING
LINE UP
INMATE ACCESS FROM VISITATION
OFFICER
INMATE PODIUM
TV
ARRAIGNMENT
INMATE ACCESS FROM INTAKE
5.2.1
Sliding Door
5.1.3
Interior Security Wall
5.9.18
Lineup
5.3.4
Security Glazing
5.9.17 similar
TV Arraignment

Figure 3.10 **Hearings and investigations designs for a small facility.**

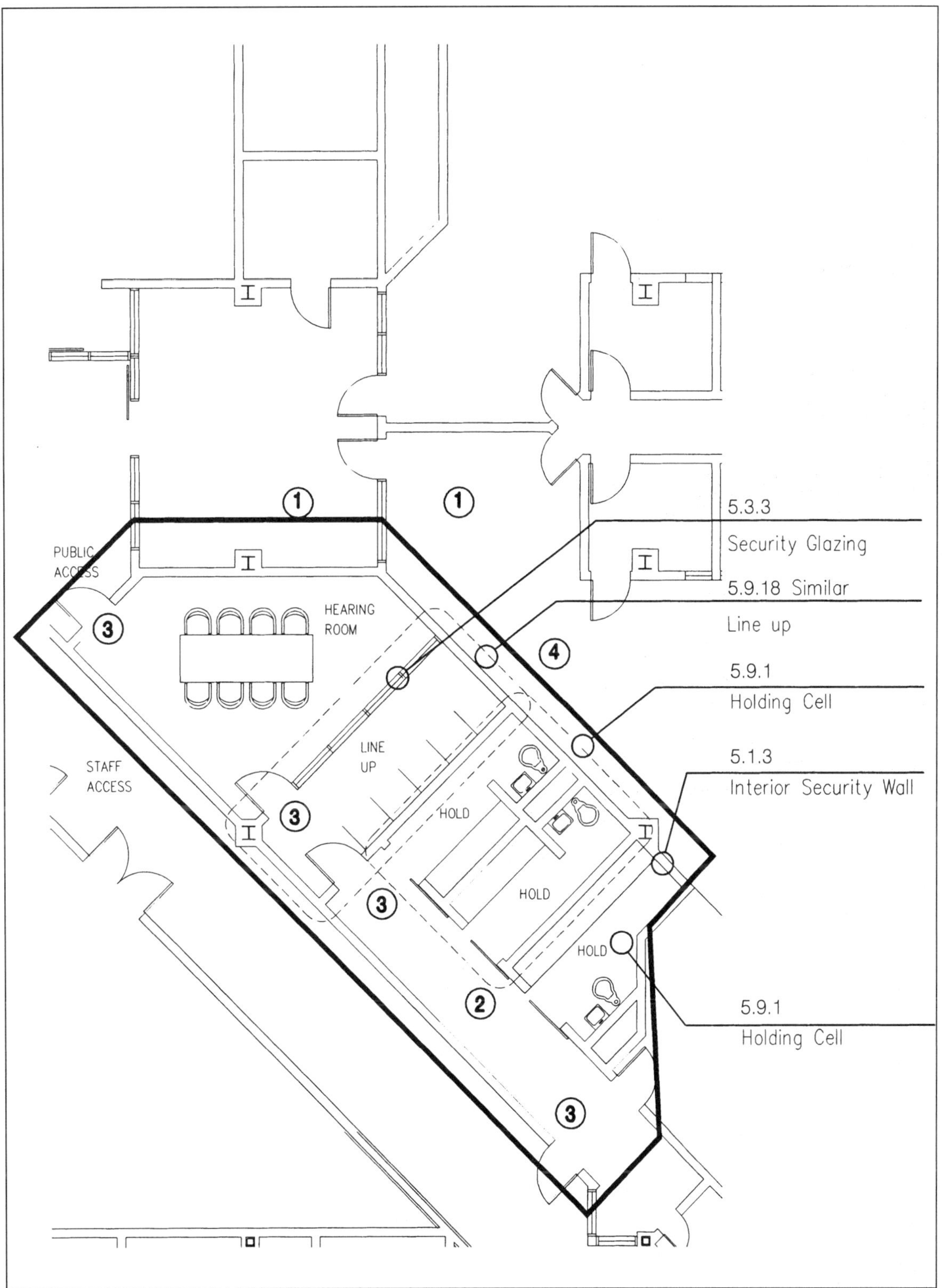

Figure 3.11 **Hearings and investigations designs for a large facility.**

- Criminal justice officials and prison officials utilize dedicated and neutral spaces to conduct proceedings, after which both criminal justice officials and inmates return in an orderly and secure fashion to their regular work/housing places.
- Inmates are given written, advance notice of hearings with which they are concerned.
- If a legal or parole board hearing, inmates are brought in small groups to a holding area prior to their appointment time.
- Inmates are called out one at a time to conduct their hearings.
- After determinations are made, inmates are returned to their housing units.
- If a facility hearing, other inmates and staff may be called as witnesses.

Staffing Implications

The number of shifts of operations: On an as-needed basis
The number of days per week: Varies

Few facilities conduct hearings on a daily basis; staffing is therefore primarily escort officers when hearings are scheduled. Investigative/case worker staff will generally be assigned to this area which may involve several staff in large facilities. In some jurisdictions, the facility is required to provide office space for employees of outside agencies (e.g., parole officers).

Design Considerations

1. Locate adjacent to the visitation area to enhance security and to limit inmate movement
2. Share inmate holding rooms, search area(s), and toilets between visitation and hearing waiting areas
3. Provide separate entrances for staff/criminal justice officials and inmates
4. Consider sharing hearing rooms between visitation and investigative areas, thereby providing flexibility in accessing the hearing rooms from two separate entrances
5. Provide natural light for staff who work in this area during normal working hours
6. Develop the architectural plan in considering the potential for future expansion

4.0 EXECUTIVE ADMINISTRATION

Program Statement

The executive administration provides leadership and support for a correctional institution to operate in an orderly and effective manner. This area is generally located outside of the secure perimeter and includes functions which support the institutional operation of the facility (see Figs. 3.12 through 3.14). Generally, these functions do not require regular interaction with functions located on the secure side of the facility. Circulation to this area is controlled by a lobby officer and/or Master Control. The departments located in executive administration that support operation are warden's (superintendent) office and support spaces, associate warden's offices and support spaces, fiscal management department, personnel department, mail room, records storage, standards coordination, and switchboard. Case management is often located there and positioned adjacent to the secure records room. Case workers are located on the secure side of the facility, adjacent to the inmates they serve, usually in the housing unit or in a unit management area.

Prototypical Spaces

4.1 Administrative waiting area/reception
4.2 Public toilets
4.3 Warden's office
4.4 Warden's toilet/shower
4.5 Warden's conference room (emergency equipment room and hospitality alcove)
4.6 Executive secretary
4.7 Associate warden of administration
4.8 Assistant to the warden
4.9 Secretary, associate warden(s)
4.10 Special investigator for internal affairs
4.11 Assistant special investigator for internal affairs
4.12 Finance director
4.13 Assistant to finance director
4.14 Inmate account stations
4.15 Payroll office
4.16 Vault
4.17 General records storage
4.18 Finance forms/supplies
4.19 Human resources secretary/waiting area
4.20 Human resources manager
4.21 Human resources assistant
4.22 Human resources clerk stations

Figure 3.12 **Main entrance for staff with three-story administration building behind.**

4.23 Conference rooms
4.24 Interview rooms
4.25 Human resources files/storage
4.26 Mail room (x-ray, staff mailboxes)
4.27 Staff lounge/vending
4.28 Staff toilets
4.29 Janitor's closet
4.30 Conference rooms/multipurpose and subdivisible
4.31 Photocopy/facsimile room

Operational Objectives

- Facilitate conduct of business
- Project image to public visitors
- Functional use of administrative spaces
- Appropriate configuration for functions

Operational Procedures

- The doors to the executive administration office area from the public and/or staff lobby should remain locked at all times. Lobby officers and Master Control should be able to electronically control these doors.
- Persons with appointments with business administration personnel will be screened in the lobby by the lobby officer. After verification of their identity and determining their need to visit with appropriate administrative staff, the officer will remotely unlock the door and direct the person to an administrative waiting area. The lobby officer will contact appropriate administrative staff to announce the arrival of the visitor.
- The offices and/or workstations will be equipped with computer terminals to network primary criminal justice and jail computer systems. This capability permits instant access to critical information and administrative reports required for managerial decisions.
- Administrative information is also maintained in departmental records that are filed in a traditional hard copy format. Space is provided for the storage of active and inactive records.
- The records include personnel files, copies of purchase orders, inventory records, and other fiscal records. This area is often restricted due to sensitive materials. A photocopier and fax machine are also provided for procedure support.
- One-on-one and group meetings (conference room) are provided.

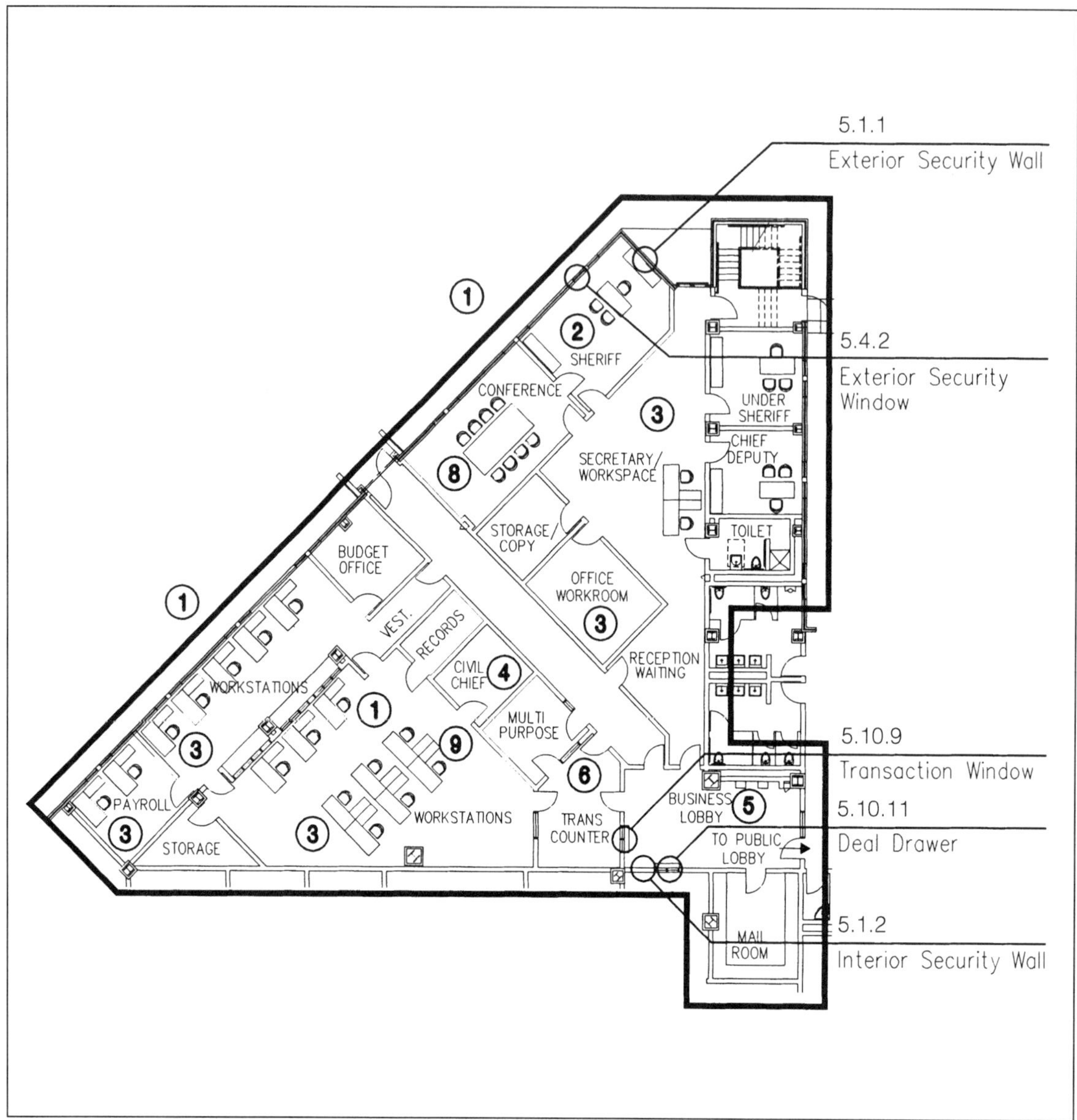

Figure 3.13 **Executive administration for a small facility.**

Staffing Implications

The number of shifts of operations: One

The number of days per week: Five, Seven for special conditions

This area is generally restricted to day use and therefore a relief factor is not required. The number of offices and personnel are determined by the number of personnel allocated to administration in the approved facility program.

Design Considerations

1. Design this area as a conventional office building and provide a generous amount of window area with exterior windows and interior door sidelights.
2. Position the warden's area to observe the overall facility or the staff/public entrances and parking lots.
3. Provide a combination of private offices for confidential activities and an open office area to create a pleasant working environment.
4. Position a senior staff office or area for observation of business activities in the office area.
5. Provide controlled direct access from public lobby to reception area, without entering business activity areas. Master Control room observation is desirable.

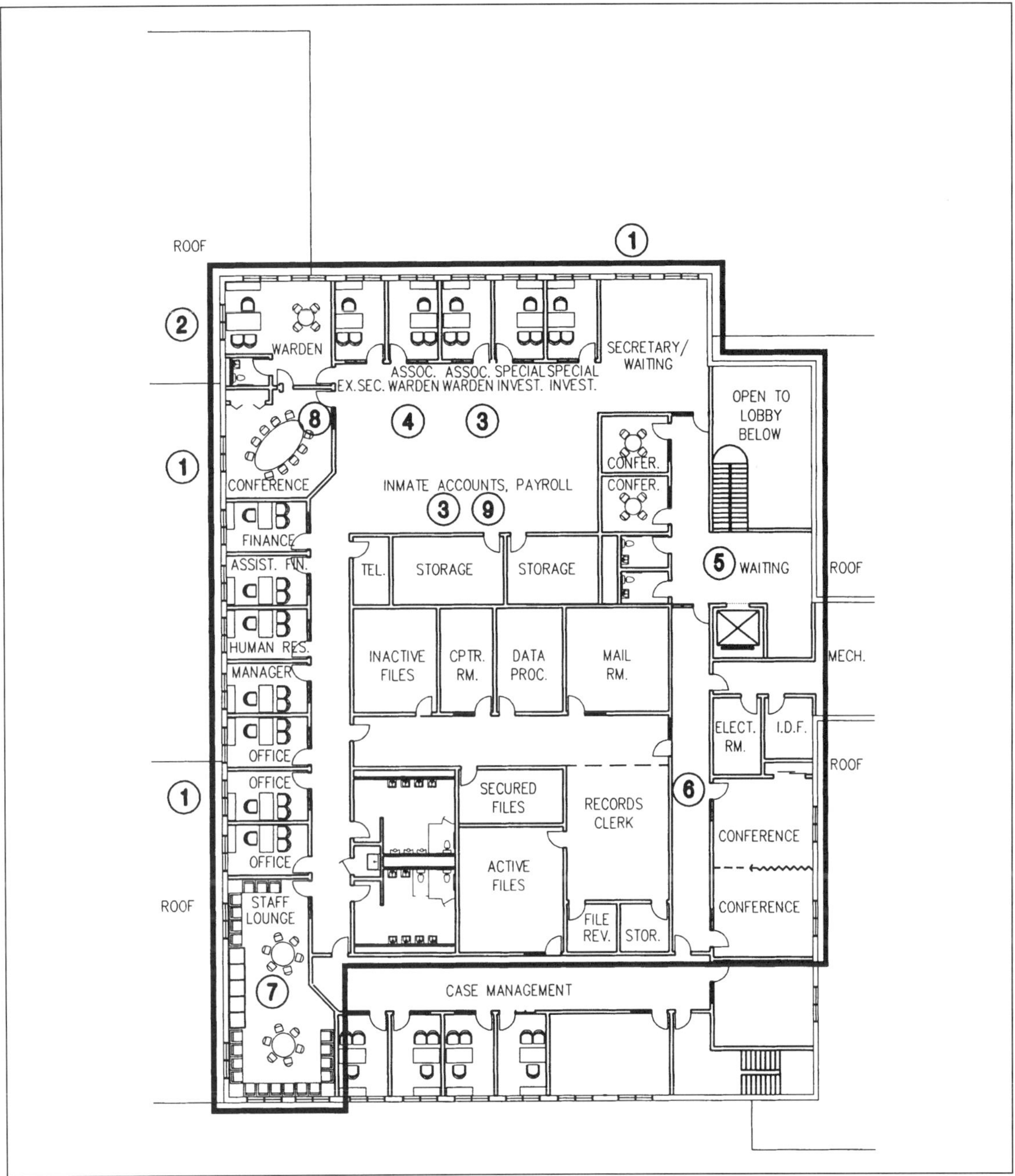

Figure 3.14 **Executive administration for a large facility.**

6. Provide public direct access from reception lobby to interview and conference rooms. Provide for official business activities. Include separate staff access to conference rooms if possible.
7. Provide staff lounge/restroom facilities away from business activities; natural light is desirable.
8. Provide warden's conference room with equipment and location for access to media for news conferences.
9. The utilization of modular office landscape design creates flexibility to accommodate changes and the opportunity to use correctional industries products.

5.0 CASE MANAGEMENT AND RECORDS

Program Statement

Case management develops inmate records. Case Management can be located in a central programs building within the secure perimeter or outside of the secure perimeter and adjacent to where inmate records are kept. At times, this area can also be located adjacent to housing units. These records maintain the most accurate information on each inmate including background in order to successfully track the inmate's progress through the system. The records department is assigned the responsibility of providing timely and accurate information to individuals responsible for making decisions regarding inmates and the operation of the facility. The need for confidentiality usually mandates that these records be kept on the outside of the secure perimeter, with case workers generally located in and/or adjacent to housing units to provide services where inmates reside. In this situation, the case workers typically use remote computer access or take in only what inmate information they need for morning or afternoon appointments with inmates (see Fig. 3.15).

Prototypical Spaces

5.1 Case management supervisor
5.2 Secretary
5.3 Clerk/typist
5.4 Staff toilet(s)
5.5 Office services supervisor
5.6 Facility information services supervisor
5.7 Data processing coordinator
5.8 Computer room
5.9 Workroom
5.10 Records clerk
5.11 Active files
5.12 Inactive files
5.13 File review room/area
5.14 Secure files (confidential records)
5.15 General storage
5.16 Staff toilet(s)
5.17 Janitor's closet

Operational Objectives

- Develop an inmate record system consistent with state requirements and the facility's policies and procedures
- Maintain a secure records storage area where all active and inactive inmate case records will be stored
- Maintain pertinent information reflecting an inmate's institutional adjustment and behavior history
- Provide safeguards to protect an inmate's right to privacy and prevent unauthorized disclosure of confidential information
- Encourage inmate access to/responsiveness of case workers since they represent their lifeline to the facility administration, program committee, and the outside world

Operational Procedures

- Inmate records are initially developed at admissions processing and continue with the classification process.
- A records clerk maintains the records in a prescribed format and performs all necessary filing and recording functions during the inmate's period of incarceration at the facility.
- When inmates are transferred to another facility or eventually released, their records will be stored in an inactive records room for a designated period of time.
- Access to inmate records area is provided to the general public and/or admissions/transfer/release area via a secure pass-through window(s) for exchange of information and/or money to inmate accounts.

Staffing Implications

The number of shifts of operations: One
The number of days per week: Five, varies on weekends

The number of offices and personnel are determined by personnel incorporated in the approved facility program. Target staffing should be on the order of one case worker per hundred inmates.

Design Considerations

1. Provide this area's general layout similar to that of commercial office building, office areas with natural light and files centralized for functional and easy access.
2. Locate the administrative staff and records on the outside of security and adjacent to the sally port leading to the secure interior of the facility. Provide for easy access to inmate case management offices located within the housing units or unit management areas.
3. Locate this area adjacent to inmate admissions (intake) for exchange of information via a secure window.
4. Consider providing an exterior window for communication with arriving official vehicles holding inmates for admissions. If paperwork presented by officer is incomplete or unacceptable, the vehicle can be turned away, denying access to the vehicular sally port.

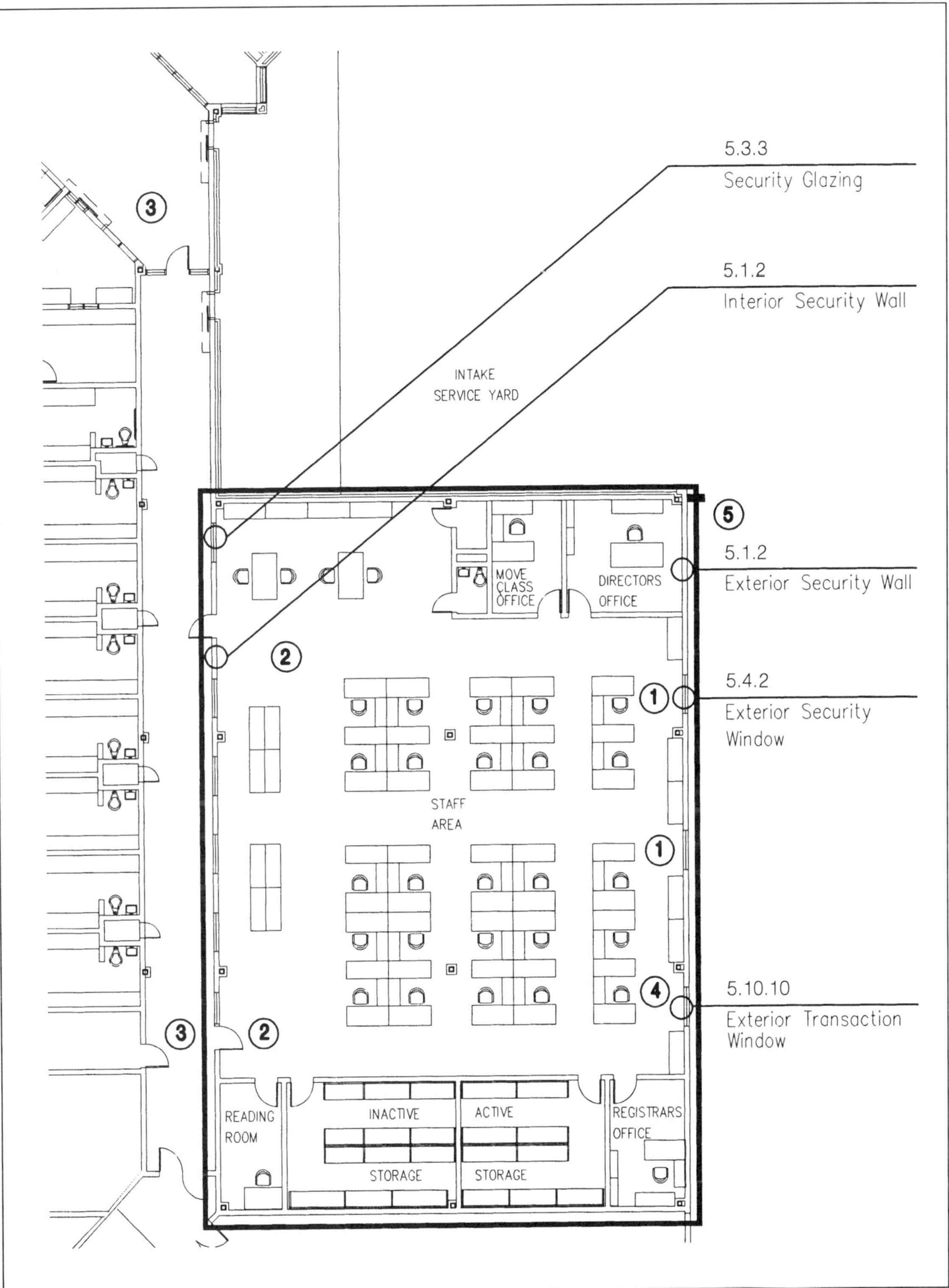

Figure 3.15 **Case management and inmate records for a large facility.**

5. Consider future expansion of this area, although most recordkeeping can be stored with computer files.

6. Design of housing units should provide interview rooms/small discussion space in or adjacent to dayroom area.

6.0 STAFF DEVELOPMENT/SERVICES

Program Statement

This area is most often located outside of the secure perimeter, adjacent to administrative lobby and executive administration. The purpose of this area is to provide staff with the necessary resources for continued growth and professional development through preservice and in-service training. These services include training in the following areas of instruction: general institution policy, training for specific job assignments, training in electronic communications, human relations and dynamics, emergency procedures, cultural diversity issues, weapons and restraints, supervision, self-defense, and security issues. This area also provides space for staff locker facilities and staff assembly for preshift briefings (see Figs. 3.16 through 3.18).

Prototypical Spaces

6.1 Training director
6.2 Assistant training director
6.3 Clerk/typist and training records
6.4 Training rooms (computer, chemical, etc.)
6.5 Training equipment storage
6.6 Assembly room
6.7 Female toilets, showers, and lockers
6.8 Male toilets, showers, and lockers
6.9 Wellness center/training room
6.10 Armory readiness room (armory located adjacent to Master Control)

Operational Objectives

- Provide adequate training to facility staff
- Promote staff development by providing access to training opportunities and materials
- Provide staff with physical fitness opportunities through fitness equipment and training
- Provide a specific area for the dissemination of information to staff
- Provide an area for staff to change into/out of uniform at shift changes

Operational Procedures

- When officers report for duty, they will access the staff development services area from a staff entrance adjacent to the main public lobby. Access is generally monitored and controlled with the use of proximity access cards.
- Staff will check in with use of time clock provided adjacent to entrance and assembly room.

Figure 3.16 **Staff services physical training room with natural light.**

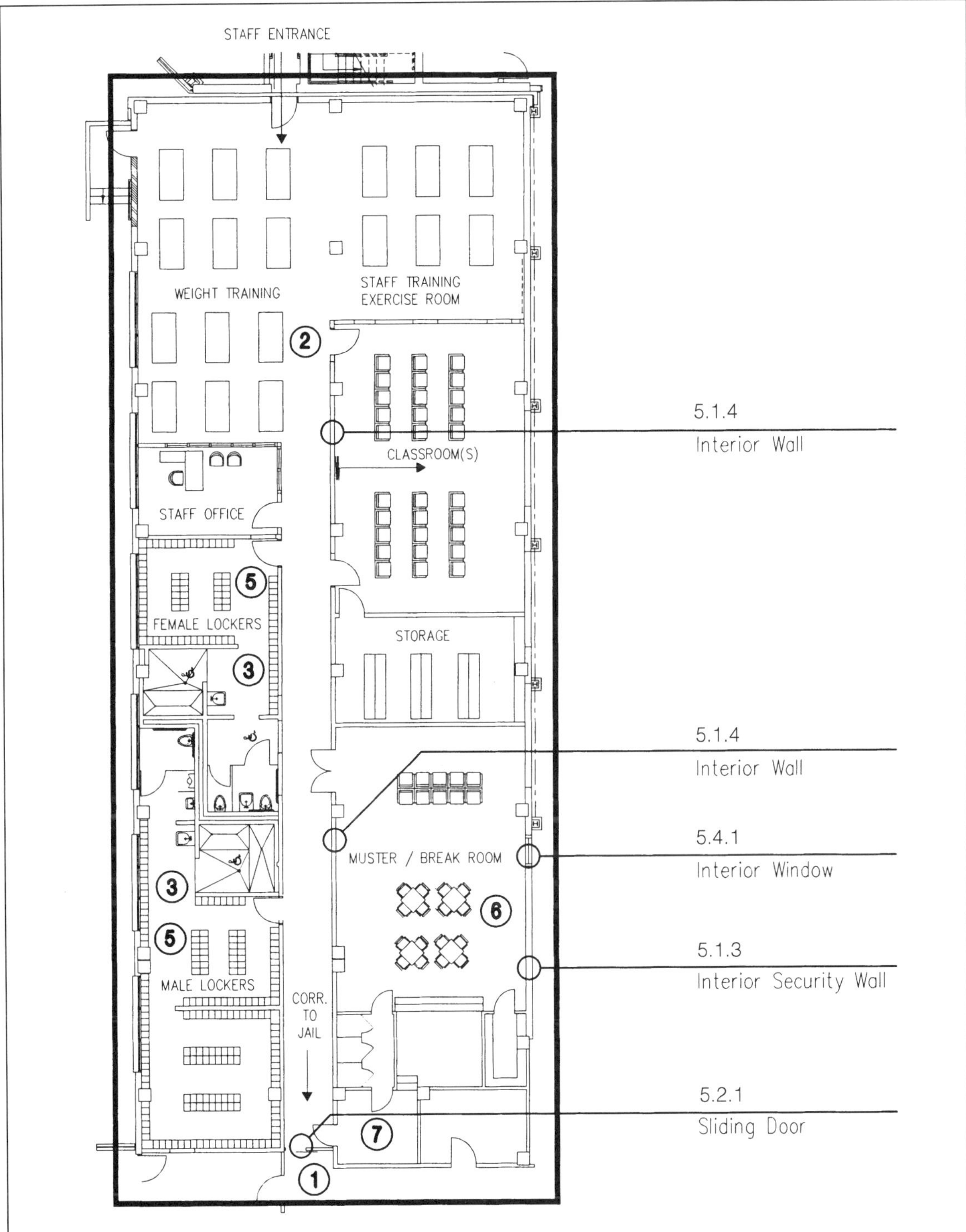

Figure 3.17 **Staff development services for a small facility.**

- Staff is usually provided with the option of wearing their uniforms to work or changing at the facility; in either case, staff lockers are needed in order to store personal property while on duty.
- Prior to taking their assignments, staff will attend a briefing in a training/briefing room to review operational information obtained from the last shift such as critical incidents, maintenance, and/or other problems that may have occurred.
- The shift supervisor will assign post positions to the staff.
- Keys will be picked up at central control.

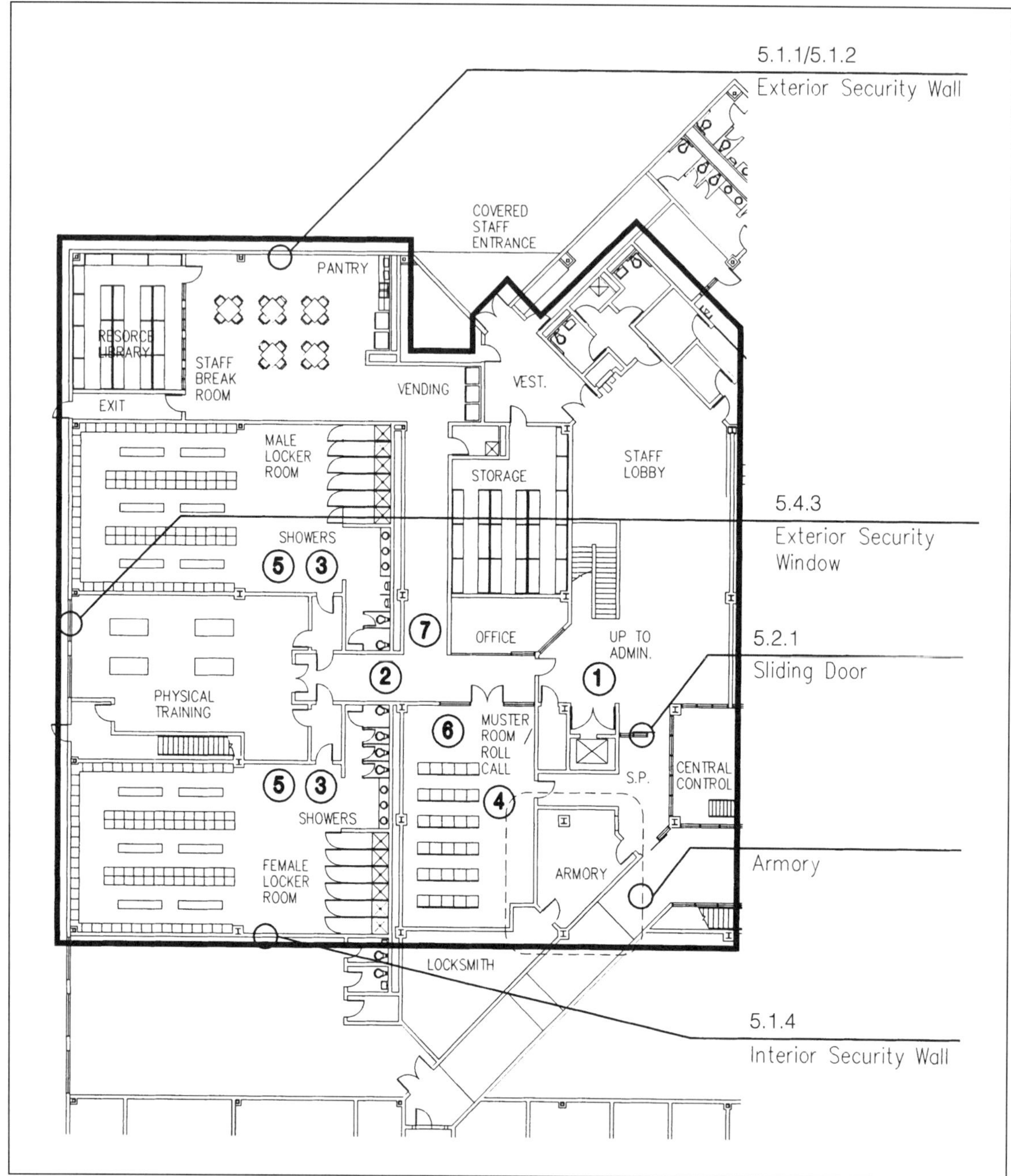

Figure 3.18 **Staff development services for a large facility.**

- After staff shift-change assignments, they will report to their assigned posts.
- Facility administrative philosophy, service, facility tours, medical procedures, personnel procedures (including rules, regulations, pay, and benefits), disciplinary hearing process, classification, educational services, substance abuse treatment programming, and physical plant operations will be given to new staff.
- Continual staff training will teach and promote professionalism to meet the goals of the facility.
- All incoming and outgoing mail is processed in the employee service area within a designated room. It is logged, opened, and inspected (except for legal mail to inmates), sorted for distribution by cart to destinations within the facility. Outgoing mail is weighed, stamped, and sent out on a daily basis, Monday through Friday.
- For Corrections Emergency Response Teams (CERT), separate locker areas are typically provided to store specialized gear and equipment; these are often located adjacent to the staff

assembly room for convenience in mustering CERT operations.

Staffing Implications

The number of shifts of operations: Three
The number of days per week: Seven

The number of offices and personnel are determined by the program and size of the facility. In-service training and continuing education activities are typically scheduled in advance during regular weekday hours. Staff lockers need to be available 24 hours per day, with the staff assembly area sized to accommodate the largest daily shift. In small facilities, the training officer may be a part-time assignment.

Design Considerations

1. Locate directly off the staff/official visitors' lobby and adjacent to the sally port which leads to the secure side of the facility.
2. Locate rooms within this component centrally. With the exception of the senior custody officers, spaces can be provided without exterior windows, since limited time is spent there.
3. Locate male and female locker/shower/restrooms on either side of the physical exercise room to provide direct access into this activity room without exposure to other persons and/or activities.
4. Locate this area adjacent to an armory (and close to Master Control room) to provide direct and controlled access to weapons for emergency response.
5. Utilize the locker room for suiting up into riot gear.
6. Utilize the assembly room (muster room) for instructions prior to the issue of weapons.
7. Provide a central location, near central control, for officers to check in, pick up mail and notices, and get keys required for their shift assignments.

7.0 INTAKE/TRANSFER/RELEASE

Program Statement

All inmates entering a detention or correctional facility must be legally admitted to the system by proper identification and physical condition, to protect the institution and inmates alike. This area involves the orderly receiving, identification, screening, and processing of all new inmates entering the facility. In detention facilities, inmates are often processed at a local police station, where an assessment can be made of their condition and for potential classification of risk. At other times, inmates are brought directly to the detention facility without prior screening. In correctional facilities, inmates are sentenced to serve time and therefore a prior history is recorded. In general, first admissions are screened for medical condition, identification records taken or updated (photography and fingerprints), and property/clothing exchanged (see Figs. 3.19 through 3.21).

The arrival point must be secure. A vehicular sally port with a drive-through opportunity is most preferred, because it eliminates a cumbersome drive-in/back-out situation. A drive-through design often creates an opportunity for other secured vehicles to be located in close proximity to operations staff.

A series of holding cells, group and individual, are generally provided. In most current direct supervision operations, open seating areas are also provided for those inmates known to behave in a general population environment. If a facility intends to operate in a direct supervision mode, the philosophy usually begins at intake.

The transfer and release area is used for processing inmates that are going to court, being transferred to another facility, and those being released from the facility. This area is located adjacent to, but separate from, the intake area. This adjacency can improve operations by sharing staff at scheduled times and the utilization of control stations and authorized transportation vehicle areas. Depending on the nature of the transfer or release, clothing exchange from jail uniform to street clothes may occur, and personal property may require reinventory.

Prototypical Spaces

7.1 Vehicular sally port
7.2 Pedestrian sally port
7.3 Intake officer's write-up area
7.4 Intake officer's toilet
7.5 Inmate search room/sobriety testing (detention)
7.6 Inmate toilet
7.7 Individual holding cells
7.8 Group holding cells
7.9 Open seating area
7.10 Shower/clothing exchange rooms
7.11 Property/clothing/linen/officer workstation
7.12 Attorney noncontact visitation room(s)—interactive TV
7.13 Medical screening/multipurpose room
7.14 Intake processing desk/area
7.15 Fingerprint/photograph area
7.16 Copier/workstation(s) area (adjacent to processing desk)

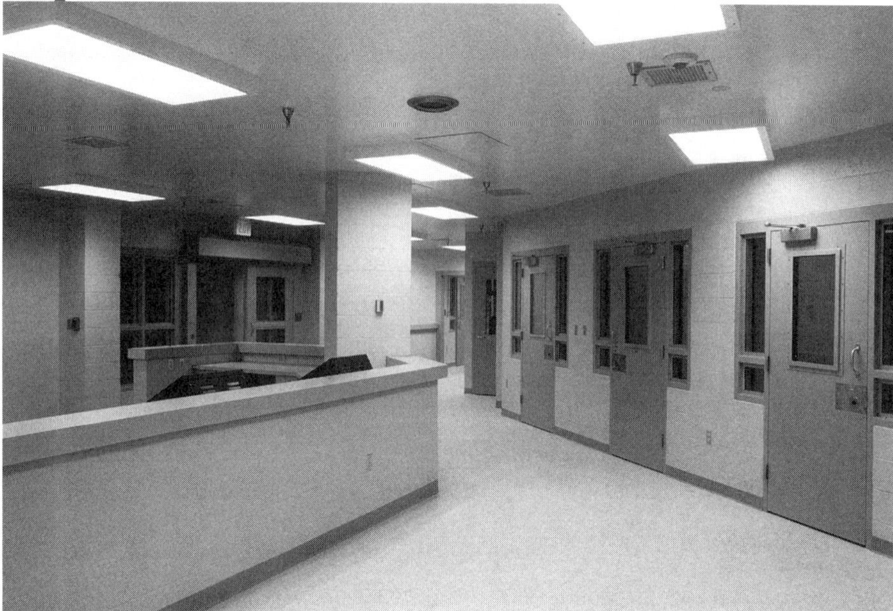

Figure 3.19 **Intake processing desk with observation of entrance sally port and holding cells.**

7.17 Staff toilet
7.18 Janitor's closet
7.19 Secure/nonsecure property storage
7.20 Clothing storage room—laundry area
7.21 Transfer officer processing area
7.22 Officer toilet
7.23 Group holding cells
7.24 Individual holding cells (detox for jails)
7.25 Open seating area
7.26 Inmate toilet(s)
7.27 Clothing exchange rooms
7.28 Search room(s)
7.29 Transportation office
7.30 Release officer processing area
7.31 Open seating area
7.32 Inmate toilet(s)
7.33 Clothing exchange rooms

Operational Objectives

- Accept custody of newly admitted inmates and ensure that they are properly and legally received into and eventually discharged from the facility
- Thoroughly search all new inmates and inventory their property
- Fingerprint and photograph all new inmates
- Store all permitted inmate property and properly dispose of property not permitted for storage
- Provide inmate orientation for their understanding of facility's rules and regulations
- Provide inmates with institutional clothing, bedding, linens, and personal hygiene items
- Prepare and store inmate records and legal documents associated with their incarceration

Operational Procedures

- The transportation vehicle will approach the sally port gate.
- The intake/release officer in control room will identify vehicle visually and audibly using an intercom, and once it is cleared, open the sally port gate.
- The vehicle enters the sally port and parks vehicle as directed.
- The transportation officer will secure his or her weapon in a gun locker before removing prisoner(s) from the vehicle.
- The processing officer will review and verify the commitment paperwork and will accept or reject the prisoner based upon medical fitness.
- An officer will search every inmate prior to processing them and place them in either an open waiting area or confinement cell, depending on their behavior.
- Each prisoner's personal property will be taken and inventoried and a receipt prepared.
- Identification officer will photograph and fingerprint each prisoner.
- Inmate records are accessed or created, including a computer file and a hard copy.
- Detention prisoners being held on bondable charges will be provided access to telephones to arrange for their release.

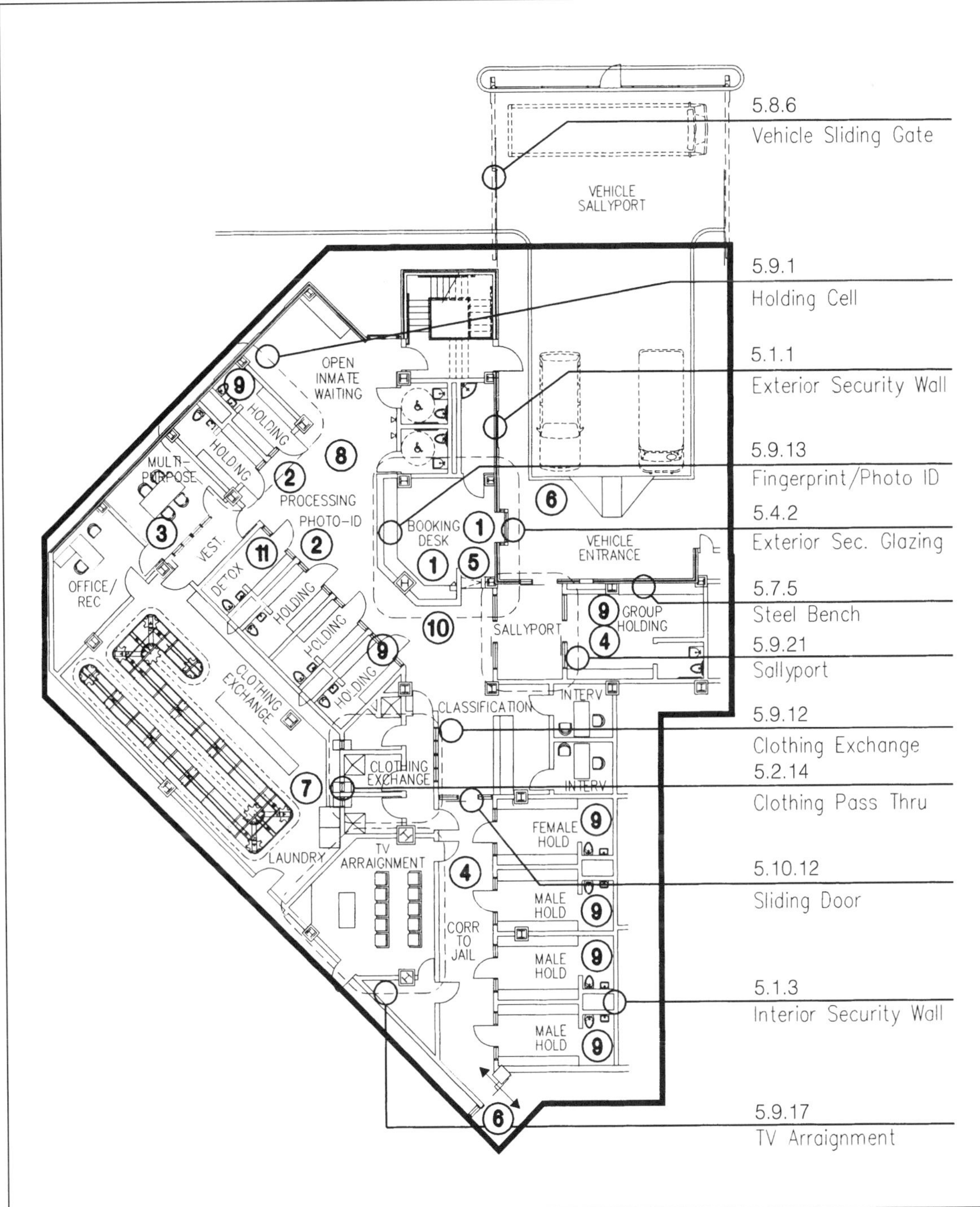

Figure 3.20 **Intake/transfer/release area for a small facility.**

- Prisoners receive an initial medical screening.
- Prisoners are escorted to shower/clothing exchange booths to receive facility clothing.
- Upon completion of processing, inmates will generally be escorted to a specific housing unit or be unescorted if observation and control along the route is physically maintained. Specific housing units are generally provided for classification and/or orientation. Those exhibiting combative or violent behavior will be housed in special management units.
- In jail facilities, within the first 72 hours of confinement, newly admitted inmates will receive an orientation and interview by a classification officer.

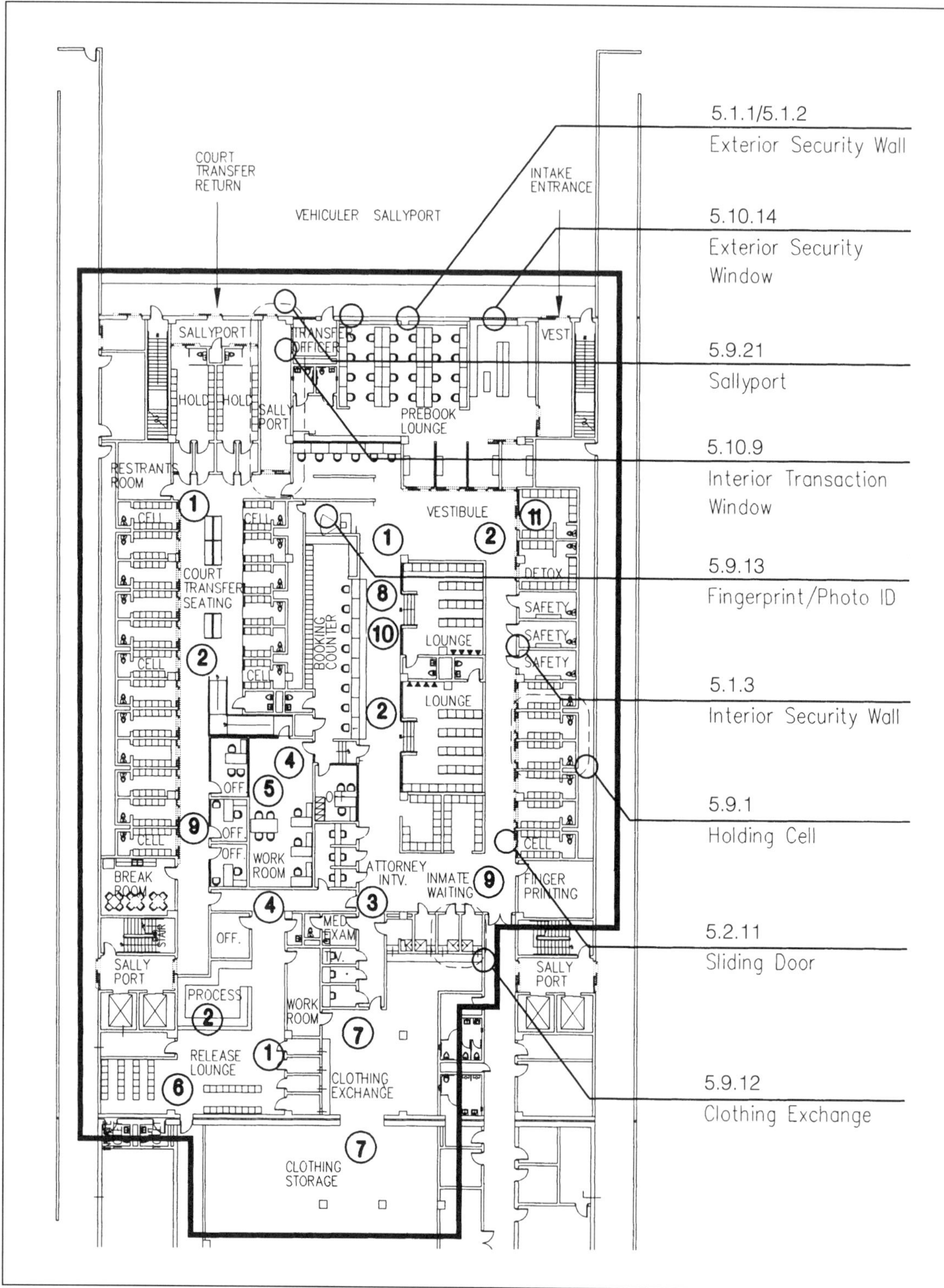

Figure 3.21 **Intake/transfer/release area for a large facility.**

- Following classification, inmates are transferred to a cell in general population or to a special management housing unit, as required.

Staffing Implications

The number of shifts of operations: Three
The number of days per week: Seven

The number of offices and personnel are determined by the requirements of the approved facility program. Capacity staffing requirements for this area are generally determined by the average high number of intake/release movements that need to be done at a given day or time. Jail intake areas typically operate 24 hours a day; prison intake areas more often operate on a scheduled daytime schedule.

Design Considerations

1. Provide the three area (intake, transfer, and release) layouts with the most optimum observation from officers' desks/stations of all inmate occupied spaces, including open seating area, holding cells, shower/clothing exchange room, and the entrance of pedestrian and vehicular sally ports.
2. Provide cell location with excellent visibility by officers, yet at the same time limit views by other inmates in open waiting and the processing areas.
3. Provide at intake (admissions), with the concern with the increase of AIDS and TB, medical screening rooms with equipment for full examinations, including x-ray capability.
4. Provide an interrelationship of intake and court/facility exchange areas that are critical and require careful separation of incoming and outgoing activities, while at the same time adjacency and flexibility to use either department for the two different functions.
5. Facilitate the sharing of custody officers, considering the scheduled nature of transfer/exchange areas; therefore, plan adjacency is essential.
6. Separate the release area, but locate adjacent to intake and transfer areas for the reasons just stated.
7. Centralize all property and clothing rooms for direct access to intake, transfer, and release functions.
8. Establish reasonable distances between seating areas, holding cells, and processing functions to enhance operations in this very busy area.
9. A range of isolation, individual, small group, large group, and open holding areas should be provided to reflect the differentiation in incoming/outgoing inmate characteristics.
10. While security is a primary consideration, contemporary jails typically strive to have this area as normative and nonthreatening as possible (e.g., open booking counter).
11. Detox cells should be provided for jails, with the capability of being hosed down for cleaning.

8.0 CLASSIFICATION (JAILS)

Program Statement

In detention facilities, this area is critical to the operations of a facility. Initial screening and interviewing generally determines an inmate's classification. Any special management issue will be taken into consideration at the initial classification process, which include inmates with known enemies, protective custody needs, psychological impairment, mental deficiency, escape risk potential, threat of serious violent behavior, known gang affiliation, substance abuse problems, known management problems, suicide risk, medical problems, and physical impairment. Classification process generally takes place initially at admissions and continues at a classification housing unit.

A small, similar activity takes place at prison facilities in terms of determining inmate housing groups and program assignments.

Prototypical Spaces

8.1 Classification officer
8.2 Assistant classification officer
8.3 Clerical/records
8.4 Program committee/conference
8.5 Interview room(s)
8.6 Staff toilet

Operational Objectives

- Classify inmates entering the facility by using an objective classification system to determine the level of custody required, an appropriate housing assignment, and eligibility for participation in inmate programs
- Provide for the separate management of male and female inmates, inmates with special problems, inmates requiring disciplinary segregation, inmates requiring administrative segregation, and juveniles
- Assign inmates to housing in one of the facility's housing pods based upon their custody level, special management needs, and institutional behavior

- Provide a thorough orientation for every inmate during their first few days in the facility concerning behavioral expectations, inmate rules, daily schedule, and available programs and services
- Provide consistent, periodic reviews and documentation of each inmate's needs, institutional behavior, and performance

Operational Procedures

- After the admissions (intake) process has been completed, inmates will typically be moved to a general population housing unit, generally designated for newly admitted inmates.
- For a period up to an average of 72 hours, inmates will be classified using an initial custody assessment scale.
- Based upon the cumulative scores of the custody assessment scale interview, inmates will be classified and assigned to a housing unit.
- Classification staff will attempt information verification during the interview process and prior to an inmate assignment to a specific housing unit.
- Reclassification will also occur on an as-needed basis consistent with state standards and facility policies and procedures.
- Reassessments may also be warranted by disciplinary actions or when an inmate's custody status changes as a result of additional charges or the disposition of charges. Inmates may appeal classification decisions and may request a reclassification review, within certain facility

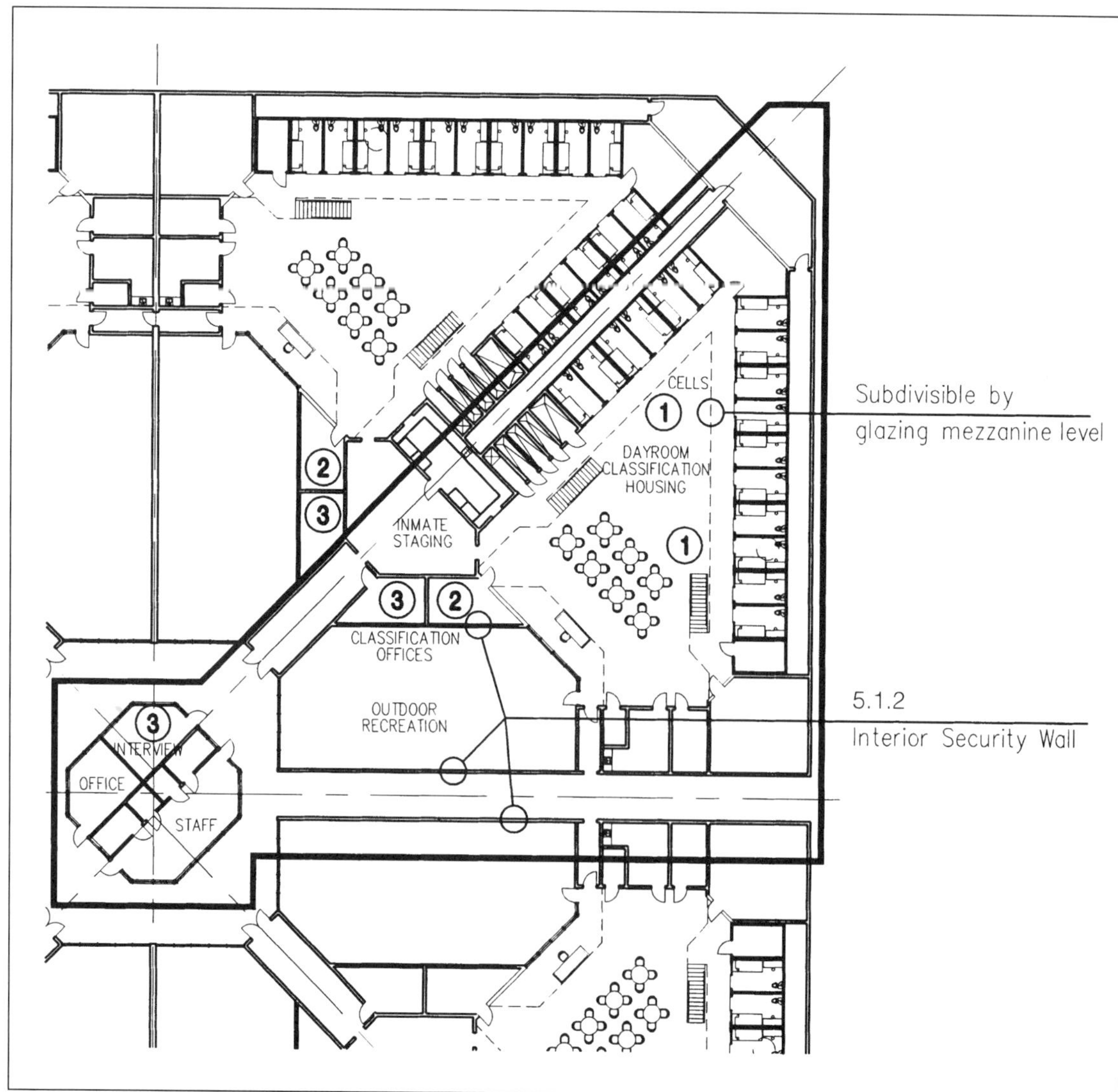

Figure 3.22 **Classification/Unit management classification and housing unit for a large facility.**

guidelines and with approval from the classification supervisor. This officer is also responsible for inmate assignment to programs.

Staffing Implications

The number of shifts of operations: One
The number of days per week: Five

The number of offices and personnel are determined by the size of the facility and requirements of the approved facility program. The classification/program assignment unit typically operates on regular business weekday hours.

Design Considerations

1. Provide flexibility in the design to accommodate large groups of inmates, with divisibility into smaller groups, with visual control from an officer station.
2. Provide multipurpose rooms within the unit for flexibility in offering a wide range of evaluation and programs.
3. Provide private, one-on-one counseling rooms out of sight and sound of general population.
4. If inmates do not come to this area for interviews, an open landscape office layout may be used.
5. A location near inmate records is beneficial.

9.0 COMMUNICATIONS

Program Statement

This component is often located within or adjacent to the Master Control center but can also be separated within its own area and component. These systems are provided to assure the necessary communications throughout the entire institution in order to maintain an orderly operation. Systems that are currently available must be flexible, serviceable, upgradable, expandable, and designed to maintain the security and privacy requirements of an institution. They must operate under the most intensive of emergency situations and therefore require 100 percent backup electric power. All workstations should be provided with, or provide for, future computer linkage to a mainframe computer system. A communication system should be capable of paging to the general population and to individual staff on a personal emergency basis. For additional information, reference Chap. 7: Security Electronics and Communications Systems (see Fig. 3.23).

Prototypical Spaces

9.1 Main distribution frame (MDF)
9.2 Intermediate distribution frame (IDF, distributed throughout the institution as required)
9.3 Main computer room
9.4 Recording equipment room
9.5 Security/safety equipment room
9.6 Communications equipment room

Operational Objectives

- To provide secure operational equipment space for the installation and maintenance of essential security, safety, and communications equipment.

Operational Procedures

- When equipment needs routine maintenance or upgrading/repair, appropriate service personnel are given access from a secure location to perform their work without getting in the middle of normal ongoing activities in a control room or other sensitive locations.

Staffing Implications

The number of shifts of operations: None
The number of days per week: None

This area provides equipment space only.

Design Considerations

1. Locate these functions adjacent to central control and on the free side of the facility.
2. Locate the IDF (intermediate distribution frame) functions at or adjacent to housing units and other program building locations.
3. Provide access to these rooms from areas where there are no inmates activities.
4. Maintaining security is an essential consideration. Communication/equipment space should be of maximum security construction, with access visually and physically controlled from a secure location.
5. Having major elements of the security, safety, and communications equipment in a separate space allows the control room design to be focused on sight lines and internal functional needs rather than accommodating equipment. Likewise, the equipment room can be designed to accommodate necessary equipment in terms of ease of access and expansion.
6. For high-security facilities, where extensive videotaping of inmate movement is done, the equipment and tape storage areas may require a significant amount of space.
7. A radio transmission tower may be required as part of the communications design.

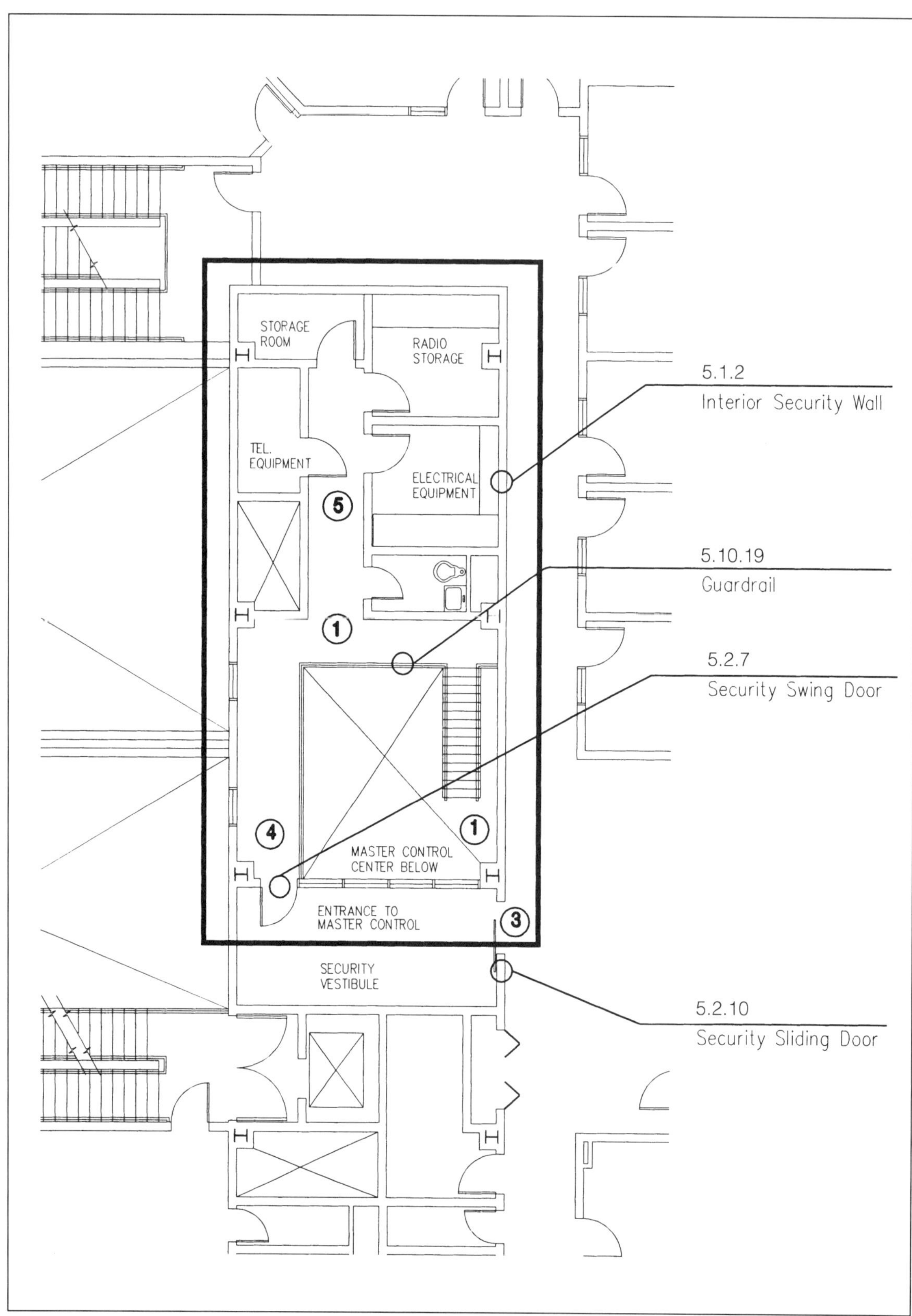

Figure 3.23 **Communications area for a large facility.**

Figure 3.24 **Master Control room with observation, supervision, and control of staff lobby on the left side and the public lobby on the right.**

10.0 MASTER (CENTRAL) CONTROL CENTER

Program Statement

The Master Control center (MCC), also referred to as *central control,* is the lifeline and nerve center of the institution. It is responsible for a successful and trouble-free operation. It oversees and monitors all facility operations and communications, including life-safety emergency equipment, procedures, and exiting. It electronically controls and monitors all movement in and out of the facility. Philosophy differs on where to locate the Master Control room. Many administrators prefer the location to be central, as one of its titles suggests, in order to see and be seen by the public, staff, and inmates alike. Others have required the location to be more remote, out of the way of traffic and hidden from public view. The latter stems from the desire to keep the control staff focused on their assignments and activities without outside distractions.

Regardless of client preference, its location should be between the nonsecure and secure areas of the institution. It's ability to visually observe critical sally port entrances is most important, although this task can also be accomplished and supported by CCTV surveillance. Since paper and other items may have to be passed between central control and individuals seeking entry into the secure part of the facility, it is desirable that it be adjacent to the main sally port entry.

During emergency situations, Master Control can often be assigned to release all cell and door locking devices and completely shut down all control panels throughout the facility (see Figs. 3.24 through 3.26).

Prototypical Spaces

10.1 Master Control center/radio distribution/ storage room
10.2 Toilet (within Master Control room preferred)
10.3 Sally port entrance into MCC
10.4 Armory (weapons storage and weapons pass)
10.5 Locksmith/key maintenance and storage room (located outside of secure perimeter)
10.6 General storage room

Operational Objectives

- Provide 24-hour control of all external security systems, including all entrances and exits

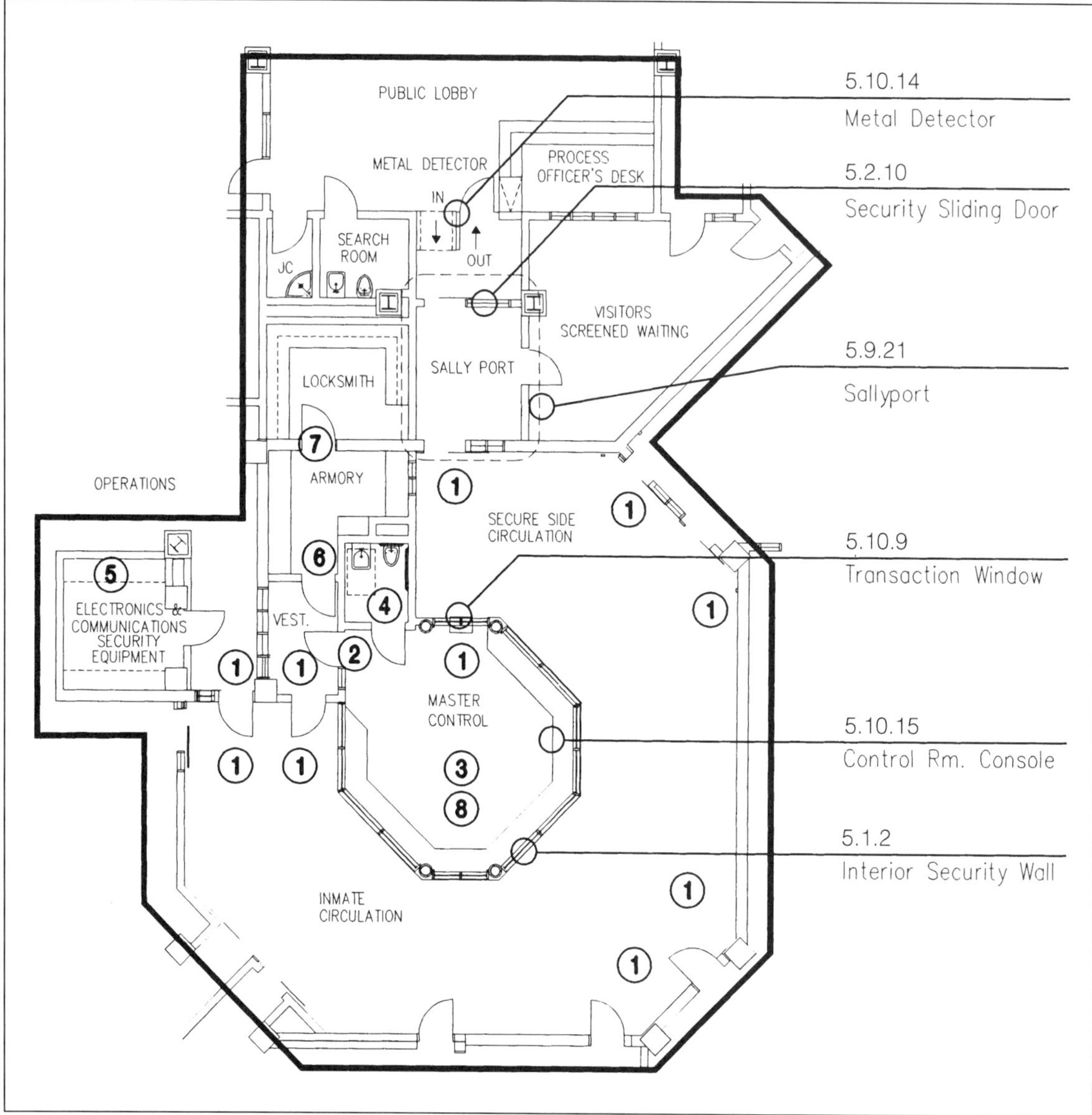

Figure 3.25 **Master Control area for a small facility.**

- Provide 24-hour control of all internal security systems, controlling movement from one area to another. Monitor all security alarm and CCTV systems
- Provide 24-hour coordination and communication of all emergency responses to events and situations in the facility
- Provide 24-hour control of all life-safety monitor and control panels
- Maintain accountability for all security keys used for access to restricted areas of the facility and maintain key control procedures

Operational Procedures

- Staff in the central control room are typically locked in for the duration of their shift, with entrance only through sally port controlled from the inside.
- Staff not assigned to central control are not permitted inside.
- For each 8-hour shift, day after day, the central control room provides supervision of all facility control, safety, and communications—coordinating staff activities within, maintaining counts, and monitoring/controlling access through security perimeters.

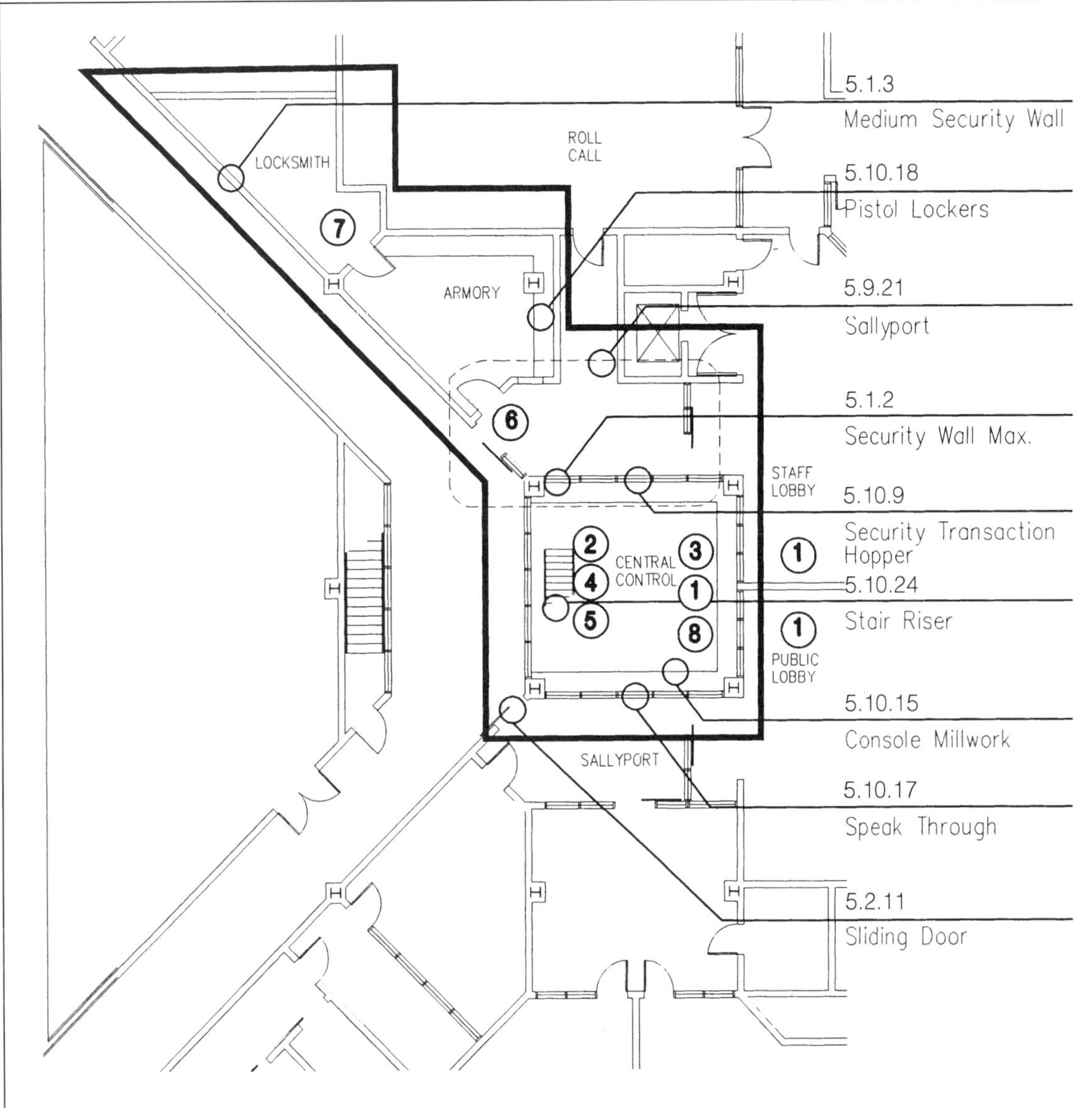

Figure 3.26 **Master Control area for a large facility.**

- CCTV systems may be utilized to supplement monitoring capability.
- Key control/operation is essential. The locksmith requires a secure workspace in or adjacent to this area with adequate storage. Central control is often responsible for handing out keys to officers and collecting them at the end of each shift.
- When weapons need to be issued to staff, that activity is controlled from this area.
- If other control rooms are provided in the facility (e.g., housing area), they should be able to be overridden from central control.

Staffing Implications

The number of shifts of operations: Three

The number of days per week: Seven

This area is staffed 24 hours a day with the number of staff for specific shifts determined by size and complexity of facility and operational policy.

Design Considerations

1. Position the control station for optimum observation to all adjacent areas. Discussion with the project team requires in-depth review of location's most important and prioritized functions.

Figure 3.27 **Unit control observation, supervision, and control of inmate corridor movement.**

2. Provide easy and direct access to an escape route from the area and secure side of the institution in cases of emergencies.
3. Elevate floor position of control room to provide unobstructed views of all physical areas for observation, supervision, and control. This can be accomplished by elevating it slightly higher than the first-floor grade (approximately 3 ft 0 in) or by positioning it at the second floor for observation of all activities below.
4. Provide access to toilet from within the control room, with visual privacy while maintaining audio monitoring of alarms and other systems.
5. Provide access to security electronics equipment from within, above, below, or adjacent to the control room.
6. Provide control of access to armory from within or adjacent to the control room.
7. Provide control of access to the locksmith area from within or adjacent to the control room.
8. Provide raised computer floor for access to all security control conduit and equipment connections.

11.0 CUSTODY OPERATIONS (COMMAND CENTER)

Program Statement

This component is responsible for the total security operations of the institution. The commanding officers, including the assistant warden of operations, heads this department and is responsible for all staff assignments and monitoring of activities. The chief of security and shift supervisors will supervise the daily security operations of the facility. The department is located on the secure side of the perimeter to continually maintain communication between housing units, programs, and other services, while assuring timely responses to all security situations (see Figs. 3.27 through 3.29).

Prototypical Spaces

11.1 Assistant warden of operations
11.2 Secretary/AWO
11.3 Case management supervisor (often located adjacent to records)
11.4 Chief of security office
11.5 Shift supervisors' office
11.6 Cell hall directors' office (unit management)

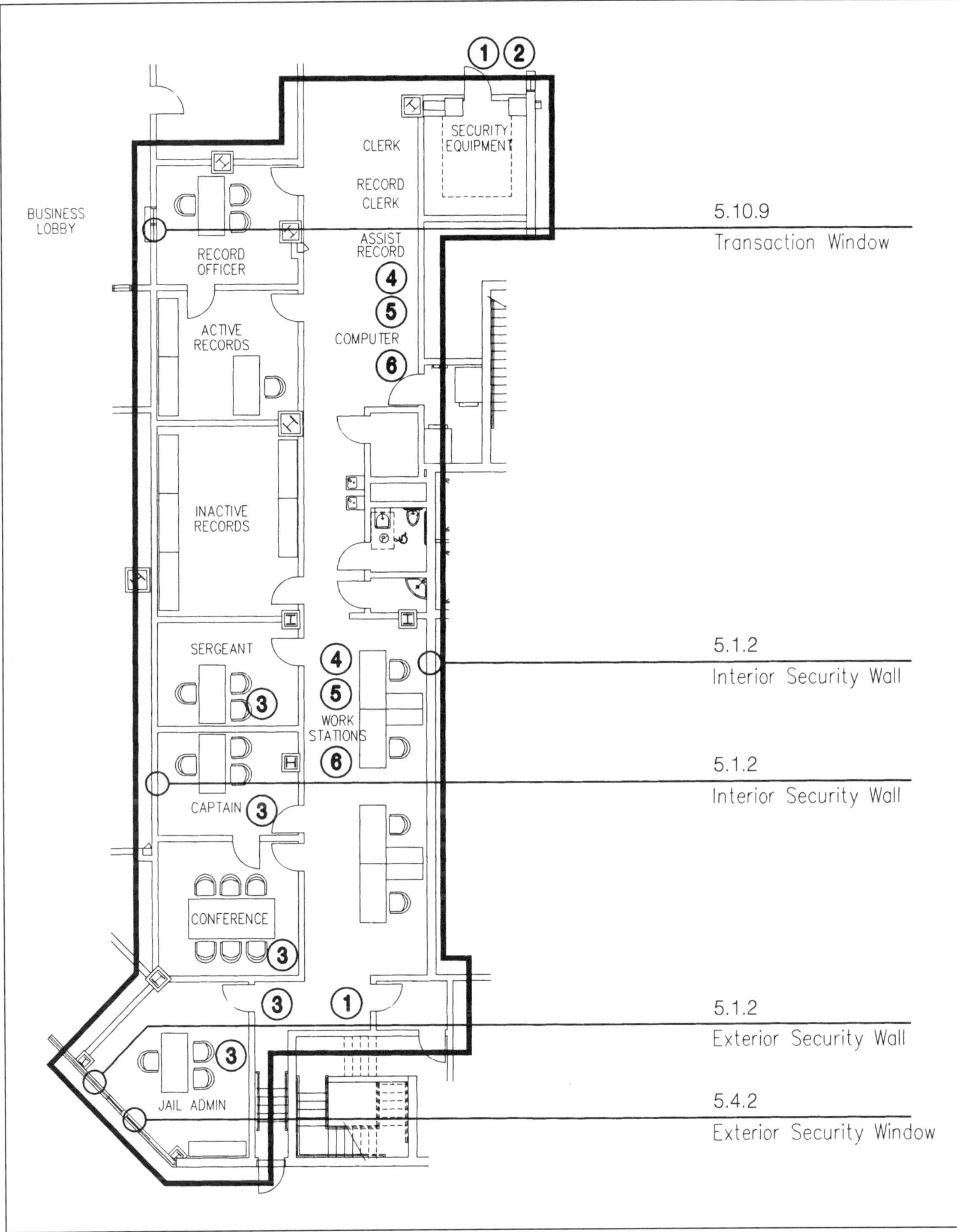

Figure 3.28 **Operations area for a small facility.**

11.7 Scheduling/coordinating officer office
11.8 Count and movement officer's office
11.9 Security squad room/general and secured storage
11.10 Secured evidence storage/lockers
11.11 Reception area/waiting
11.12 Coat closet
11.13 Clerk's workstation
11.14 Supplies/copier/coffee station room (area)
11.15 Conference room
11.16 Staff toilets
11.17 Janitor's closet

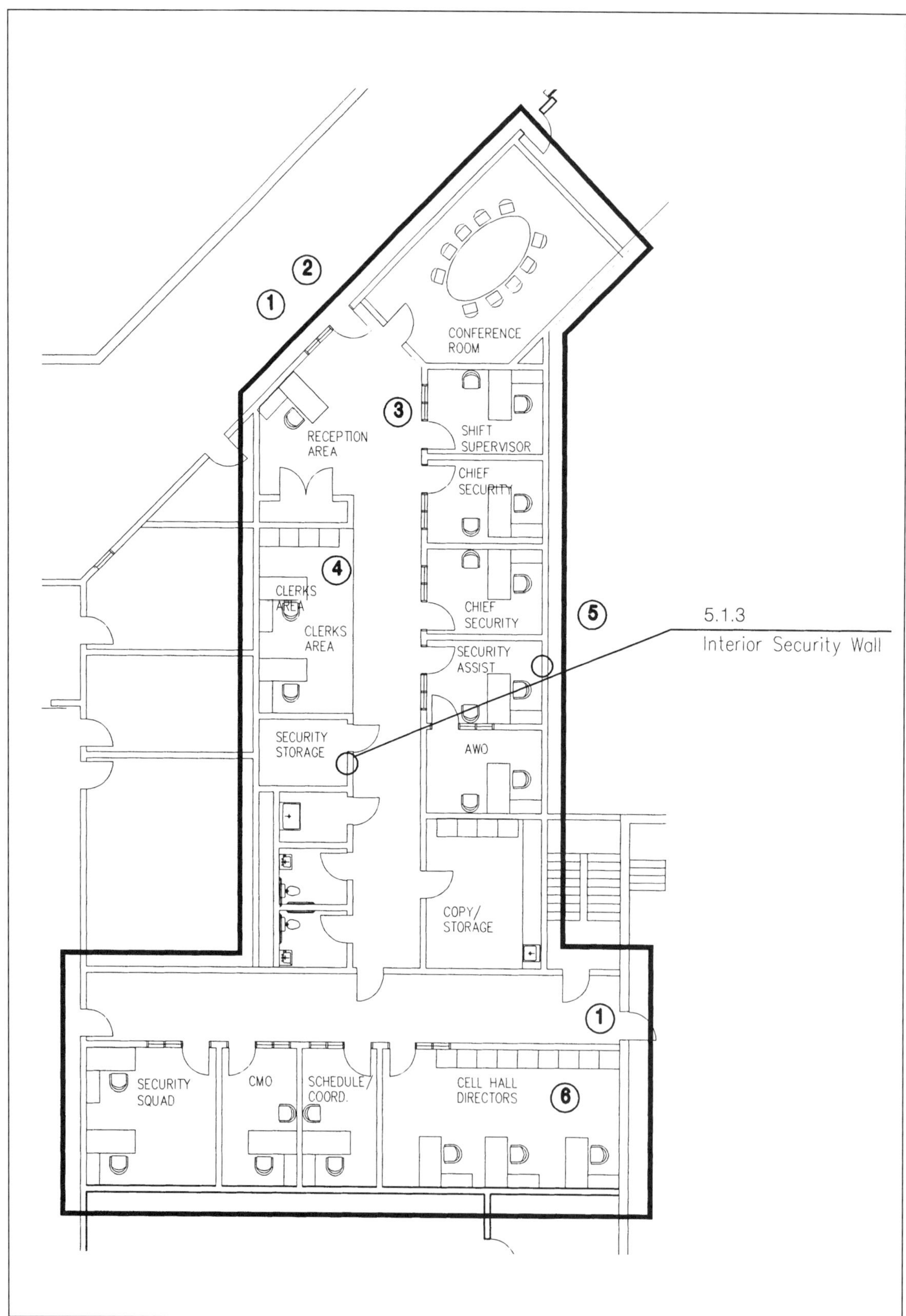

Figure 3.29 **Operations area for a large facility.**

Operational Objectives

- Ensure compliance with the facility's established policies and procedure for all line staff
- Provide line staff with assistance and guidance in the completion of their assigned duties
- Conduct routine safety and security inspections to ensure a high level of safety and security
- Take control of all critical situations and incidents that are exceeded by line staff authority and/or experience
- Monitor and improve employee behavior to create a high level of staff professionalism
- Provide opportunity for staff improvement and development with training facilities
- Conduct emergency operations drills to ensure prompt and appropriate response to all emergency situations

Operational Procedures

- Shift supervisor will gather information prior to shift change and make shift assignment in preparation for shift change briefings. A record of proceedings will be kept on file in this department.
- Shift supervisors should spend as much time as possible within the facility monitoring operations and addressing potential problem issues and areas where situations may arise.
- They should spend as much time as possible with unit managers at housing units and with pod (living unit) officers.
- Supervisors will routinely spend time monitoring safety, security, and sanitary conditions of the facility.
- Written reports will also be kept in the custody operations department. Corrective action for issues identified will be coordinated and kept on record in this department.
- Operations is responsible for the distribution of fully charged radios and maintaining of battery charges which may be issued to incoming officers from this area or from central control. Records of distribution will also be kept in this department.

Staffing Implications

The number of shifts of operations: Three
The number of days per week: Seven

This area is staffed 24 hours a day with the number of staff for each shift determined by size and complexity of facility and by operational policy. Typically, shift supervisors will be staffed 24 hours a day; other security supervisors may work regular weekdays/evenings to provide staggered coverage.

Design Considerations

1. Locate this position to optimize observation of, with quick responses to, critical areas, such as visitation, inmate housing, programs, and service areas.
2. Locate in close proximity to intake/transfer/release areas on a line between nonsecure and security perimeter. It is desirable, but not often easily achieved.
3. Provide privacy for senior officers and conference areas.
4. Create open office space for flexible work areas and provide observation of activities by senior custody staff.
5. Providing internalized space without natural light is acceptable, since officers are encouraged to move about and interact with unit managers and pod officers.
6. Work area design is often related to several functions; providing five small desks within a single office space for the individuals who will at various times be the shift supervisors saves space.

12.0 GENERAL INMATE HOUSING

Program Statement

The housing area for the inmate population is the heart of every institution since it provides the living area for inmates for the majority of a typical day. Numbers also typically represents 50 percent or more of the total area required for a facility. Thus, this area deserves considerable time and attention to assure proper design (see Figs. 3.30 through 3.35).

In the early days of new generation facility planning and design, housing units provided normative living environments. Smaller numbers of inmates were grouped together in contrast to the traditional linear housing unit designs of the previous 100 years. Initially, groups of 32 cells per housing unit were commonly grouped together, with implied, internal subdivisions into even smaller groups of four, eight, and sixteen. They were arranged around a dayroom area, in forming a shape referred to as a pod. Rectangular, square, and triangular shapes in plans often produced the most efficient uses of space and permitted observation from an officer's control room or desk position of all activity spaces. When direct supervision

Figure 3.30 **Dayroom upper-cell-level balcony looking toward dining platform with outdoor recreation area in rear.**

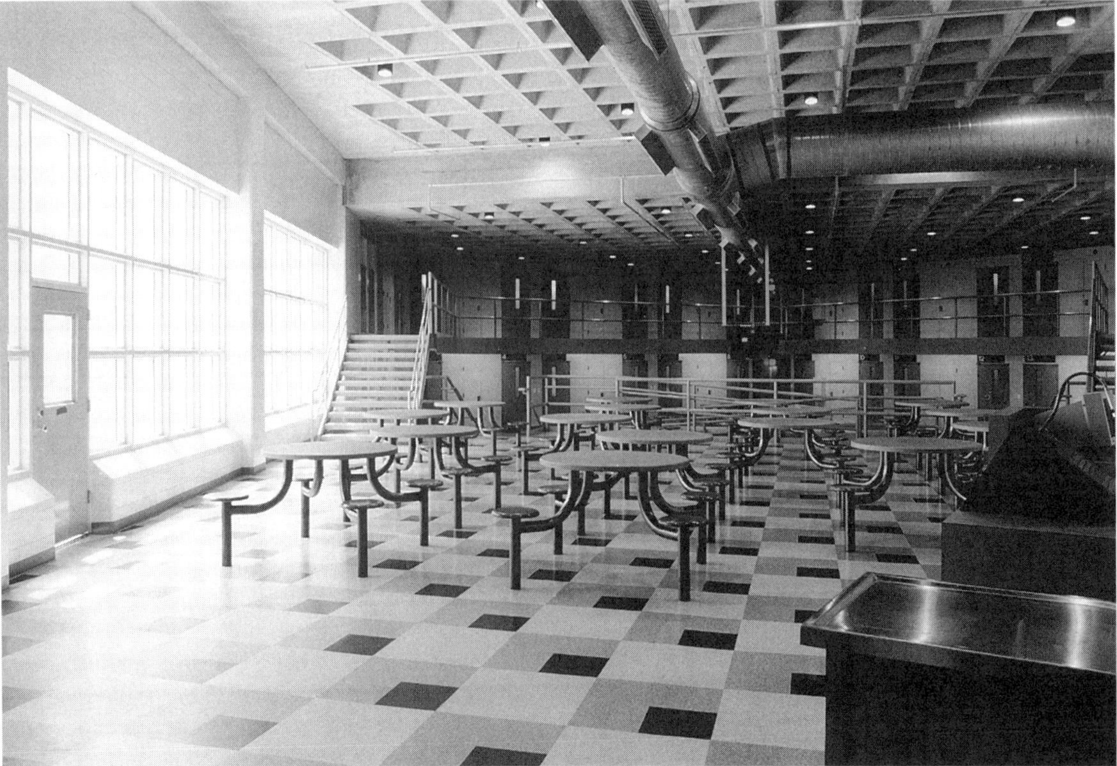

Figure 3.31 **Housing unit dayroom with dining tables, the officer's desk up front, and an adjacent outdoor recreation glass wall.**

became the preferred choice of many administrators, shapes and sizes of housing units changed. Currently client requirements for maintaining a cost-effective relationship between the numbers of officer's needed to supervise, control, and provide inmates services has resulted in varying unit sizes from 48 to 128 cells (beds). For the purposes of this section of the text, a housing unit of 56 cells has been selected to provide design continuity with the facility design section that follows.

Individual cells should be secure and private. However, national trends toward double bunking and, in some jurisdictions, providing four-bed cells creates a unique design challenge in grouping cells and dayrooms together without compromising observation or producing excessive square foot area. The cells should be relatively soundproof and include a toilet and lavatory with hot and cold running water. There should be provisions for personal property storage, and all furnishings should be designed to prevent materials used in construction to be made into weapons. Cells should be climate controlled and made of indestructible materials which are fireproof. Many administrators request that cells be equipped for two-way communications, cable TV, and radios. Each cell should allow for staff observation through a secured glazed window or an opening in each inmate door. While doors are generally electronically and remotely controlled from an officer's station, during daytime hours, some administrators will request the option of inmate's own access in and out of their cells to maintain personal privacy and safety. Each cell should be provided with direct or indirect natural light, with size of window generally directed by local codes and the American Correctional Association (ACA) Standards. These standards are accepted by most administrators as their compliance guide in determining sizes and amount of cells, dayroom area, showers, outdoor exercise area size, and the like.

Multipurpose/interview rooms are generally provided in a housing unit for individual and group activities and should be equipped for multimedia functions having the capacity for central monitoring. Reading areas should be quiet in nature for reading and study purposes. Other areas are provided for TV viewing and require careful attention to sound transmission. Inmate telephones are also often provided.

Dining is generally provided in the dayroom as a preference by many clients for jail facilities and in some prison facilities, too. Prisons generally gather inmates from several housing units to eat their meals in larger dining rooms, adjacent to a central kitchen. When dining occurs in the dayroom, it is often preferred to design the tables for use for passive recreation activities, such as reading and table games as well. Recognize the impact of hygiene requirements for dining in dayrooms.

Access to adjacent outdoor exercise areas is often requested to provide one of the most important activities in reducing tension. This space should be observed and accessed from the dayroom. Initially designed for jails, it currently has become requested by prison facility administrators as well. The principal benefit is to permit outdoor recreation without the necessity of movement off the housing unit to do so.

Prototypical Spaces

12.1	Entry vestibule (sally port)
12.2	Officer's control station
12.3	Individual cells with toilet, lavatory, beds, desk, and stool (single or double occupancy)
12.3*a*	Cells with toilet, lavatory, beds, desks, and stools (three- or four-inmate occupancy)
12.3*b*	Sleeping areas with beds, desks, and storage (for multiple-inmate occupancy, 48–75)
12.4	Individual showers
12.4*a*	Group shower areas, adjacent to grouped toilets and lavatories for multiple-occupancy dorms for minimum security
12.5	Dayroom
12.6	Beverage area
12.7	Inmate telephones
12.8	Laundry facilities (or located in unit management area)
12.9	General storage
12.10	Interview/meeting room (or located in unit management area)
12.11	Janitor's closet(s)
12.12	Trash room (recycling area)
12.13	Medical exam/screening room
12.14	Multipurpose/program space
12.15	Outdoor recreation
12.16	Staff toilet
12.17	Inmate toilet(s) (optional)

Operational Objectives

- Provide a safe and secure environment for inmates confined to housing units.
- Provide manageably sized groups of inmates in each housing unit.
- Provide separation of inmate types by classification determined at admissions.

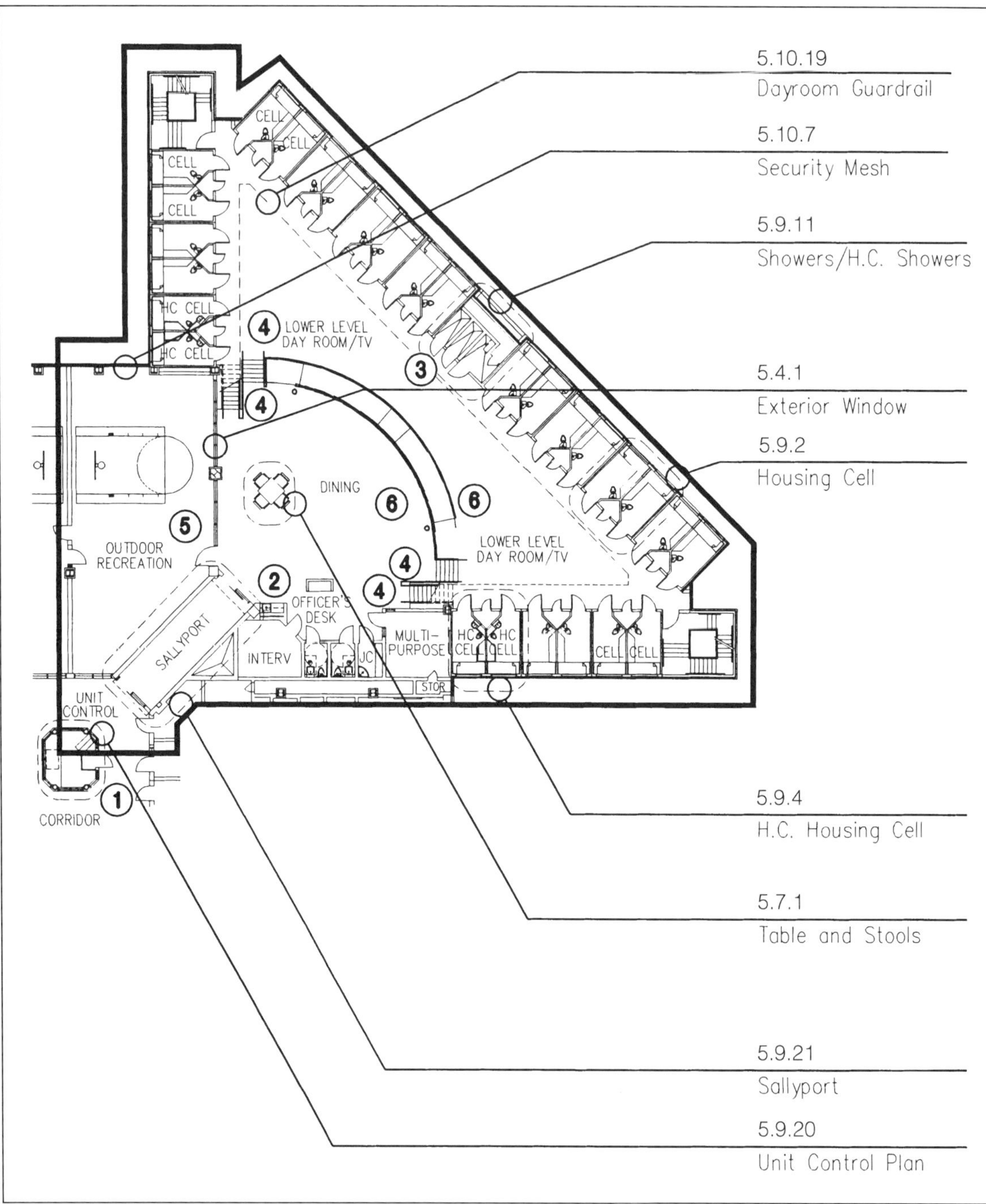

Figure 3.32 **General inmate housing area with split-level dayroom/dining area.**

- Provide programs and services to inmates within their housing unit and/or adjacent to it to limit movement (jail orientation and in some prisons where inmate classification levels require limited movement) and to be able to maintain essential services where some portion of the facility must be locked down.
- Provide appropriate number and quality of staff to efficiently operate each housing unit.
- Provide housing unit design that meets all applicable local and state standards and Life Safety Code requirements.
- Provide housing unit design that meets the national ACA Standards.
- Provide staff and inmates with an environment that is free of physical and psychological danger.

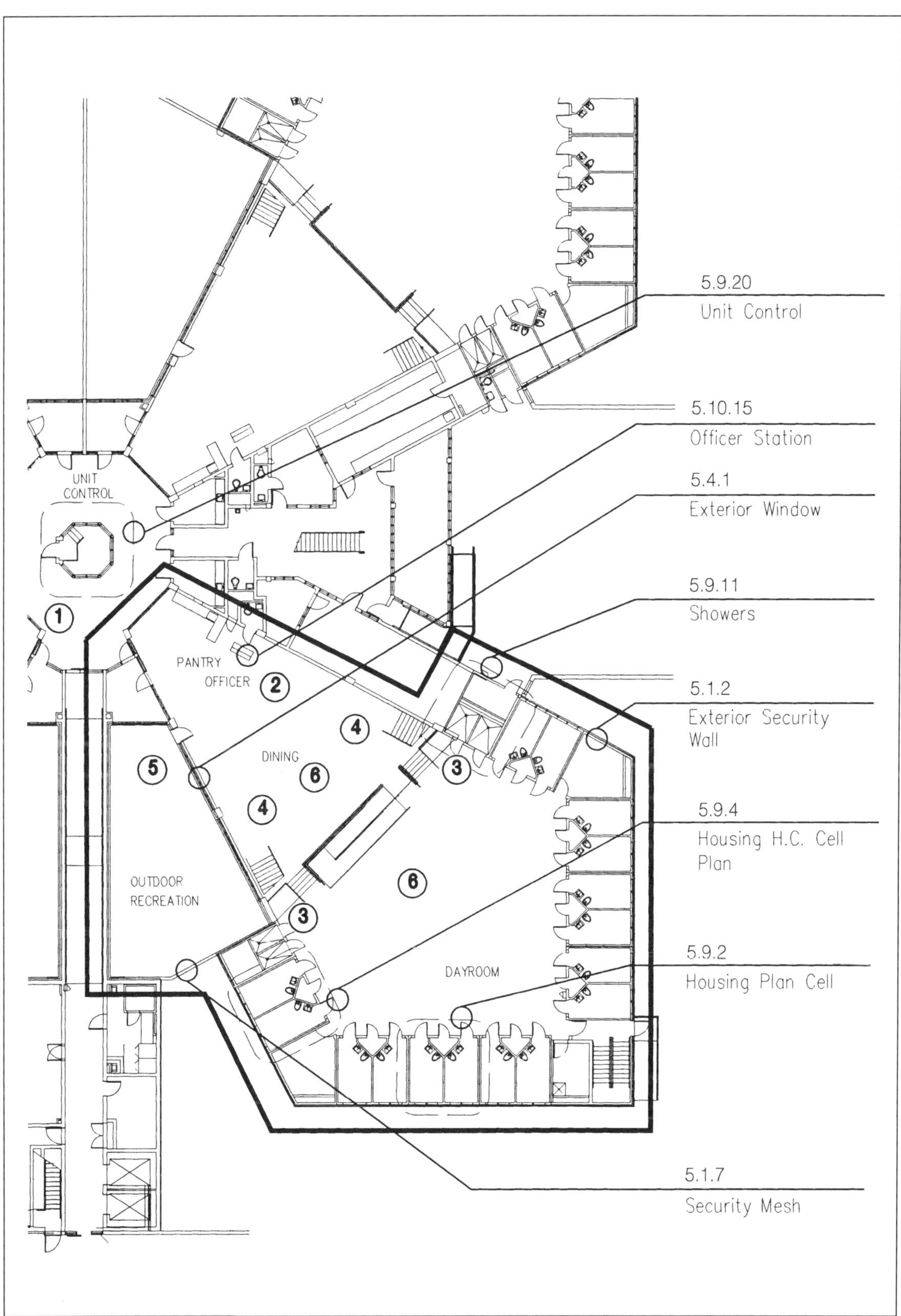

Figure 3.33 **General inmate housing for a large facility.**

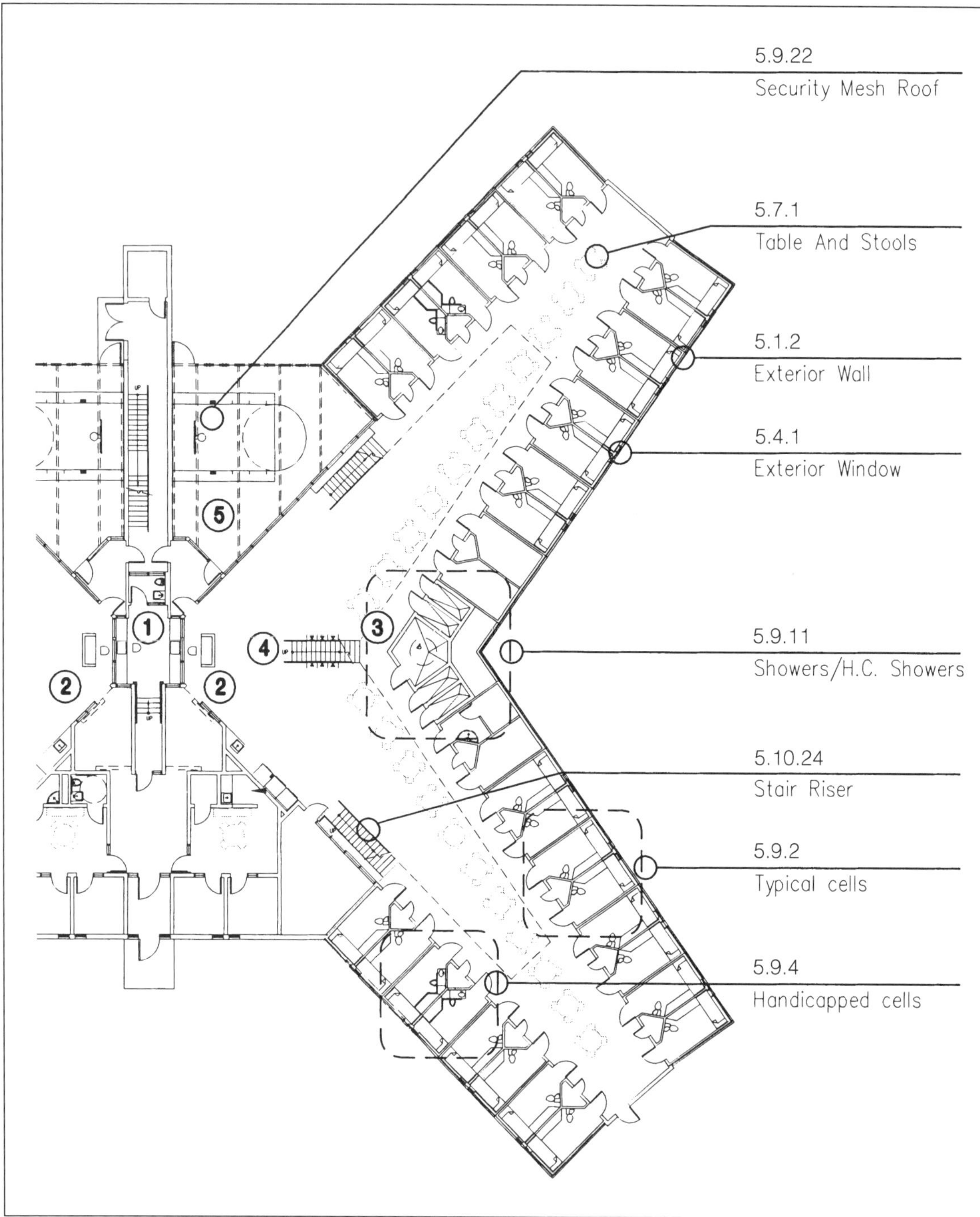

Figure 3.34 **General inmate housing for a large facility.**

- Provide housing unit environments within the overall facility capacity with different privilege opportunities to encourage a positive attitude and behavior and to discourage unacceptable or disruptive behavior.
- Within each housing unit, each cell or dormitory cubicle should be identical to minimize favoritism.

Operational Procedures

- In grouping individual housing units, with supervision by unit management operations staff, a unit management control station will monitor and control all doors into and out of housing units and adjacent related functions, such as triage, counseling, and so forth.

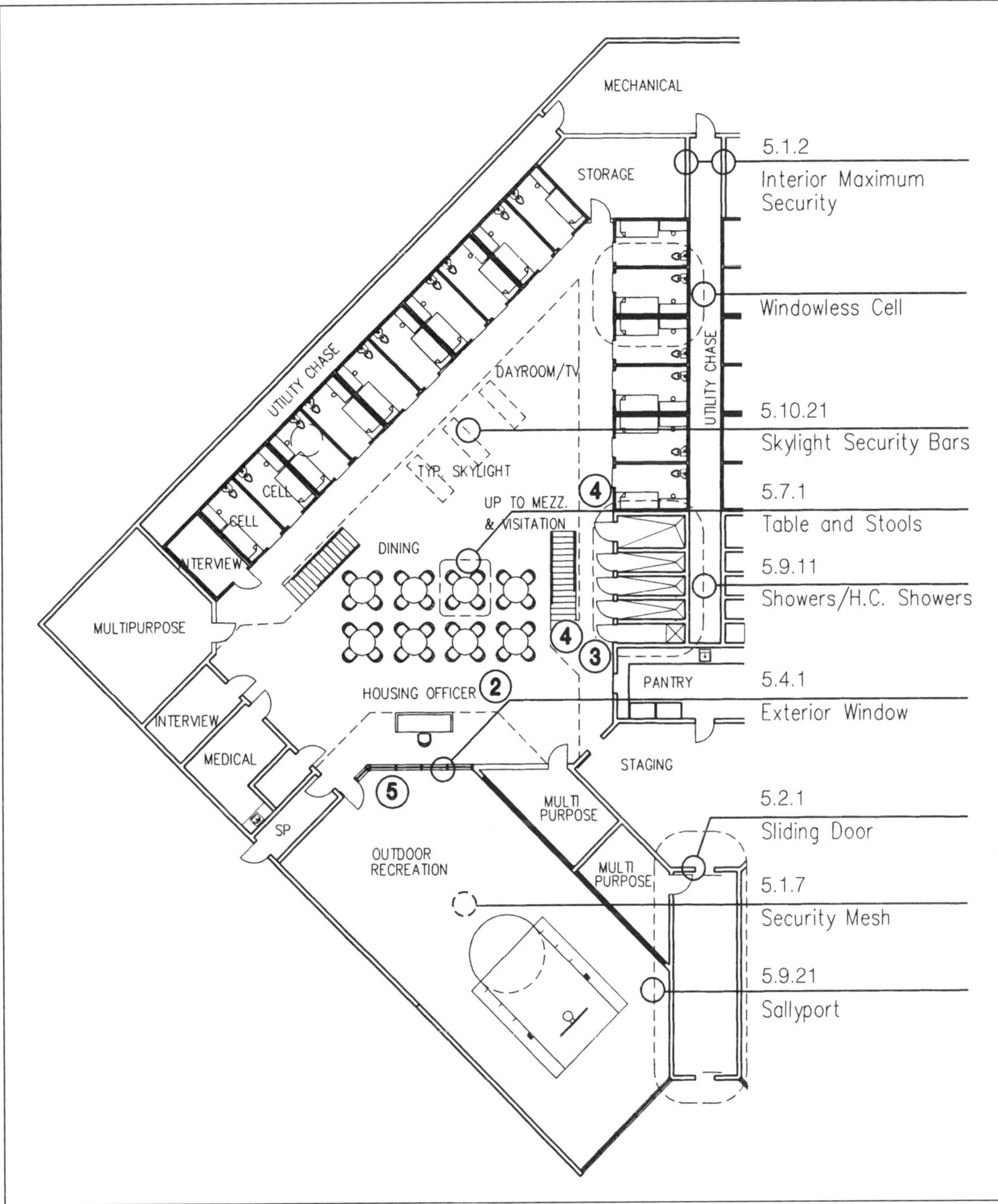

Figure 3.35 **General inmate housing with flat-floor dayroom, a dining area, and 32 windowless cells (double-bunked).**

- The outer door of the sally port leading into housing will be controlled by unit control or central control, but the inner door of this same sally port will be controlled by the housing unit officer. Typically, housing units must be staffed whenever there are inmates in the unit.
- Access in and out the housing unit is through a sally port which is used as an area for staging inmates arriving and leaving the housing unit.
- In summary, all activities within a housing unit are the responsibility of the housing officer; those outside of the unit are under control of the unit management control staff.

Staffing Implications

The number of shifts of operations: Three, Two if backup rover is legally approved

The number of days per week: Seven

This area is active 24 hours a day. The number of staff and operational procedures are determined by size of facility and client operational objectives. The number of housing control officers is determined by the number of housing units in a facility; four are used as example for small institutions (200+), and 20 may be used for large institutions (1000+). Reduced pod officer staff is indicated for jurisdictions that permit morning shift sharing. This area is the largest user of custody staff and all reduction opportunities should be explored with governing authorities and code enforcers to provide a safe, secure facility, but with a reduced staff.

Design Considerations

1. Position housing unit control officer's station to optimize observation of all entrance doors, outdoor exercise areas, and in some situations, to observe the entire interior of housing pods.
2. Position housing officer's desk/station to observe all internal wall surfaces enclosing and defining the dayroom, including cell fronts, showers, outdoor recreation's glazed wall, support space entrances, and sally port.
3. Group showers together, at lower- and upper-cell levels and in close proximity to the housing officer station for ease of visual supervision.
4. Observe through stairs accessing the mezzanine levels and down to lower levels without obscuring views from any position within the dayroom; utilize open risers with mesh for code compliance requirements.
5. Provide housing officer's observation of outdoor recreation area as a primary focus and responsibility and within a clear range of visual supervision.
6. Provide, whenever possible, designs with split-level environments, whereby the bottom cell floor is lowered by two to three feet from the entrance level where food service, interview rooms, access to outdoor recreation, and the like are located. Three basic advantages for this design provide improved observation, spacial-diversity, and reduced volume as the following describes:
   - ***Improved observation*** of the upper-cell level (mezzanine), reducing its height from the main entrance level from nine feet to approximately six to seven feet.
   - ***Spacial diversity*** is offered in separating the lower-level dayroom from the entrance level, creating an opportunity for special architectural treatment of activities, such as TV viewing with carpeted floors versus dining areas with tile or hardened concrete floors.
   - ***Reduced volume*** produces an interior character of residential living, rather than institutional, whereby inmate behavior may be improved and provide an environment for counselors to help change inmate behavior in preparation for their return to society.

However, some administrators prefer a flat floor plus mezzanine floor design to eliminate dropped floor for straight sight-line observation and quicker staff response.

13.0 SPECIAL INMATE HOUSING

Program Statement

In many institutions, the general population is represented by approximately 90 percent of the total population. The other 10 percent, on average, has special needs. The typical categories of special needs range from protective custody to punitive segregation. The number and size of these units differ per jurisdiction; generally speaking, a typical housing unit design is often used with subdivisions provided to accommodate most conditions and inmate types. On the other hand, there are many administrators who prefer a specially designed unit. Since a significant number of administrators prefer the flexibility of using a typical housing unit design for the general population and for special housing conditions, the prototypical space listing is similar to those listed in the general housing individual cell condition (see Figs. 3.36 through 3.38).

Prototypical Spaces

13.1 Safety vestibule (sally port)
13.2 Officer's control station
13.3 Individual cells
13.4 Showers
13.5 Dayroom
13.6 Beverage area
13.7 Inmate telephones
13.8 Laundry facilities
13.9 General storage
13.10 Interview/meeting room(s)
13.11 Janitor's closet(s)
13.12 Staff toilet
13.13 Trash room (recycling area)
13.14 Inmate toilet(s) (optional)

Figure 3.36 **Segregation housing with glazed enclosure for stairs/balcony level for divisions into smaller cell groups.**

Operational Objectives

- Provide a safe and secure environment for inmates confined to special housing units
- Provide manageably sized groups of inmates in each housing unit
- Provide separation of inmate types by classification, determined at admissions into small groups for improved flexibility of containment and movement
- Provide limited, if any, programs and services to inmates within their housing unit and/or adjacent to it to restrict and limit movement
- Provide appropriate number and quality of staff to efficiently operate each housing unit
- Provide housing unit design that meets all applicable local and state standards and Life Safety Code requirements
- Provide housing unit design that meets the national ACA Standards for special housing
- Provide staff and inmates with an environment that is free of physical and psychological danger
- Provide housing units with a less normative environment and without privilege opportunity to encourage movement toward a change in attitude and behavior

Operational Procedures

- Typically, inmates are brought to special housing as a result of participating in an incident or otherwise violating a major facility rule.
- Typically, they will be held in administrative detention, awaiting due process hearings.
- When their cases have been determined, they may be assigned to punitive segregation for a specific time.
- Inmates in segregation status are typically locked in their cells 23 hours per day, with an hour per day out of cell for recreation.
- Special housing for protective custody or other program (rather than behavior) reasons operate under the same procedures as general housing units with the exception of reduced/no exposure to the rest of the general inmate population.

Staffing Implications

The number of shifts of operations: Three

The number of days per week: Seven

This area is active 24 hours a day. The number of staff and operational procedures are determined by the size of facility and client operational objec-

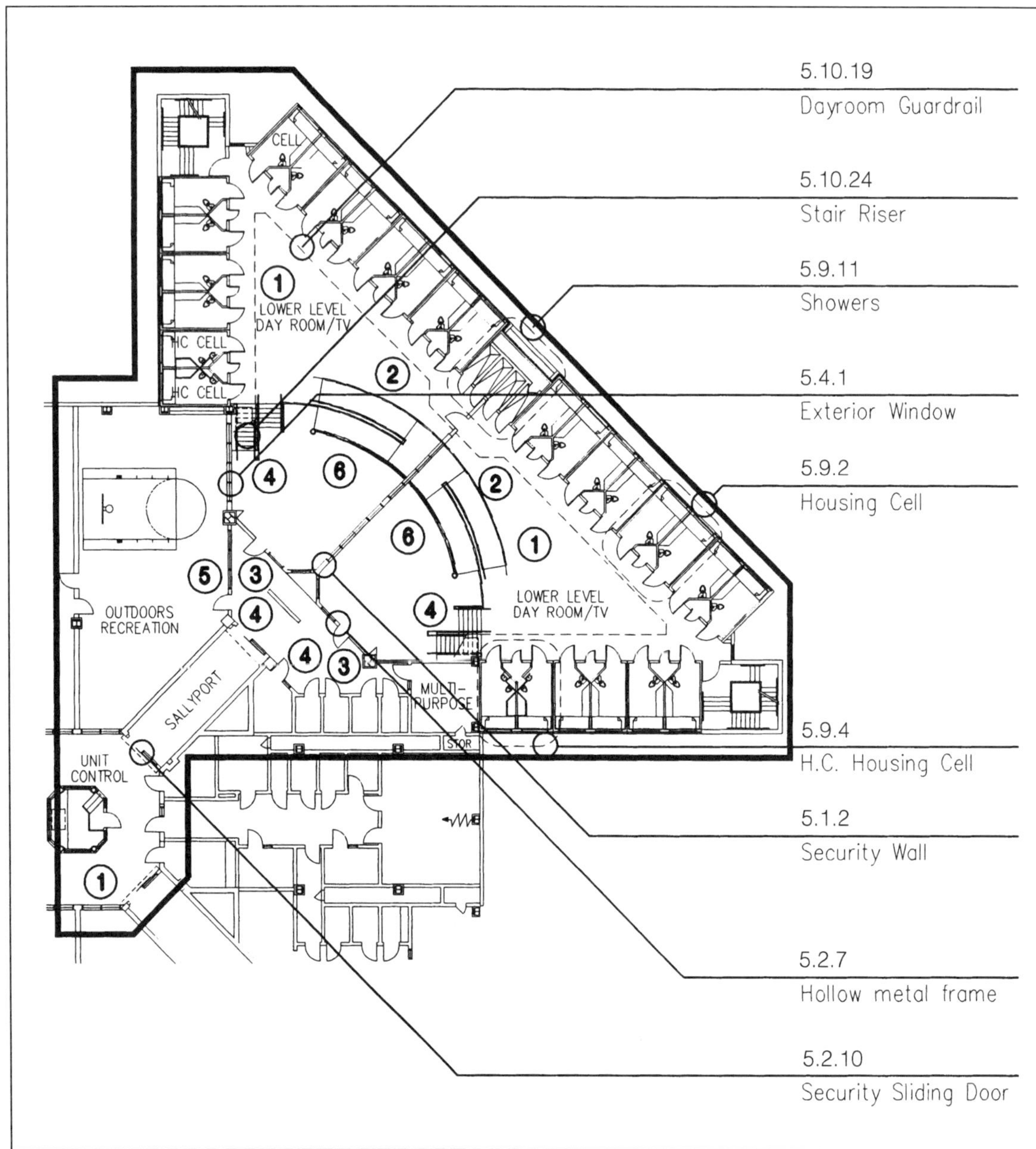

Figure 3.37 **Special inmate housing units with split-level dayroom/dining area with horizontal separation by walls.**

tives. The number of pod control officers is determined by the number of housing units in a facility. While most general housing units operate very well under direct supervision, special housing units often use indirect or floor officers with indirect backup, since inmates in special housing may represent definite behavior/security risks.

Design Considerations

1. Consider the use of a general population housing unit design for use in special management conditions. Test the design to determine if it yields the following: (1) easy subdivision into units of 8, 16, and 32; (2) observation from the officer's control station which is not compromised and which can view all cell fronts, dayroom spaces, and access to all functions; and (3) whether the security risk posed by inmates can be accommodated without use of a harder housing unit design.
2. Provide separate shower facilities for individual showering.
3. Provide inmate access to individual housing units without compromising security by passing through or by another inmate unit/cell area.

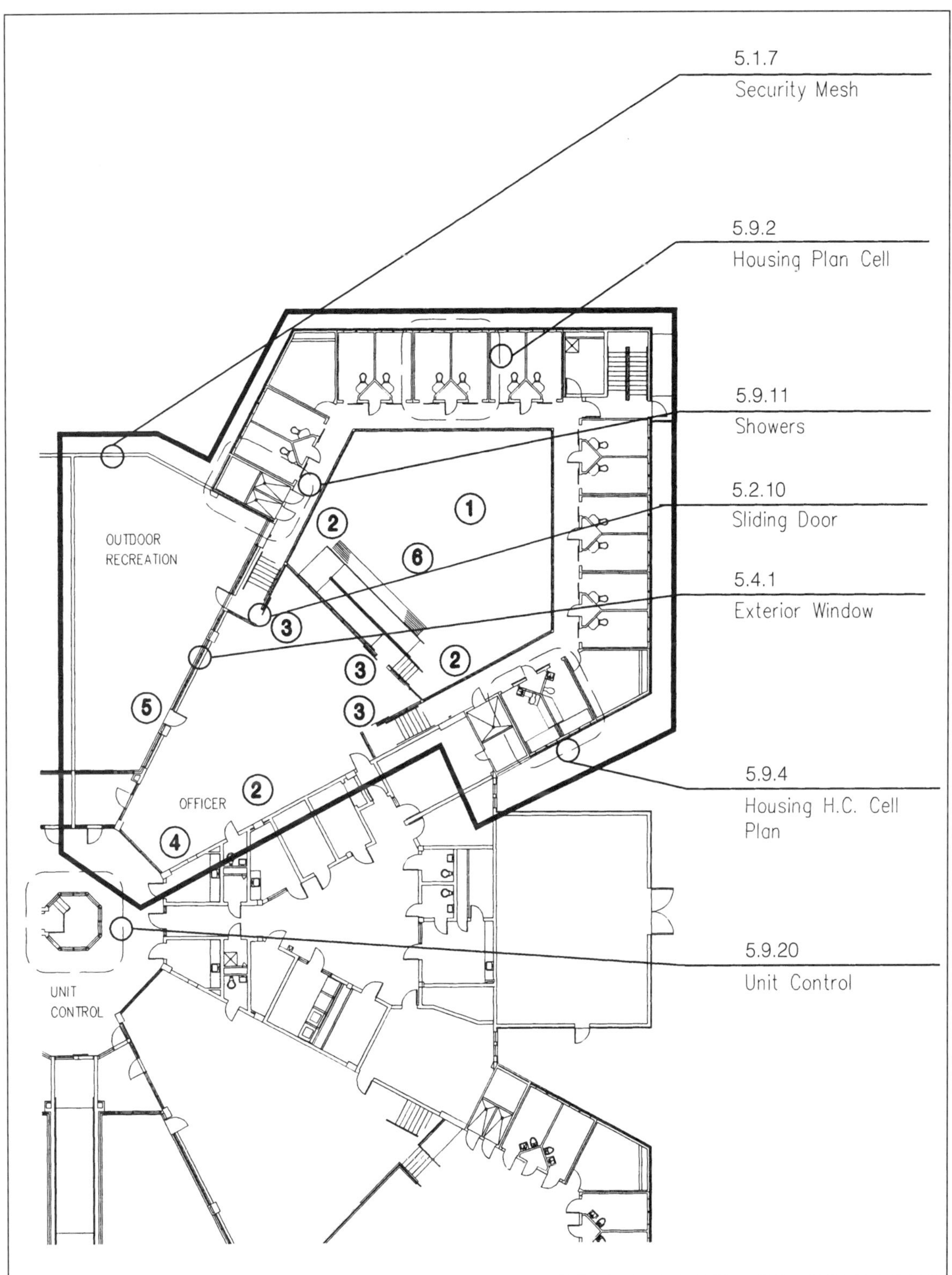

Figure 3.38 **Special inmate housing units for a large facility with vertical separation by balcony glazing.**

Figure 3.39 **Unit control station with observation of housing unit entrances.**

4. Provide food delivery to cells for easy access from sally port.
5. Provide access to outdoor exercise activity as directly as possible and without disruption to adjacent units, but that is observable by unit and/or housing control officer station.

14.0 UNIT MANAGEMENT

Program Statement

The concept of providing unit management for inmate population groups ranging from 200 to 300 is currently used more consistently as a preferred management technique. Twenty years or so ago, ACA considered an entire facility population comprised of 300 to 400 inmates a manageable size. With recent national trends toward larger facilities, ranging from 800 to 2000, the need to create groups of smaller numbers of inmates together within the larger total institution has led to a need for the concept of unit management. The staff assigned to this area is responsible for all inmate activities associated within the housing unit population located there. Recently, some jurisdictions have constructed facilities of more that 3000 beds, but have utilized the concept of a multiple-facility complex such as three 1000-bed facilities, with shared central support. The concept of assigned responsibility through unit management (200–300 beds) is equally applicable, if not more important (see Figs. 3.39 through 3.41).

Prototypical Spaces

14.1 Sally port
14.2 Secure control room/rest room
14.3 Unit manager office
14.4 Assistant UM office
14.5 Staff offices
14.6 Case managers/interview rooms
14.7 Meeting room/multipurpose room
14.8 Medical exam (triage)
14.9 Laundry facilities
14.8 Staff toilet(s)
14.9 Inmate toilet
14.10 Janitor's closet
14.11 General storage

Operational Objectives

- To provide ongoing personal involvement with the conditions, needs, and activities in the housing areas that comprise the unit management area
- To provide for the safety of officers and inmates by facilitating communication with the unit
- To provide a level of understanding and communication with inmates in the unit that is not otherwise possible in a large facility

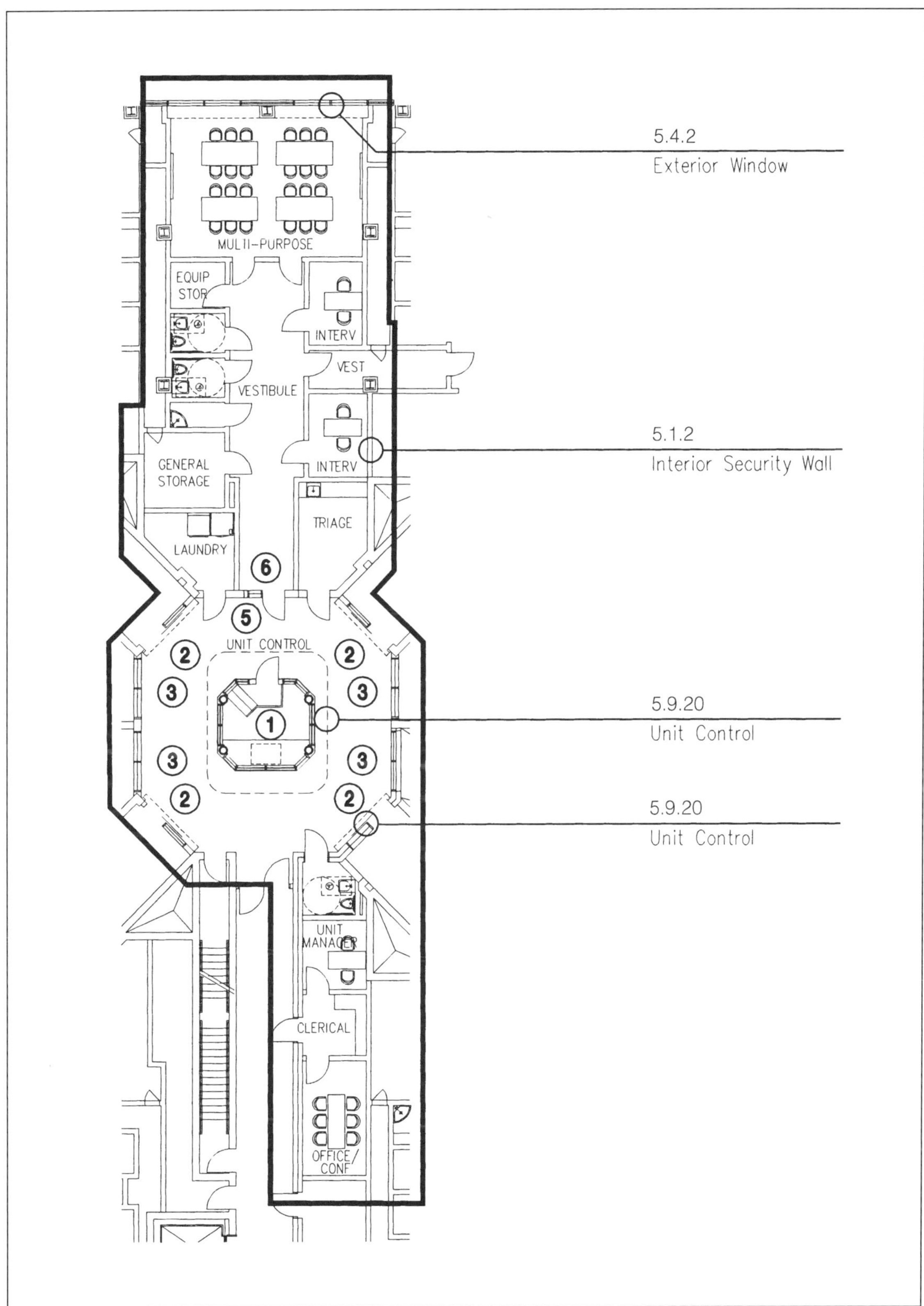

Figure 3.40 **Unit management for a small facility.**

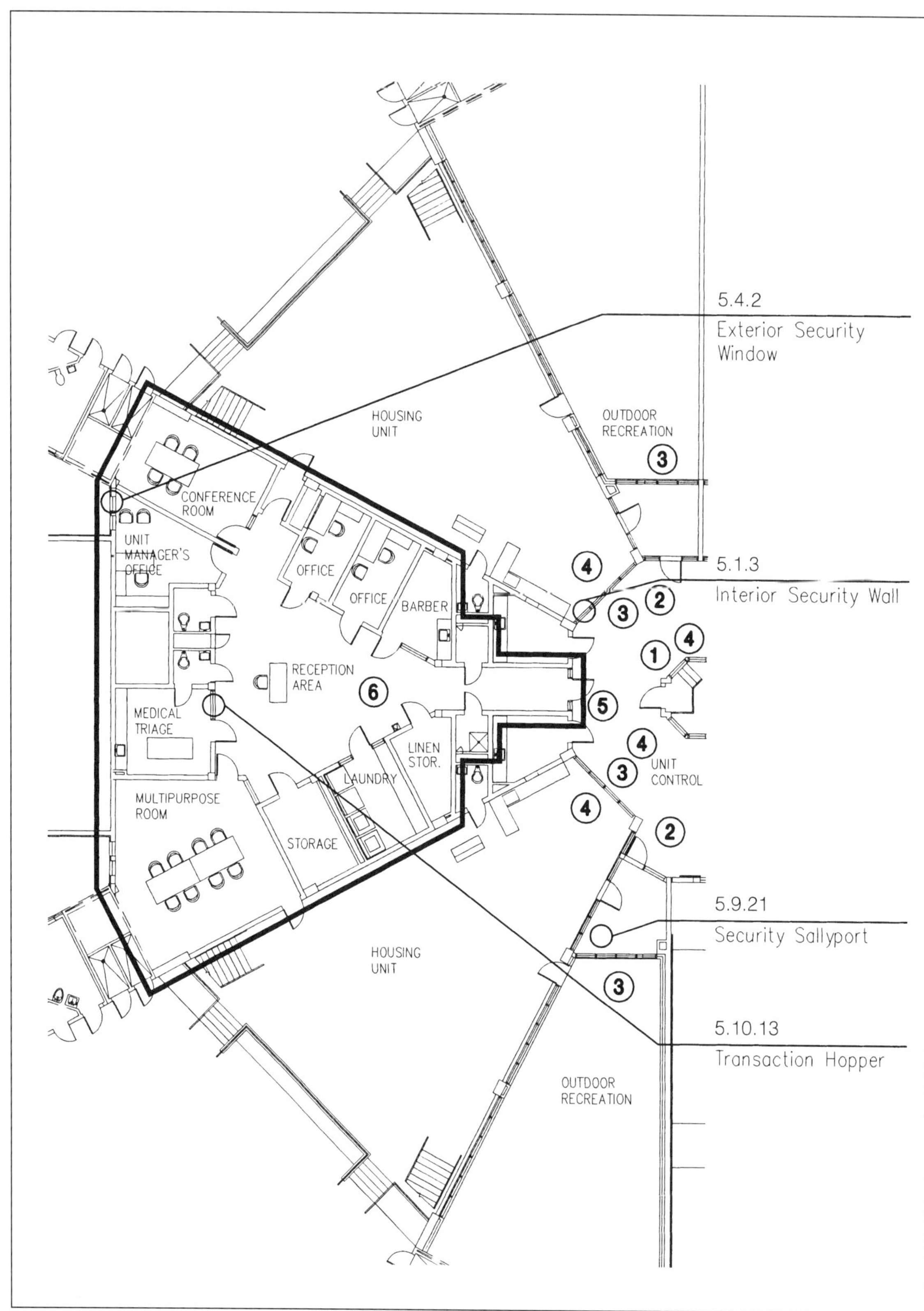

Figure 3.41 **Unit management for a large facility.**

Operational Procedures

- The unit manager meets regularly with staff assigned to the unit to discuss events, policy, and direction and to foster a professional and consistent approach to managing the unit.

Staffing Implications

The number of shifts of operations: Three
The number of days per week: Seven

This area is active 24 hours a day. The number of staff and operational procedures are determined by size of facility and client operational objectives for each unit management area.

Design Considerations

1. Determine the appropriate number of housing units for grouping together in order to provide secured entrances/exits from each unit area and observation from one area control position.
2. Provide visual surveillance of all housing unit entrances.
3. Provide direct observation of all housing outdoor recreation areas. It is highly desirable and can often justify a staffing position reduction in rovers, as well as minimizing movement in the facility.
4. Explore the potential for a unit control officer's location to observe all activities within the dayroom in each housing unit. Although this is a geometric challenge, a solution will provide a security backup position for officers within each housing unit. In some jurisdictions, it is permitted to reduce the number of staffing positions, during the evening shift, based upon this additional availability of visual supervision from outside the unit.
5. Position the unit management area with direct access from each of the housing units under direct unit control station observation, thereby eliminating or reducing the need for staffing escorts, which in turn can reduce operational costs.
6. Strive for the colocation of other inmate activities such as triage, interview rooms, law library, and arts and crafts, and potentially, indoor recreation in close proximity to housing units. This feature can further limit and control inmate movement in reducing distance and time from the housing units and thereby lower operational costs, since escorting inmates to these functions may not be required.

15.0 INMATE/SOCIAL SERVICES PROGRAMS

Program Statement

Many institutions provide this important service to inmates from outside community-based groups in addition to facility staff. These inmate/social services program staff and volunteers work with inmates by providing reentry programming, coordination of legal activities, assisting in self-improvement activities, and educational and cultural opportunities. This program is designed to create an improvement to the quality of life while serving time in a correctional facility. A home base area for volunteers should be provided on the outside of the secure perimeter, with activity with inmates provided in the education area, on the inside of the secure perimeter (see Fig. 3.42).

Prototypical Spaces

15.1 Social services director's office
15.2 Volunteer service coordinator
15.3 Clerical/support area
15.4 Small multipurpose room(s)
15.5 Group activity room(s)
15.6 Staff toilet

Operational Objectives

- To improve inmate access to positive, rehabilitative reinforcement activities and ties to the community
- To prepare inmates for reentry into the community

Operational Procedures

- Staff makes rounds of housing units to solicit interest and conduct inmate-oriented programs on a schedule basis.
- Volunteers are screened, then scheduled for specific activities within the facility. This area provides a base for volunteers to work from, typically using multipurpose areas to conduct activities.

Staffing Implications

The number of shifts of operations: One
The number of days per week: Five

This area is usually active during the day shift but may also operate in the evening. The number of staff is determined by size of facility and client operational objectives.

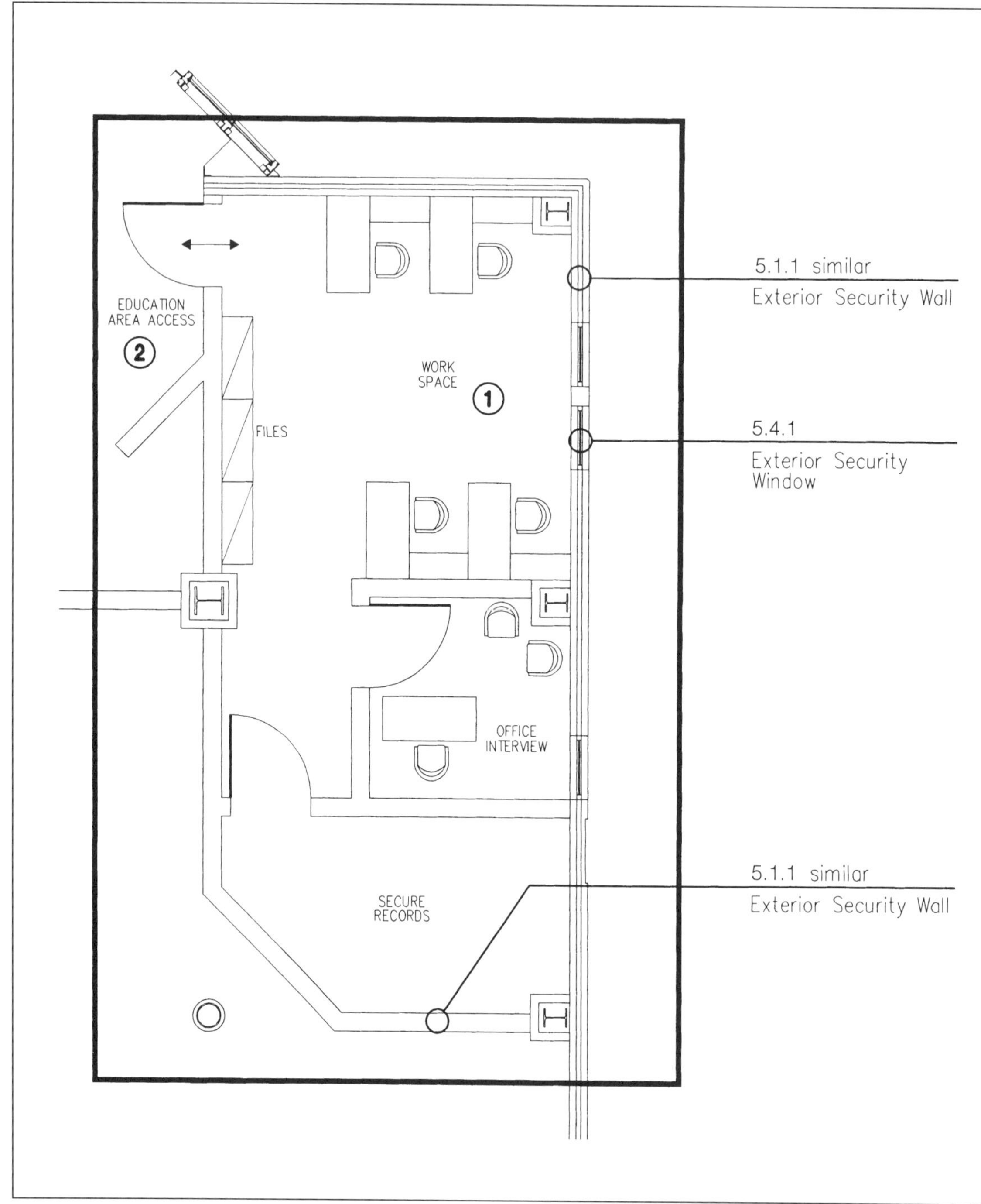

Figure 3.42 **Inmate/social services for a small facility adjacent to the education area.**

Design Considerations

1. Provide area that is comfortable with an environment of normative character, including natural light, to promote a sense of community for staff while working with inmates.
2. General proximity to inmate records is desired to facilitate staff review of inmate participation information.

Figure 3.43 **An education area classroom (CPR demonstration) with natural light and security observation from access corridor.**

16.0 EDUCATION

Program Statement

This area provides spaces for a variety of inmate activities oriented toward self-improvement, education, and group interaction (see Figs. 3.43 through 3.45). Services include education, vocational education, library services, and administrative/support services. Academic education and vocational education are given to provide inmates with competency-based functional mathematics, reading, and writing skills with Adult Basic Education (ABE) courses. Instruction in each of the five areas of the high school equivalency examination are provided with a General Equivalency Degree (GED). Post-secondary education programs in cooperation with a local institution of higher learning are also provided. Skill training, combining lab and classroom instruction, are also generally provided.

Library functions are provided for comprehensive library services for the inmate population, including reference, information referral, interlibrary loan, periodicals, and audio visuals. Recreational reading materials appropriate to the interests and reading levels of the inmates are also provided. Access to continuing education and career materials and resources encourage growth and development for future opportunities in society.

The library also serves as the learning center and should become the nucleus of the education department. Legal library materials are also provided as part of the general reference collection, although usually separated into its own area or room. Library materials should be kept relevant to inmates' needs and should reflect a variety of languages, reading levels, and interests.

Vocational training areas operate in conjunction with adjoining classrooms to provide comprehensive skill training which incorporates both technical (classroom) and hands-on (training labs) experiences and opportunities. Security of tools requires control of these areas and this is kept separate from other educational activities. Consideration should be given to provide all classrooms with provisions for interactive TV instruction and the ability to be cabled or wired for computers.

Prototypical Spaces

16.1 Officer station
16.2 Inmate toilet(s)
16.3 Janitor's closet
16.4 Education director
16.5 Secretary/file room
16.6 Teacher preparation area
16.7 Staff toilets
16.8 General storage (secured)
16.9 Interview room(s)
16.10 Testing cubicles
16.11 Academic classrooms
16.12 Education office(s)/workroom
16.13 Business classroom(s)/computer learning lab
16.14 General library
16.15 Legal library
16.16 Librarian office
16.17 Work area/general classroom
16.18 Storage (books and materials)
16.19 Audio-visual room/material storage
16.20 Vocational education classroom(s)
16.21 Instructor office
16.22 Tool storage (secured)
16.23 Materials storage

Operational Objectives

- Provide classrooms with supplies and materials to support the academic program
- Provide programs of interest to inmates
- Provide basic literacy assessment and remedial academic training for interested inmates
- Provide community involvement with the utilization of volunteers

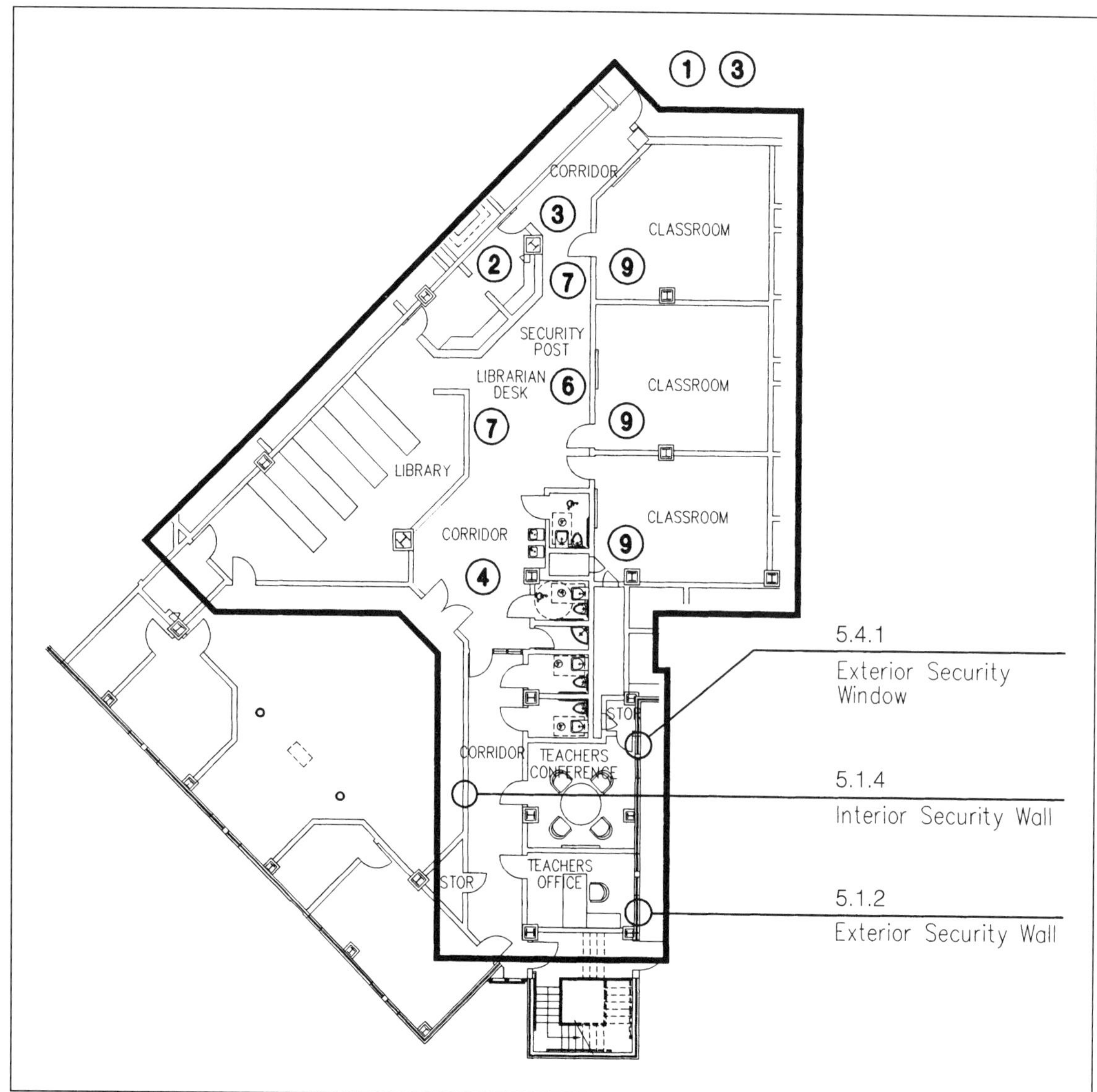

Figure 3.44 **Education/vocational programs area for a small facility.**

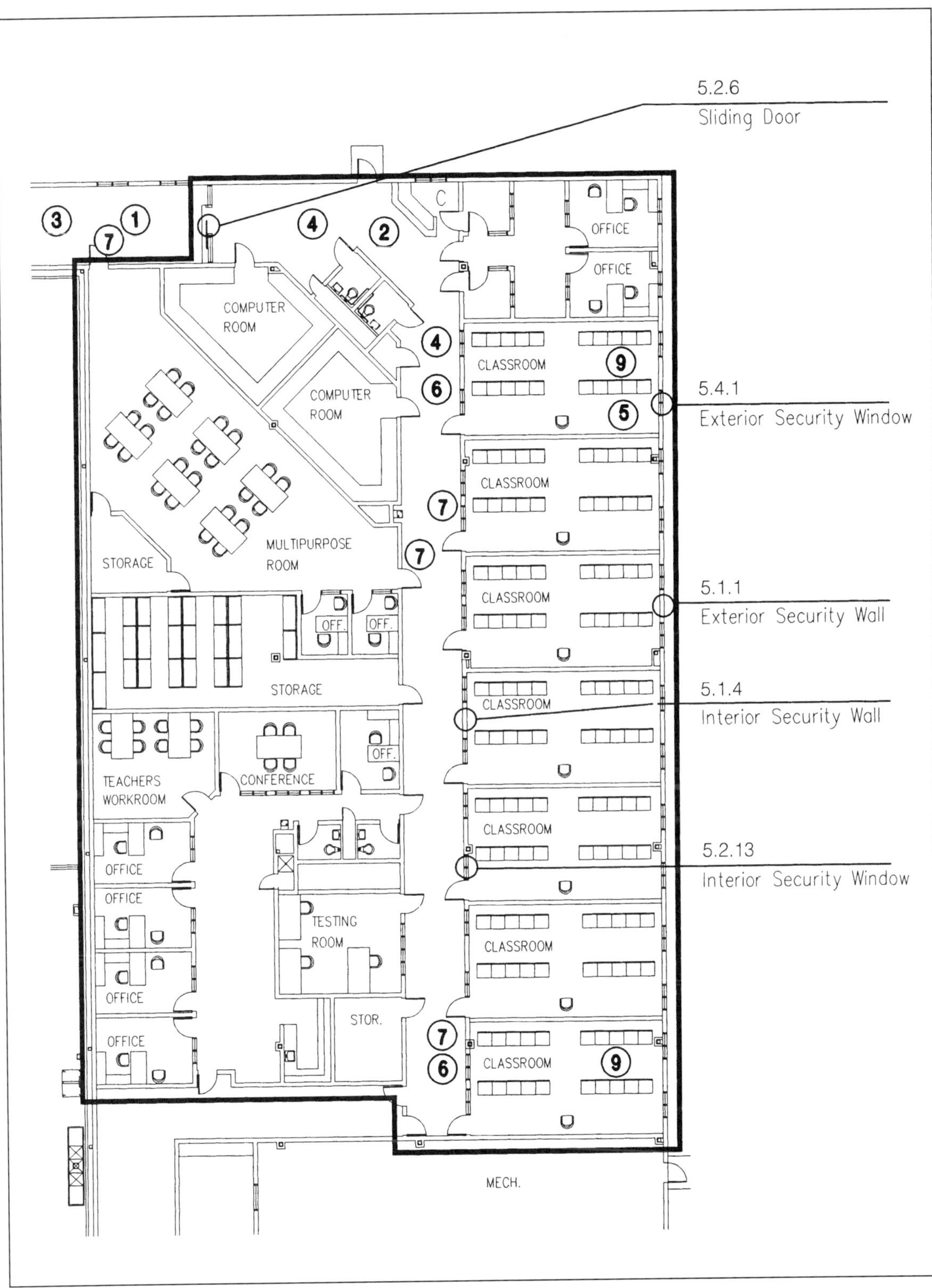

Figure 3.45 **Education area for a large facility.**

- Provide Adult Basic Education (ABE) and General Educational Development (GED) programs through the local school district

Operational Procedures

- Inmates will either be escorted or travel on their own, with a pass identification system, to the general educational area.
- A control officer's station (or room) is often located at the entrance to this area to observe, supervise, and control movement in and out of area.
- Inmates are observed during activities from the corridor leading to all rooms.
- Inmate program assignments to this area may be for morning, afternoon, and/or evening sessions.

Staffing Implications

The number of shifts of operations: One or Two
The number of days per week: Five

This area is active essentially during the day shift, occasionally with evening programs available. The number of staff is determined by size of facility and client operational objectives.

Design Considerations

1. Locate the education area central to all inmate activity, with relative equality of access to/from all housing units and/or housing complexes.
2. Provide education, vocational education, and industry spaces with security control and observation of all inmate activity from one central position.
3. Provide corridors for the staging of inmates from different housing units/complexes or different classified population groups in accessing these functions in an orderly manner. It should also provide for metal detection/security screening when necessary.
4. Provide individual toilet room(s) adjacent to control position for monitoring and control.
5. Provide natural light into classrooms and library reading areas in support of creating a normative environment, similar to that found in educational facilities in society.
6. Provide simple, straight-line corridor access into and out of each and every activity space, for maintaining observation from control posts or positions.
7. Provide roving officer's with direct observation into each activity space by creating a generous amount of glazed areas to each room from windows in the corridor. Typically, officers are not positioned inside the education space and therefore the direct observation of movement within the corridor can assist in providing for the safety of instruction staff and inmates alike.
8. Dirty vocational shop areas (e.g., masonry or carpentry) may need to be located off to one side of the educational area or colocated with correctional industries areas in order to minimize noise disruption in academic and library areas.
9. Academic, vocational classrooms are typically designed for 15 to 20 students.
10. In vocational shops, provide the instructors office, tool crib, and material storage within the overall shop area, similar to those in vocational schools. Provide a service/delivery access for receiving large or bulky materials.
11. While most jails do not have correctional industries areas, vocational shops are often use to undertake community service projects (e.g., building park benches), which has positive impact in the area.

17.0 RELIGIOUS SERVICES

Program Statement

This area should provide inmates with an opportunity to express their religious beliefs in a space conducive to this quiet activity. The right of religious expression is a constitutional guarantee, and courts have upheld these rights of inmates to engage in this activity during their confinement. The space should provide flexibility for many religious dominations with a character of environment which is serene (see Figs. 3.46 through 3.48).

Prototypical Spaces

17.1 Chapel
17.2 Chaplains's office(s)
17.3 Receptionist/secretary
17.4 Meeting room(s)
17.5 Religious storage room
17.6 Multipurpose chapel
17.7 Staff toilet
17.8 Sweat lodge (where required)

Operational Objectives

- Provide inmates with regularly scheduled religious access to programs to fulfill their individual spiritual needs and requirements

Figure 3.46 **Chapel with flexible inmate seating, movable wall for room division, CCTV, and access to chaplin offices.**

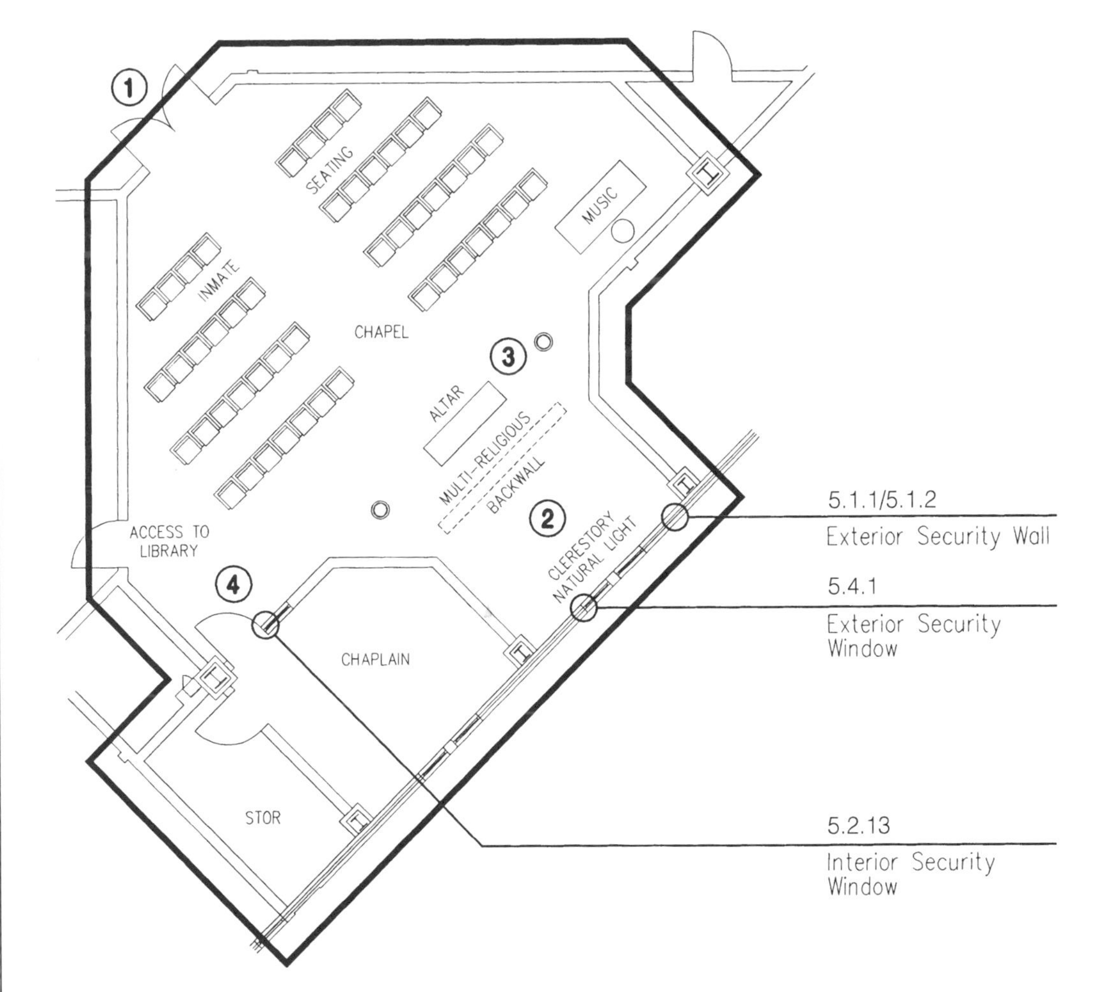

Figure 3.47 **Religious services area for a small facility.**

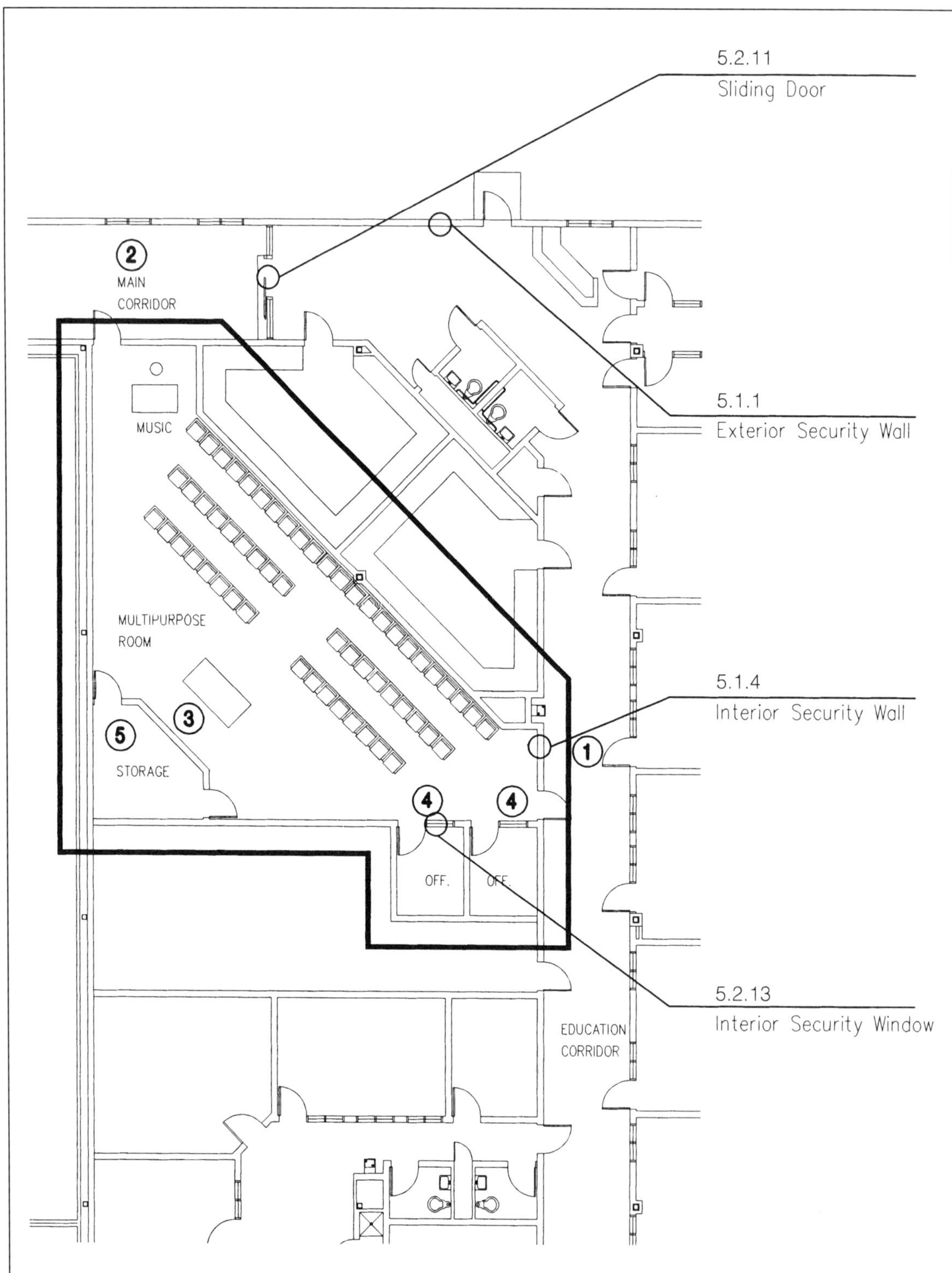

Figure 3.48 **Religious services area for a large facility.**

- Provide inmates with the opportunity for individual religious, spiritual, and crisis-prevention counseling
- Provide an appropriate architectural environment to conduct these activities
- Provide and encourage community religious volunteers to support the facility's religious programs
- Accommodate a variety of religious denominations/orientations with acceptable physical space

Operational Procedures

- Religious services are scheduled for specific days and times—usually once a week.
- Counseling is performed on a daily basis.

Staffing Implications

The number of shifts of operations: One
The number of days per week: Varies

This area is typically active only during the day shift. The number of staff is determined by the size of the facility and the requirements of the approved facility program. Large facilities may have full-time staff, others rely on volunteers.

Design Considerations

1. Locate the chapel area and its support spaces adjacent to the education area to create a flexibility of spacial use when religious activities are not programmed.
2. Provide natural light to this space to support the normative environment of this space.
3. Provide a flexible lectern/podium area to support a variety of religious beliefs. A rotating panel or rear wall design can provide for the display of appropriate religious symbols or icons; in order to have a multidenominational chapel work well, each religious group needs to have an adjacent storage room in which to store their religious supplies and materials.
4. Provide direct access from chapel to religious offices for one-on-one counseling and crisis intervention.
5. Where there is a significant Muslim population, it is preferred to have a separate mosque space, since shoes are not permitted to be worn.

18.0 INDUSTRY (PRISONS)

Program Statement

Industry programs provide the benefit for comprehensive work to the inmate population who are willing and able to work. Generally, this space should be designed with flexibility in size and shape to provide for a variety of industrial activities. It should be designed to accommodate production schedules which include swing shifts and weekend activity.

Future expansion of the industry area is highly desirable, without disruption to ongoing operations of activity initially built. Allow 25 to 50 percent, over any current need as your guide in planning expansion. There should be sufficient space for raw material storage and finished products (see Figs. 3.49 and 3.50).

Figure 3.49 **Industries shop with large interior windows for observation, supervision, and control of inmates.**

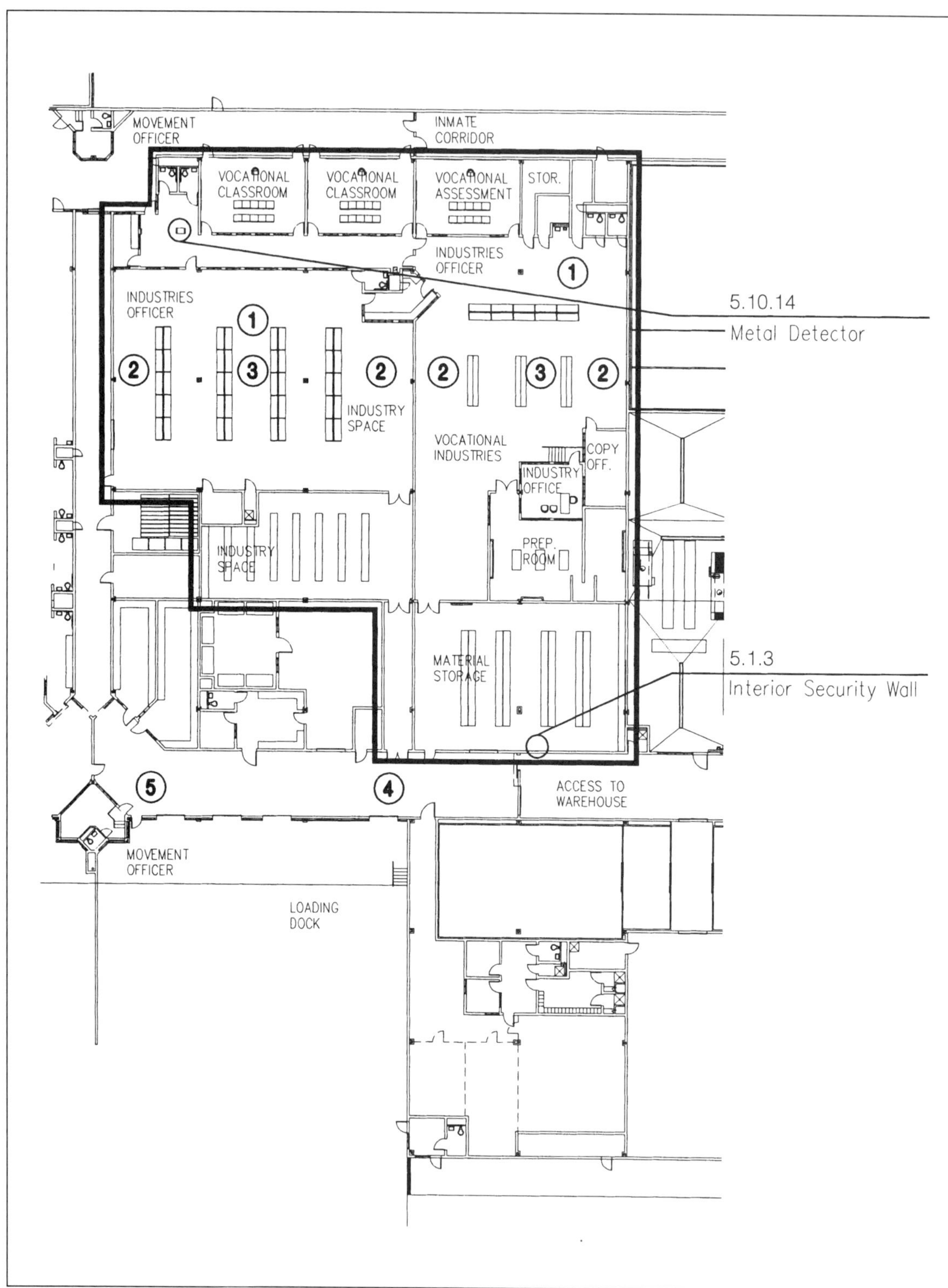

Figure 3.50 **Industry area for a small facility.**

Layout should permit observation of production area from a central position, without compromising equipment layout, wherever possible. The work area should be OSHA approved, safe, and quiet.

Prototypical Spaces

18.1 Sally port to loading dock
18.2 Industry production area(s)
18.3 Raw material storage
18.4 Finished product storage
18.5 Industry director office
18.6 Industry clerical support staff office(s)
18.7 Staff toilet(s)
18.8 Secured tool storage
18.9 Security screening area/metal detection
18.10 Search room
18.11 Inmate toilet(s)
18.12 Janitor's closet

Operational Objectives

- Provide inmates with work opportunities with industry programs similar to those available in the community.
- Provide inmates with industry training opportunities, with associated vocational programs.
- Provide useful products for use by government agencies that can be sold to cover the costs of running the industries program.
- Correctional industries assignments are typically for a full day.

Operational Procedure

- As the best program assignment in prison facilities, inmates are generally screened to ensure academic and/or vocational skill requirements are met for each specific job.
- Inmates come to this area, either escorted or on a pass system, for a full program day. Metal detection and screening may be required when inmates leave the area, depending upon the materials and tools in use.

Staffing Implications

The number of shifts of operations: One or Two
The number of days per week: Five

This area is typically active during the day shift. The number of staff is determined by size and types of correctional industries provided. In terms of program assignments, correctional industries often provides 25 percent or more of the available program slots.

Design Considerations

1. Provide for flexibility of use of the shape of space layout for a variety industry production processes.
2. Consider carefully the utilities placement of all listed spaces since, generally, the industry is not known at the time of design and often not until the facility is completed in construction and ready for occupancy. Therefore, general capability only can be provided.
3. Provide a minimum clear height within the space of 14 feet to anticipate functional use for all anticipated industry activities.
4. Locate industry space adjacent to warehouse, providing an opportunity for shared access to loading docks which can enhance security.
5. Control and monitor access to/from sally port to receiving dock and/or warehouse in maintaining security.

19.0 RECREATION

Program Statement

This activity is a fundamental program in providing a physical activity to the inmate population. Providing inmates with constructive means for relieving and challenging their tensions inherit in institutional living can provide for an improvement in the operation of a facility. Recreational activities provide inmates with an opportunity to improve their physical and mental health, develop good sportsmanship, and improve morale (see Figs. 3.51 through 3.53).

Prototypical Spaces

19.1 Recreational director office
19.2 Athletic equipment storage room
19.3 Chair storage room/area
19.4 Staff toilet
19.5 Inmate toilet(s)
19.6 Gymnasium space (basketball, volleyball, etc.)
19.7 Exercise/weight lifting area
19.8 Activity room(s)
19.9 Outside recreational activities: baseball, basketball, handball, running track, and so forth

Operational Objectives

- Provide inmates with a variety of healthy and safe recreational activities
- Provide inmates with leisure time recreational activities
- Maintain inmate safety and security in delivering these recreational programs

Figure 3.51 **Gymnasium with mezzanine activity space and clerestory for natural light.**

- Provide inmates housed in segregation housing the opportunity for at least one hour of daily recreational (exercise) activity

Operational Procedures

- For many facilities, there is early evening recreation to expand available time each day.
- Utilization of indoor and outdoor recreation is typically scheduled by housing unit on a rotating basis. Inmates that are interested are called out and escorted to recreation for the allocated time period.

Staffing Implications

The number of shifts of operations: Two
The number of days per week: Seven

This area is typically active during the day and early evening shift. The number of staff is determined by size of facility and client operational objectives. However, every facility should have some indoor recreation area and at least one staff person should be assigned to run the recreation program.

Design Considerations

1. Locate the gymnasium space(s) centrally to provide equal access for the general inmate population.
2. Locate gymnasium adjacent to other centralized services to improve security observation by utilizing staff already assigned and positioned for other functions.
3. Provide complete visibility into the activity space(s) to observe inmate behavior during this very physical activity and provide supervisor with backup opportunity.
4. Locate multipurpose rooms, weights, and other activities to the rear or sides of open court (basketball) areas to improve observation.
5. Locate director's office in a position to monitor and control access to support spaces, storage rooms, and toilets.
6. If showers are provided they should have privacy screens but be generally open to the main activity areas for ease of supervision.

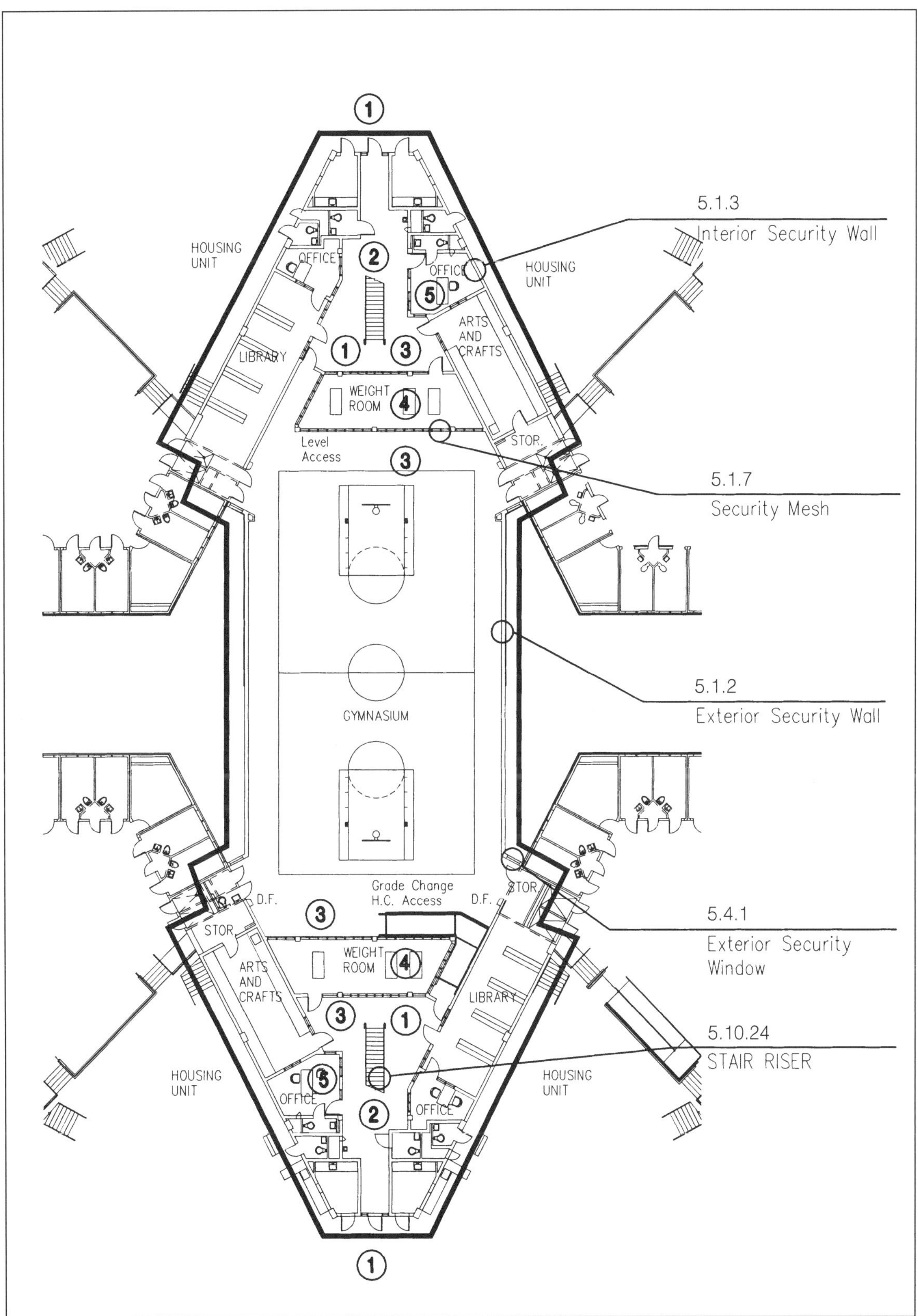

Figure 3.52 **Recreation area for a large facility.**

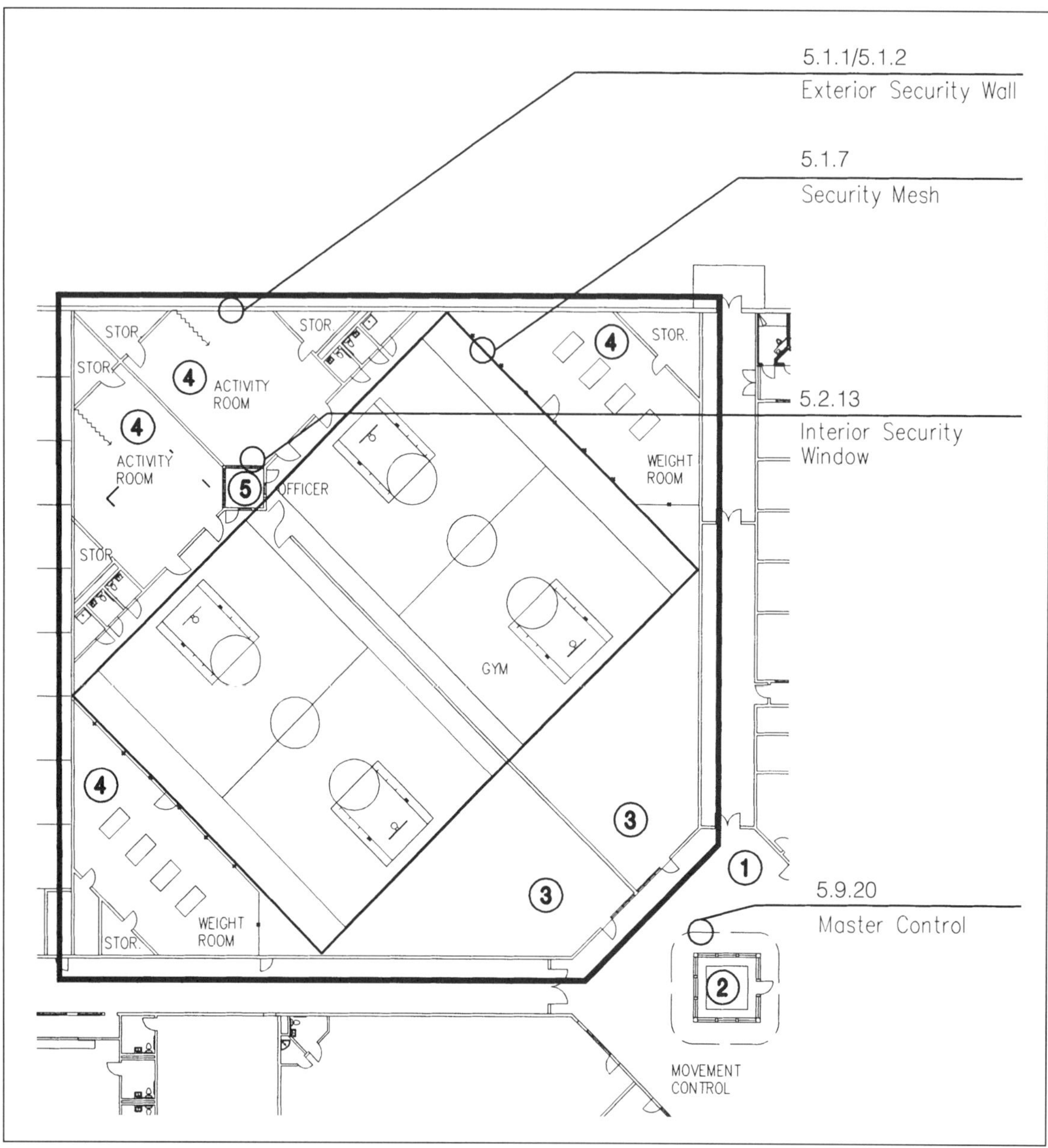

Figure 3.53 **Recreation area for a large facility.**

20.0 HEALTH SERVICES

Program Statement

A wide range of medical and mental health services are normally provided for the inmate population to assure care and treatment opportunities and to contain potential contagious diseases. The health service area generally consists of an outpatient medical clinic, medical health inpatient infirmary, and a mental health infirmary. Each of these areas is interrelated in terms of operations, requiring free access throughout the area by staff with controlled access to each by inmates and observable from a control position.

Inmate movement to and from the clinic and dental areas should not cross and provide for separate arrival and exiting patterns. Clinic areas should be separated from administrative areas, where inmates are denied access to secure area where records, supplies, and pharmacy items are generally located. An officer's station should observe all waiting and treatment areas, including visual access into each treatment room to observe inmate behavior. Convenient ambulance access to health services should be provided.

The mental health infirmary should be in close proximity to the medical infirmary, to share nursing, security, and support services. This area should include space for acute patient care/confinement, group and individual therapy, and infectious disease controlled environments. A substance abuse treatment area is often located adjacent to, and sometimes within, the health services area to utilize multipurpose rooms and other support functions.

Prototypical Spaces

Medical Administration

20.1 Health care administrator
20.2 Nurse supervisor
20.3 General medical offices
20.4 Records/clerical/files
20.5 Dental office
20.6 Dental storage
20.7 Conference room
20.8 Staff toilet(s)

Medical Clinic

20.9 Officer's duty station
20.10 Inmate medical waiting
20.11 Dental waiting
20.13 Secure inmate waiting
20.14 Inmate toilet(s)
20.15 Nurse's station
20.16 Examination rooms
20.17 Examination/trauma room
20.18 Physical therapy
20.19 Tub room
20.20 Laboratory
20.21 Laboratory storage
20.22 X-ray room
20.23 X-ray file storage
20.24 X-ray development room
20.25 Storage room
20.26 Central sterile supply room
20.27 Clean room
20.28 Dirty linen room
20.29 Janitor's closet
20.30 Dental examination room(s)/operatory

Medical Infirmary

20.31 Nurse's station
20.32 Officer's duty station
20.33 Staff toilet
20.34 Pharmacy

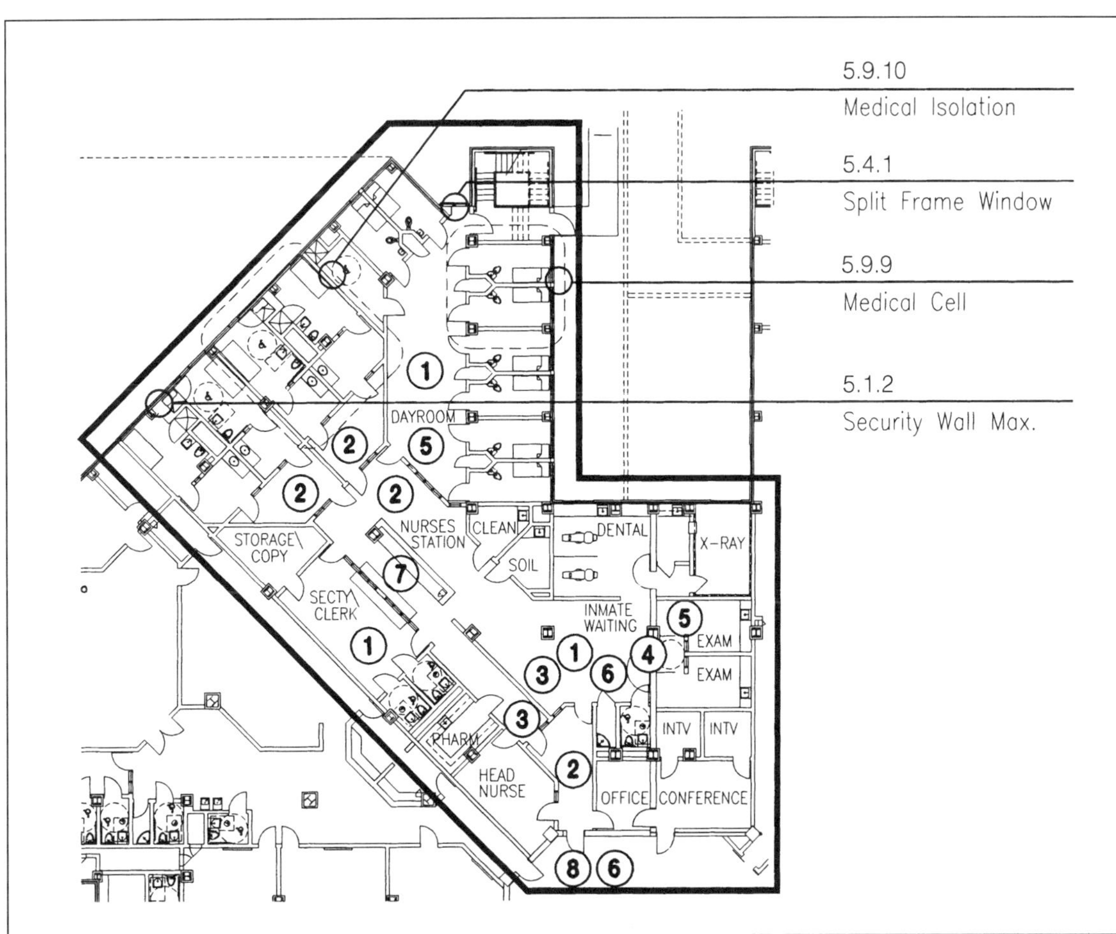

Figure 3.54 **Health services for a small jail.**

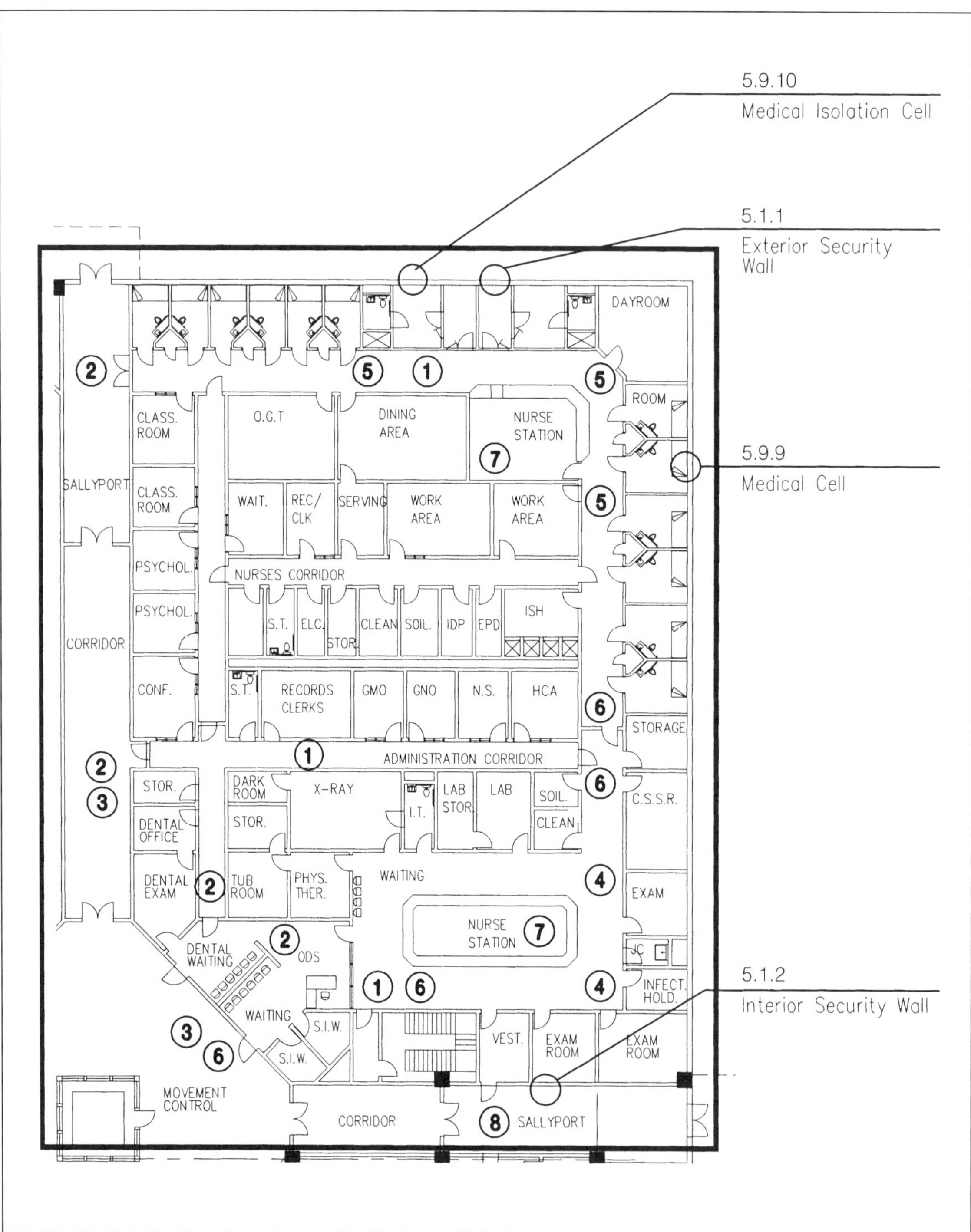

Figure 3.55 **Health services for a large facility.**

20.35 Individual patient rooms
20.36 Infirmary ward (4-bed rooms)
20.37 Infectious disease rooms (negative pressure air controlled)
20.38 Dayroom/dining
20.39 Pantry
20.40 Showers
20.41 Clean linen
20.42 Soiled linen
20.43 Infectious waste
20.44 Bedpan rinse room
20.45 Laundry room
20.46 Janitor's closet
20.47 General storage

Operational Objectives (Medical)

- Provide medical screening of all inmates entering (admissions) the facility to determine medical condition requiring special needs or treatment
- Provide inmates confined to the facility with medical and dental general services in a secure environment
- Provide inmates with special medical needs in separated housing units
- Provide inmates with continual medical assessment to promote early identification of problems/conditions in support of medical care and maintenance programs
- Provide inmates with emergency medical and dental services
- Provide pharmacy, laboratory, and other support functions in the day-to-day health care of the inmate population
- Provide appropriate medical, dental, and mental health staff for inmate examination and treatment services
- Maintain medical records and provide for security control of inmate information
- Provide inmates with legally approved medication as required for treatment
- Provide physically disabled inmates with continual health assessments and appropriate care
- Provide inmates with adequate nutrition and therapeutic diets as medically required
- Provide for the functional and operational interrelationship of the three areas of medical clinic, medical/mental housing, and medical administration

Operational Objectives (Mental)

- Provide inmates with continual mental health assessments and treatment for serious mental disorders
- Provide assessment to prevent potential suicides and homicides
- Provide aggressive inmates with appropriate isolation and treatment
- Assess sudden inmate behavioral changes that pose a threat or danger to institutional safety and order
- Provide inmates who arrive at the institution with mentally impaired conditions with evaluation and treatment
- Identify inmates with developmental disabilities and provide them with proper classification and referrals
- Provide inmates those who require psychopharmacological intervention and programs with medication review and treatment
- Provide 24-hour supervision of inmates requiring crisis intervention

Operations Procedures

- The administration area is located adjacent to the medical clinic to provide office space for the facility's medical and nursing staff in support of completing medical paperwork.
- Nursing services and stations are primarily responsible for inmates' medical assessment, planning, implementation, evaluation, revisions, and maintenance of health care programs.
- They will also administer medications and treatment while maintaining updated records.
- All services associated with patient care, such as infection control, lab specimens, blood sugar checks, blood pressure checks, diets, prenatal care, and suicide prevention procedures, among others, fall under the nursing staff's responsibilities.
- Triage services, also known as *sick call,* are generally decentralized and located at the housing unit. Inmates requiring medical attention contact their housing unit officer, and in turn this officer will contact the medical staff who will schedule visits to the housing unit to determine inmate treatment beyond that administered at the housing unit. This activity can be provided within a multipurpose room shared for counseling or other activity.
- The medical clinic generally provides services during the day shift on a Monday to Friday basis.
- Visits by inmates are scheduled after screening at the housing unit. The coordination of scheduled visits is between the housing unit officer (or unit management officer) and the medical staff.
- A waiting area at the medical clinic is observed with movement controlled by a locally positioned officer's station.
- Acute care/emergency medical needs are typically handled via contact with local hospitals.

Staffing Implications

The number of shifts of operations:
Outpatient Clinic: One
Inpatient Infirmary: Three

The number of days per week:
Outpatient Clinic: Five
Inpatient Infirmary: Seven

This area is active during the day shift. The number of staff is determined by size of facility and client operational objectives. The outpatient clinic typically operates on a normal weekday schedule, while the inpatient infirmary will operate 24 hours a day, 7 days a week if it has any patients. Outside medical assignments may be required to have officers supervise inmates in local hospital or emergency rooms.

Design Considerations

1. Provide arrangement of spaces to produce a solution that maintains separation of the three areas, while providing adjacencies for functional use and security observation
2. Provide separate entrances into these areas, so one does not pass through the other
3. Provide separate entrance routes into the clinic, physically and visually, from the exiting one, while maintaining total observation from a control position of all spaces and entrances to all patient service spaces
4. Provide each treatment room with a vision panel in the door and/or sidelight to observe inmate activity from the corridor side
5. Provide a plan layout that groups all infirmary-type rooms (medical and mental health) into one area for easy staff access for routine activities and quick emergency response situations
6. Locate the clinic department adjacent to infirmary, but closer to main corridor for routine inmate access on a daily basis
7. Combine nurses' station and security control post to observe the same inmate treatment areas
8. Provide a location in close proximity to intake/release or make other provisions for emergency ambulance access.

21.0 FOOD SERVICE

Program Statement

This component should provide wholesome, nutritious meals to inmates, three meals per day, seven days a week. Provide therapeutic diet meals or special meals to inmates requiring diet therapy for medical reasons and religious reasons, respectively. The meals should be delivered in a most efficient manner with palatable meals served at the correct temperature. The food service facility and equipment must meet all federal, state, and local codes and regulations and ACA standards.

The food service area provides a central food preparation area, supply storage area, and dispensing area, all in close proximity to each other and on one level. Warehouse with coolers and freezers should be included. The loading dock area should be designed to separate supply delivery from garbage recycling pickup. The kitchen office should be located to observe the entire preparation area and service corridors, where inmates may work. An inmate break area should also be provided (see Figs. 3.56 through 3.59).

Prototypical Spaces

Receiving and Delivery

21.1 Dock
21.2 Receiving refrigerator
21.3 Receiving freezer
21.4 Receiving dry food/supply storage
21.5 Secure storage
21.6 Walk-in freezer
21.7 Meat freezer
21.8 Walk-in produce refrigerator
21.9 Walk-in meat refrigerator/tempering box
21.10 Walk-in daily refrigerator
21.11 Cool commodity storage
21.12 Garbage/grease refrigerator

Production

21.13 Vegetable preparation/cold food mixing
21.14 Cooks' prep/meat prep
21.15 Hot food production
21.16 Bakery

Tray Assembly

21.17 Cart parking
21.18 Tray parking

Sanitation

21.19 Pot and pan washing
21.20 Dishwashing
21.21 Cart wash
21.22 Janitor's closet
21.23 Recycling areas, sort, and store

Cafeteria

21.24 Serving line
21.25 Beverage/condiment line
21.26 Dining room(s)
21.27 Inmate toilet(s)
21.28 Control platform/position
21.29 Staff dining room/staff break room/toilets

Office/Staff Area

21.30 Manager's office
21.31 Supervisors'/chef's office
21.32 Staff toilet
21.33 Inmate employee break room
21.34 Inmate toilet

Figure 3.56 **Kitchen cooking area with refrigerator/freezer on back wall.**

Figure 3.57 **Central dining room with fixed stainless steel tables/seats and natural light.**

Operational Objectives

- Provide inmates with nutritious meals three times daily, seven days a week
- Provide inmates requiring special therapeutic diets for medical and/or religious dietary restrictions with appropriate menus
- Provide and ensure all meals are prepared and delivered under sanitary conditions, consistent with regulations of local and state jurisdictions governing institutional food service operations
- Provide inmates with work opportunities in food service, an important cadre assignment

Operational Procedures

- The areas of the food service area, including food storage, food preparation, meal tray assembly, meal distribution, and return cart/dishwashing functions, are under supervision and control of the food service manager and supported by a security officer's station or rover.
- Food product and trash removal occur at the loading dock of the warehouse, often located on the free side of the facility; include provisions for recycling programs.
- Product is stored in bulk in the warehouse and delivered to daily/weekly storage areas located within the kitchen area.
- Meals are prepared by inmate workers and supervised by cooks, with an assembly-line operation, and then are placed on carts for delivery to housing units, in *detention* facilities, and brought to pantries adjacent to the kitchen to serve directly to centralized dining rooms, in most *correctional* facilities.
- Returned trays (carts) enter a separate dishwashing area adjacent to and separated from the food preparation area to maintain sanitary conditions. Carts, trays, flatware, pots, and pans, and so forth, are cleaned and stored after each meal.
- A staff dining area is generally located adjacent to the kitchen.
- The supervisor's office should be able to observe the entire food service area, including inmate break/restroom facilities.

Staffing Implications

The number of shifts of operations: Two or Three, depending on system

The number of days per week: Five or Seven, depending on system

This area is active during the day and evening shifts. The number of staff is determined by size of the facility and client operational objectives. Dining areas are typically sized to seat the total number of inmates in two to three shifts of 20 to 30 minutes each.

Design Considerations

1. Locate kitchen adjacent to each dining room to reduce staffing/operations by monitoring inmate movement within the space while providing security observation of both kitchen and dining rooms.
2. Locate, if possible, the kitchen central to the program center to take advantage of the dining rooms for other functions at off meal times. This can be achieved only occasionally due to other design conditions.
3. Provide inmate access and observation from a central point with kitchen delivery access from an opposite side from inmate entry and in close proximity to the warehouse.
4. Provide natural light into the dining area to create a normative environment, which can promote positive inmate behavior.
5. Locate office space to observe as much of the food service operation as possible.
6. Elevate office via a raised platform.
7. Locate the inmate break area adjacent to the office area(s) to permit total observation of activity including restroom facilities.
8. Limit partition heights to a minimum, including those for the pot washing and/or dishwashing area.
9. Provide vision panels in walk-in refrigerators, freezers, and in storage rooms.
10. Eliminate breaks in wall lines to increase visual observation.
11. Maintain high lighting levels, especially in refrigerated and dry storage areas.
12. Provide fluorescent lighting in the walk-in refrigerators and freezers to lower energy costs.

Food service design for correctional facilities requires the understanding of the design considerations for observation, as the preceding describes. Security and durability are essential to a successful operation. Once these critical areas are maintained, all other good food service design practices can occur.

Additional Design Security Considerations

- Access to the food service department should be kept to a minimum number of entrances to ensure control and security.

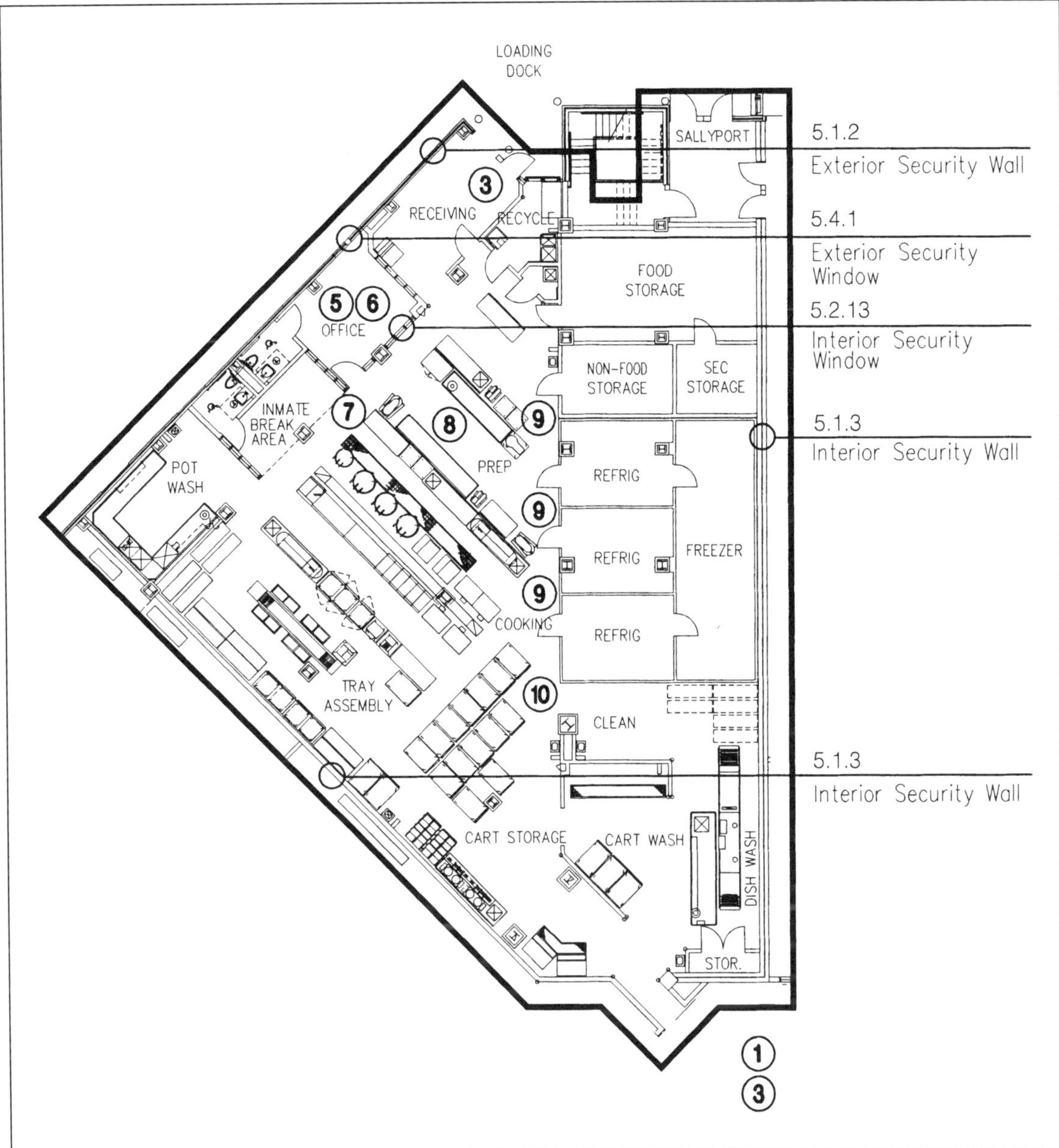

Figure 3.58 **Food service area for a small facility.**

- Equipment must be constructed to limit the possibility of tampering with and/or taking it apart.
- Storage areas should have shelving that is all welded and not constructed of wire.
- Screws on all equipment should be tamper-proof.
- Moving parts should be kept to a minimum.
- Control devices, such as ventilator water wash control panels, should be located in an office.
- Vision panels should be made of nonbreakable materials.
- Provide only two (2) access points to the food service space, in receiving and delivering products.
- Good lighting levels should be maintained in all food service spaces.
- Ceiling heights should be maintained at a minimum of 10 feet 0 inches, whenever possible.
- Ceiling system should be of a secure type.

Provisions for securing utensils such as knives should be provided. A *shadow board* is one method used in achieving security control of knives and other sharp food service utensils. All items are

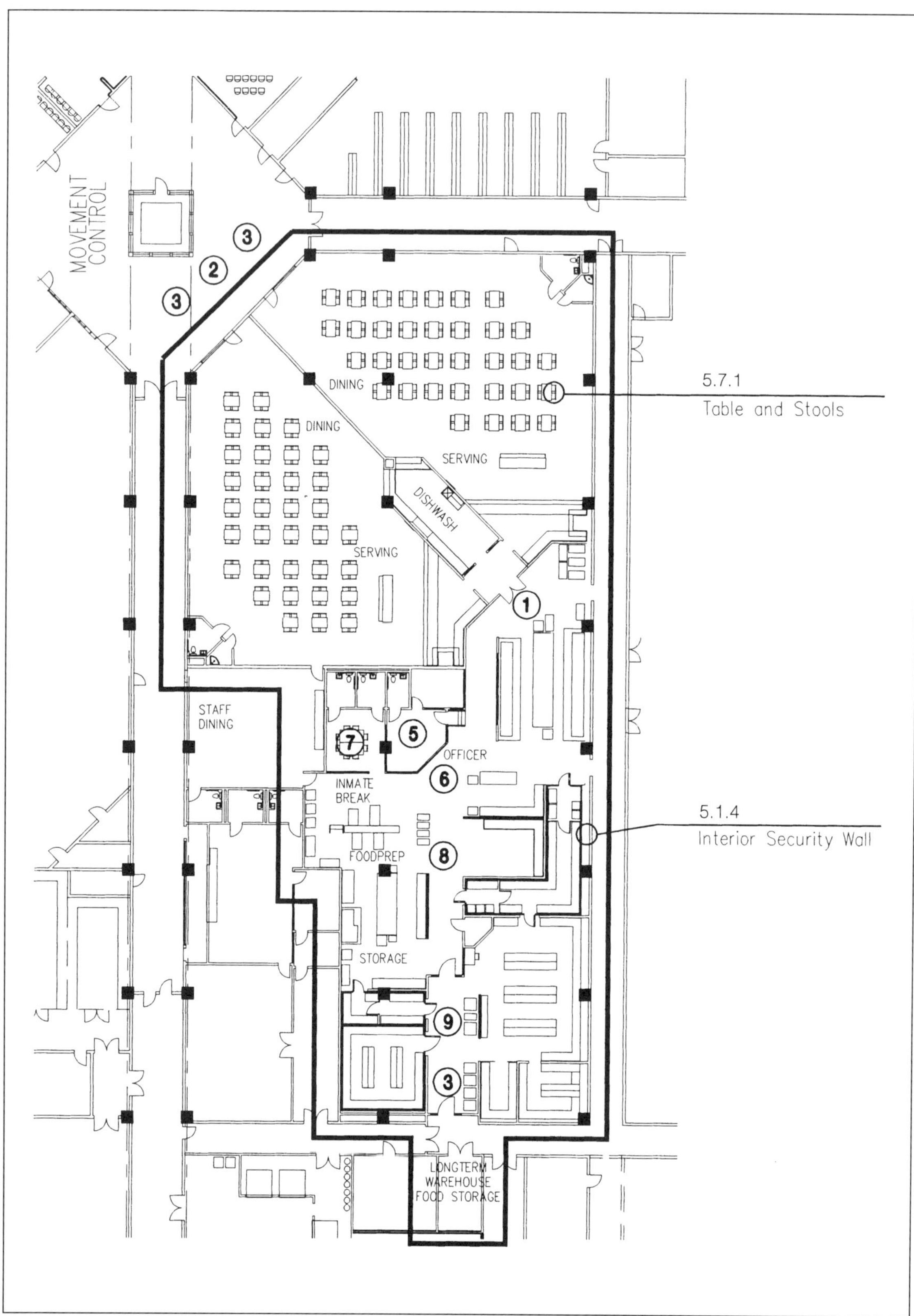

Figure 3.59 **Food service area for a large facility.**

placed on a board that has an outline of the utensil that is being stored. With a glancing observation of the board, a missing item can be identified and perhaps the individual responsible identified. This unit is always kept under lock and key. Another security issue relates to limiting access to certain ingredients that are considered possible contraband or can be used for making bathtub gin or causing bodily harm, such as pepper which could be thrown in someone's eyes.

Additional Design Durability Considerations

- Equipment must be durable to prevent damage that can occur from rough handling and misuse. Wherever possible, secure equipment to floor and walls.
- Walls should be constructed of masonry block.
- Doors should be constructed of stainless steel.
- Ceilings should be constructed of metal pan.
- Floors should utilize quarry tile or equally durable material and should be skid-proof.
- Doors to walk-in refrigerators and freezers should be clad with diamond plate.
- All undershelves of tables and counters should be of welded construction.
- Shelving in storage areas should be of stainless steel with welded construction.
- Compressor housings/controls should be protected by stainless steel louvered or perforated guards.
- Tangent draw off to kettles should be provided with a welded step guard over them.
- Hand sinks should be fully enclosed with stainless steel material.
- Wall shelves should be minimized or eliminated.
- Drawers should be eliminated from work tables.

By keeping a facility design simple, you can provide an opportunity for good security and observation. It can become user-friendly and easier to operate, which can result in improved equipment maintenance and lower operational costs.

22.0 COMMISSARY (CANTEEN)

Program Statement

The commissary, also known as the *canteen* in some facilities, provides inmates with items for purchase for personal use and convenience. Sufficient storage is essential within the space permitting efficient and low-cost operation of the facility. Since food items are also stored in the commissary, the space should provide refrigeration and meet appropriate health codes.

Inmates often are scheduled to work in the canteen assisting correctional supply officers, stocking shelves, and bagging orders for delivery to the inmate population. The commissary sells items not routinely issued to inmates by the institution, such as candy, cookies, soda, deodorant, greeting cards, radios, and sundries. Often commissary hours are in the evening to limit interference with inmate daytime work and program schedules.

Commissary is generally provided to inmates on a regular (weekly) basis. The purchasing/delivery method is a required choice decision by the facility. Rewarding inmates with special purchases is another aspect of inmate behavioral control.

The commissary component may also provide for a central storage and issue point of institutional supplies that are used on a daily basis, such as paper goods and nonhazardous cleaning supplies. A correctional supply officer should manage this operation, with all items being delivered through loading dock/receiving and staging areas (see Figs. 3.60 and 3.61).

Prototypical Spaces

22.1 Receiving/staging
22.2 Storage area (cold and dry)
22.3 Correctional supply supervisor
22.4 Staff support room (clerical/files)
22.5 Staff toilet
22.6 Inmate work area
22.7 Inmate toilet

Operational Objectives

- Provide inmates with a procedure to purchase approved items for personal use
- Deliver products to inmates at their housing units in jail facilities, and, generally, have items picked up by inmates at the commissary in prison facilities
- Maintain an automated inmate account system for order deductions
- Maintain inventory records
- Maintain special account for profits obtained from commissary operations for purchasing items for inmate welfare, such as recreational equipment
- Mitigate against providing unfair advantages to wealthy inmates by limiting the total amount of weekly, monthly purchases

Operational Procedures

- Commissary items, as well as institution-issued materials, will be transported to the facility by outside vendors in their vehicles.
- All arriving goods, after proper screening, will be taken off delivery trucks and placed on the loading dock, inventoried, and then placed in commissary storage area.
- Generally, commissary items may be delivered to the housing units, or inmates come to the commissary to pick up orders, depending on facility management. In the case of central pickup, the inmate is assured of receiving the order as requested; in the case of bag and deliver, there is less movement of inmates within the facility.

Staffing Implications

The number of shifts of operations: One
The number of days per week: Five

This area is active during the day shift. The number of staff is determined by the size of the facility and client operational objectives, such as the fre-

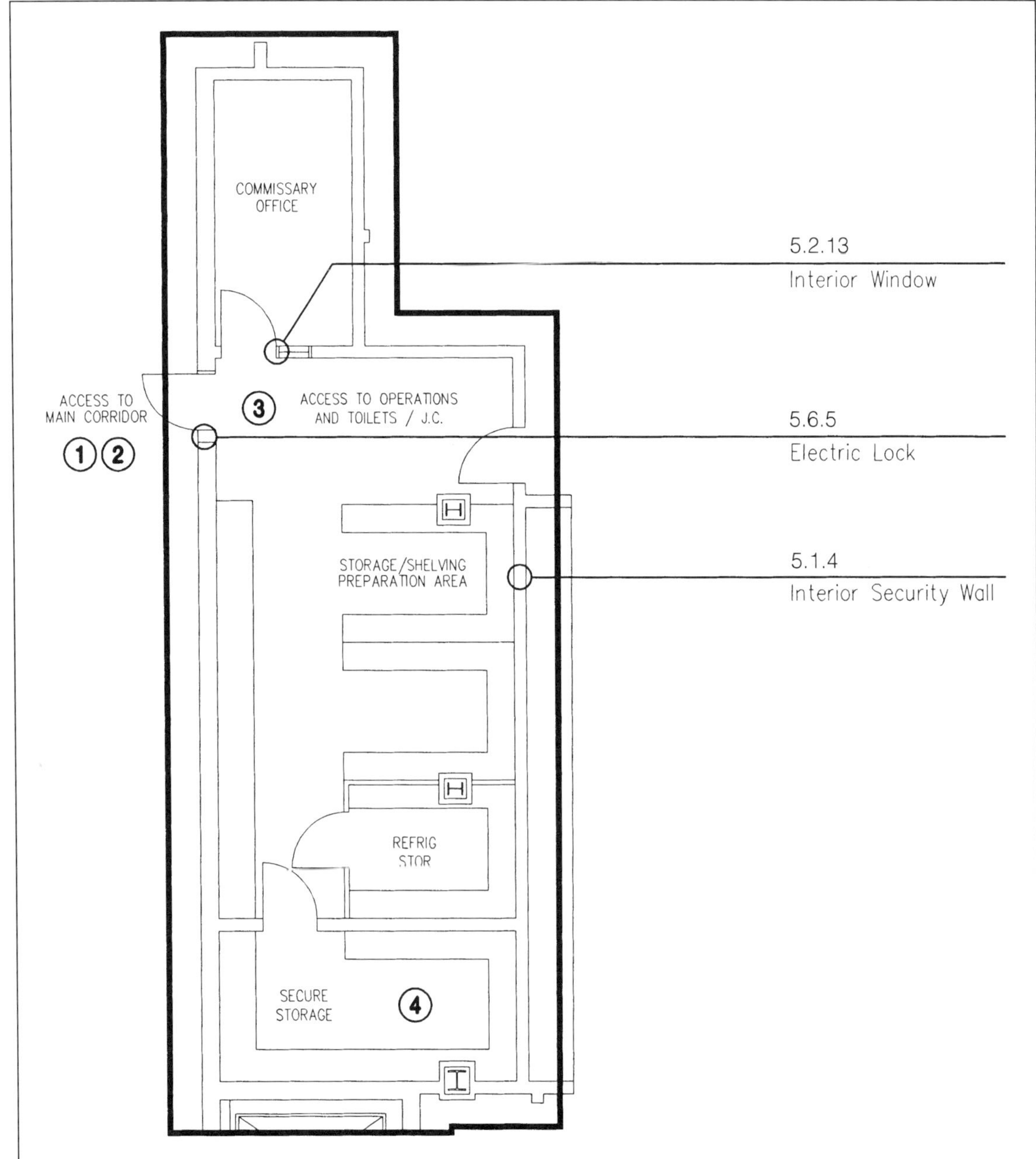

Figure 3.60 **Commissary for a small facility.**

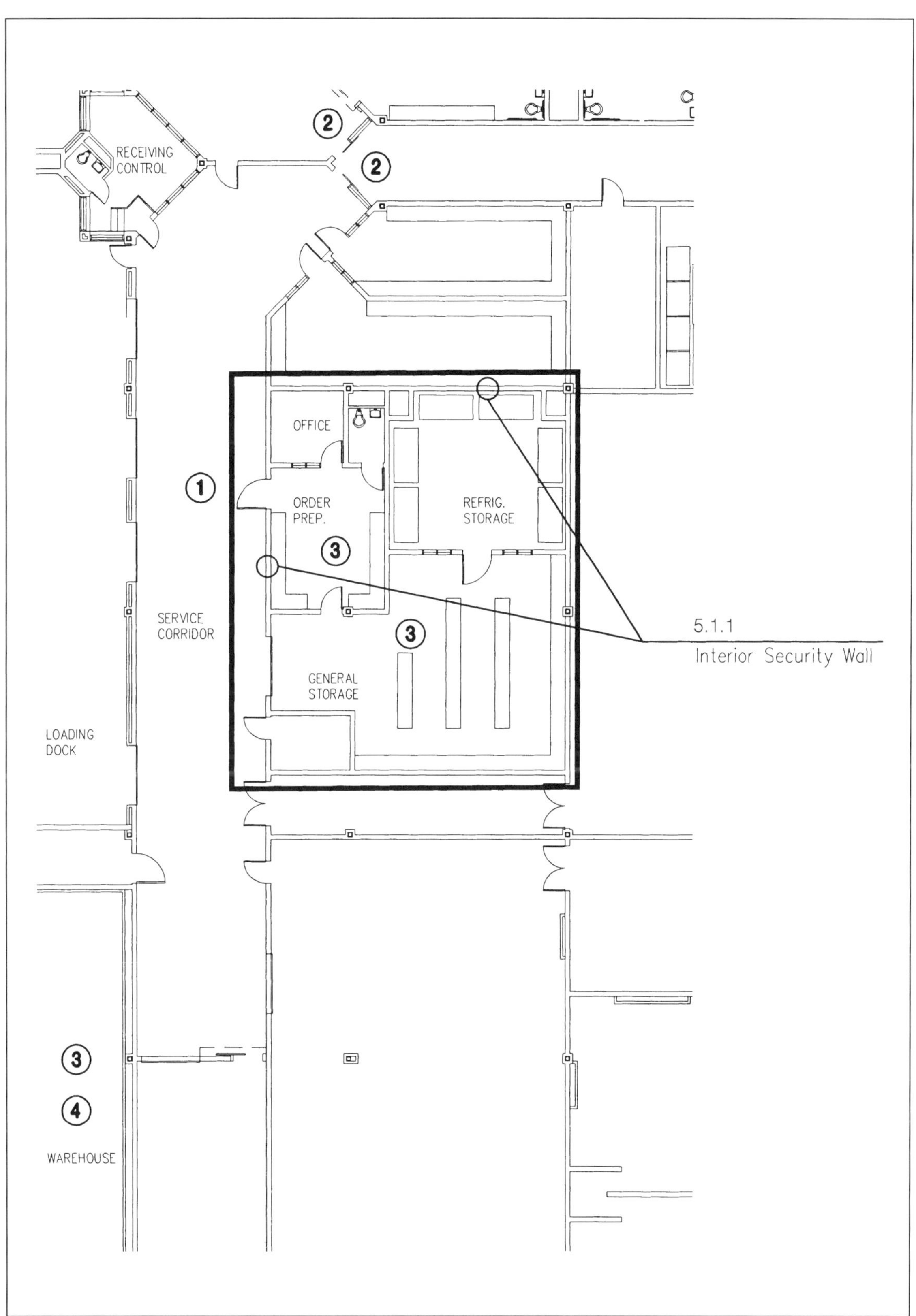

Figure 3.61 **Commissary for a large facility.**

quency and size of commissary purchases permitted. Due to the nature of having supplies of desirable materials on hand, security staff participation in maintaining order and accountability is essential.

Design Considerations

1. Locate the commissary adjacent to warehouse, kitchen, and laundry services to take advantage of inmate work programs, the sharing, screening, and inventory of goods, and for security control.
2. Locate the commissary adjacent to the inmate corridor to facilitate pickups if items are not delivered to housing units.
3. Separate the commissary purchasing area from warehouse storage of goods to facilitate the delivery of items to inmates. As an example, the purchasing area can be located adjacent to centralized dining room(s) in prison settings, or gymnasium(s), to provide inmate pickup of items before or after these activities.
4. Provide separate, secure storage space for commissary materials in the warehouse in order to maintain control of inventory.

23.0 CENTRAL LAUNDRY

Program Statement

Provide adequate laundry services for all inmates. Provide a procedure whereby state- or county-issued clothing, linens, and bedclothes are collected from the housing units on a regular basis and taken to the central laundry. Clothing, when cleaned, is returned to inmates promptly or to the clothing supply room.

Inmate clothing can be collected by manual carts from each housing unit and operations areas, such as medical, and brought to the central laundry. Institutional grade washers and dryers should be used. State- or county-issued clothing being laundered is returned to inventory including regular and special items such as outdoor clothing and kitchen whites.

In addition to a supervisor's office, provide areas for loading dock, receiving, sorting, washing, drying, pressing, packaging clean laundry, storage, mending, and chemical storage.

Institutional laundry services often offer the opportunity for shared services to reduce overall operational cost (e.g., doing all county institution laundry at the facility since it requires major capital investment to construct a proper laundry and because it is a recurring workload that can be handled in manageable pieces (see Fig. 3.62).

Prototypical Spaces

23.1 Receiving/staging area
23.2 Shipping
23.3 Laundry office(s)
23.4 Staff toilet
23.5 Laundry area (washers and dryers)
23.6 Laundry issue
23.7 Mending area
23.8 Secure detergent storage
23.9 Inmate break area
23.10 Inmate toilet
23.11 Janitor's closet

Operational Objectives

- Provide a procedure for regularly scheduled collection of inmate clothing, bedding, and towels for cleaning
- Provide inmate distribution of clean clothing, bedding, and towels on a regular basis
- Maintain an adequate supply of clean inmate clothing, bedding, and towels to support the facility's daily operations and intake facilities
- Provide work opportunities to inmates who express interest in an active work program

Operational Procedures

- At intake (admissions) area, inmates are issued clean clothing, bedding, and towel(s) from the property storage room.
- Staff will supervise collection of dirty laundry and distribution of clean products to inmates at their housing units, on a regularly scheduled basis.
- Storage of additional and/or new items such as mattresses, pillows, bedding, blankets, facility uniforms, and towels is in the warehouse.
- Clean items are stored in the laundry and the property room in the intake/release area.
- Typically, inmates are required to exchange items one for one to maintain inventory control and accountability for damages.

Staffing Implications

The number of shifts of operations: One
The number of days per week: Five

This area is usually active during the day shift. The number of staff is determined by the size of the facility and client operational objectives including whether or not the secure facility provides central laundry services for other facilities and jurisdictions.

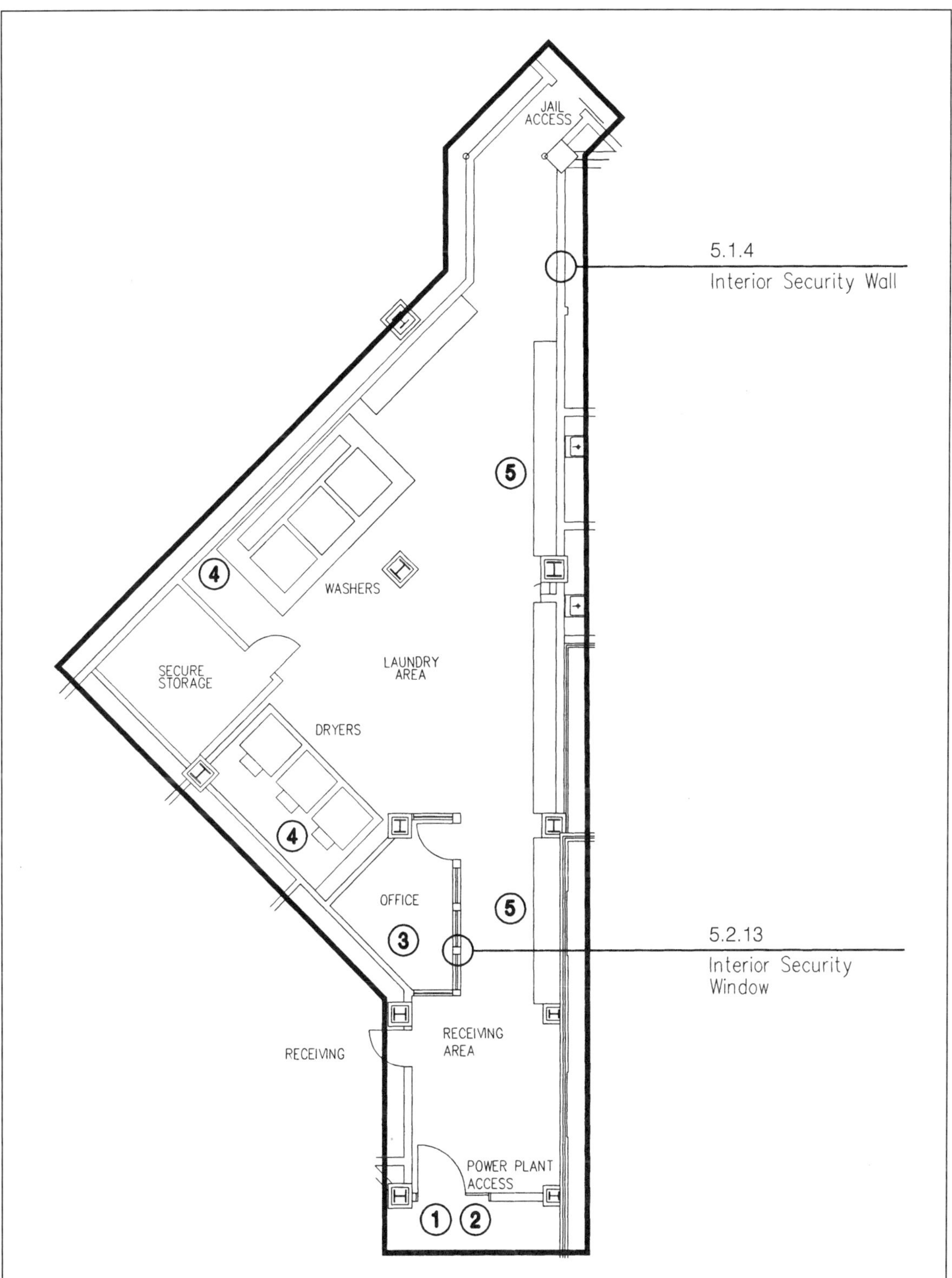

Figure 3.62 **Laundry service area for a small facility.**

Design Considerations

1. Locate the laundry near the kitchen and adjacent to the central power plant to reduce construction and operating costs with the supply of steam to specific equipment for these functions
2. Locate the laundry adjacent to the warehouse and loading docks to facilitate delivery and waste removal
3. Locate the laundry supervisor's office centrally within the space to observe and control in-

Figure 3.63 **Services control station with 100 percent observation, supervision, and control of loading/unloading area.**

mate workers' activities in the laundry operation

4. Locate equipment against walls to provide an open view of operations
5. Separate dirty item delivery access from clean item delivery access
6. Provide adequate ventilation and sanitary drainage capacity

24.0 WAREHOUSE

Program Statement

The space includes storage for all dry goods, material storage, secure storage, and inactive inmate files. Space is also provided for office personnel, staff, and inmate restrooms. Some provisions are included for refrigerated and freezer storage for kitchen and canteen items. Industry usually has provisions for raw material and finished product storage in the warehouse.

A key issue is location of the warehouse with respect to the security perimeter. For high-security facilities, design professionals tend to promote leaving the warehouse on or outside of the perimeter because it reduces the cost and effort for deliveries. A location inside the perimeter requires vehicles to be searched in and out, but may be better in terms of maintaining security and staff efficiency (see Figs. 3.63 and 3.64).

Prototypical Spaces

24.1 Materials manager's office
24.2 Secretary office/area
24.3 Secured storage
24.4 Buyer's office
24.5 Dock control office/area
24.6 Male toilet
24.7 Female toilet
24.8 Janitor's closet
24.9 Inmate toilet
24.10 Receiving docks
24.11 Staging area (includes fluoroscope)
24.12 General warehouse storage (partial use by industry)
24.13 Refrigerated storage
24.14 Freezer storage
24.15 Hazardous material storage
24.16 Crusher/compactor
24.17 Covered recycling storage

Operational Objectives

- Provide bulk storage space for all facility supplies, inmate clothing, bedding, paper products, office supplies, long-term food goods, and so forth

- Search all incoming items for contraband
- Log all items received and delivered to the facility and maintain records
- Maintain an inventory of items on-hand to meet projected needs

Operational Procedures

- Access to the central storage/warehouse area should be strictly monitored and controlled by a staff supervisor, and in some cases by a civilian.
- Communications, and often control, is supported from the central control station.

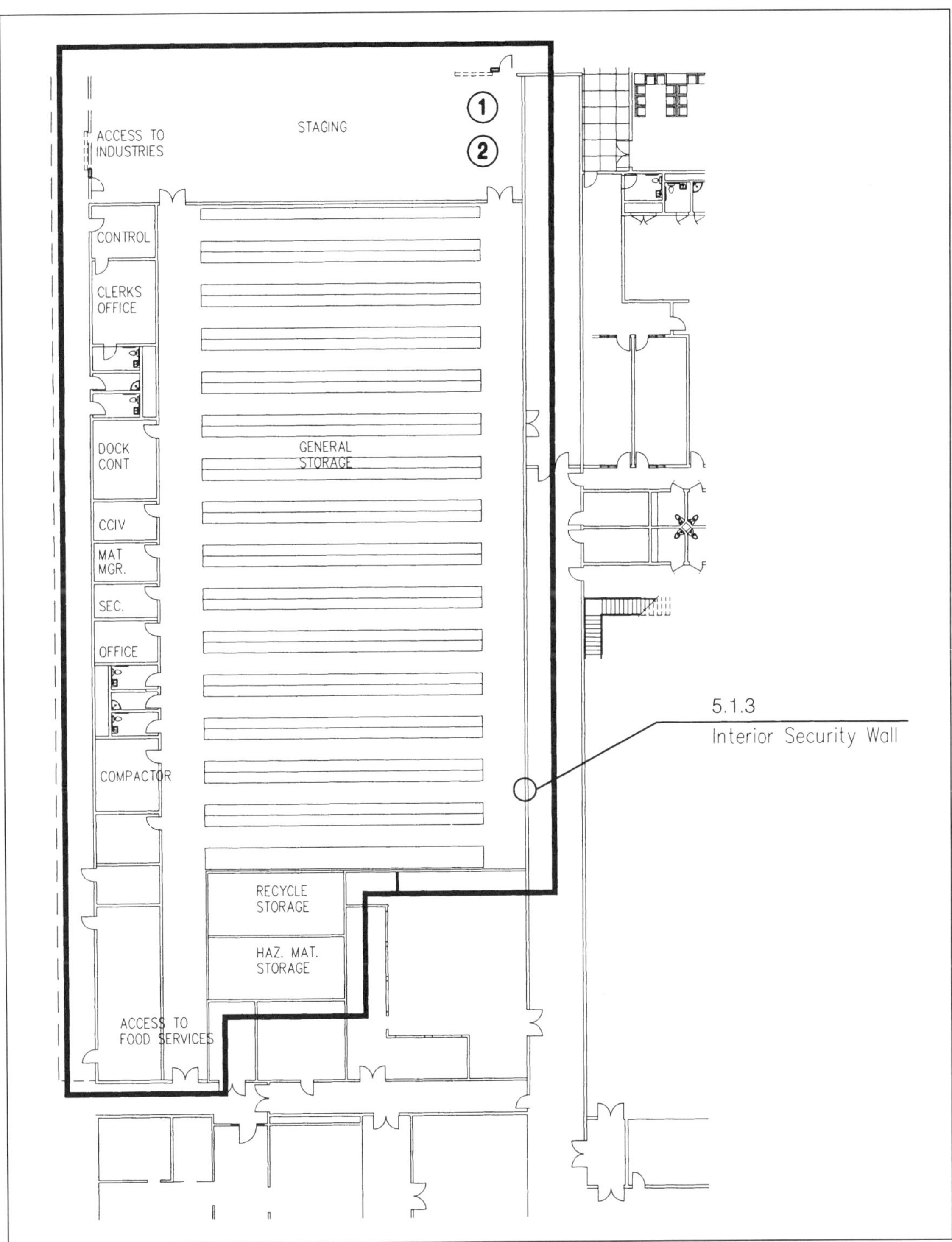

Figure 3.64 **Warehouse area for a large facility.**

- Inmates working in the warehouse will be carefully monitored under direct staff supervision.
- While a single central warehouse area for all types of goods and materials utilized by the facility would generally be the most efficient, administrative and/or financial reasons (e.g., inmate funds generated by the commissary) may require that discrete, secure areas be provided for general stores, commissary, food service, education, or industries.

Staffing Implications

The number of shifts of operations: One or Two
The number of days per week: Five or Seven

This area is normally active during the day shift. The number of staff is determined by the size of the facility and client operational objectives. Inmate supervision may be by civilian personnel if within the security perimeter.

Design Considerations

1. Locate this area based upon a detailed discussion with the project team. Its location has experienced a variety of positions as expressed by administrative operational preferences. If located completely on the free side of the facility, daily deliveries of products require a major traffic flow through the security perimeter albeit utilizing institutional vehicles and personnel. Although reduction of vendor contact inside the perimeter is best with this delivery method, the double handling of inventory may outweigh its benefits.
2. A location completely on the secure side of the facility provides vendors with penetration of the secure perimeter of the facility on a daily basis which can often be staff-intensive, including vehicle search and rover escorts.
3. Consider current thinking, which focuses on splitting the function and appears to have benefits in addressing both concerns: a staging area for vendors located on the free side can be limited, while providing the bulk of storage on the secure side of the facility for ease of daily delivery of materials and improved operations.

25.0 ENGINEERING/PLANT MAINTENANCE

Program Statement

This department maintains the physical plant and its equipment to create an environment required for an institution to function. Maintenance of equipment and services should cause a minimal intrusion on the operations of the institution.

This department should create a program whereby a preventative maintenance program is developed and maintained. A secured supply room must be controlled and maintained. In addition, this department must maintain the mobile patrol vehicles in good working order, as well as the institution's other vehicles and emergency generators (see Fig. 3.65).

Prototypical Spaces

25.1 Building maintenance supervisor's office
25.2 Electrical maintenance supervisor's office
25.3 Secretary office/area
25.4 Safety officer's office
25.5 Office/record room
25.6 Open work area
25.7 Staff toilet
25.8 Inmate toilet
25.9 Supply room office/clerical area
25.10 Supply room
25.11 Tool room
25.12 Maintenance shops area (or individual shops as follows)
Carpentry shop
Masonry shop
Electrical shop
Plumbing shop
Metal shop
Paint shop
General repair shop
25.13 Hazardous material storage
25.14 Paint storage
25.15 Compressor room
25.16 Locked storage
25.17 Maintenance materials storage
25.18 Receiving area

Operational Objectives

- Provide a comprehensive preventative program for the maintenance of the facility's mechanical, electrical, and plumbing systems
- Maintain the physical plant, equipment, and facility grounds in good condition
- Ensure daily maintenance and cleaning of the facility

Operational Procedures

- Civilian staff is typically responsible for staffing, operation, and maintenance of primary utility systems and physical plant (powerhouse, emergency power). During the normal activities of operation the central plan, regularly scheduled maintenance, and emergency repairs are accomplished to keep the facility operational. Relatively few inmates are used in central powerhouse plant operations.

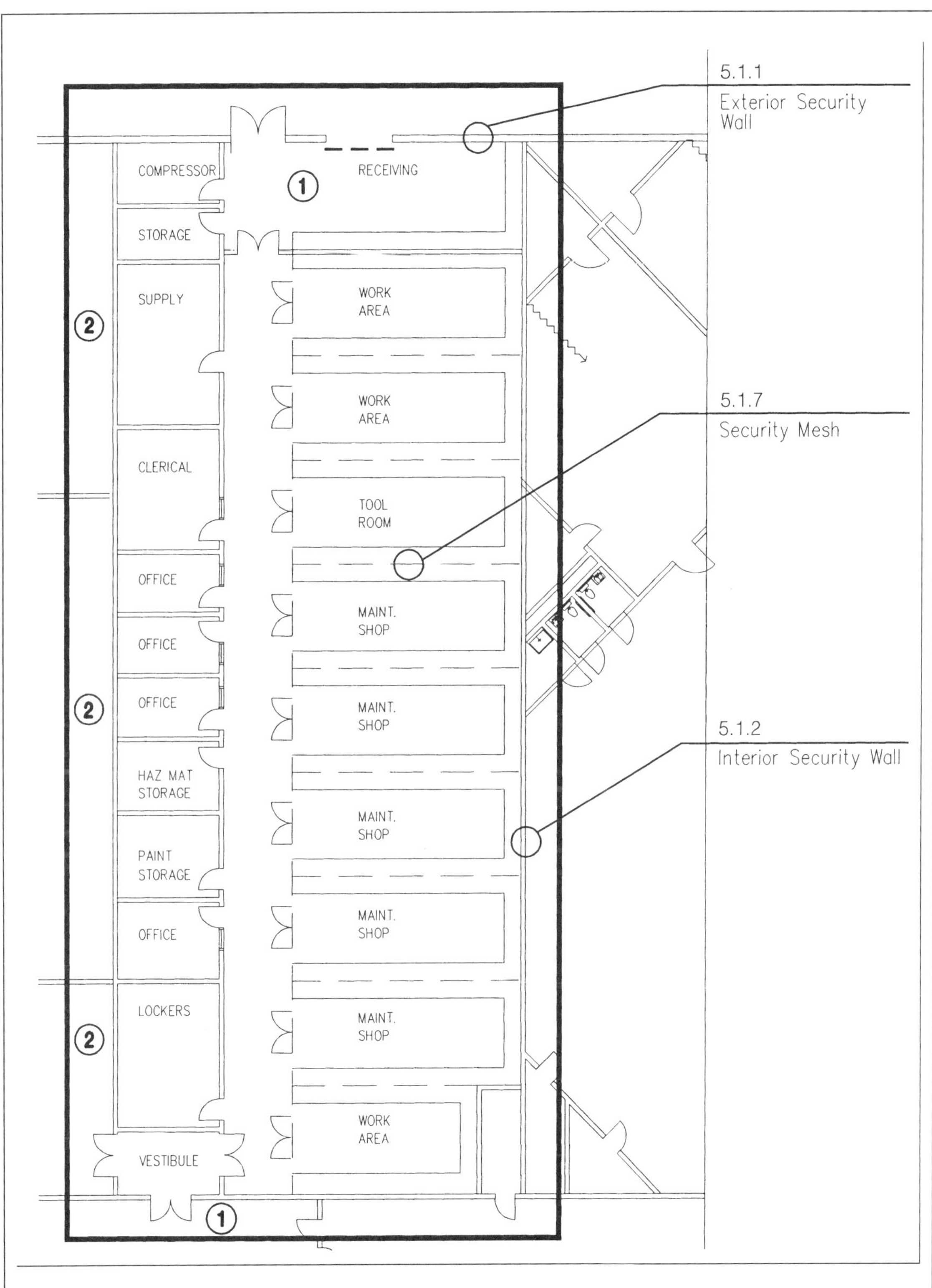

Figure 3.65 **Engineering/plant maintenance for a large facility.**

- Civilian staff is also responsible for daily maintenance and cleaning of the entire facility; inmate cadre assignments, particularly in housing units, play an important part of getting this accomplished. For long-term maintenance and general repairs, a work-order system is generally established with the work assigned to the shop supervisor that has the largest role in performing the project. The quality and skill demonstrated by in-house staff is frequently amazing.

Staffing Implications

Staffing in this component is significantly affected by size, age, and condition of existing buildings. The failure to maintain adequate staffing to perform regular maintenance over time poses a threat to the ability to keep the facility online.

The number of shifts of operations: Three
The number of days per week: Five, Seven

This component area is most active during the day shift. The expense of maintaining adequate facility maintenance is significantly aided by use of inmate work assignments. Daily cleaning is normally accomplished by inmate cadres. Similarly, time-consuming and difficult maintenance assignments are often performed by civilian shop supervisors with inmate work crews.

Design Considerations

1. Locate the maintenance area on the inside of the secure perimeter side of the institution for daily routine repairs within the facility, particularly since the civilian staff may not be immediately available at night for emergency repairs
2. Provide space adjacent to the central power plant, since the staff that work in the maintenance area are often those who also maintain the central plant
3. Provide a space for the maintenance of vehicles outside of the secure perimeter

26.0 PHYSICAL PLANT

Program Statement

The physical plant is the energy center of the institution. Included in this area are the boilers, chillers, electrical switchgear, and so forth to provide power, water, and electricity to the institution. Generally, the physical plant is located on the outside of the security perimeter. However, some administrators in lower-security or open campus facilities prefer its location on the inside of security and adjacent to the maintenance area, where staff are located and can operate and maintain the plant and its equipment.

While the central plant provides power for the institution as a whole, localized mechanical and electrical rooms are generally required at housing buildings and support buildings. Local conditions generally dictate the systems, conditions, and energy source based upon economic considerations. Since the facility cannot evacuate its inmates without great difficulties, the proper operational capacity is essential to maintain light, heat, power, water, and sanitary drainage for the facility to stay up and running (see Figs. 3.66 and 3.67).

Prototypical Spaces

26.1 Mechanical equipment room
26.2 Chiller equipment room
26.3 Fan room
26.4 Electrical room
26.5 Emergency generator room
26.6 Sewage treatment plant
26.7 Water treatment/storage
26.8 Staff toilet
26.9 Janitor closet

Operational Objectives

- Provide all essential utility services to all areas of the facility 24 hours a day, 7 days a week, 365 days a year
- Maintain an appropriate comfort level of heat in the winter and coolness in the summer for visitors, staff, and inmates alike
- Maintain security control of this area

Operations Procedure

- For each of the primary utility generation and distribution systems provided on site, a schedule for routine maintenance and repair must be prepared and carried out.
- Action plans and other provisions need to be made in advance for emergency situations (e.g., failure of a boiler or the water supply).

Staffing Implications

The number of shifts of operations: Three
The number of days per week: Seven

The number of staff is determined by size of facility and client operational objectives. In most facilities, there is at least one full-time qualified plant engineer on duty at all times to maintain operation of primary utility systems.

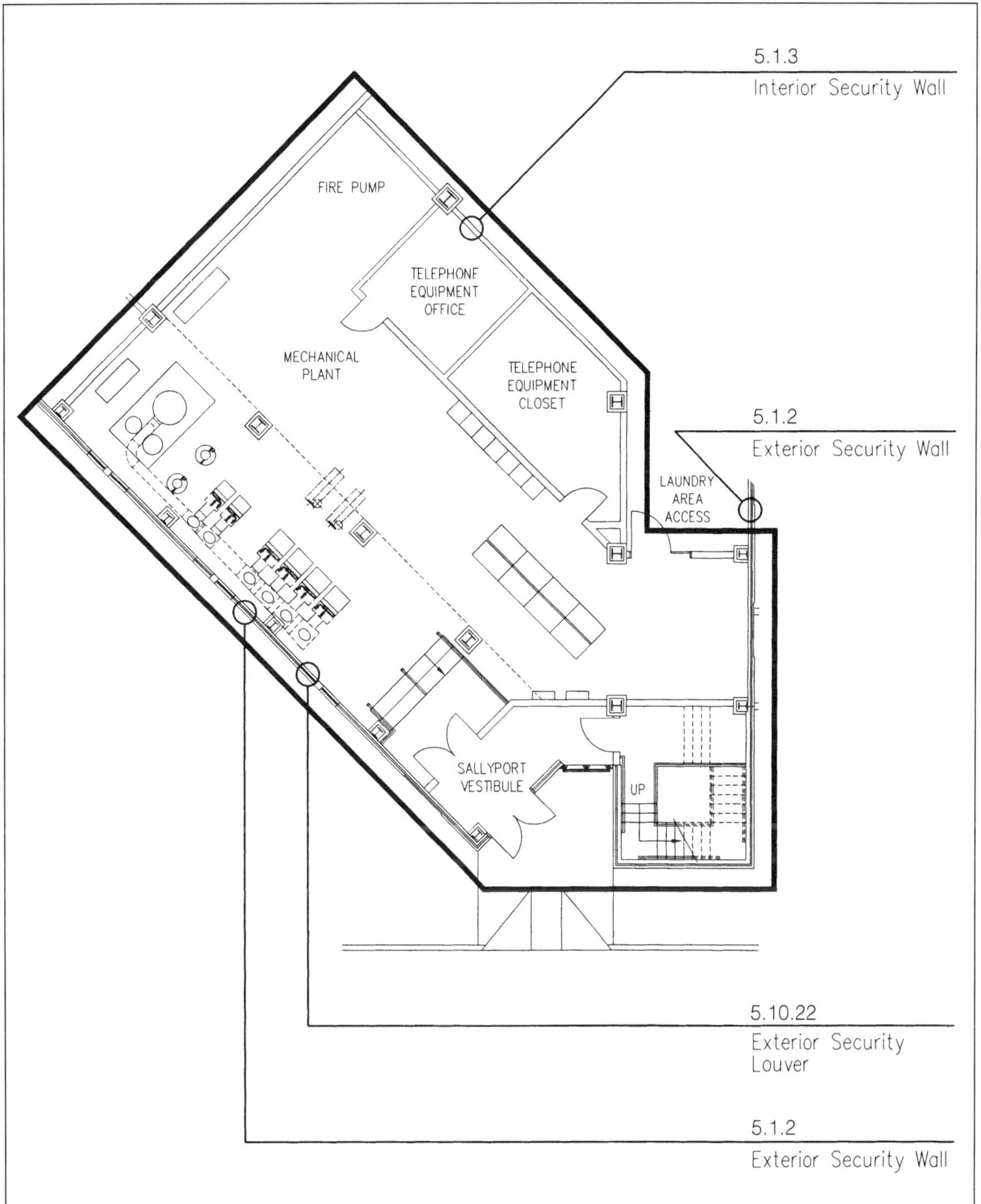

Figure 3.66 **Physical plant design for a small facility.**

Design Considerations

1. Locating the central physical plant is generally a decision by your client representative group based on a variety of reasons as identified in the previous section.
2. A location within the secure perimeter, when secured within itself and close to maintenance shops, may outweigh the reasons to locate it outside of the secure perimeter.
3. A central location could equally distribute utilities to all buildings and areas of an institution, and thereby provide cost savings in the initial construction of a facility.

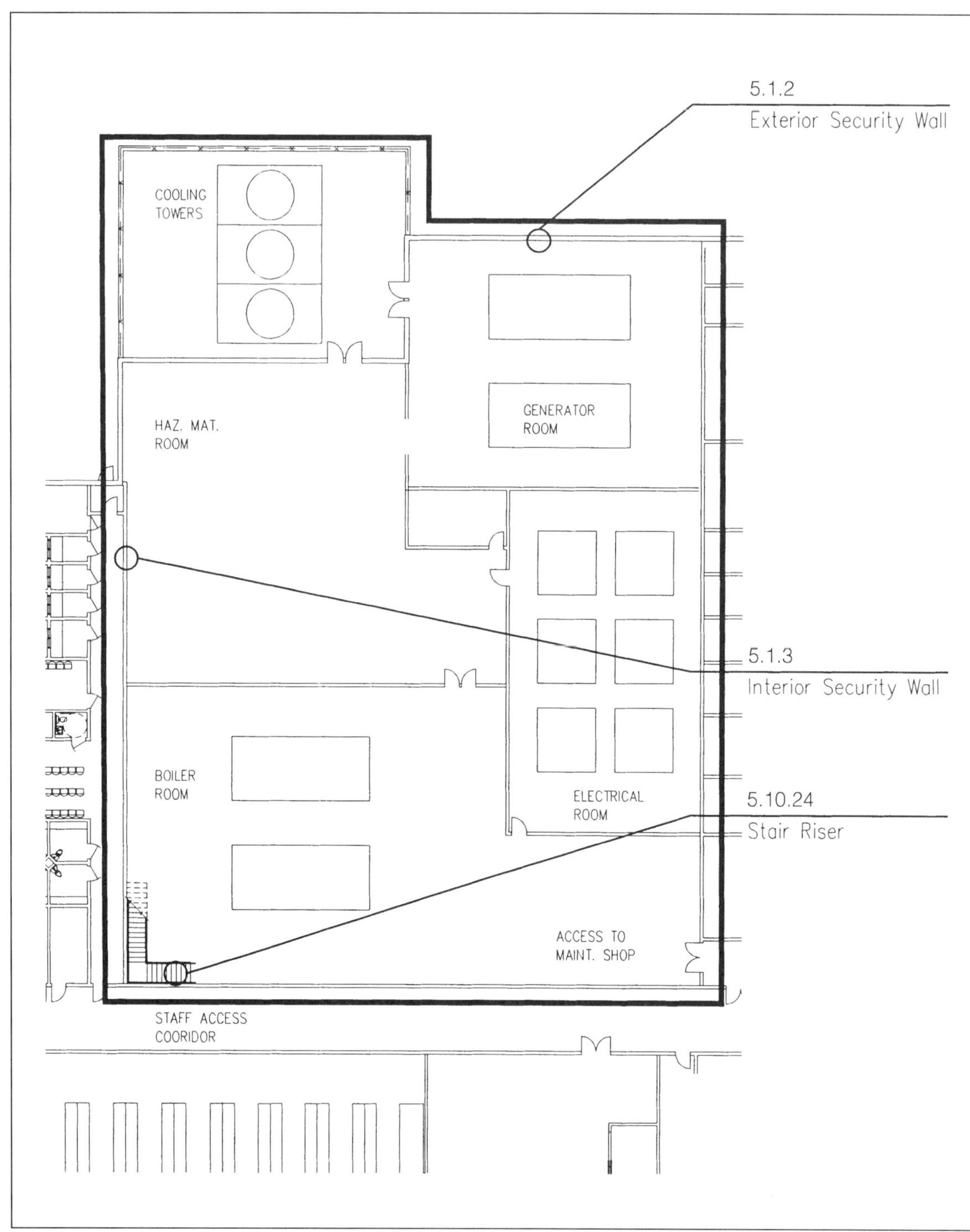

Figure 3.67 **Physical plant design for a large facility.**

27.0 TRANSPORTATION/SECURITY PERIMETER ACCESS

Program Statement

Safe, secure, and timely transportation of inmates to and from (and often within) the institution is provided from this component. In addition, transportation needs of staff, public officials, visitors, and vendors are the responsibility of the staff who are assigned to this department.

Entry into the institution should be provided in an orderly, timely, and secure manner for inmates, staff, visitors, vendors, public officials, and others to maintain the institution's security. An orderly release and/or exit from the institution of persons authorized to leave must be maintained.

Ideally, there are only two points of penetration of the facility perimeter for entry—one for pedestrians (staff, visitors) and one for vehicles (inmate transportation, goods/materials). The ability to maintain the integrity of the perimeter security is significantly affected by having additional penetrations, since each requires staffing when in use (see Fig. 3.68).

Prototypical Spaces

27.1 Visitor parking area
27.2 Public transportation waiting shelters
27.3 Staff parking area
27.4 Vehicular sally port(s) (drive-through preferred)
27.5 Pedestrian sally port(s)
27.6 Traffic manager's office
27.7 Transportation staff office
27.8 Motor pool garage (multiple bays)
27.9 Auto repair (one hydraulic lift)
27.10 Parts storage room
27.11 Tire storage area
27.12 Staff toilet
27.13 Janitor closet

Operational Objectives

- Provide a secure area for transportation vehicles to unload inmates being admitted to and transferred from the facility
- Provide secure gun lockers for officer's use to prevent them from entering the facility and from inmate access
- Provide a secure area for transportation vehicles entering the secure perimeter with a sally port of size for the largest anticipated delivery vehicle
- Provide convenient parking areas for staff, visitors, and handicap-accessible, public transportation discharge and loading areas

Operational Procedures

- In terms of general facility access, visitors and staff should be able to approach the parking areas and pedestrian walks to the facility entry without impediment.
- Security controls are then initiated once an individual enters the facility.
- The perimeter security system, including any perimeter patrol perimeter road, should be relatively inaccessible from the perspective of the general public.

Staffing Implications

The number of shifts of operations: One

The number of days per week: Five

This area is active during the three shifts. The point of pedestrian entry needs to be staffed 24 hours per day, 7 days a week. The vehicular sally port is typically manned during the day, but capability to operate it must be maintained around the clock in the case of emergency vehicles or, in the case of jails, for inmate intake.

Design Considerations

1. Locate this component always on the outside of the secure perimeter to facilitate easy access by staff and for vehicle maintenance.
2. Locate fuel pumps in this location. The area should be designed to function similar to a gasoline filling station in providing vehicular access and a garage area for official vehicles.
3. Provide space to accommodate the facility's largest vehicle size, both in terms of sally port entries and in terms of maneuvering space for vehicular roads.
4. Locate staff and public parking areas conveniently with respect to the point of pedestrian entry to the facility. Some jurisdictions prefer staff and visitor parking to be separate areas; in this case, the staff parking area should not be located in the path between visitor parking and the facility entrance.
5. Provide clarity of vehicular and site graphics which is essential for people unfamiliar with the facility to have a clear understanding of where they should go.
6. Locate the point of vehicular sally port entry through the facility perimeter to require intentional decisions to approach (minimizes accidental approach by inappropriate vehicles). Similarly, access to the perimeter patrol road should be designed to discourage unauthorized vehicle entry.

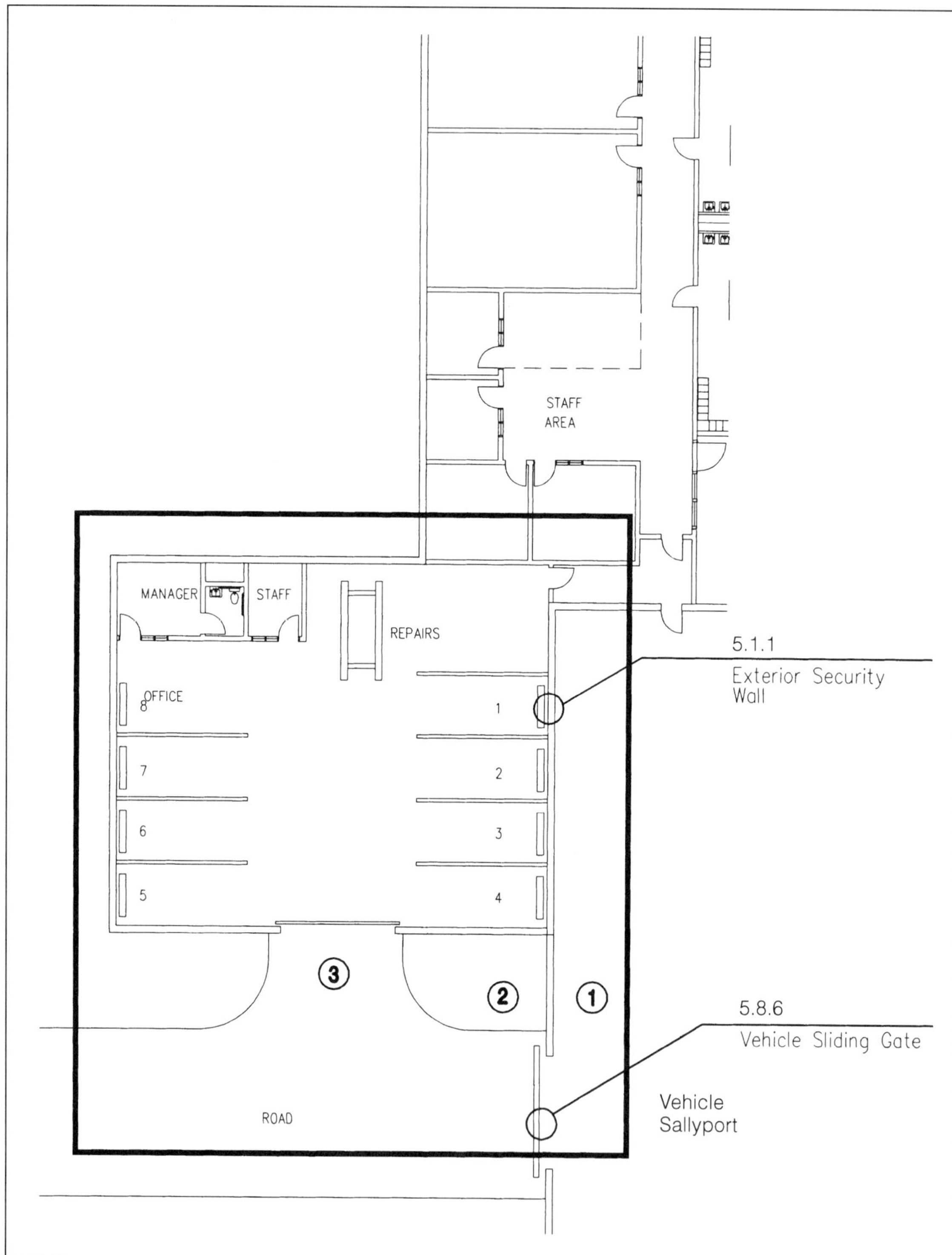

Figure 3.68 **Transportation/perimeter access for a large facility.**

7. Locate control of the vehicle sally port gates, for high-security facilities, on the outside of the sally port at a point that provides visual supervision of activity within the sally port.
8. While sight lines from any perimeter patrol road in toward the facility must be maintained, the opportunity exists outside that zone to utilize landscaping and planting to provide a visual buffer for activities at the facility.
9. Within a facility security perimeter, building configuration and design must permit relative ease of access for fire and other emergency vehicles.

SUMMARY

The challenge of architectural space planning is in the assemblage of the various component parts that form an architectural plan. Each component's relationship to an adjacent area becomes the fundamental and driving force in determining a final arrangement of spaces in support of a facility's operational philosophy. Many facility operators establish operational policy and goals that can directly affect a design's final planned arrangement of spaces. Each component may not be required or desired as part of every jail or prison project's program.

The following two facility designs (Figs. 3.69 and 3.70) represent a small-scale jail (with housing stacked over administrative and support spaces located at grade) and a large-scale prison (with housing units stacked over housing units, and administrative and support spaces located at grade and adjacent to housing units). Program component areas of each are graphically outlined to indicate adjacency relationships. Facility designs are addressed in the next chapter identifying key design issues for consideration for incorporation into correctional facilities. Eighteen facility designs are presented, highlighting housing plan arrangements, facility plan layouts, and specific design features.

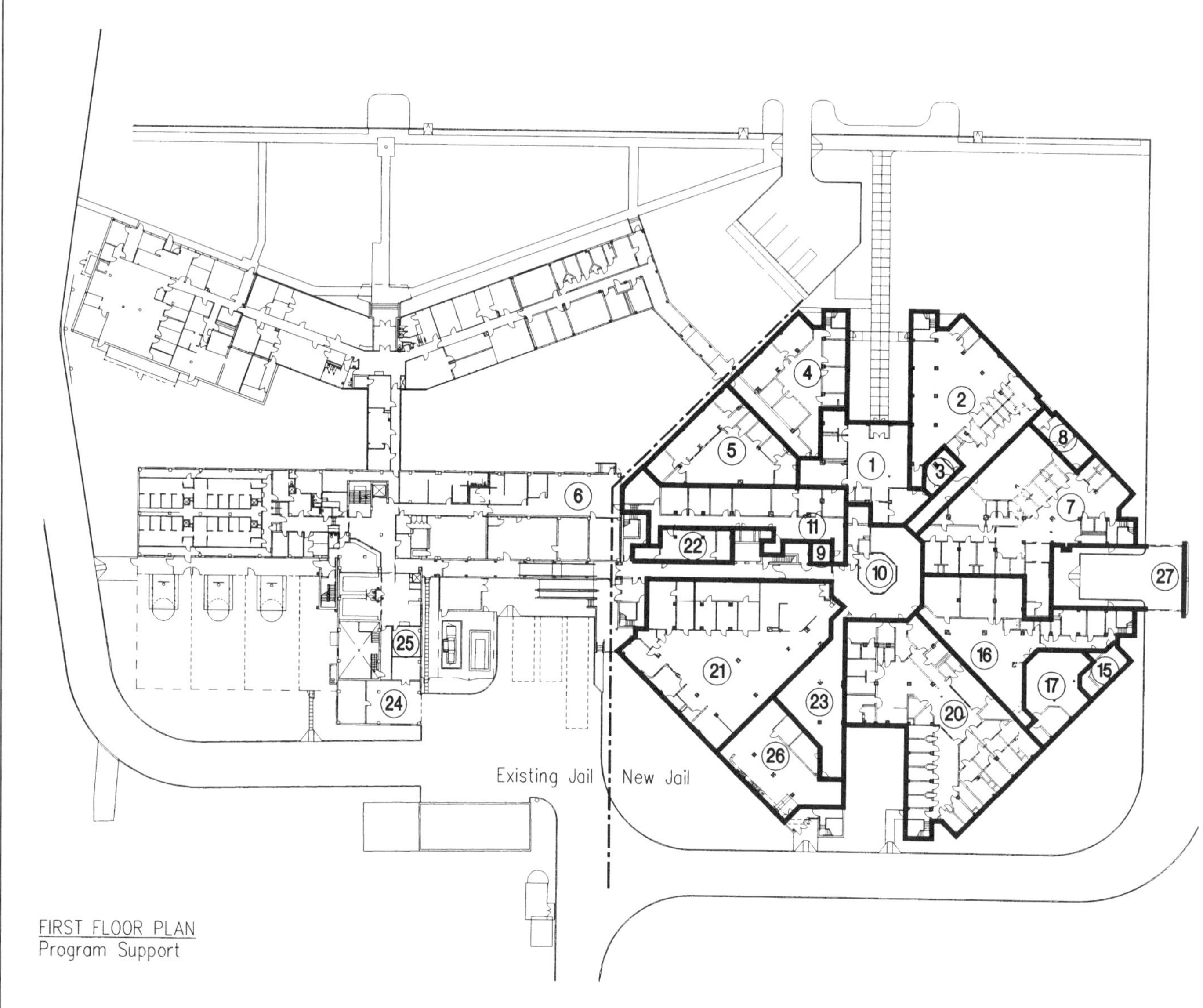

Figure 3.69 **Components assembled into facility floor plan for a small jail facility.**

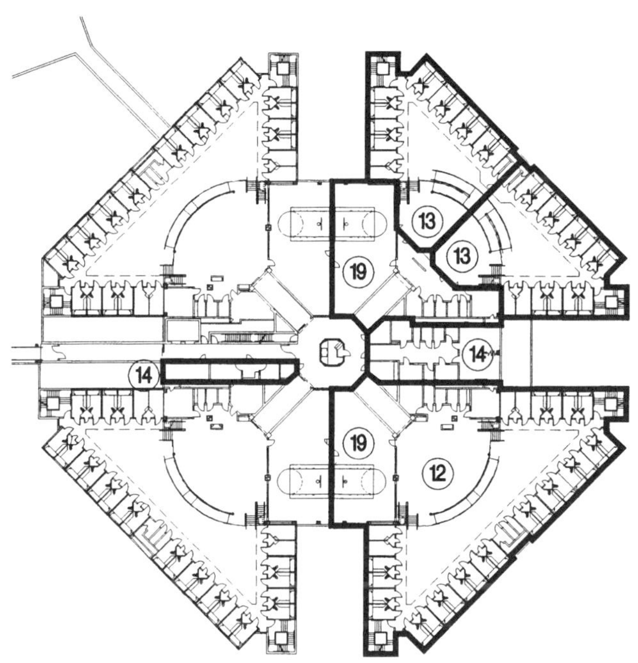

1 = Public Lobby
2 = Visitation
3 = Hearings/Invest.
4 = Exec. Admin.
5 = Case Management
6 = Staff Development
7 = Intake/Transfer
8 = Classification
9 = Communications
10 = Master Control
11 = Operations
12 = General Housing
13 = Special Housing
14 = Unit Management
15 = Inmate/social services
16 = Education
17 = Religious Services
18 = Industry
19 = Recreation
20 = Health Services
21 = Food Service
22 = Commisary
23 = Laundry Service
24 = Warehouse
25 = Engineering/Maint.
26 = Physical Plant
27 = Transport./access

SECOND FLOOR PLAN
Housing

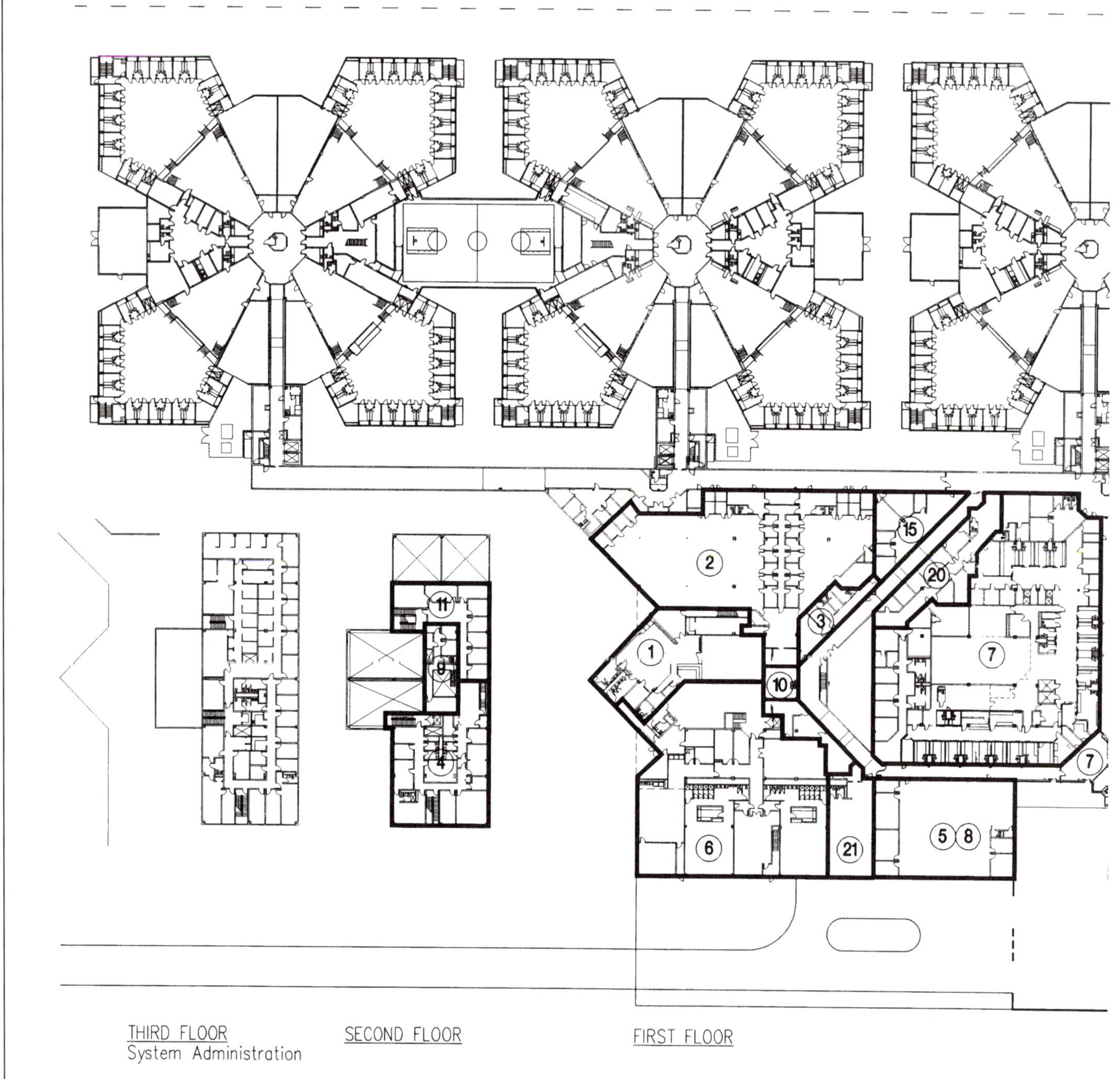

Figure 3.70 **Components assembled into facility floor plan for a large prison facility.**

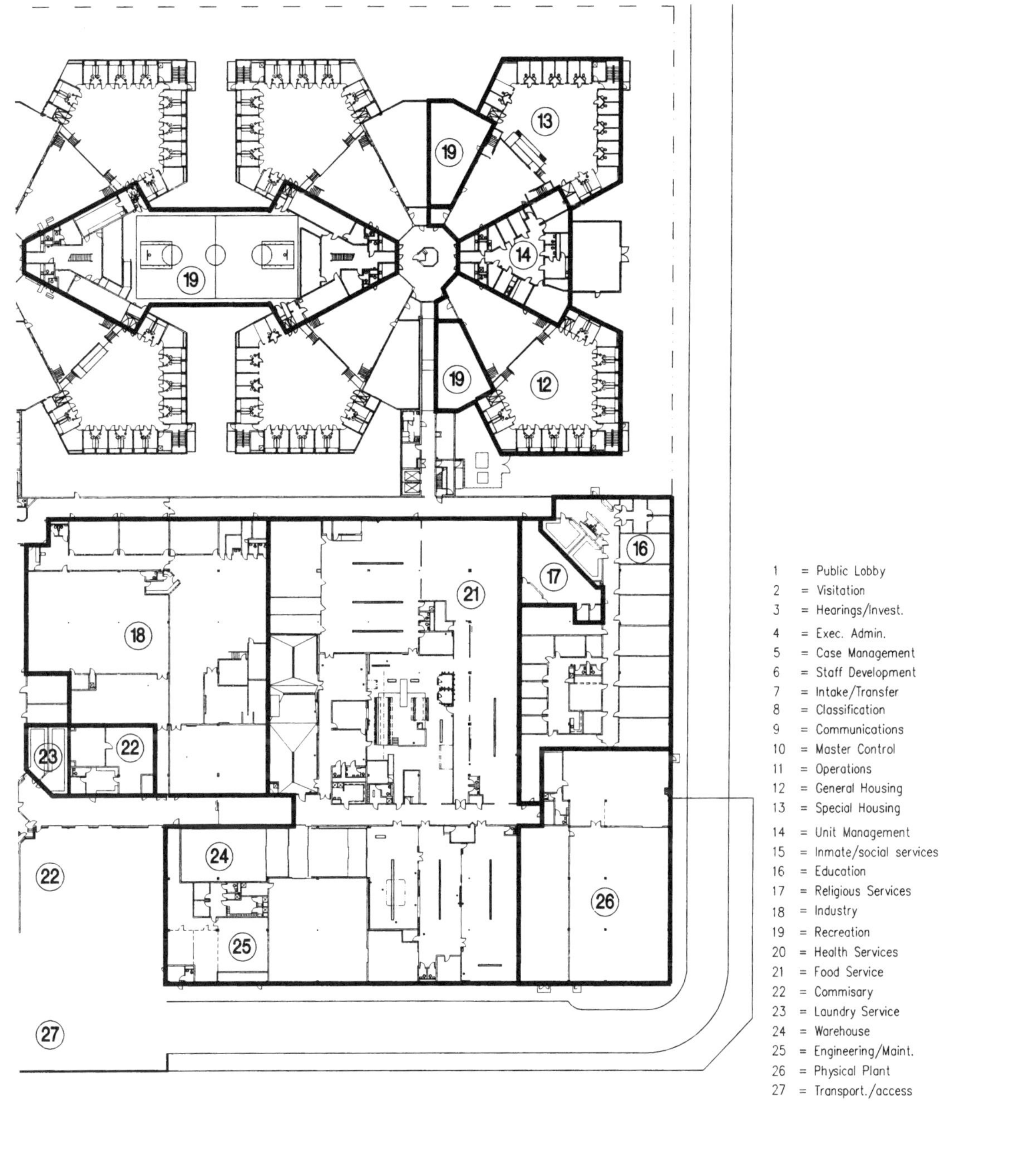
1 = Public Lobby
2 = Visitation
3 = Hearings/Invest.
4 = Exec. Admin.
5 = Case Management
6 = Staff Development
7 = Intake/Transfer
8 = Classification
9 = Communications
10 = Master Control
11 = Operations
12 = General Housing
13 = Special Housing
14 = Unit Management
15 = Inmate/social services
16 = Education
17 = Religious Services
18 = Industry
19 = Recreation
20 = Health Services
21 = Food Service
22 = Commisary
23 = Laundry Service
24 = Warehouse
25 = Engineering/Maint.
26 = Physical Plant
27 = Transport./access

4 Facility Design

Architectural plans illustrating program component relationships in forming complete facility designs: major types of correctional facilities are illustrated: municipal/county/regional detention facilities (jails); federal/state correctional facilities (prisons). Small-, medium-, and large-scale facilities (from campus plans to high-rise urban facilities) are shown to provide a visual comparison of issues and solutions.

The following pages illustrate a variety of facility designs for jails as well as prisons for sites requiring low-rise, mid-rise, and/or high-rise buildings, and for direct and indirect supervision modes of operation. The facility plans describe the major building components of a correctional facility and their adjacency relationships. These design examples pictorially contrast physical differences of jails, which are generally more compact in plan, with prisons, which are generally more open in plan (often campuslike in layout). Understanding these designs can assist a project team in addressing a project's specific programmatic goals, with opportunities to choose an appropriate design solution based upon an institution's major objectives, practices, and preferences.

The first series of diagrams describe the general relationship of components in creating facility types: campus, modified campus, interconnected, contained, contained and linear, and contained and stacked. Each diagram indicates relationships of the main elements of a correctional facility: public/staff entrance and parking, administration, program/service support, inmate housing, outdoor exercise/recreation spaces, and secure perimeter. These relationship diagrams are followed by examples of facility housing unit plans and floor plans of completed institutional designs which are currently in operation. In some cases, facilities have experienced changes with new administrative executive staff, changes in operational philosophy, and shifts in inmate population type and size. Current demands from these shifts in inmate profiles and the need for additional bed space can have a significant impact on a facility's design.

A facility that remains flexible and continues to function as planned is often a good test of a successful design. Many of these designs have withstood years of operation with support of the original architectural plan design. These plans typically exhibit a simplicity in the plan layout that provides clear sight lines for ease of staff response to incidents; normally, they also enjoy flexibility of spatial use, including the provision of multipurpose rooms.

Generic to all functional layouts are elements which allow the architect to create design features that can support a client's operational philosophy and mode of operation. In the previous chapter, design considerations were indicated for each program space component. In this chapter, design features are indicated for each of 18 different facilities supported with architectural floor plans. The following are correctional design–related issues offered for consideration and discussion by any project team. They provide a design perspective of exterior, interior, housing, and other related correctional facility conditions.

EXTERIOR ISSUES

- ***Exterior perimeter*** fences or buildings should be simple in form. Uniformity can be achieved with a continuous, fence line/patrol road and a minimum of directional changes and breaks in form. Alignment of buildings should follow the same criteria.
- ***Exterior view of perimeter*** should allow the officer to observe large portions of the fence configuration and buildings. Maximum views should be available from a minimum number of vantage points. Although CCTV and other monitoring devices can be utilized, visual supervision by direct personal observation also enhances security. (See Fig. 4.1.)
- ***Guard towers*** often provide additional security for a large prison facility in observing, control-

Figure 4.1 **Housing dayroom window view to exterior, with guard tower located on fence line in background to control perimeter.**

ling, and preventing penetration of the perimeter fences of the institution. Placing the towers in line with the outer fence can provide views of the entire length along a fence line. Placing the towers on the inner fence line will provide observation of the secure side of the facility where inmates potentially may attempt escape. Utilizing a single, centrally located tower to observe the entire perimeter can also be supported by perimeter patrol vehicles on chase roads for quick response to incidents.

- ***Facility patrol vehicles*** should be considered in lieu of guard towers for improved response to all incidents, when utilizing perimeter fence security detection systems. The annual cost of operating guard towers may not provide the value for the dollars expended when compared with roving patrol vehicles.
- ***Distance from inner perimeter security fence*** to buildings should be as great as possible. In campus building layouts, where housing buildings form the perimeter envelope, a distance of 200 to 300 feet is highly recommended.
- ***Distance from exterior building surface*** in cases of more urban-type designs generally cannot yield a significant distance from building face to fence or the property line. One should consider a distance of 25 to 50 feet as a minimum. The primary use of this fence is to prevent persons outside the facility (the neighborhood) from physical access to the building's exterior wall, especially when the exterior building wall is the perimeter enclosure of the facility. Design parameters need to minimize the ability of outsiders to throw contraband over the security perimeter to where it may be reached by inmates. (See Fig. 4.2.)
- ***Exterior building walls*** containing inmate housing units located at grade present an additional concern, since physical, visual, and audible contact between inmates in the facility and persons on the outside must be prevented. Cell windows located in a building's exterior wall should be placed at the highest possible position, limiting observation in or out of rooms or areas, but permitting natural light to enter inmate spaces.
- ***The number of penetrations*** should be limited from the free side of an institution into and through the secure perimeter of a facility. Generally, limiting entrances/exits to a single point of entry for pedestrians (public and staff) and another for official vehicles is preferred for improving security control. When separate vehicle areas for intake/transfer and services are required, a control station should be positioned between areas to observe both activities and control entry/exit sally ports. Whenever possible, the main control station should be similarly positioned between public and staff lobbies.

Figure 4.2 **Limited distances from secure building exteriors with low security fence configuration.**

- ***Inmate views from housing units*** of service entry points and pedestrian approaches to a facility's main entrance should be limited to minimize visual and physical contact between inmates and visitors on the free side.
- ***Fences and buildings*** should be illuminated to detect pedestrian access to buildings, minimizing the lighting of adjacent areas and the neighborhood. Exterior surface-mounted building lighting should be supported by pole lighting located in parking and surrounding areas. (See Fig. 4.3.)
- ***Graphic signage*** can enhance appropriate access to the facility by directing different groups of people toward intended functions and areas. Likewise, it can be used to limit access to areas reserved for authorized personnel and vehicles only.
- ***Art programs*** often become part of a project's budget in meeting facility goals and/or requirements. Choosing an appropriate art form for public, staff, and inmates can enhance a building's architecture for exterior and interior appreciation. (See Figs. 4.4, 4.5, and 4.6.)

Figure 4.3 **Low security fence utilizing a base of chain-link, a top of nonclimbable mesh, and a top band of barbed razor wire.**

INTERIOR ISSUES

- ***Building components*** should be aligned with great care. A simple form provides maximum observation, supervision, and control. The fewer the breaks and turns in corridors, the greater the observation and control of inmate and staff movement. Facility designs that appear simple in plan generally function best. Plans that present a clear pattern of movement support operations by allowing quick staff response to incidents and by offering visual observation of critical points in an institution. (See Fig. 4.7.)
- ***Grouping of inmate programs and services in one area*** is generally preferred for inmate access and control. In jails, locate program space adjacent to housing units, where unit management staff is positioned. In prisons, locate programs and services in a single building accessible by several housing buildings or unit management groups. This also offers the ability to shut down and close off major portions of the facility when not in use.
- ***Recreation is an important inmate program in jail and prison facilities.*** Spaces available for exercise and recreational activities are often located either at housing units (decentralized) and/or are centralized in providing interior and

Figure 4.4 **Housing exterior utilizing precast cells with public art program (bird nesting) placed for public/inmate view.**

Figure 4.5 **Inmate art program/lobby location.**

Figure 4.6 **Inmate graphics noting philosophy placed in main circulation corridor and highlighted by clerestory for natural light.**

exterior recreation programs. Recreation keeps inmates busy, promotes good health, reduces personal tension and anxiety, and reduces assaults by inmates on other inmates and staff. (See Fig. 4.8.)

- ***Exterior exercise location is preferably adjacent to each housing unit*** (or shared between units) for jails and prisons alike. This location, with proximity to housing officer and unit management control/staff, allows longer periods of activity each day without escorting inmates to the activity. Centralized outdoor playing fields for basketball, handball, and softball-related activities are generally provided for a prison population where sentenced inmates spend more time in an institution. These activities are usually located on the interior (within an area formed by detached or connected housing buildings) or exterior (outside an area formed by detached or connected housing buildings).
- ***Interior recreation activity is generally centralized for prisons*** and in some instances for jail facilities, when construction budgets permit. In jails, locating the activity adjacent to housing units is preferred in order to limit inmate movement. In prisons, indoor recreation (gymnasium) is best located centrally and adjacent to other inmate programs to facilitate officers'

Figure 4.7 **Interior natural light for offices borrowed from corridor clerestory.**

observation and supervision utilizing one control post.

- ***Visitation activity is located in various positions*** in correctional facilities, depending on facility type and physical design (low-, mid-, or high-rise layouts). In jails, it is generally best located at or adjacent to housing units, in unit management support areas, or between housing units on a shared schedule. Such an adjacency will limit inmate movement from living/housing units to visitation areas. Generally, visitation in jails is limited to noncontact types of visiting. However, many jails allow and provide contact visitation, either in a central location or at the housing/management unit level. Careful attention to inmate screening and search areas should eliminate opportunities for contraband to enter the facility and prevent inmates from leaving the secure perimeter. In prisons, where inmates spend a longer period of incarceration, movement from housing to a centralized location is preferred. Visitors are thereby limited to a facility's entrance/lobby area. Visitation is generally located between the public lobby (free side) and inmate areas (secure side) and is secure within its own enclosure. Many facilities provide outdoor visitation accessible via the contact visitation room and observed, supervised, and controlled by the visitation officers. The need to have visitors in medical and segregation housing areas must be considered in the overall design of the facility.
- ***Ceilings in corridors and program spaces*** can be eliminated when considered in conjunction with lighting, utilities, and equipment located at suitable height above the floor to prevent inmates from contact. Eleven feet clear is recommended with ten feet clear as a minimum. Appropriate acoustical treatment is generally required for maintaining low noise levels. (See Fig. 4.9.)
- ***Services unloading/loading docks for outside facility vendors*** require observation, supervision, and control of activity with interlock/sally port control of any movement to the secure side of the institution. Limiting the number of vehicular entrances reinforces control and enhances security. The unloading/loading location should be close to services on the secure side, such as warehouse, kitchen/laundry, industry, and maintenance activities and should provide minimal inmate views of the area.
- ***Trash and garbage storage and removal*** requires adequate space to handle recyclables,

Figure 4.8 **Housing unit exterior courtyard enclosed by buildings with projected window eyebrows for security containment.**

Figure 4.9 **Inmate corridor with natural light, floor markings to estimate distance, and utilities mounted 11 feet above inmate reach.**

and other trash and storage adjacent to exterior for easy maintenance vehicle pickup. Centralizing this area and locating it adjacent to the industries activity space can provide a useful inmate activity.

HOUSING ISSUES

- ***Inmate housing units or buildings*** form the heart of a facility. The design issues of observation, supervision, and control are paramount in creating a successful solution for security operations. Operating costs are often a direct result of design decisions related to officer(s) location and numbers of staff required. (See Figs. 4.10 and 4.11.)
- ***Cells fronts*** (entrances doors) should be in view of the housing unit officer's desk or control room. The officer should be able to observe all inmate activity within, and adjacent to the dayroom (counseling, pantry, laundry, outdoor exercise, etc.), even when moving throughout the space.
- ***Housing unit officer*** is often observed, and supervised directly by a centralized control position, either unit management or a central control room. Some jurisdictions permit housing officer post shutdown during the morning shift if inmate cells can be observed directly from a centralized control station.
- ***In a modified direct supervision operation,*** the housing unit officer is often supported by a unit management control room officer for all shifts. It is ideal if this control room is positioned to observe, supervise, and control several housing units and/or entrances . . . two or more. This can minimize staffing positions and result in reduced operating costs. (See Fig. 4.12.)
- ***Split-level housing unit designs*** can provide improved observation, supervision, and control of inmate activities and movement within a housing unit. The split level provides separation of activities into three distinct areas by level, with group activity participation located at midlevel between lower and upper cell floors. This midlevel is often used for dining activity with floor surface suitable for cleaning. The lower housing floor can similarly be treated with appropriate material, such as carpeting, for quieter activities. (See Fig. 4.13.)
- ***Individual showers*** are preferred to group showering, for all levels of inmate management, from minimum to maximum security. They are best located within close proximity to a housing

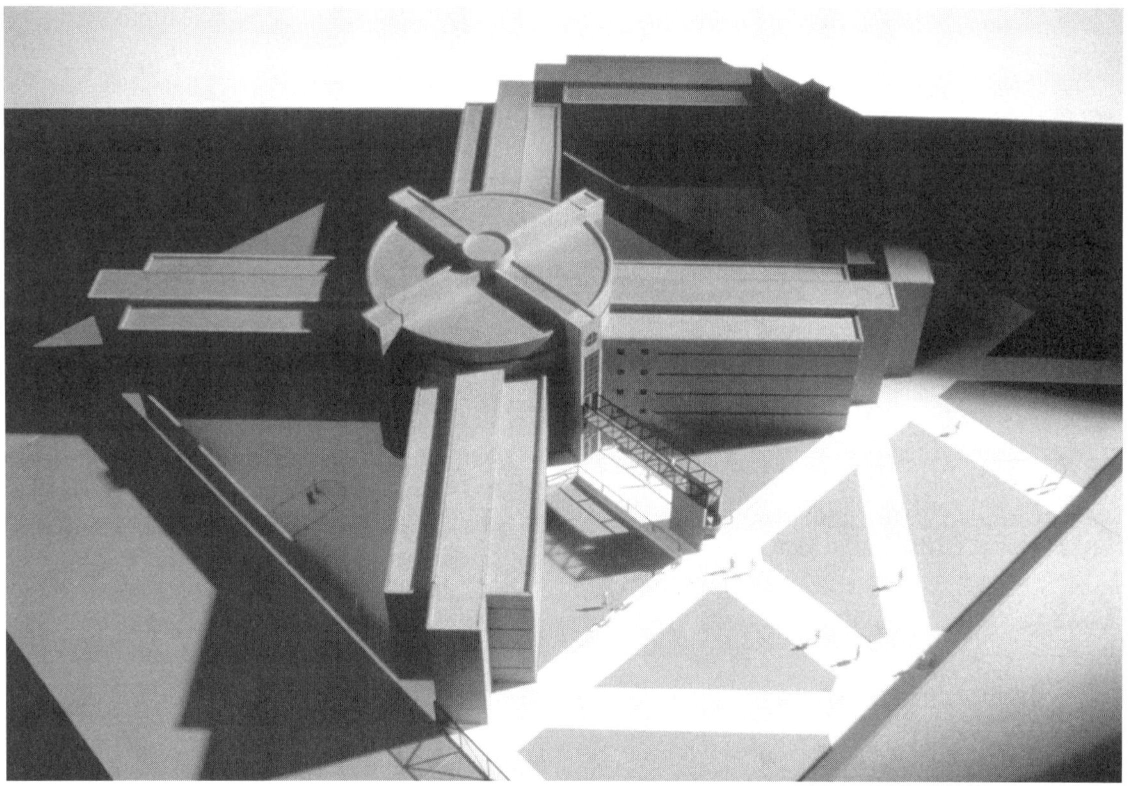

Figure 4.10 **Two-story (with mezzanines) housing unit study model describing separate entrances, shortened cell wings, and outdoor recreation courtyard.**

Figure 4.11 **Single-story (with mezzanine) podular housing unit study model describing five attached units, interior recreation yards, and unit management control.**

Figure 4.12 **Stacked housing units/separate first- and second-story access.**

Figure 4.13 **Split-level dayroom design utilizing continuous carpeted steps for access and seating.**

Figure 4.14 **Housing dayroom utilization of large window areas for natural light.**

Figure 4.15 **Typical inmate cell with window for natural light and views of exterior.**

unit control officer's desk or room to monitor a potentially interactive and dangerous activity.

- ***Natural light into dayroom activity and cell space*** should be a design goal in providing a normative environment to inmates and staff alike. Even when it may not be a local code requirement, it is important to remember that an officer spends his/her eight-hour shift assignment in a dayroom space. (See Figs. 4.14 and 4.15.)
- ***Acoustics*** is a major issue to be concerned with in a correctional environment. All areas where inmates gather in large groups should be carefully designed to minimize noise levels and reverberation. Reference Chap. 8: Acoustical Design Guidelines.

OTHER DESIGN-RELATED ISSUES

- ***Appropriate levels of security electronics and communications systems*** throughout an institution must be reviewed early in the design process. Experienced engineers can lead team discussion with appropriate, current, and available technologies in support of a facility's operational objectives and procedures.
- ***Food service component analysis*** in the program and early design phases can provide an opportunity for the appropriate level of facility service, in conventional cook/serve or cook/chill methods of food preparation, delivery, and service. An experienced consultant can support a project team in the selection of a system of food service that is appropriate for a facility's inmate population, method of food delivery that is most suitable to facility operations, and an efficient system that limits the cost of food operations.
- ***Appropriate architectural aesthetics*** cannot be overlooked. Good architecture is the result of a careful balance between program and art, whereby building designs are functional, physically attractive in form, and visually pleasing to the eye. Selection of materials, colors, and details contribute to an aesthetically pleasing edifice. Commercial, governmental, and other edifices often bring high aesthetic standards and expectation to a project and its team members. Often jails and prisons do not consider aesthetics unless the edifice is linked or incorporated into a justice center or adjacent to a courthouse facility. Jails and prisons, from a public and often from a client's directive and perception, provide the opportunity for an appropriate aesthetic solution, without opulence. It is generally understood that correctional clients intend to show the community a frugality with the expenditure of their tax dollars

for this basically unpopular building type. (See Fig. 4.16.)

- ***Project documentation*** is a prerequisite to satisfying client and architectural requirements and limiting liability for all parties. The creativity of an architect is valuable in providing clients with design opportunities and suggesting improvements of operations through skillful design. Clients will generally make final decisions on all issues affecting operations and design. The architect is advised to record all related issues and be sure that all decisions are well documented to provide information for future reference.
- ***Current public perception*** persists that the incarcerated population is undeserving of programs and activities, which are often considered amenities, such as TV, recreational activities, air-conditioned spaces, and so forth. The public believes that these programs are inappropriate for individuals who have committed crimes against society. The misunderstanding is that these programs and conditions are *amenities*, when, in fact, they provide the staff operational benefits in keeping inmates busy and/or comfortable and thereby prevent incidents. Staff also occupy these spaces on a 24-hour basis, and their comfort is important to consider in support of managing inmate activities and behavior properly. Also, electronic security system equipment performance can be improved, requiring less maintenance, when placed in air-conditioned dayroom spaces.

Figure 4.16 **Facility entrance canopy with architectural theme carried into facility for inmate horticultural program in background.**

- ***Designing in a political environment*** can often become a difficult situation. Many projects begin without a facility operator aboard. At times, even with a facility director in place, transition teams are difficult to fund during the design process and thereby limit future operational staff participation in the project's program and design phases. Whenever possible, the facility director and operating staff should participate in the entire design process to ensure continuity of programming, operational, and design consistency, the *buy-in* concept.

In many instances, a facility director may join the project when it is well along in its development, making changes difficult and potentially costly. One should appeal to a neutral source (arbitrator) to provide guidance for project direction to satisfy all team members without causing delays to a project's schedule. This condition is growing more widespread among building jurisdictions as funding for facility staff early in the design process is minimized or eliminated due to limited project budgets.

FACILITY COMPONENT RELATIONSHIPS AND BUILDING DESIGNS

Assembling the components of any facility program offers a design team choices and opportunities in meeting an institution's goals and objectives. The factors of site location (rural to urban), site size, neighborhood context, user operational preferences, and construction costs are all influences on program component selection and facility layout design. However, the choices can be narrowed to several basic facility configurations, which can be described as follows:

4.1 Campus
4.2 Campus modified
4.3 Interconnected
4.4 Contained
4.5 Contained and linear
4.6 Contained and stacked

The following listings summarize descriptions for each facility type, followed by a series of facility plan layouts (footprints) as examples of facilities built and operating. Three examples are presented in each category to indicate differences in approach with specific design solutions. These facilities are identified by name, location, owner, and architect in a summary listing, following the examples, in order to focus attention on the issues which are relevant to design and remain contemporary. The year of occupancy is also listed, as an historical reference, providing a chronological perspective and sequential understanding of new generation designs for jails and prisons. The total number of staff is also included for reference only, although many factors can influence these numbers: additional inmate population from double-bunking; additional adjacent/existing facility beds/cells; jurisdictional mandates; and added staff by client, related to an institution's specific security concerns.

4.1 Campus

(Reference: Figs. 4.17, 4.18, 4.19, and 4.20)

a. Separated buildings for administration, program, services, and housing
b. Single-story building heights
c. Single floor for dorms or single floor plus mezzanine option for dormitories and cells
d. Exterior circulation to all building functions
e. Outdoor recreation between or behind buildings
f. Perimeter security fence(s) with detection, depending on inmate population classification

4.2 Campus Modified

(Reference: Figs. 4.21, 4.22, 4.23, 4.24)

a. Combined buildings for administration, program, and services—one or several buildings
b. Separate housing buildings
c. Single- or two-story building hcight for admin istration building
d. Single- or two-story building height for support building
e. One-story (grade level + mezzanine) or two-story housing buildings (two stacked units)
f. Exterior circulation from housing to all other building functions
g. Outdoor recreation between or behind buildings
h. Perimeter security fence(s) with detection, depending on inmate population classification

4.3 Interconnected

(Reference: Figs. 4.25, 4.26, 4.27, and 4.28)

a. Combined buildings for administration, program, and services—one or several buildings
b. Connected housing buildings
c. Multiple-story administration building
d. Two-story building height for support buildings
e. One-story (grade level + mezzanine) or two-story housing buildings (two stacked units)
f. Interior circulation from housing to all other building functions. Exterior access, too
g. Outdoor recreation location internalized between or behind buildings
h. Housing buildings form the first line of security perimeter
i. Perimeter security fence(s) with detection, depending on inmate population classification

4.4 Contained

(Reference: Figs. 4.29, 4.30, 4.31, and 4.32)

a. Combined and centralized administration, program, and services functions into one building
b. Connected housing buildings
c. Multiple-story administration building
d. Two-story building height for support buildings
e. One-story (grade level + mezzanine) or two-story housing buildings (two stacked units);
f. Interior circulation from housing to all other building functions
g. Outdoor recreation location internalized and localized between building components
h. Support and housing buildings form the security perimeter
i. Optional perimeter security fence(s) with detection (user preference)
j. Compact footprint for limited site-area conditions
k. Limited inmate movement, maximizes staff observation, supervision, and control

4.5 Contained and linear

(Reference: Figs. 4.33, 4.34, 4.35, and 4.36)

a. Megastructure; all building functions connected
b. Combined and centralized administration, program, and services functions
c. Single or multiple building heights for administration, program, and services functions
d. One- or multistory housing buildings (one or multiple stacked units)

e. All circulation internalized between housing and all other building functions
f. Interior recreation (gymnasiums) centralized and shared between housing units
g. Outdoor recreation location internalized and located adjacent to housing units
h. Support and housing buildings form the security perimeter
i. Optional perimeter security fence(s) with detection; user preference
j. Optimum compact footprint for limited site area conditions
k. Limited inmate movement, maximizes staff observation, supervision, and control

4.6 Contained and Stacked

(Reference: Figs. 4.37, 4.38, 4.39, and 4.40.)

a. Megastructure; all building functions connected
b. Combined and centralized administration, program, and services functions
c. Mid-rise/high-rise building
d. Multiple-story housing buildings (two or more stacked units)
e. Housing units (building) stacked over administrative, programs, and services functions
f. All circulation internalized between housing and all other building functions
g. Vertical circulation (elevators) and limited inmate movement
h. Interior recreation (gymnasiums) centralized and shared between housing units
i. Outdoor recreation location internalized and located adjacent to housing units
j. Support and housing buildings form the security perimeter
k. Perimeter security fence(s) with detection optional (user preference)
l. Optimum compact footprint for limited site area conditions and urban locations

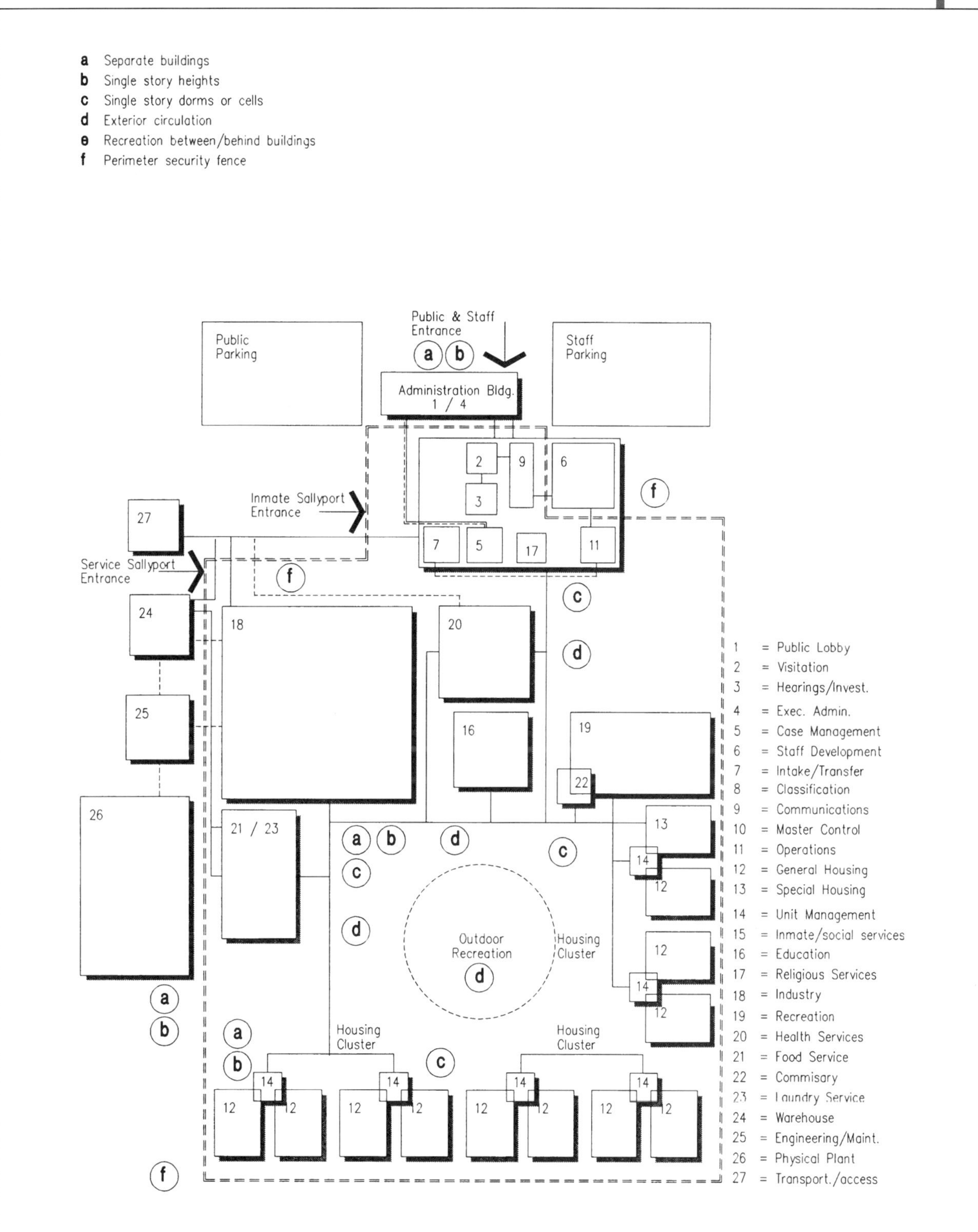

Figure 4.17 **Campus facility diagram.**

4.18 Campus	Statistics
Site:	800 acres
Type:	State prison, men and women
Stories:	Low-rise, single-level support, one-story housing (with mezzanine)
Building area:	329,789 gsf
Population:	1400 single cells—medium; planned expansion to 1600
Housing:	Two, 48 cells per control
Management:	Indirect supervision
Staff:	754 (for inmate population of 2463)
Operational:	1981

Design Features

1. Four separate, self-contained facilities—400 cells each.
2. Facilities buffered by distance and with natural farmland development.
3. Women's facility further separated from others by main access road.
4. Design utilizes year-long mild weather, providing outdoor covered activity areas.
5. Visitors movement to each facility is by complex official vehicle.
6. Facility architecture incorporated rural scale and desertlike materials and colors.

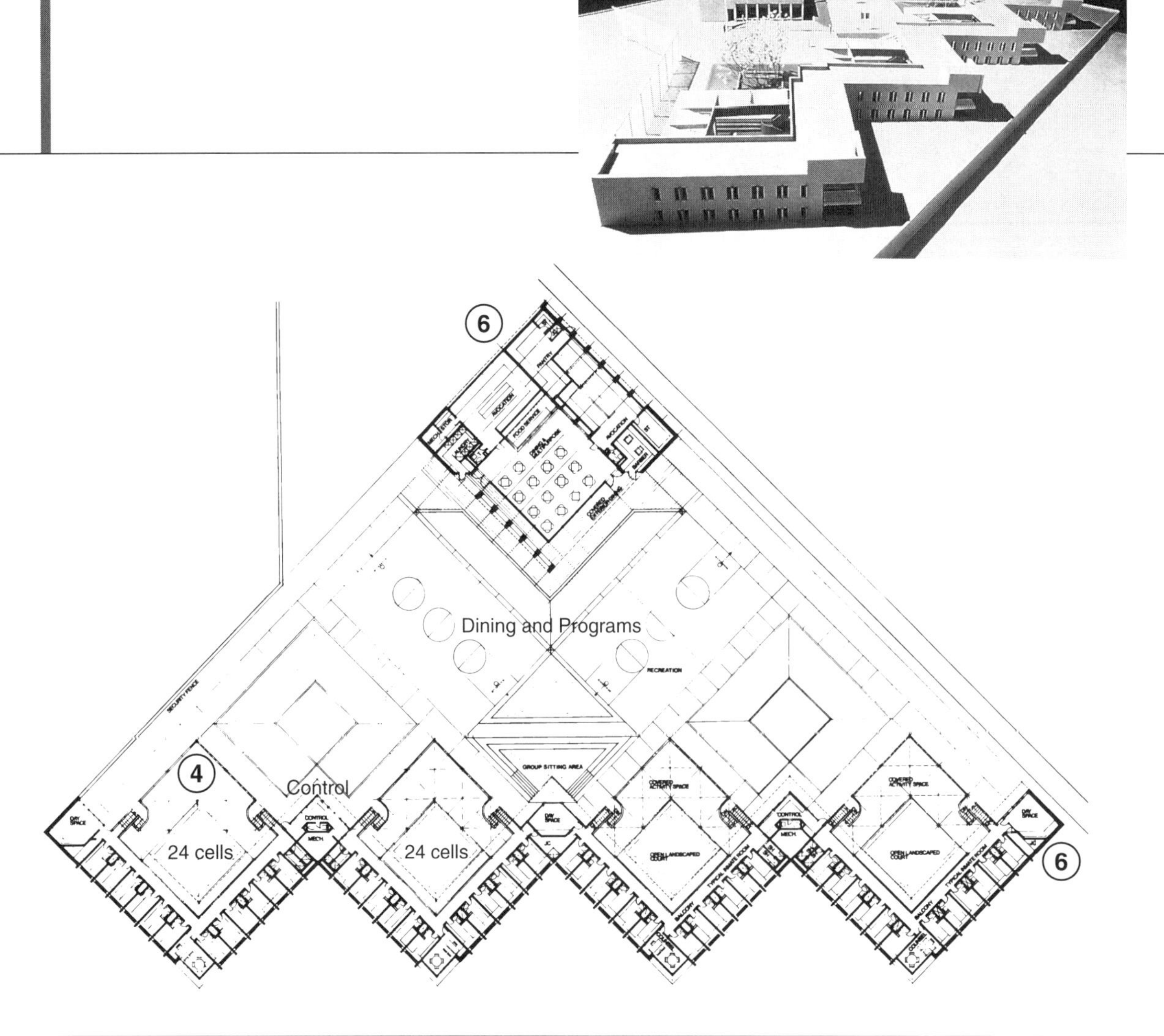

Figure 4.18*a* **Housing plan.**

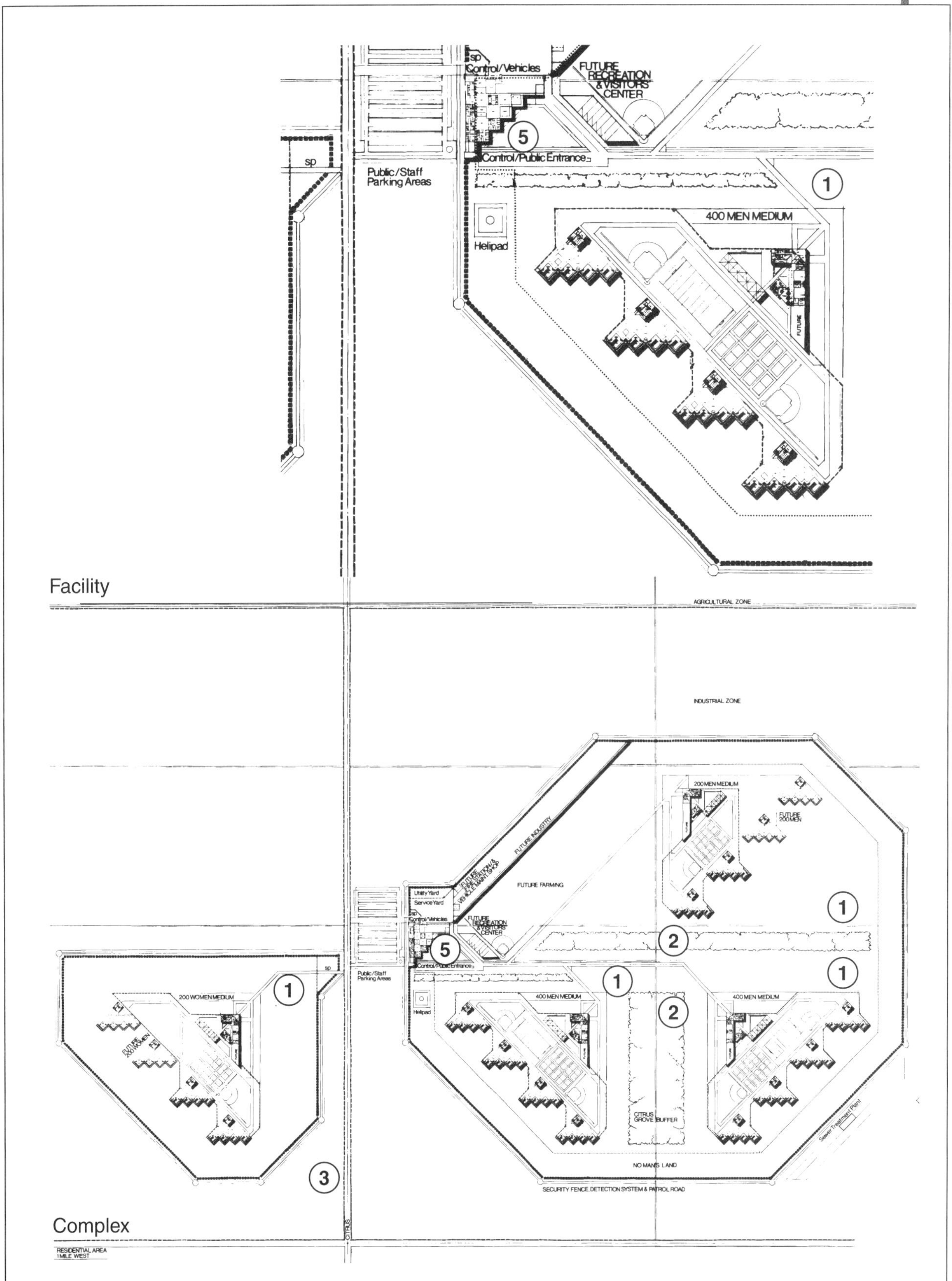

Figure 4.18*b* **Facility and complex plans.**

4.19 Campus Statistics

Site:	50 acres
Type:	State prison
Stories:	Low-rise, single-level support, one-level housing
Building area:	250,000+ gsf
Population:	900 beds—minimum
Housing:	Two 75-bed dormitories per building, each with control center
Management:	Indirect supervision
Staff:	340
Operational:	1990

Design Features

1. School-type campus environment, with housing surrounding open space.
2. Maximizes inmate free movement to all program activities and visitation.
3. Reconstruction buildings program, without operational interruption.
4. Construction phased over a 7-year period.
5. Administration/visitors' buildings screen public views of inmate activities.
6. Architectural plan and aesthetics respectful of suburban neighborhood.

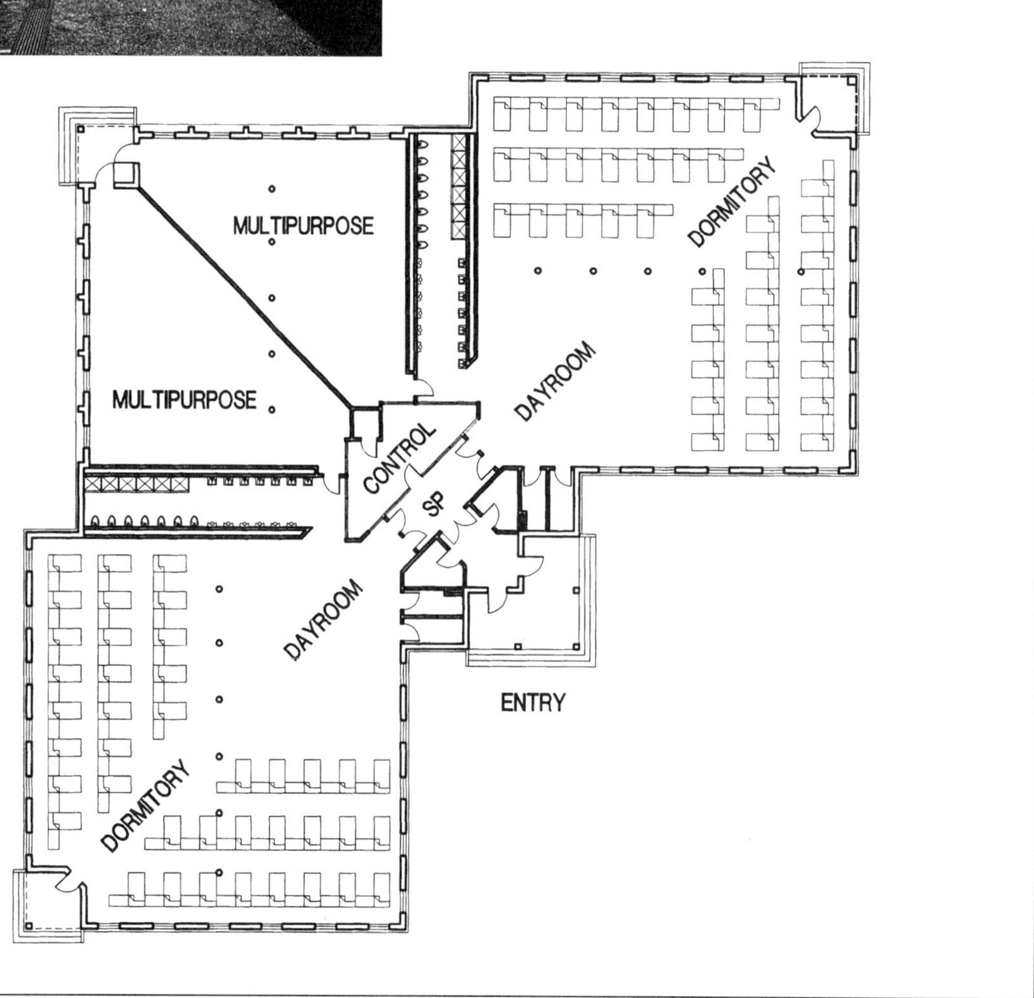

Figure 4.19*a* **Housing plan.**

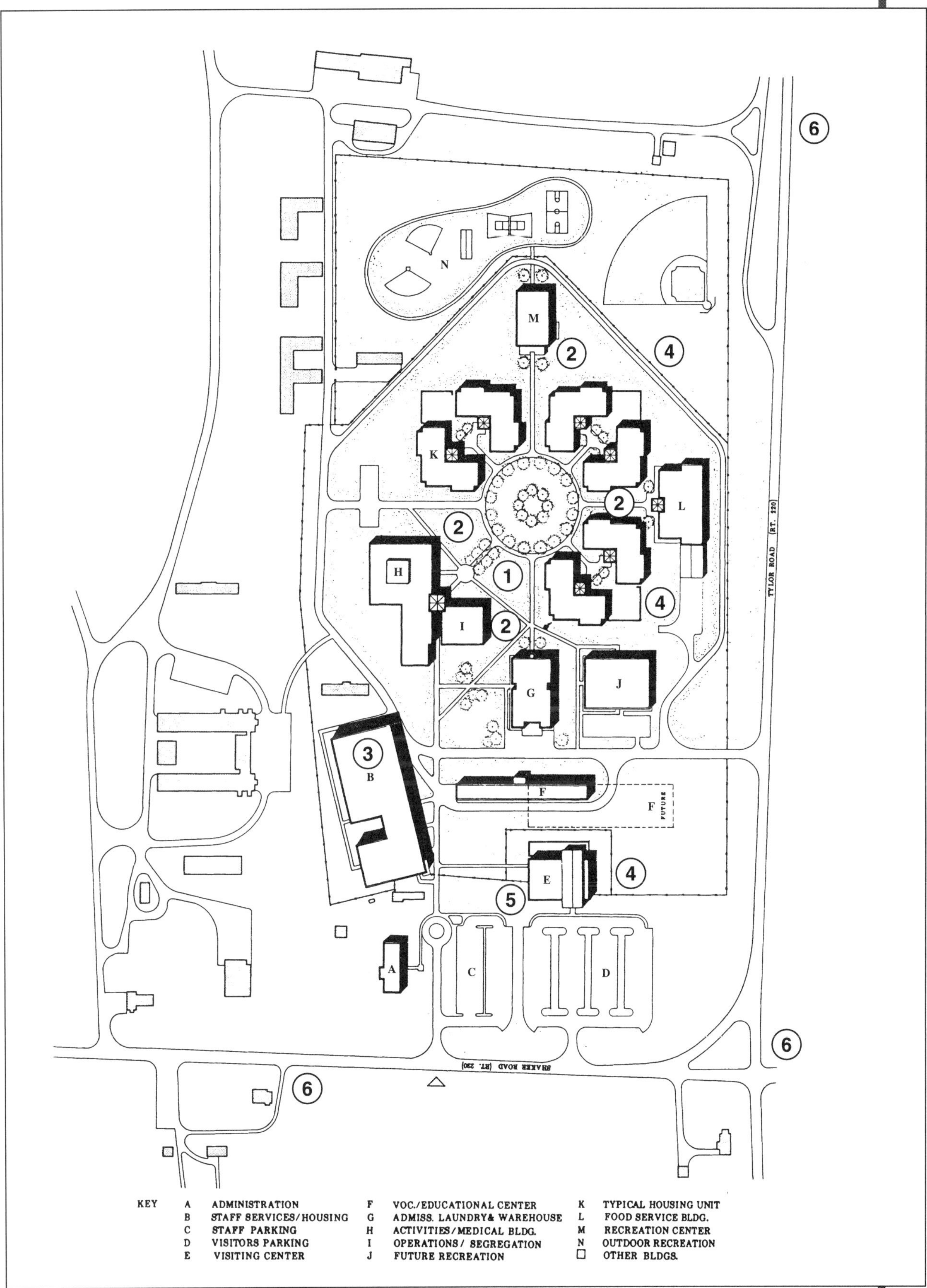

Figure 4.19*b* **Facility plan.**

4.20 Campus	Statistics
Site:	130 acres
Type:	State prison; multiple campuses
Stories:	Low-rise, single-level support, two-story housing (with mezzanines)
Building area:	892,000+ gsf
Population:	1780: three, 516 cells—close custody; 192 cells—seg.; 40 beds—medical
Housing:	Two, 43 cells per control; 172 cells per building; 516 cells per facility
Management:	Indirect supervision
Staff:	910
Operational:	1990

Design Features

1. Large, three-facility campus, with defined and separated populations.
2. Separate and central to three facilities—medical and segregation housing buildings.
3. Each facility's security perimeter individually fenced.
4. Control towers observe each facility's exterior and interior yards.
5. Administration, warehouse, power plant located outside of the secure perimeter.
6. All inmate activities screened from public view.

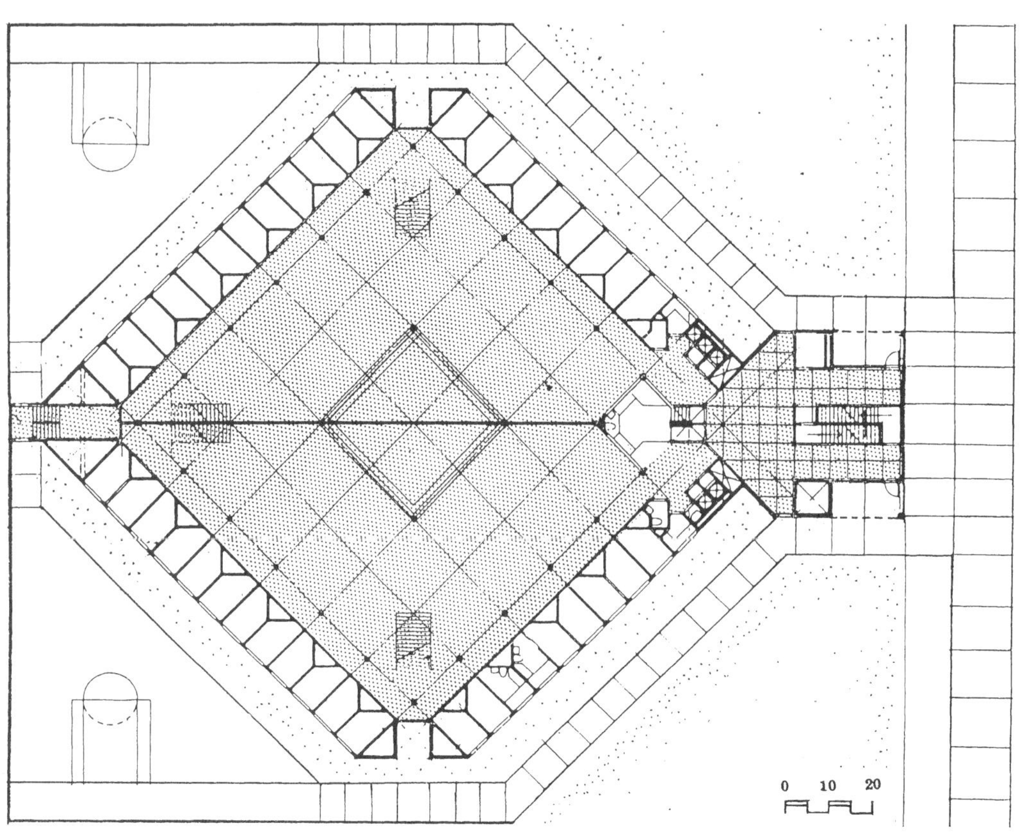

Figure 4.20*a* **Housing plan.**

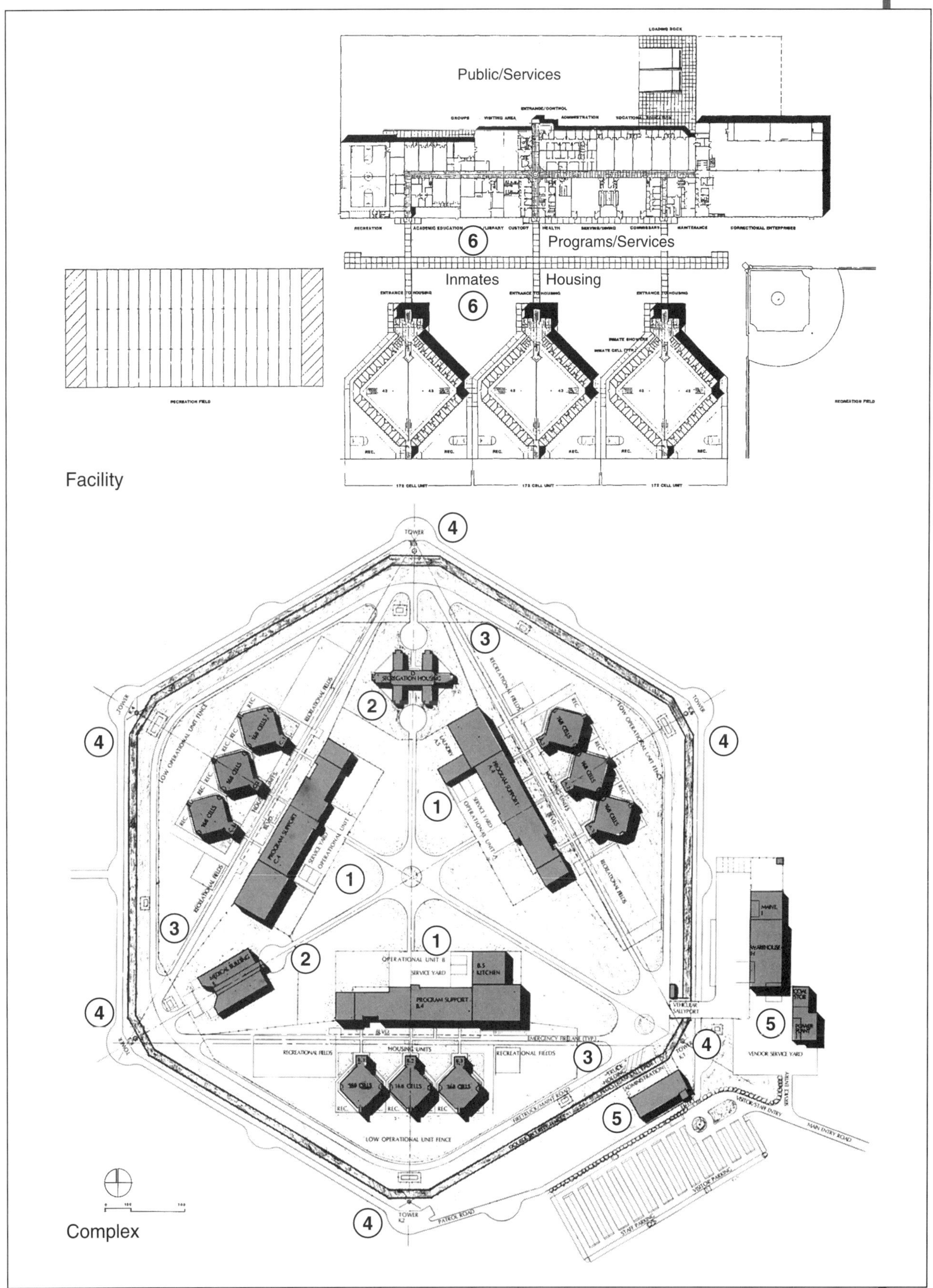

Figure 4.20*b* **Facility and complex plans.**

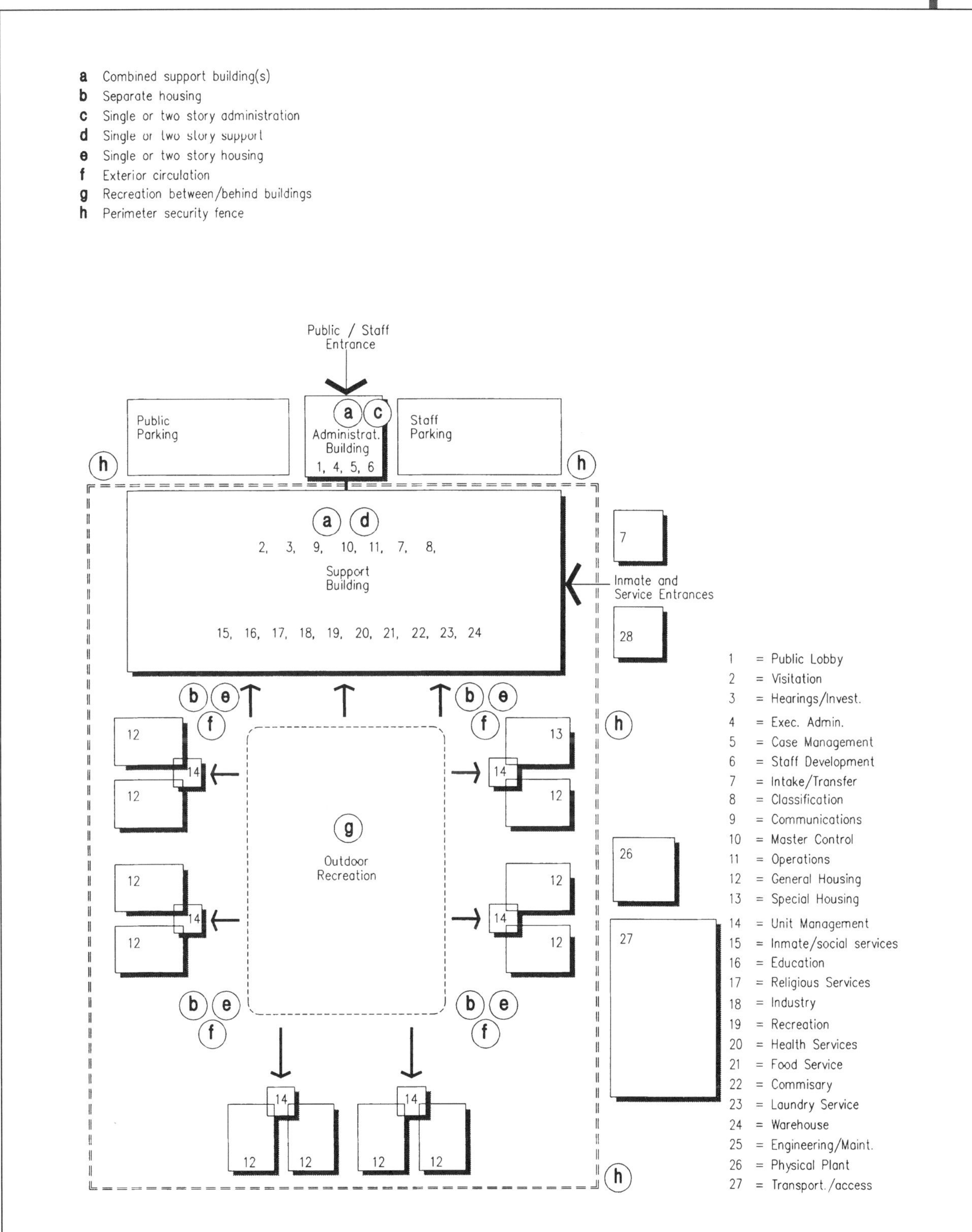

Figure 4.21 **Campus modified facility diagram.**

4.22 Campus Modified

Statistics

Site: 20 acres for main facility—interior/secured perimeter; 35-acre development
Type: State prison
Stories: Mid-rise, two-level support, two-story housing (with mezzanines)
Building area: 560,000 gsf
Population: 1125: 1024 single cells—medical; 48 beds—minimum; 48 cells—maximum
Housing: One, 128 cells per control, two stacked units, 256 per building
Management: Direct and indirect supervision
Staff: 400 (total inmate population of 2000—partially double-bunked)
Operational: 1990

Design Features

1. Two separate 512-cell facilities, separated by central support building.
2. Separated, second-story exterior housing unit entrances access by stairs (see Figure 4.12, page 126).
3. Large housing unit population, with efficient staff ratio—direct observation.
4. Housing units planned for future subdivision into smaller groups.
5. Housing mechanical equipment rooms access from behind units.
6. Housing and support buildings form intimate, controllable passive activity spaces.

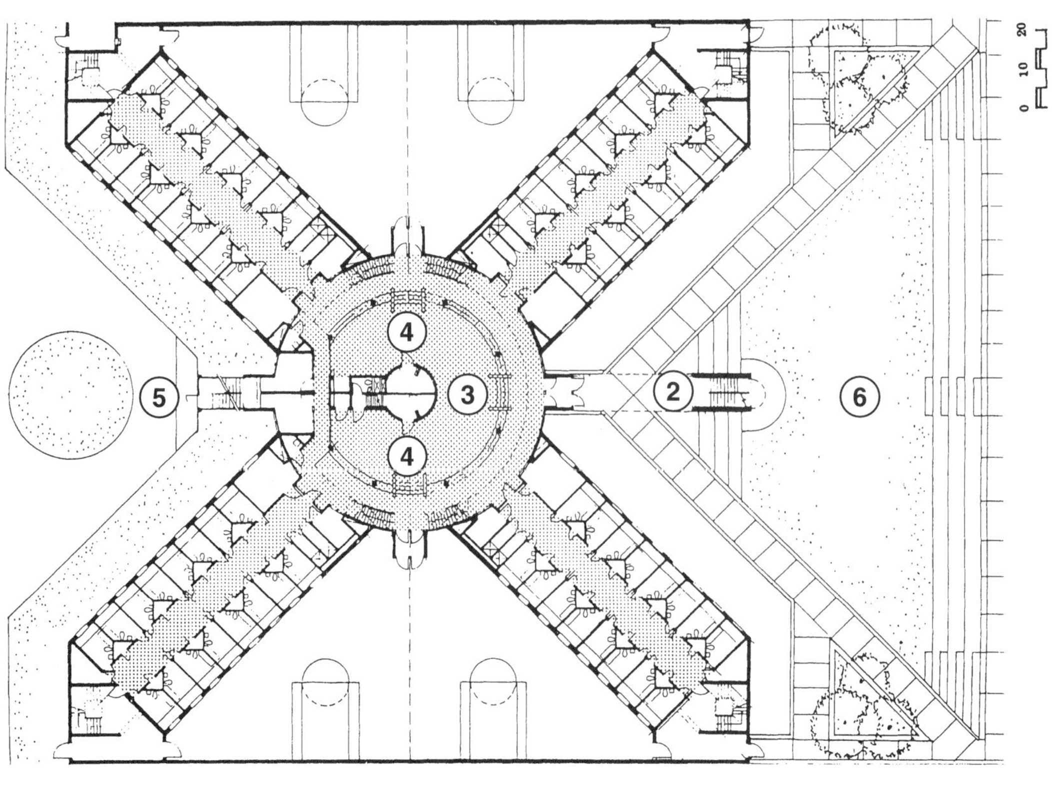

Figure 4.22*a* **Housing plan.**

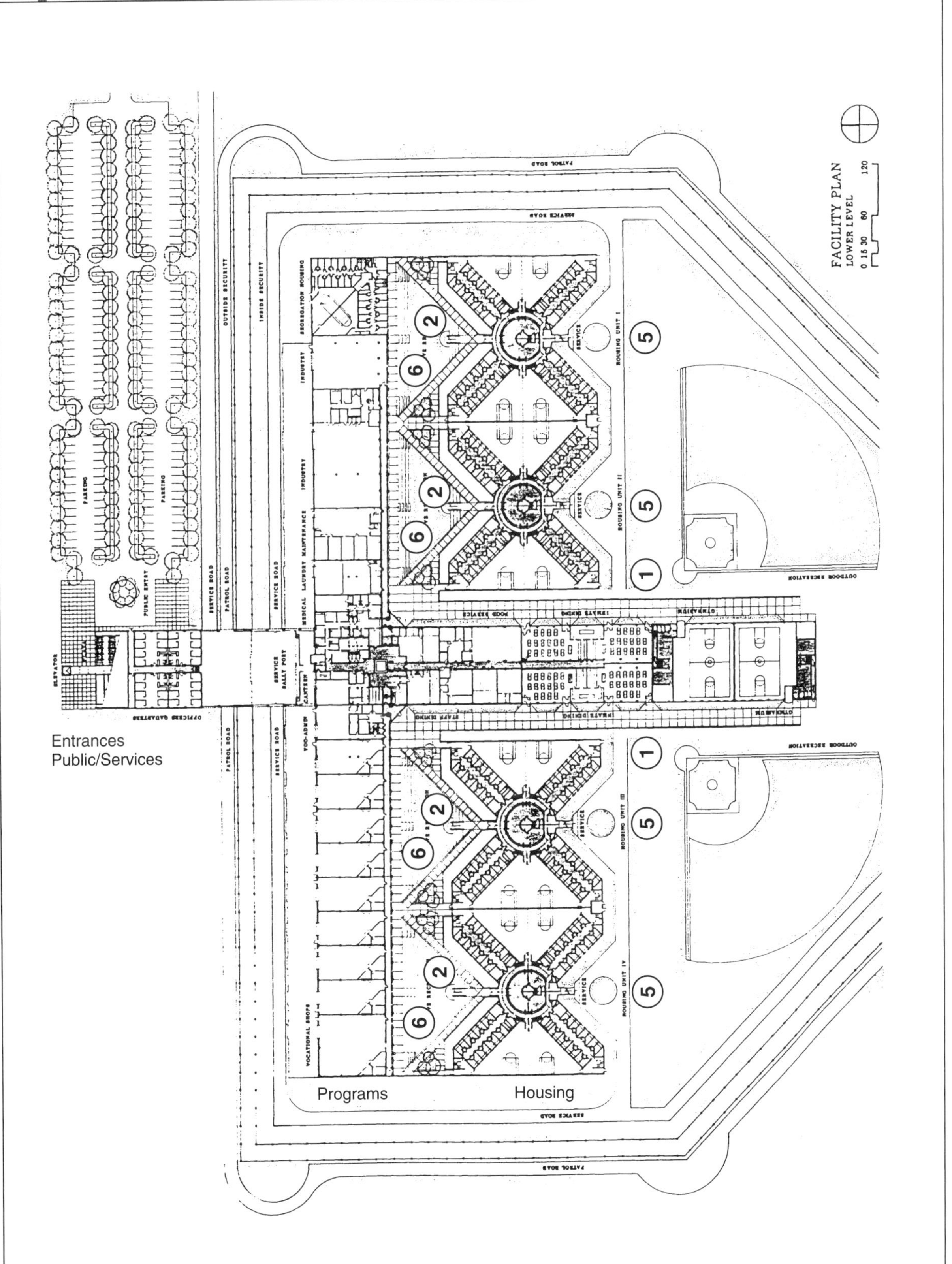

Figure 4.22*b* **Facility plan.**

4.23 Campus Modified

Statistics

Site:	45 acres—main facility (shown); 5 acres—satellite facility (see site examples)
Type:	Federal prison
Stories:	Low-rise, single-level support, one-story housing (with mezzanine)
Building area:	554,663 gsf
Population:	816: 512 cells—medium; 256 beds—minimum; 48 cells—maximum
Housing:	One 64-cell unit per control; two 64-cell units per building
Management:	Direct supervision
Staff:	250 (total inmate population of 1588—double-bunked)
Operational:	1992

Design Features

1. Client design model modified, improved, and site adapted.
2. Centralized campus amphitheater focus for passive inmate activities.
3. Architecture utilized natural site conditions (mountain) to separate two facilities.
4. Administration building located outside of secure perimeter.
5. Public views of inmate campus screened at entrance.
6. Relaxed architectural plan layout and aesthetics for public, staff, and inmates.

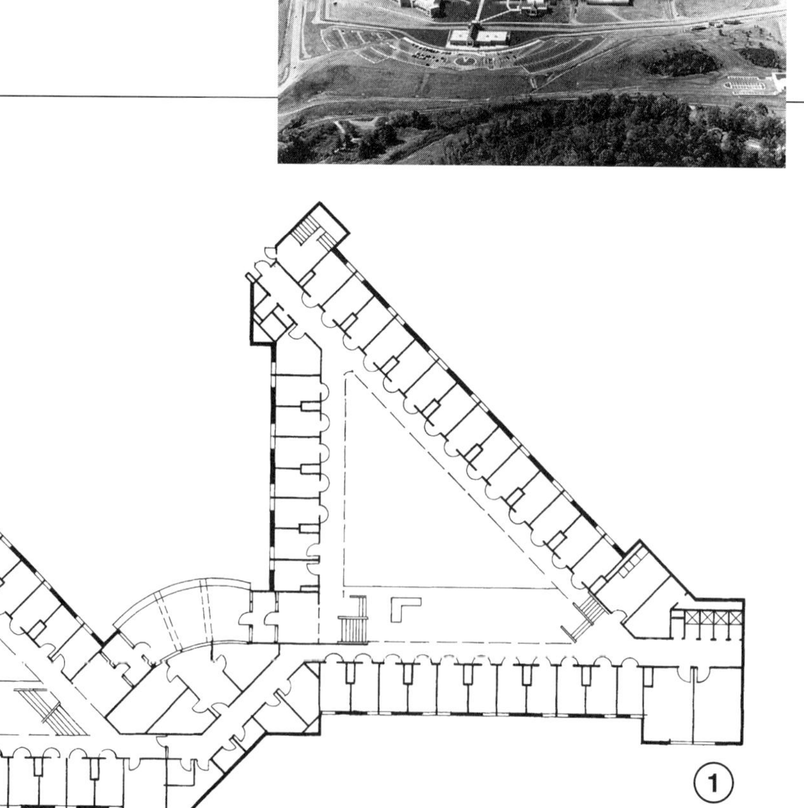

Figure 4.23*a* **Housing plan.**

Figure 4.23*b* **Facility plan.**

4.24 Campus Modified

	Statistics
Site:	35 acres
Type:	U.S. island commonwealth prison
Stories:	Mid-rise, two-level support, three-tiered housing units
Building area:	187,860 gsf
Population:	504 single cells—maximum; two separated 250-cell facilities
Housing:	Two 48-cell units per control; three units per facility (neighborhood)
Management:	Indirect supervision
Staff:	376
Operational:	1986

Design Features

1. Two separated facilities, sharing central programs and support buildings.
2. Each facility provides centralized recreation surrounded by housing.
3. Covered walkway for inmate movement to central programs and housing.
4. Three tiers of housing stacked, with covered exterior access and control.
5. Inmate cells with operable windows take advantage of tropical winds.
6. Kitchen building screens public view of inmate housing at entrance.

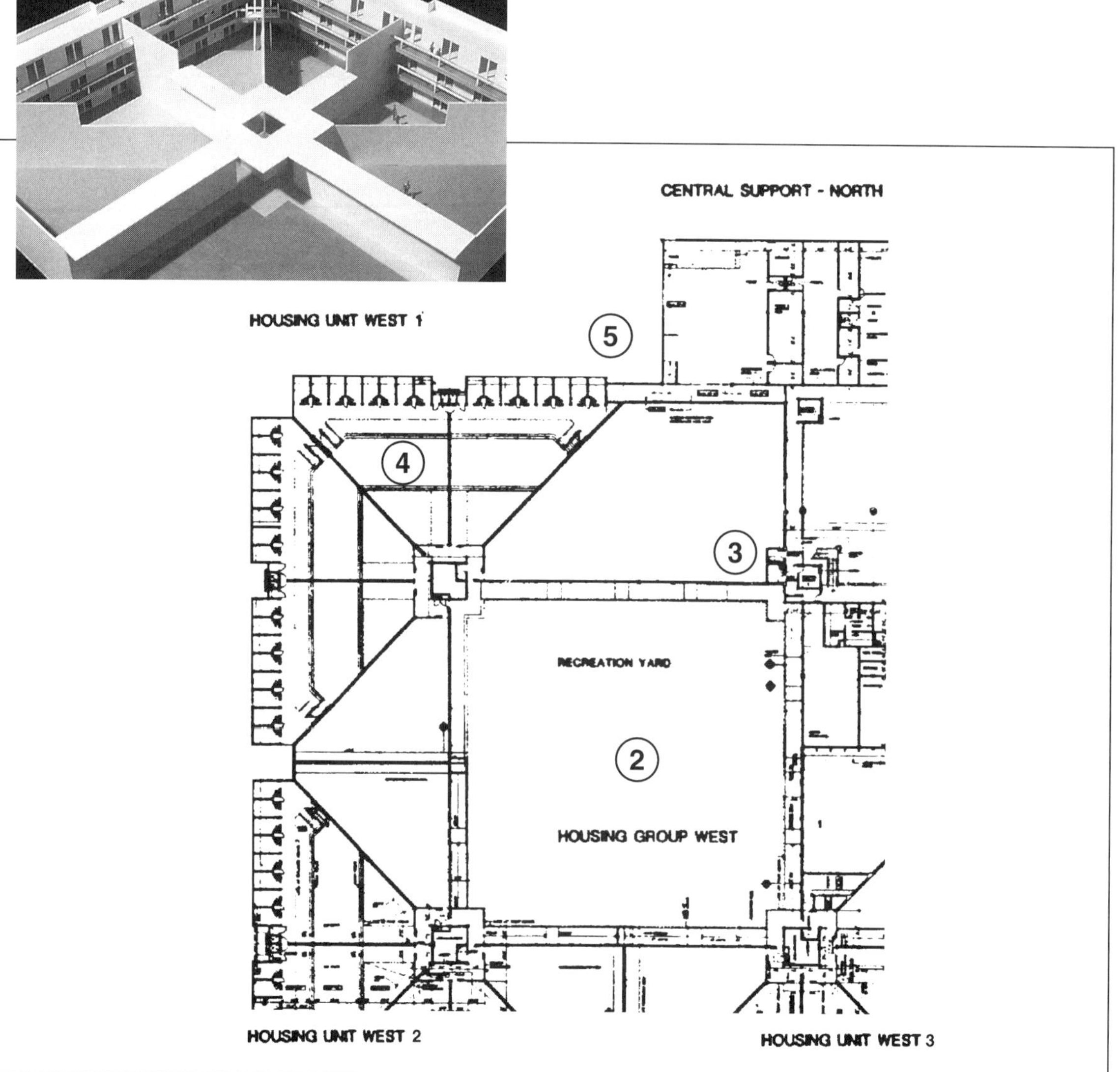

Figure 4.24*a* **Housing plan.**

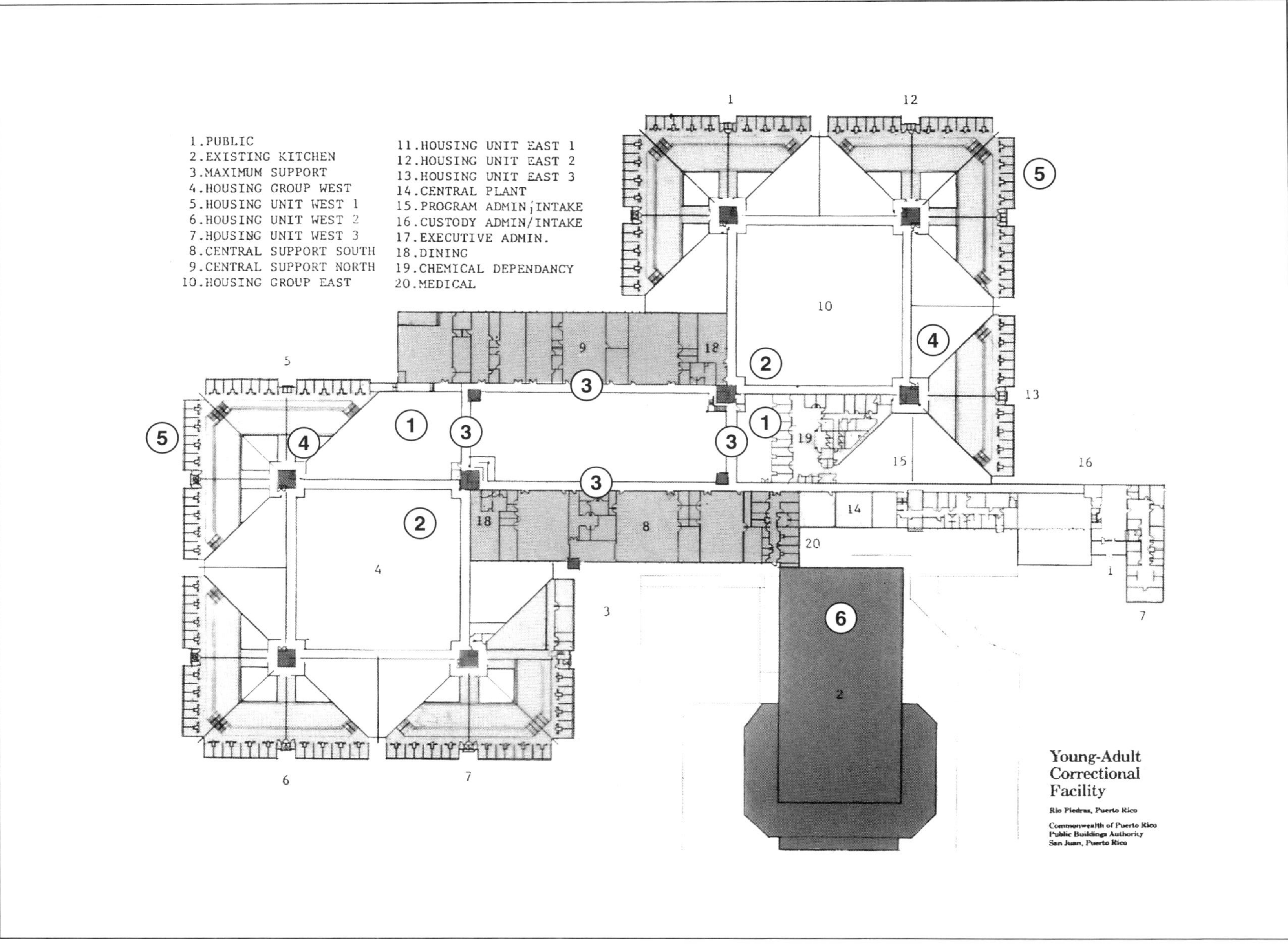

Figure 4.24*b* **Facility plan.**

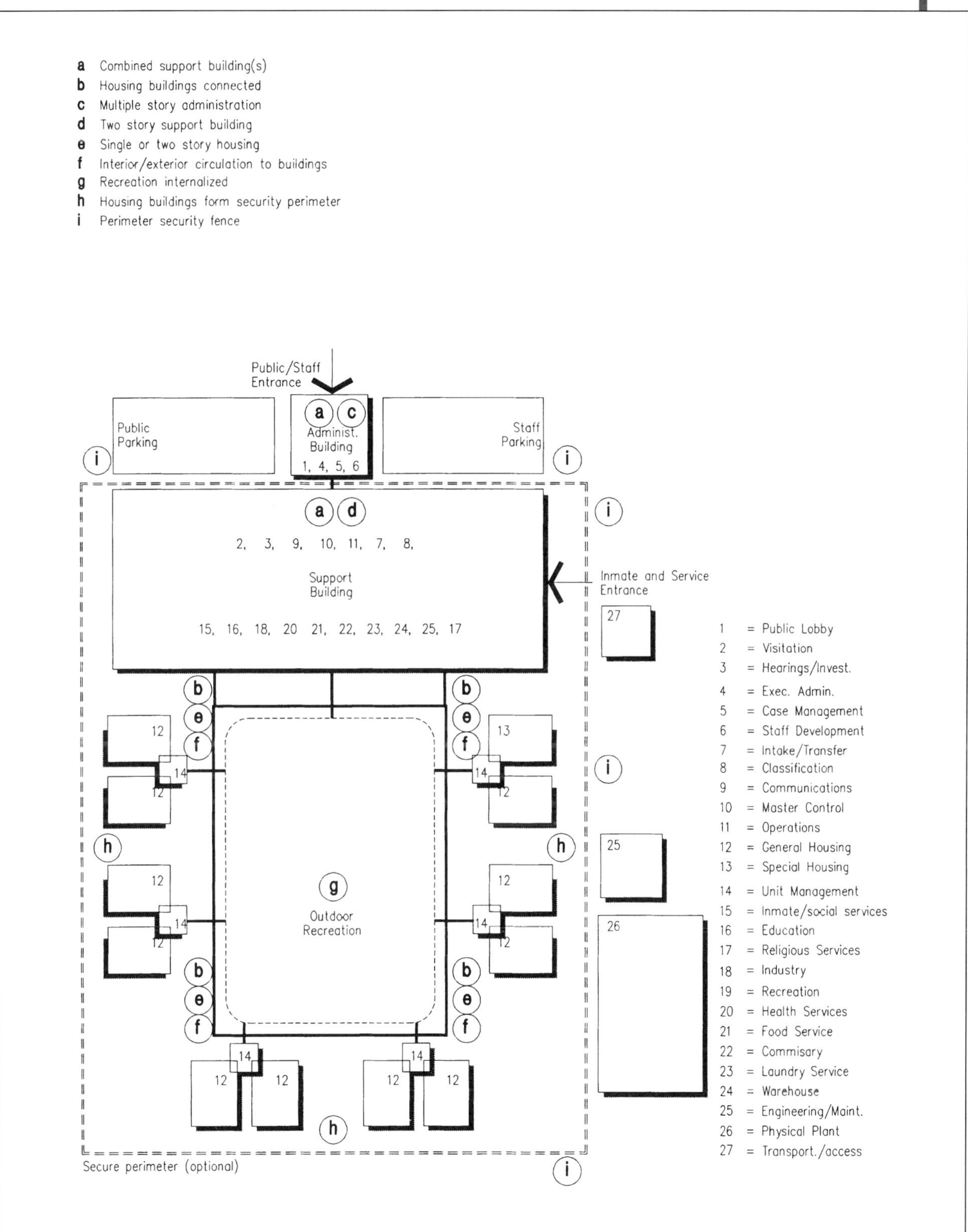

Figure 4.25 **Interconnected facility diagram.**

4.26 Interconnected

Statistics

Site:	50 acres
Type:	State prison
Stories:	Low-rise, two-level support, one-level housing (with lower level and mezzanine)
Building area:	128,917 gsf
Population:	320 single cells—medium/maximum
Housing:	Two 32-cell units per control in one building
Management:	Direct supervision (day), indirect supervision (night)
Staff:	196
Operational:	1979

Design Features

1. Small inmate groupings in housing design configuration.
2. Variety of level changes within housing units.
3. Second-story inmate/staff corridor creates access underneath to central court.
4. Circulation corridor forms internalized recreation courts at each housing unit.
5. Centralized courtyard activities contained by building walls.
6. Grade-level support services building connection to adjacent diagnostic facility.

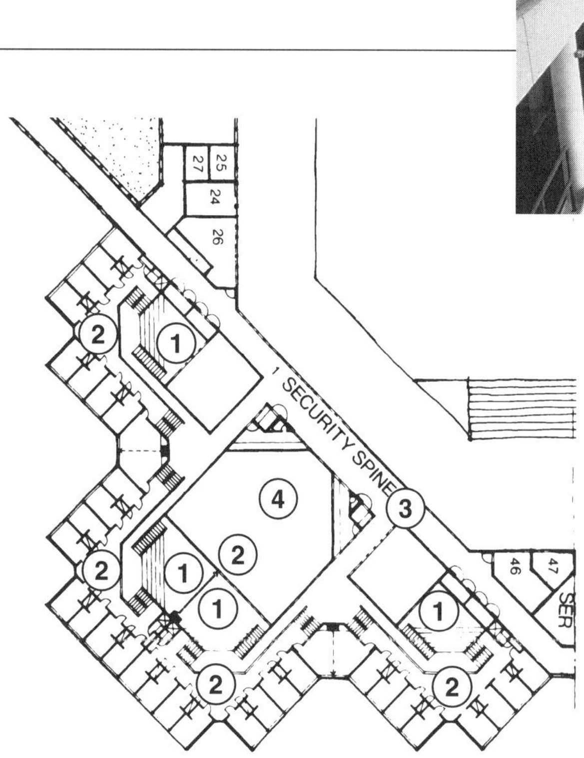

Figure 4.26*a* **Housing plan.**

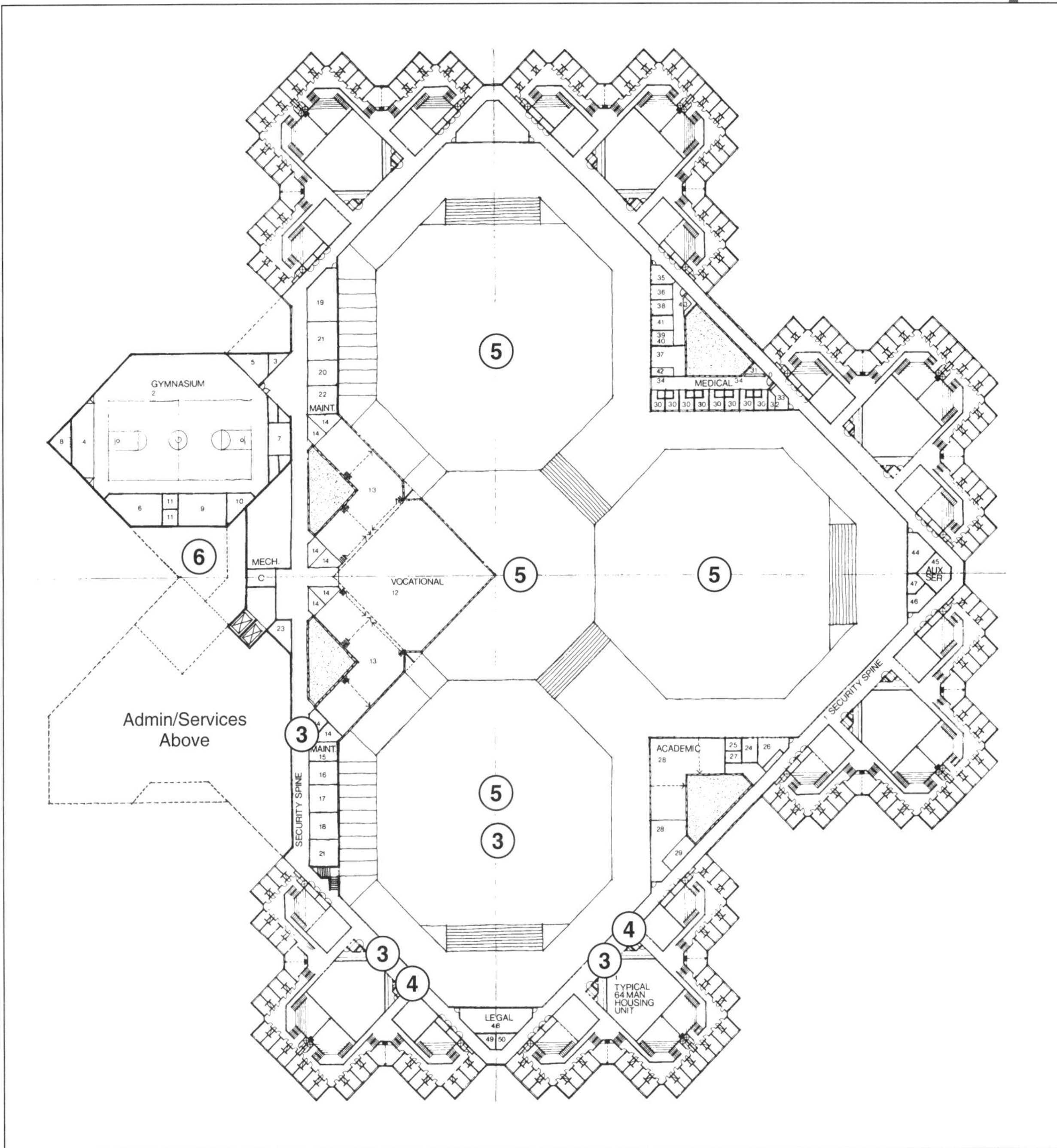

Figure 4.26*b* **Facility plan.**

4.27 Interconnected

Statistics

Site:	45 acres
Type:	State prison
Stories:	Low-rise, single-level support, one-level housing (with mezzanine)
Building area:	285,260 gsf
Population:	512 single cells—maximum; planned expansion to 640 single cells
Housing:	Two 64-cell units per control
Management:	Indirect supervision
Staff:	463
Operational:	1985

Design Features

1. Facility exterior walls without windows; windows internalized for natural light.
2. Curvilinear exterior wall provides continuous quick response via road for vehicles.
3. Continuous observation and control of inmate corridor movement from elevated station.
4. Passive and active recreation activities located between three building masses.
5. Programs located adjacent to each housing complex.
6. Single control tower observes entirety of security perimeter.

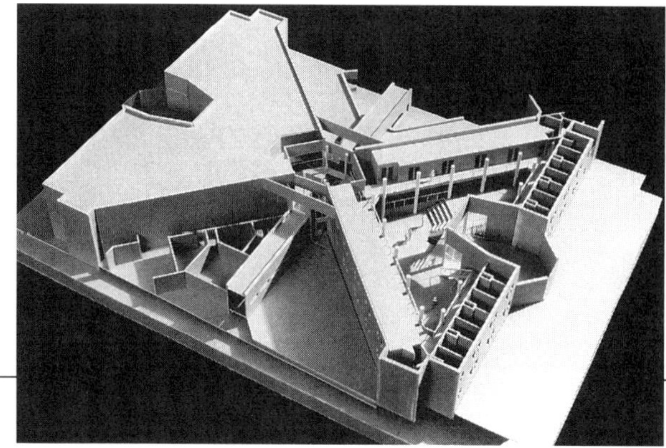

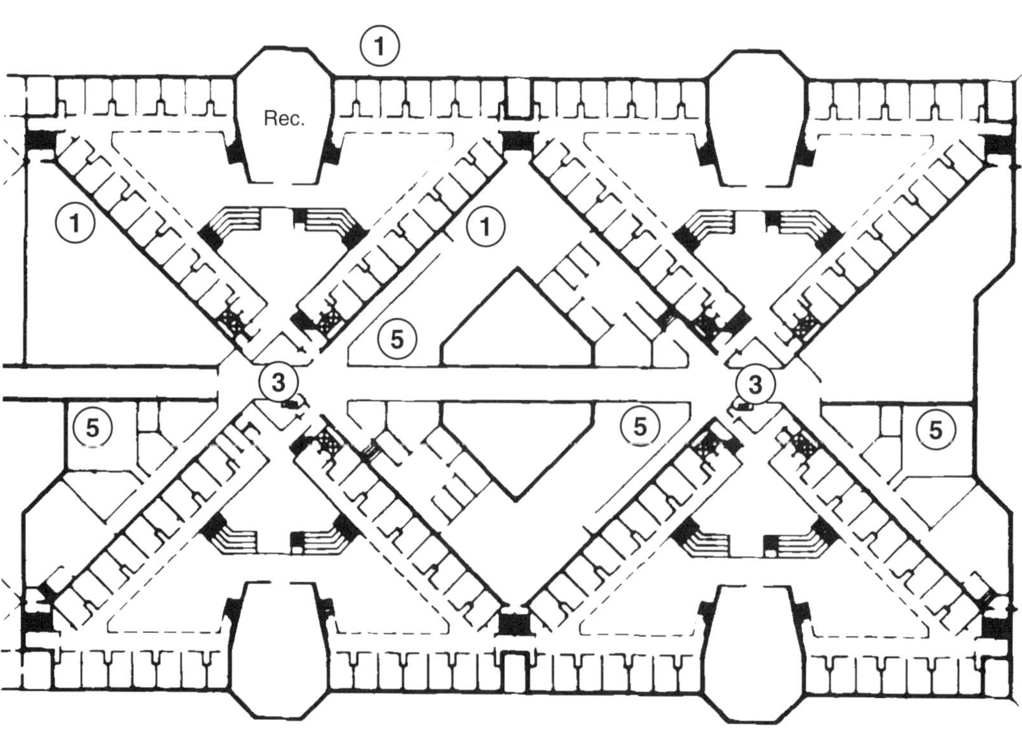

Figure 4.27*a* **Housing plan.**

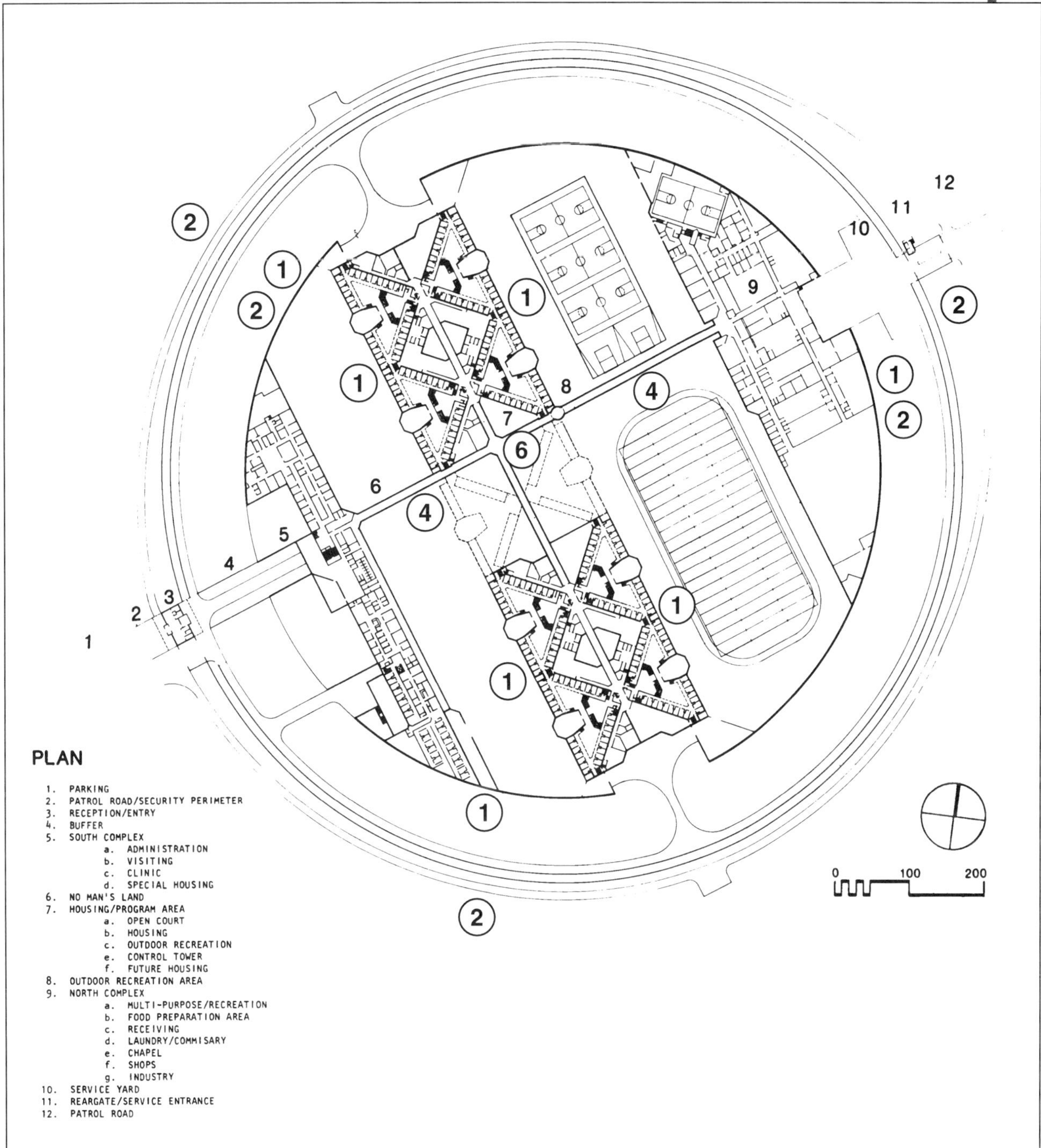

Figure 4.27*b* **Facility plan.**

4.28 Interconnected

Statistics

Site:	60-acre building development—208 acres of rugged terrain
Type:	State prison
Stories:	Mid-rise, single-level program support on top of one-story housing (with mezzanine)
Building area:	330,000 gsf
Population:	400 single cells—maximum
Housing:	Seven 52-cell units per control; one 42-bed medical/mental health unit
Management:	Indirect supervision
Staff:	353
Operational:	1982

Design Features

1. Building exterior buried into hill on three sides, bridged and open on other.
2. Majority of facility hidden from neighborhood views.
3. Housing and support windows face internally onto courtyard for natural light.
4. Programs stacked above each housing unit to minimize inmate movement.
5. Each housing unit's outdoor recreation leads to centralized recreation space.
6. Building exterior walls, at grade-level courtyard, form facility's secure perimeter.

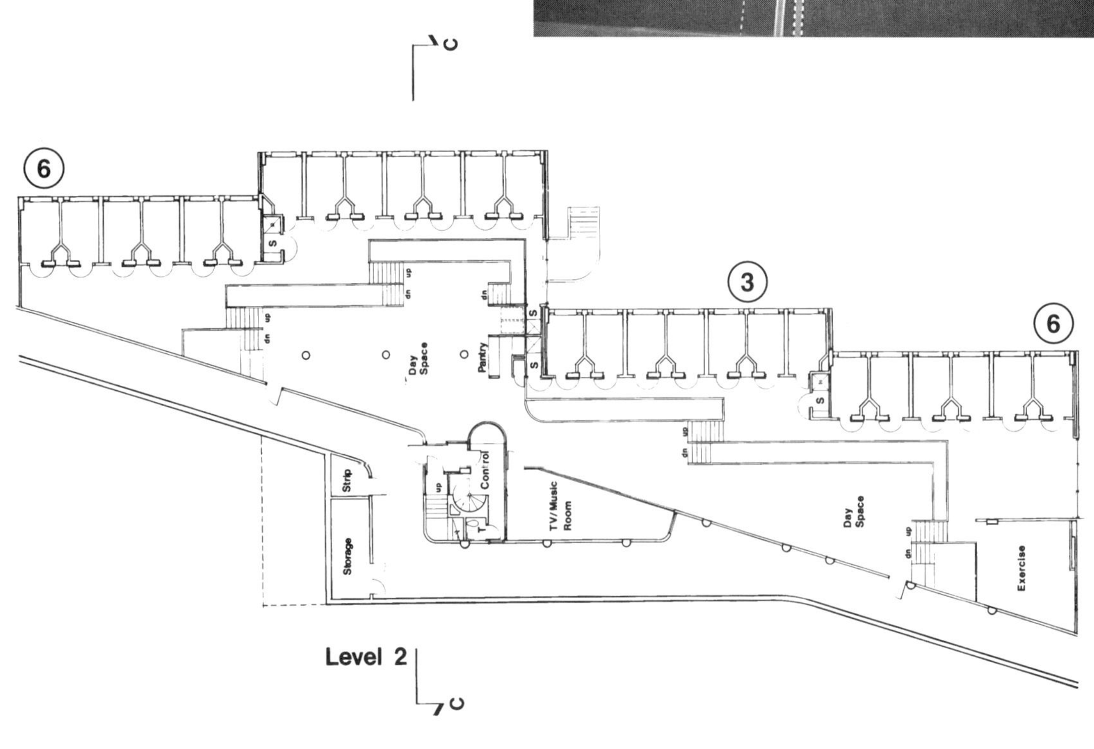

Figure 4.28*a* **Housing plan.**

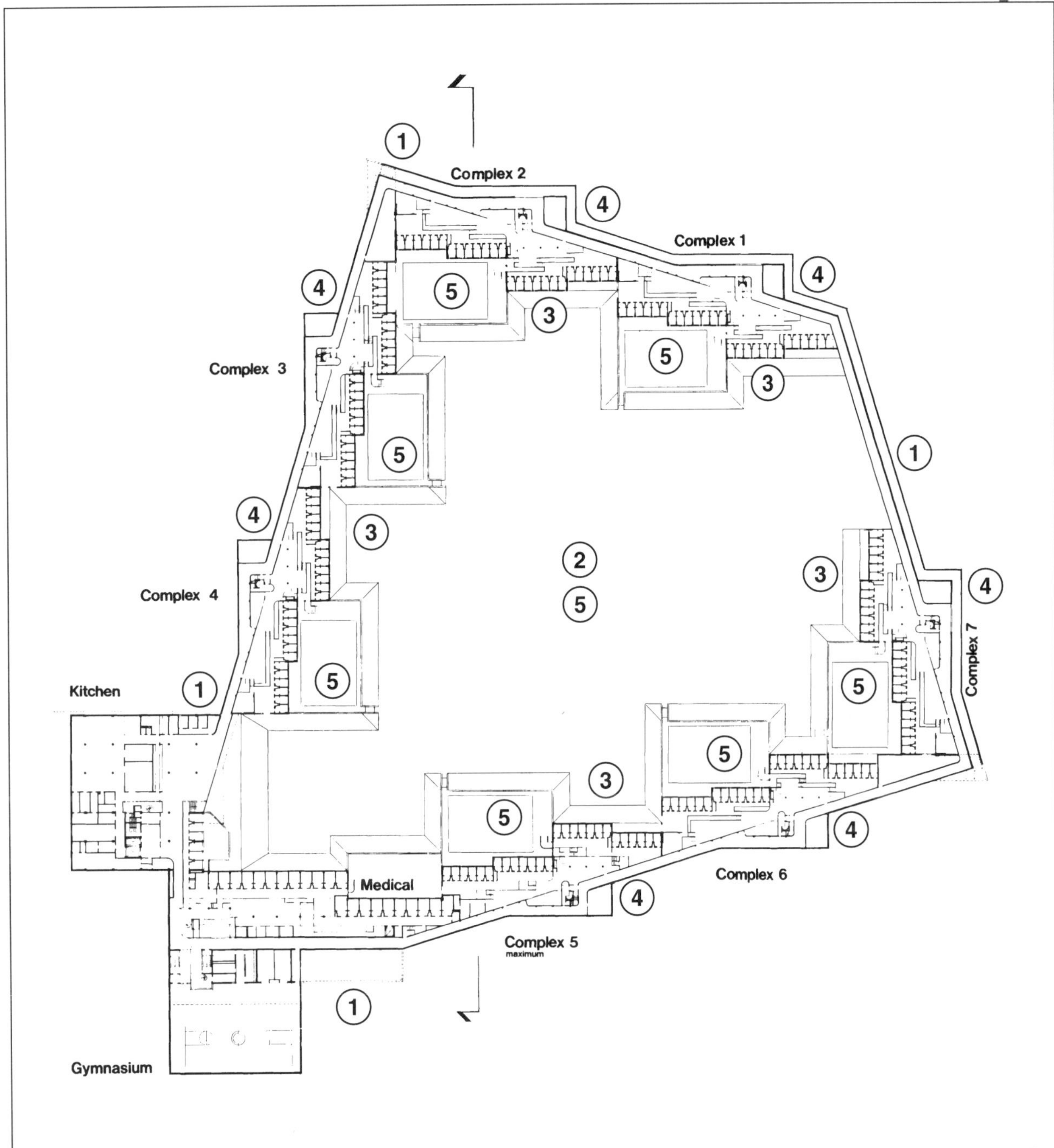

Figure 4.28*b* **Facility plan.**

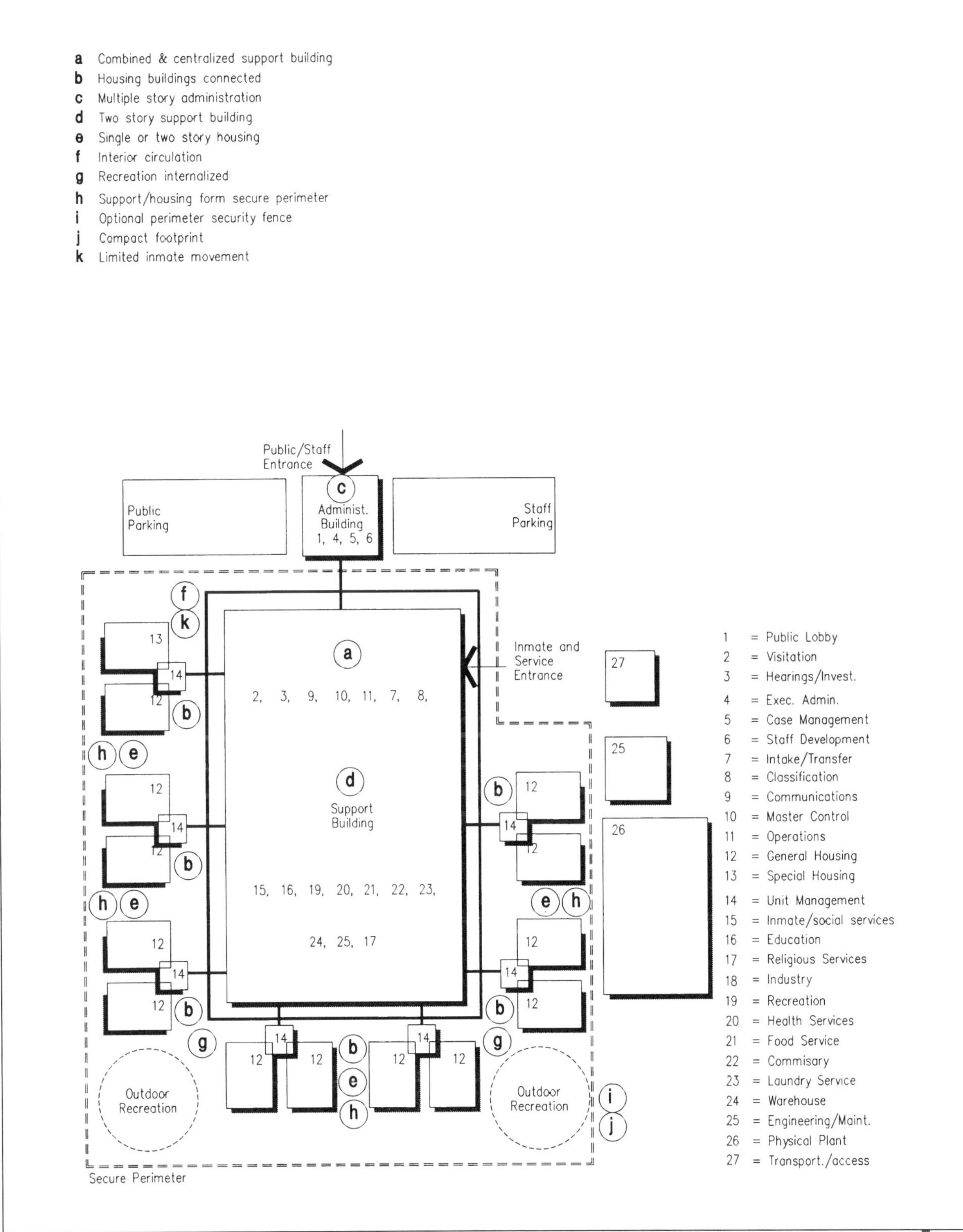

Figure 4.29 **Contained facility diagram.**

4.30 Contained

	Statistics
Site:	5.5 acres
Type:	State prison system's diagnostic and reception center
Stories:	Low-rise, two-level support, one-level housing (with mezzanine)
Building area:	76,293 gsf
Population:	160 single cells—maximum; 16 medical cells
Housing:	One 32-cell unit per control
Management:	Indirect supervision
Staff:	119 (intensive classification program)
Operational:	1979

Design Features

1. Separate facility, connected by tunnel to adjacent state prison.
2. Lower-level treatment functions central to all housing units.
3. Small facility, yet provides centralized gymnasium and outdoor exercise spaces.
4. Complete observation, supervision, and control of inmate corridor movement.
5. Each housing unit's control station's observation of adjacent unit's station.
6. Upper-level public entrance screens public view of adjacent housing exteriors.

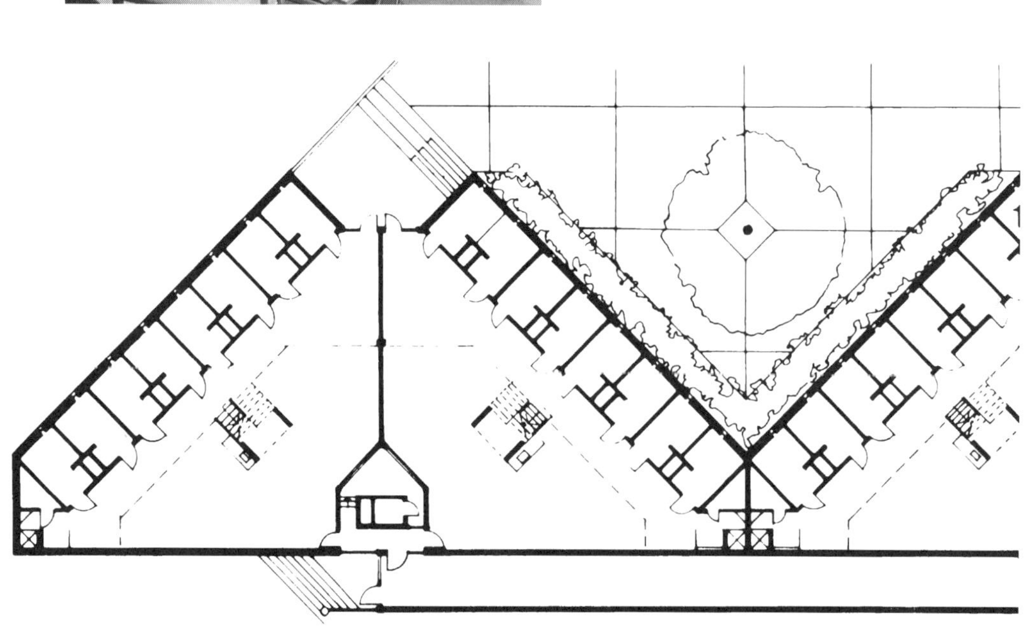

Figure 4.30*a* **Housing plan.**

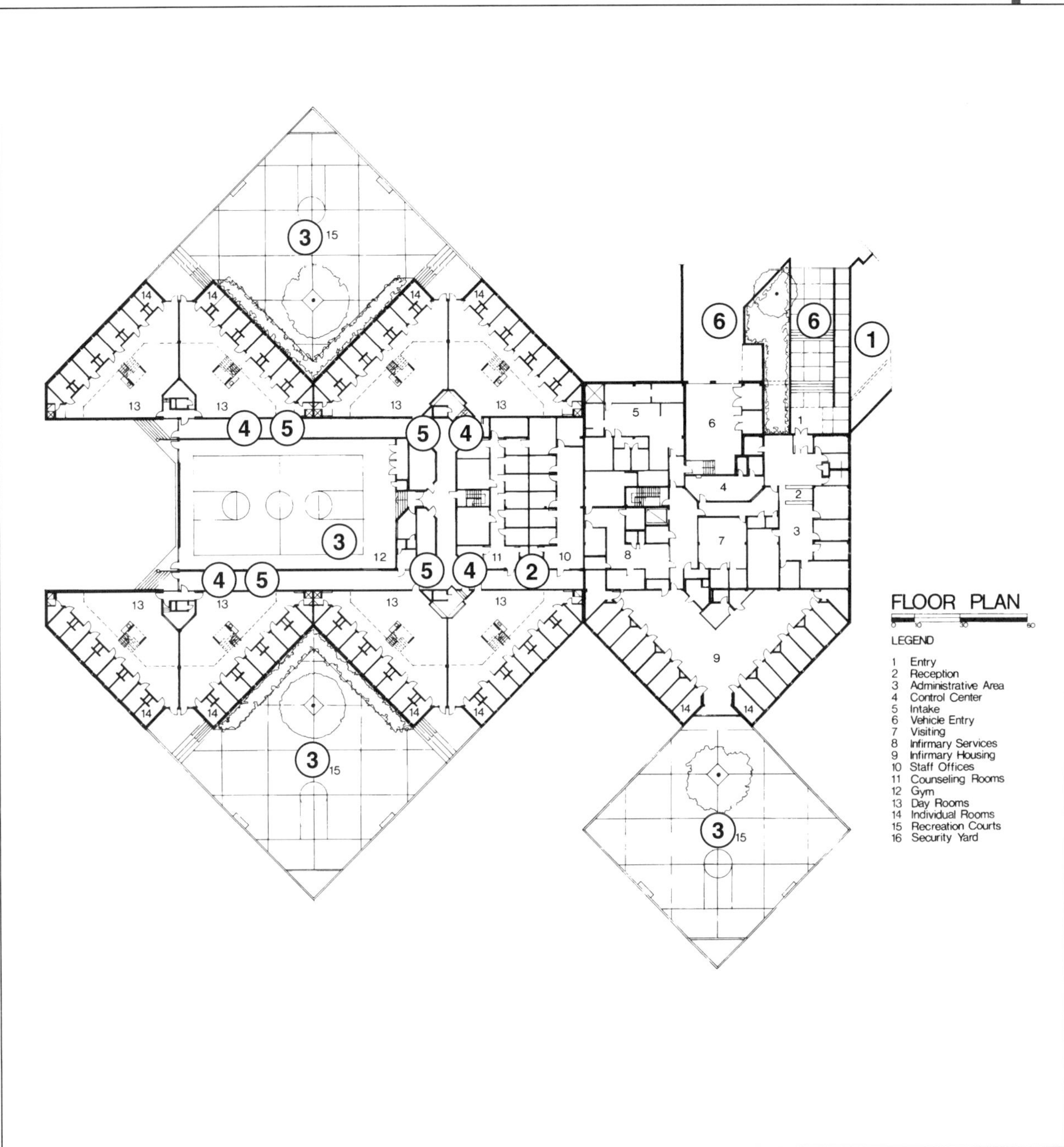

Figure 4.30*b* **Facility plan.**

4.31 Contained Statistics

Site:	50 acres
Type:	Seven-county regional jail facility
Stories:	Low-rise, two-level support, one-level housing (with mezzanine)
Building area:	571,000 gsf
Population:	720 single cells—maximum/medium; planned expansion to 1200
Housing:	Five 48-cell housing units per unit management control
Management:	Direct supervision
Staff:	259
Operational:	1997

Design Features

1. Separate, public (upper) and inmate (lower) level circulation centrally observed.
2. Unit management groups of 240, include programs and visitation.
3. Unit management housing with equal distance linkage to central functions.
4. Each housing unit has separate outdoor recreation, screened from public view.
5. Architectural plan and aesthetics appropriate to neighborhood context.
6. Facility location adjacent to federal facility and public park.

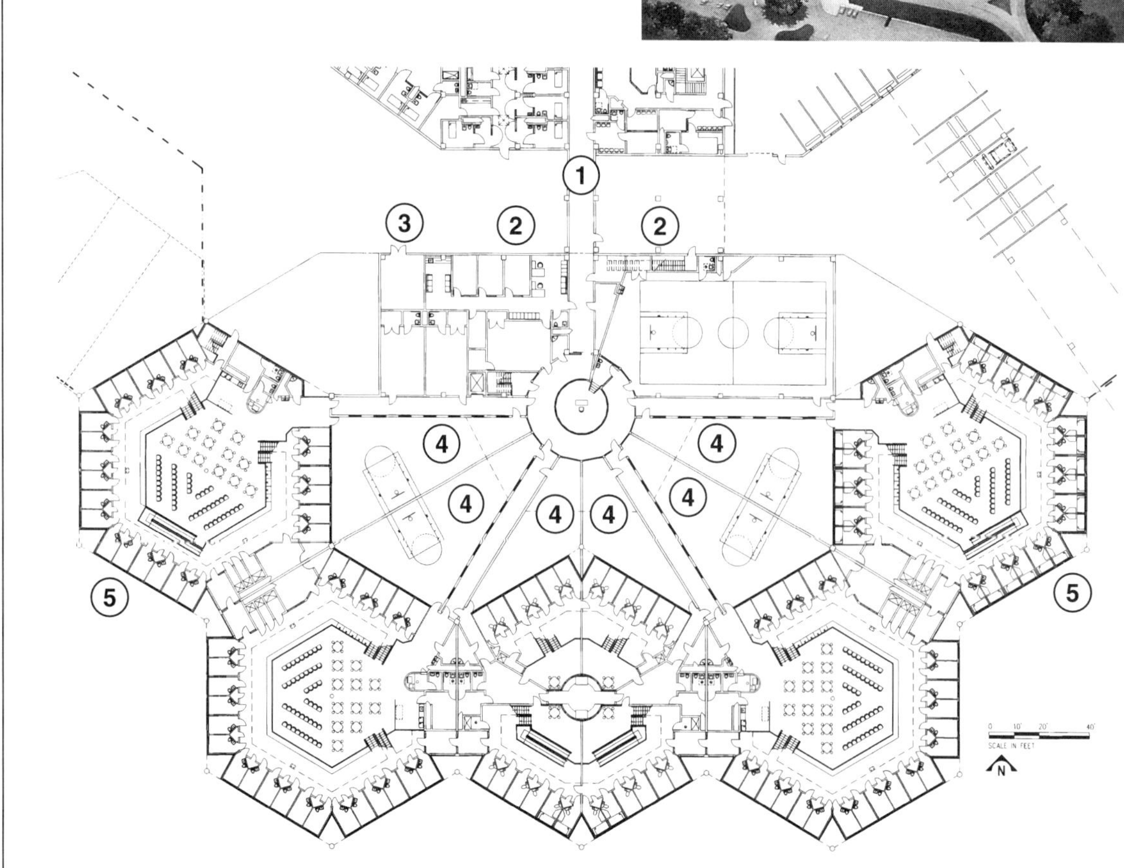

Figure 4.31*a* **Housing plan.**

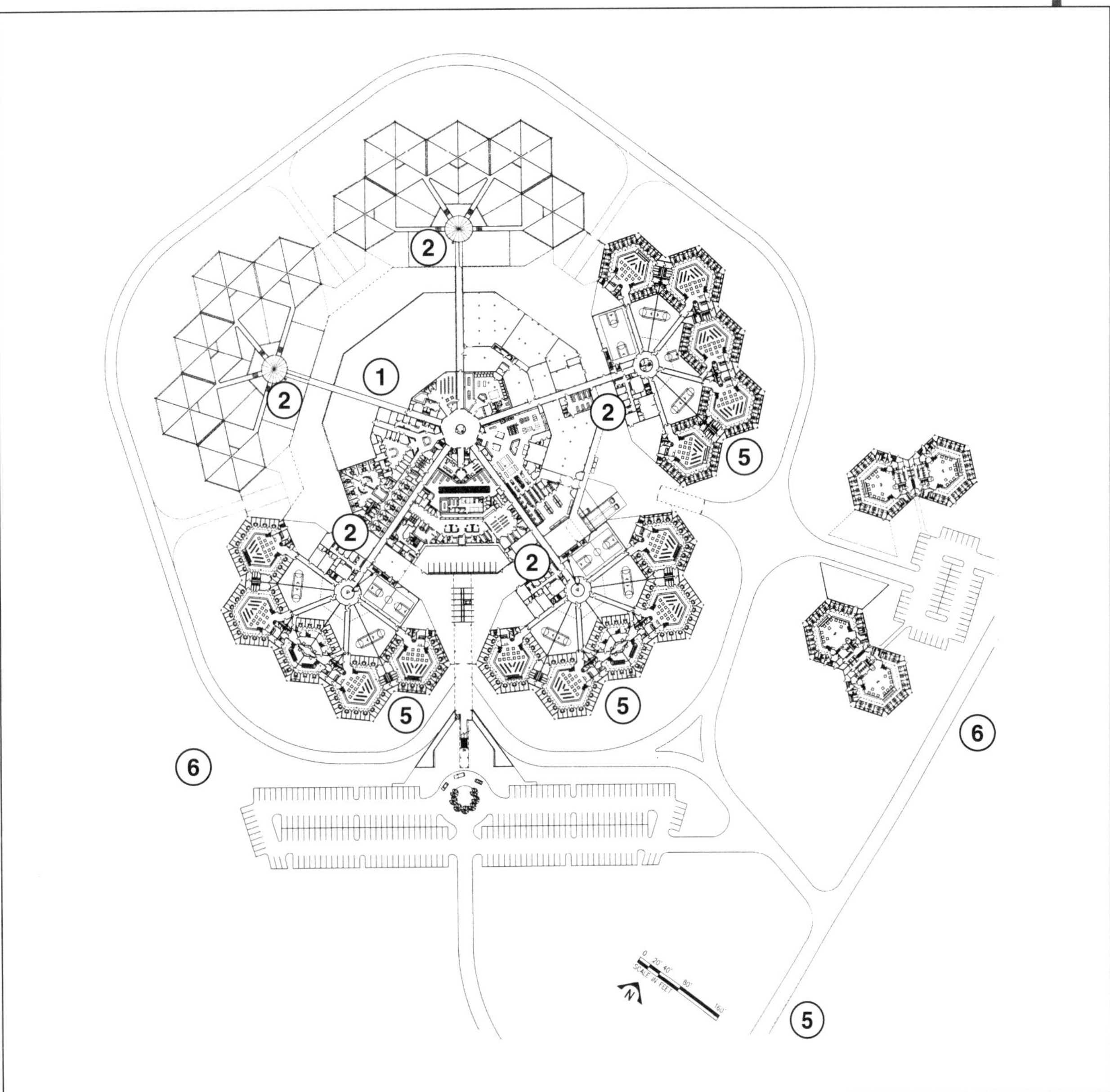

Figure 4.31*b* **Facility plan.**

4.32 Contained

Statistics

Site: 5 acres—new facility; 20 acres jail development

Type: County jail

Stories: Low-rise support, two-story housing (with mezzanines)

Building area: 155,000+ gsf

Population: 448 single cells—maximum; planned double-occupancy cells

Housing: Four 56-cell housing units per floor; two-story housing building

Management: Direct supervision

Staff: 151 (total inmate population of 592, new + existing jail)

Operational: 1997

Design Features

1. Separated administration and support building from housing complex.
2. Unit management groups of 224, linked to central support and existing facility.
3. Connection to, and renovation of, adjacent existing operational facility.
4. Housing units planned for double-bunking opportunity.
5. Housing units are grouped to share localized unit management programs.
6. Architectural plan and aesthetics sensitive to existing building architecture.

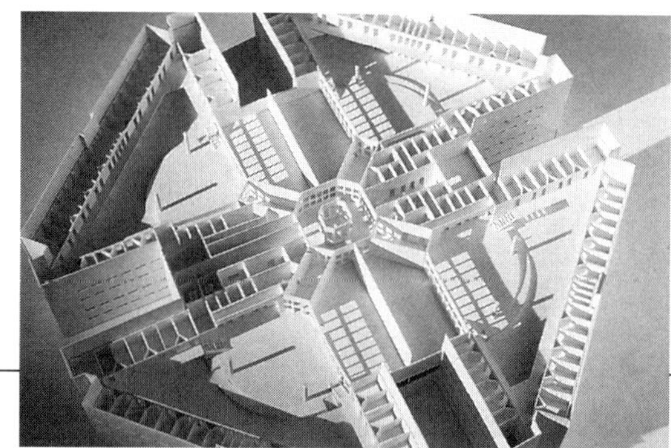

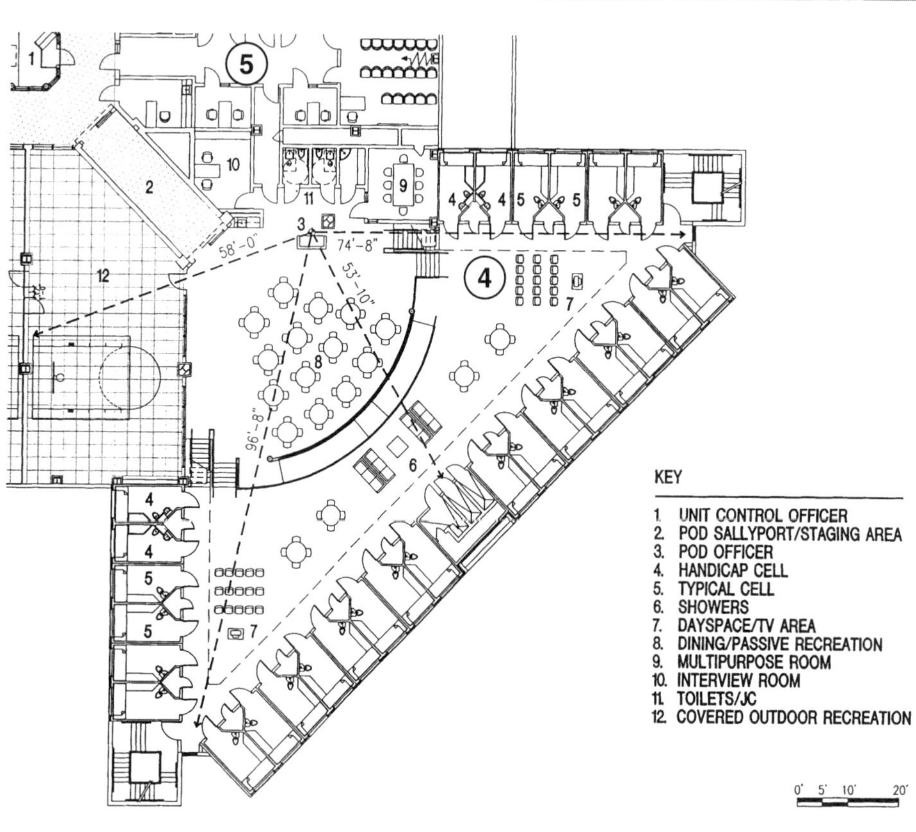

Figure 4.32*a* **Housing plan.**

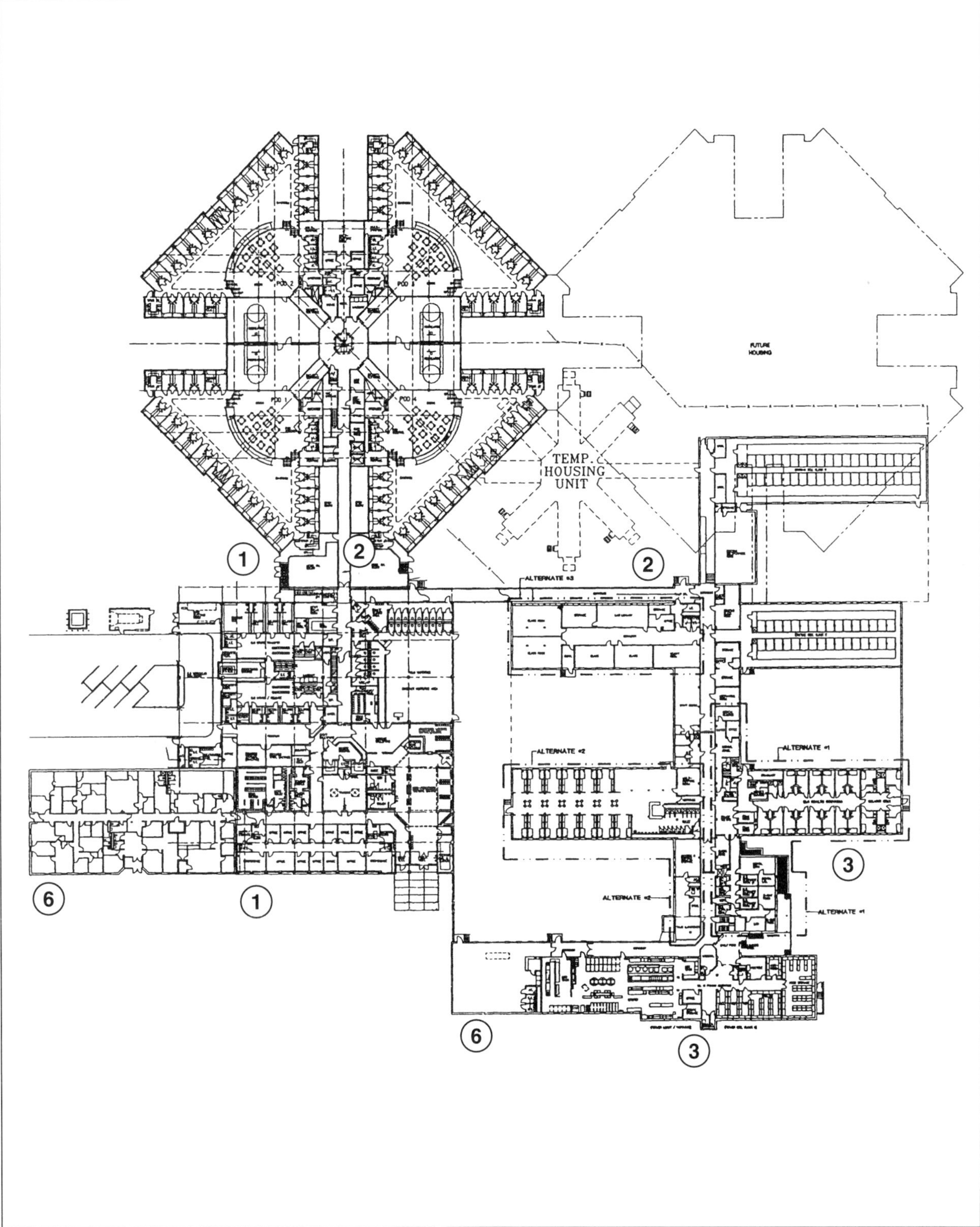

Figure 4.32*b* **Facility plan.**

a Mega structure
b Combined & centralized support
c Multiple story support
d Multiple story housing
e Circulation internalized
f Indoor recreation centralized
g Outdoor recreation internalized (optional)
h Support/housing form secure perimeter
i Optional perimeter security fence
j Optimum compact footprint
k Limited inmate movement

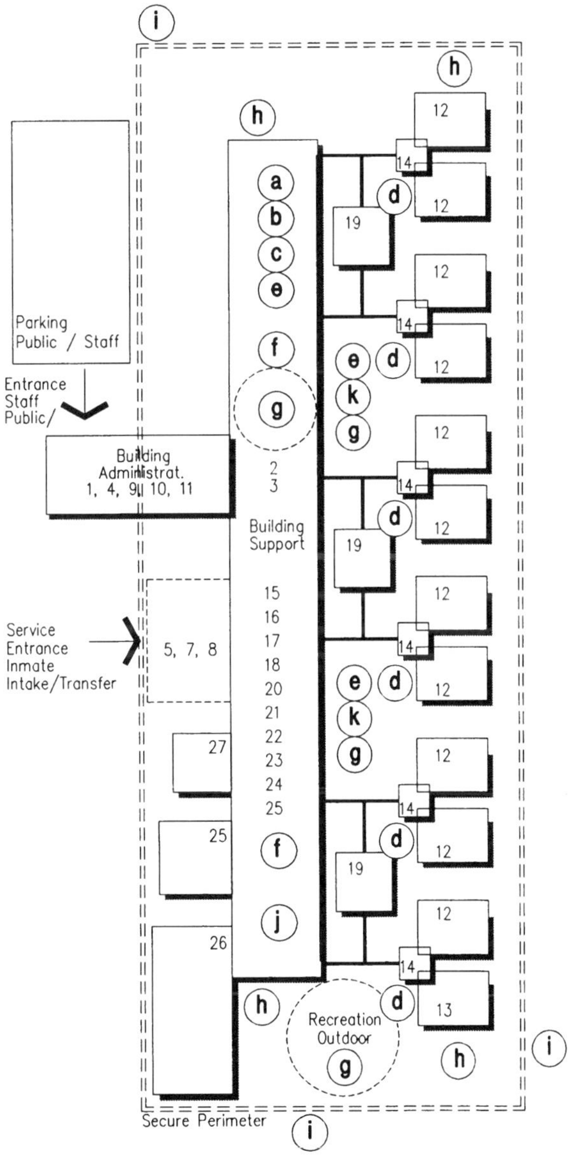

Parking Public / Staff
Entrance Staff Public/
Building Administrat. 1, 4, 9, 10, 11
2 3
Building Support
15 16 17 18 20 21 22 23 24 25
Service Entrance Inmate Intake/Transfer
5, 7, 8
Recreation Outdoor
Secure Perimeter

1 = Public Lobby
2 = Visitation
3 = Hearings/Invest.
4 = Exec. Admin.
5 = Case Management
6 = Staff Development
7 = Intake/Transfer
8 = Classification
9 = Communications
10 = Master Control
11 = Operations
12 = General Housing
13 = Special Housing
14 = Unit Management
15 = Inmate/social services
16 = Education
17 = Religious Services
18 = Industry
19 = Recreation
20 = Health Service
21 = Food Service
22 = Commisary
23 = Laundry Service
24 = Warehouse
25 = Engineering/Maint.
26 = Physical Plant
27 = Transport /access

Figure 4.33 **Contained and linear facility diagram.**

4.34 Contained and Linear

Statistics

Site:	20.5 acres
Type:	Municipal reception center, presentenced-sentenced
Stories:	Mid-rise, single-level support, three-level administration, two-story housing (mezzanines)
Building area:	750,000 gsf
Population:	1000 cells (doubled-bunked yielding 2000 beds)—close custody
Housing:	64-bed unit per control, four units per unit management control
Management:	Direct supervision
Staff:	525
Operational:	1995

Design Features

1. Large population located on a limited acre site.
2. Unit control observes all four housing unit interiors/supports housing officer.
3. Each housing management group separated by level and building.
4. Two housing buildings (two stories + mezzanine each) share large gymnasium-programs.
5. Unescorted inmate movement to decentralized inmate programs.
6. Separate public and staff lobbies, observed and supervised by central control.

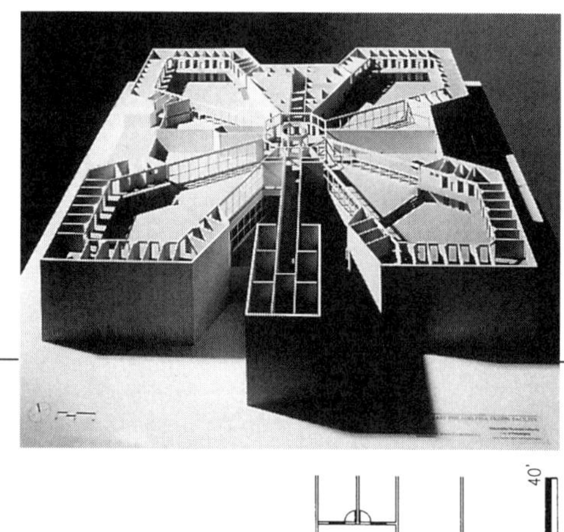

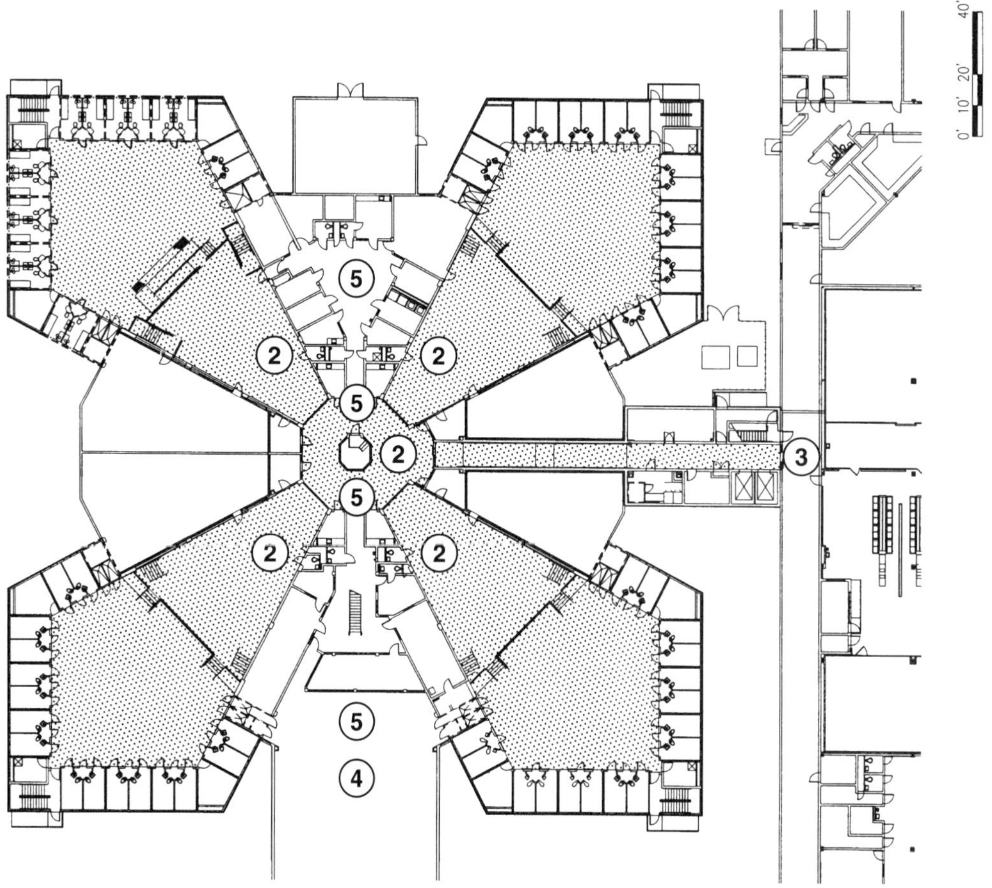

Figure 4.34*a* **Housing plan.**

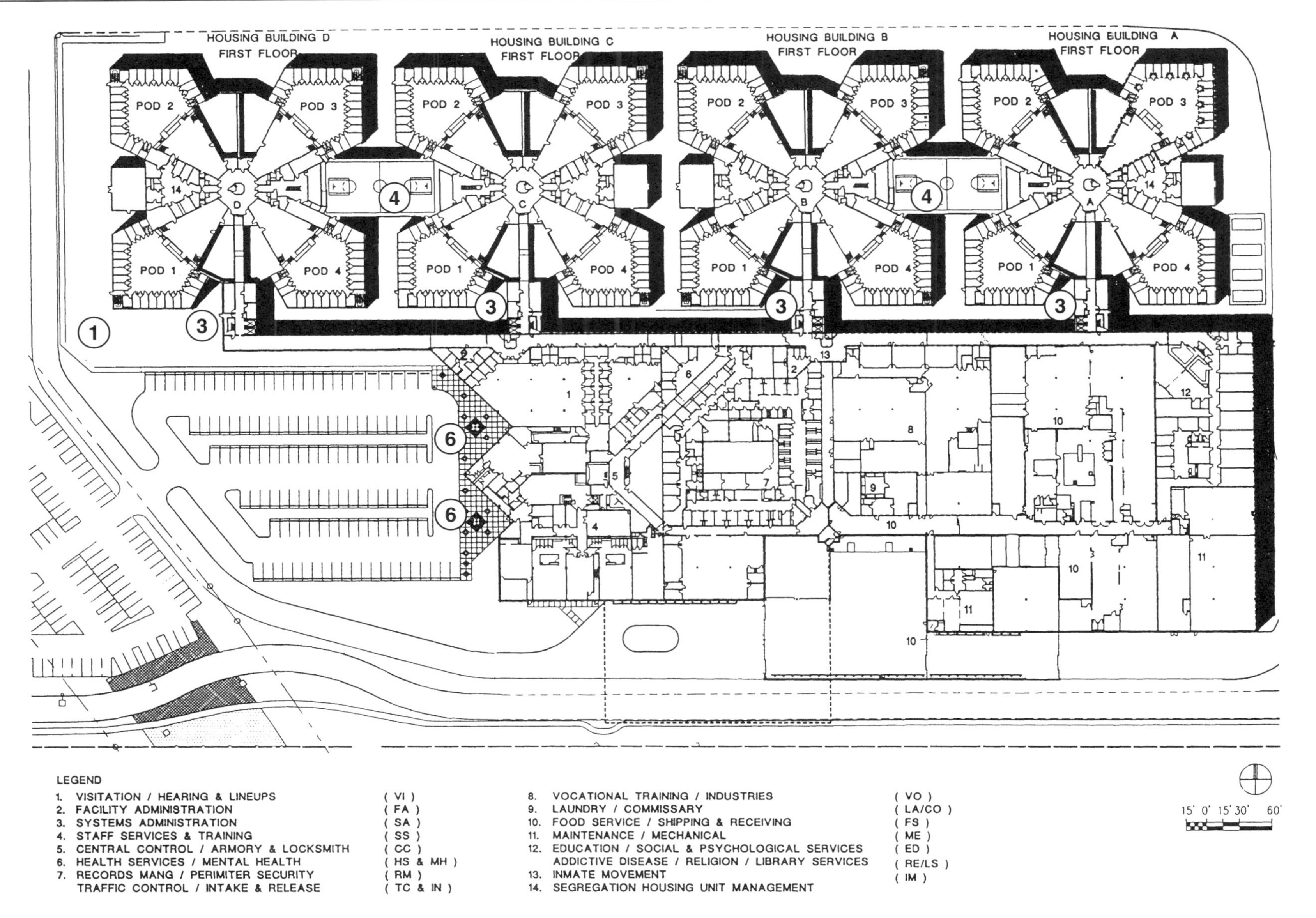

Figure 4.34*b* **Facility plan.**

4.35 Contained and Linear

	Statistics
Site:	20 acres
Type:	State prison
Stories:	High-rise, multiple-level administration/support, three-story housing (with mezzanines)
Building area:	359,518 gsf
Population:	850 single cells—maximum
Housing:	One 48-cell unit per control; three units per floor; three floors per building
Management:	Indirect supervision
Staff:	949 (total inmate population of 2059 new + existing prison)
Operational:	1983

Design Features

1. New facility constructed while existing prison remained operational.
2. All inmate exterior activities hidden from residential neighborhood views.
3. Natural light in inmate corridors, above eye level; inmates screened from public view.
4. All inmate cell windows focus internally toward the compound site.
5. Preserved original 1836 prison facade, centrally located in new facility.
6. Overcrowding prevented planned demolition of existing prison buildings.

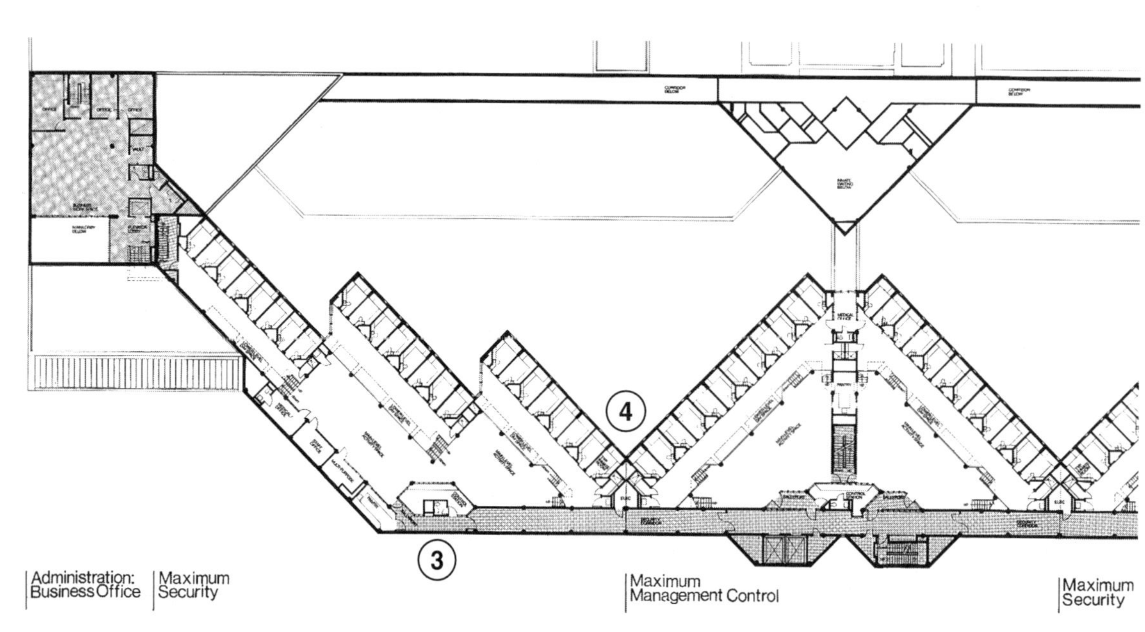

Figure 4.35*a* **Housing plan.**

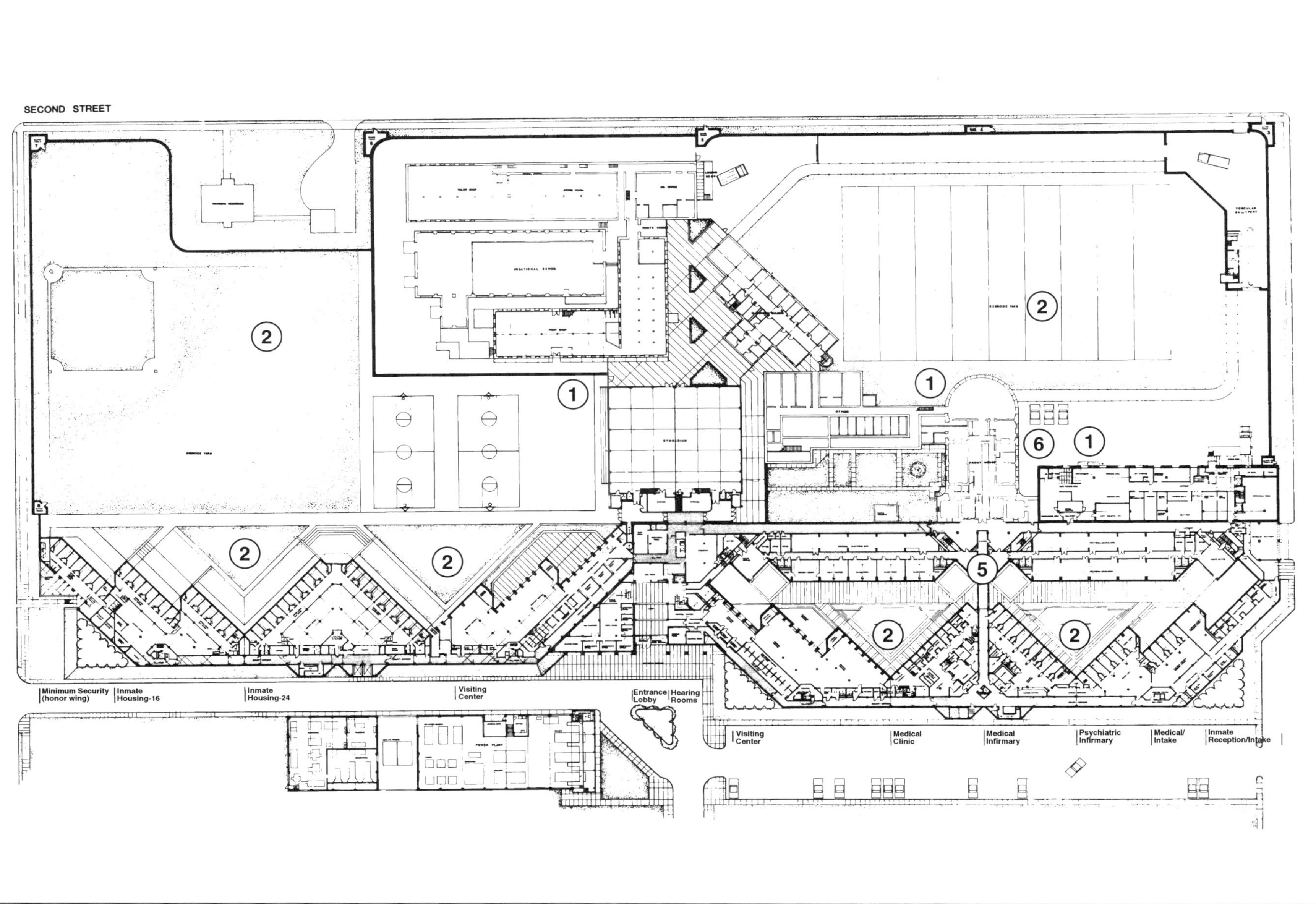

Figure 4.35*b* **Facility plan.**

4.36 Contained and Linear

	Statistics
Site:	5 acres
Type:	State prison
Stories:	Low-rise, administration, support, and one-level housing
Building area:	73,000 gsf
Population:	300 beds—minimum
Housing:	Four 75-bed dormitory buildings, each with control
Management:	Direct supervision
Staff:	102
Operational:	1991

Design Features

1. New facility constructed adjacent to existing prison.
2. Centralized circulation corridor provides inmate movement observation and control.
3. Internal corridor utilized clerestory for natural light.
4. Outdoor recreation located between or adjacent to housing and support building.
5. Preengineered structure supported a 4-month construction program.
6. Aesthetic exterior utilized unit masonry construction with textures and colors.

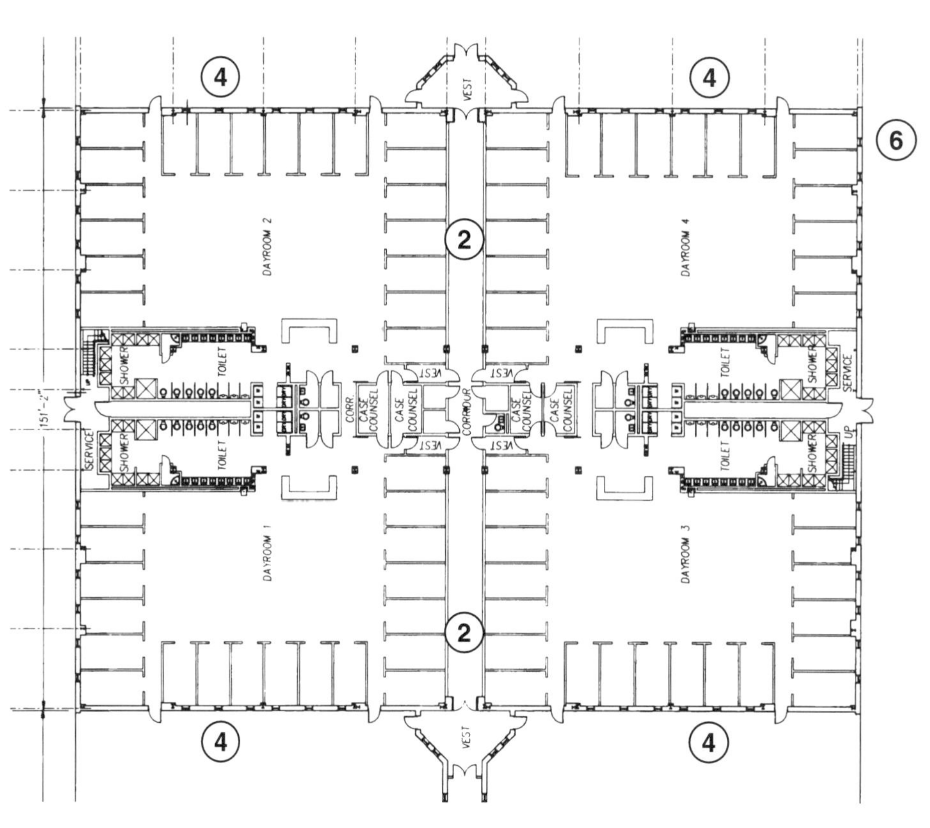

Figure 4.36*a* **Housing plan.**

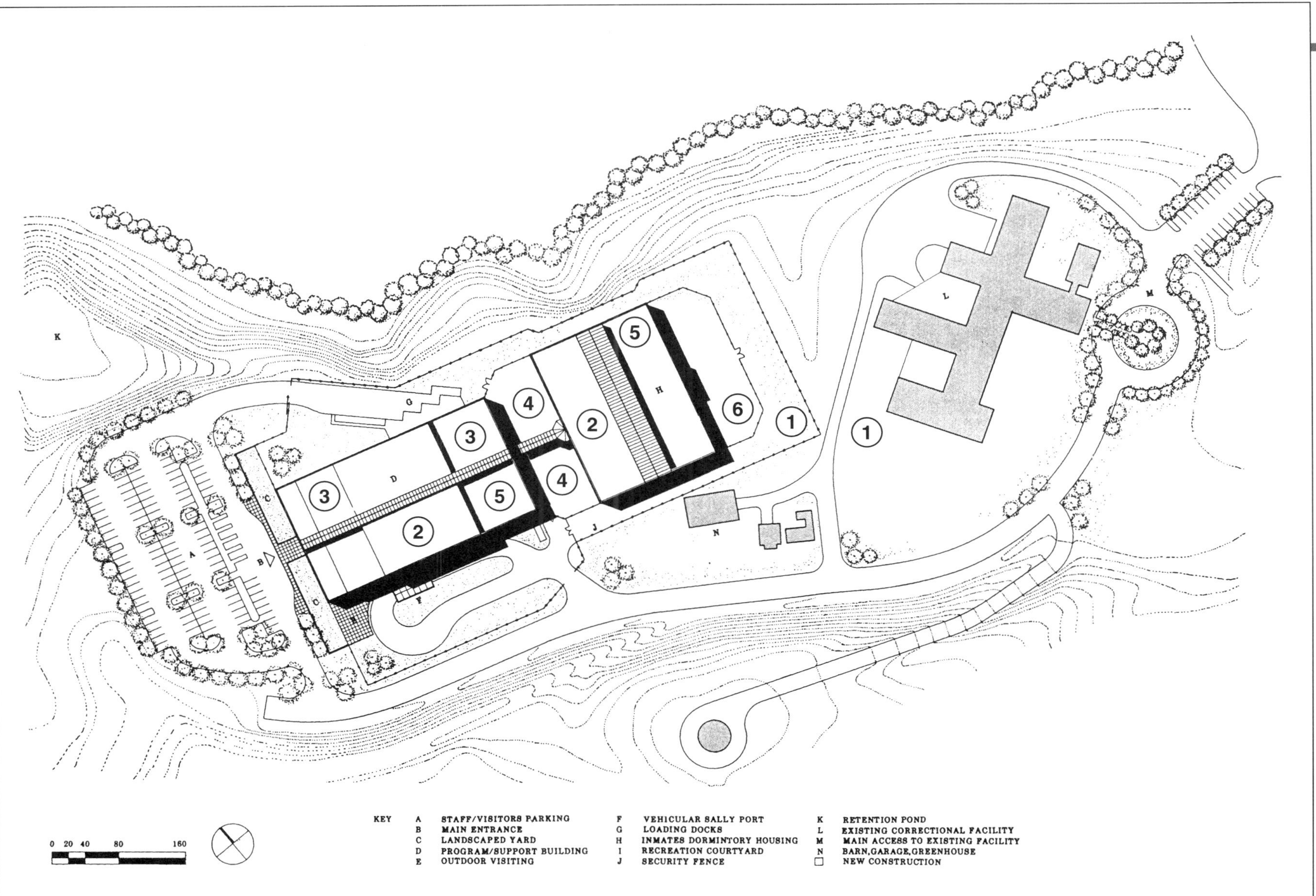

Figure 4.36*b* **Facility plan.**

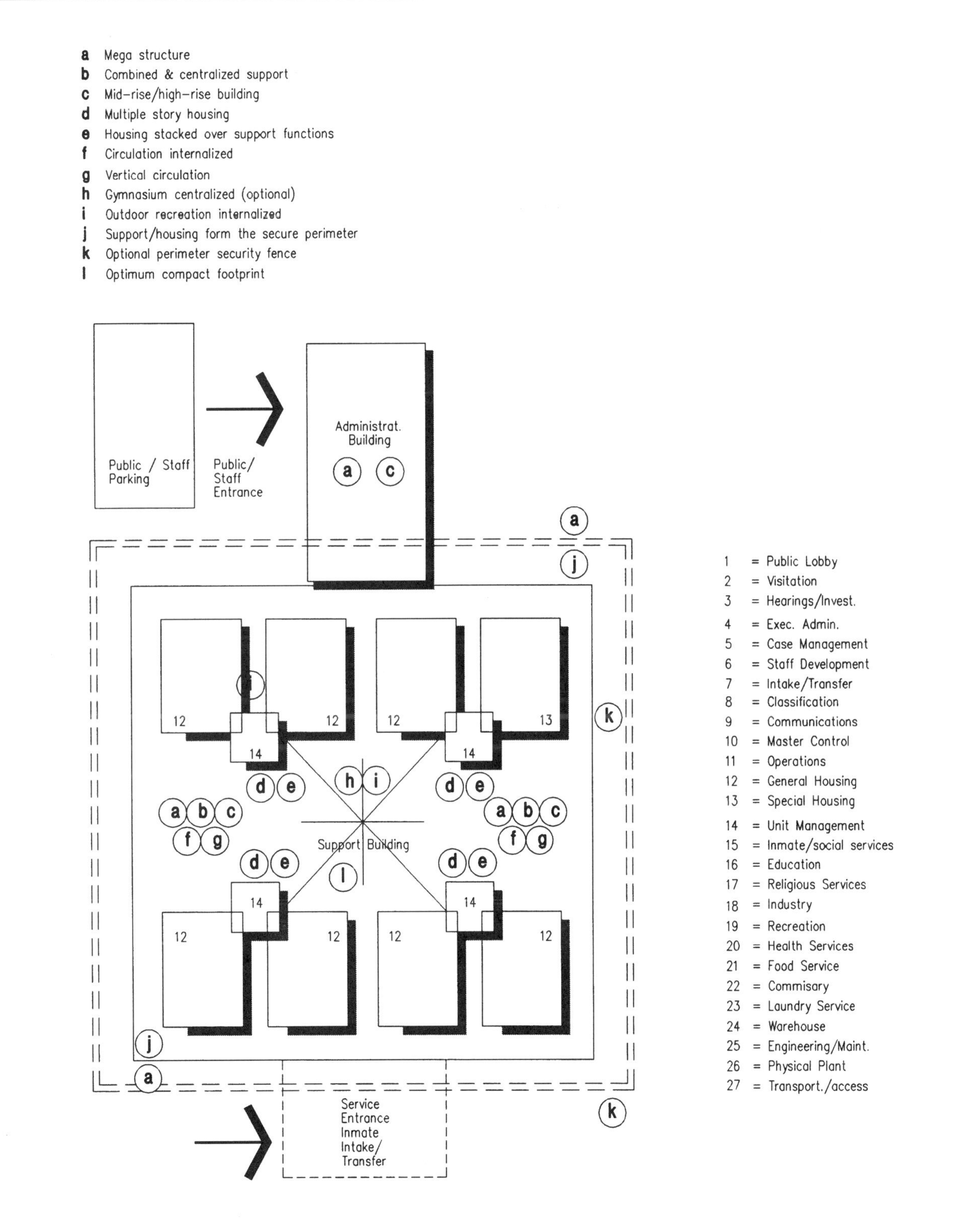

Figure 4.37 **Contained and stacked facility diagram.**

4.38 Contained and Stacked

Statistics

Site:	3 acres
Type:	Municipal jail and sentenced facility connected to existing courthouse
Stories:	High-rise, multiple-level support with three-story housing (with mezzanines) above
Building area:	512,000 gsf
Population:	848 single cells—maximum
Housing:	One 56-cell housing unit per control and four per floor (two per separate buildings)
Management:	Indirect supervision
Staff:	326
Operational:	1983

Design Features

1. Separated jail and sentenced population buildings, linked to each other and existing courthouse.
2. Public plaza created between buildings with interior lobby artwork display.
3. Jail facility built above new courts and support functions.
4. Separate drive-through, service, and intake sally ports are screened from public view.
5. Building exterior walls are only security perimeter barrier.
6. Urban area commercial building aesthetics; linear facade and window treatment.

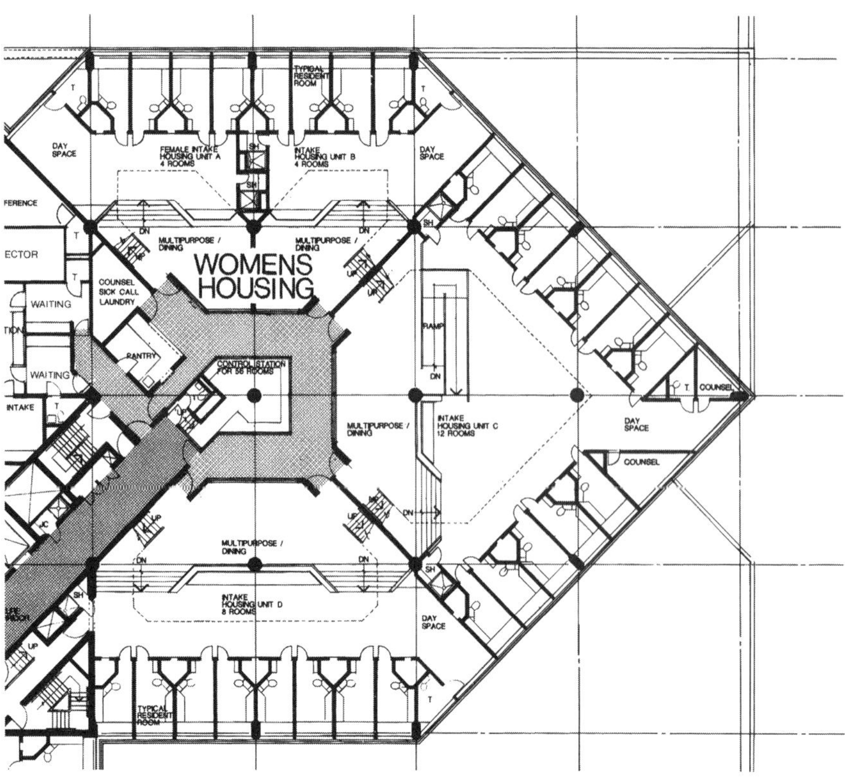

Figure 4.38*a* **Housing plan.**

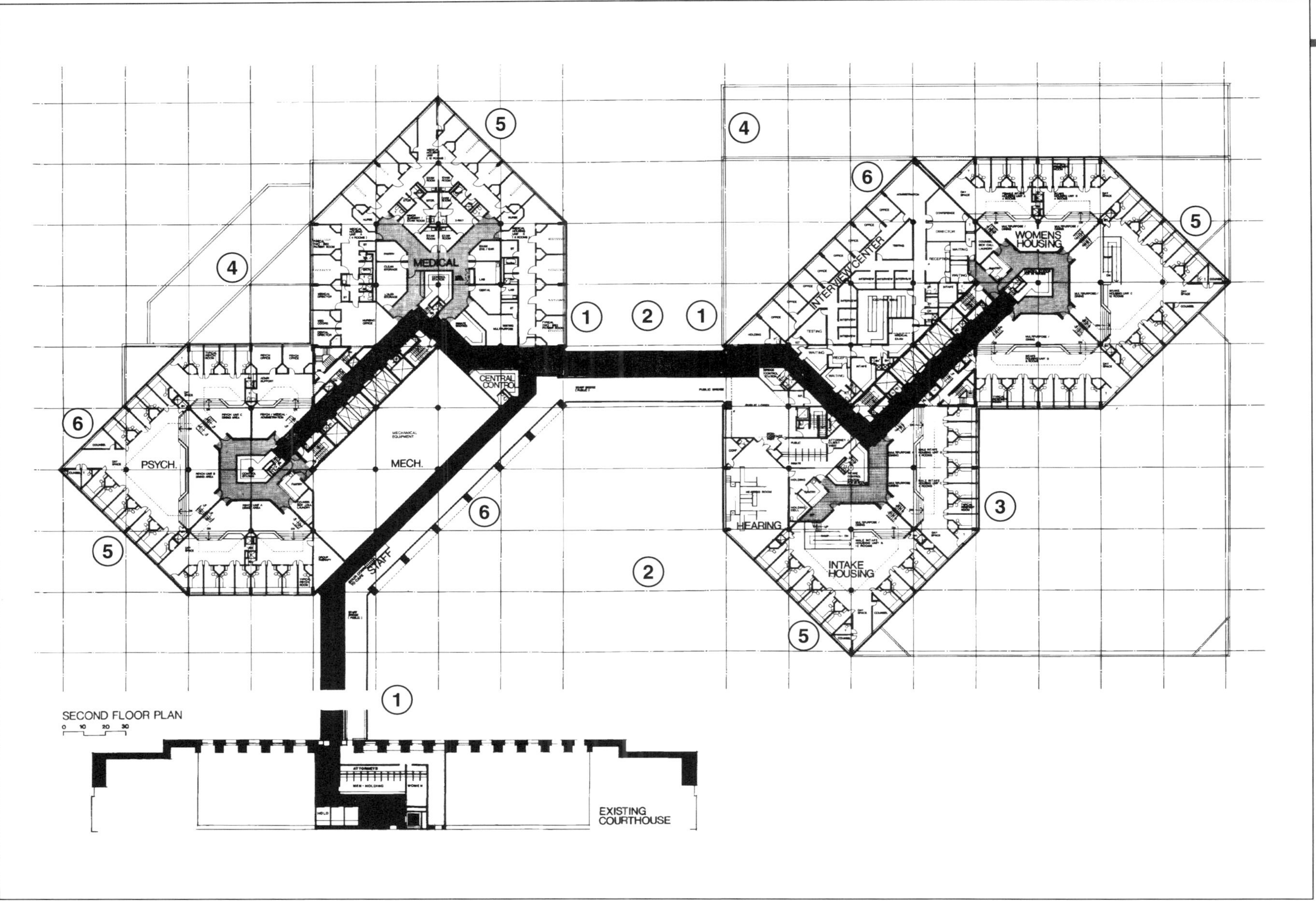

Figure 4.38*b* **Facility plan.**

4.39 Contained and Stacked

Statistics

Site:	3 acres; 18.5-acre future site development
Type:	County jail
Stories:	Mid-rise, single-level support with one-story housing above (with mezzanine)
Building area:	186,530 gsf
Population:	192 single cells—maximum; partial double occupancy
Housing:	Four 48-cell units per unit management control
Management:	Direct supervision
Staff:	204 (total inmate population of 805, new + existing jail)
Operational:	1994

Design Features

1. Noncontact visitation adjacent to each housing unit; dayroom-level access.
2. Multiple, internalized outdoor exercise yards for each housing unit.
3. Connection to existing jail and county building maintained continuous operations.
4. All services are located in basement, taking advantage of sloped site grade access.
5. Drive-through intake/transfer sally port is screened from public view.
6. Multiple facilities are master-planned for future jail expansion.

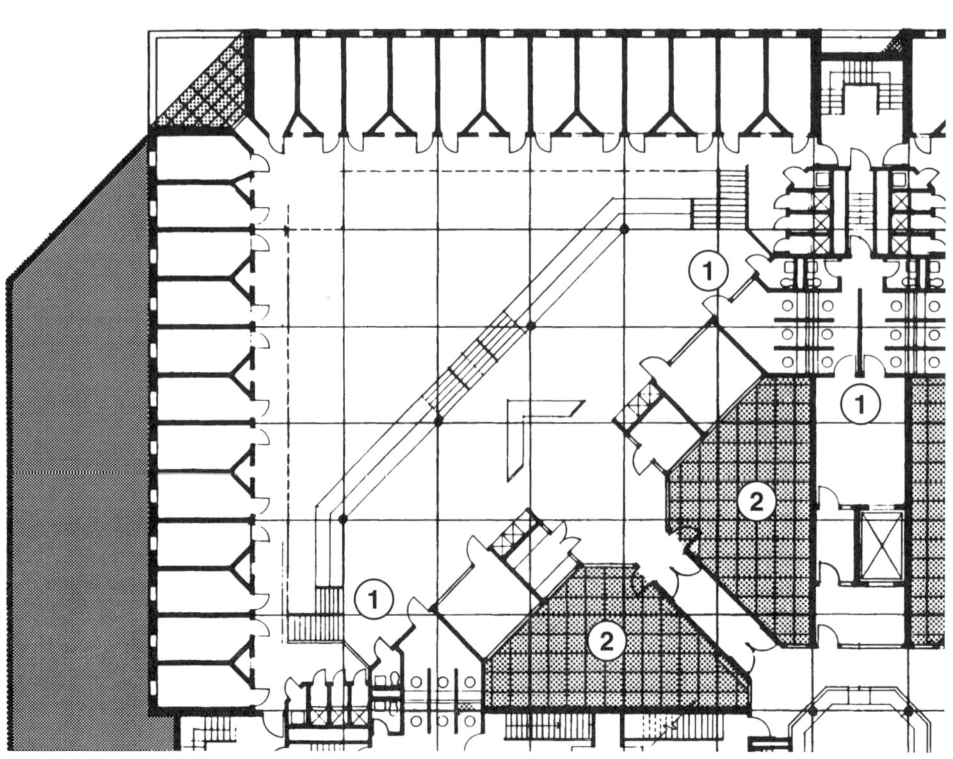

Figure 4.39*a* **Housing plan.**

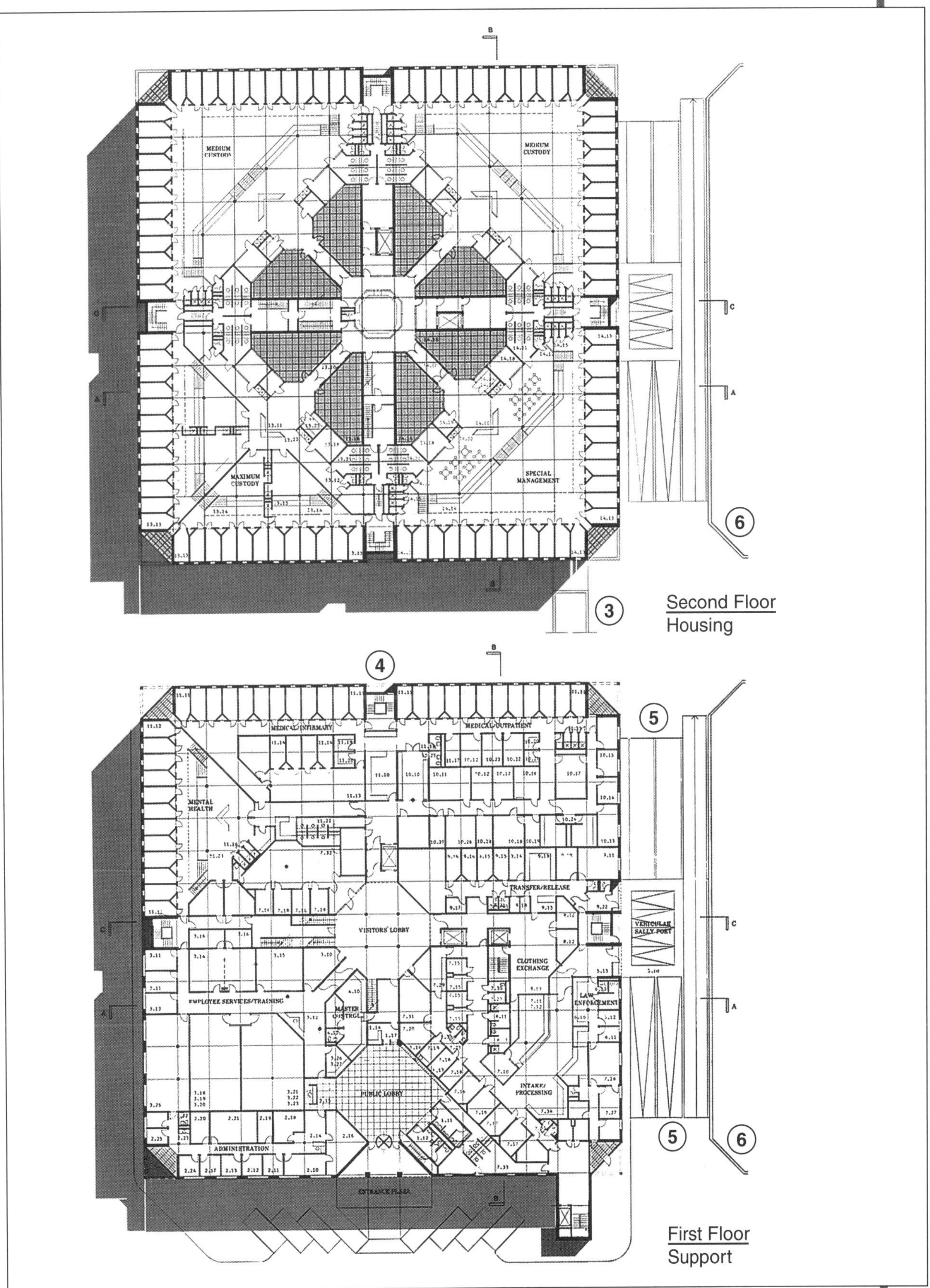

Figure 4.39*b* **Facility plan.**

4.40 Contained and Stacked

Statistics

Site:	5 acres
Type:	County jail
Stories:	Mid-rise, single-level support with one-story housing (with mezzanine) above
Building area:	150,000+ gsf
Population:	224 single cells—maximum; planned for double occupancy
Housing:	Four 56-cell units per unit management control
Management:	Direct supervision
Staff:	112 (total inmate population of 404, new + existing jail)
Operational:	1996

Design Features

1. Prototypical design; modified and site adapted from neighboring county.
2. Unescorted and limited inmate movement to programs and services.
3. Connection to existing jail facility; remained operational during construction.
4. Design planned for double-bunking anticipated change in state regulations.
5. Housing cells are adaptable for HC accessibility utilizing identical cell design and dimensions.
6. Split-level housing design improves visibility of all inmate activities.

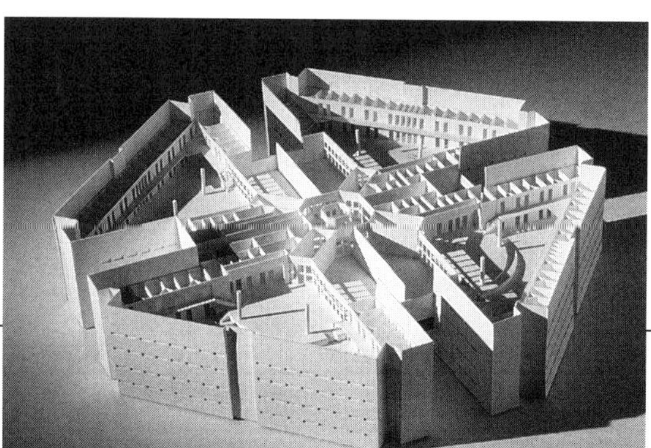

KEY

1. UNIT CONTROL OFFICER
2. POD OFFICER-56 CELLS
3. OUTDOOR RECREATION
4. UNIT MANAGEMENT ADMIN. AND PROGRAMS
5. CORRIDOR TO EXISTING JAIL

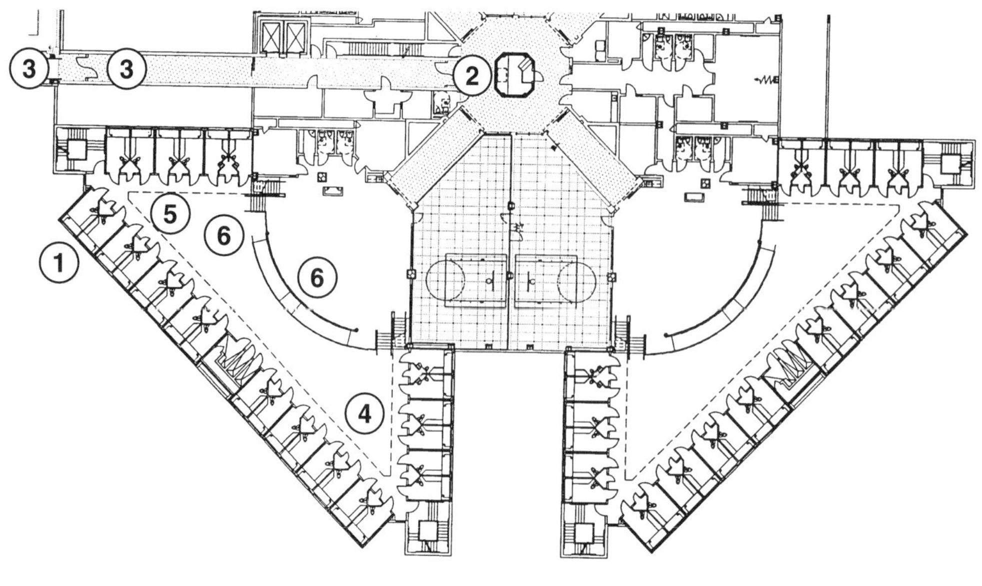

Figure 4.40*a* **Housing plan.**

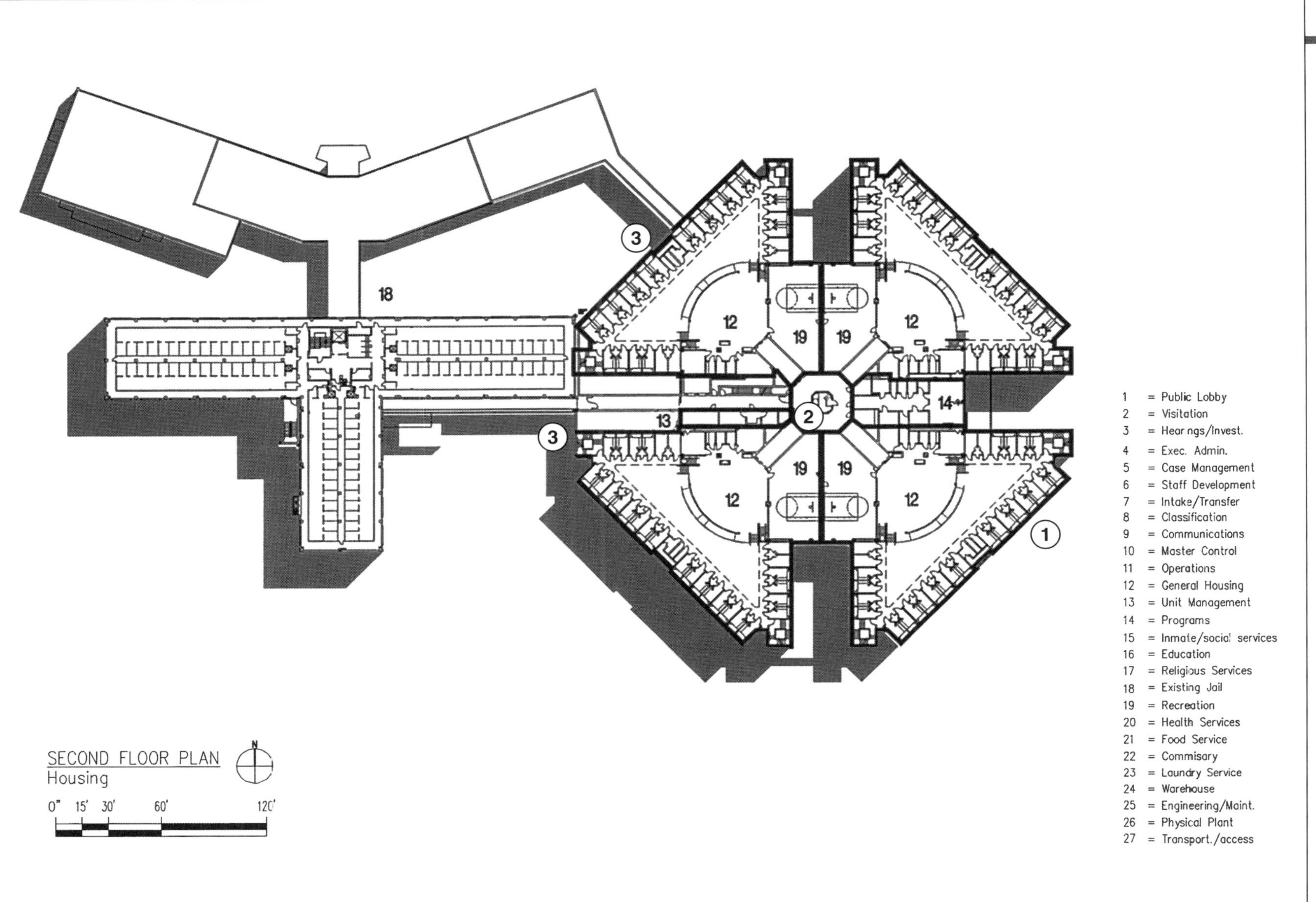

Figure 4.40*b* **Facility plan.**

SUMMARY FACILITY REFERENCE

Fig. no. cells/staffing building area	**facility name, location** operational/facility type/housing design	**client name,** location design/architect of record
4.18	**Arizona State Prison, Perryville and Tucson Facilities, Arizona**	**Dept. of Admin./Corrections**
1600/754	1981, low-rise prison, open campus style plan, individual buildings,	Phoenix, Arizona
329,789 gsf	two 48-cell housing units per control	Gruzen/Varney-Sexton
4.19	**Carl Robinson Correctional Institution, Connecticut**	**Dept. of Public Works**
900/340	1990, low-rise prison, support and dormitory separated buildings,	Hartford, Connecticut
250,000 gsf	six 150-bed housing buildings; two 75-bed units per control	DMJM
4.20	**Greensville Correctional Center, Jarratt, Virginia**	**Dept. of Corrections**
1780/910	1990, mid-rise prison housing, low-rise support buildings	Richmond, Virginia
892,000 gsf	three separate facilities; one segregation unit; one medical unit	DMJM/DMJM-VVKR
4.22	**Eastern Kentucky Correctional Complex, West Liberty, Kentucky**	**Commonwealth of Kentucky**
1125/400	1990, mid-rise prison, stacked housing units, centralized support,	Frankfort, Kentucky
535,236 gsf	two 256-cell housing floors; 128-cell housing units per control	DMJM/DMJM-GRW
4.23	**Federal Correctional Institution, Manchester, Kentucky**	**Federal Bureau of Prisons**
816/250	1992, low-rise prison, site adaptation of federal design model,	Washington, DC
554,663 gsf	two 64-bed housing units per building; 64-bed unit per control	DMJM/DMJM-GRW
4.24	**Young Adults Correctional Facility, Rio Piedras, Puerto Rico**	**Commonwealth of Puerto Rico**
504/376	1986, low-rise prison, three-level housing tiers, campus style plan,	San Juan, Puerto Rico
187,860 gsf	two 48-cell housing units per control; two housing neighborhoods	Gruzen/G Z Mark
4.26	**Lincoln Correctional Center, Lincoln, Nebraska**	**Dept. of Corrections**
320/196	1979, low-rise prison, connected campus style environment,	Lincoln, Nebraska
128,917 gsf	two 32-cell housing units per control, shared outdoor exercise	Gruzen/Kirkham-Michael
4.27	**Sullivan Maximum Security Prison, Woodbourne, New York**	**Office of General Services**
640/463	1985, low-rise prison, connected buildings, internalized windows,	Albany, New York
285,260 gsf	two 64-cell housing units with one control; separate exercise	Gruzen & Partners
4.28	**Oak Park Heights Maximum Security Prison, Minnesota**	**Dept. of Corrections**
400/353	1982, mid-rise prison, continuous circulation corridor on two levels,	St. Paul, Minnesota
330,000 gsf	seven 52-cell housing units each with control	Gruzen/Winsor Faricy
4.30	**Diagnostic and Evaluation Center, Lincoln, Nebraska**	**Dept. of Corrections**
160/119	1979, low-rise prison, compact plan, one building, single building,	Lincoln, Nebraska
76,293 gsf	one 32-cell housing unit per control	Gruzen/Bahr Vermeer Haecker
4.31	**Riverside Regional Jail, Prince George County, Virginia**	**RRJ Authority**
720/259	1997, low-rise jail, all housing and support connected buildings,	Chesterfield, Virginia
571,000 gsf	five 48-cell housing units per unit management control (1200 future)	DMJM
4.32	**Oneida County Jail, Oriskany, New York**	**Oneida County DPW**
448/151	1997, mid-rise jail housing; single-story support; existing renovation,	Utica, New York
155,000 gsf	four 56-cell housing units per control; two stories (592 N/E)	DMJM/Harza Northeast
4.34	**Curran Fromhold Correctional Facility, Philadelphia, Pennsylvania**	**Dept. of Public Properties**
2000/525	1995, mid-rise jail/reception and sentenced facility; connected bldgs,	Philadelphia, Pennsylvania
750,000 gsf	four 64-bed housing units per unit management control (1200 future)	DMJM
4.35	**Trenton State Prison, Trenton, New Jersey**	**Division Building Construction**
850/949	1983, high-rise prison, compact plan, connected buildings,	Trenton, New Jersey
359,518 gsf	three 48-cell housing units per floor, (2059 N/E)	Gruzen/Gruzen-Grad

SUMMARY FACILITY REFERENCE (*Continued*)

Fig. no. cells/staffing building area	**facility name, location** operational/facility type/housing design	**client name,** location design/architect of record
4.36	**Montville Correctional Facility, Connecticut**	**Dept. of Public Works**
300/102	1991, low-rise prison; single-story housing and support building,	Hartford, Connecticut
73,000 gsf	four 75-bed dormitories, each with a control officer	DMJM
4.38	**Hamilton County Justice Center, Cincinnati, Ohio**	**County Commissioners**
848/326	1983, high-rise separated detention; sentenced with courts connection,	Cincinnati, Ohio
512,000 gsf	four 56-cell housing units per floor (2 jail; 2 sentenced with controls)	Gruzen/Glaser Myers/Haupt
4.39	**Greenville County Jail, Greenville, South Carolina**	**County Commissioners**
288/204	1994, mid-rise jail, housing stacked above admin/program/services,	Greenville, South Carolina
186,530 gsf	four 48-cell housing units per control; (805 N/E)	DMJM/Craig Gaulden Davis
4.40	**Niagara County Jail, Lockport, New York**	**Niagara County DPW**
224/112	1996, mid-rise jail, housing stacked above admin/program/services,	Lockport, New York
150,000 gsf	four 56-cell housing units per unit management control; (420 N/E)	DMJM/DMJM-Mesch

5
Correctional Details

Specific architectural details with illustrations, architectural working drawings, and photography representing the most appropriate and current industry standards. Details are supported by text to provide an understanding of architectural, engineering, and security-related issues.

INTRODUCTION

In this chapter, descriptions of correctional building components are accompanied by illustrations, working drawings (plans and sections), and photographic images. They provide the basis for understanding security areas by category and are often keyed to facility plans illustrated in Chap. 3: Program, Operations, and Design. The following are essential areas for the design, development, and the coordination of correctional facilities.

Security and codes must be an integral part of the initial design process for all correctional facility projects. A correctional facility is a building type that encompasses many different occupancies and often different construction classifications. It requires visual observation through vision panels and doors which may cause parts of a building to be noncompliant to code requirements. Many codes are aware of correctional building design and have specifically addressed the issues by providing information with dedicated chapters related to a correctional environment and its operations. A correctional building, like all other building types, must be designed to respond to and resolve all code and life-safety issues. However, because of the complexity of this building type and specific security requirements, there are occasions where full compliance with the code cannot be met.

During the initial design phase, continuing through the construction document phase, a code analysis is essential and critical to the success of obtaining a certificate of occupancy. One must identify all life-safety issues, including the establishment of a list of materials permitted and not permitted by code. With this prepared information gathered during the earliest design phase, code variances should be applied for on the basis of a correctional facility's requirements for observation, supervision, and control of an inmate population. The variance should identify all noncompliant code issues and offer the variance board alternate solutions, through the use of other materials and/or personnel, of how the intent of the code will be met. Variances are often obtained by describing the operations of many areas within the institution requiring 24-hour staff positions. Coupled with noncombustible construction and life-safety alternative solutions, this condition can support the case for a code agency granting a variance.

Security manufacturers supplying materials and security products to a correctional facility must be experienced, with a proven track record of supply and installation. This is not a standard building type and therefore conventional materials and construction often do not apply to secure areas of this facility type. Materials must be carefully researched to determine whether they have been tested and approved for use according to industry standards and testing agencies. Manufacturers providing these materials must be totally familiar with the standards and methods of testing and must comply with having their products tested to ensure compliance. Upon request, a reputable manufacturer should always be able to provide the design team with comprehensive information. Architects are responsible for providing materials, devices, and security-related products to create a secure facility. The architect's technical background is a prerequisite for providing a client with a comfort level for receiving a facility design that is secure in its containment of an inmate population from a neighboring community. Experienced manufacturers can often be of valuable assistance to architects/clients in providing technical information and services in delivering security products.

The detention equipment contractor (DEC) should be the single point of responsibility for the close coordination between security hollow metal, security hardware, and security electronics. One way of achieving this coordination is by providing the addition of a Detention Equipment section to the project's specification. Although the overall coordination of the project is the responsibility of the general contractor the addition of this specific section will place the burden for the coordination of these specific security items with the DEC. It is the DEC's responsibility to ensure that all security components are properly interfaced with other trades, are installed according to industry standards, and are in accordance with the construction documents. Once the construction phase of the project is completed—but before the facility is occupied—the DEC is responsible for training staff for security systems functions and performance. The DEC is also responsible for the maintenance of the various components of the system(s) for the duration of time as stated in the specifications. Once this period of maintenance responsibility is fulfilled, the facility owner has the option of renewing the contract or seeking a new contract with another DEC.

The DEC must provide the knowledge required for the means and methods of construction, consistent with industry standards for the security components specified. To assure that a subcontractor properly performs the work required for this specialized area of technology, specific qualifications should be included in the specifications as fundamental requirements:

- The DEC should have a minimum of five years of experience.
- The DEC should have a minimum of two projects completed of the same type, size, and complexity as the project being constructed.
- One of the DEC's completed projects must be in operation for a minimum of one year.
- The DEC's list of project references should include the name and telephone number of the architect, contractor, construction manager, owner, and operator of each completed facility.
- The DEC must provide proof of being fully bonded and financially stable.

A DEC should have a proven track record with this facility type to ensure the technical performance for this complex building type. The security system must operate properly and consistently to restrict movement in and out of security areas and to protect those who are responsible for the facility's daily operations and activities, 24 hours a day, every day of the year.

Security/detention equipment coordination between architectural and engineering disciplines is an essential element to ensure a project with an outstanding facility design. It is imperative that close attention be paid to all security products and issues to ensure that systems operate effectively and efficiently in preventing breaches in security. As an example, all ducts passing through security walls must be provided with a security grille sized to prevent inmate penetration. (See Figs. 5.10.20, 5.10.21, and 5.10.22.)

Security hardware and security electronics must be thoroughly coordinated and work in combination with the equipment at a control station to alert an officer of a breach in security, leading to a potential escape. Claims for liability can be avoided if documents are complete and thoroughly coordinated.

The matrix on page 183 is offered as a guide for the coordination of all security systems/detention equipment items. Its most appropriate use is in the early design development phase of the project, once all architectural floor plans are finalized and approved by the client.

5.1 SECURITY WALLS

Materials

Security walls are one of the most important components forming a perimeter. Walls must be constructed of materials that are impenetrable and can withstand environmental decay, as in long-term exposure to salts and corrosive elements. The location of security walls is determined by the level of security demanded by the facility and should be reviewed early in design. Poured-in-place concrete, concrete masonry units, precast concrete, and steel panels have proven track records of meeting the security requirements for most correctional facilities. Other determining factors to be considered include the cost of material, environmental conditions, proximity to a precasting plant, and the aesthetic preferences of the architect/client.

Levels of Security and Construction

In detailing a security wall, the architect should maintain continuity and application of the product to ensure that no breech in the security of the wall construction occurs. All reinforcing must be continuous, in the horizontal and/or vertical planes. The following wall types identify specification elements for consideration:

- ***Poured-in-place concrete or precast concrete*** should have a minimum compressive strength of 4000 PSI and have a minimum thickness of four inches with an amount of reinforcing required for structural integrity. (Reference: Fig. 5.1.1.)
- ***Concrete masonry units*** should be reinforced based on the degree of security required.

  Maximum security walls should fill the voids with grout and provide no. 4 reinforcing steel bars at 8 inches on center, both horizontally and vertically. Horizontal joint reinforcement may be substituted for horizontal rebars.

  Medium security walls should fill the voids with grout and provide no. 4 reinforcing steel bars at 16 inches on center vertically.

  Minimum security walls should fill the voids solidly with grout only. In both medium and minimum security walls, joint reinforcement should be provided at 16 inches on center vertically.

All masonry mortar shall be type M (2500 PSI). All rebars provided in concrete and masonry walls must be securely anchored to the floor slab and the ceiling deck. See Figs. 5.1.1, 5.1.2, 5.1.3 for methods of attachment.

- ***Steel bar security walls*** have been used for decades for cell front maximum security enclosures and they provide complete visibility into cells. They are used in other areas of correctional facilities to provide secure barriers when resisted inmate movement is desired and where total visibility of spaces or corridors is essential. They are constructed of tool-resistant steel and welded to embedded steel plates in adjacent walls. Typical applications include

  Corridor movement control
  Security enhancement to control stations
  Sally ports

  See Fig. 5.1.5.

- ***Steel panels*** should be a minimum of 3/16 inches thick or could be fabricated of hollow metal steel similar to door construction, meeting design criteria requirements. (See Fig. 5.1.6 and the following section.)
- ***Woven wire mesh*** can also be used for cell fronts but is not constructed of tool-resistant steel and therefore offers less than maximum security enclosures. The level of security obtained from woven wire mesh is dependant on the gauge of the woven mesh. The mesh is welded to a minimum of 10-gauge steel tubes which in turn are welded to supporting walls or other members. Typical applications include:

  Holding cells
  Tool crib storage
  Partitions separating functions within a program space, as in gymnasiums where separation of weight-lifting area from the basketball court is desirable

  See Fig. 5.1.7.

- ***Security gypsum board*** by itself does not provide any type of security. However, when used in conjunction with a heavy expanded wire mesh between layers, a level of security can be achieved. A minimum of a 20-gauge steel stud should be used to provide stiffness to the wall. This type of construction should be limited to areas where inmates are occupying spaces for short durations. (See Fig. 5.1.8.)
- ***Glass blocks*** are available in several sizes and have been used successfully in correctional facilities to provide natural light into spaces and for clear or obscured visibility from interior spaces to the outside. Glass blocks are manufactured in two types: a hollow unit two-wall product and a solid one-piece product. Hollow-type units should be used only in nonsecure areas where preventing wall penetration is not a requirement. Solid-type glass block units can be used in secure areas with the product strengthened for security by placing the units into a window frame assembly provided with steel grids that allow the units to be inserted and mortared in place. Several manufacturers have tested their products for ballistics and physical penetration properties with satisfactory results. (See Fig. 5.1.9.)

5.2 SECURITY HOLLOW METAL (DOORS AND FRAMES)

Testing of Doors and Frames

Security hollow metal, similar to security glass but unlike standard hollow metal, experiences rigorous testing to meet the physical abuse that the doors and frames often receive in a correctional environment. The following tests measure the performance of security doors and frames to meet most correctional facility requirements:

- ***Static load test*** and the rack test (that follows) subject a door to a specific loading. In the static load test, the door is placed in a horizontal position. Loads are applied at quarter points to determine maximum deflection and door strength.
- ***Rack test*** fixes the door at one end and ridgedly fixes a third corner. A specified load is applied to the unsupported corner to determine the maximum allowable deflection. Both tests use a plain hollow metal door, 3 × 7 feet in size, without any door hardware. This test is performed to determine an inmate's ability to pry a door open at the corners.
- ***Impact load test*** is a more realistic test on how a door will actually behave under riot conditions. The door is tested in a vertical position complete with hardware and its performance is evaluated under conditions when a ramming device impacts the door at certain points.
- ***Removable glazing stop test*** is performed to ensure that the glass stop is as strong as the glass it holds in place. Similar to the impact test, a ramming device is used to perform this test.
- ***Bullet-resistant test UL 742*** is conducted to prevent the loss of life caused by glass failure. UL considers the test successful only if protection is provided against complete penetration of the material; it stops the passage of fragments of projectiles; or if the spalling (fragmentation) of the protective material would cause injury to a person standing directly behind the bullet-resistive barrier.

Gauge of Metal

For doors to pass these tests, the gauge of the face sheet should be a minimum of 14. The internal reinforcement of a door should also be spaced at close intervals to provide the stiffness required in resisting the loads applied during testing. Security door construction should also provide the strength necessary to resist most types of attacks and abuse that can occur in a correctional setting. Doors must be designed to prevent inmates from hiding weapons and contraband within their construction. The edges of doors should have a continuous flush closure channel welded and dressed smooth. The door must not have any visible gaps. (See Fig. 5.2.16.)

Door frames are an equally important component of the assembly. Frames must be a minimum of 14 gauge and be securely fastened to the wall. There are several ways of anchoring frames to walls that resist escape attempts. A few common attachments for consideration are as follows:

- ***Precast concrete*** or ***poured-in-place concrete***—Weld on stud anchors (such as Nelson Anchors). (See Fig. 5.2.1.)
- ***Masonry walls***—Strap anchors shall be a minimum of 12 gauge and no less in size than 2 × 10 inches. (See Figs. 5.2.2 and 5.2.3.)
- ***Existing masonry walls***—Care should be taken when installing a frame with this application. The frame should be dimpled to receive a ½-diameter expansion bolt and a conduit spacer welded to the frame. After the frame has been properly installed, the bolt should be welded to the frame and then grinded, dressed, and finished smooth. (See Fig. 5.2.4.)
- ***Prefinished masonry, precast concrete, or poured-in-place openings***—With these conditions, a two-piece frame should be used. This will permit a contractor to provide weld plates around the opening and install the frames at a later date. (See Fig. 5.2.5.)

See Figs. 5.2.6 through 5.2.16 for more door-frame-related details.

5.3 SECURITY GLASS

Design Considerations

A correctional facility requires natural light to meet most local, state, and national building code requirements. A correctional facility also requires additional use of interior glazing in support of security observation, supervision, and control; however, unlike other buildings, they require glazing to have specific degrees of security. It is important to understand that security glazing will fail when exposed to sustained periods of attack with objects such as sledge hammers, fire extinguishers,

Figure 5.1 **Glass testing with sledge hammer.**

chisels, fire axes, and battering rams. The intent of specifying the appropriate type and thickness of glass is to prolong the time of an escape (not to prevent it) by providing an officer (or riot squad) time in order to regain control of a facility.

Security glazing is also specified for areas as a barrier to prevent the passage of contraband. Two areas most commonly utilizing glazing as a barrier are noncontact visitation booths and between the interior and exterior functions of a building. During the design process, an architect should determine the sizes of glazed openings, the locations of glazing, and the degree of security required. Security-sensitive areas, such as exterior walls, and officer control rooms require a much higher level of security glazing to withstand physical impacts and ballistics.

Other areas may require vision panels in walls and doors (inmate program spaces) but require a lesser degree of security since they are generally for supervised inmate activities. It is important to discuss and review the types of glazing being considered and recommended for spaces with the project team, including the facility operations staff. The discussion and documentation of final recommendations will ensure the owner and the architect that the glazing specified will provide the appropriate level of security of areas of the facility's security zones.

Types of Security Glass

There are several types of glazing currently manufactured that provide the appropriate level of security desired in meeting specific security requirements. The following is a summary of the most often specified security glass:

- ***Polycarbonate plastics*** are comprised of a single or multiple layers of material and offer a high degree of security. (See Fig. 5.3.1.) They provide one of the lowest material and replacement costs of all security glass currently available. However, like most plastics they scratch and can easily burn. Some manufacturers offer an assembly, when used in conjunction with a specific sprinkler system, provides a protected fire opening for a period of up to 2 hours.
- ***Glass laminates*** are comprised of multiple layers of glass bonded with an interlayer material. While this type of glass also offers a moderate degree of security, the required assembly can become thick and heavy. Consideration should be taken in detailing and specifying this glazing type since, under heavy attack with sharp metal objects, glass penetration is possible. (See Fig. 5.3.2)
- ***Replacement glass systems*** are composed of a layer of polycarbonate, an air gap, and a sacrificial piece of heat-treated glass. The polycarbonate and the glass are held together by a perimeter piece of foam tape. The system is not hermetically sealed and therefore should not be used in an exterior application. (See Fig. 5.3.3.)
- ***Glass-clad polycarbonates*** are comprised of a combination of polycarbonate and glass bonded together using a urethane interlayer. This is one of the most widely used types of security glass in this country. Care should be taken when using this material in an exterior application because of its composition. The combination of plastic and glass, creates a material with two different coefficients of thermal expansion. The expansion and contraction may cause stresses in the glass that can cause it to break. (See Fig. 5.3.4.)

In selecting the appropriate glazing for a particular application, as with other building materials, it would be prudent to consult with the manufacturer. Its information can often assist in determining which product should be used for a particular area meeting specific security requirements.

Testing of Security Glass

Security glazing has an extensive history of testing to ensure its performance and to provide the user with a product that offers security for and safety from most physical threats. The types of testing performed evaluates the ballistic and forced-entry resistance of a particular glass. Several independent testing agencies offer certification for security glazing. In addition, there are several methods of testing currently available that offer different information and results:

- ***Bullet-resistant test UL 742*** considers the test successful only if the following criterion is met: protection against complete penetration of the material; if it resists passage of fragments of projectiles; or if spalling (fragmentation) of the protective material would cause injury to a person standing directly behind the bullet-resistive barrier.
- ***UL 972 burglary-resistant glazing material*** considers the test successful if the glazing material resists penetration when a steel ball weighing 5 pounds is dropped from a distance of either 10 or 40 feet.

- *HP White test* is conducted with a procedure requiring multiple blows by different objects, such as a chisel, sledge hammer, and/or fire extinguisher. The more blows applied to a glass without penetration, the higher the degree of security. (See the previous Fig. 5.1.)
- *WMFL test* is similar to the HP White, except a time limit is established to determine the degree of security. The result is measured in either a 30-minute attack, 60-minute attack, or 60-minute attack plus bullet-resistant quality.
- *ASTM1233 test* measures the ballistic impact, blunt tool impact, sharp tool impact, thermal stresses, and chemical decay of a glass. This test evaluates both force entry penetration and duration.

Each of these testing agencies has conducted extensive testing on security glass. The architect should review with the facility owner/operations staff the product and testing results to decide which material is most appropriate for the intended use.

5.4 SECURITY WINDOWS

Types and Anchorage

As with any building component, the material is only as strong as its connection. A window must be positively anchored to a wall to ensure that a frame cannot be removed from its opening. The anchors must also be of sufficient strength to hold a window in place. There are several methods which have been successfully utilized in secure attachments, depending on the following wall construction types:

- *Split window frames* are used when a window is required to be installed after an opening has been made. Weld plates are provided around the opening to secure the window in place. The frame has factory-installed clip angles which are welded to the weld plates. Once the window is installed, the closure plates are attached to the frame with security-type fasteners. (See Figs. 5.4.1 and 5.4.3.)
- Casting the frame into a *precast concrete panel* is another method of attachment. The frame is provided with weld-on type anchors. The frame is than fastened to the form work. Once the form work is stripped, the frame becomes an integral part of the precast concrete panel. (See Fig. 5.4.2.)

All window frame assemblies should be fabricated to meet industry standards. This includes, but is not limited to, adding weep holes where required and insulation with thermal breaks for cold regions.

Exterior security windows offer a potential area for escapees from correctional facilities. Therefore, windows must be constructed to withstand considerable abuse from inmates and the environment. They can be fabricated of either 12-gauge steel or 14-gauge stainless steel. Security windows have a history of testing to ensure their strength and performance against wind-driven rain and air infiltration.

Security

The size of the window opening is one of the most critical parts of any assembly. Inmates have the ability to create makeshift tools for taking window assemblies apart in support of their escape. Means must be provided to prevent an inmate from removing or breaking components of a window assembly. Following are several ways of preventing escape through a window wall:

- ***Security glazing*** specified for windows should provide the appropriate degree of security for an intended program and/or activity space.
- ***Tool-resistant bars*** should be provided with a maximum opening between stops of 5 inches. In this application, tool-resistant bars must be welded to a flat bar installed within the frame itself. This will maximize the security of the window and offer a strong and integral building component which should be equal in strength to the adjacent wall. All security bars should be tested in accordance to ASTM A 627 and ASTM A 629.

See Figs. 5.4.4 and 5.4.5.

5.5 SECURITY CEILINGS

Security ceilings have experienced a change from when concrete, security plaster, and steel plates were used as security barriers. While older traditional ceilings provided a sense of security, the new lighter ceiling materials and assemblies offer similar security but at lower costs. The intent of a security ceiling is to prevent an inmate from gaining access into an interstitial space located between the ceiling and structure and/or for hiding contraband and weapons. Exterior walls, roofs, and security ceilings form the security perimeter for a building which can prevent inmate escapes. In addition, some ceiling systems offer an acoustical value which are an improvement over older materials. Acoustical considerations are discussed in Chap. 8: Acoustical Design Guidelines.

The following criteria should be considered in determining the appropriate locations for security ceilings and their requirements:

- The supervision within a space (direct or indirect) and related hours of observation
- The clear height of the interior space, from floor to underside of ceiling
- Inmate accessibility to the ceiling surface and its materials
- Type of inmates using a particular area (general or segregation population)

Appropriate materials can be chosen from the following systems.

Types

- ***Metal security ceilings*** provide a system that is durable and economical. A plank system is usually fabricated of either 14-, 16-, or 18-gauge steel and is available in 12-inch widths. The planks must be interlocked or mechanically fastened together to prevent the removal of individual planks and/or the concealment of contraband. Wall and intermediate supports are provided to add additional strength to the system. There are several minimum requirements that should be specified:

  Uniform live load: 40 PSF
  Concentrated load of 400 lbs., either in up or down applied positions
  Maximum deflection: 1/240

  Access panels in a plank system should be fabricated of the same material as the ceiling. They should include heavy-duty hinges and tamper-resistant fasteners to prevent inmates from removing the planks and gaining access to the ceiling plenum. When acoustics is a concern, perforated planks can be utilized that include an insulation material backing. This insulating material should be encapsulated in a polybag to prevent inmates from destroying the insulation material from access through the perforations. (See Fig. 5.5.1.)

- ***Security gypsum board systems*** require two layers of Sheetrock with an expanded mesh interlayer. This can be assembled and utilized in less than maximum security environments and when accessibility to a ceiling surface is minimal or within a supervised activity space. A third layer of glued/adhered acoustical tile can be applied for spaces requiring quiet environments. Where access panels are required, a security-type access panel should be used. These panels are generally fabricated of either 14- or 12-gauge steel or stainless steel with a heavy-duty continuous hinge. A security-type lock should also be installed with the panel. (See Figs. 5.5.2, 5.5.7.)

- ***Metal panel ceilings*** may be used in lieu of a Sheetrock system. These panels are fabricated of 18- or 20-gauge steel or aluminum and are available in either 2 × 4 foot panels or 2 × 2 foot panels. The installation of these panels is similar to the installation of commercial metal pan ceilings. The one difference between the two is that a metal ceiling panel is installed to prevent inmate access into the ceiling plenum. Similar to a metal plank ceiling, this type of ceiling is available with perforations and insulation to add an acoustical value to a ceiling surface. (See Fig. 5.5.3.)

- ***Hollow metal ceilings*** can be used for maximum security applications. They are fabricated similar to hollow metal door construction, with the internal reinforcement either as truss-type or high-hat sections. Similar to metal panel ceilings, they can be fabricated with or without perforations and sound insulation material, depending on the acoustical requirements of the space. (See Fig. 5.5.4; Fig. 5.5.5—plaster type; Fig. 5.5.6—steel plate.)

5.6 SECURITY HARDWARE

Design Considerations

The selection of security hardware is based upon the degree of security required for a particular opening. The locks and hinges are tested with the door during the impact load test, previously discussed. Careful consideration should be given to the function of each door depending on whether the facility requires a minimum, medium, or maximum security level and whether the door is in sight of an officer's post.

Inmate classification use of a given space should be continually accessed. Codes often govern the type of locks that are permitted for use on specific doors. For example, the Life Safety Code 101 requires remote release of doors in sleeping areas or other spaces with a door count greater than 10. This requirement is driven by emergency situations where doors need to be opened from a remote location without requiring staff to open individual doors.

The fire rating of the opening must also be considered. Not all security hardware is manufactured with a UL label. The architect should provide a code analysis for each project to determine which doors require fire ratings.

During the design development phase of a project, the architect should establish which doors require security hardware. A meeting is recommended between the agency and user group, the architect, and a security electronics engineer. The following criteria should be considered:

- Determine which doors require security hardware
- Determine which doors require electrical operation or mechanical operation
- Determine points of control for electrically operated doors: primary and secondary locations
- Determine level of security required
- Determine type of key required: paracentric or mogul
- Determine which doors are interlocked
- Establish an emergency exiting plan

These are the primary hardware issues that require early discussion and finalization. Other design-related issues are generally discussed during these sessions; however, these issues will provide the architect with the opportunity of finalizing a door and hardware schedule. Coordination of these schedules is required with the hollow metal section of a project. (See the following matrix.)

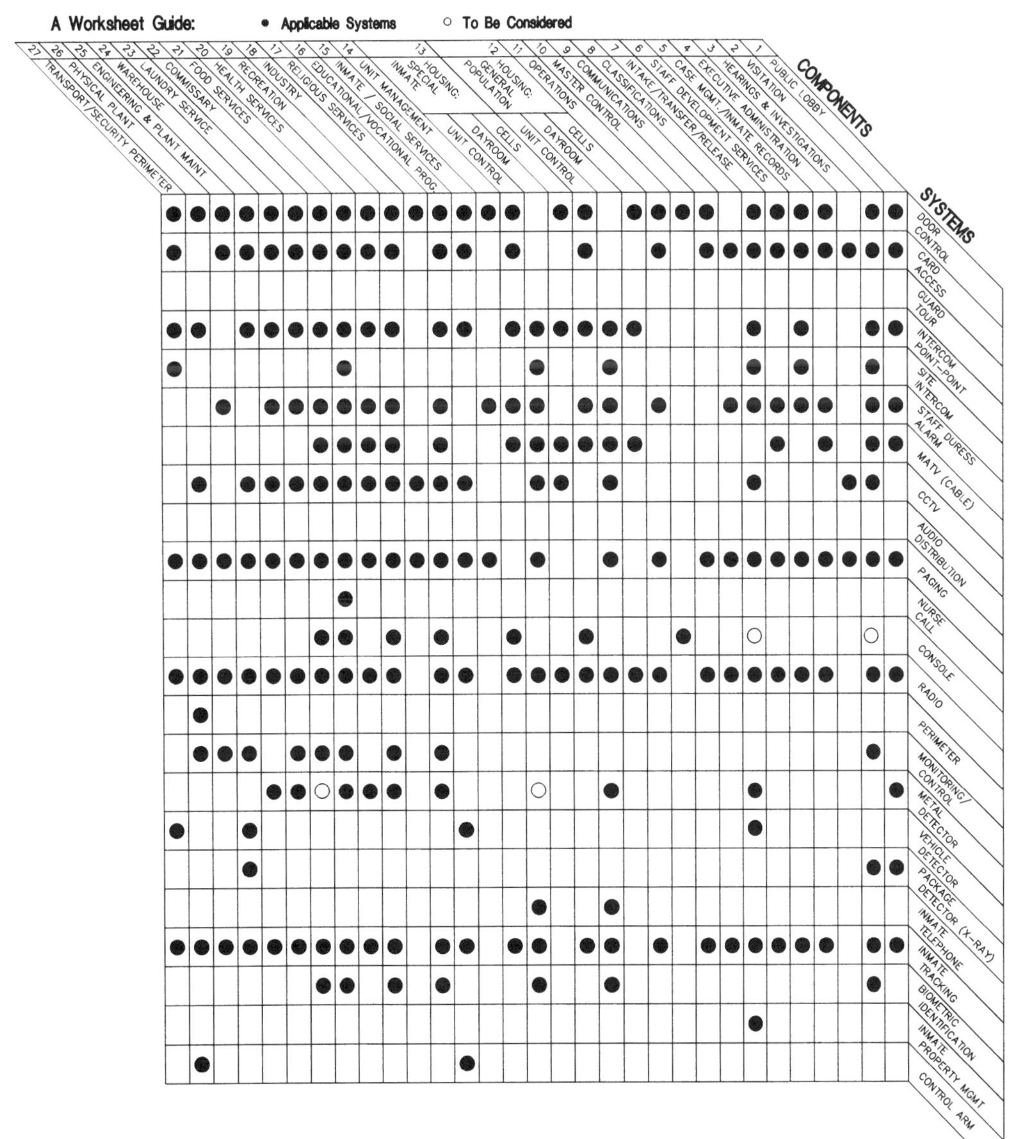

A Worksheet Guide: • Applicable Systems ○ To Be Considered

Systems \ Components	27 Transport/Security Perimeter	26 Physical Plant	25 Engineering & Plant Maint	24 Warehouse	23 Laundry Service	22 Commissary	21 Food Services	20 Health Services	19 Recreation	18 Industry	17 Religious Services	16 Educational/Vocational Prog.	15 Inmate / Social Services	14 Unit Management	13 Housing: Special Inmate – Unit Control	13 Housing: Special Inmate – Dayroom	13 Housing: Special Inmate – Cells	12 Housing: General Population – Unit Control	12 Housing: General Population – Dayroom	12 Housing: General Population – Cells	11 Operations	10 Master Control	9 Communications	8 Classifications	7 Intake/Transfer/Release	6 Staff Development Services	5 Case Mgmt./Inmate Records	4 Executive Administration	3 Hearings & Investigations	2 Visitation	1 Public Lobby
Door Control	●	●	●	●	●	●	●	●	●	●	●	●	●	●	●		●	●		●	●	●	●		●	●	●	●		●	●
Card Access	●		●	●	●	●	●	●	●	●		●	●		●			●			●		●	●	●	●	●	●	●	●	●
Guard Tour																															
Intercom Point-Point	●	●		●	●	●	●	●	●	●		●	●		●	●	●	●	●	●					●		●			●	●
Site Intercom	●							●								●			●						●		●			●	
Staff Duress Alarm			●		●	●	●	●	●	●		●		●	●	●		●	●		●			●	●	●	●	●		●	●
MATV (Cable)							●	●	●	●		●			●	●	●	●	●	●						●		●		●	●
CCTV		●		●	●	●	●	●	●	●	●	●	●			●	●		●						●				●	●	
Audio Distribution																															
Paging	●	●	●	●	●	●	●	●	●	●	●	●	●	●		●			●		●		●	●	●	●	●	●	●	●	●
Nurse Call								●																							
Console							●	●		●		●			●			●				●			○					○	
Radio	●	●	●	●	●	●	●	●	●	●		●	●		●	●	●	●	●	●	●		●	●	●	●	●	●		●	●
Perimeter		●																													
Monitoring/Control		●	●	●		●	●	●		●		●																		●	
Metal Detector					●	●	○	●	●	●		●				○			●						●						●
Vehicle Detector	●			●									●												●						
Package Detector (X-Ray)				●																										●	●
Inmate Telephone																●			●												
Inmate Tracking	●	●	●	●	●	●	●	●	●	●		●	●		●	●		●	●		●		●	●	●	●	●	●		●	●
Biometric Identification							●	●		●		●				●			●											●	
Inmate Property Mgmt																									●						
Control Arm		●											●																		

The security lock industry has conducted numerous tests of its locks to ensure that they operate in a manner which has been specified. The architect should become familiar with these industry standards in order to specify the appropriate type of lock; it is critically important to the security of a project to determine the appropriate type of lock for each area application. The consequences of specifying a commercial-grade lock where a security-type lock is required must be avoided. Security locks are manufactured with a heavier gauge, dead bolt, or latch assembly than standard commercial locks.

Types of Security Locks

Security locks are manufactured with a variety of functions that can support a facility's operational requirements.

- *Mechanical-type locks* are generally used in areas where officers are required to manually open doors for inmates where remote operation is not a requirement. They are manufactured with a dead bolt or a latch bolt. In areas where double doors are required, a Cremone bolt is used. This type of lock is similar to a head and foot bolt but provides a greater degree of security. As previously mentioned, check code requirements for the permitted use of mechanical locks. (See Figs. 5.6.1 and 5.6.2.)
- *Electric-type locks* are used in areas where remote locking and/or unlocking is required. The advantage of electric locks is that doors can be opened and closed individually or in groups and provide emergency release for egress in emergency situations. Doors can be locked or unlocked by key without jeopardizing the electrical function of the lock. Locks are manufactured with either electromechanical or solenoid specifications. Electromechanical locks are generally for interior use only; solenoid locks can be used for both interior and exterior building applications. As with any system, discussion between the manufacturer and architect is valuable in determining appropriate lock applications.

  Unlike standard commercial locks, most electric security locks are manufactured for door jamb application. Careful coordination is required between the hollow metal and detention hardware manufacturer. Depending on the security required, door jamb dimensions vary from 2 to 12 inches. (See Figs. 5.2.6, 5.6.3, 5.6.4, and 5.6.5.)
- *Sliding door–type mechanisms* are another form of electric hardware most commonly used for sally ports. This type of door operation permits doors to slide open and closed without a person physically pushing or pulling the door. Similar to swinging door locks, sliders can be opened from a remote location and/or by key operation at the door itself. A two-point locking mechanism can add an additional degree of security to an opening. (See Figs. 5.2.9, 5.2.10, and 5.2.11.)
- *Pneumatic-type locks* have gained popularity for correctional facility use in recent years. Their operation requires air compressors located in a remote secure room. Air is sent through a nylon tube which activates the locking mechanism. As a result of this type of operation, fewer moving parts are in the lock assembly itself, suggesting less maintenance, according to industry manufacturers. The air tubes, however, must be kept dry and free of moisture in order to maintain proper operation. It is recommended that client and architect work closely with a reputable manufacturer to assure quality control of product and installation. (See Fig. 5.6.6.)

For cylinder types, see the glossary for mogul lock and paracentric lock types.

Degree of Security

Determining which type of lock to use is directly connected to the level of security required by a particular facility operator and is often determined by personal preference. When discussing maximum security locks, one should determine what characteristics are critical in terms of a locking device and the level of abuse an inmate may render the lock. Generally, the higher the level of facility security required, the more secure and heavier the construction of the locking device. Although, there are maximum security facilities that have successfully utilized narrow-type jamb locking devices. A determining factor may be as simple as, if an inmate were to neutralize a locking device and leave a resisted area (such as the cell), where would that inmate be contained? For example, leaving a cell in a housing unit, an inmate is observed by an officer and is contained within the secure walls of a dayroom.

There are other determining factors, outside of housing units, for providing maximum security locks. These include areas where large inmate populations gather with a potential for disturbances and in spaces that use locks as a means of isolating and confining an incident to a specific area. Dining rooms, recreation spaces, industry areas, and vocational shops are often candidates for greater inmate containment.

Many facilities overbuild and therefore overspend, in the perception of security, without greatly enhancing their operations. The level of locking devices specified for a facility should be a subjcct for discussion in the initial project meetings regarding all doors, locks, and control conditions.

Hardware Accessories

Hardware accessories should have the same resistance to abuse and strength as doors and locks. They should act as part of a unit to ensure the security integrity of an opening. The following is a list of hardware accessories which are generally part of a detention door assembly:

- ***Security door pulls*** come in a variety of sizes and shapes. The architect should determine which type of door pull is appropriate for the intended use (general population, segregation, and suicide-type conditions), degree of security, and the type of door (swinging or sliding type) to be used. (See Fig. 5.6.7.)
- ***Indication switch*** monitors the position of the bolt. It is placed in the strike of a door and is wired back to a control station panel. It will alert an officer to the condition of the bolt in either an extended or retracted position. This type of indication switch is accessible to inmates and therefore can be manipulated to indicate false information at the control panel.
- ***Door position switch (DPS),*** unlike an indication switch, can monitor the position of a door. It is also wired back to a control station panel which will advise an officer of an unauthorized breach of a particular door. Because it is concealed from inmates, it provides a much more reliable means of monitoring the position of a door. (See Figs. 5.6.8 and 5.6.9.)
- ***Door closer*** should be fabricated of heavy-gauge steel with security-type fasteners. Some manufacturers produce security-type closers with built-in door position switches that can be wired directly to a control point.
- ***Wood door strike reinforcement*** is used for solid-core wood security doors. They are fabricated of 12-gauge steel and are approximately 24 inches in length. This type of reinforcement can prevent inmates from opening a door by destroying the door material adjacent to the strike. The reinforcing strike is attached to the door with security-type fasteners. (See Fig. 5.6.10.)

5.7 INMATE FURNISHINGS

Design Considerations

Correctional facilities, unlike other buildings, require furnishings that are capable of sustaining a tremendous amount of abuse. Depending on the type of contract, the architect is often required to specify the furniture package. Careful evaluation of program requirements often determine the location and the appropriate type of furniture to be used. For example, inmate cells may require double-bunking, but current jurisdictional law prohibits the second occupant; therefore, the architect is often requested to provide weld plates or inserts to support future bunk installation. These are questions that should be addressed before selecting furniture types and locations. See Figs. 5.7.1 through 5.7.8 for types of furnishings and Figs. 5.9.1 through 5.9.10 for typical and HC-accessible cell layouts and location of furnishings.

Locations

Furnishings in inmate-occupied areas are generally limited to simple, strong, durable materials which are difficult to use as weapons or to cause physical abuse to other inmates and staff. Cells are equipped with a toilet and sink fixture and the following other furnishings:

Bunk(s) with a mattress(es)
Table with a secured stool or loose chair
Book shelf(s)
Personal locker(s)

- ***Cell furniture*** is generally fabricated of steel or stainless steel, even though some facilities have successfully used butcher-block wood desktops. The mattress material must be flame resistant to prevent inmates from starting fires in cells. All cell furnishings, with the exception of the mattress, must be securely anchored to the walls and/or floors. Depending on the type of construction, the type of anchors will vary. Masonry construction utilizes strap anchors with weld plates that are generally acceptable.
- ***Precast concrete construction*** utilizes either embedded weld plates or threaded anchors. The bolts for threaded anchors have snap-off heads. After installation of a particular piece of furniture, the head of the bolt is snapped off to prevent inmates from tampering with or removing the bolt.
- ***The day space*** in a typical housing unit is where inmates spend the majority of their time on a daily basis. This area requires a certain mini-

mum amount of furniture. Activities such as card playing, television, reading, and conversation occur in the dayroom. Some day spaces provide a separate area for dining, which requires dining tables often secured in place. Dayroom furniture is generally constructed of molded plastic, and often includes fire-resistant cushions. Other furniture is fabricated out of wood furniture which is highly resistant to physical abuse. Dining areas, whether located within a day space or in a separate dining room, often located adjacent to the main kitchen, require dining tables with either stools or benches. All furniture should be securely anchored to the floor slab and is generally fabricated of painted steel or stainless steel. Tables are fabricated in different configurations.

Other areas throughout a facility where furniture and furnishings are required include

- Stools and counters at inmate noncontact visitation booths
- Benches at inmate waiting areas in various program spaces and medical services
- Benches in holding cells

Materials

Stools and benches specified throughout a facility should also be constructed of either steel or stainless steel and be securely anchored to walls and floors. Although wood desks, chairs, and benches have been used successfully in many facilities, wood is susceptible to gauging and cigarette burns. When wood furniture is selected, a very low flame spread must also be specified. Oak butcher block, because of its durability, has been used, successfully resisting abuse. Like any piece of furniture used in a correctional environment, it must be securely fastened to its supports. Dayroom furnishings are generally limited to molded plastic and wood furniture with solid sides and backs and may include cushions.

Because of the variety of correctional furniture available in the market today, the project team should discuss the appropriate types and location of furniture required for the specific institution and let the decision be driven by the level of inmate population incarcerated. Each area should be viewed carefully to ensure that the appropriate furniture is selected for the space's occupants and intended use.

Figure 5.2 **Dayroom passive activity loose tables and chairs.**

Figure 5.3 **Dayroom individual lounge furnishings.**

5.8 PERIMETER SECURITY FENCING

Design Considerations

When viewing most low-rise correctional facilities from the perimeter, one first observes a continuous fence line with barbed tape. This forms the primary barrier between the outside free world and the secure side of an institution. The security perimeter is there to prevent inmate escapes and to prevent people from entering the secure perimeter. Inmates who are prone to escape, with plenty of time for planning, must be physically and visually deterred. Therefore, fencing must be designed to maintain a high level of security and provide physical height and materials to be effective. Fence height and configuration must be carefully studied and devised to prevent inmates from climbing over, digging under, and cutting through the fence material and its supports. When a fence line is interrupted by a building, additional devices and/or barriers should be provided to maintain the integrity of the security perimeter. This can be accomplished by continuing the fence construction up to buildings and over roofs. Appropriate means of attaching a fence to the structure must be provided to ensure the structural integrity of the fence. (See Figs. 5.8.1 through 5.8.8 for fencing details.)

- ***Two separate (double) fences with barbed tape*** are most commonly used for facilities as the primary security perimeter. The inner fence forms the first line of defense. Some facilities provide an additional means of security by mounting a motion detection system in front of or on this inner fence. There are a variety of sophisticated security electronic detection systems available which will sound an alarm when tampering with or when an inner fence penetration occurs. For specific detection systems information, refer to Chap. 6: Perimeter Security Systems.
- ***Continuous concrete grade beam at the inner fence*** is provided for most perimeter conditions. This forms a barricade to prevent inmates from digging under the fence and gaining access into the area between the inner and outer fence. The depth of the grade beam is dependent on soil conditions with softer soils requiring deeper grade beams.
- ***Continuous embedment of the fence fabric into the soil*** is another means of accomplishing this barrier. Care should be taken when using this detail since a high probability of fabric corrosion can occur causing a failure to the barrier.

The outer fence is generally higher than the inner fence and contains multiple barbed tape rolls from the base to the top of the fence to prevent access to and penetration of the fence as a final barrier. The amount of rolls specified is determined by a facility's inmate classification level and client preference. The rolls of razor wire cause considerable delay to inmates attempting escape and provide an opportunity and the time for an officer's patrol vehicle car to respond to a situation. If guard towers are utilized along the perimeter, the delay to inmate fence penetration can also provide time for these officers to contact central control for the appropriate response to a situation. The area between the two fences should be sterile and treated to prevent future growth of vegetation.

Types of Materials

Fabric. Materials used for security fencing must be durable enough to withstand the punishment from the environment and from inmates. All components of the fence must be weather-resistant. A maximum of a two-inch opening and a nine-gauge wire is the general standard chain-link fabric used for most facilities' perimeter fencing material. Maximum-security facilities and program areas requiring greater security have used higher-gauge fabric. Nonclimbable fabric fencing is manufactured consisting of a mesh size opening of ¼ or ⅜ inch. This type of fabric is sometimes used in conjunction with a standard two-inch fabric with the lower half of the assembly consisting of the two-inch fabric and the upper half of the nonclimbable type. Another assembly type available utilizes a bent post support system. According to the manufacturer of this assembly type, a nonclimbable fence system can be obtained. Careful attention must paid to the fabric attachment to the supporting post to prevent inmates from removing the ties for use in producing weapons.

Some other types of fabrics that have been used successfully for fence applications are expanded metal and welded wire mesh. As with the standard chain-link mesh, a heavy gauge and a noncorrosive material must be used.

Barbed tape is a key component to a security fence assembly, is the visually intimidating, and can be physically lethal. Galvanized steel or stainless steel are available for the barbed tape material for protection against corrosion. It is manufactured in several different configuration as follows:

- ***Spiral coil*** is a single helical coil of barbed tape available in several different diameters.
- ***Single-coil concertina*** is a single coil of barbed tape clipped together at certain intervals around the diameter to form a smaller opening, also available in several different diameters.
- ***Double-coil concertina*** is two coils of concertina, one inside the other, and is generally manufactured with a 30-inch coil on the outside, with a 24-inch coil on the inside. This type of barbed tape produces a high degree of entanglement and is used on many facilities in this country.

5.9 PLAN ENLARGEMENTS

Correctional facilities often require a series of *plan enlargements* to clarify functional and security-related issues and equipment location. Different from conventional construction, correctional facilities require careful study of all areas, corners, and vision opportunities to provide custody staff with optimum observation, supervision, and control of inmates. Figures 5.9.11 through 5.9.23 described in this section provide this kind of information.

5.10 MISCELLANEOUS DETAILS

This section of details (Figs 5.10.1 through 5.10.24) is an addition to those covered in the previous sections and is keyed to component plans and plan enlargements for typical applications. These items are generally distributed throughout a correctional facility in areas that are most related to areas of security concern.

5.11 INMATE CELL COMPONENT CONSTRUCTION METHODS

The housing unit portion of any correctional facility represents the largest percentage of gross building area of the project (approximately one-half of the gross square footage) and is the most expensive to construct (approximately two-thirds of total facility cost). For these reasons, it is important for the project team and its cost estimator to evaluate the cost in considering the type of construction to use for a housing unit's most repetitive component, *the cell.* Five of the most currently used types of inmate cell construction utilized for correctional facilities have significant characteristics that can be summarized as follows:

Reinforced unit masonry construction is the most often used type where masons are readily available in a particular region. The masonry trade workforce can contribute to limiting construction cost with a competitive bidding climate. The issues are

- Consistency in construction for all walls of an institution—interior and exterior
- A variety of security levels using the same unit product—core reinforcement
- Scale added to interior spaces with their small-sized units, but mortar joints can be picked at to create voids

Poured-in-place reinforced concrete construction is not often utilized unless offered as an alternative to a construction bid document package's base method of cell construction. It may be the preferred method of construction indigenous to a region or specifically requested by an owner for a specific maximum-security facility. The issues are

- Homogeneous interior wall surfaces, without joints to pick at or voids to hide contraband
- Consistency in construction with foundation and superstructure if poured in place, too
- Durable material requiring low maintenance

Precast concrete modular cell unit construction is currently a popular choice for cell construction when considering the overall cost of construction, the shorter time for construction, and improved quality control. The issues are

- Homogeneous interior wall surfaces, without joints to pick at or voids to hide contraband
- Components structurally support up to six units in height and adjacent dayroom framing
- Utilized during long cold winter climate conditions
- Cell can be fully equipped with fixtures and furnishings at the manufacturer's plant

Precast concrete panel construction can be used as an alternative to precast concrete modular cell unit construction offering even tighter product quality control in its connections and finishes. The issues are

- System purchased from a manufacturer or constructed on-site as tilt-up precast approach
- Offers flexibility in providing the production of the panels adjacent to their final location
- Consistency in construction used for interior and exterior walls

Steel modular cell unit construction is a system that can be used as an alternate to precast concrete modular cell unit construction and offers good quality control. Modules are available in stainless steel and painted galvanized-like steel finishes. The issues are

- Can be used for both new construction and for renovations in retrofitting existing buildings
- Cells can be stacked and are approximately one-third the weight of concrete
- Requires exterior material application for building facade
- Utilized during long cold winter climate conditions
- Cell can be fully equipped with fixtures and furnishings at the manufacturer's plant

Figure 5.4 **Precast concrete modular cell construction.**

SUMMARY LIST OF DETAILS

5.1 Security Walls

5.1.1 Poured-in-place concrete
5.1.2 Concrete masonry units—maximum security
5.1.3 Concrete masonry units—medium security
5.1.4 Concrete masonry units—minimum security
5.1.5 Steel bars
5.1.6 Steel panels
5.1.7 Woven wire mesh
5.1.8 Security gypsum board
5.1.9 Security glass block

5.2 Security Hollow Metal

5.2.1 Precast concrete poured-in-place
5.2.2 Masonry walls/flush frames
5.2.3 Masonry walls/wrap-around frames
5.2.4 Masonry walls/existing wall (opening) condition
5.2.5 Masonry walls/prefinished masonry, precast, and poured-in-place
5.2.6 Frame types
5.2.7 8-inch frame with vision panel
5.2.8 12-inch frame with vision panel
5.2.9 Sliding-type head
5.2.10 Sliding-type with vision panel
5.2.11 Sliding-type door jambs
5.2.12 Frame with fixed panel
5.2.13 Frame with vision panel
5.2.14 Clothing exchange window
5.2.15 Noncontact visitation
5.2.16 Door closure

5.3 Security Glass

5.3.1 Glass laminates
5.3.2 Replacement glass systems
5.3.3 Glass-clad polycarbonates
5.3.4 Polycarbonate plastics

5.4 Security Windows

5.4.1 Split window frame with security bars
5.4.2 Casting the frame into precast concrete
5.4.3 Split frame—cell window
5.4.4 Operable window sash
5.4.5 Jalousie window

5.5 Security Ceilings

5.5.1 Metal type
5.5.2 Security gypsum board
5.5.3 Downward-locking metal panel
5.5.4 Hollow metal type
5.5.5 Plaster type
5.5.6 Steel plate
5.5.7 Acoustical ceiling panels

5.6 Security Hardware

5.6.1 Mechanical—typical type
5.6.2 Mechanical—cremone type
5.6.3 Electric—minimum security
5.6.4 Electric—medium security
5.6.5 Electric—maximum security
5.6.6 Pneumatic type
5.6.7 Security door pulls
5.6.8 Door position switch (DPS)—surface-mounted
5.6.9 Door position switch (DPS)—concealed
5.6.10 Wood door strike reinforcement

5.7 Furnishings

5.7.1 Built-in dining table and stools—single pedestal
5.7.2 Built-in dining table and stools—multiple supports
5.7.3 Built-in stool
5.7.4 Built-in wood bench
5.7.5 Built-in steel bench
5.7.6 Inmate cell bunks
5.7.7 Inmate cell steel desk and stool
5.7.8 Inmate cell wood desk and stool

5.8 Security Fencing

5.8.1 Minimum-security configuration section
5.8.2 Medium-security configuration section
5.8.3 Maximum-security configuration section
5.8.4 Man-type swinging gate
5.8.5 Vehicle-type swinging gate
5.8.6 Vehicle-type sliding gate
5.8.7 Low building configuration
5.8.8 High building configuration

5.9 Plan Enlargements

5.9.1 Holding cell plan
5.9.2 Housing cell plan
5.9.3 Housing cell section/elevations
5.9.4 Housing HC-accessible cell plan
5.9.5 Housing HC-accessible cell sections/elevations
5.9.6 Housing HC-accessible cell sections/elevations
5.9.7 Segregation housing cell plan
5.9.8 Segregation housing cell plan with shower
5.9.9 Medical cell plan/observation (suicide) cell plan
5.9.10 Medical isolation cell plan
5.9.11 Inmate shower/HC shower plans
5.9.12 Clothing exchange (shower and pass-through window) plan
5.9.13 Fingerprinting area plan/photographic area plan
5.9.14 Inmate visitation waiting area plan
5.9.15 Noncontact visitation booth plan

5.9.16 Contact visitation room plan
5.9.17 TV arraignment room plan
5.9.18 Lineup room plan
5.9.19 Master Control room plan
5.9.20 Local control room plan
5.9.21 Sally port plans
5.9.22 Outdoor exercise security mesh roof plan
5.9.23 Guard tower

5.10 Miscellaneous Details

5.10.1 Inmate cell toilet/lavatory attachment
5.10.2 Inmate cell safety clothing hook and shelf
5.10.3 Inmate cell secure food/handcuff pass
5.10.4 Inmate cell mirror
5.10.5 Inmate cell toilet paper holder
5.10.6 Inmate cell light fixture
5.10.7 Security grab bars attachment
5.10.8 Inmate shower door types
5.10.9 Interior transaction hopper, window, and communications device
5.10.10 Exterior transaction hopper, window, and communications device
5.10.11 Deal drawer
5.10.12 Package receiver
5.10.13 Transaction hopper
5.10.14 Metal detector and side exit door assembly
5.10.15 Control room console millwork details
5.10.16 Control room escape hatch access to roof
5.10.17 Communications speak-through
5.10.18 Pistol lockers
5.10.19 Dayroom balcony guardrail options
5.10.20 Security grille in walls
5.10.21 Security grille in slab
5.10.22 Security louver
5.10.23 Acoustical wall panels
5.10.24 Wire mesh stair riser

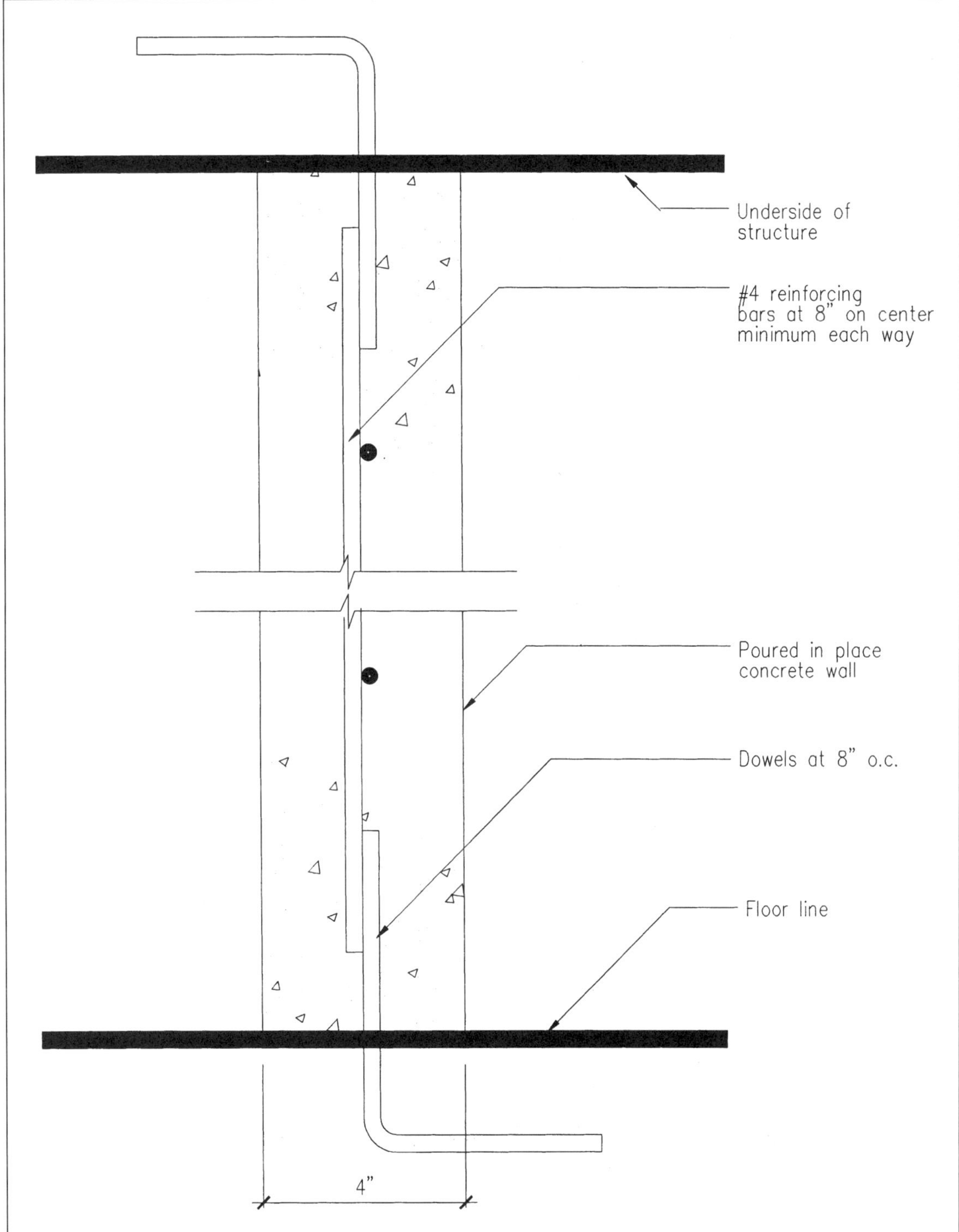

Figure 5.1.1 **Poured-in-place concrete wall.**

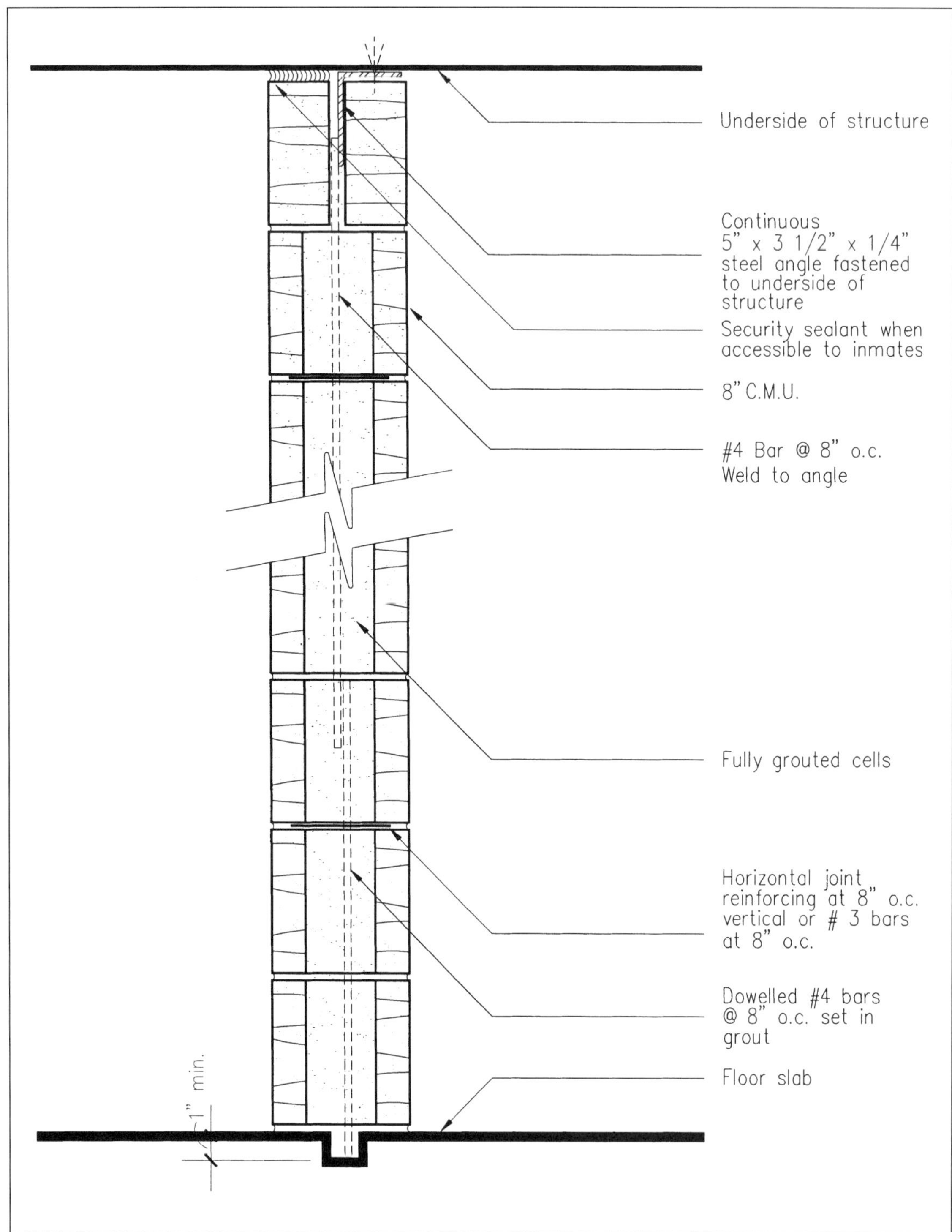

Figure 5.1.2 **Concrete masonry units—maximum security.**

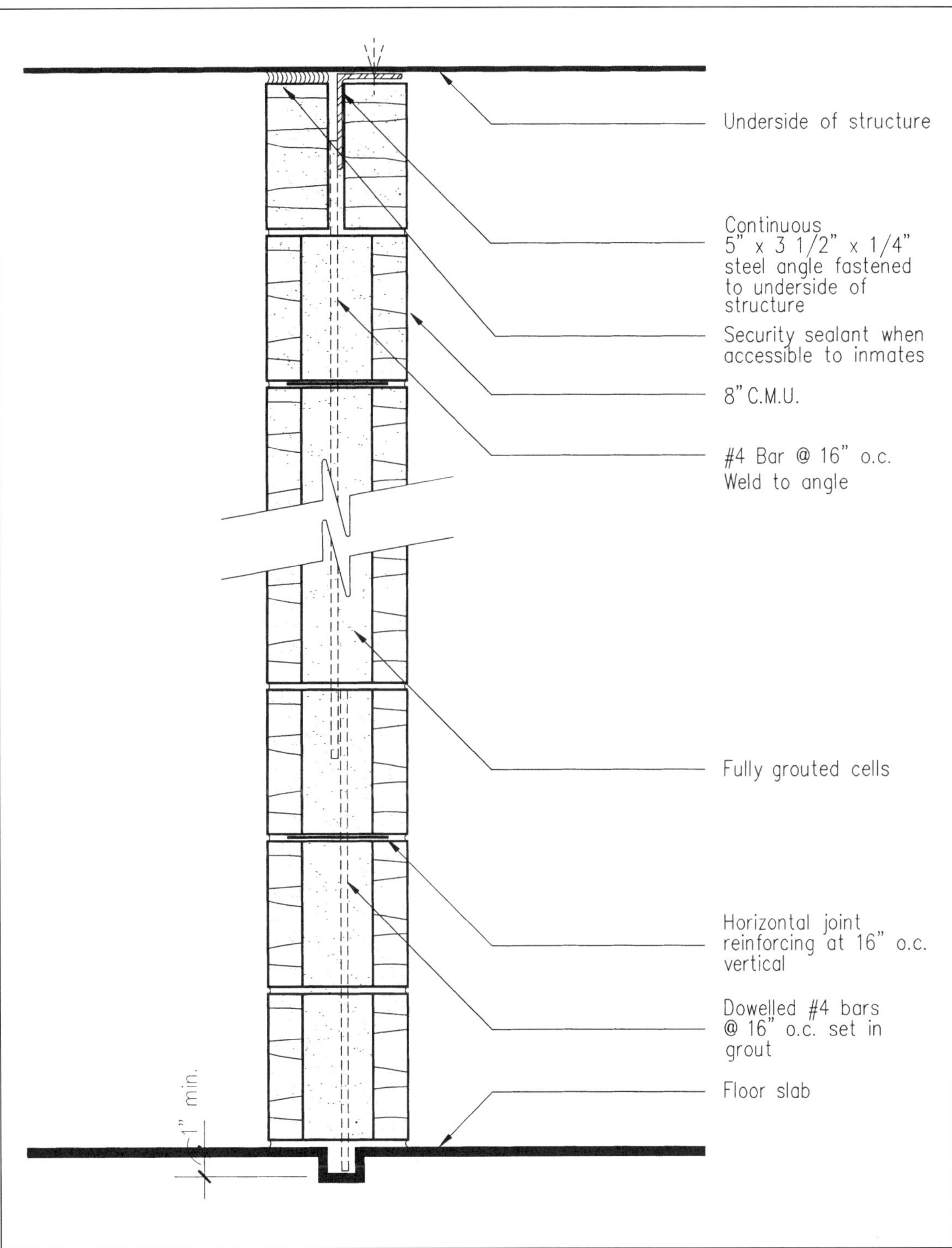

Figure 5.1.3 **Concrete masonry units—medium security.**

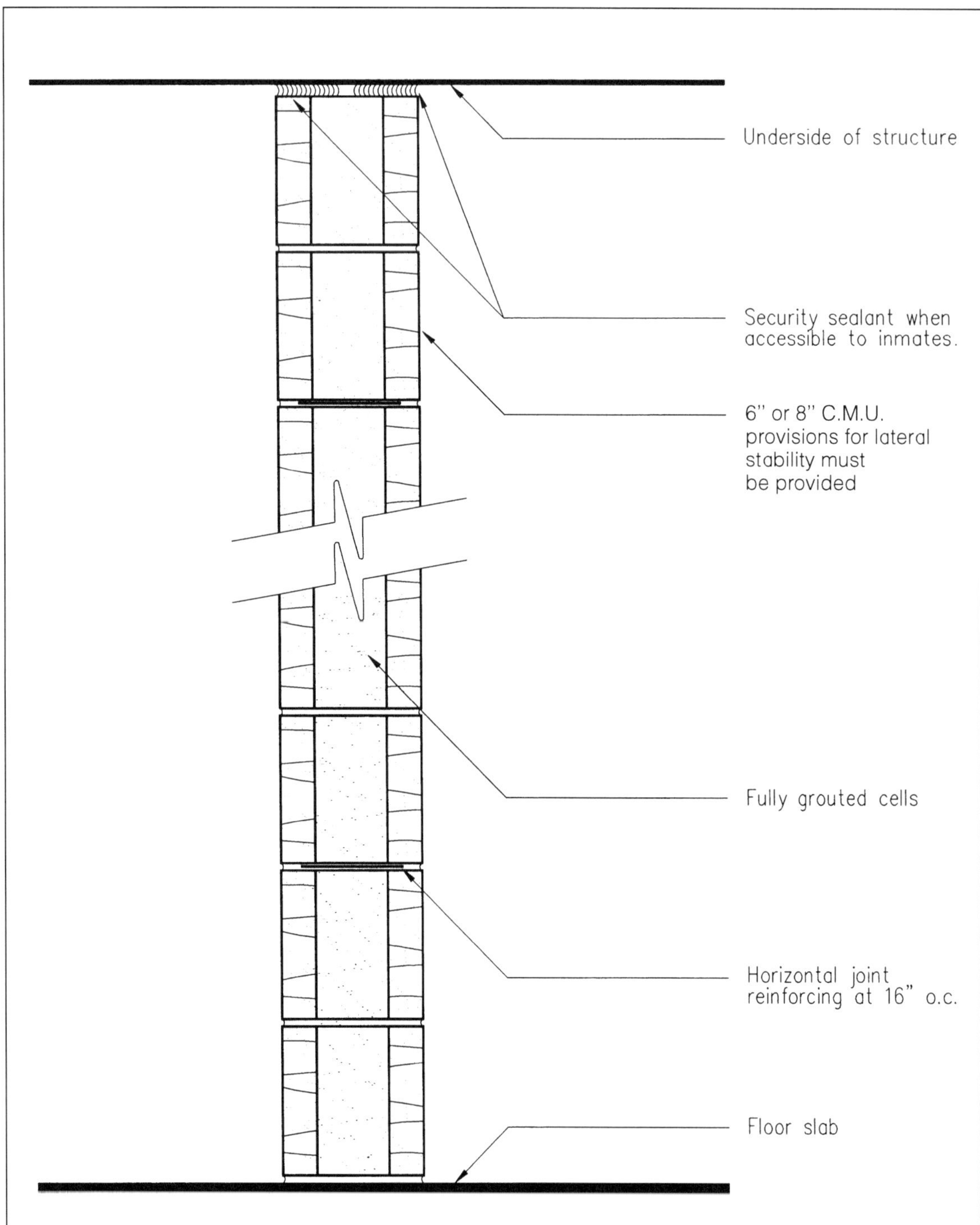

Figure 5.1.4 **Concrete masonry units—minimum security.**

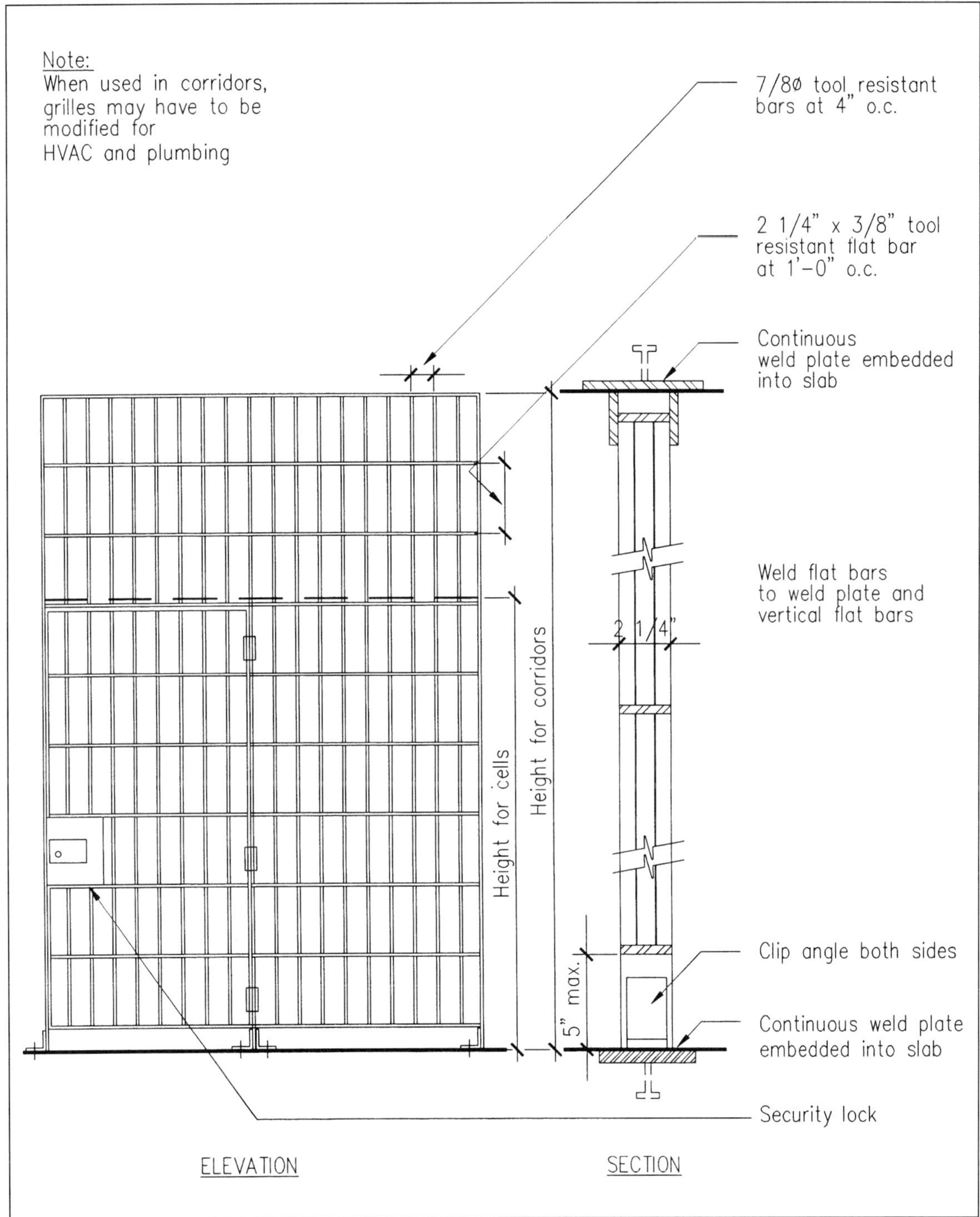

Figure 5.1.5 **Steel bars.**

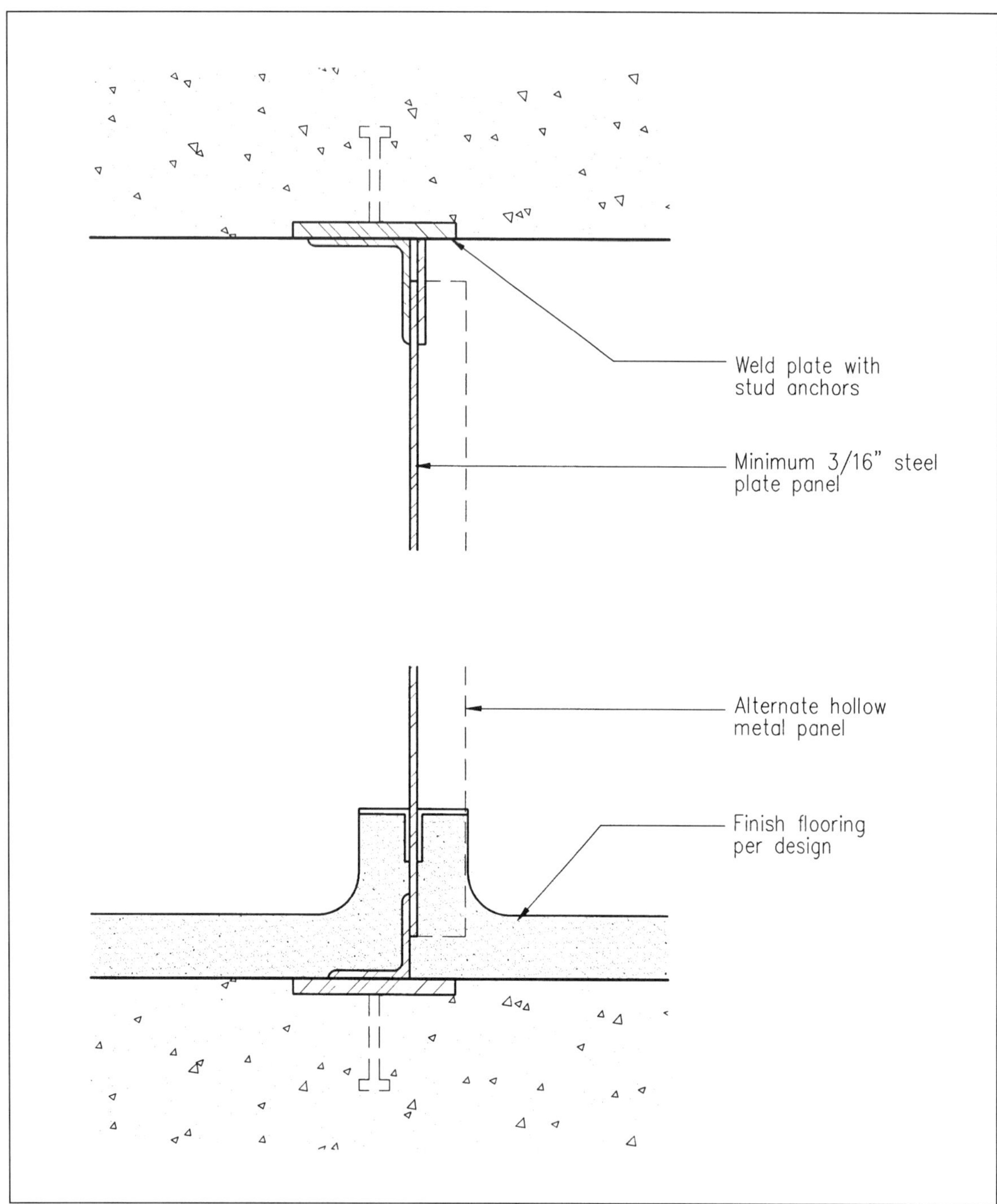

Figure 5.1.6 **Steel panels.**

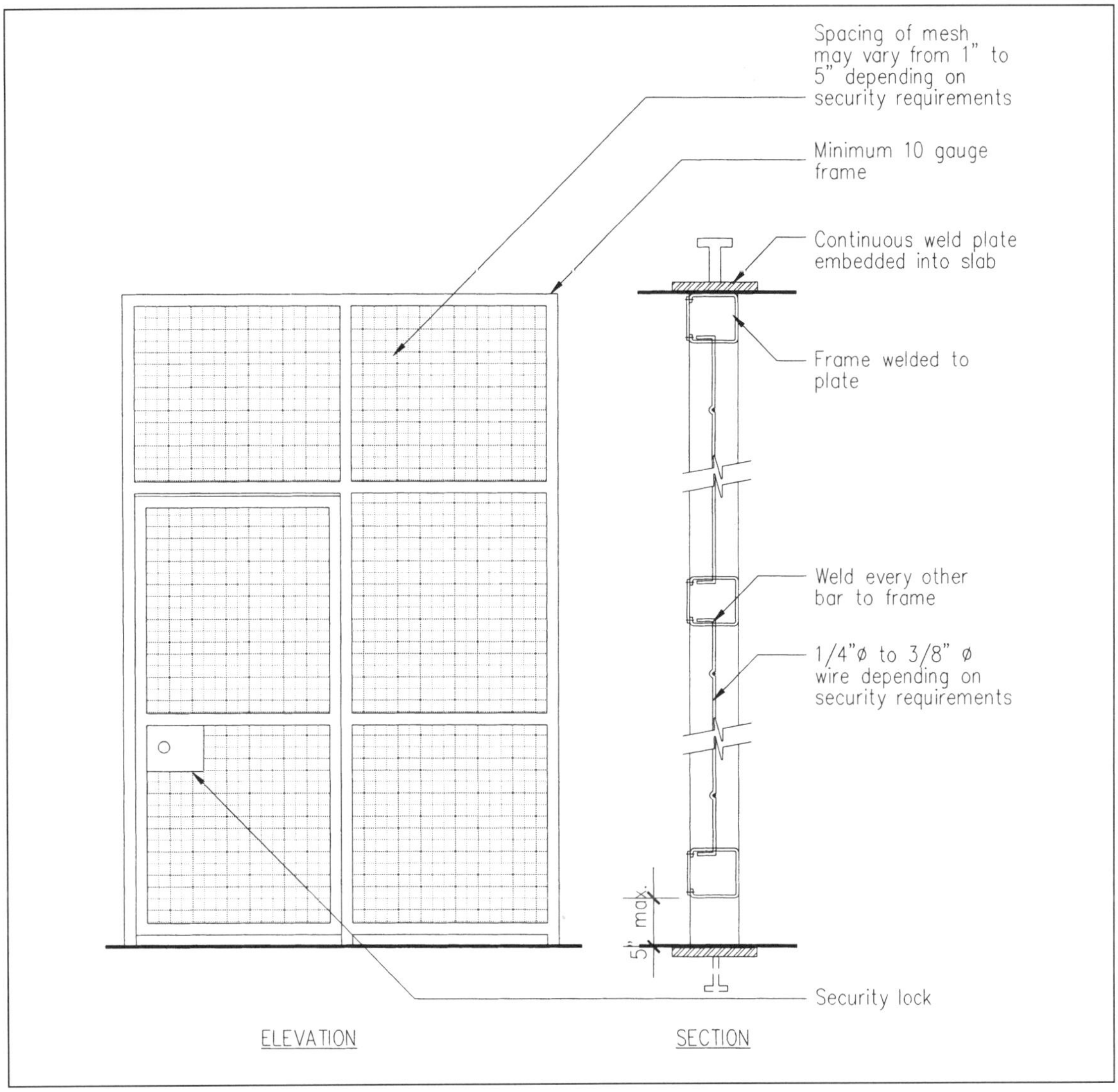

Figure 5.1.7 **Woven wire mesh.**

Outdoor recreation security mesh screen wall adjacent to inmate cell windows.

Exterior window with security woven wire mesh.

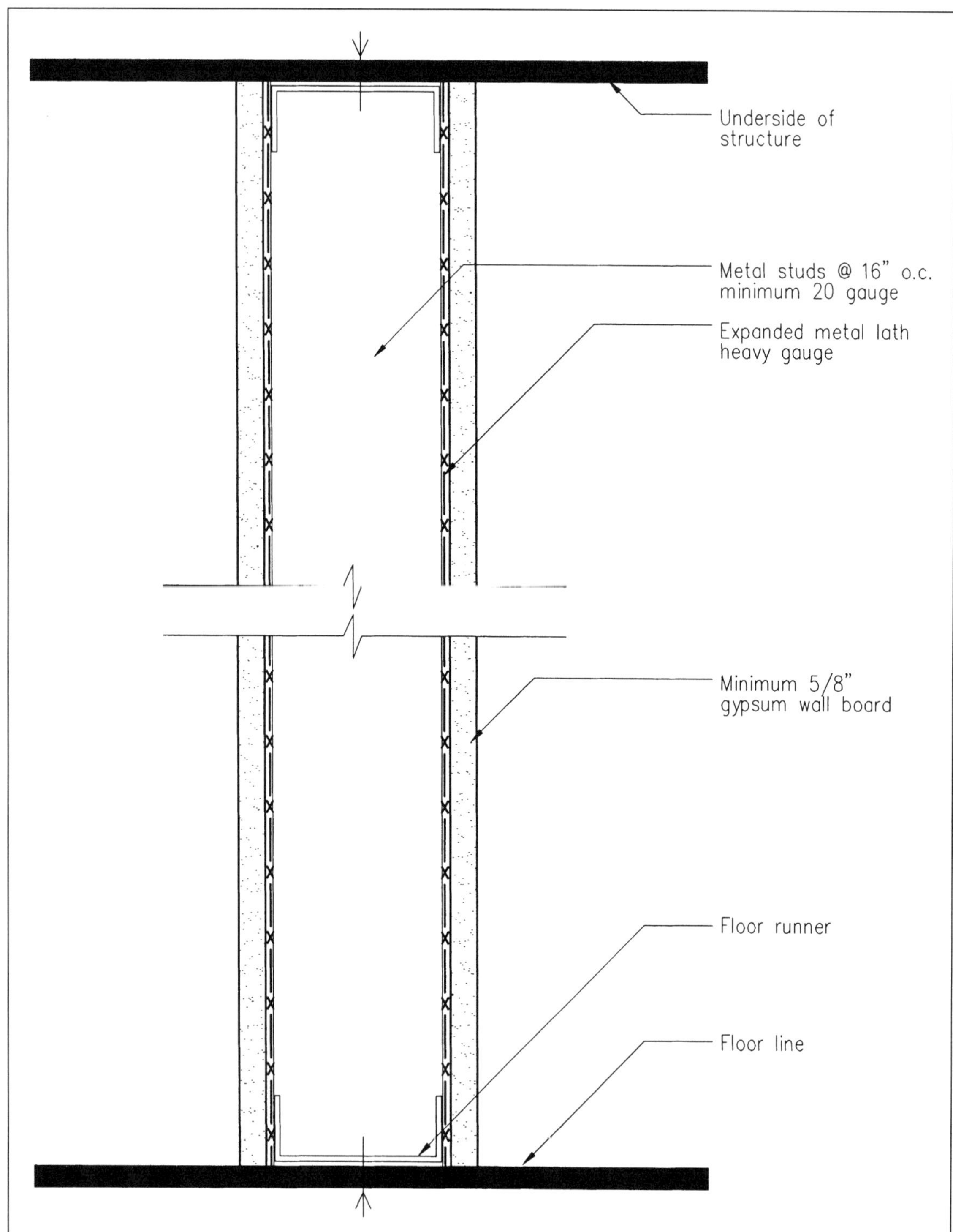

Figure 5.1.8 **Security gypsum board.**

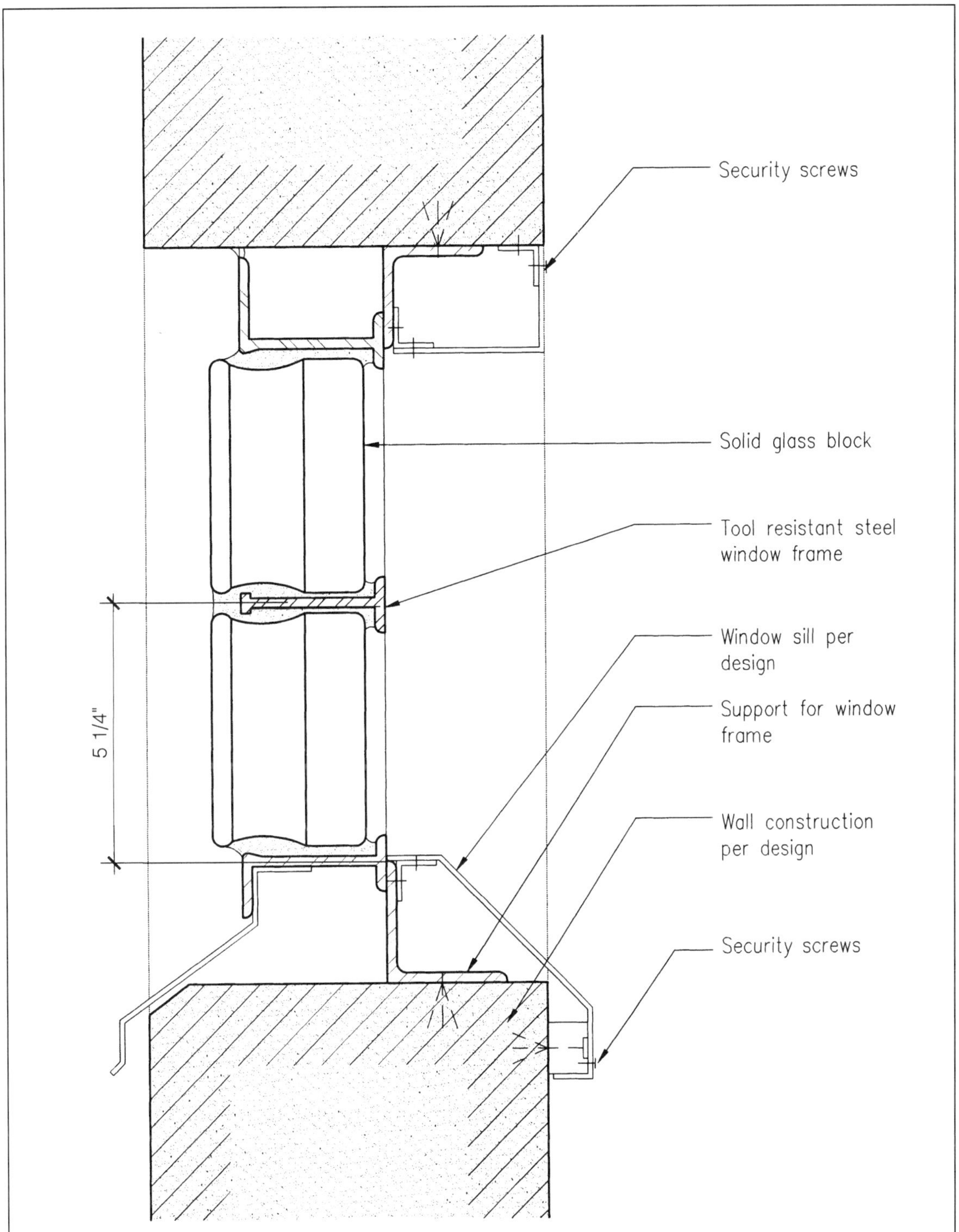

Figure 5.1.9 **Security glass block.**

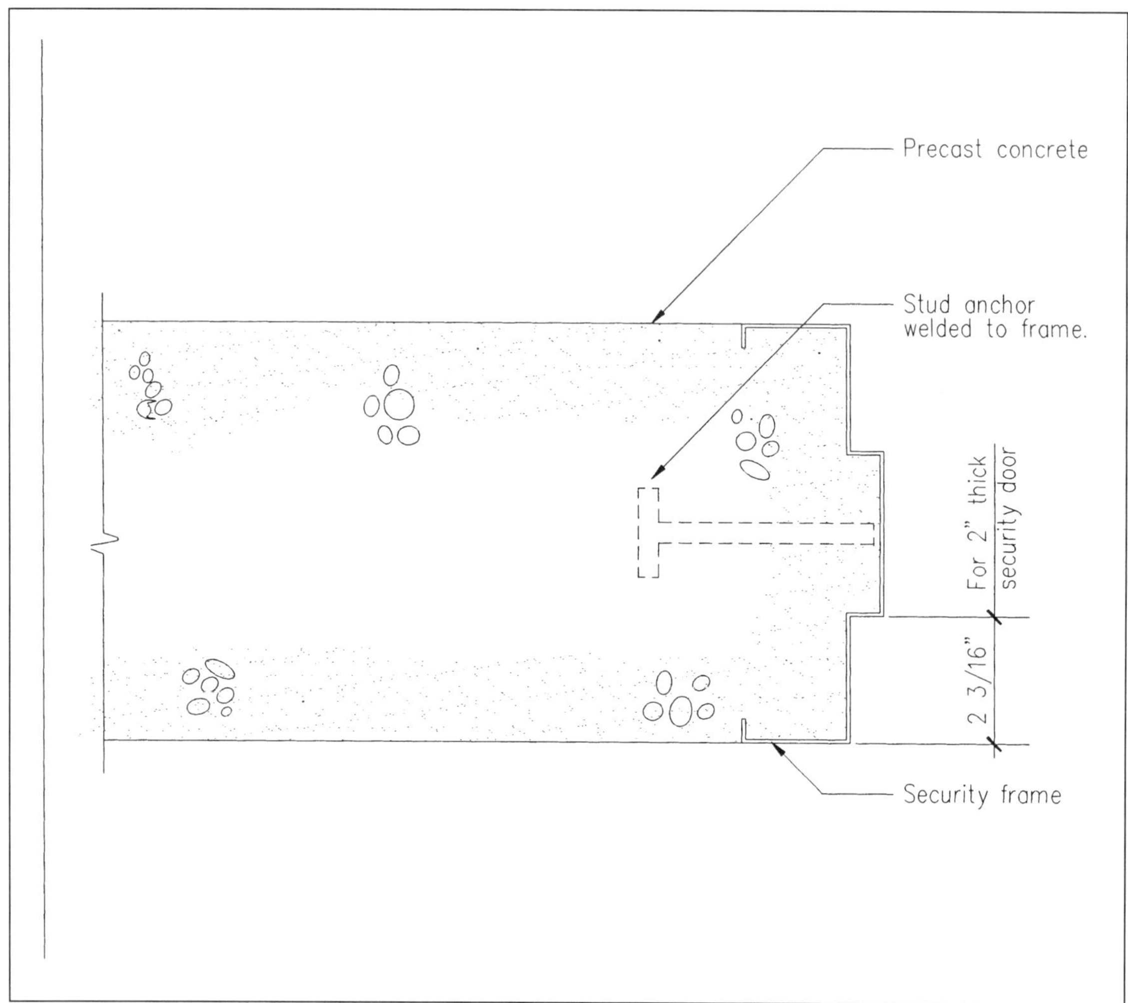

Figure 5.2.1 **Precast concrete/poured-in-place concrete.**

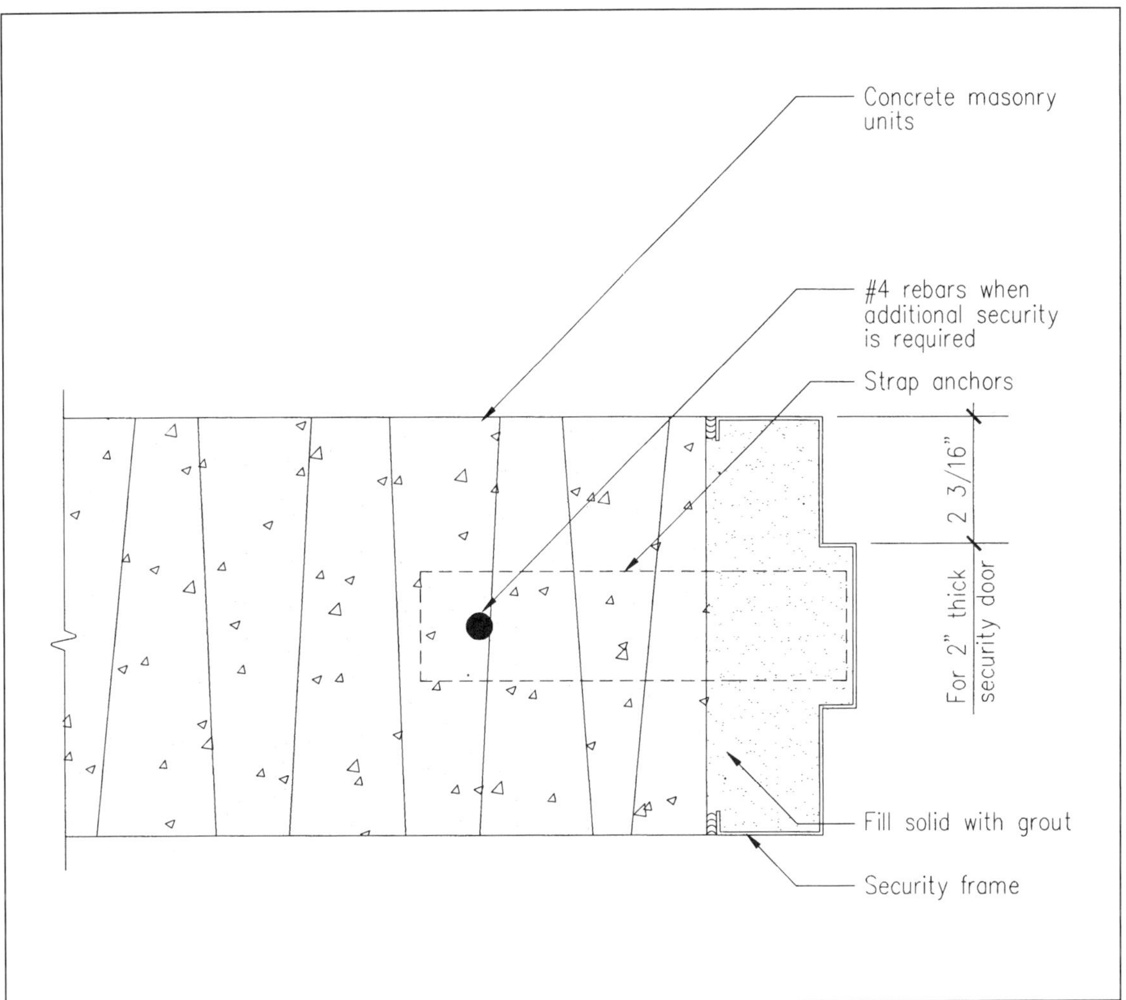

Figure 5.2.2 **Masonry walls/flush frames.**

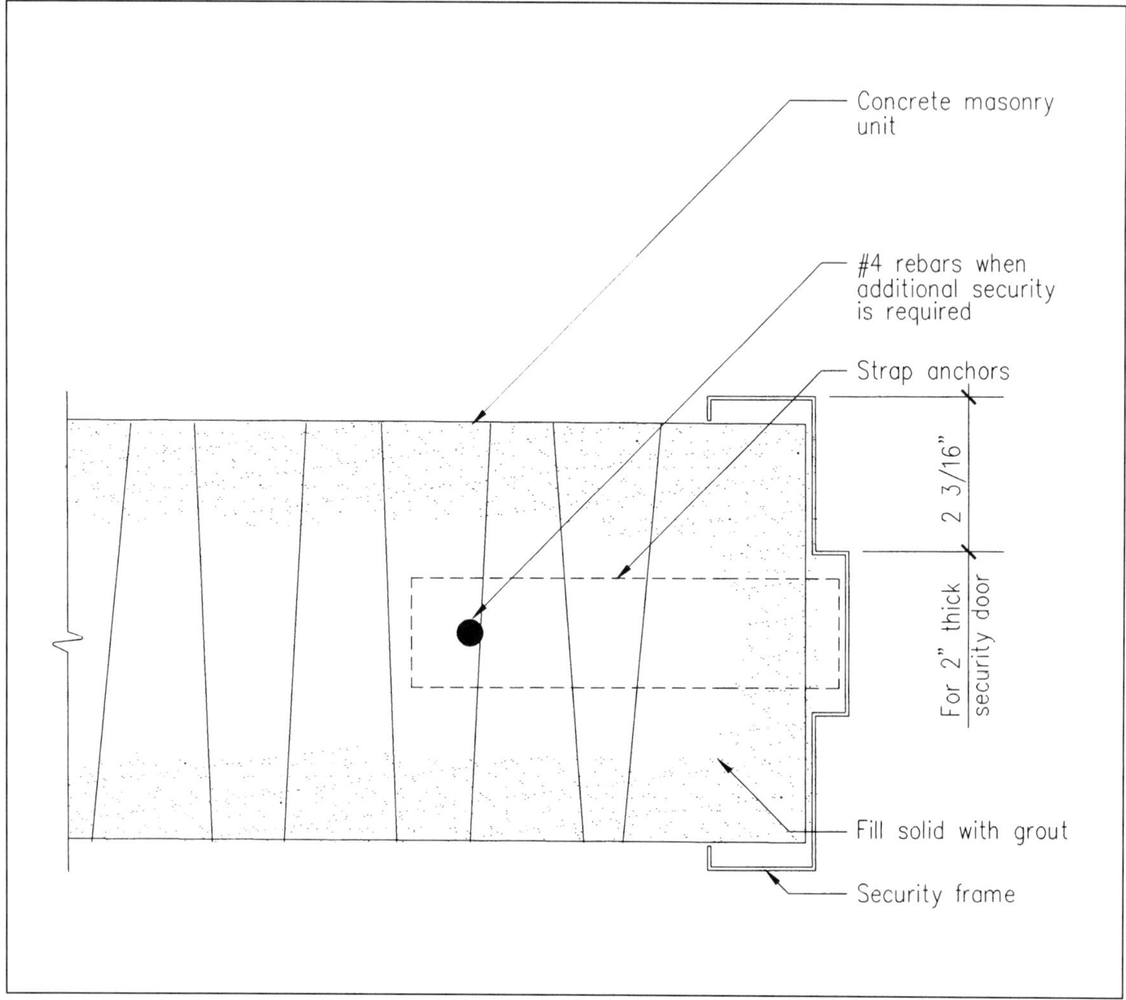

Figure 5.2.3 **Masonry walls/wrap-around frames**

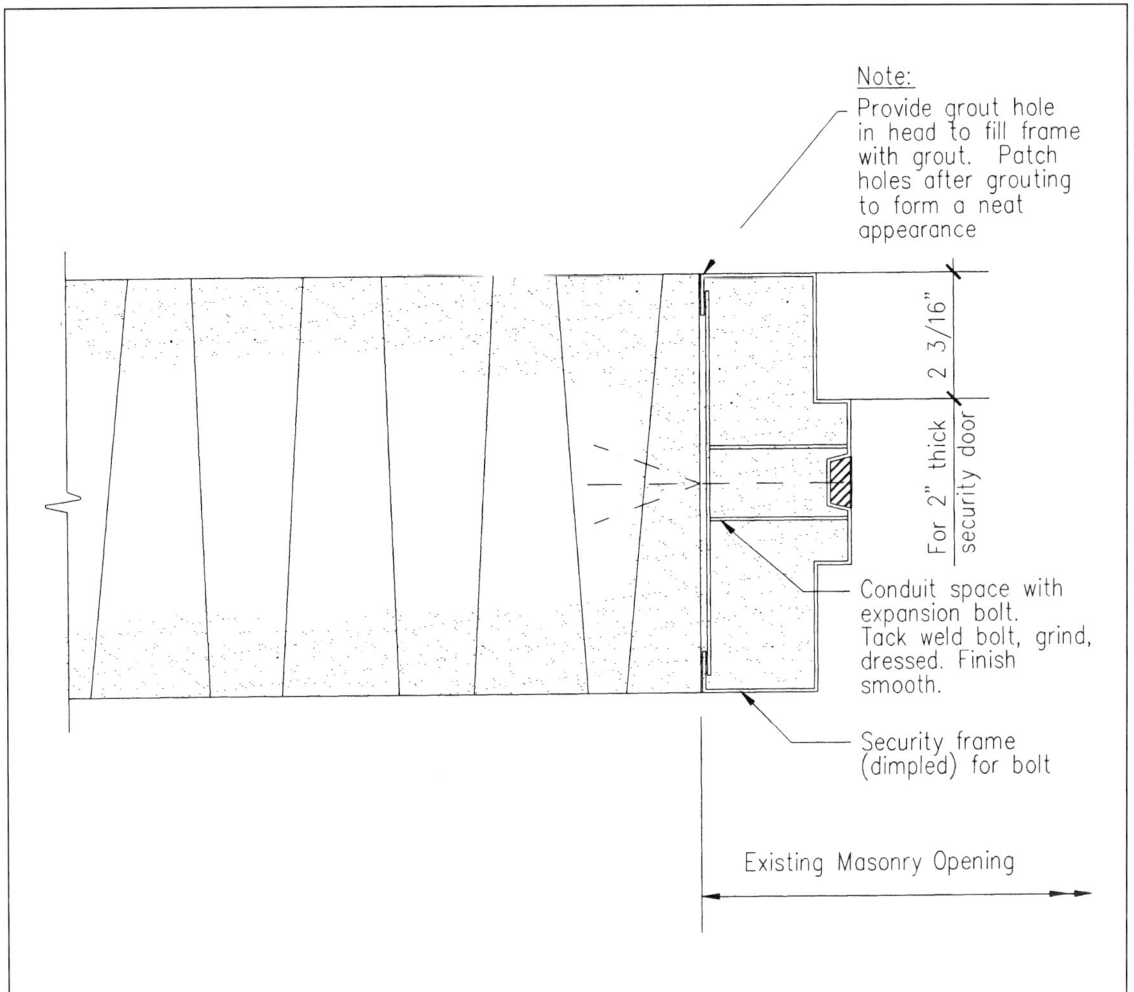

Figure 5.2.4 **Masonry walls/existing wall (opening) condition.**

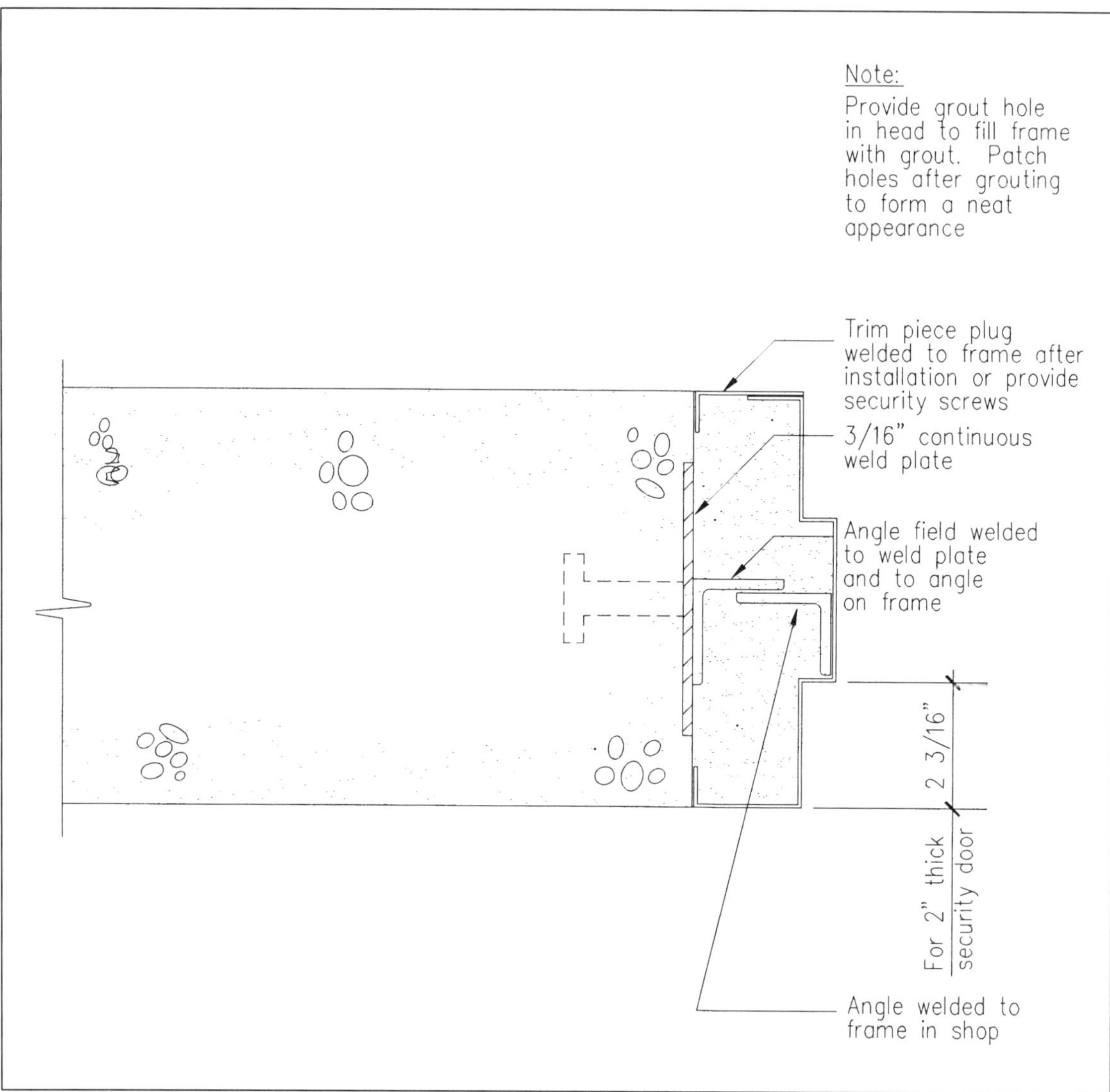

Figure 5.2.5 **Masonry walls/prefinished masonry, precast, and poured-in-place.**

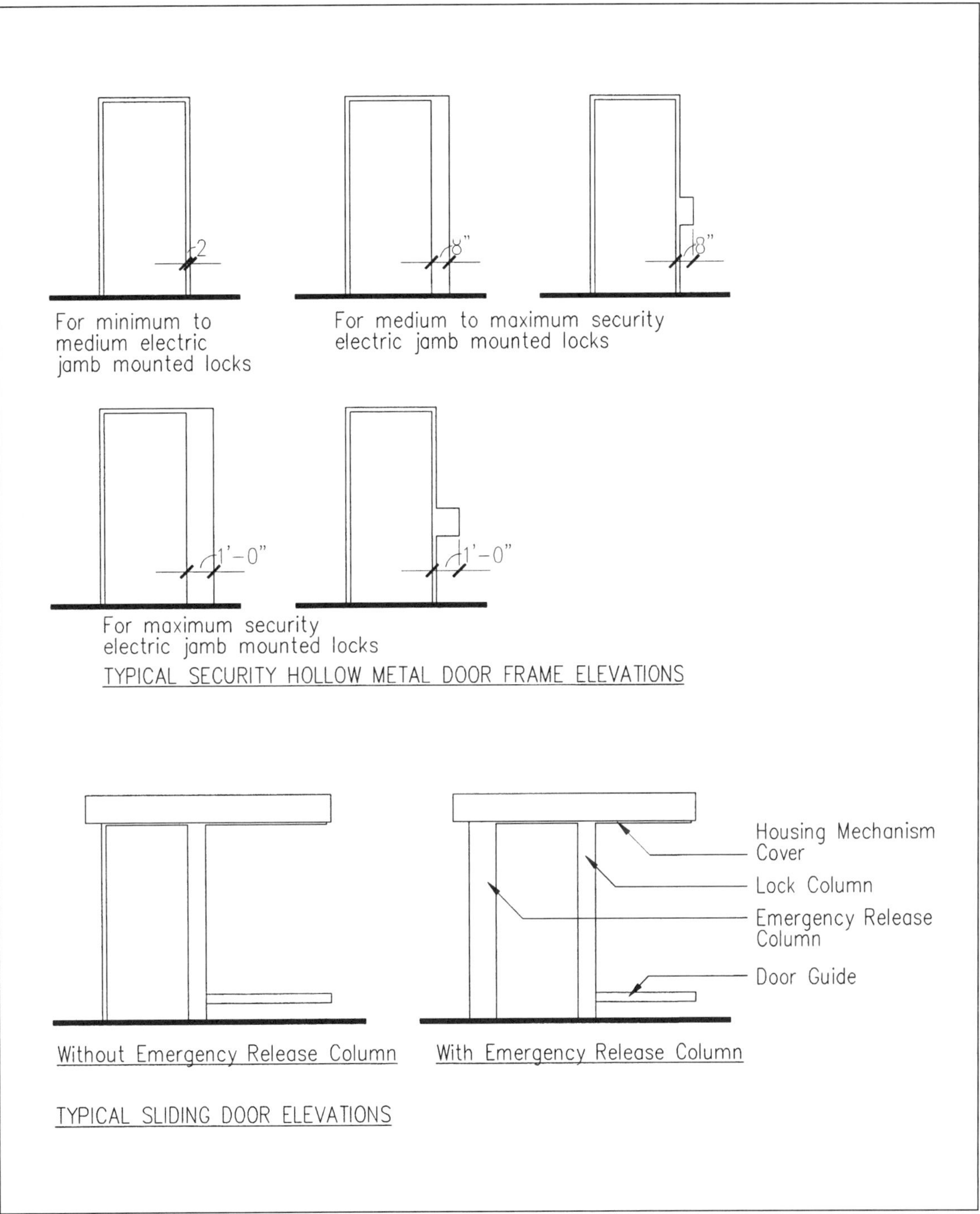

Figure 5.2.6 **Frame types.**

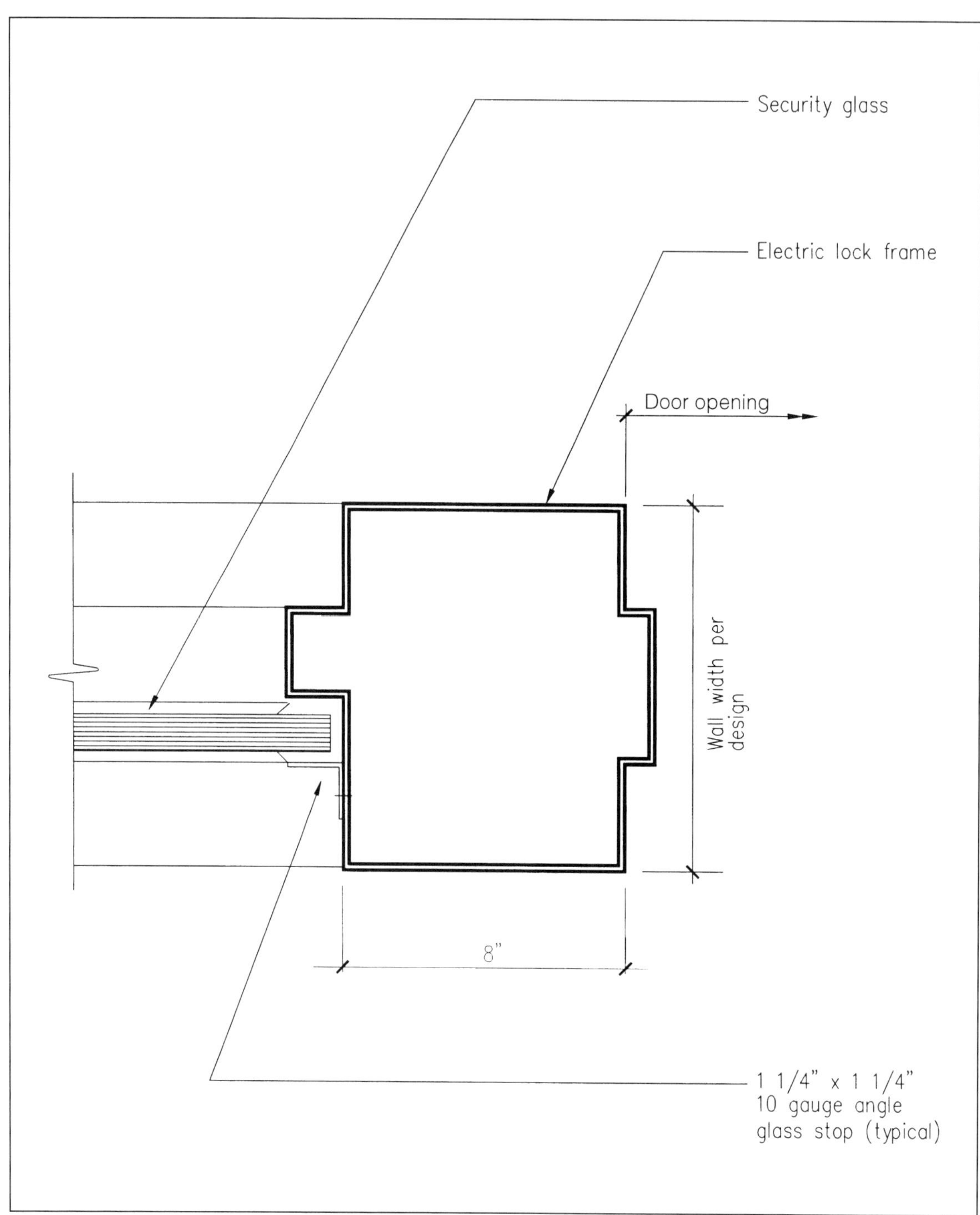

Figure 5.2.7 **8-inch frame with vision panel.**

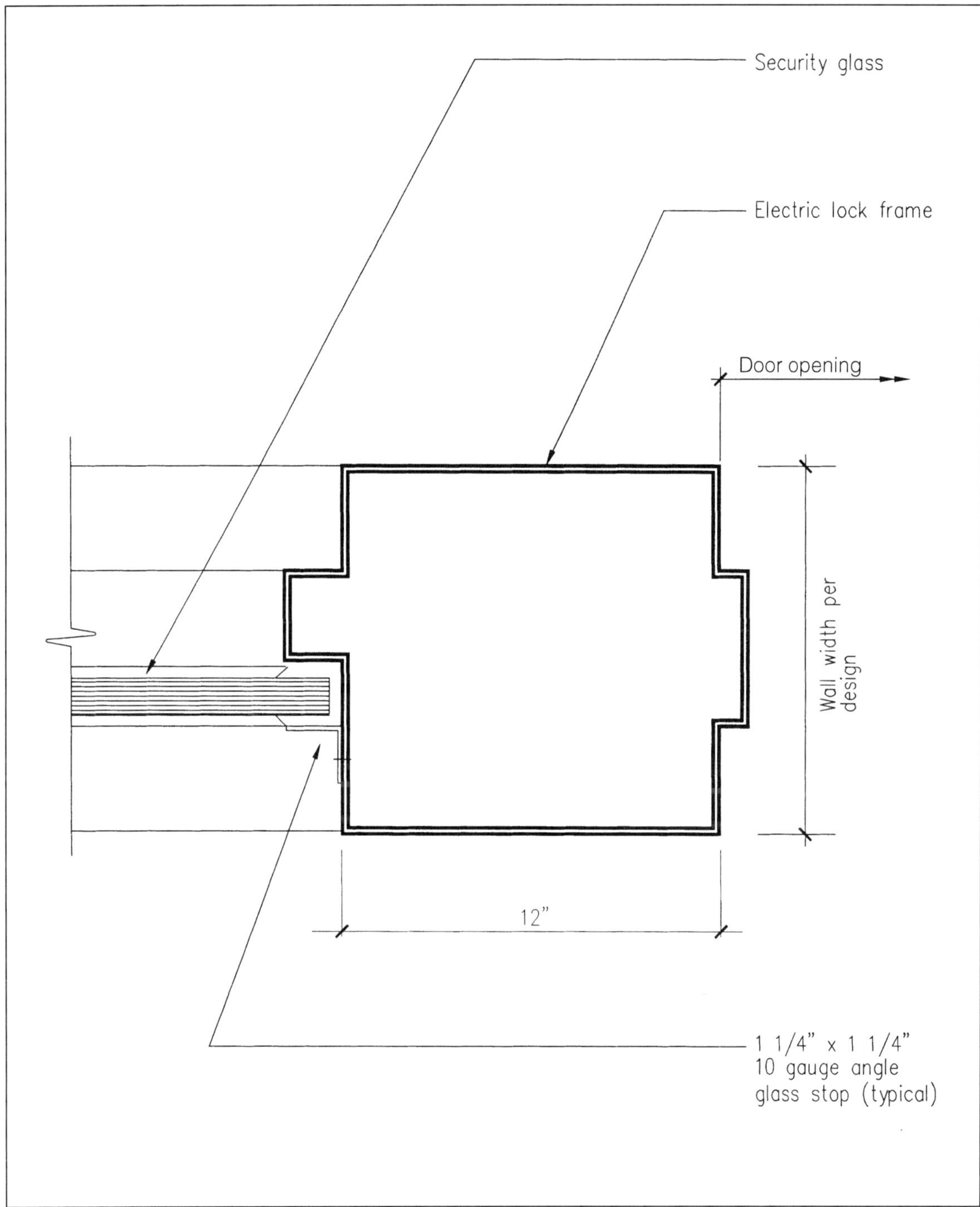

Figure 5.2.8 **12-inch frame with vision panel.**

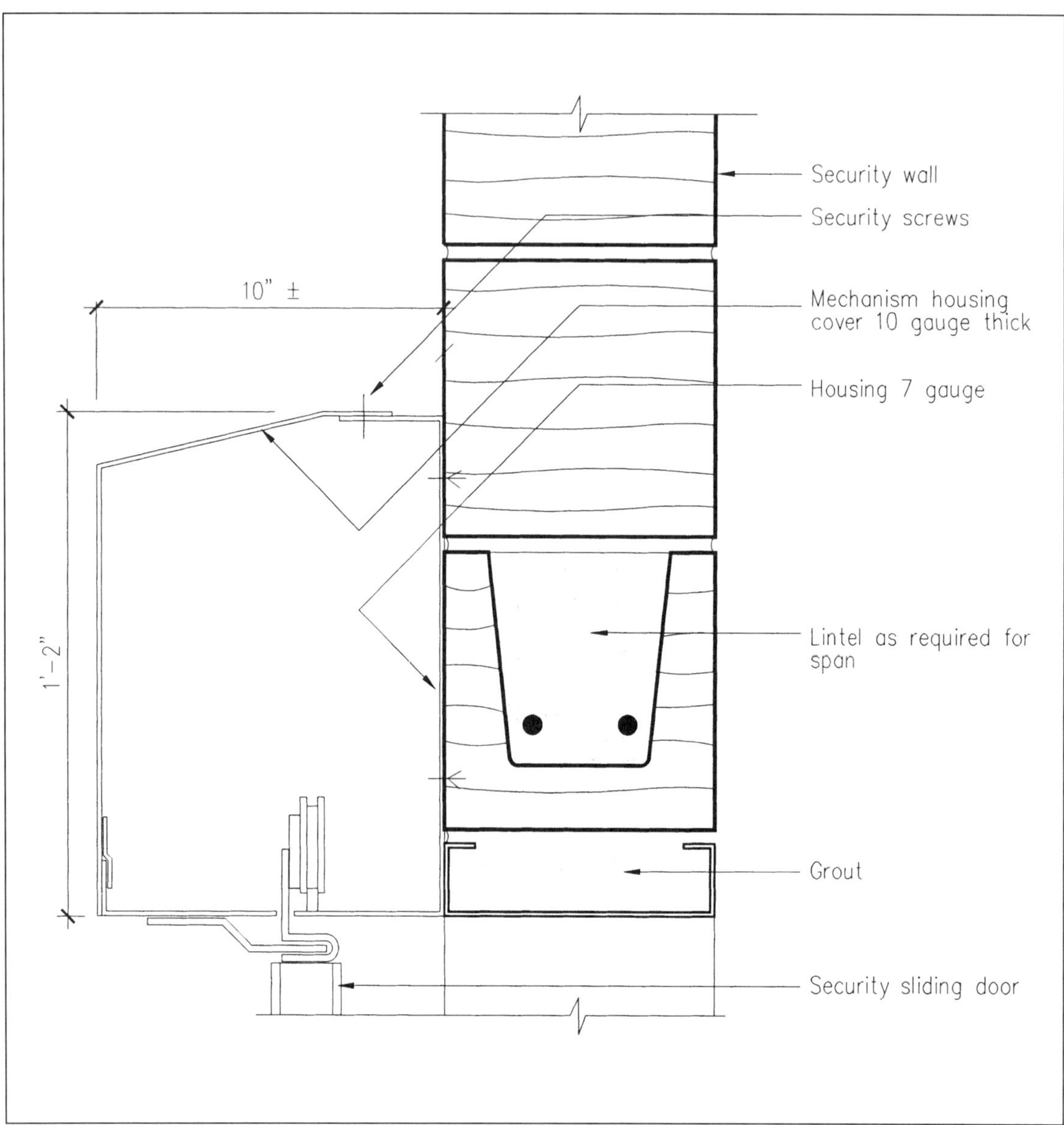

Figure 5.2.9 **Sliding-type head.**

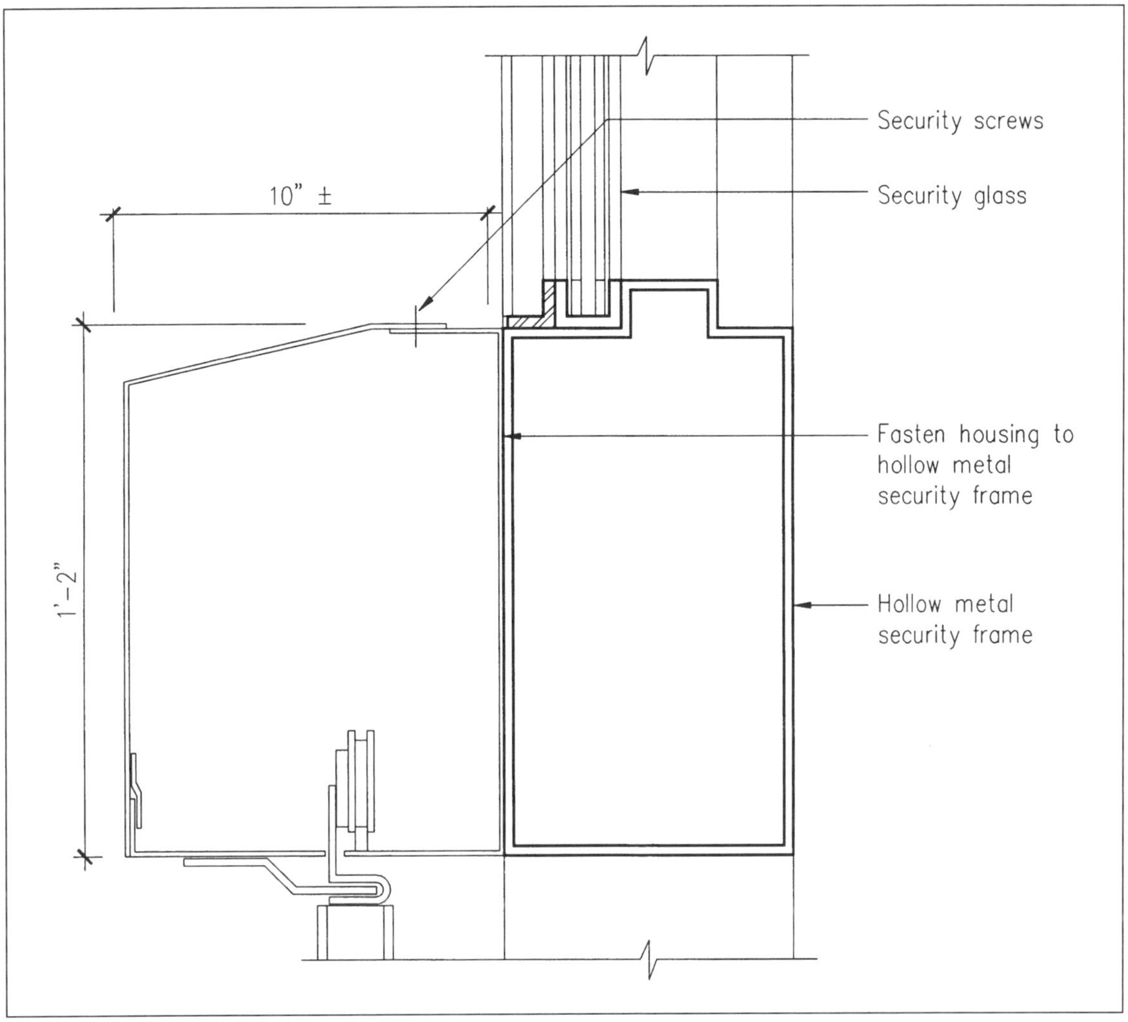

Figure 5.2.10 **Sliding type with vision panel.**

Master Control with observation and control of adjacent sally port sliding doors.

Sliding door assembly with jamb and head glazed panels.

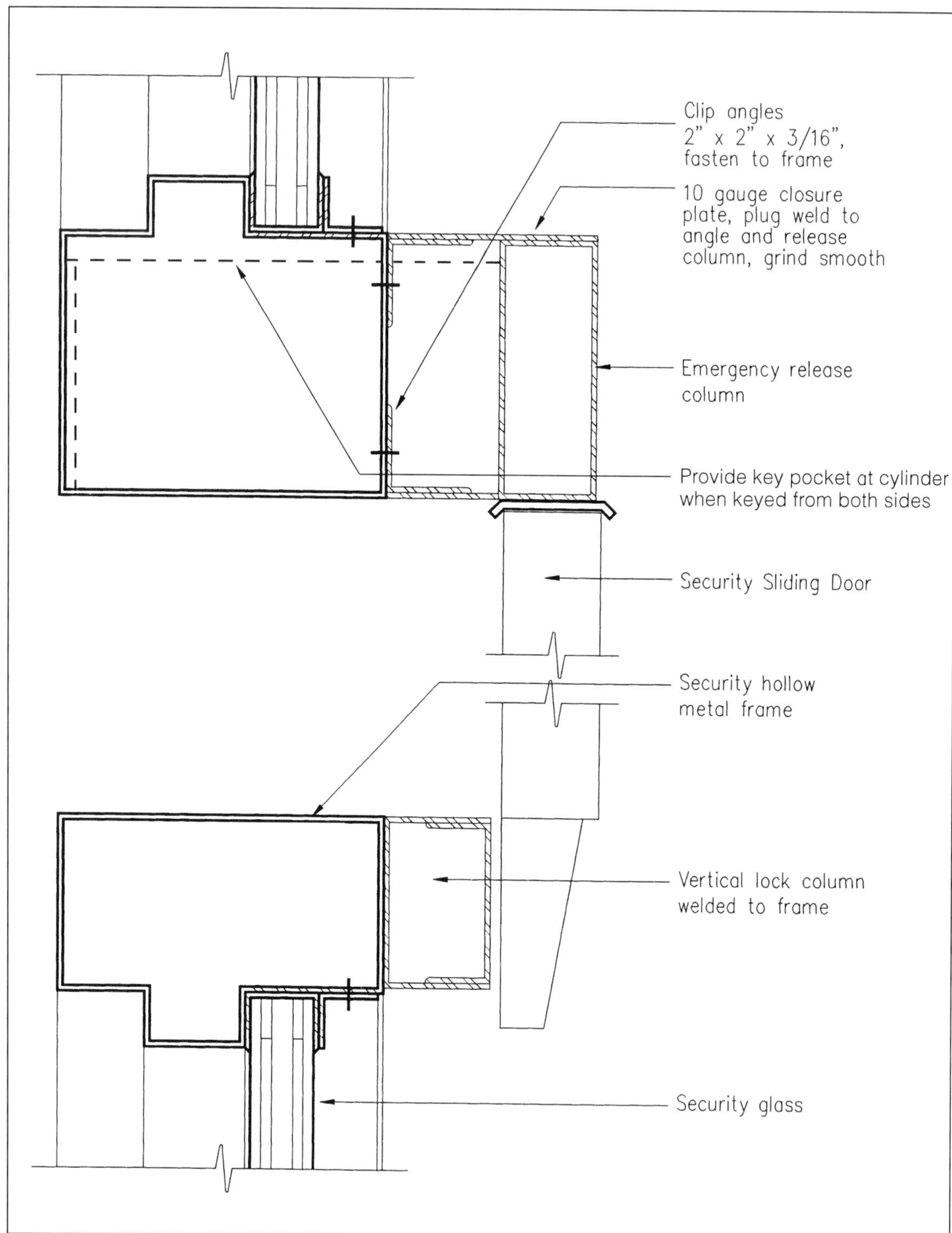

Figure 5.2.11 **Sliding-type door jambs.**

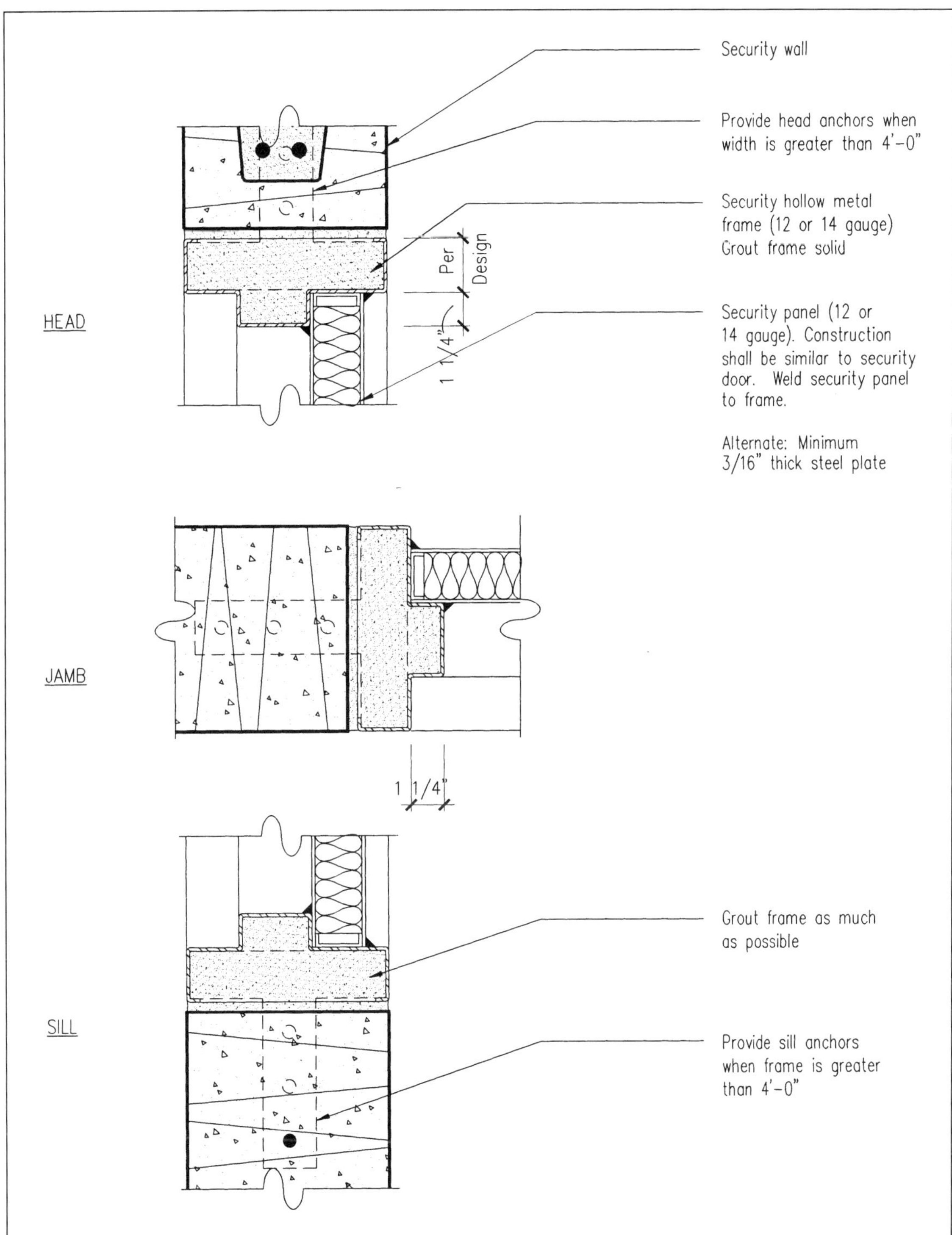

Figure 5.2.12 **Frame with fixed panel.**

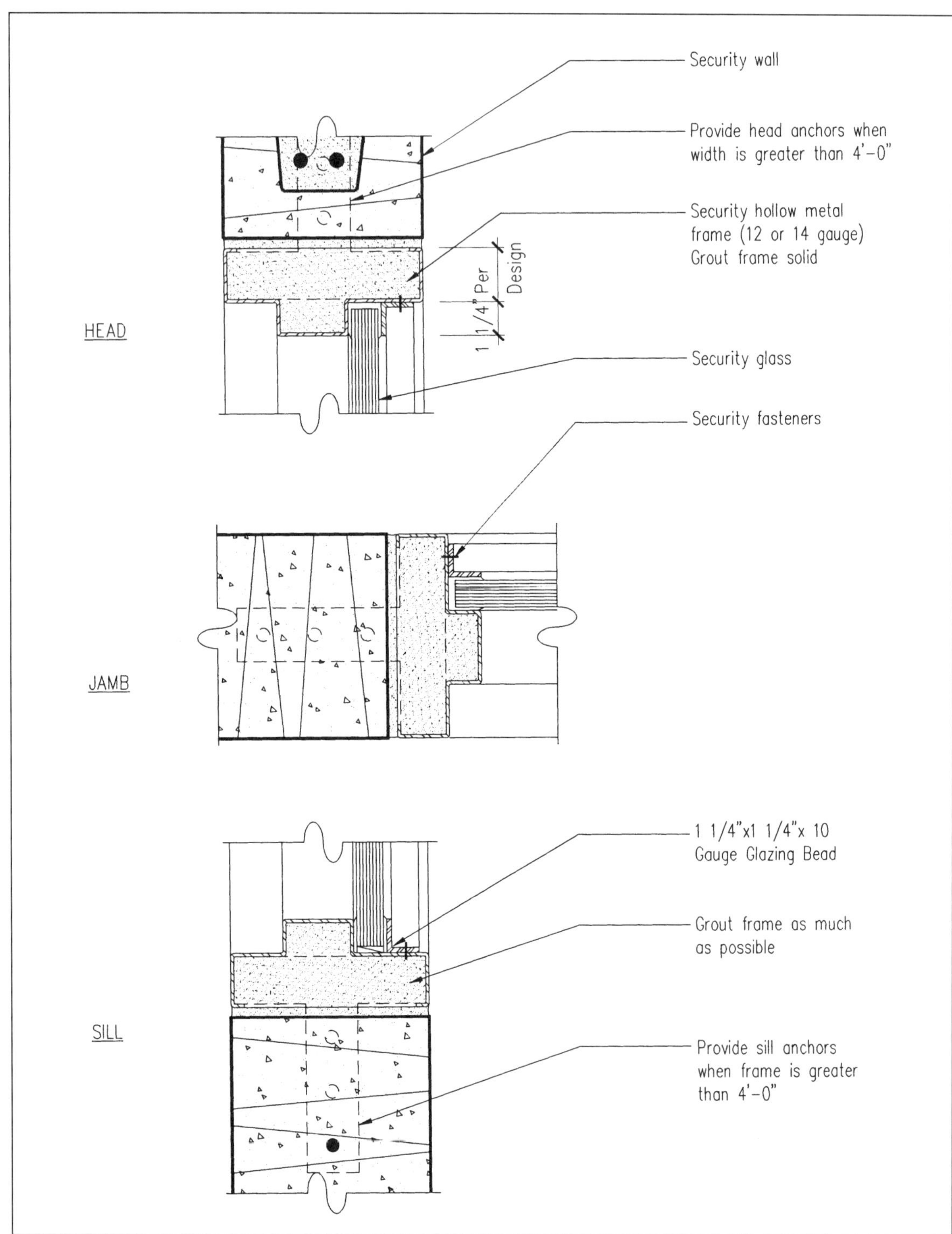

Figure 5.2.13 **Frame with vision panel.**

Clothing exchange room window with shower enclosure.

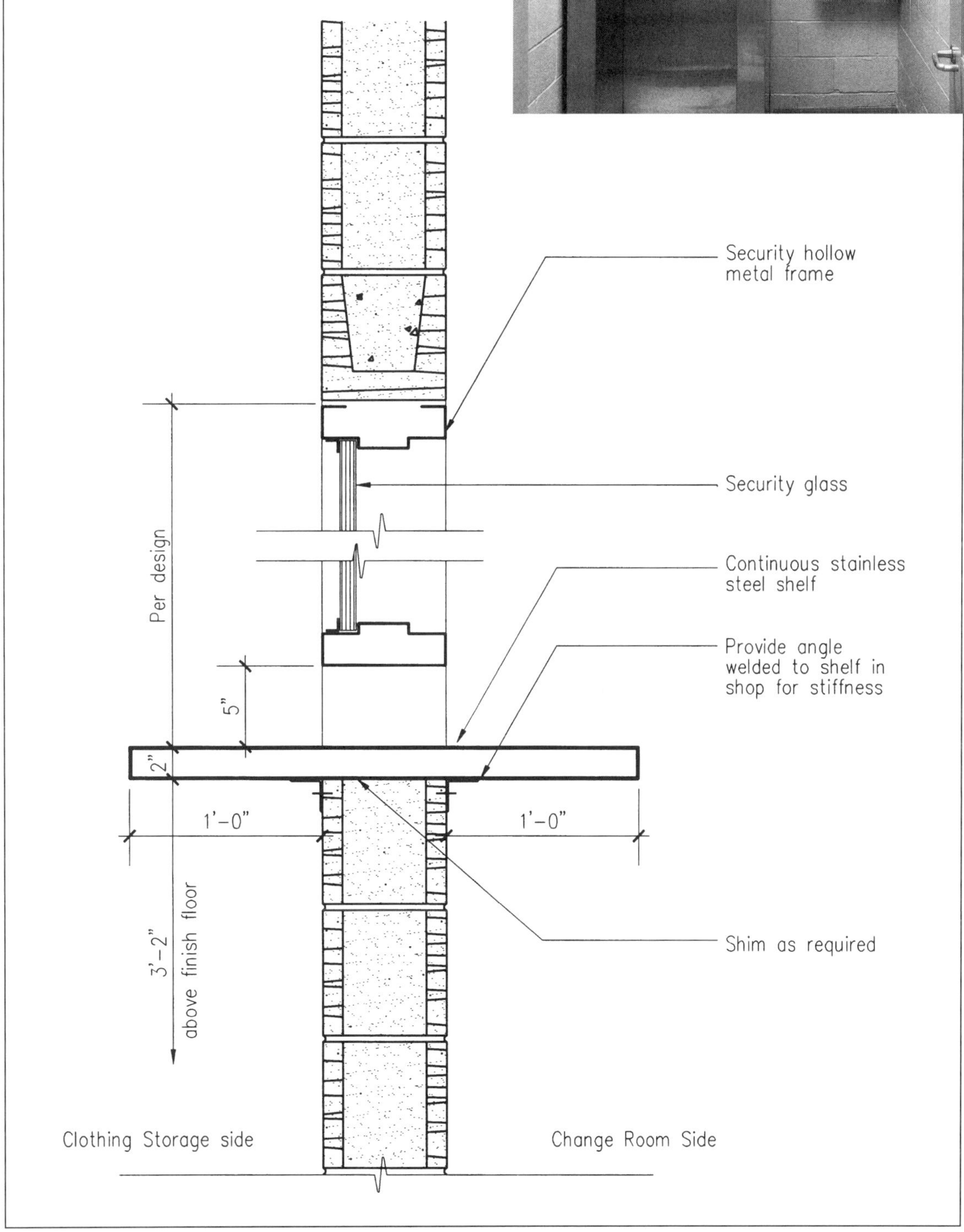

Security hollow metal frame
Security glass
Continuous stainless steel shelf
Provide angle welded to shelf in shop for stiffness
Per design
5"
2"
1'-0"
1'-0"
Shim as required
3'-2" above finish floor
Clothing Storage side
Change Room Side

Figure 5.2.14 **Clothing exchange window.**

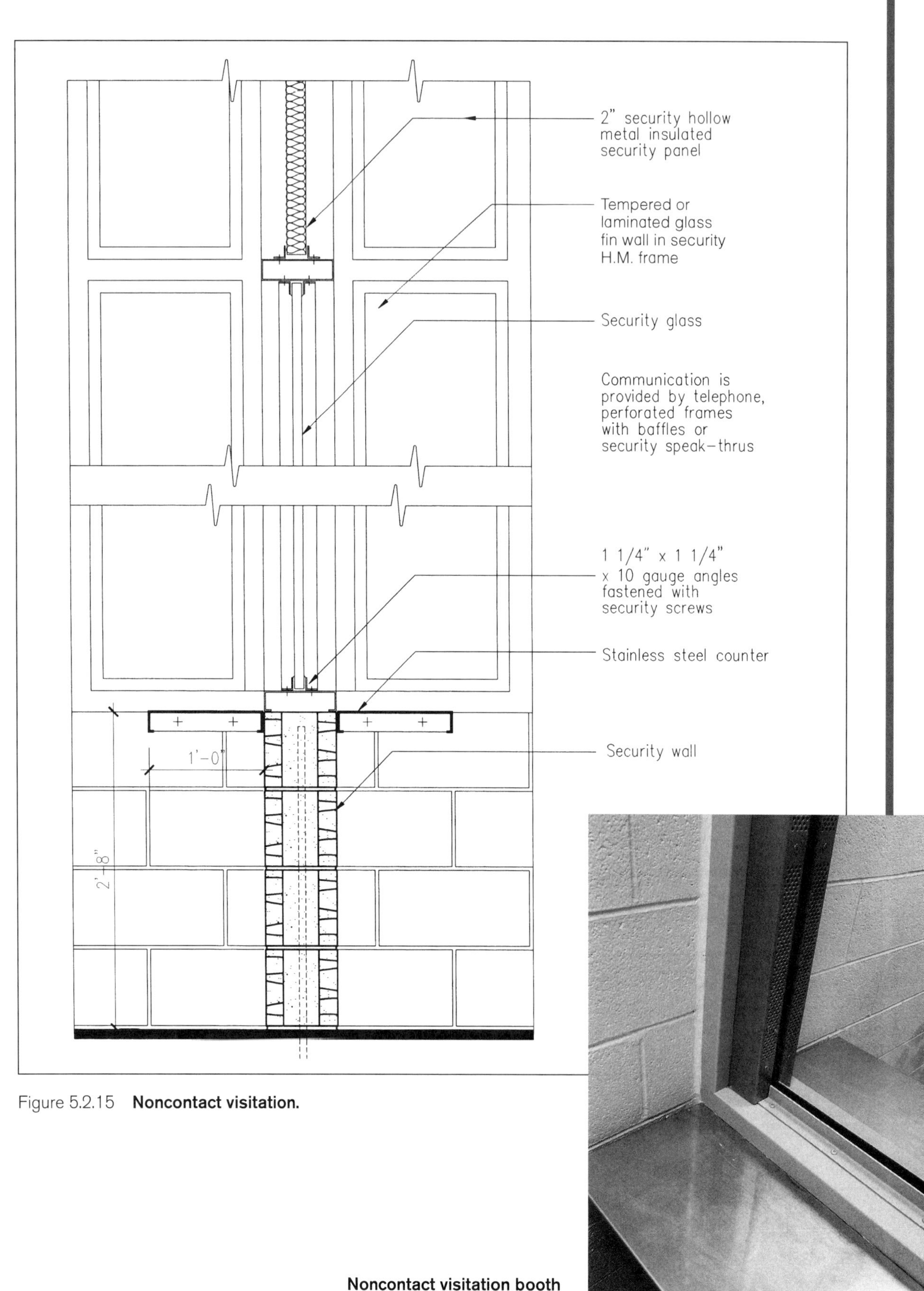

Figure 5.2.15 **Noncontact visitation.**

Noncontact visitation booth with a speak-through jamb frame.

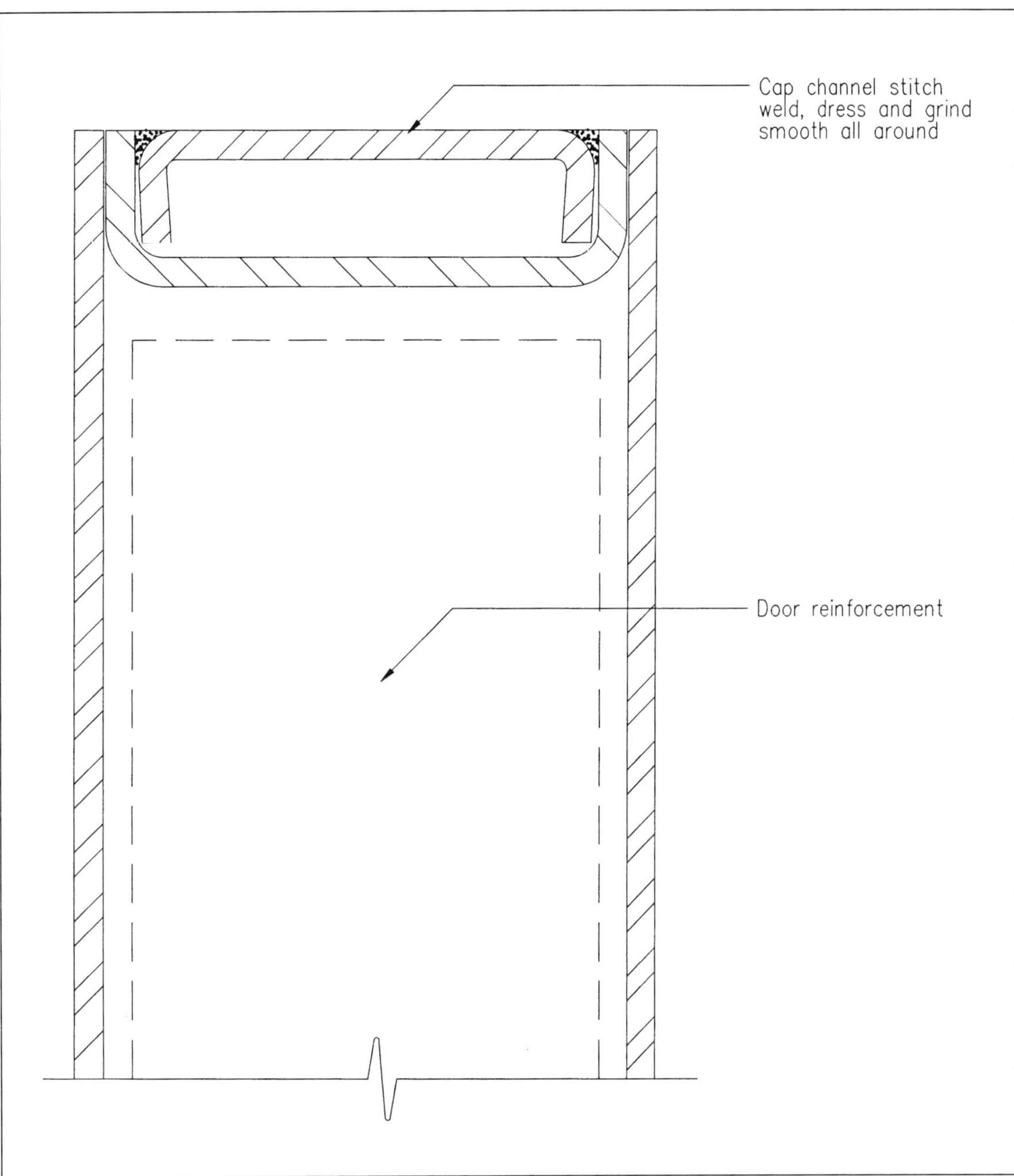

Figure 5.2.16 **Door closure.**

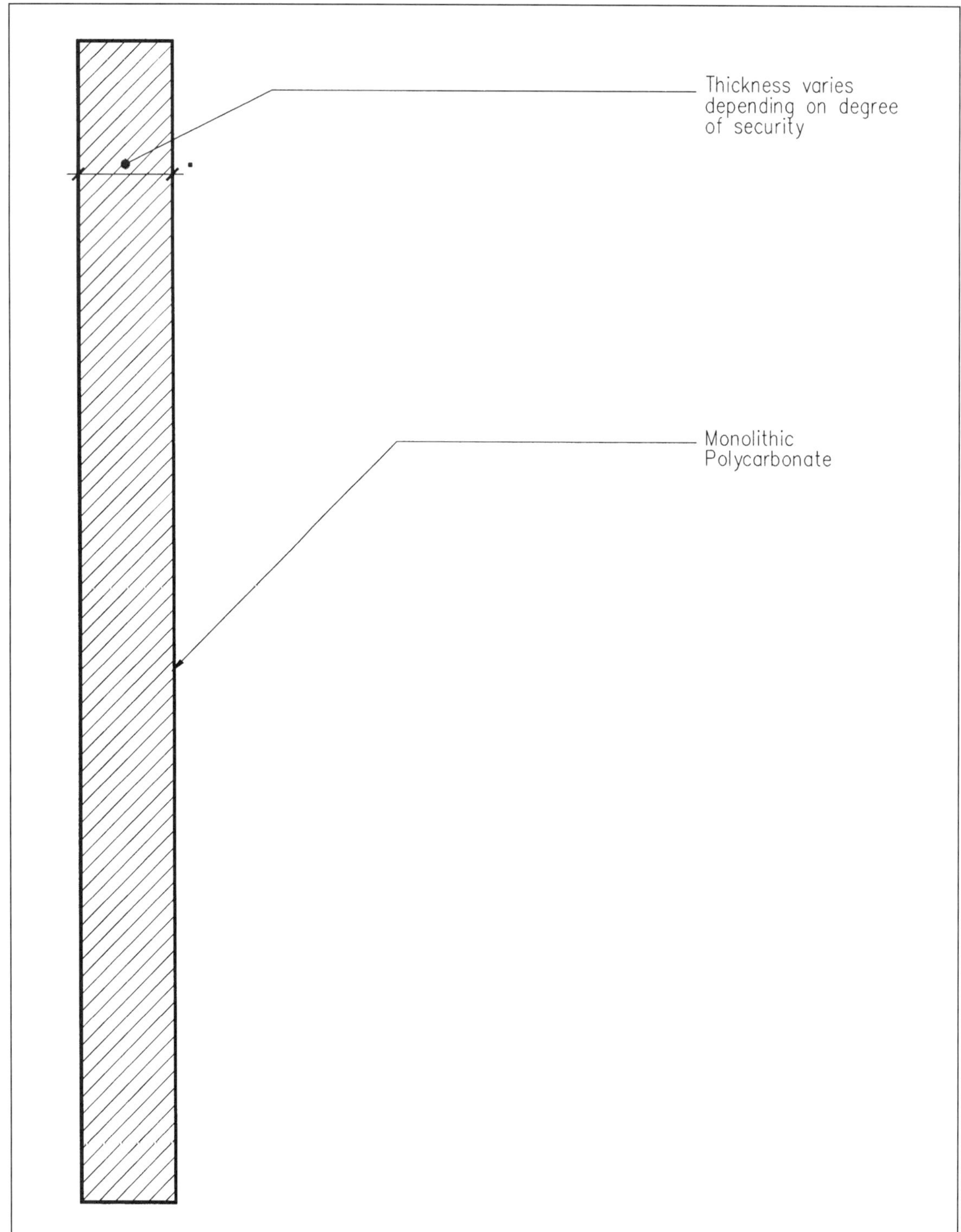

Figure 5.3.1 **Polycarbonate plastics.**

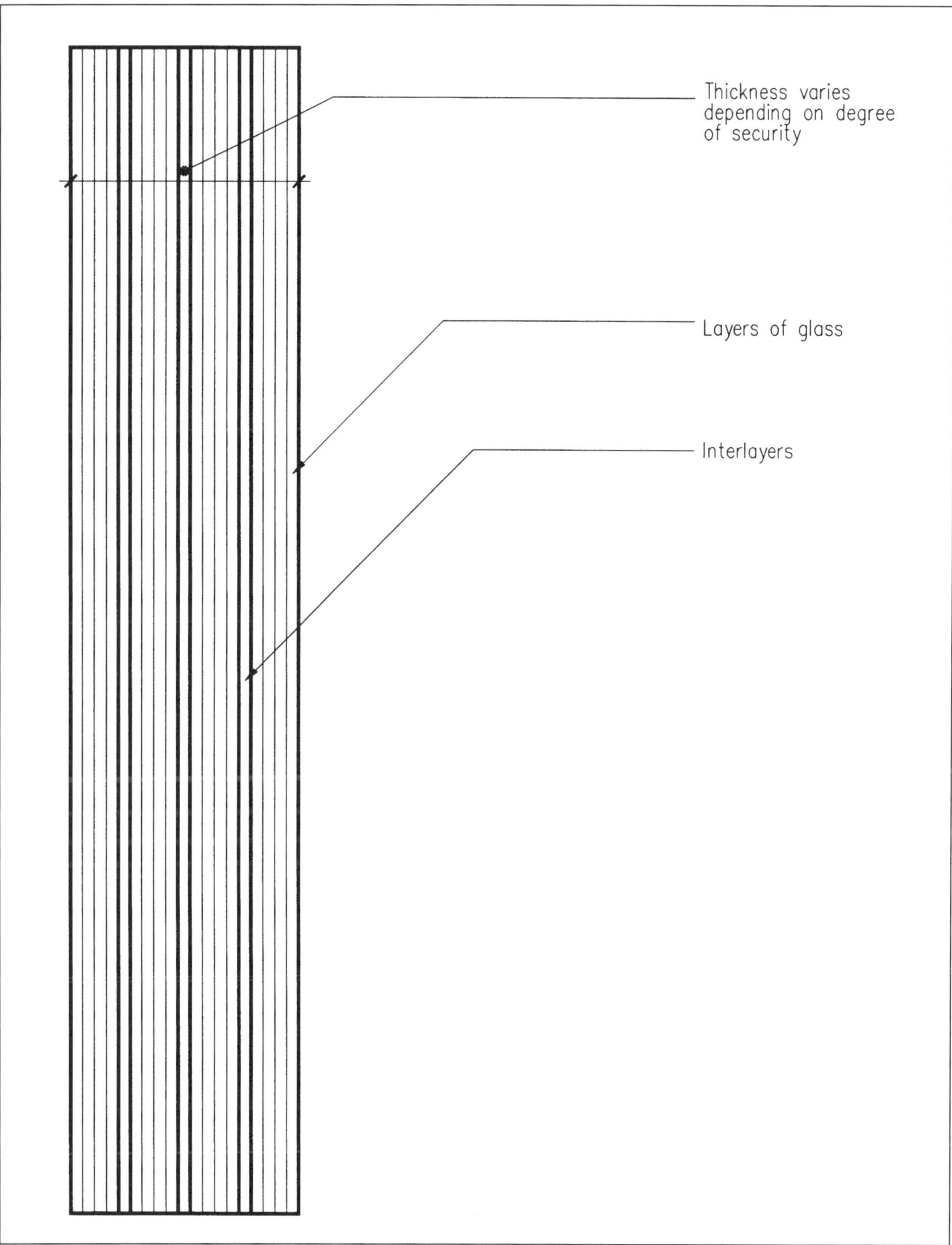

Figure 5.3.2 **Glass laminates.**

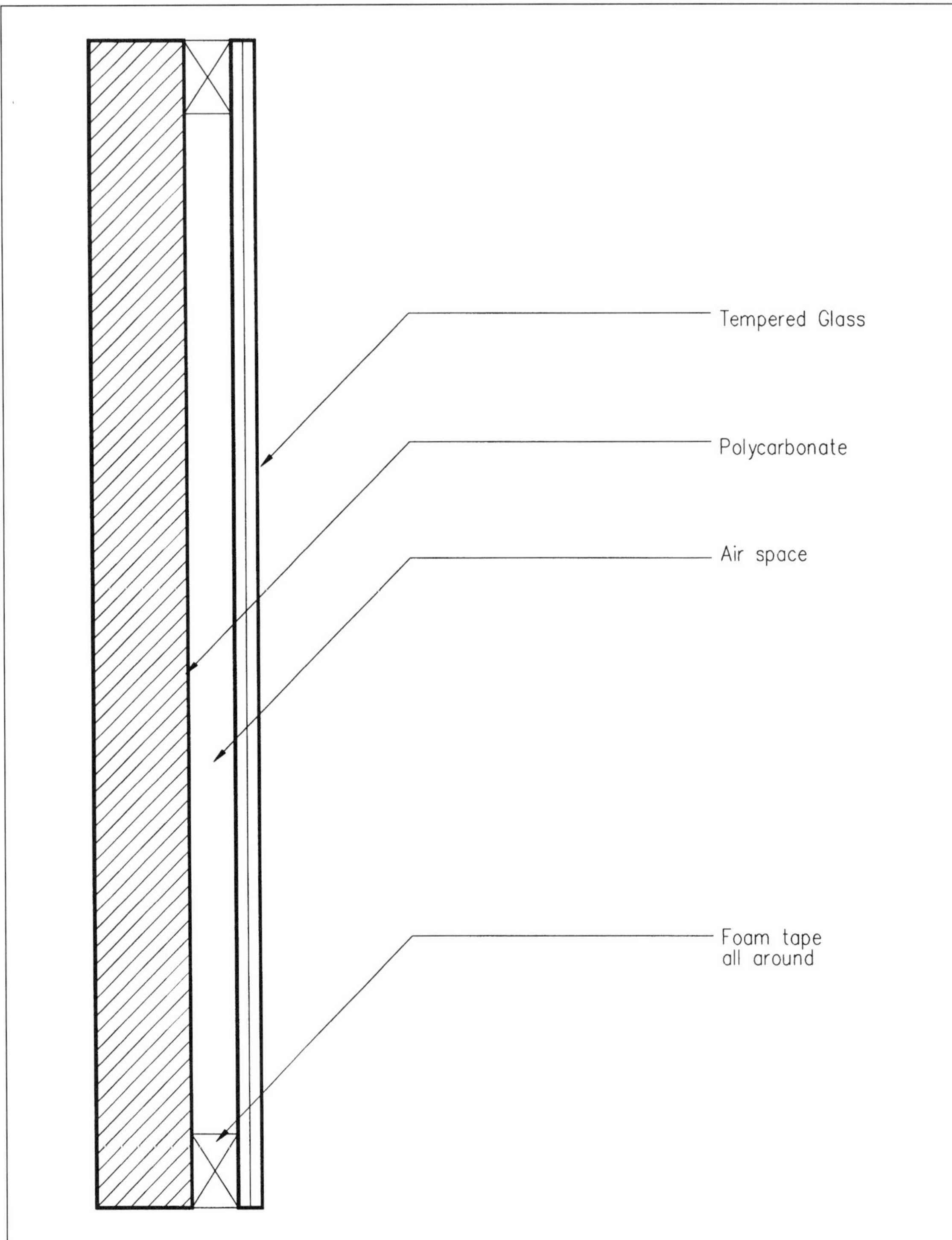

Figure 5.3.3 **Replacement glass systems.**

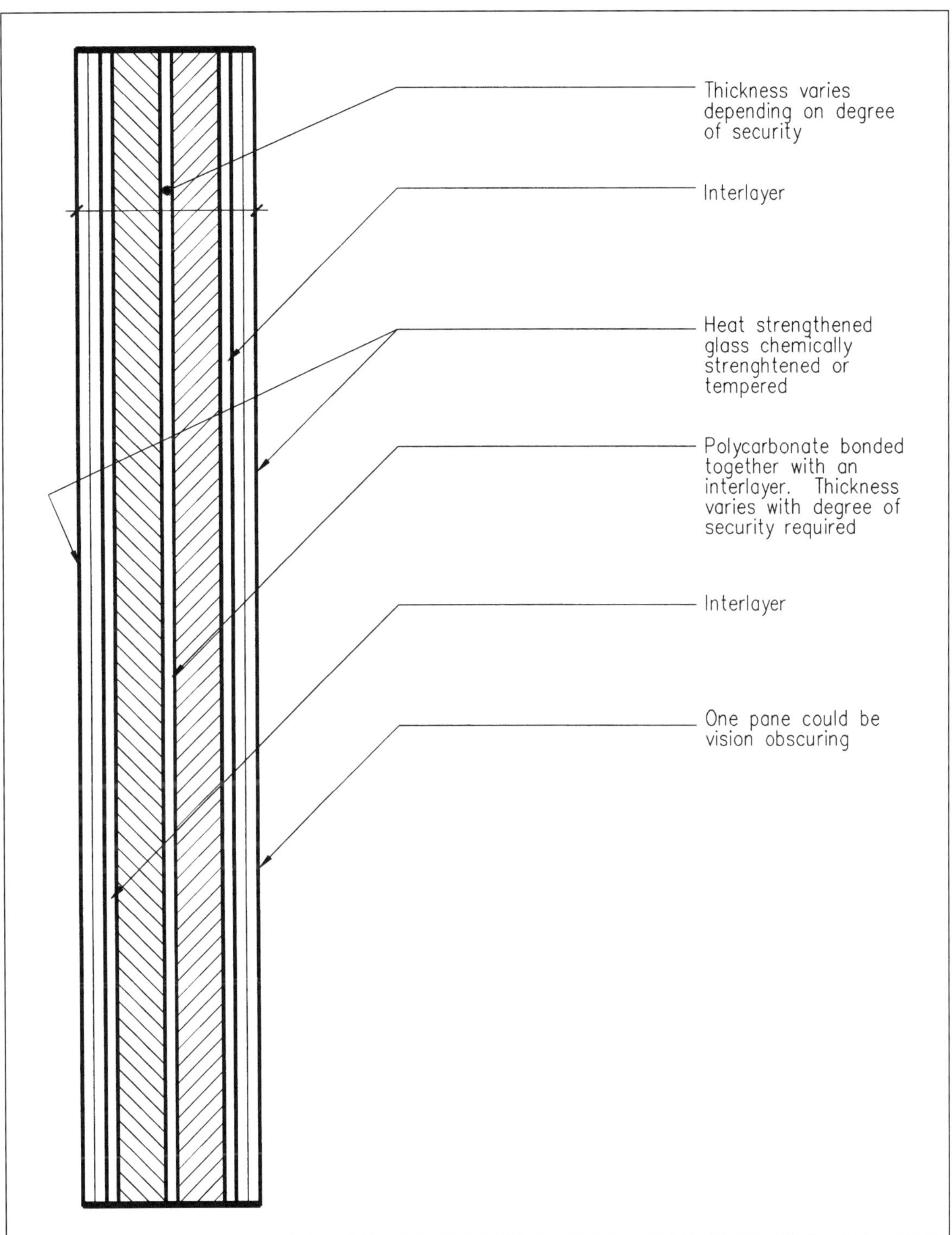

Figure 5.3.4 **Glass-clad polycarbonates.**

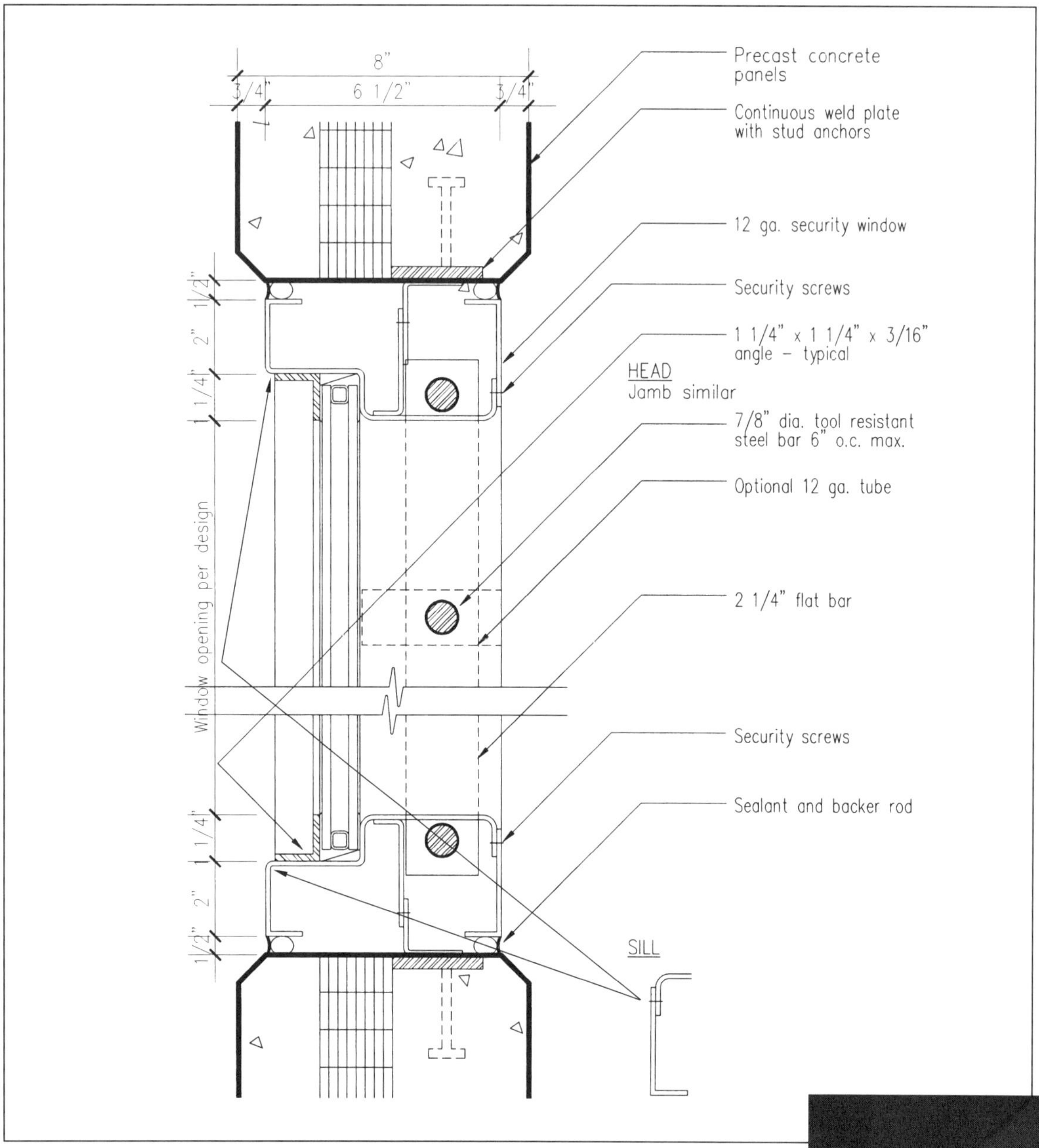

8"
3/4" 6 1/2" 3/4"
1/2" 2" 1 1/4"
Window opening per design
1 1/4" 2" 1/2"

Precast concrete panels
Continuous weld plate with stud anchors
12 ga. security window
Security screws
1 1/4" x 1 1/4" x 3/16" angle – typical
HEAD
Jamb similar
7/8" dia. tool resistant steel bar 6" o.c. max.
Optional 12 ga. tube
2 1/4" flat bar
Security screws
Sealant and backer rod
SILL

Figure 5.4.1 **Split window frame with security bars.**

Exterior split-frame window with security bars.

Exterior window with security bars in vertical position.

Precast exterior panels with horizontal inmate cell windows and fenestration reveals to reduce visual mass.

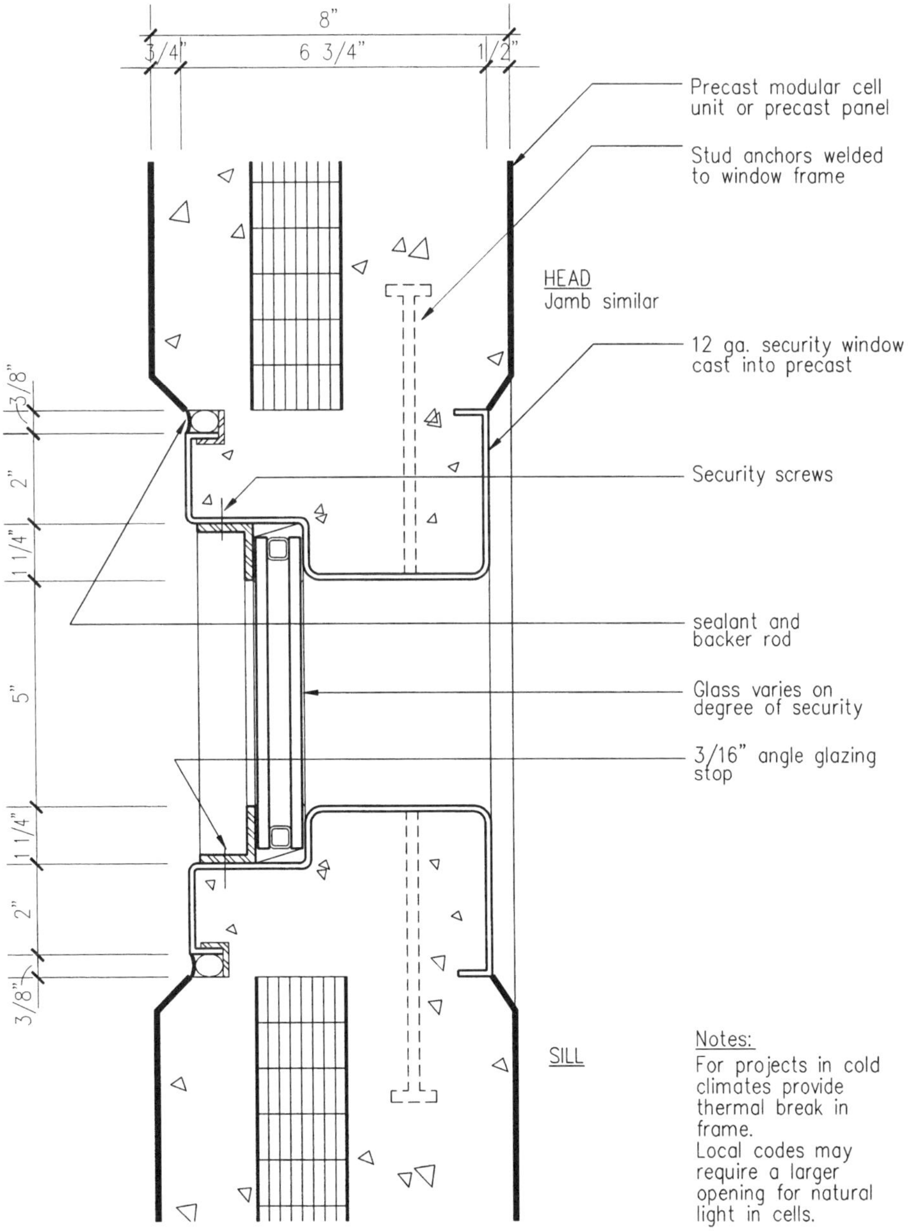

8"

3/4" 6 3/4" 1/2"

Precast modular cell unit or precast panel

Stud anchors welded to window frame

HEAD
Jamb similar

12 ga. security window cast into precast

Security screws

sealant and backer rod

Glass varies on degree of security

3/16" angle glazing stop

3/8" 2" 1 1/4" 5" 1 1/4" 2" 3/8"

SILL

Notes:
For projects in cold climates provide thermal break in frame.
Local codes may require a larger opening for natural light in cells.

Figure 5.4.2 **Casting the frame into precast concrete.**

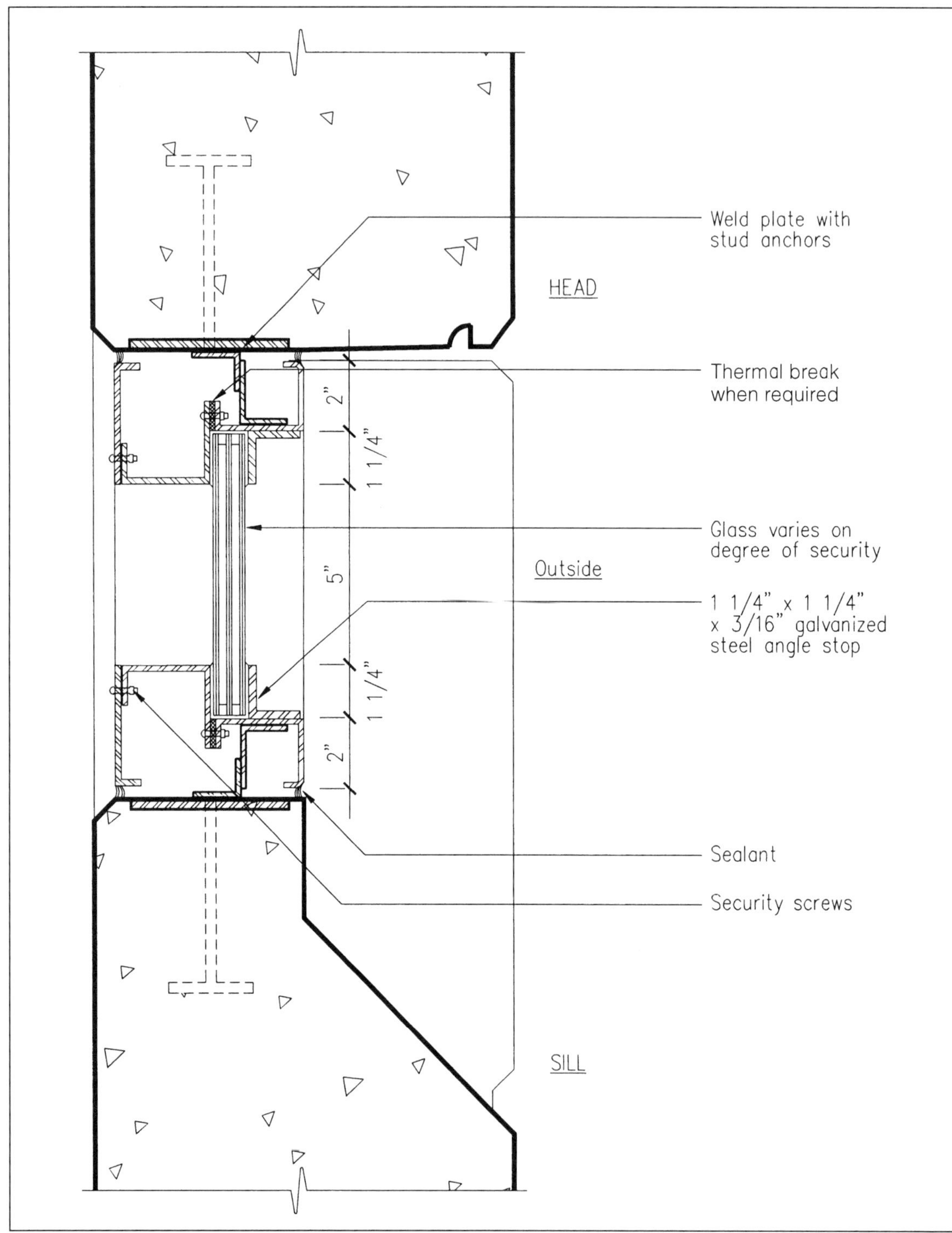

Figure 5.4.3 **Split-frame cell window.**

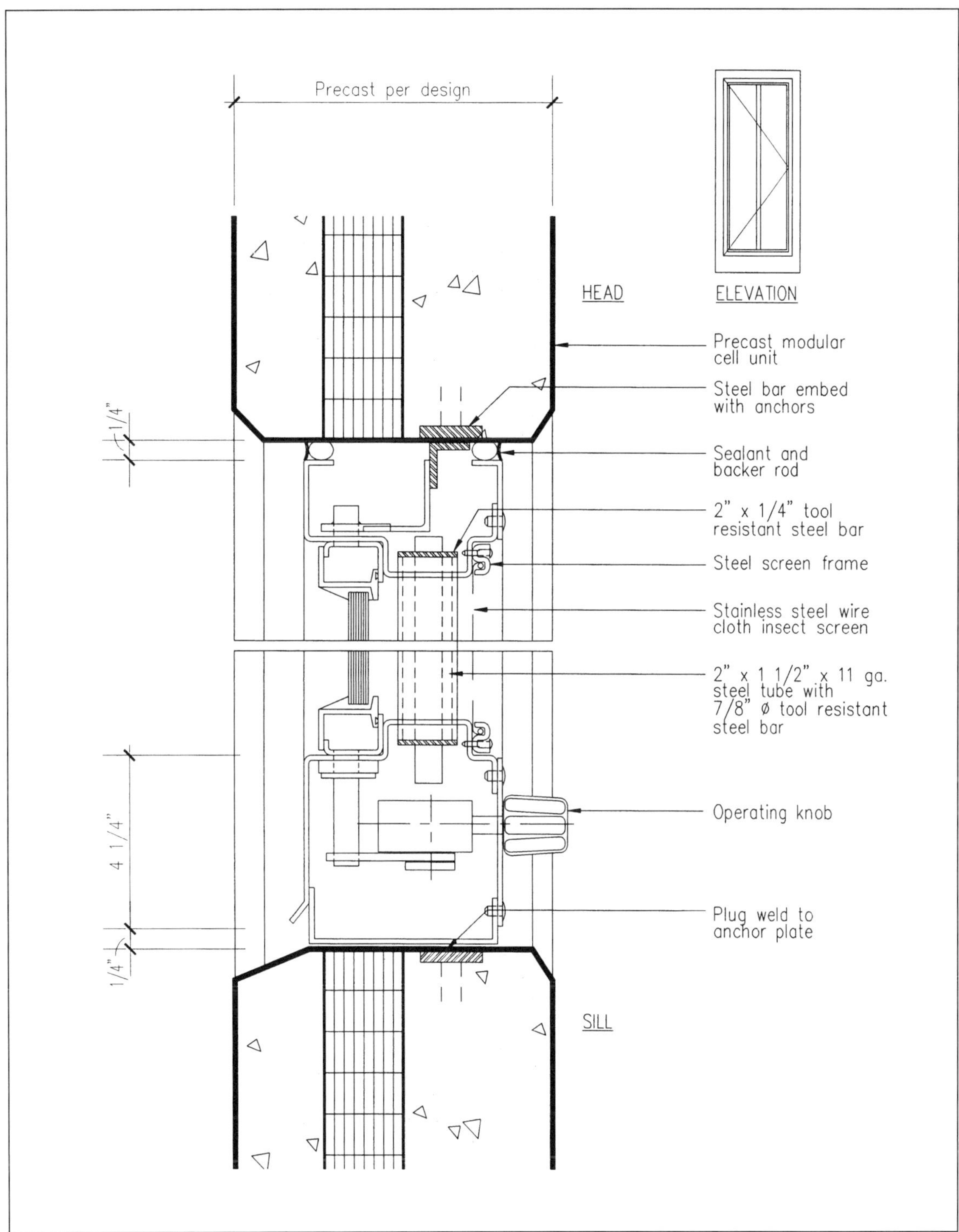

Figure 5.4.4 **Operable window sash.**

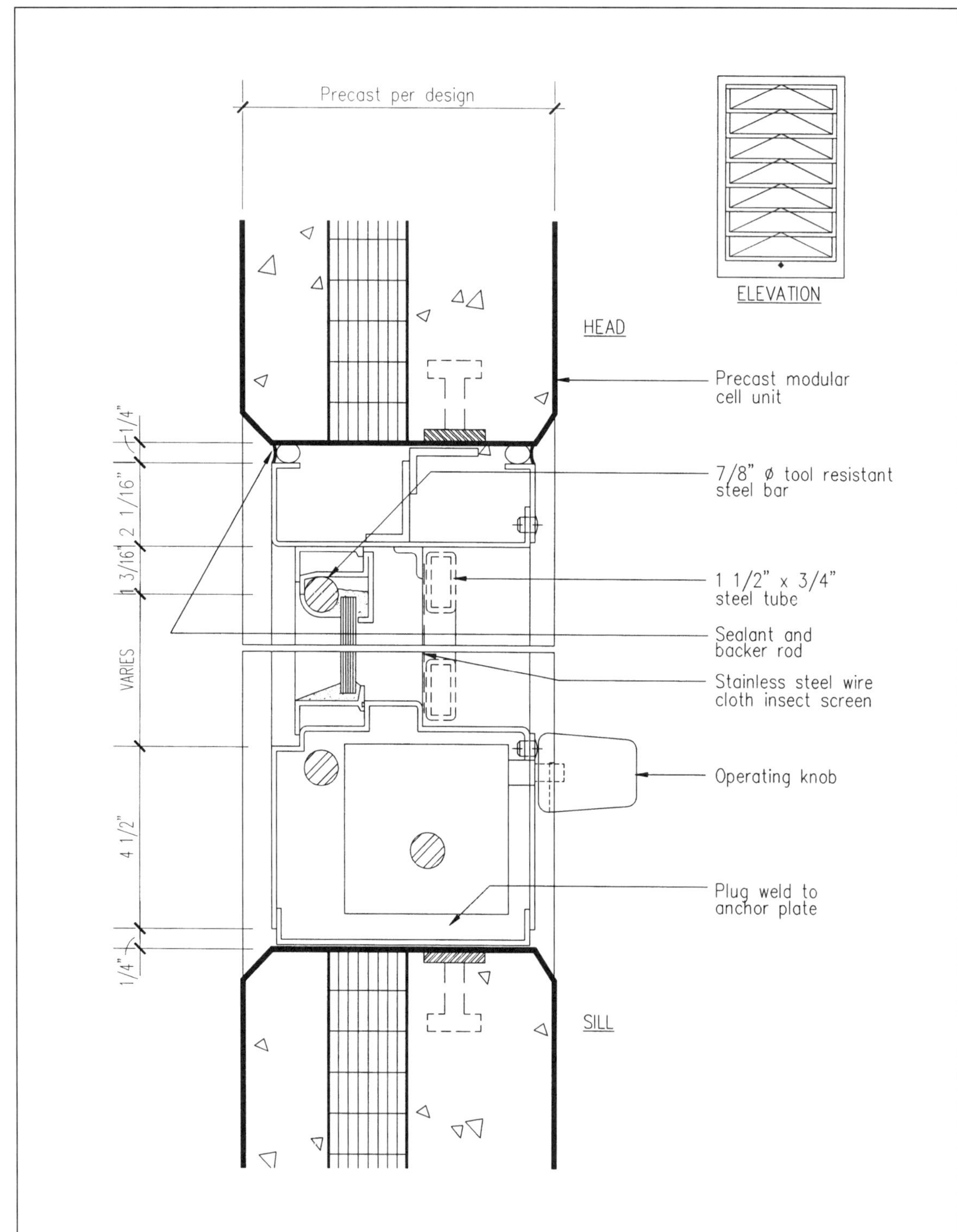

Figure 5.4.5 **Jalousie window.**

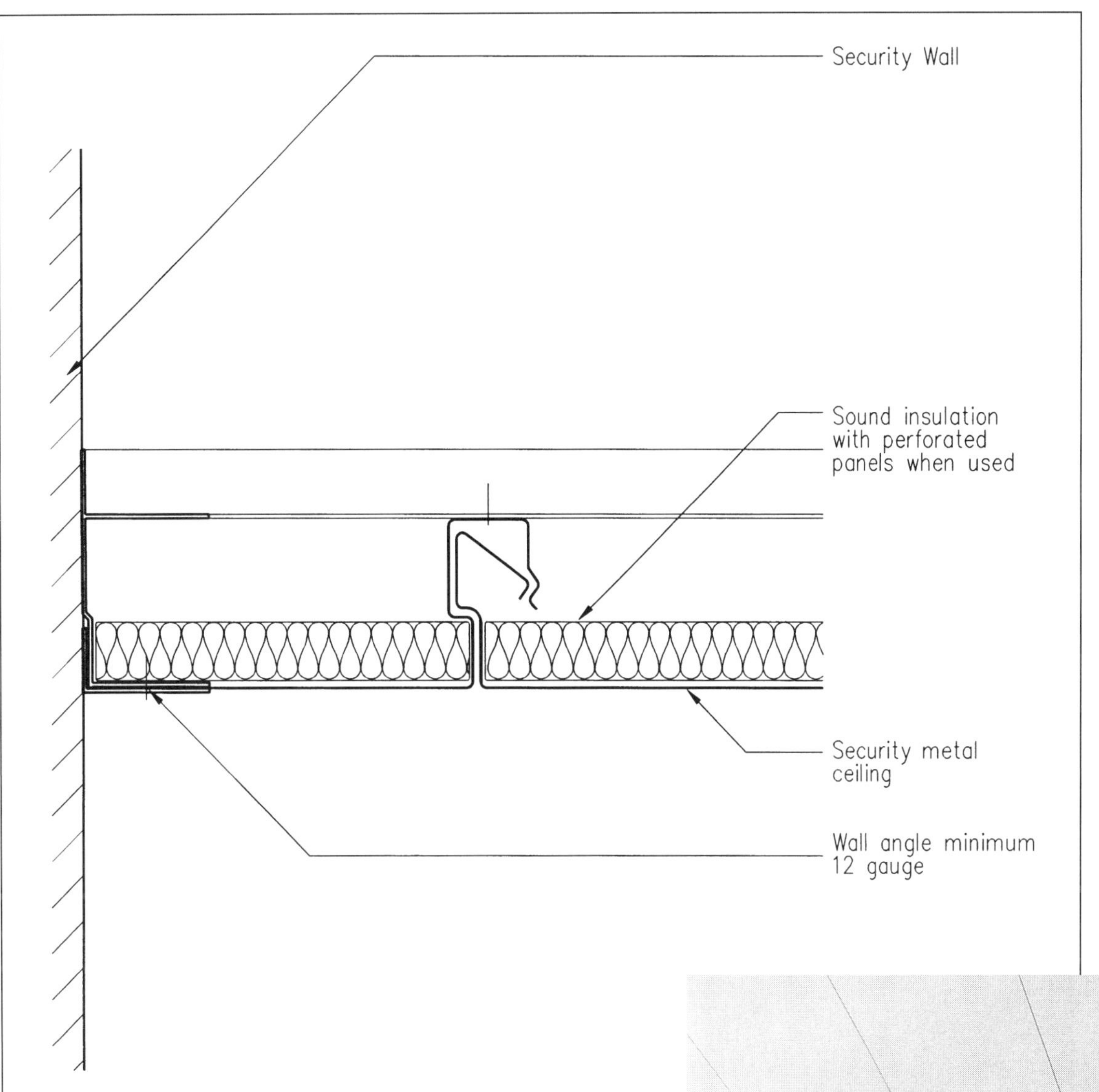

Figure 5.5.1 **Metal type.**

Shower compartment with suspended security metal ceiling.

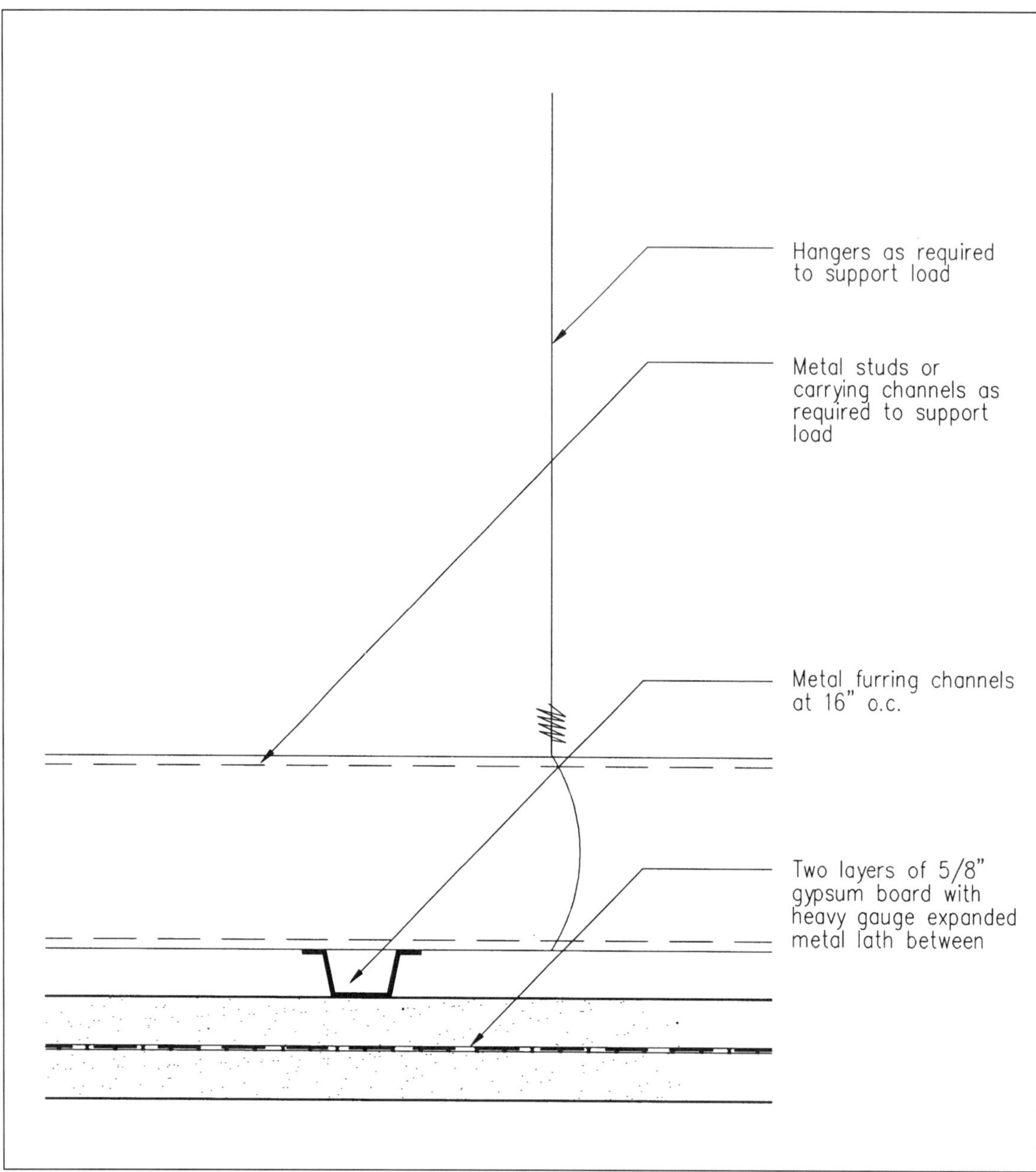

Figure 5.5.2 **Security gypsum board.**

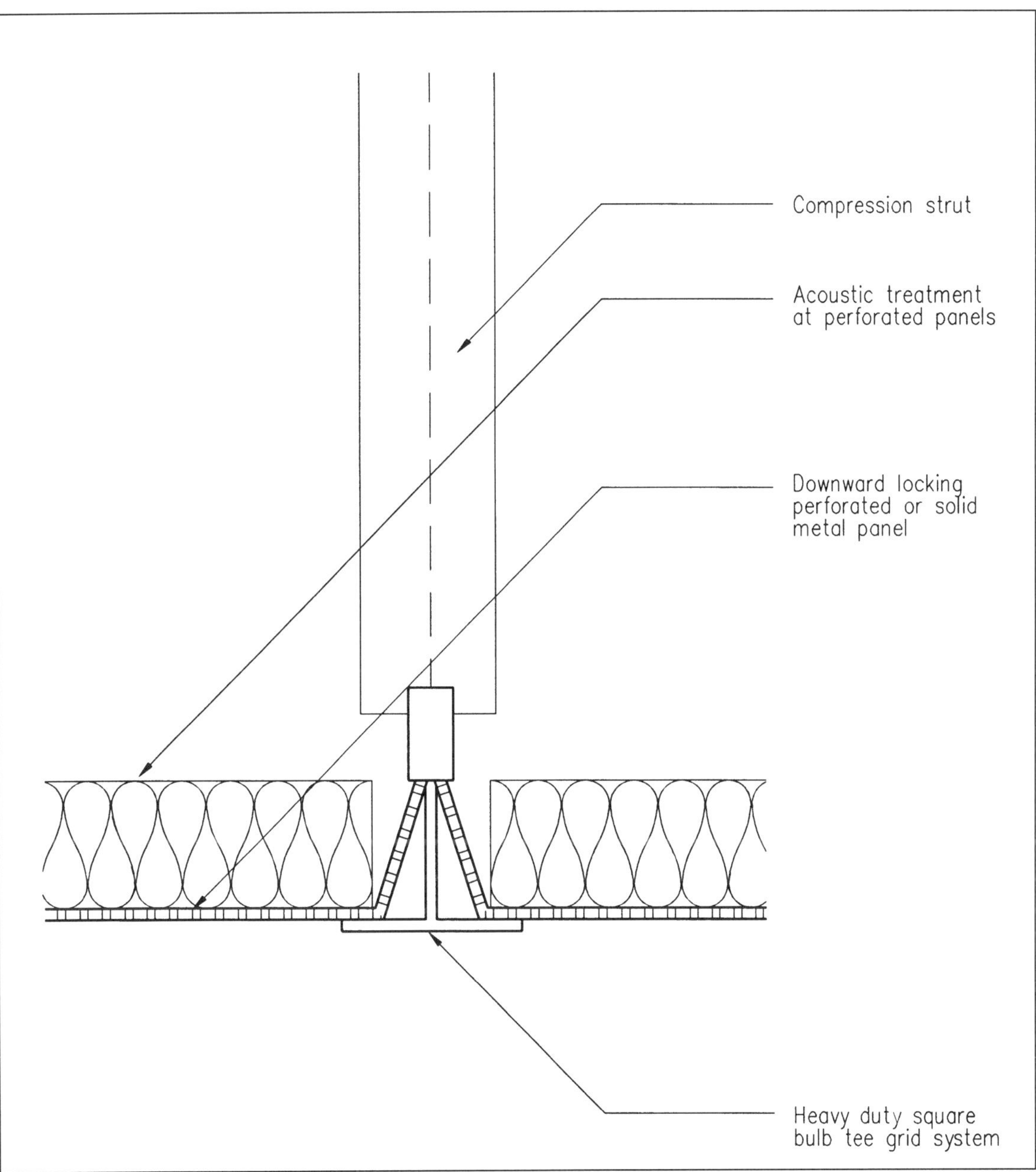

Figure 5.5.3 **Downward-locking metal panel.**

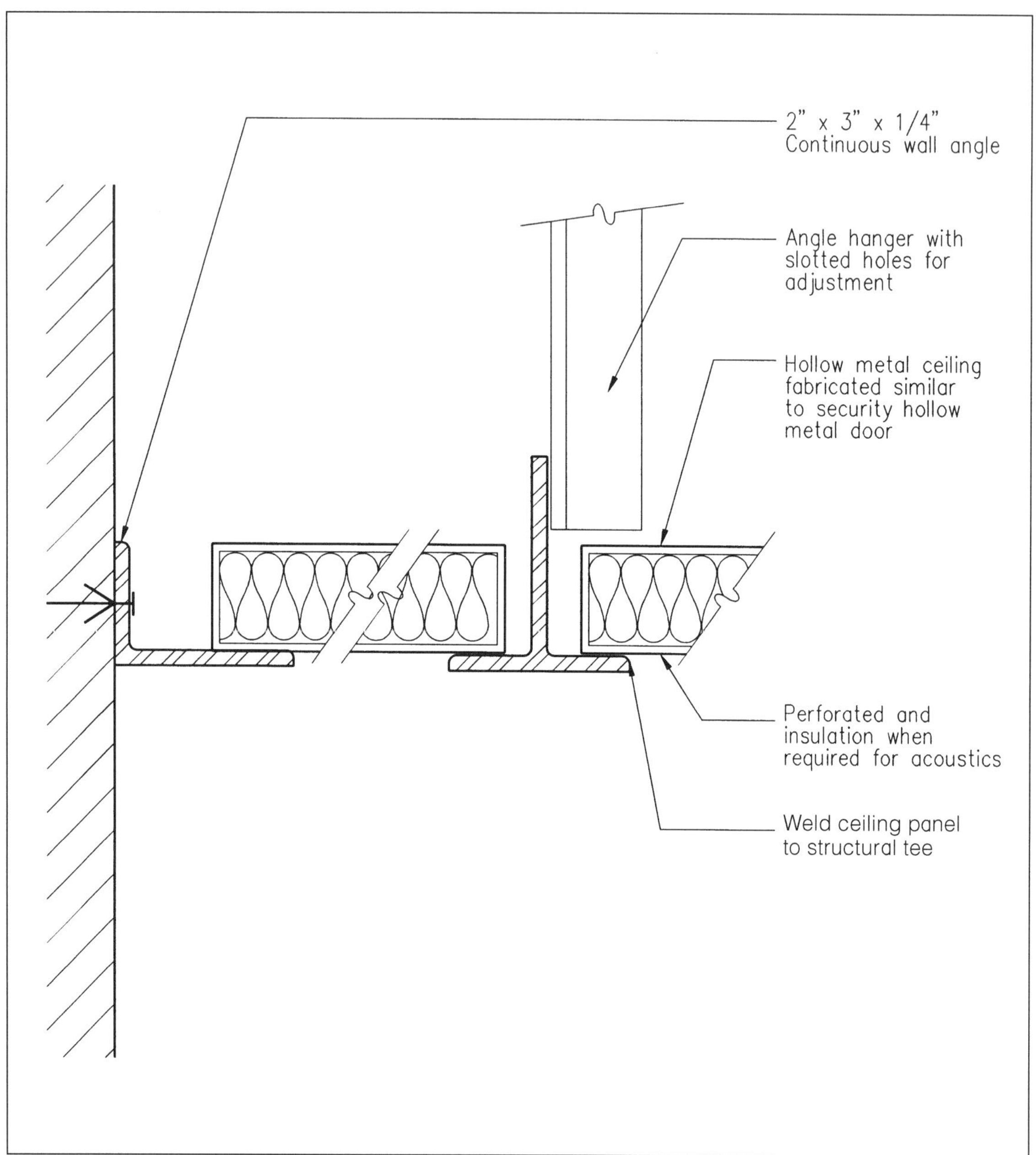

Figure 5.5.4 **Hollow metal type.**

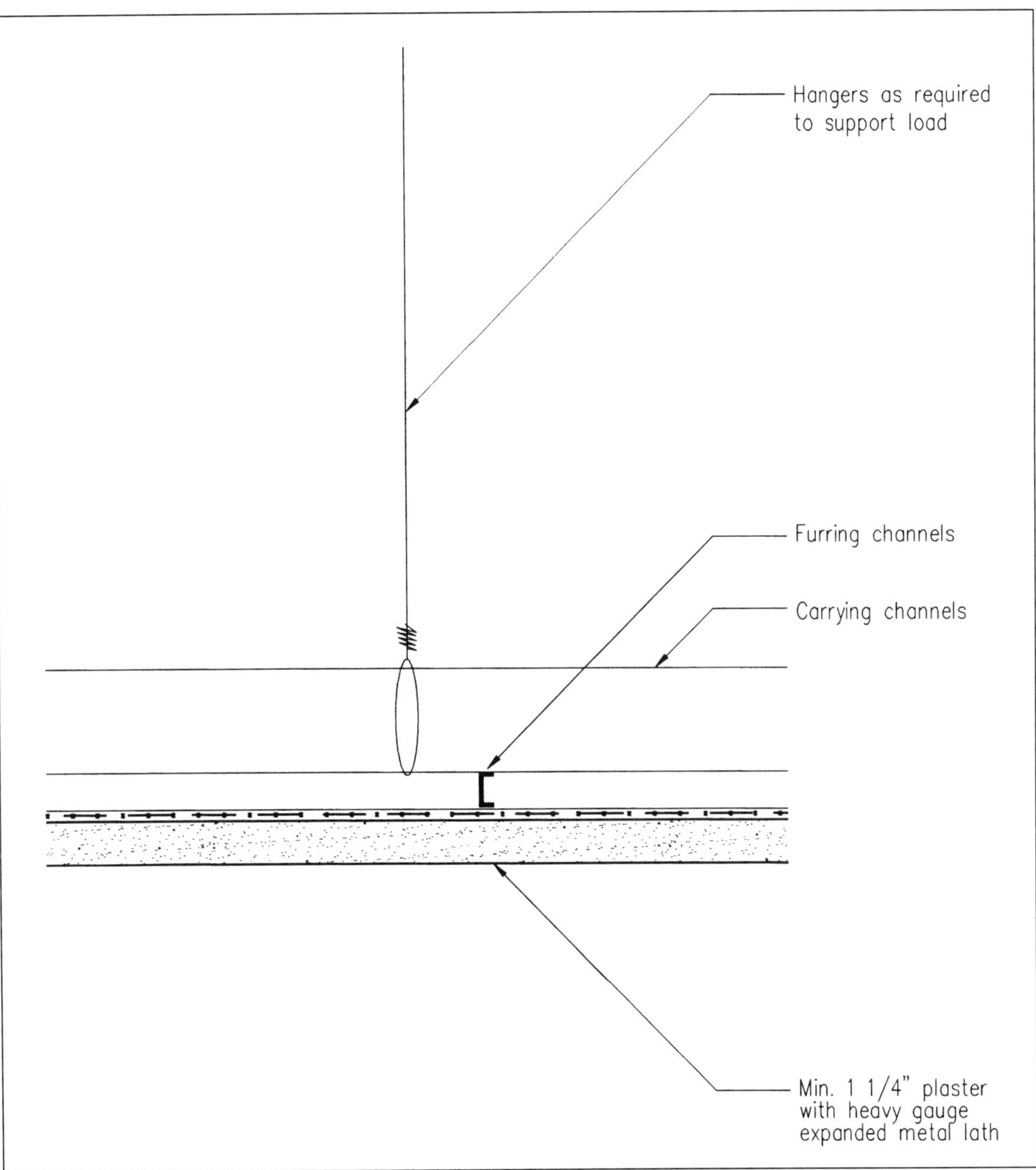

Figure 5.5.5 **Plaster type.**

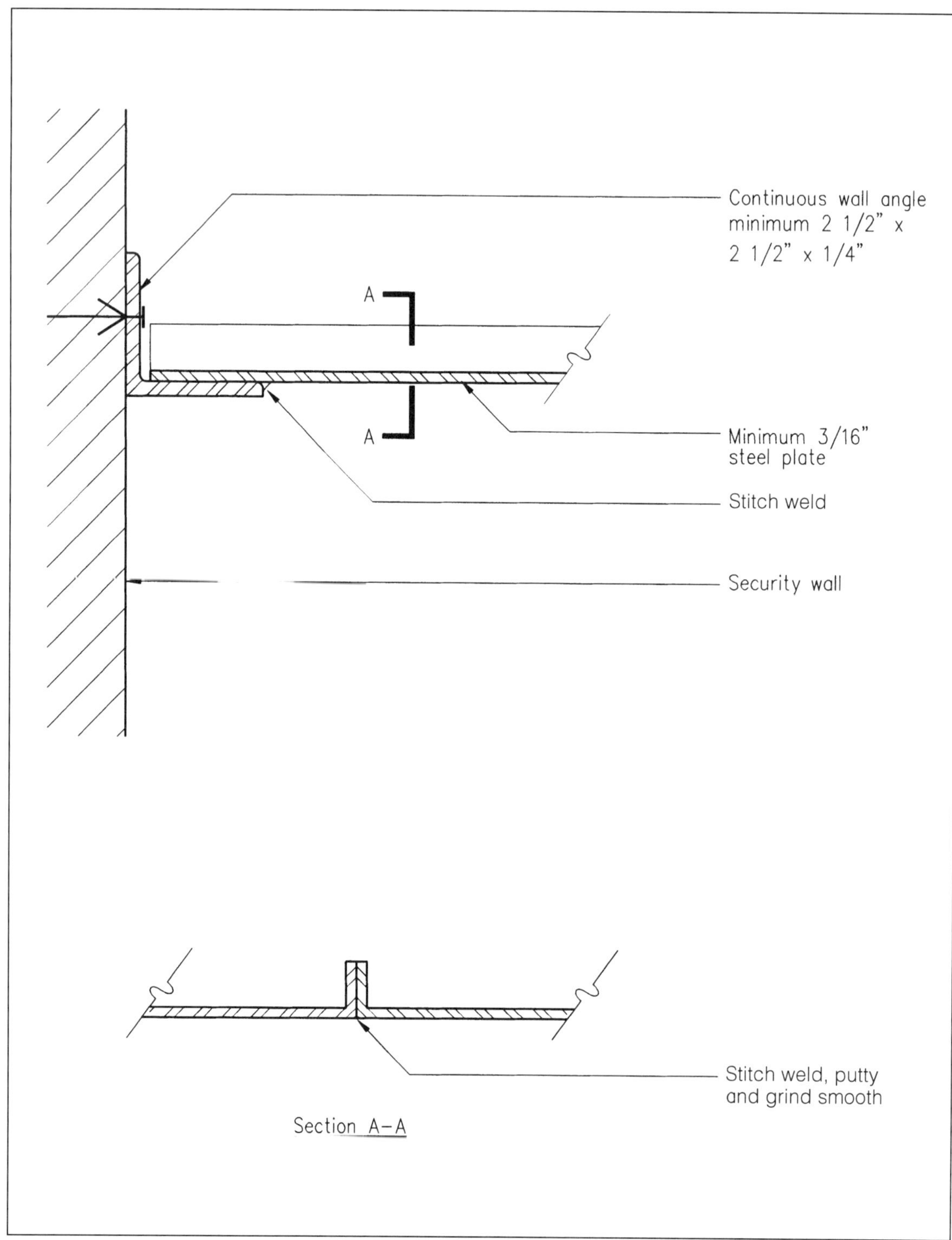

Figure 5.5.6 **Steel plate.**

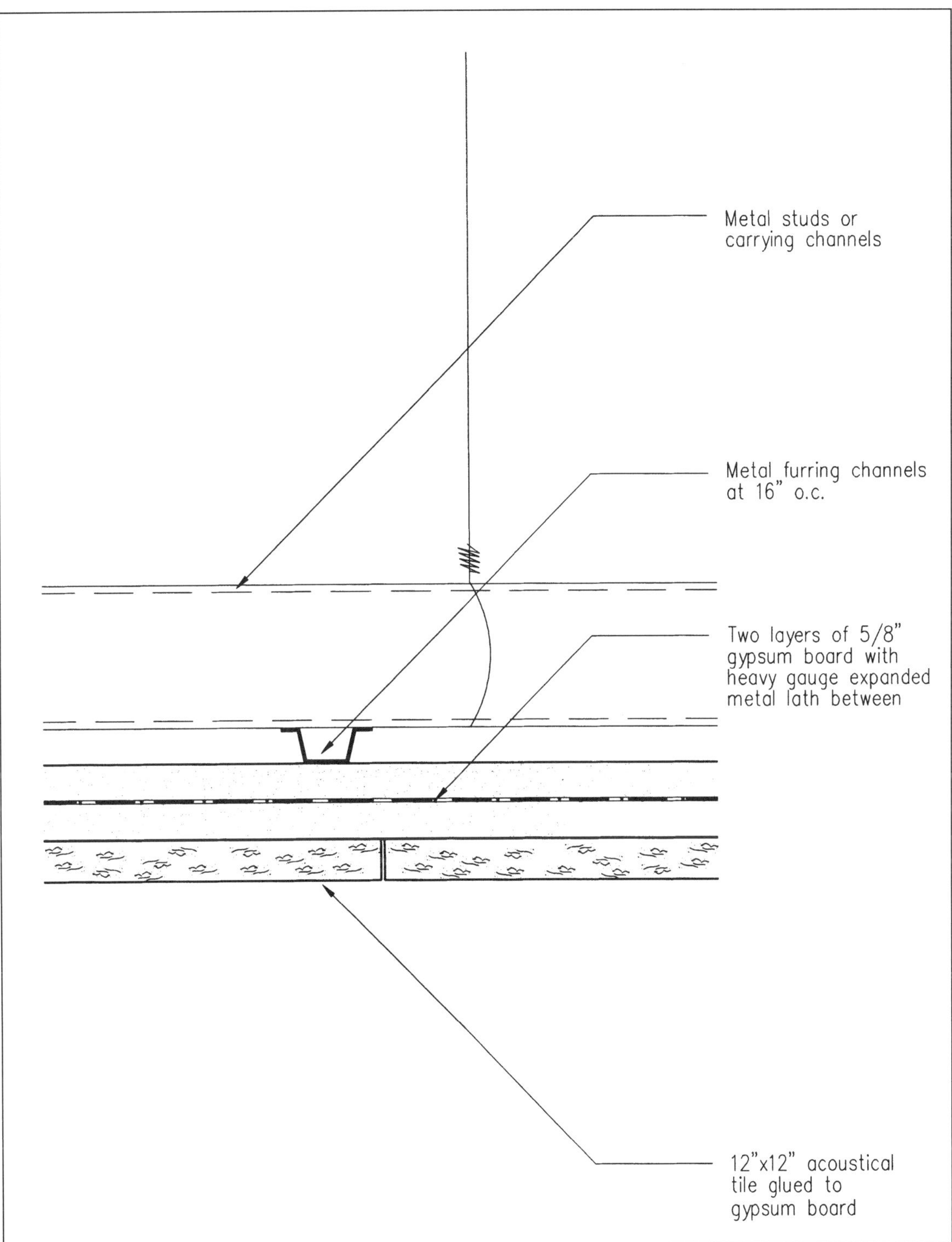

Figure 5.5.7 **Acoustical ceiling panels.**

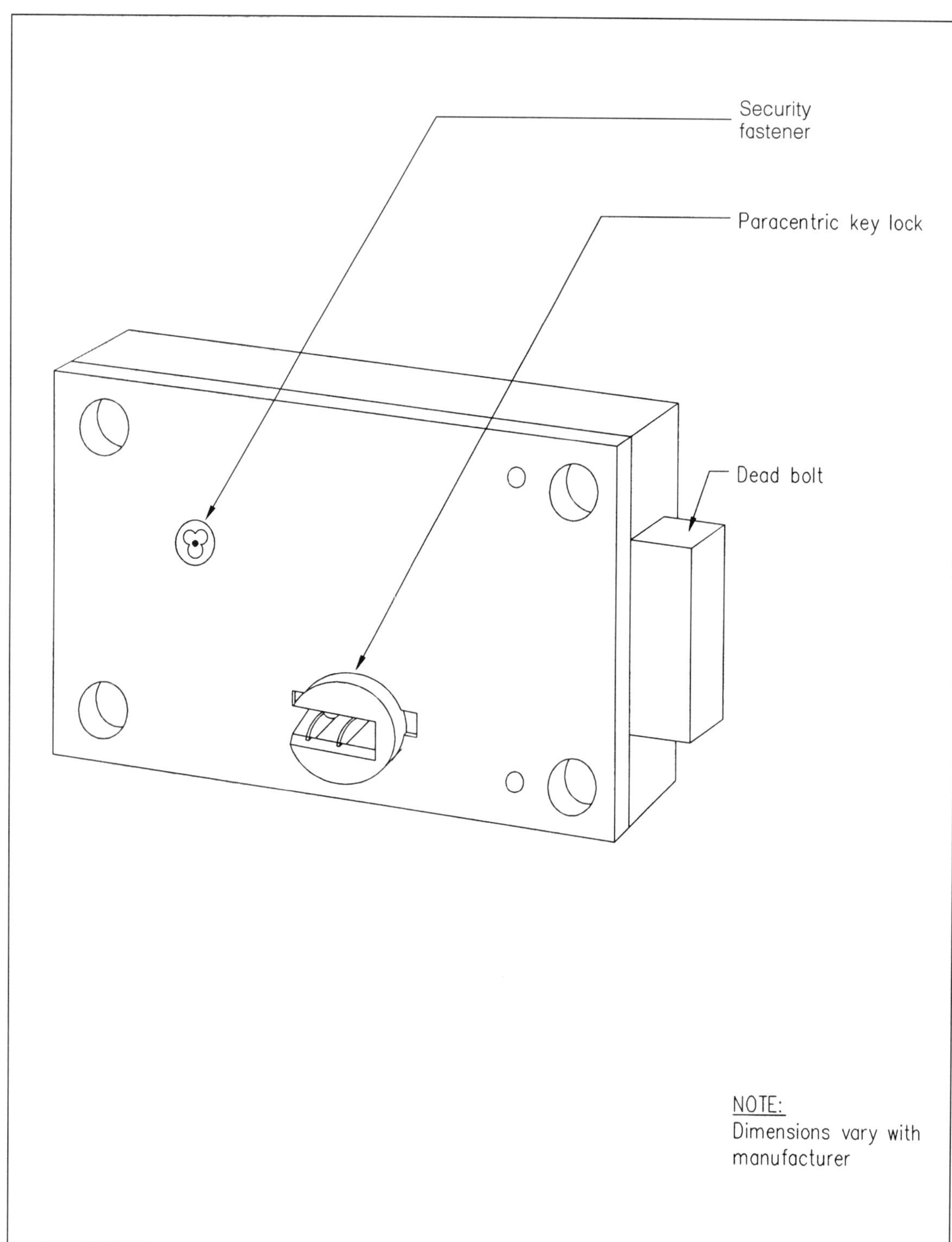

Figure 5.6.1 **Mechanical–typical type.**

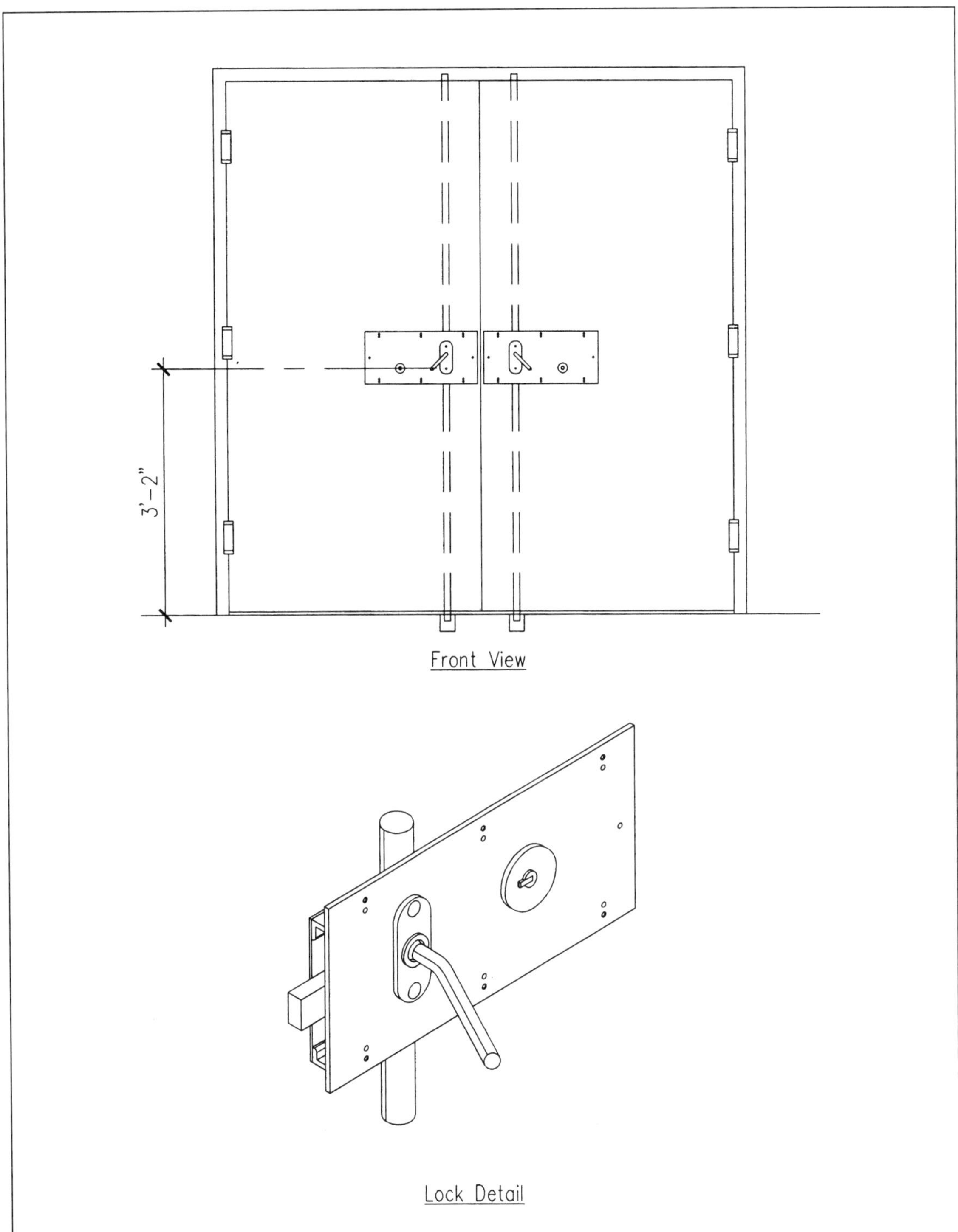

Figure 5.6.2 **Mechanical–Cremone type.**

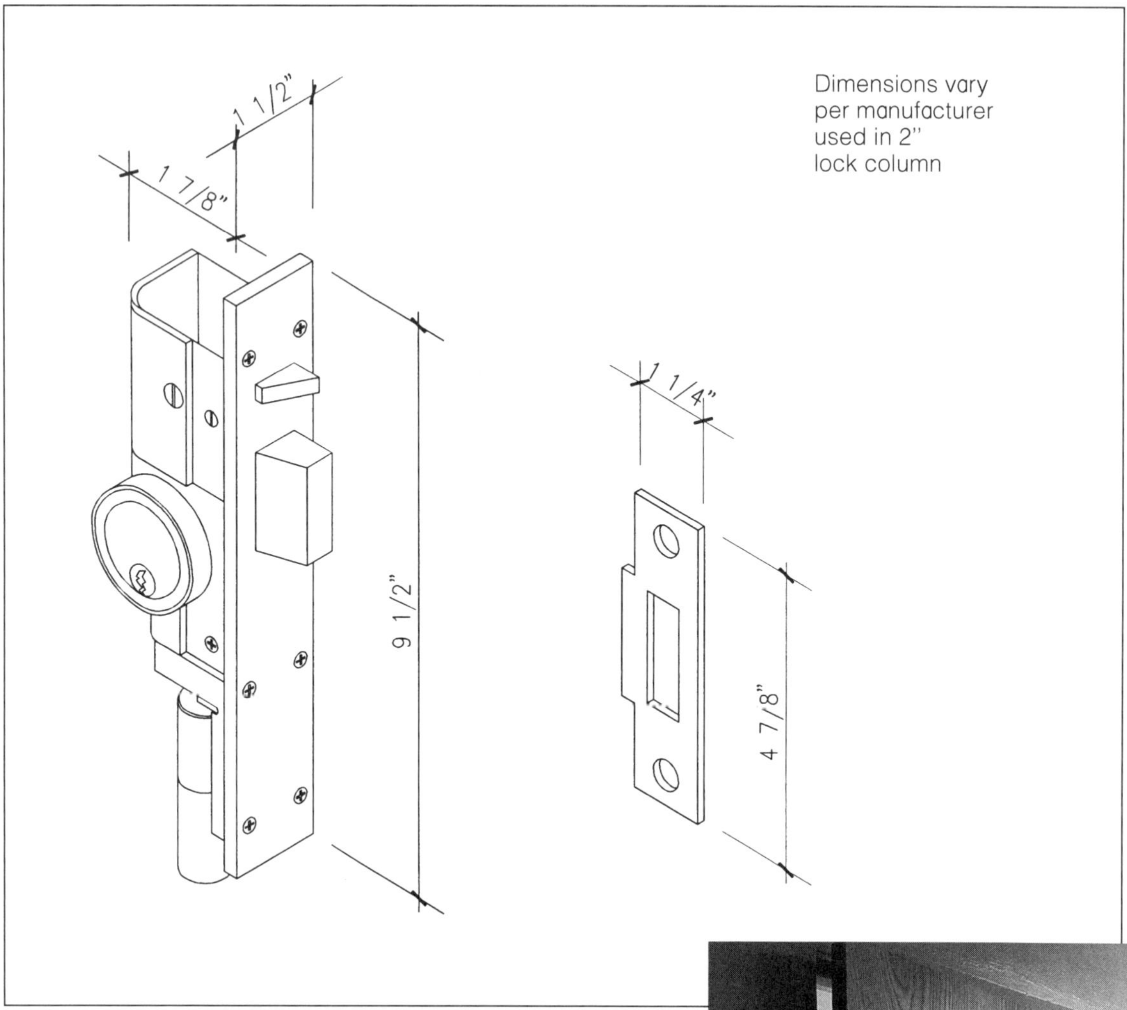

Dimensions vary per manufacturer used in 2" lock column

1 1/2"

1 7/8"

9 1/2"

1 1/4"

4 7/8"

Figure 5.6.3 **Electric–minimum security.**

Inmate wood cell door with vision panel assembly with speak-through panel.

Inmate cell door, 8-inch jamb lock with door pull and security-type control switch for inmate cell light.

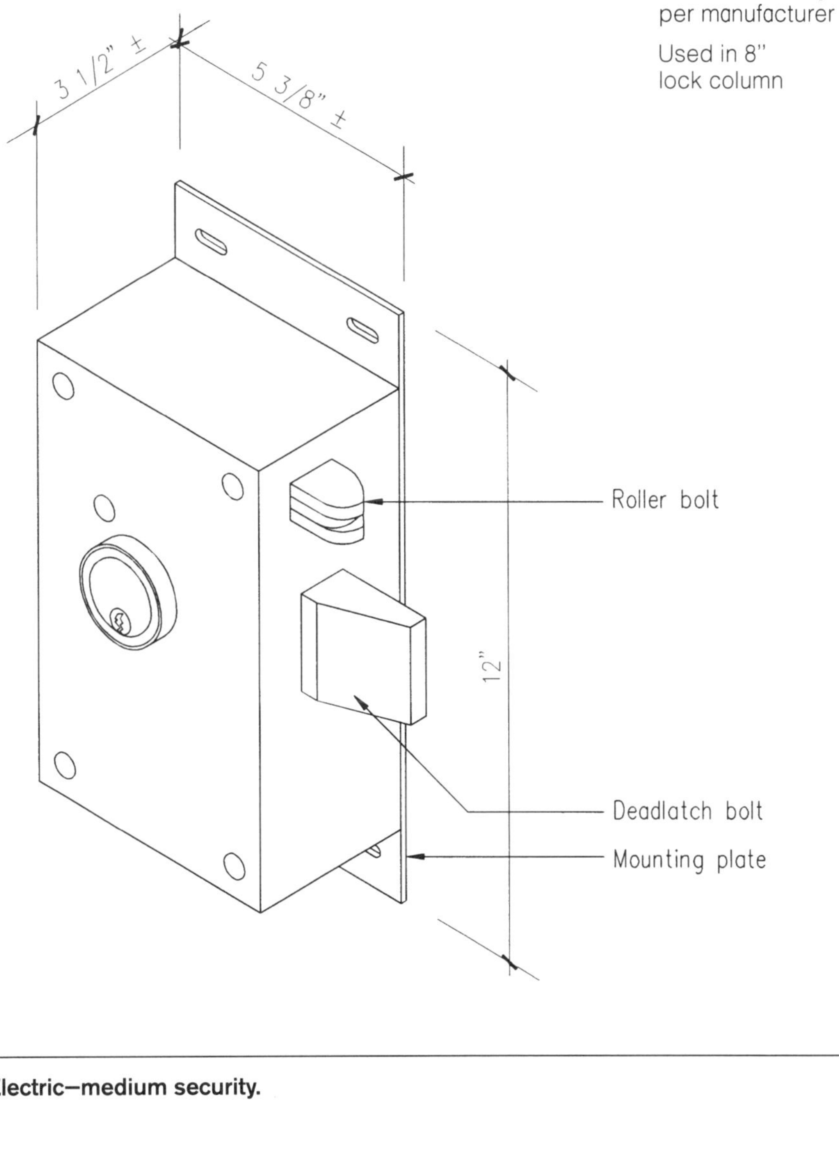

Dimensions vary per manufacturer

Used in 8" lock column

3 1/2" ±

5 3/8" ±

12"

Roller bolt

Deadlatch bolt

Mounting plate

Figure 5.6.4 **Electric—medium security.**

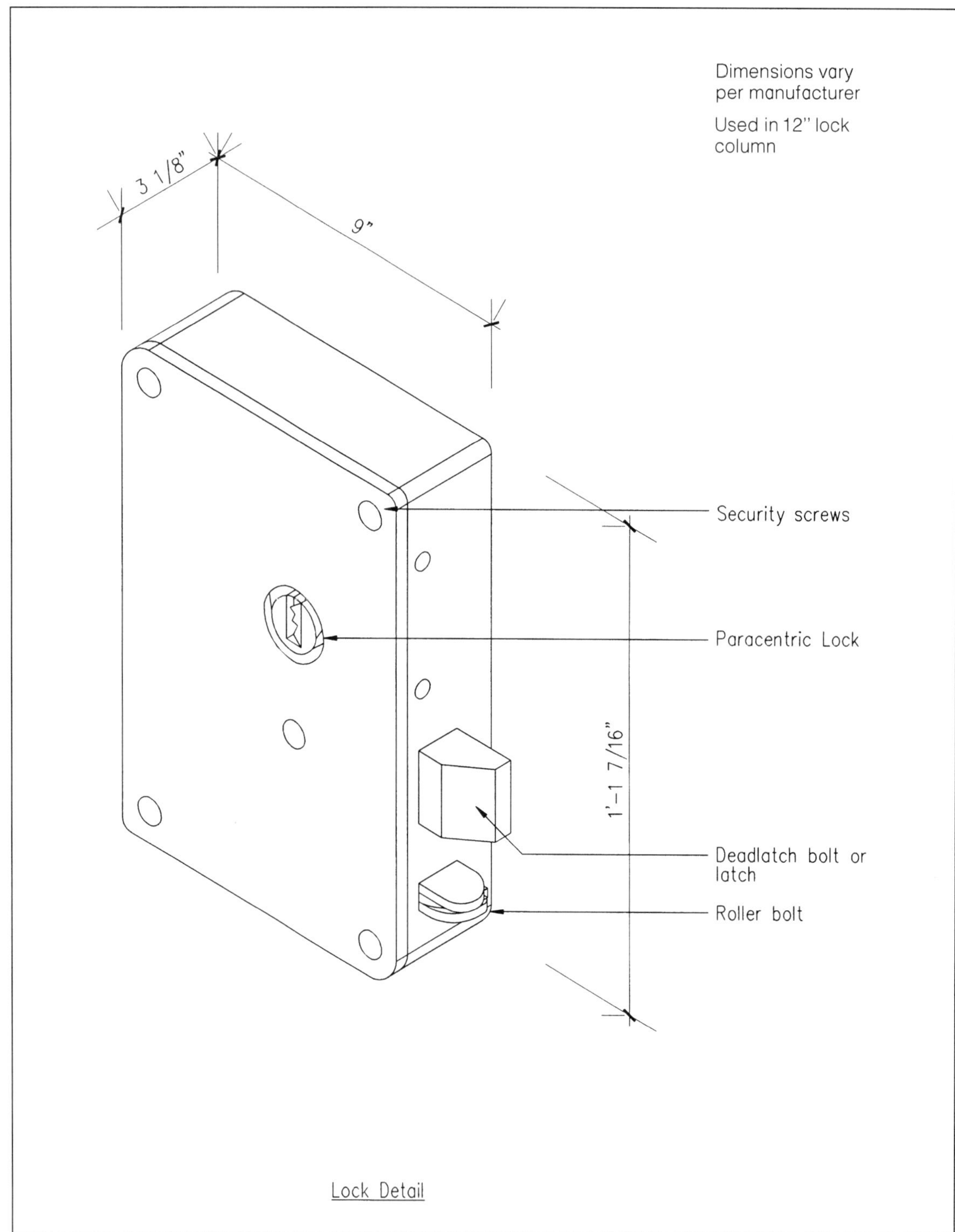

Figure 5.6.5 **Electric—maximum security.**

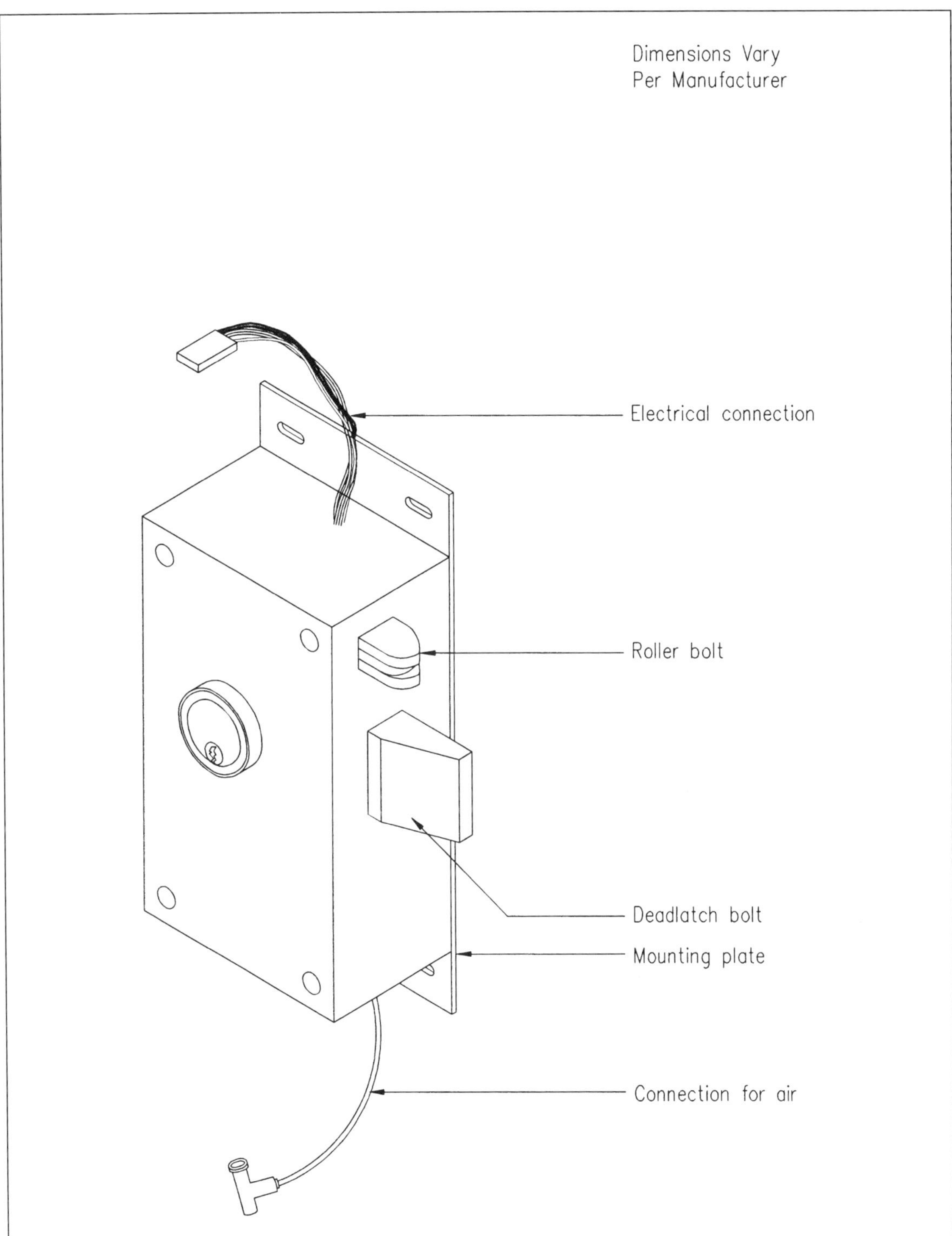

Figure 5.6.6 **Pneumatic type.**

Inmate cell interior with bed, desk, stool, combination toilet/lavatory, mirror, light fixture, and exterior window.

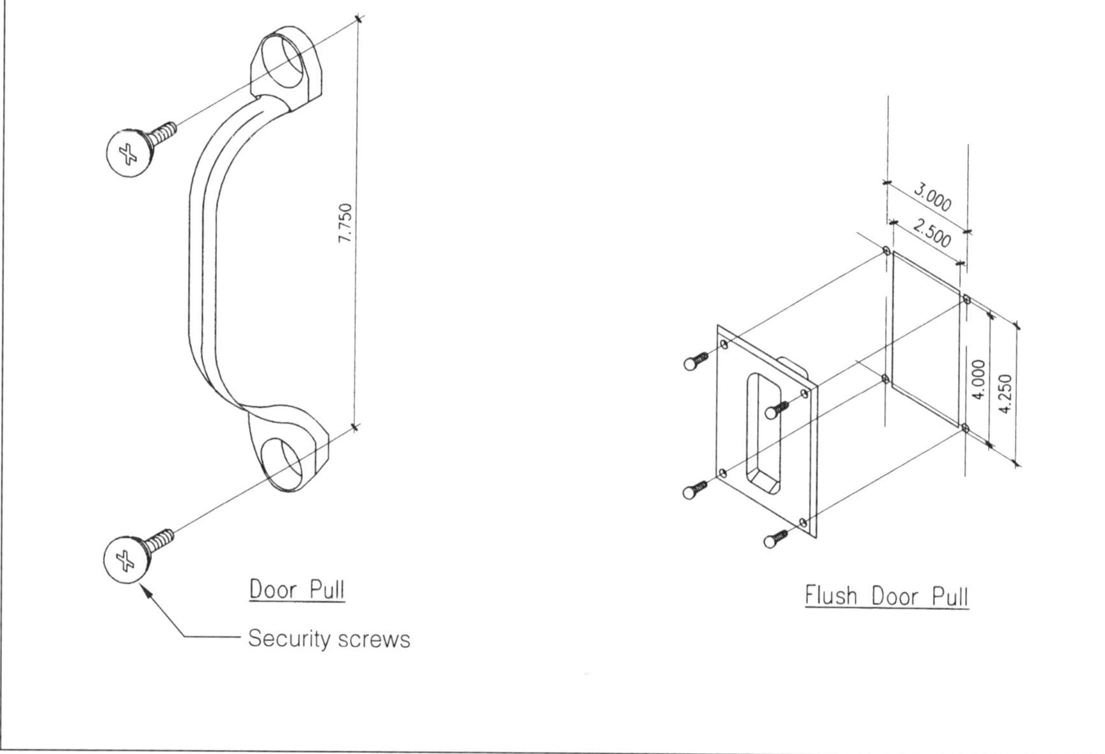

Figure 5.6.7 **Security door pulls.**

Inmate cell door position switch.

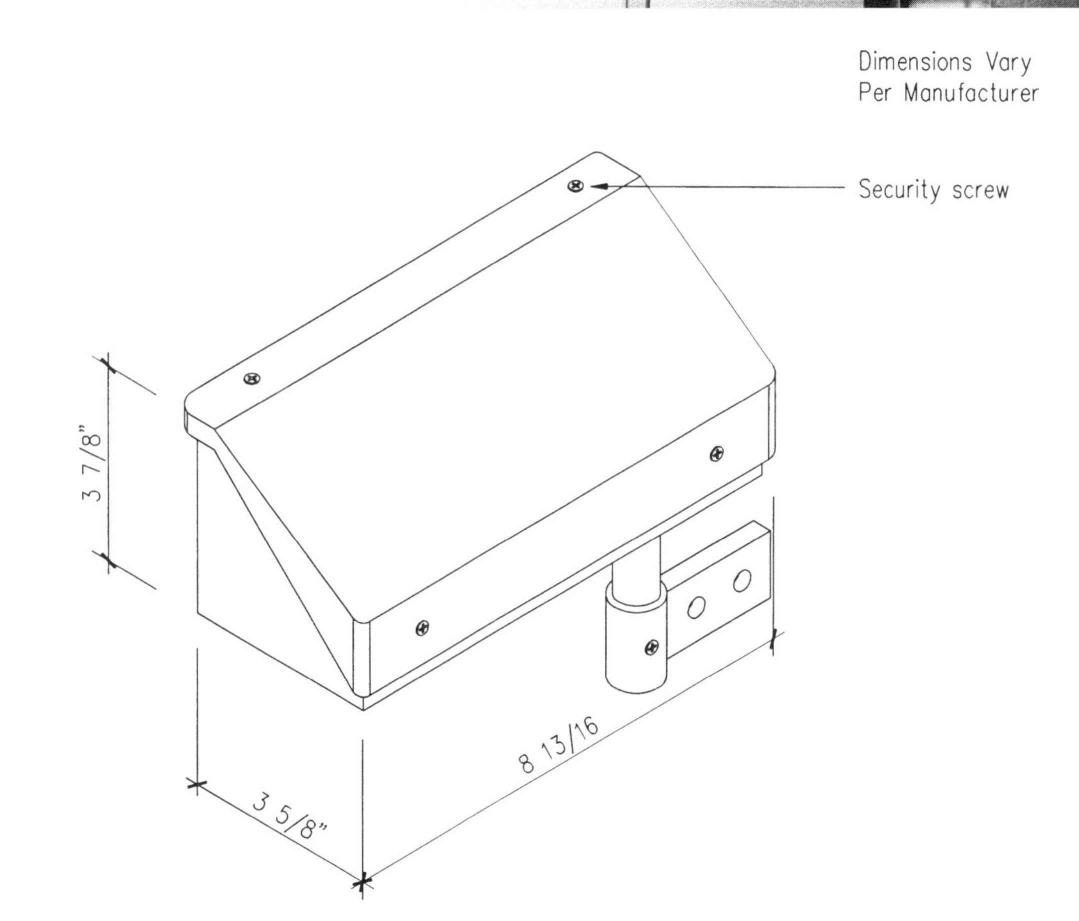

Figure 5.6.8 **Door position switch (DPS)—surface mounted.**

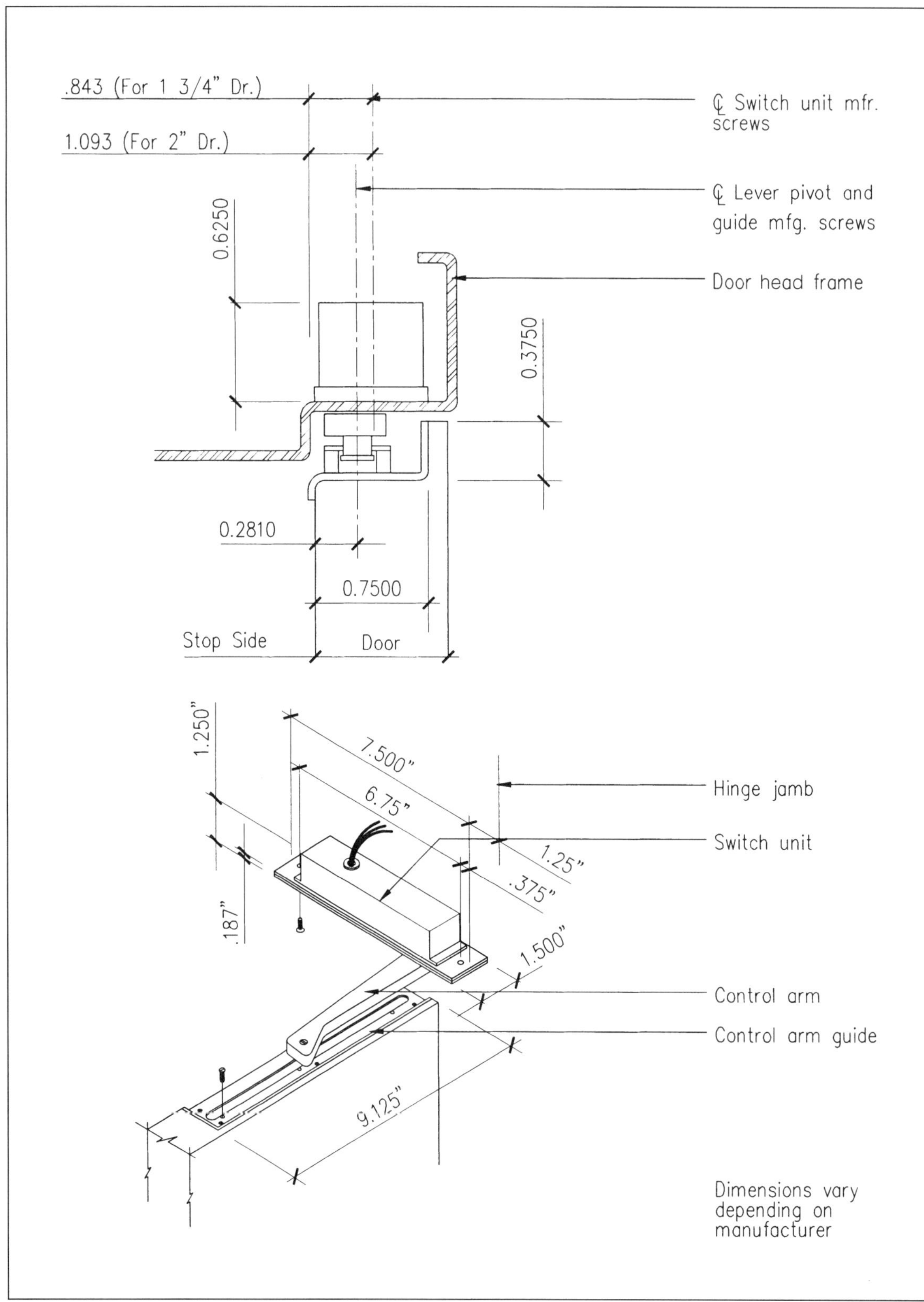

Figure 5.6.9 **Door position switch (DPS)—concealed.**

Inmate cell wood door with strike, 2″ jamb lock, door pull, and vision panel.

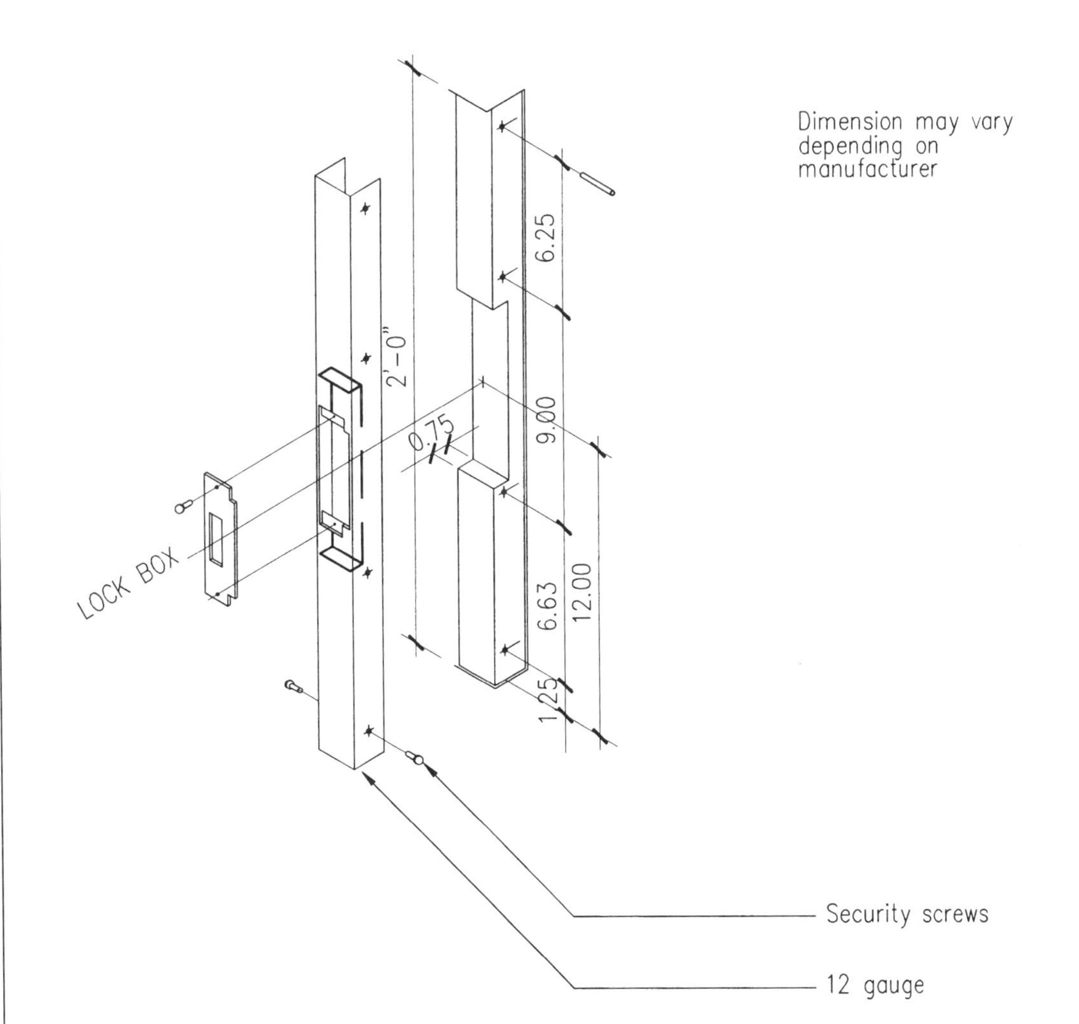

Figure 5.6.10 **Wood door strike reinforcement.**

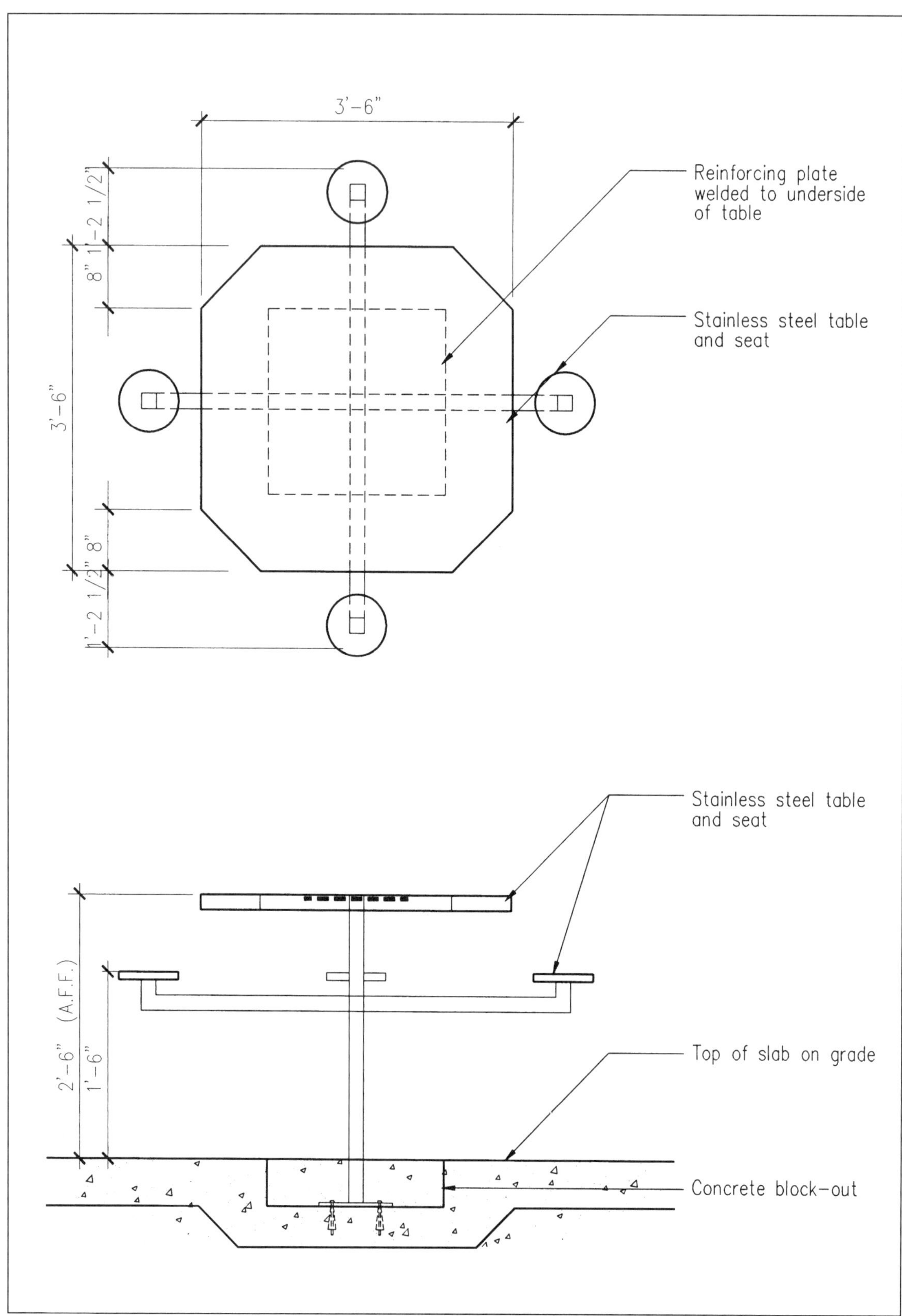

Figure 5.7.1 **Built-in dining table and stools, single pedestal.**

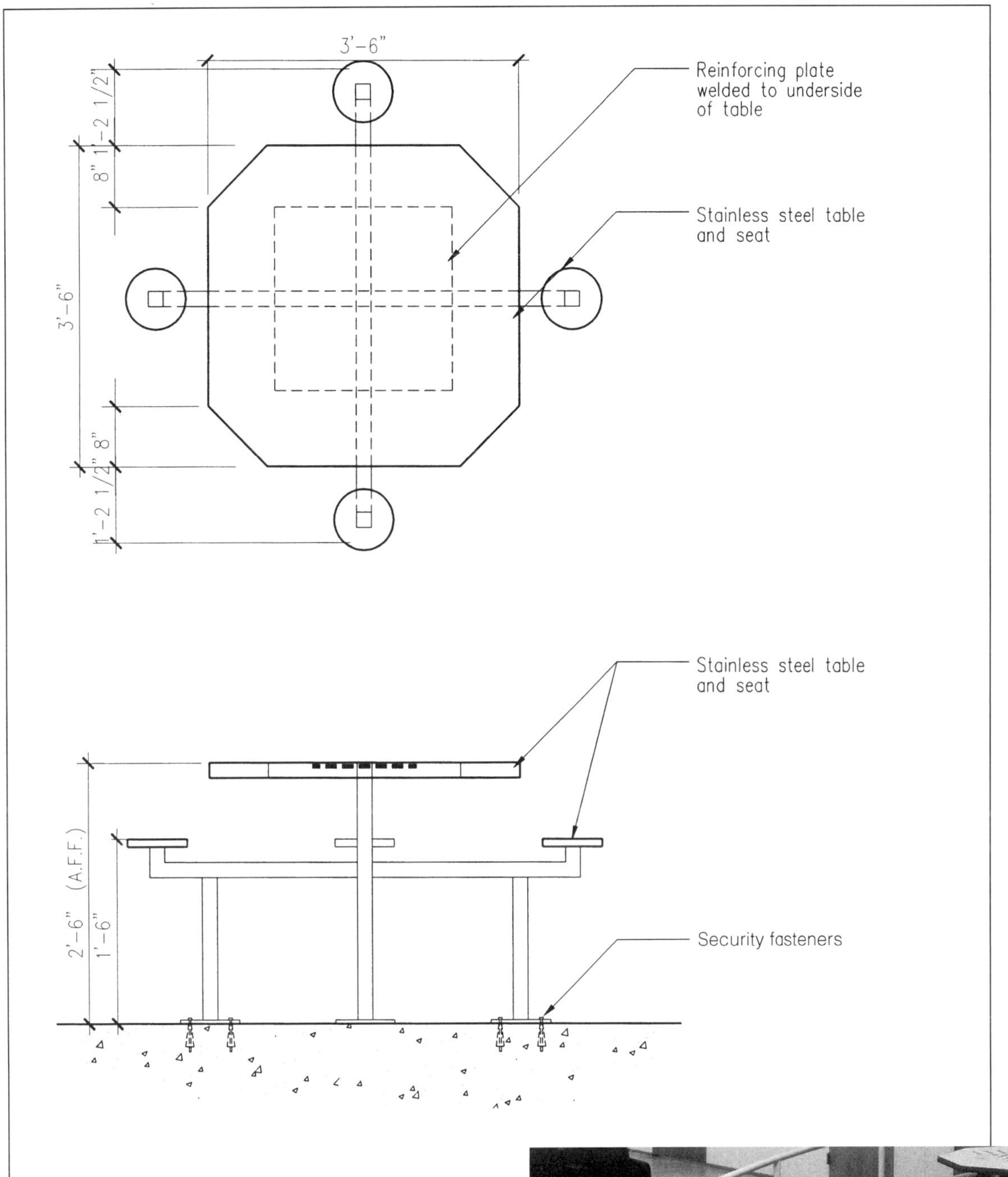

Figure 5.7.2 **Built-in dining table and stools, multiple supports.**

Dayroom dining tables with fixed stools.

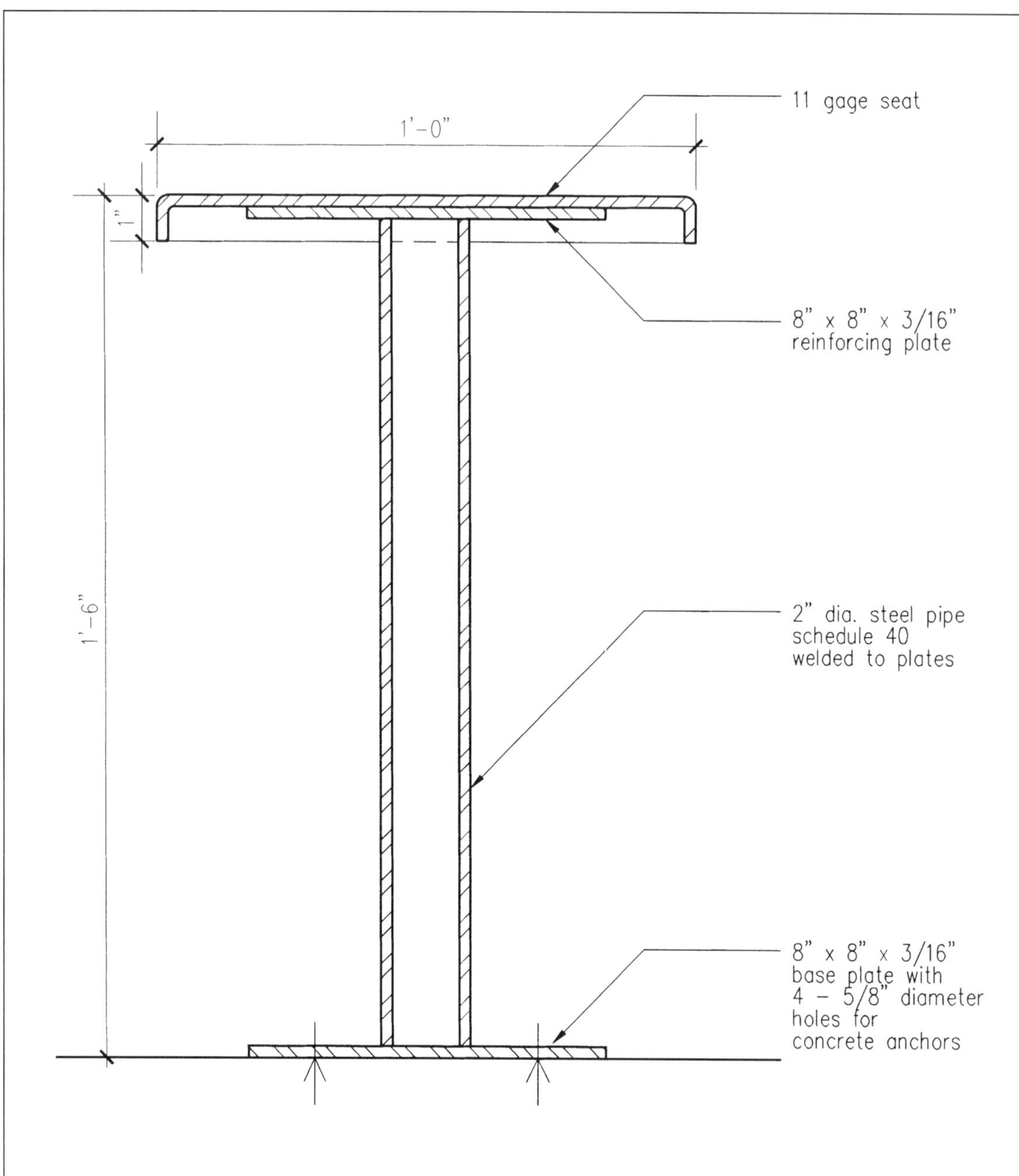

Figure 5.7.3 **Built-in stool.**

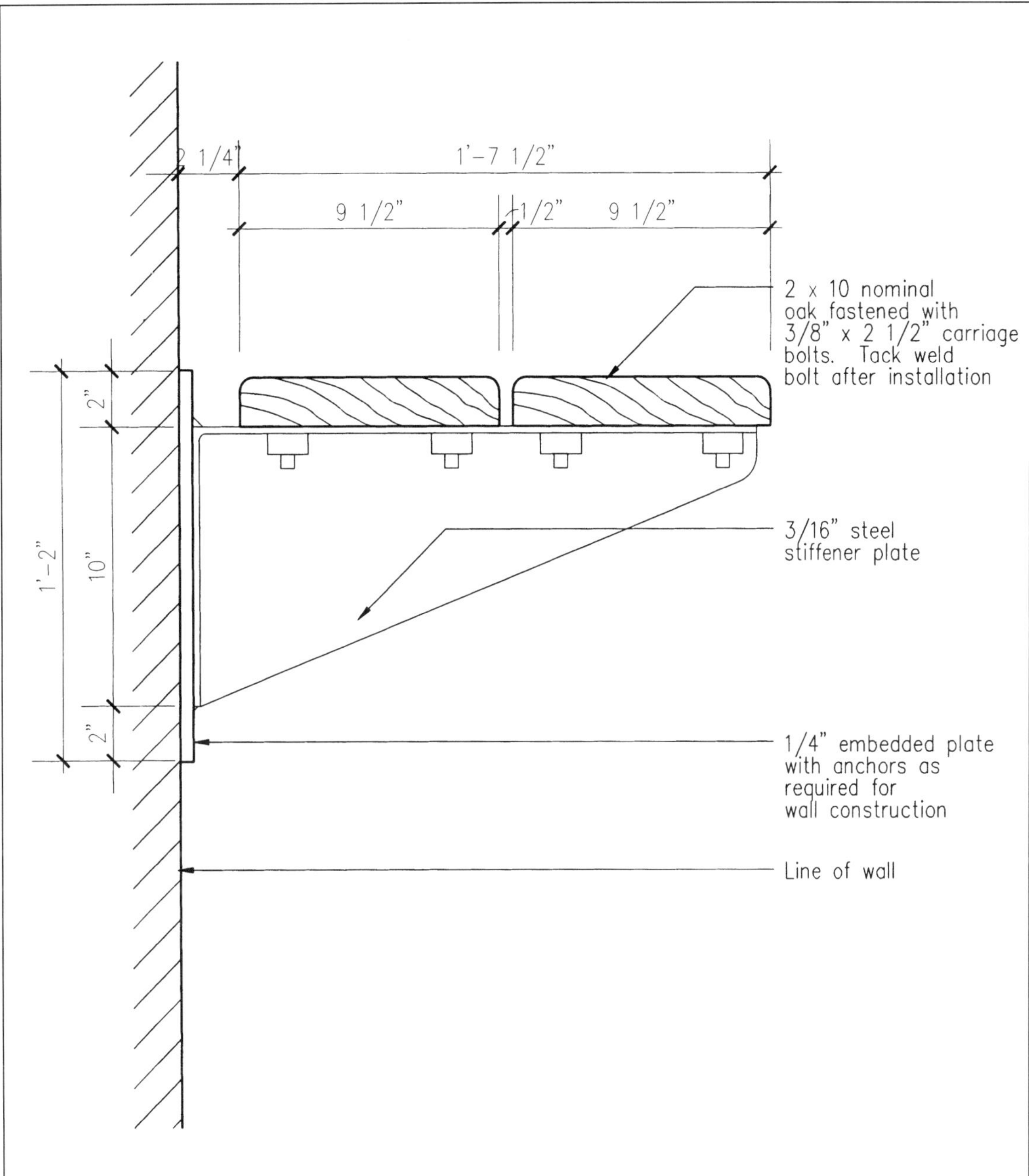

Figure 5.7.4 **Built-in wood bench.**

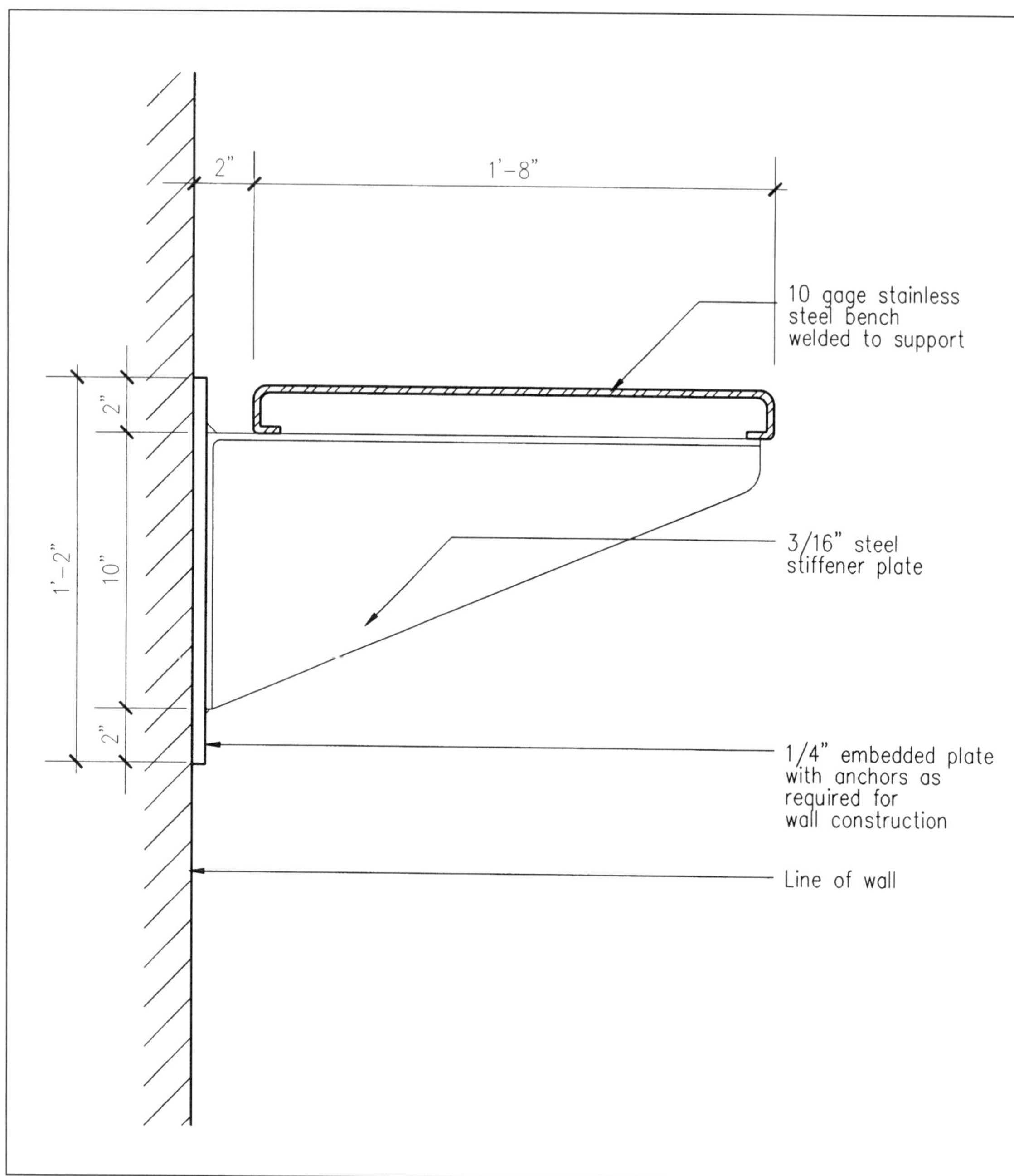

Figure 5.7.5 **Built-in steel bench.**

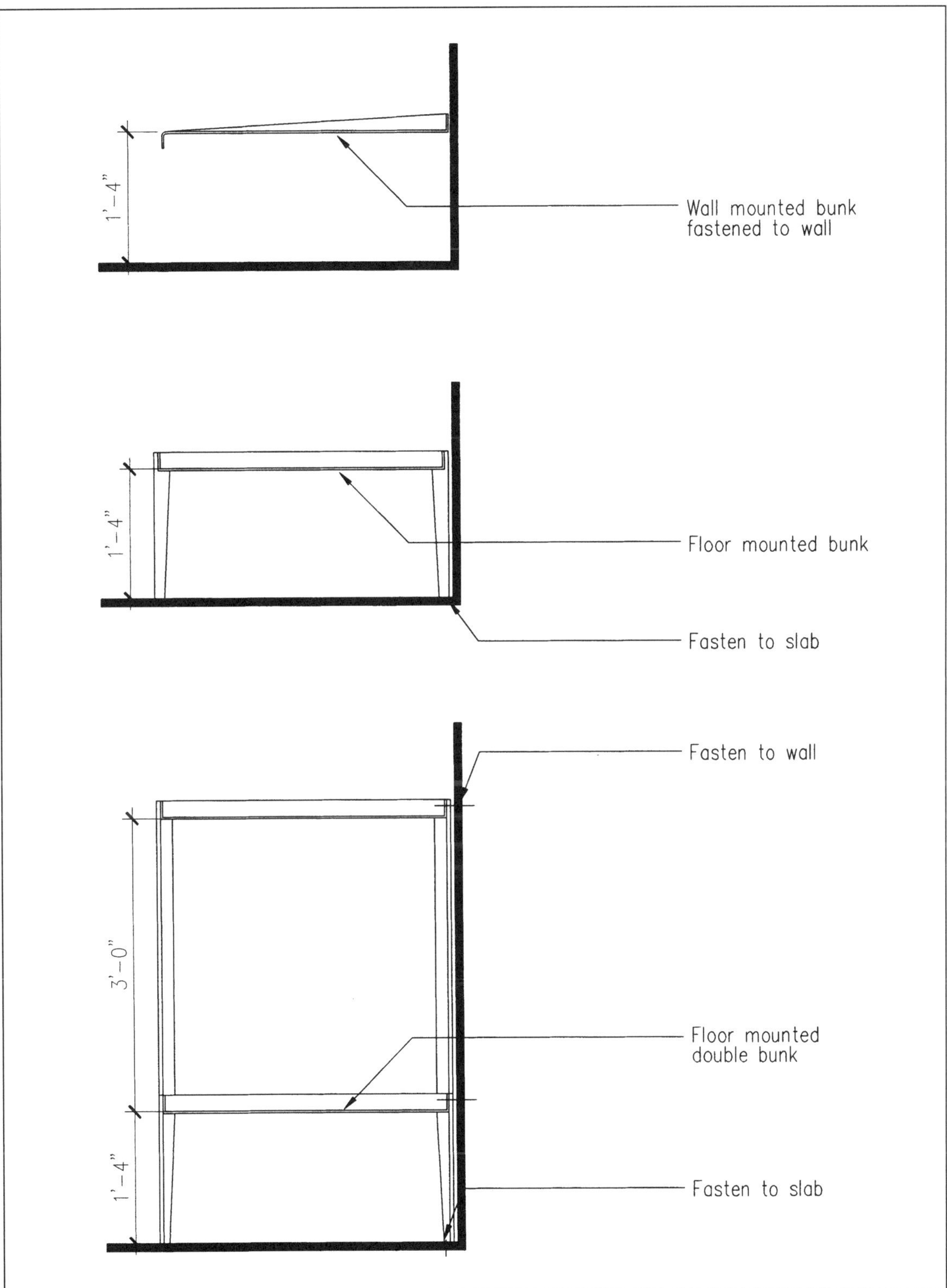

Figure 5.7.6 **Inmate cell bunks.**

Cell painted steel desk and fixed stool.

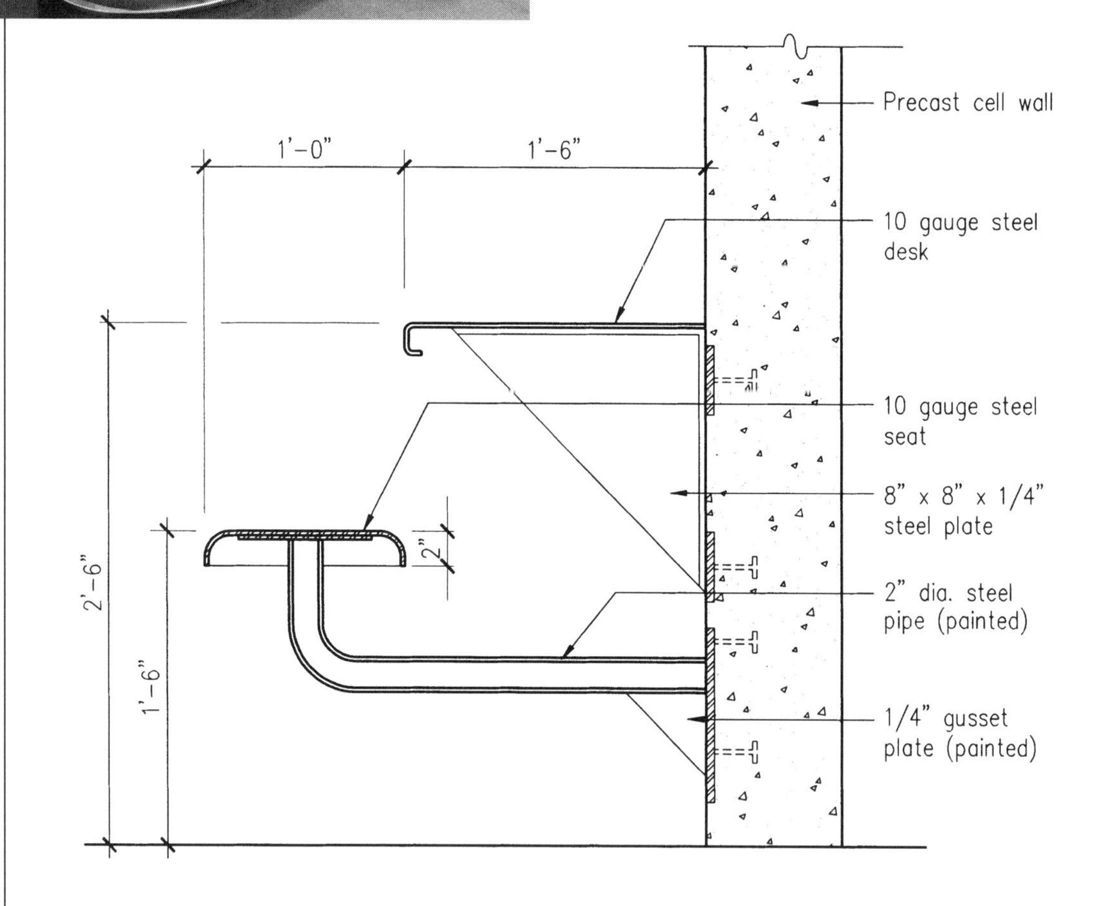

Figure 5.7.7 **Inmate cell steel desk and stool.**

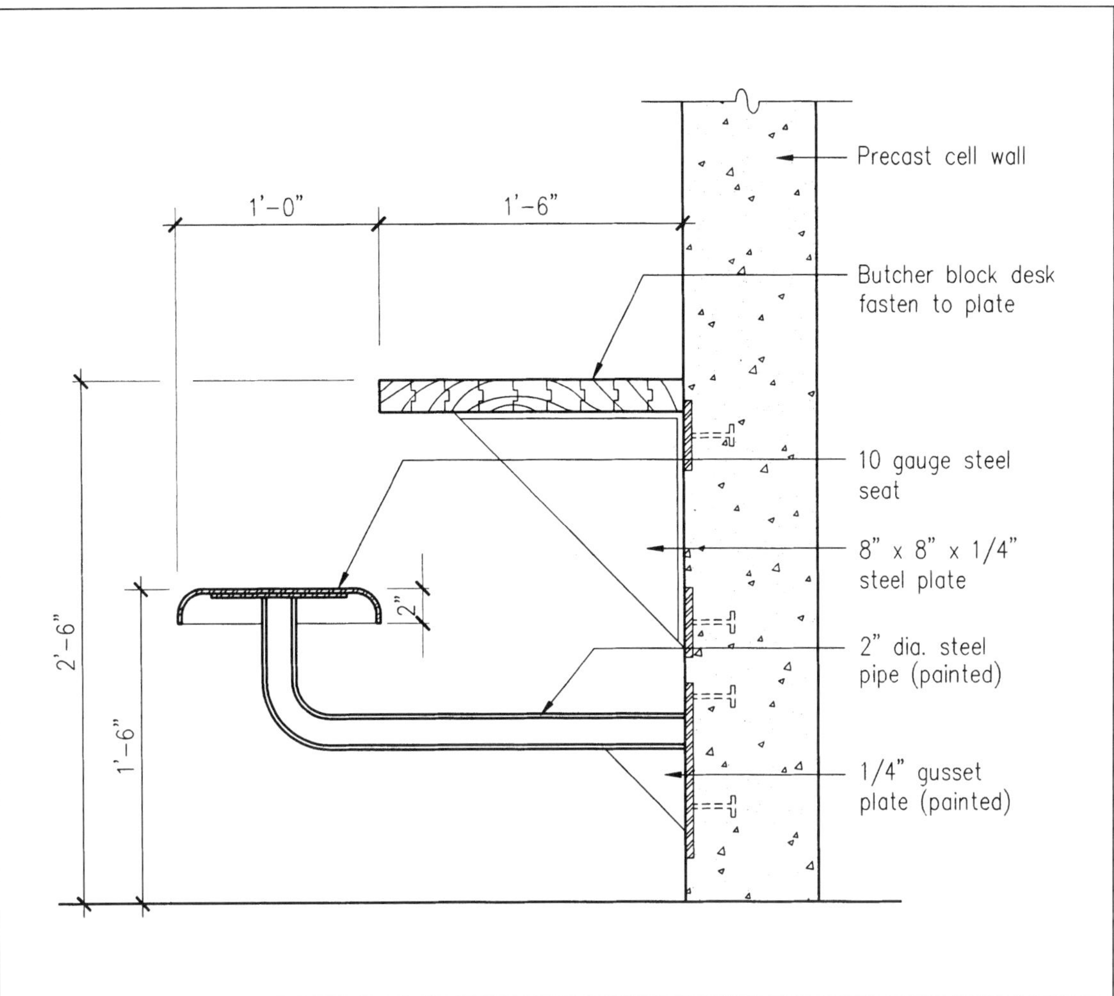

Figure 5.7.8 **Inmate cell wood desk and stool.**

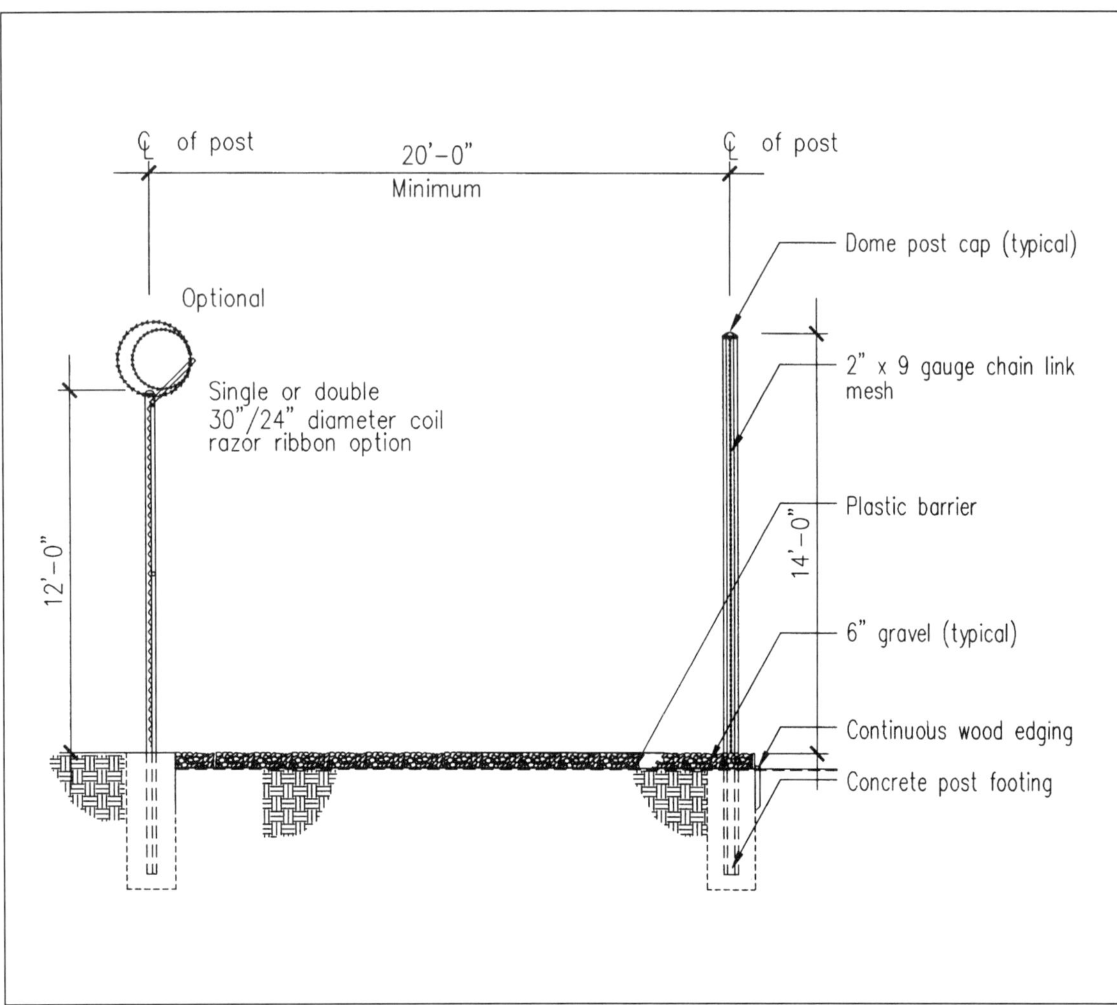

Figure 5.8.1 **Minimum-security configuration section.**

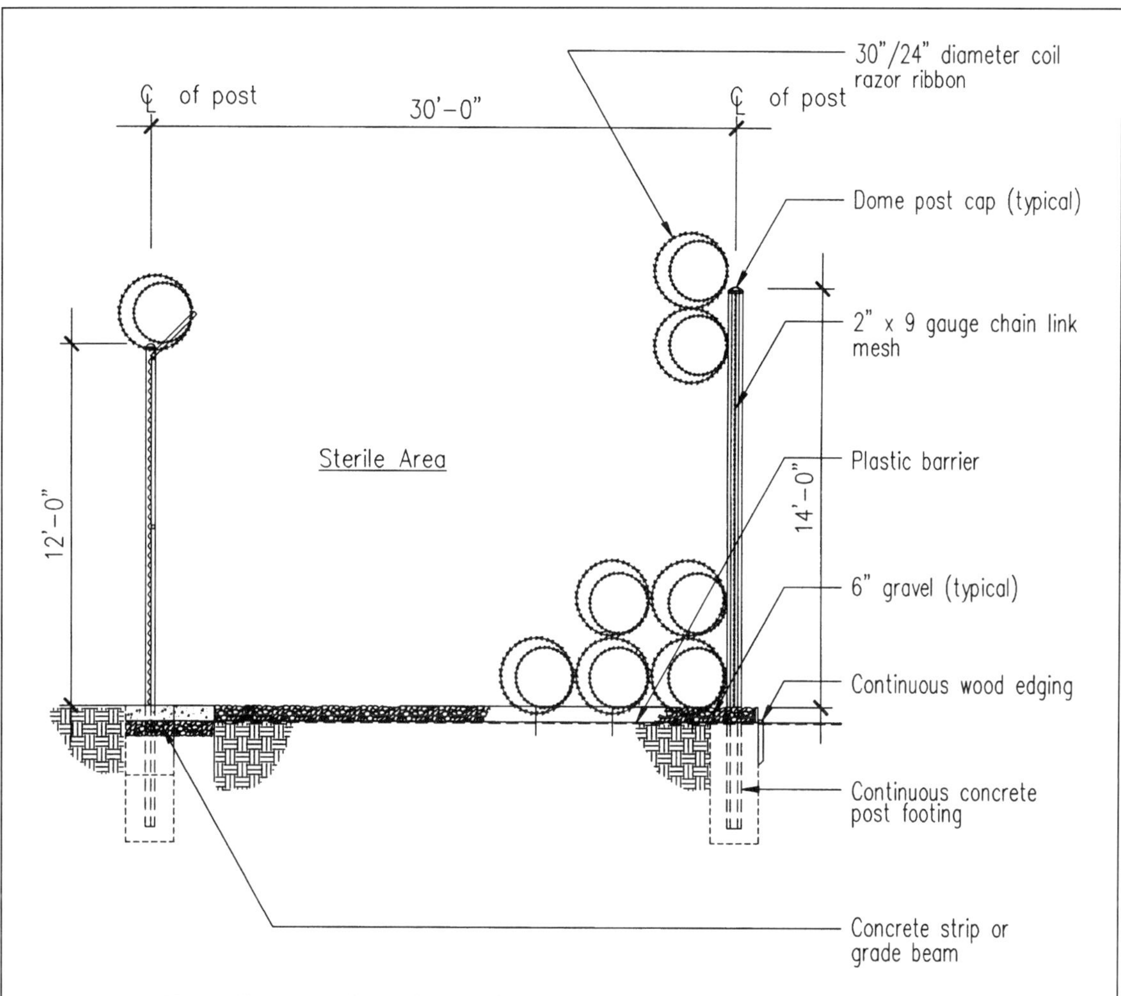

Figure 5.8.2 **Medium-security configuration section.**

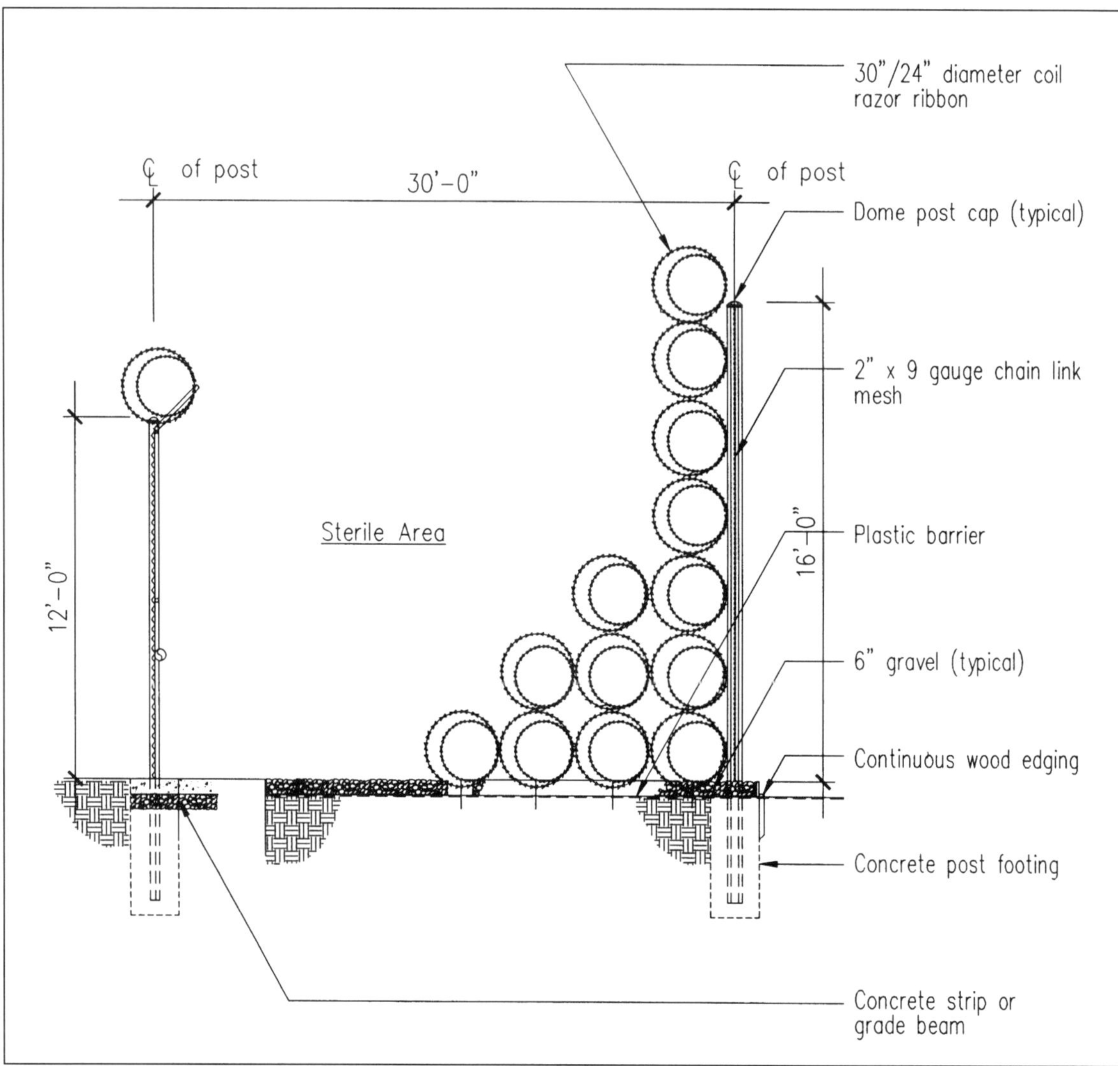

Figure 5.8.3 **Maximum-security configuration section.**

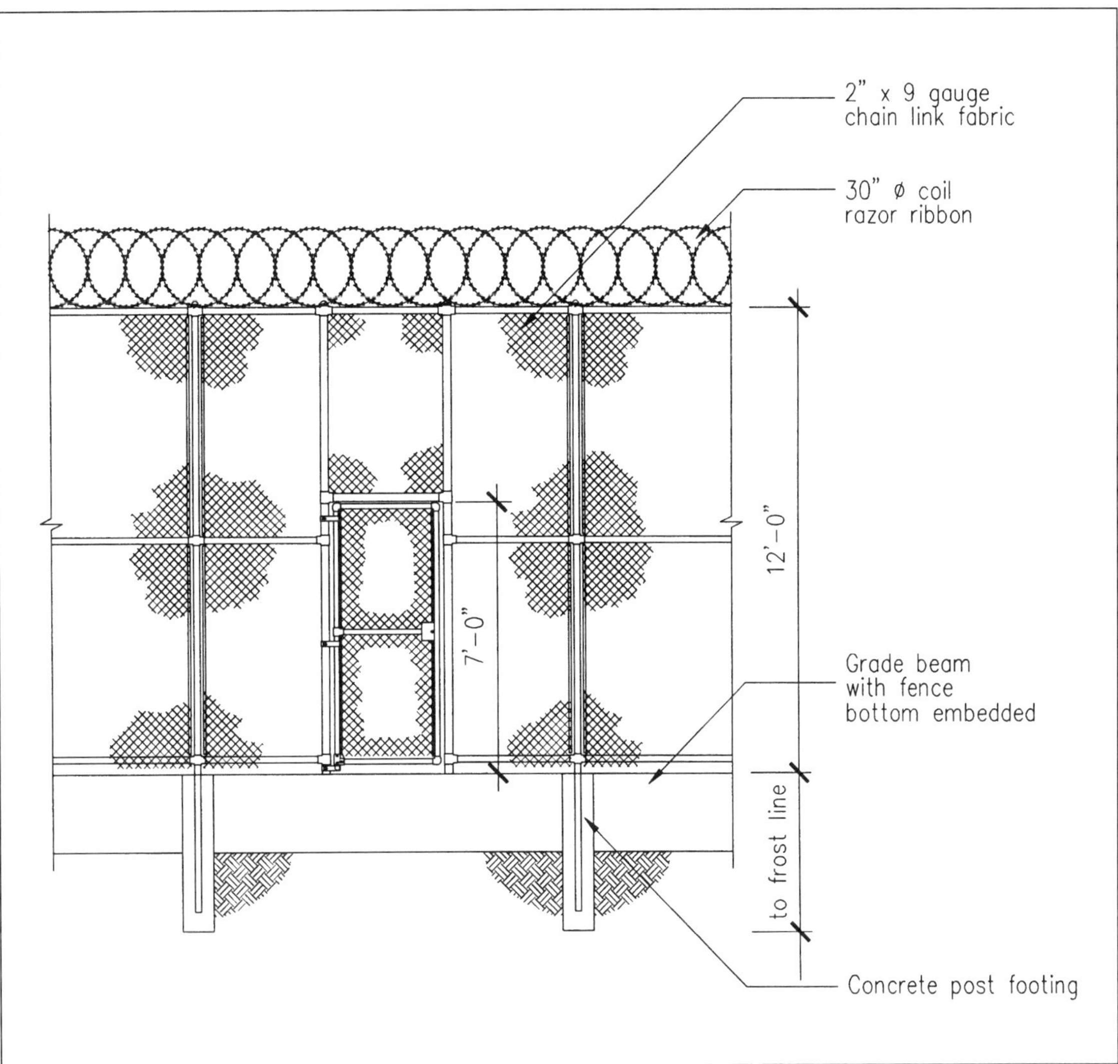

Figure 5.8.4 **Man-type swinging gate.**

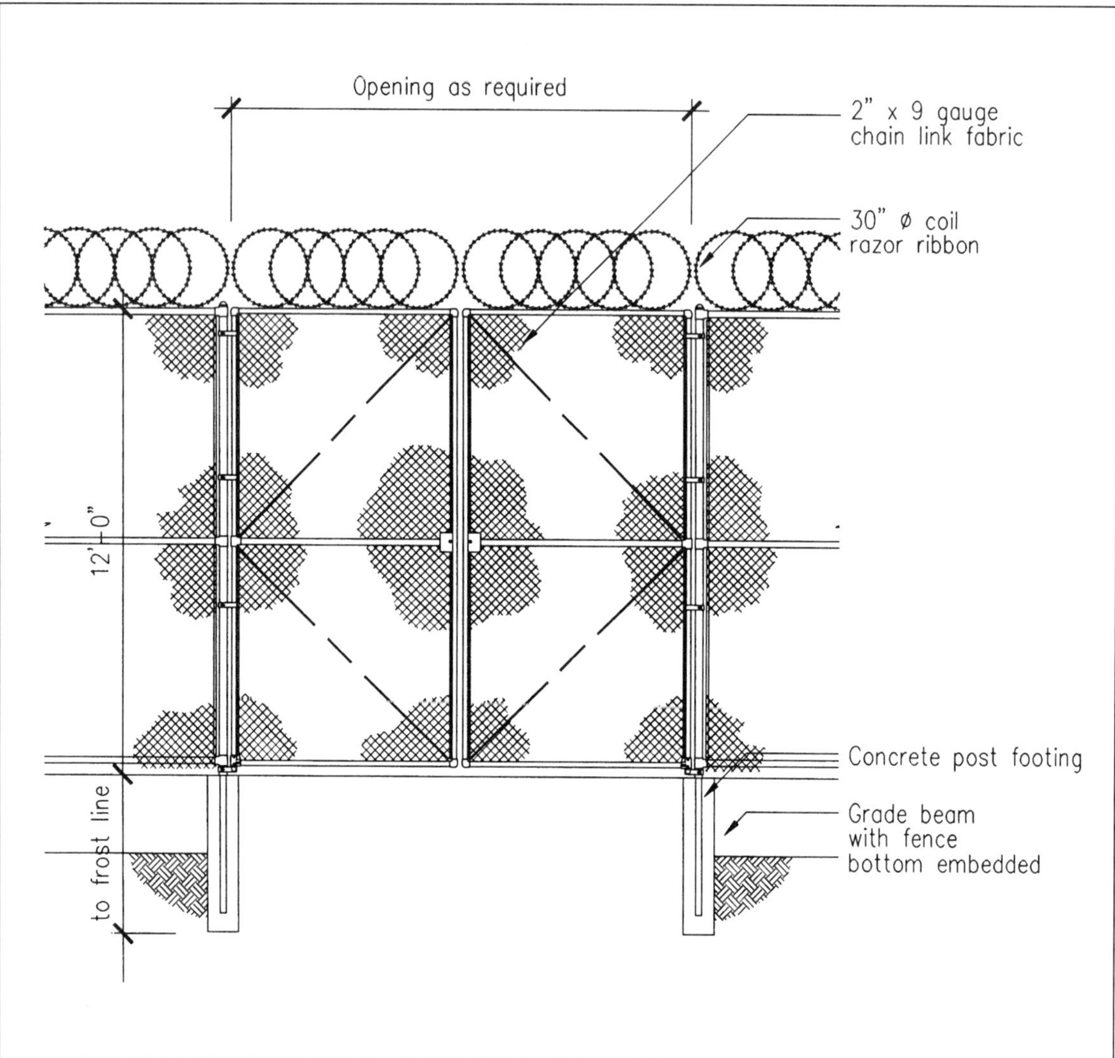

Figure 5.8.5 **Vehicle-type swinging gate.**

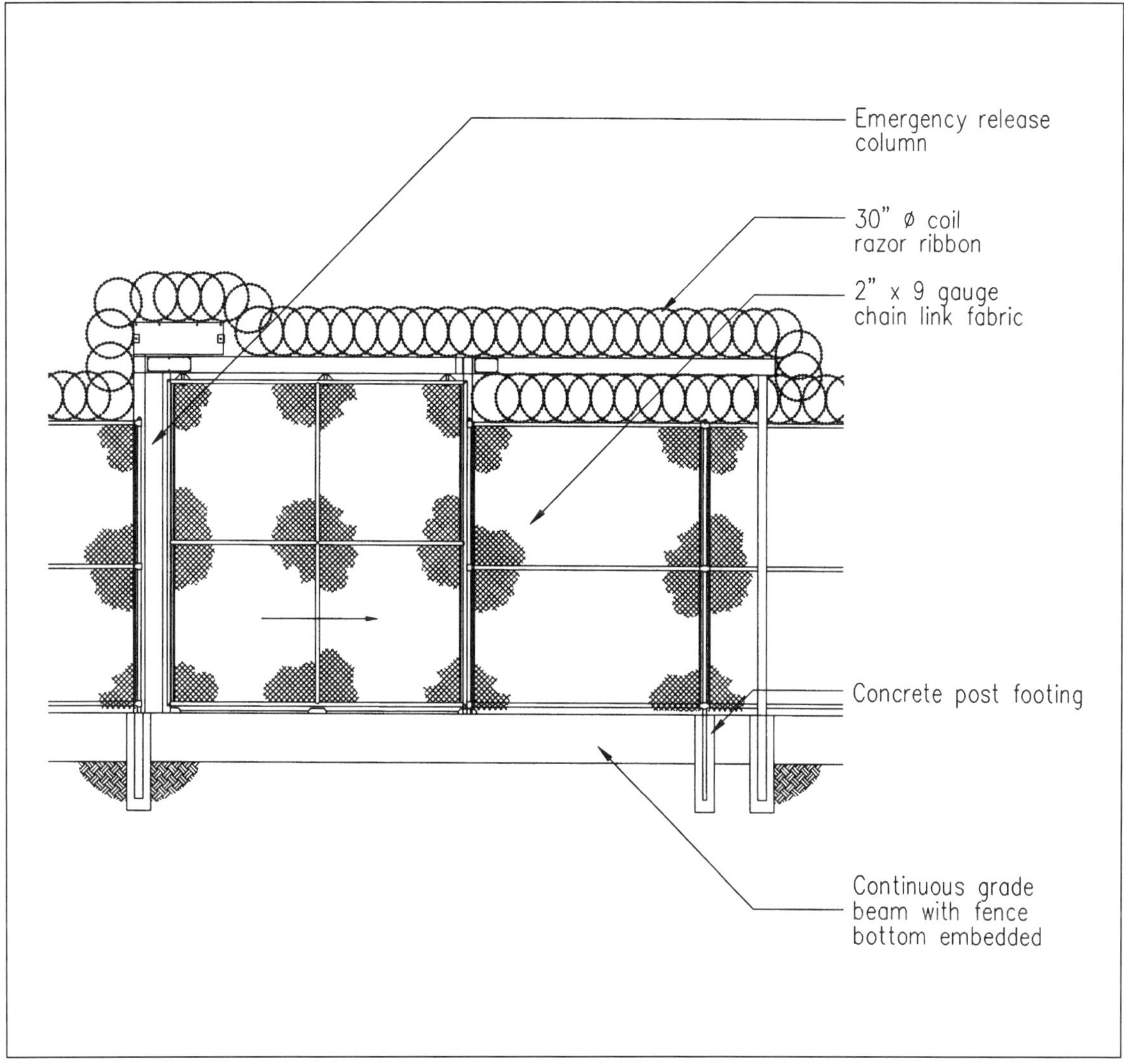

Figure 5.8.6 **Vehicle-type sliding gate.**

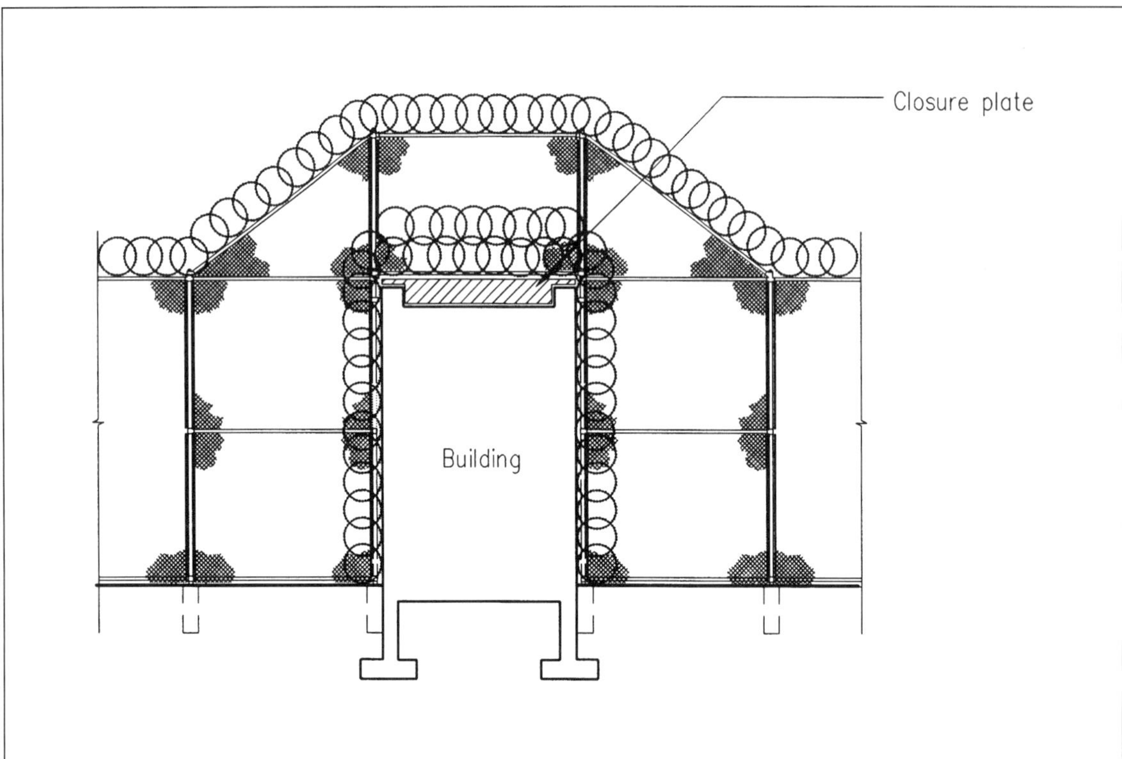

Figure 5.8.7 **Low building configuration.**

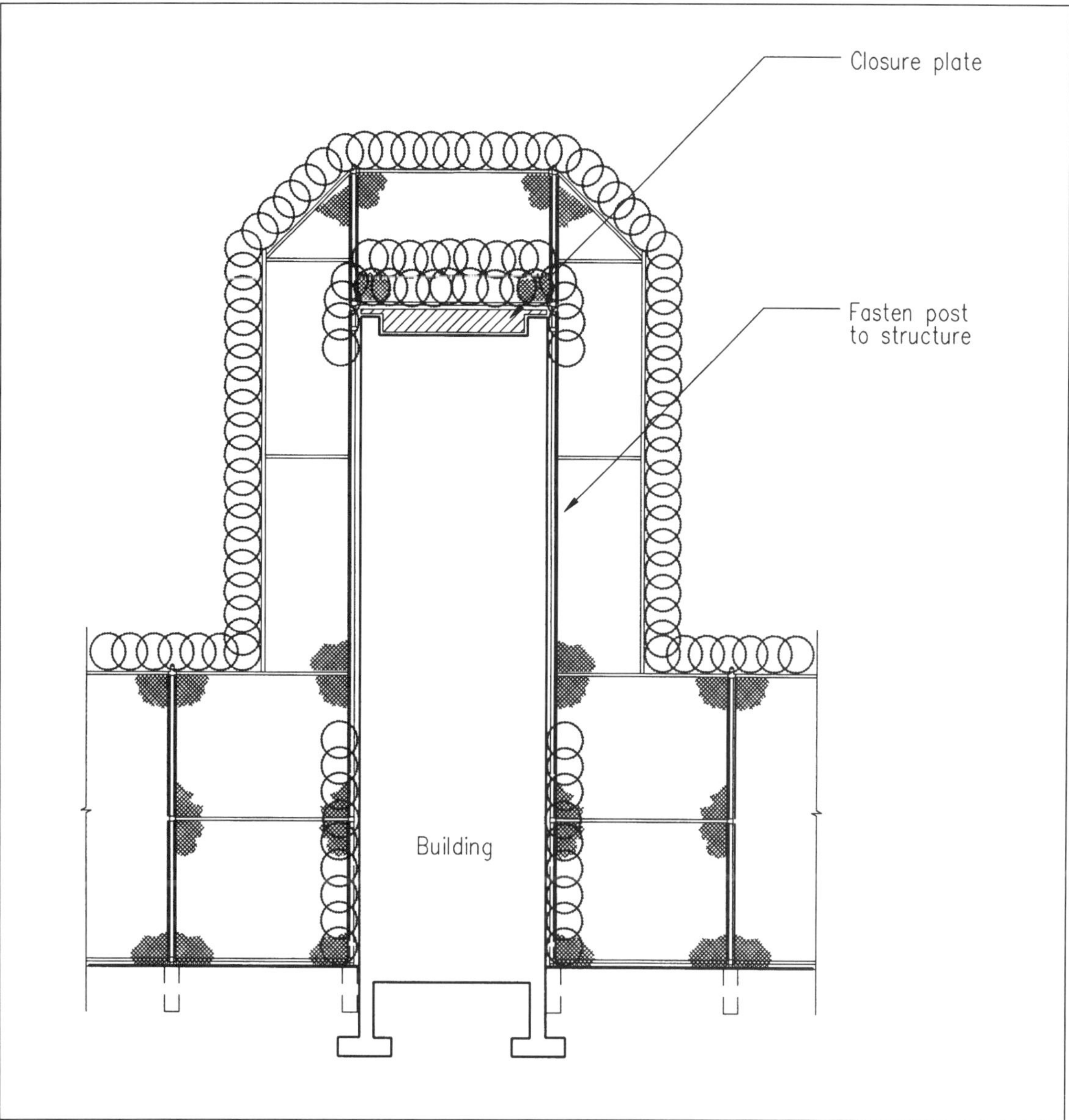

Figure 5.8.8 **High building configuration.**

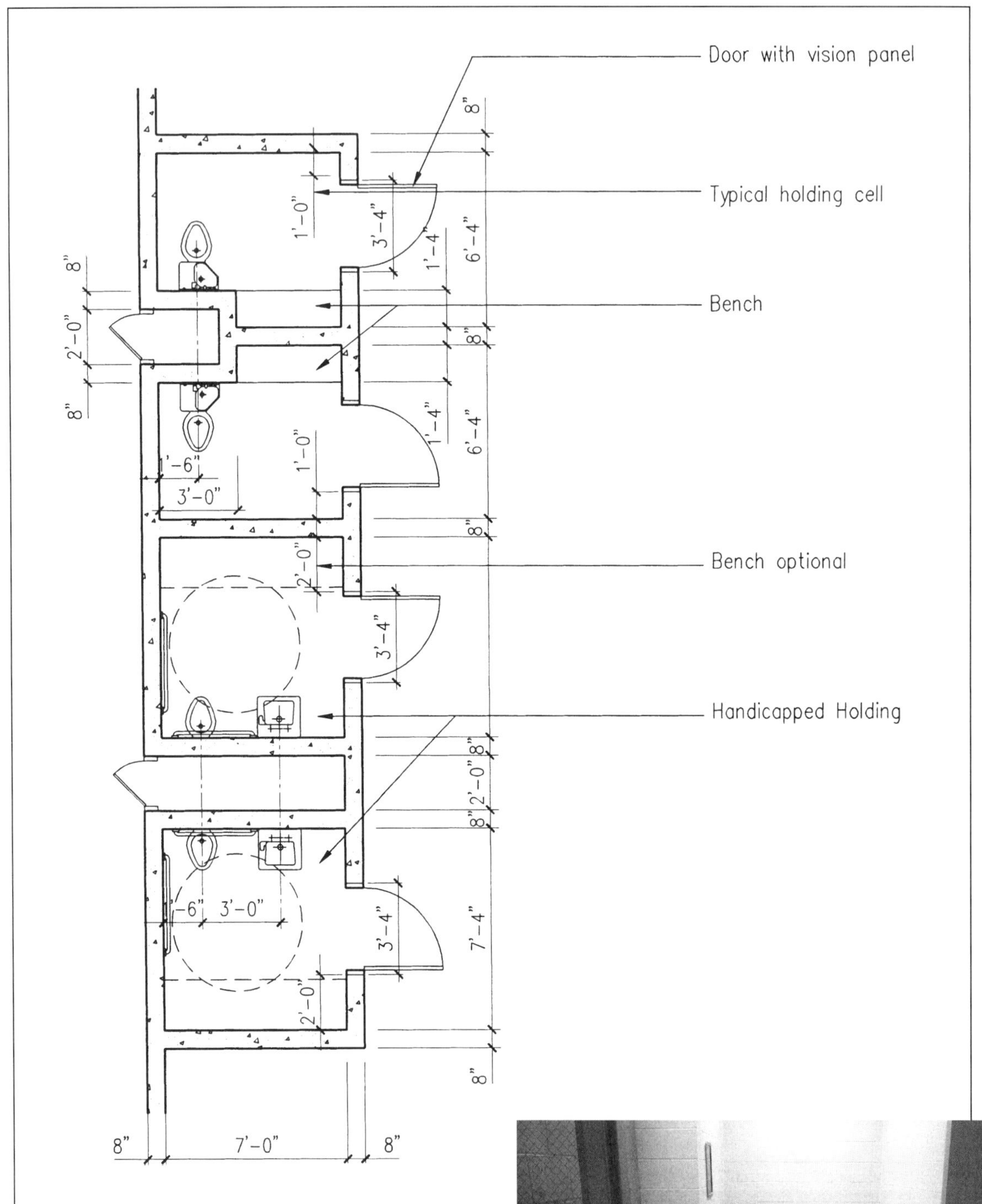

Figure 5.9.1 **Holding cell plan.**

Intake holding cell.

Typical inmate cell door arrangement on lower and upper levels.

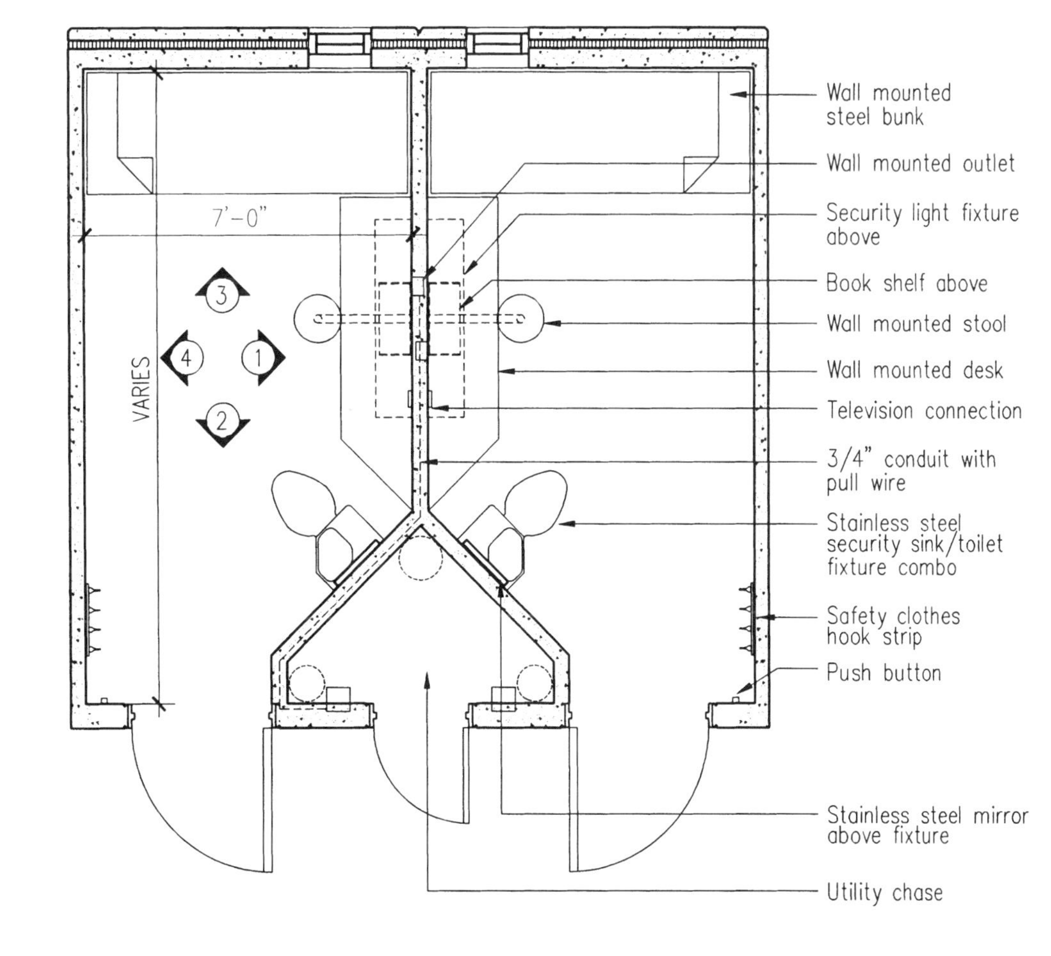

Figure 5.9.2 **Housing cell plan.**

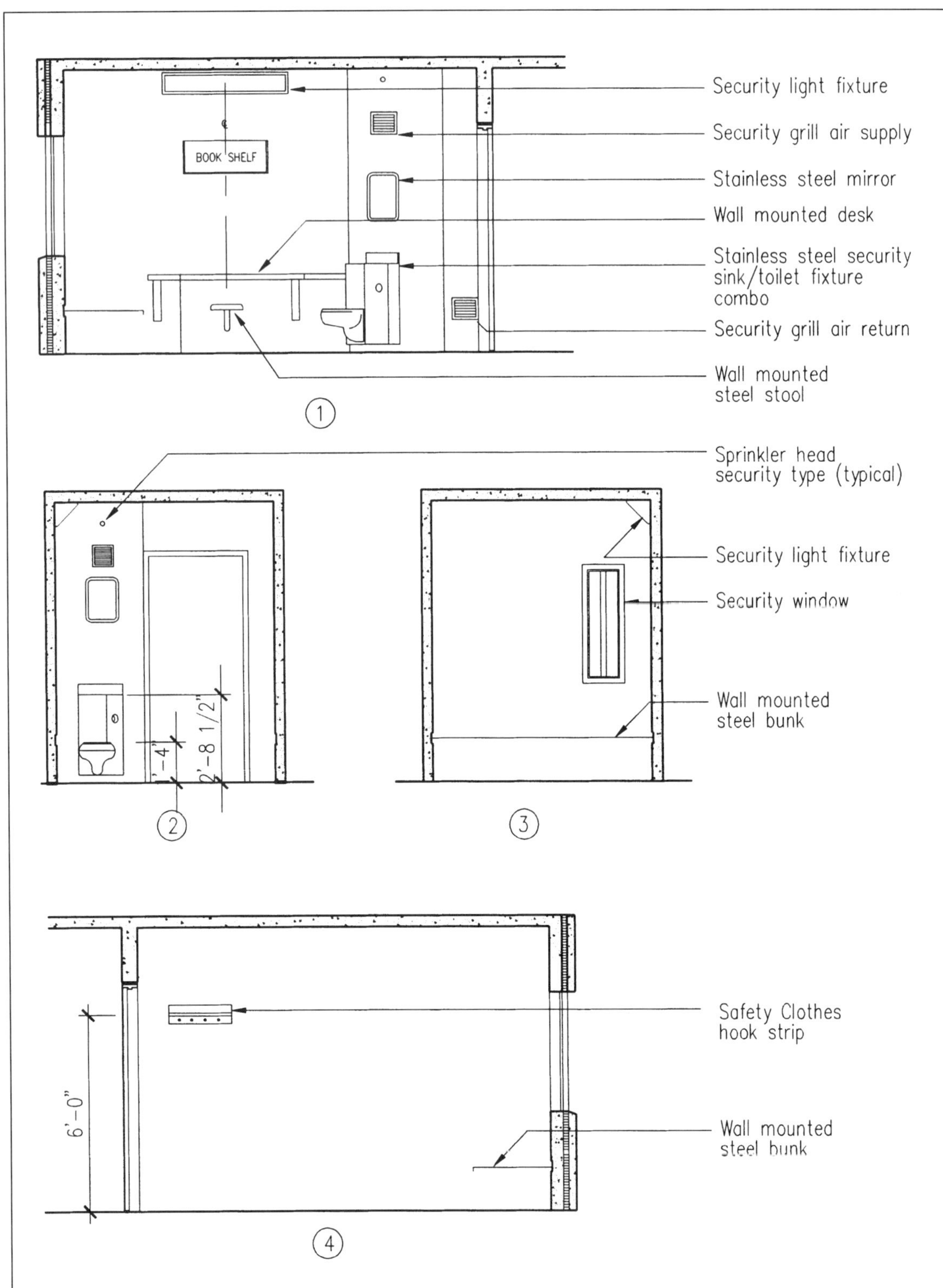

Figure 5.9.3 **Housing cell sections/elevations.**

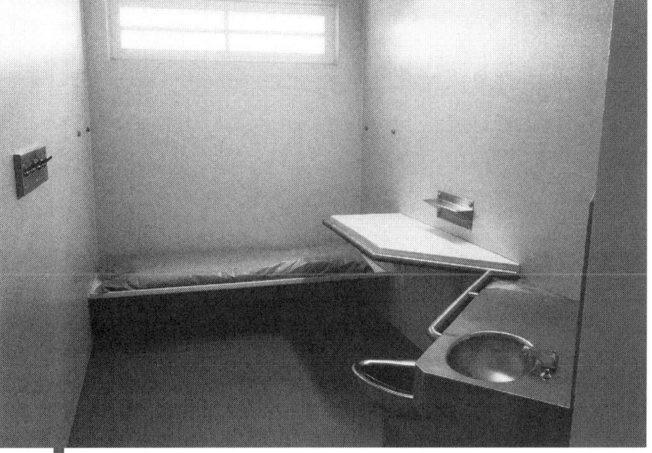

HC cell interior with bunk, desk, and toilet/lavatory unit.

HC cell's desk and stainless steel combination toilet/lavatory unit, mirror, and shelf.

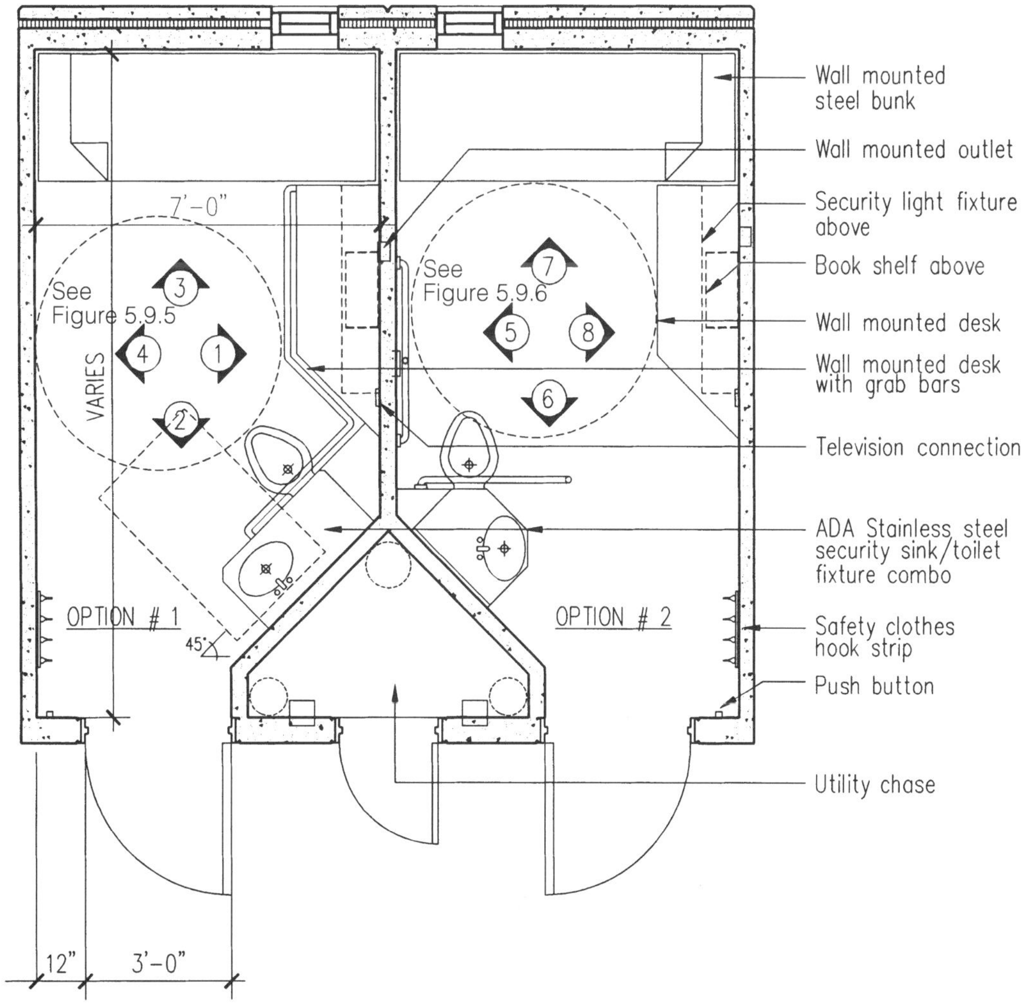

Figure 5.9.4 **Housing HC-accessible cell plan.**

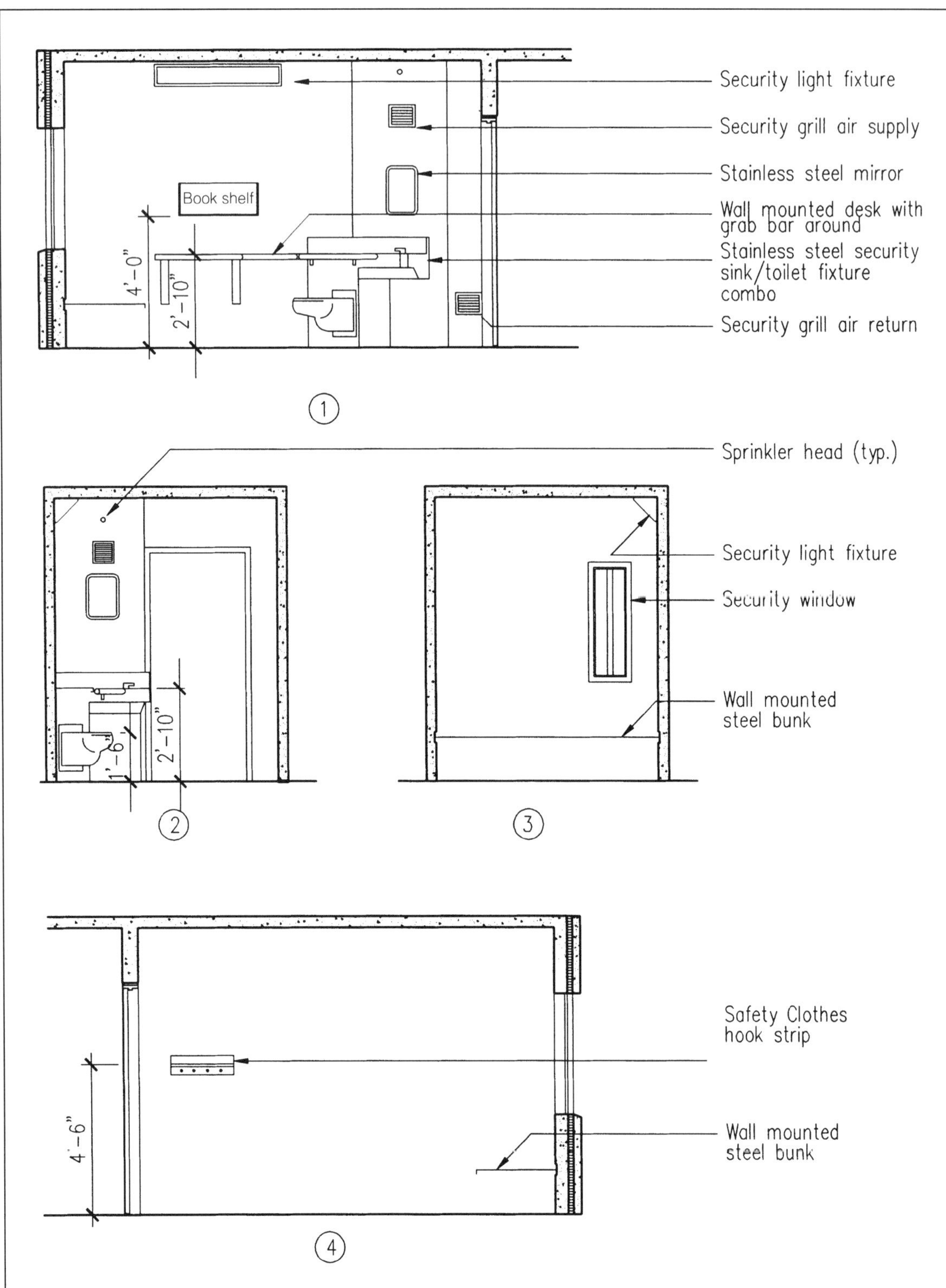

Figure 5.9.5 **Housing HC-accessible cell sections/elevations.**

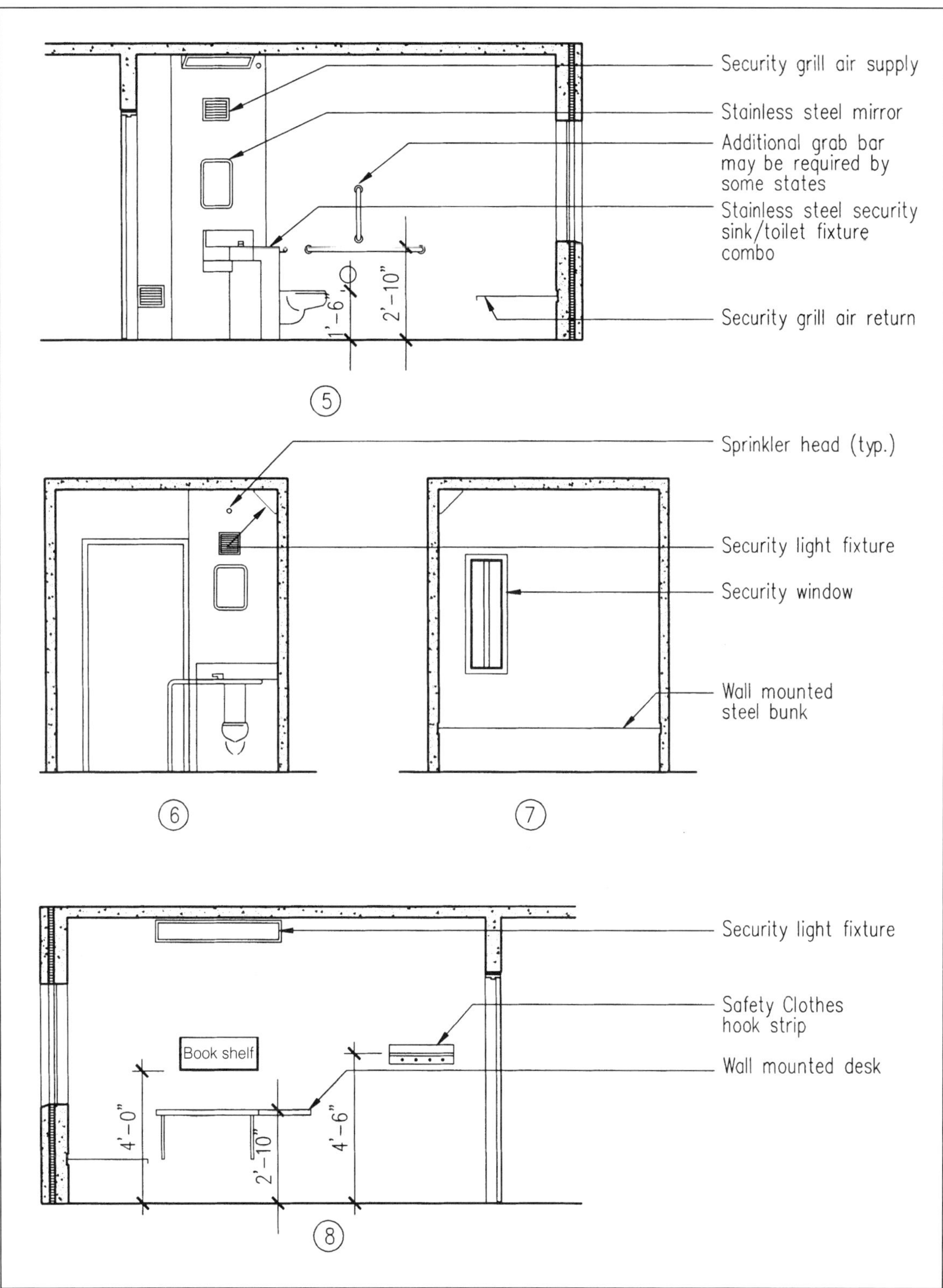

Figure 5.9.6 **Housing HC-accessible cell sections/elevations.**

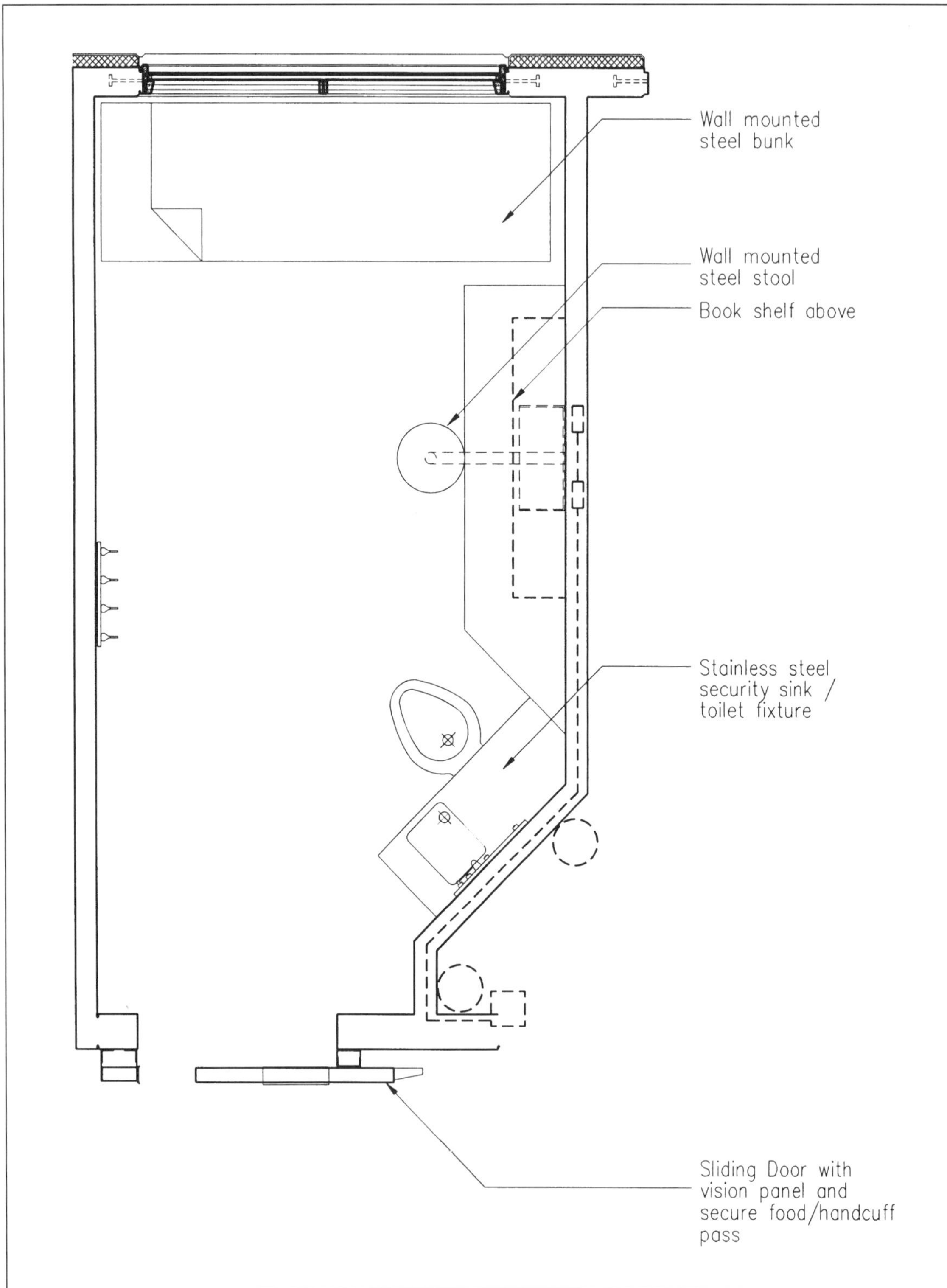

Figure 5.9.7 **Segregation housing cell plan.**

Inmate cell sliding door with vision port and food/handcuff pass.

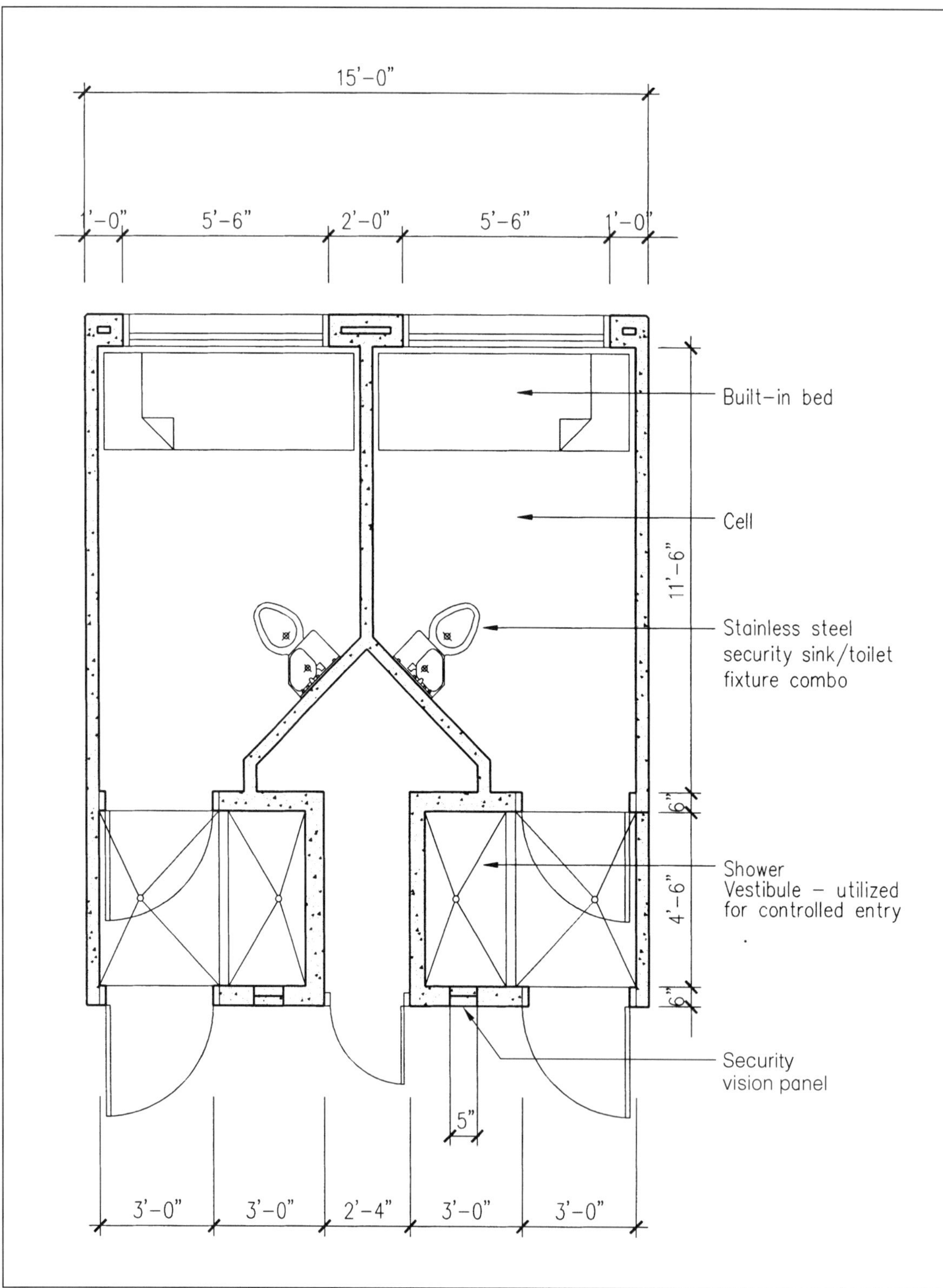

Figure 5.9.8 **Segregation housing cell plan with shower.**

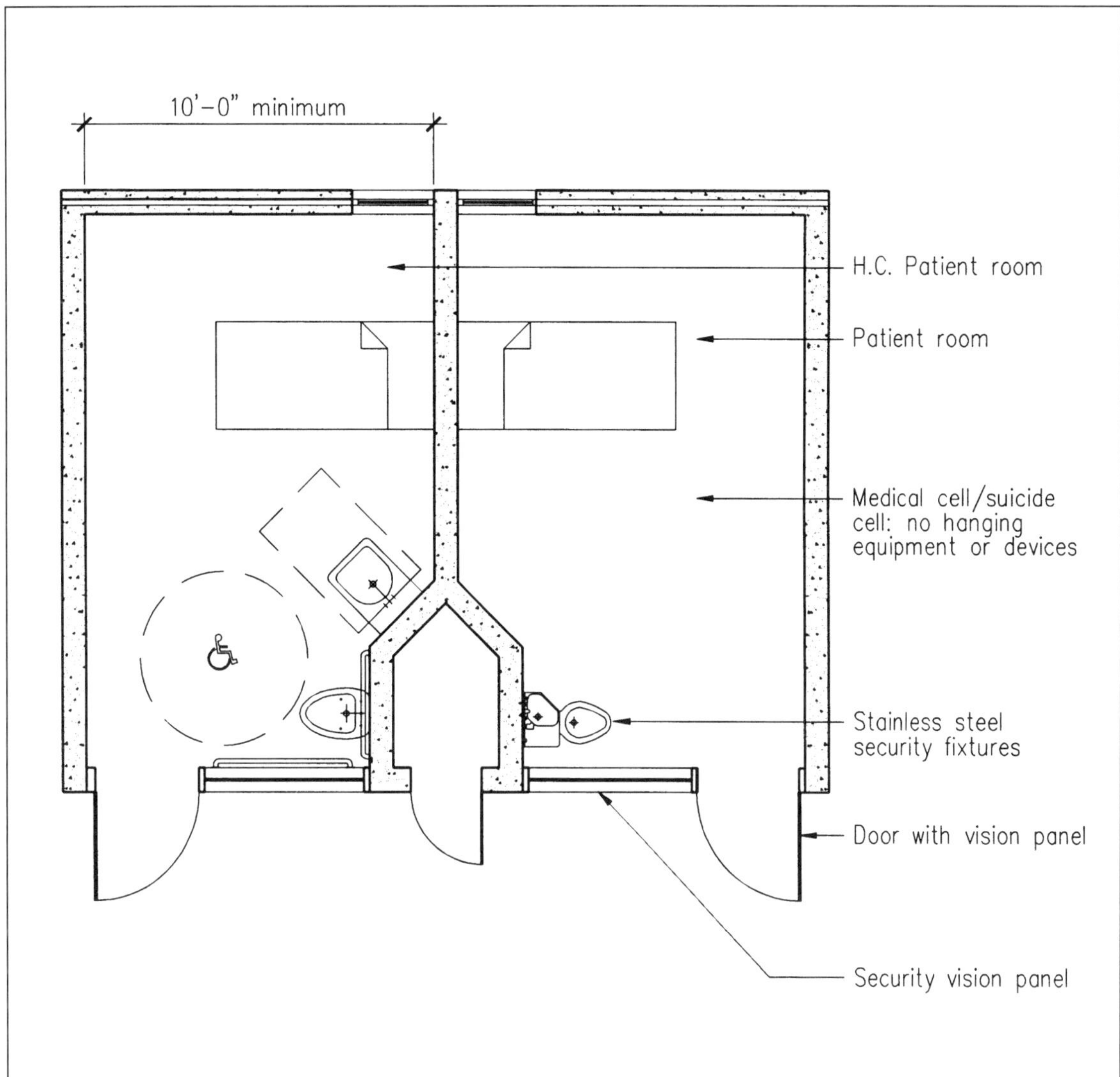

Figure 5.9.9 **Medical cell plan/observation (suicide) cell plan.**

Medical isolation cell with toilet, sink, and shower.

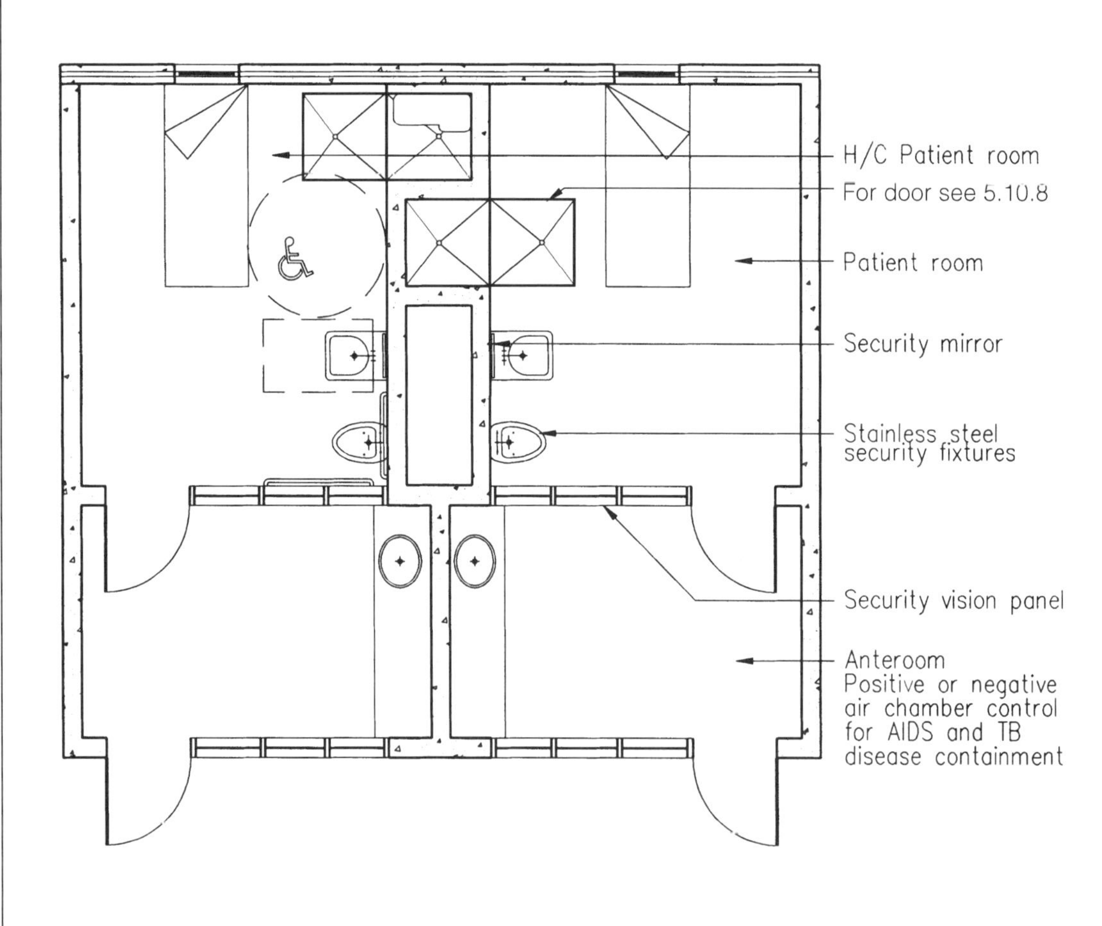

Figure 5.9.10 **Medical isolation cell plan.**

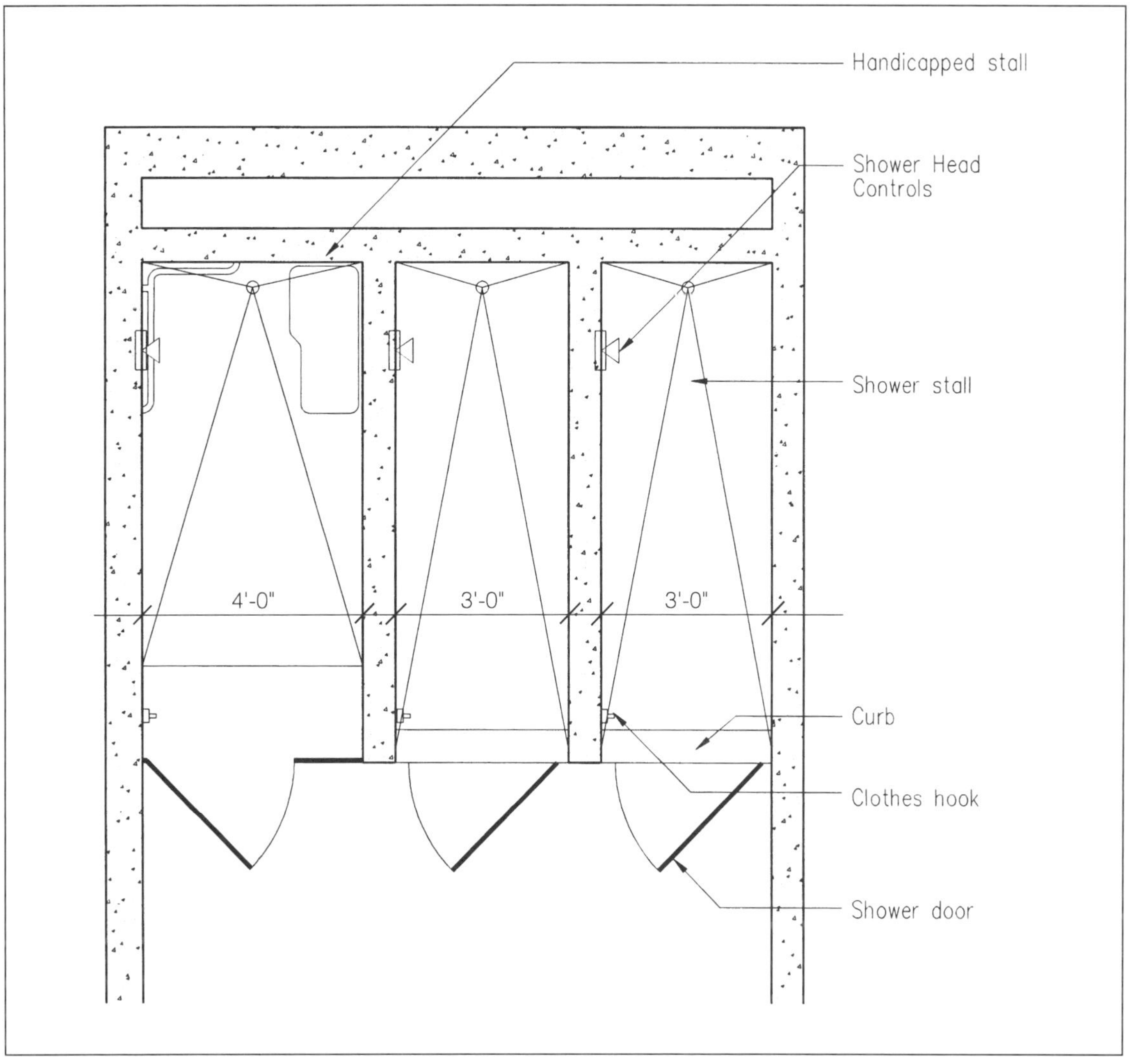

Handicapped stall
Shower Head Controls
Shower stall
4'-0"
3'-0"
3'-0"
Curb
Clothes hook
Shower door

Figure 5.9.11 **Inmate shower/HC shower plans.**

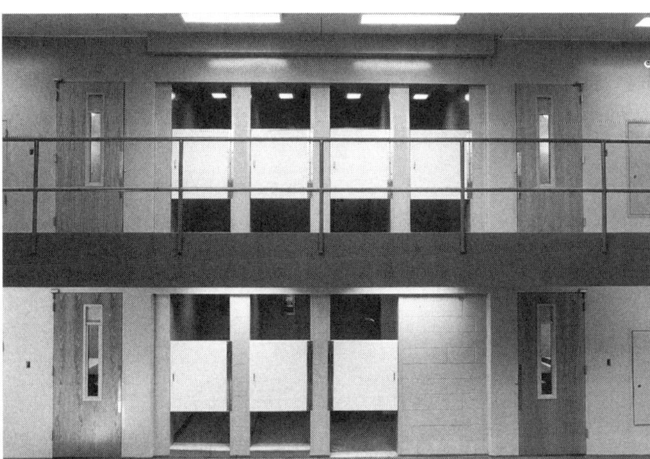

Lower- and upper-level groups of inmate showers with modesty panels.

A-147
Shower 1
Shower 2

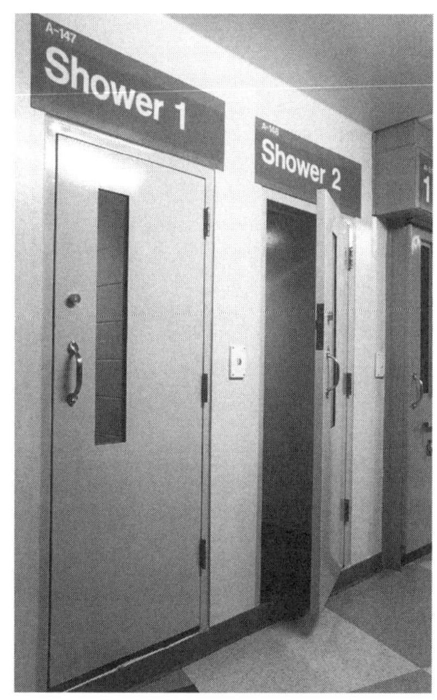

Showers with security doors.

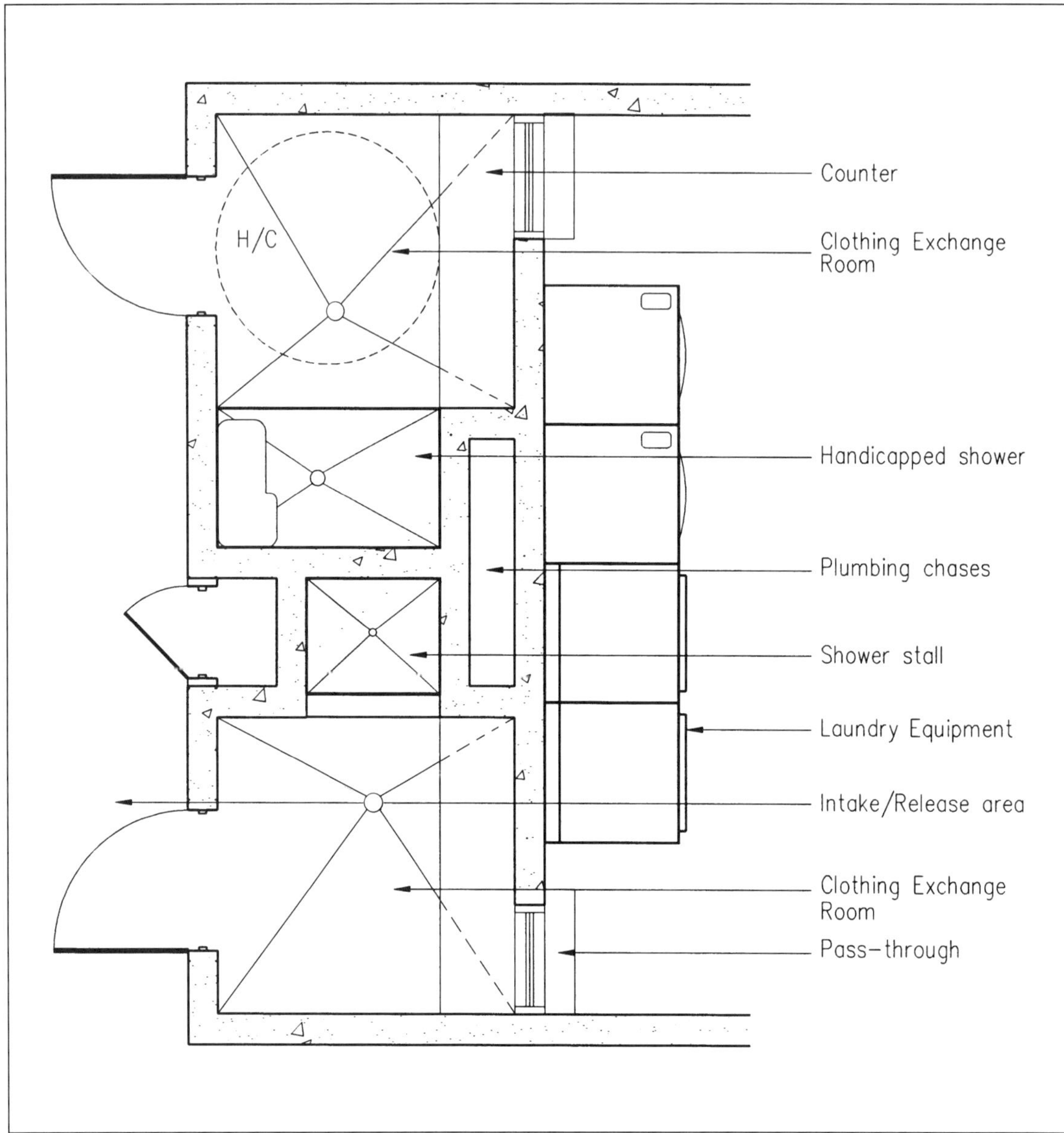

Figure 5.9.12 **Clothing exchange (shower and pass-through window) plan.**

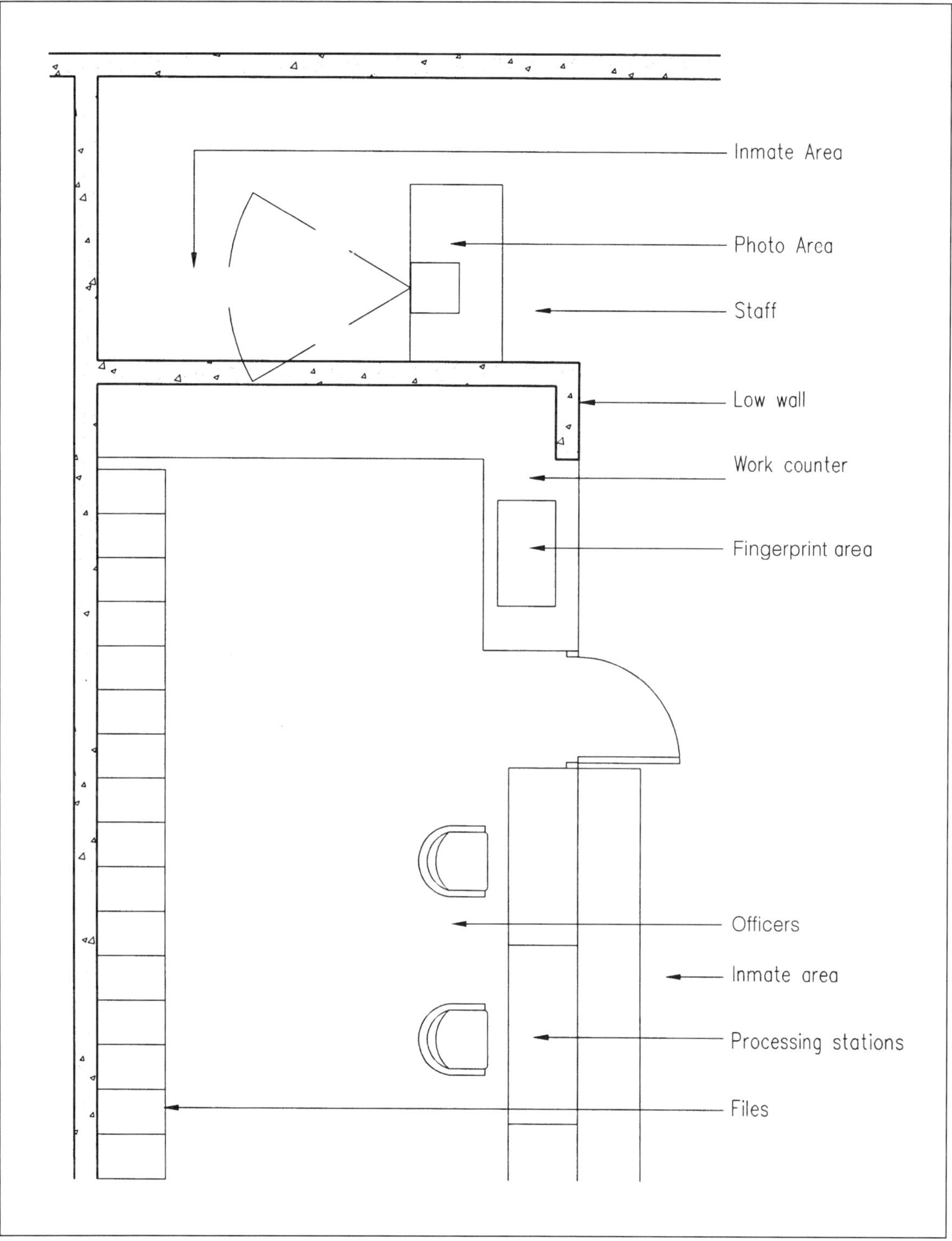

Figure 5.9.13 **Fingerprinting area plan/photographic area plan.**

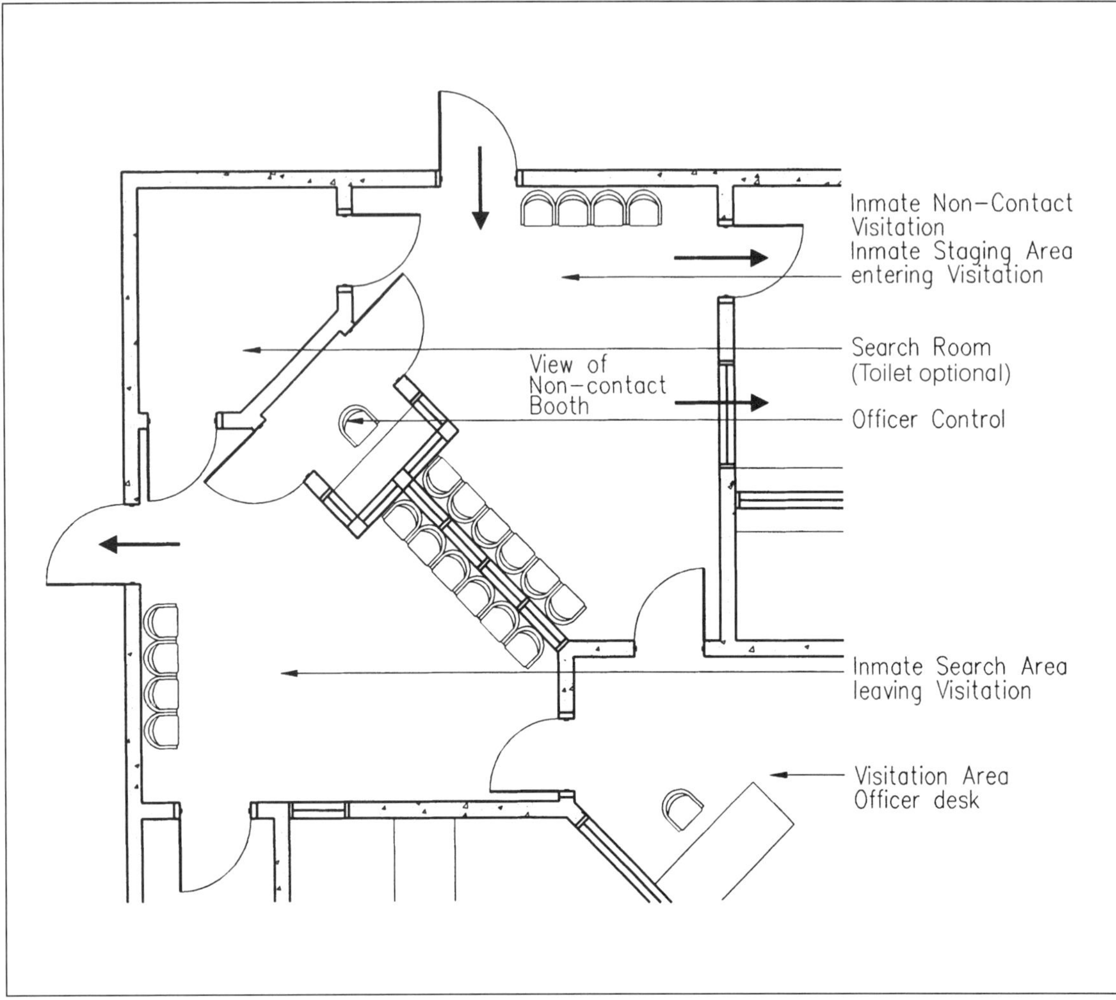

Figure 5.9.14 **Inmate visitation waiting area plan.**

Noncontact visitation booth with speak-through jamb frame.

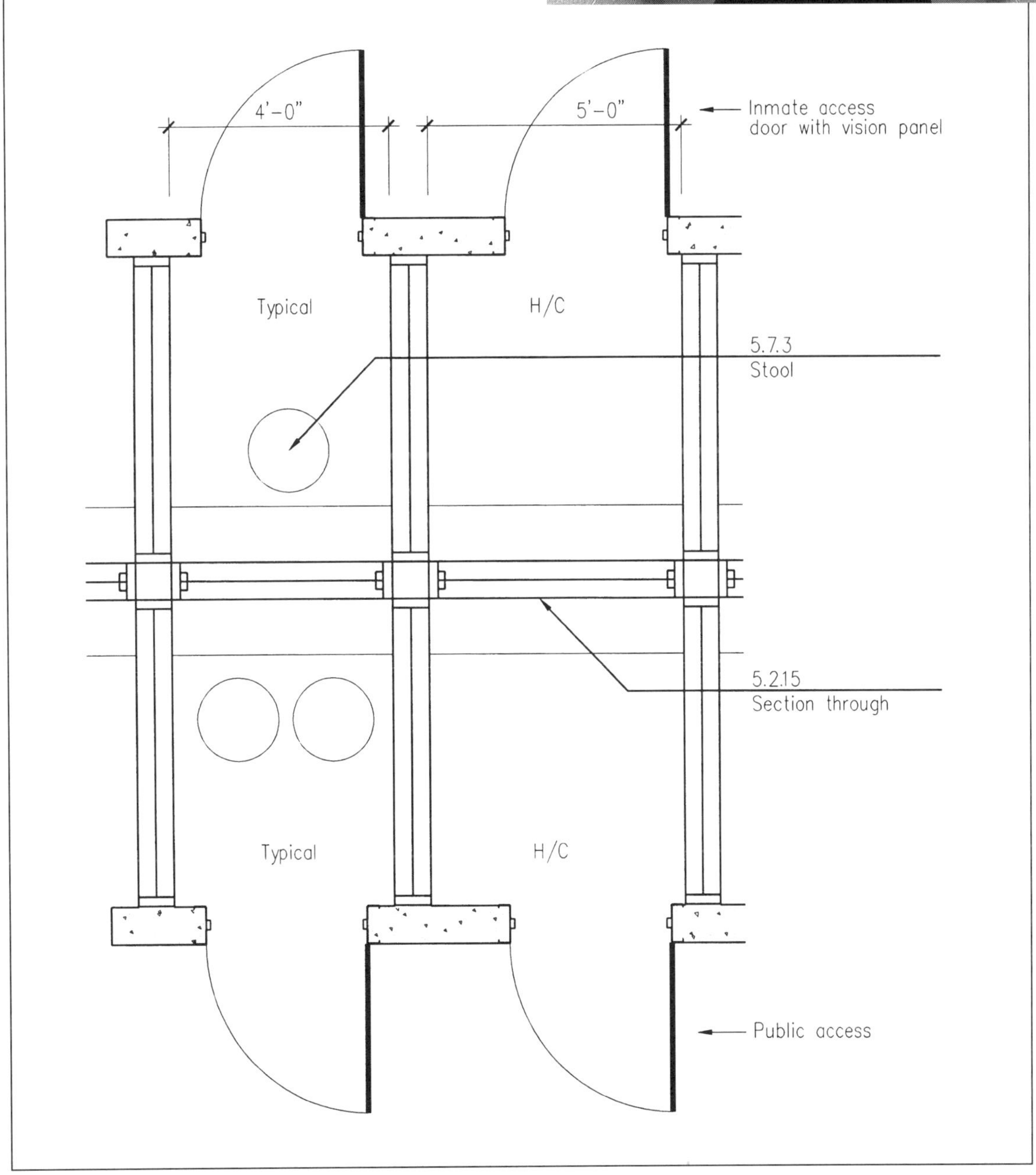

Figure 5.9.15 **Noncontact visitation booth plan.**

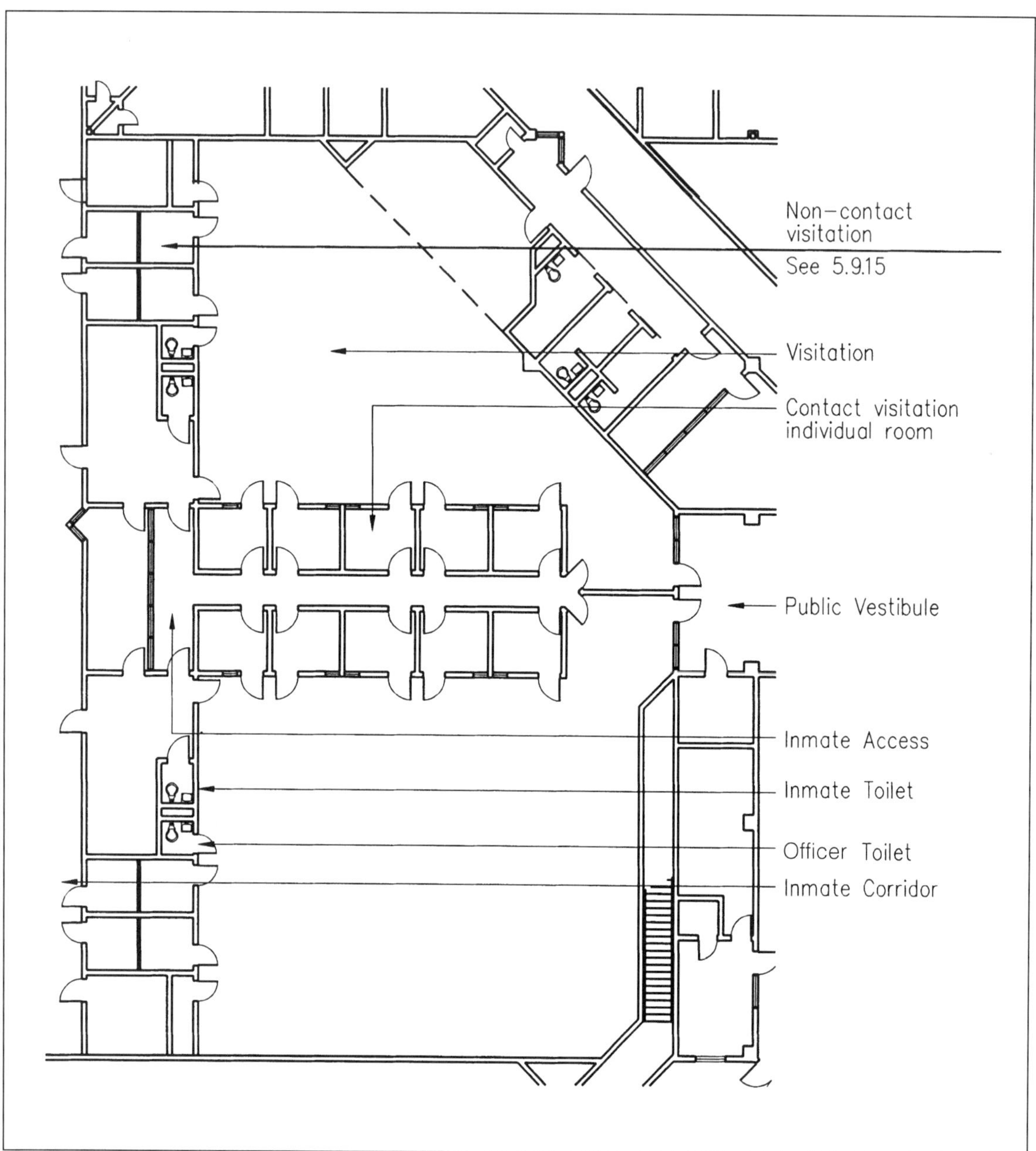

Figure 5.9.16 **Contact visitation room plan.**

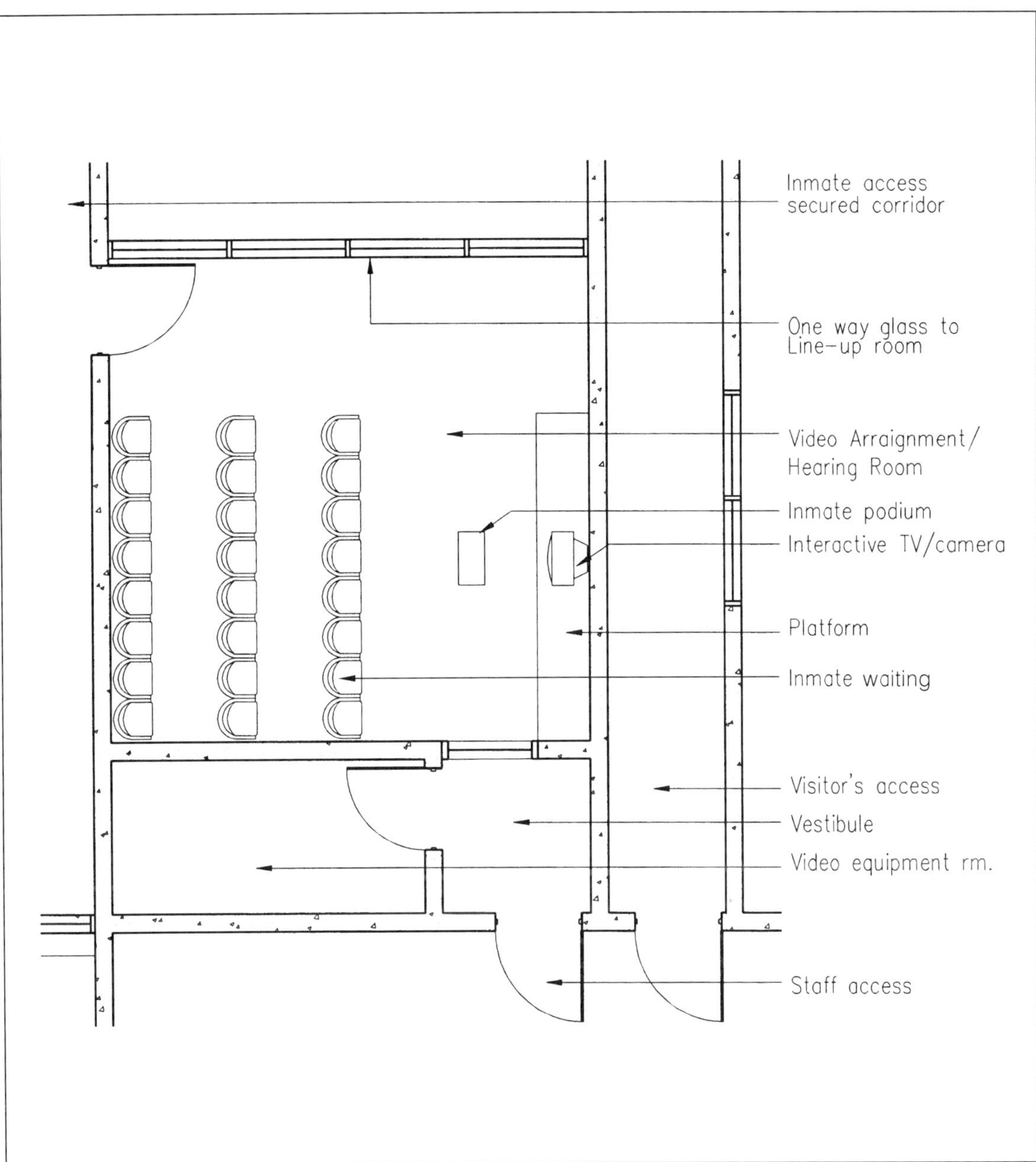

Figure 5.9.17 **TV arraignment room plan.**

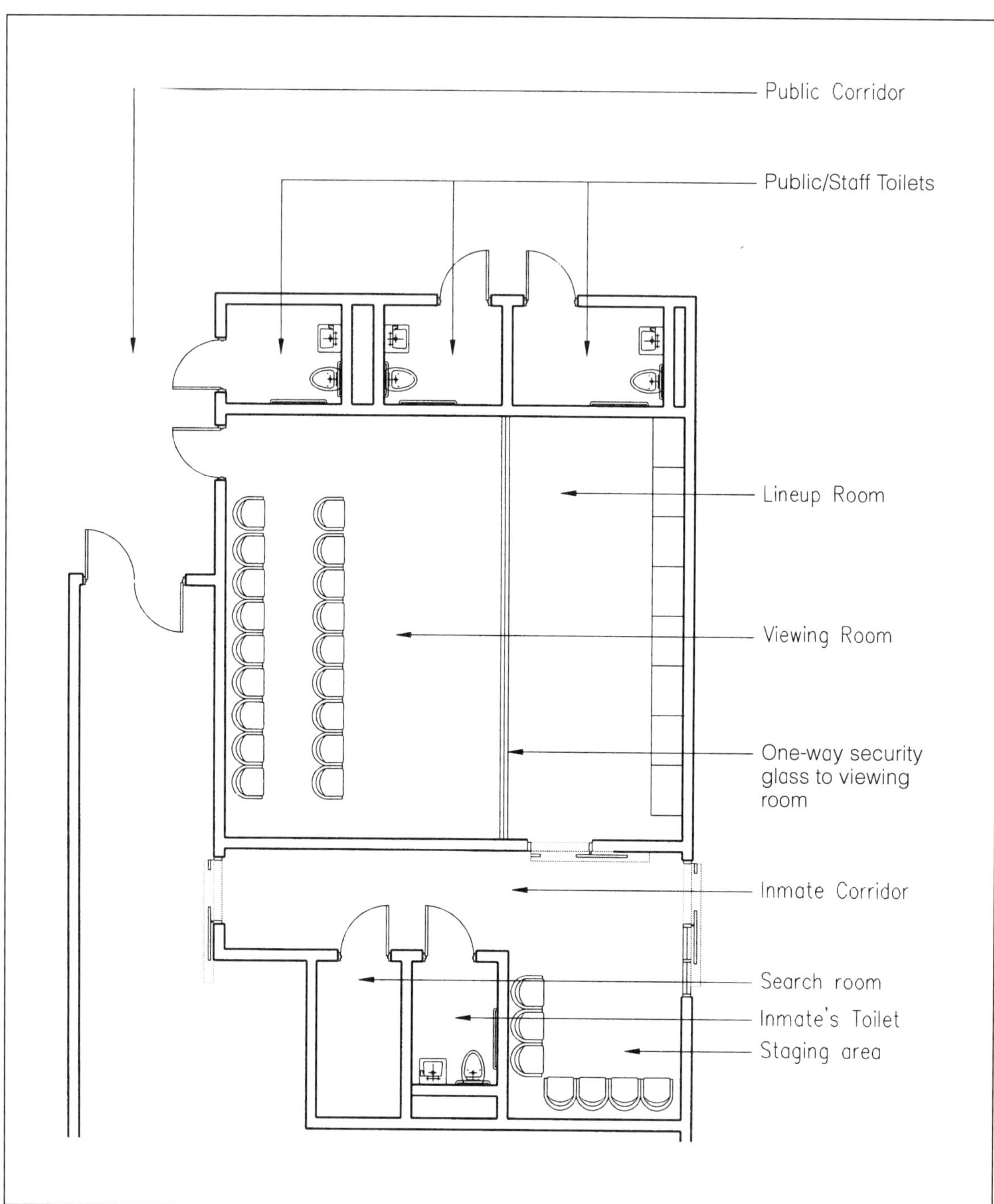

Figure 5.9.18 **Lineup room plan.**

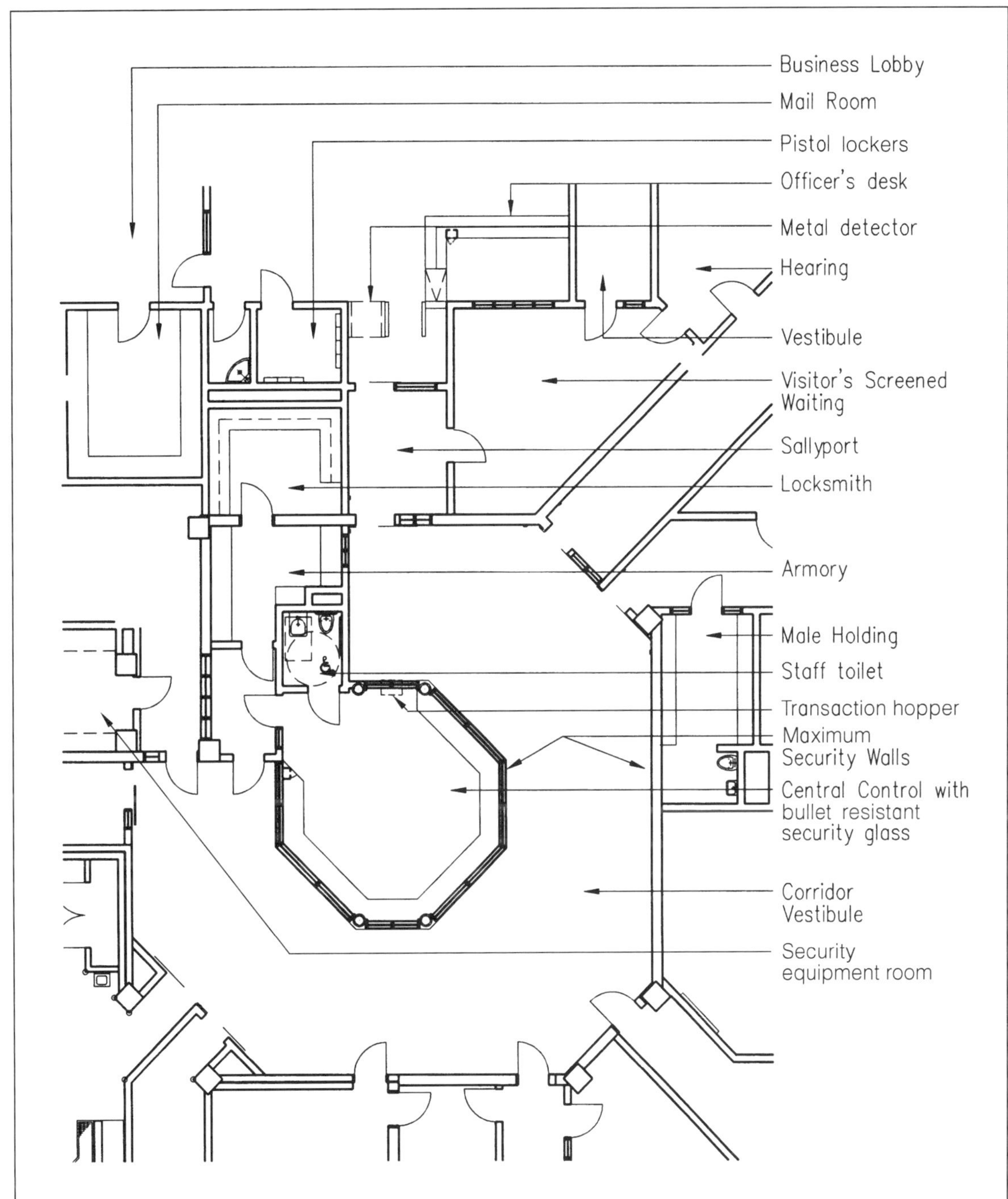

Figure 5.9.19 **Master control room plan.**

Unit control station with observation, supervision, and control of inmate housing unit entrances, dayrooms, and outdoor recreation yards.

Outdoor Recreation Yards
Sallyport to cells
Security vision panel
Laundry
Door with vision panel
Unit Control with security glass
Corridor
Transaction hopper
Staff Toilet
Triage
Sallyport to cells
Outdoor Recreation Yards

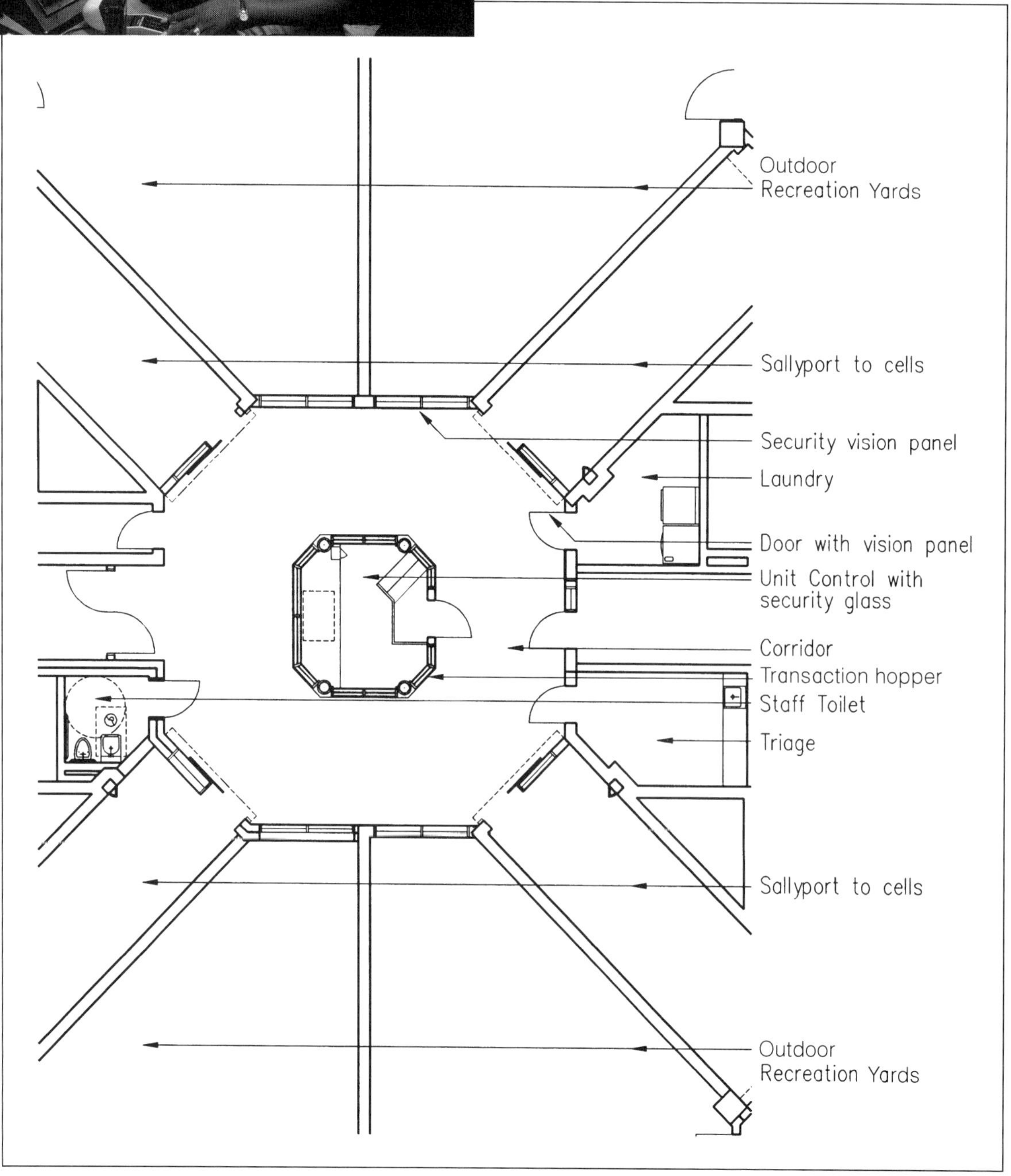

Figure 5.9.20 **Local control room plan.**

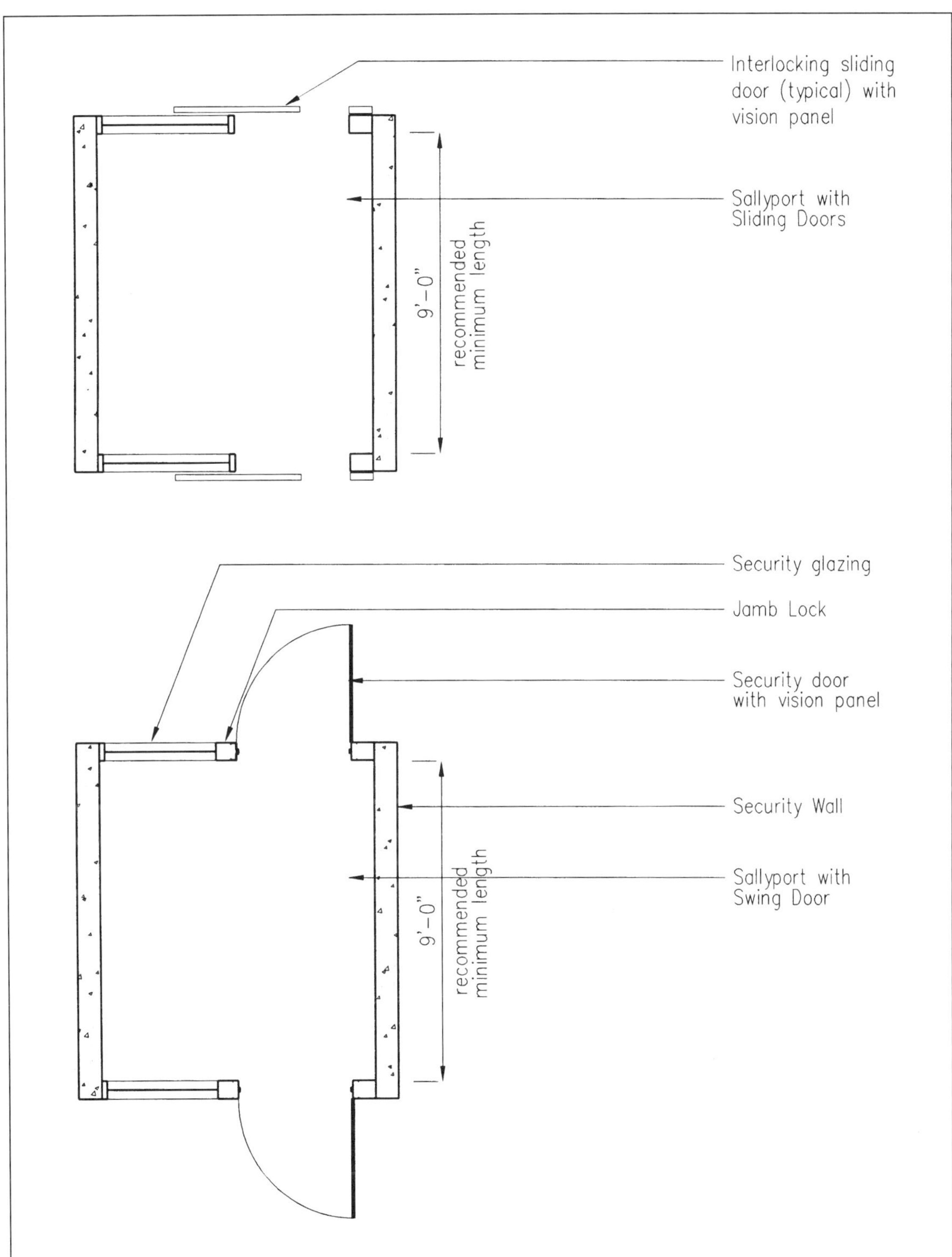

Figure 5.9.21 **Sally port plans.**

Outdoor recreation adjacent to housing building with observation from central control tower.

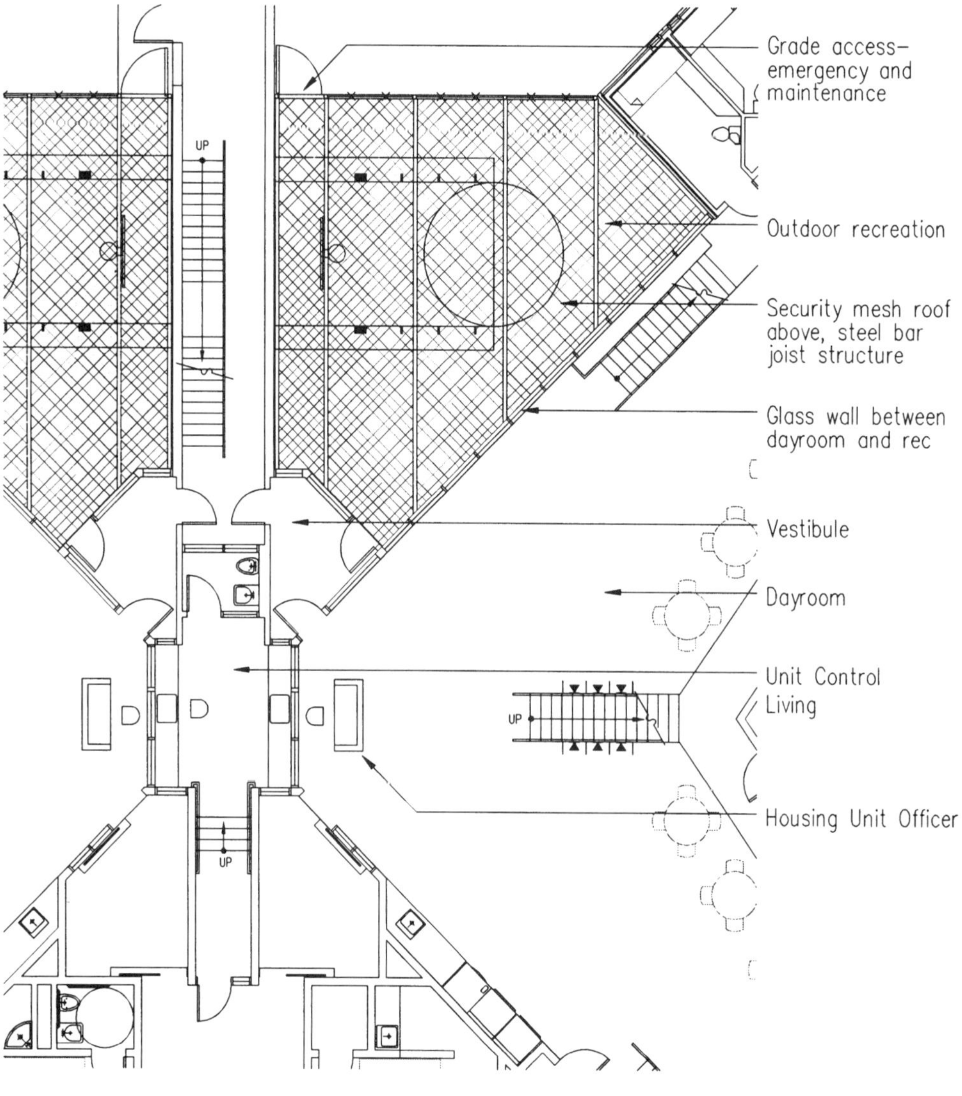

Grade access–emergency and maintenance

Outdoor recreation

Security mesh roof above, steel bar joist structure

Glass wall between dayroom and rec

Vestibule

Dayroom

Unit Control Living

Housing Unit Officer

UP

Figure 5.9.22 **Outdoor exercise security mesh roof plan.**

Outdoor exercise court with security mesh in horizontal application, security light fixture, and paging device.

Unit control of inmate movement to living unit entrances and observation of outdoor recreation courts.

Outdoor recreation security mesh in vertical and sloped applications.

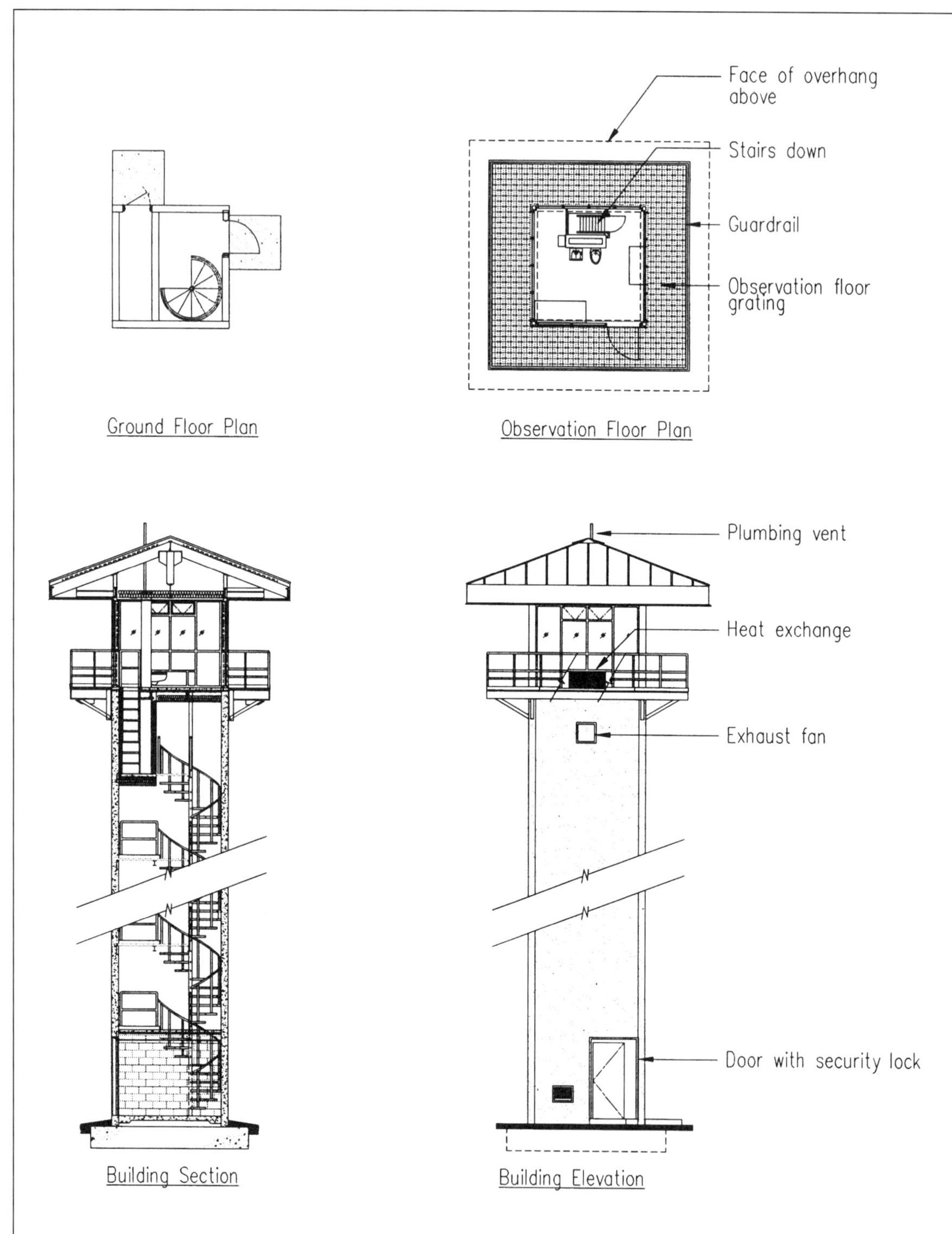

Figure 5.9.23 **Guard tower.**

Inmate cell interior with desk, stool, combination toilet/lavatory, and mirror.

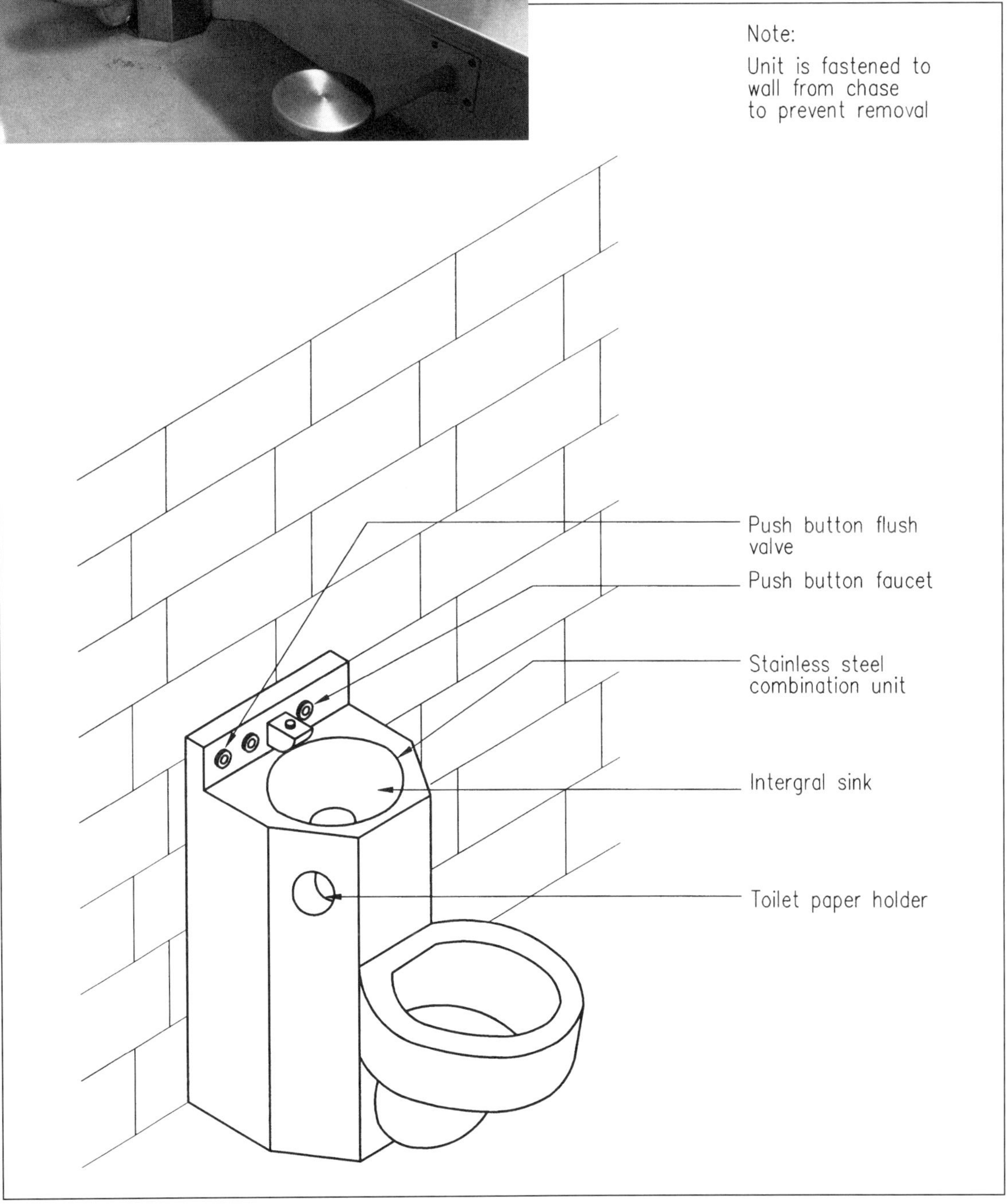

Note:
Unit is fastened to wall from chase to prevent removal

Push button flush valve

Push button faucet

Stainless steel combination unit

Intergral sink

Toilet paper holder

Figure 5.10.1 **Inmate cell toilet/lavatory.**

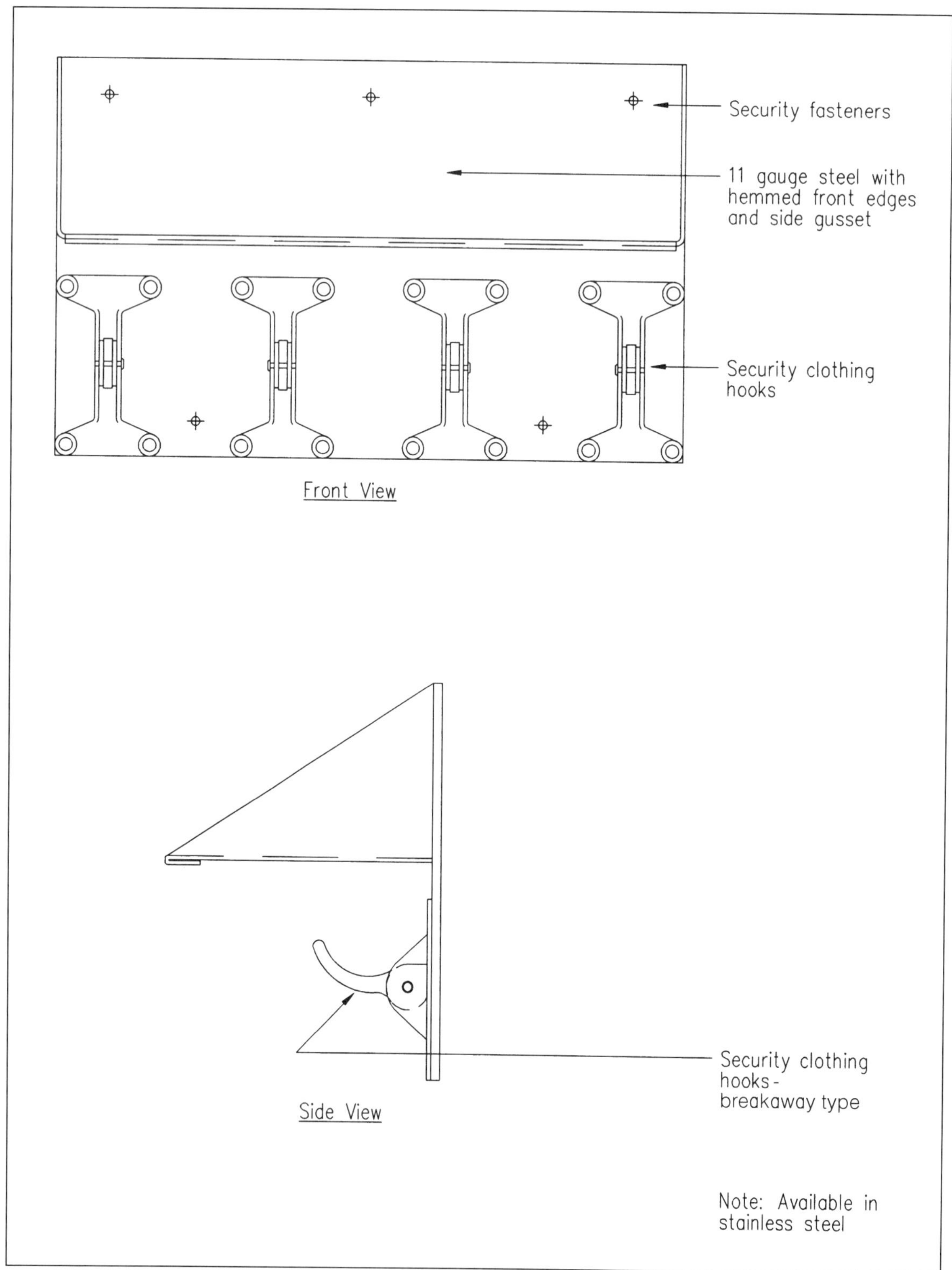

Figure 5.10.2 **Inmate cell safety clothing hook and shelf.**

Cell breakaway hook assembly.

Individual breakaway hook attachment.

Cell stainless steel shelf.

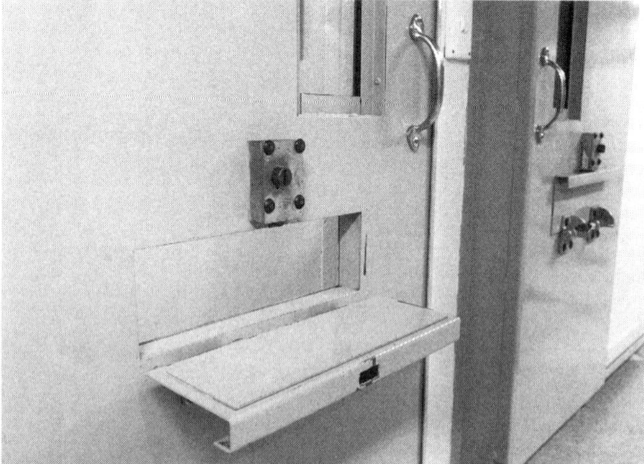

Inmate cell door food and cuff pass, in opened and closed position.

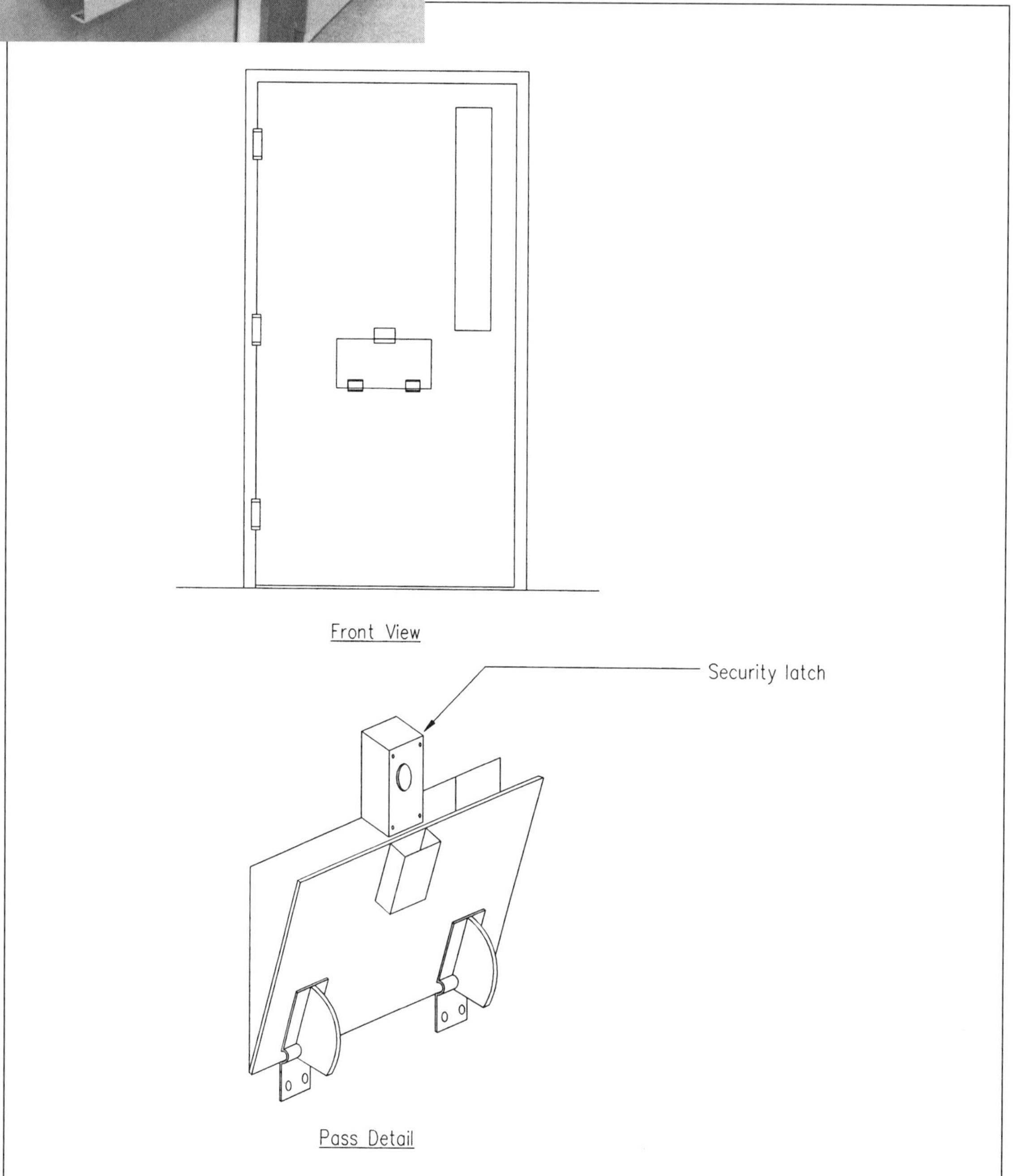

Front View

Security latch

Pass Detail

Figure 5.10.3 **Inmate cell secure food/handcuff pass.**

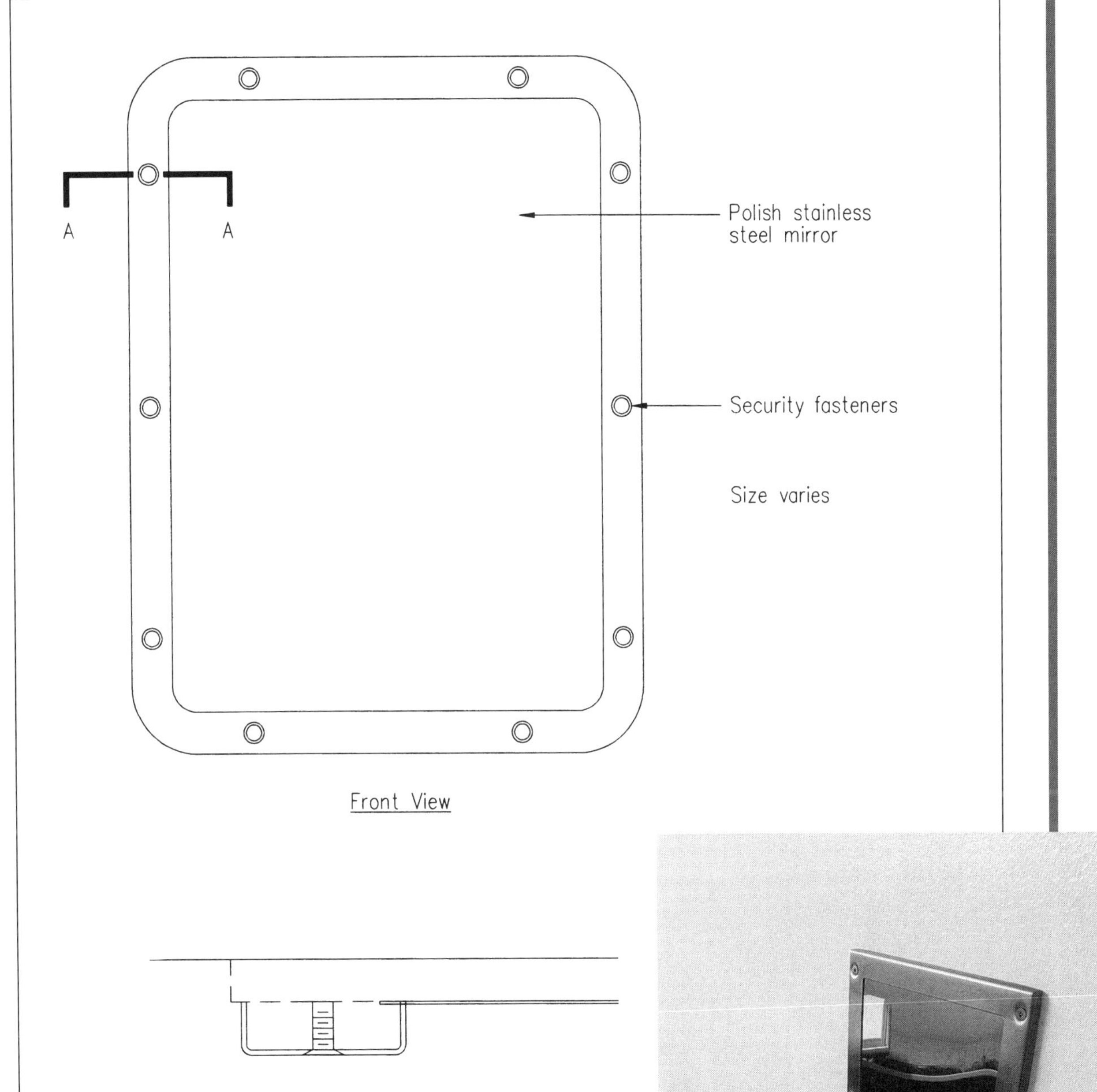

Figure 5.10.4 **Inmate cell mirror.**

Security mirror positioned in HC cell.

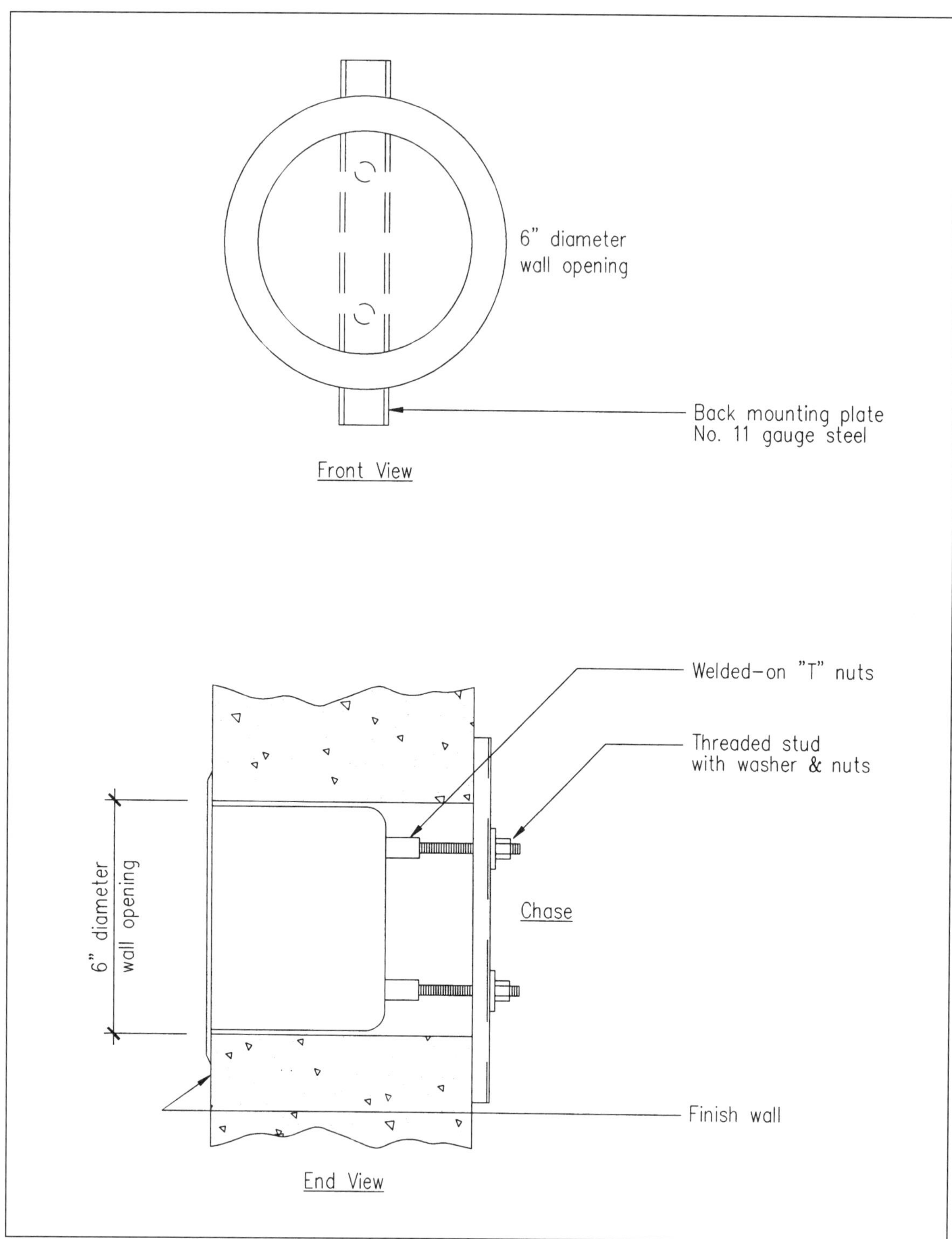

Figure 5.10.5 **Inmate cell toilet paper holder.**

Security-type light fixture attached to underside of mezzanine balcony.

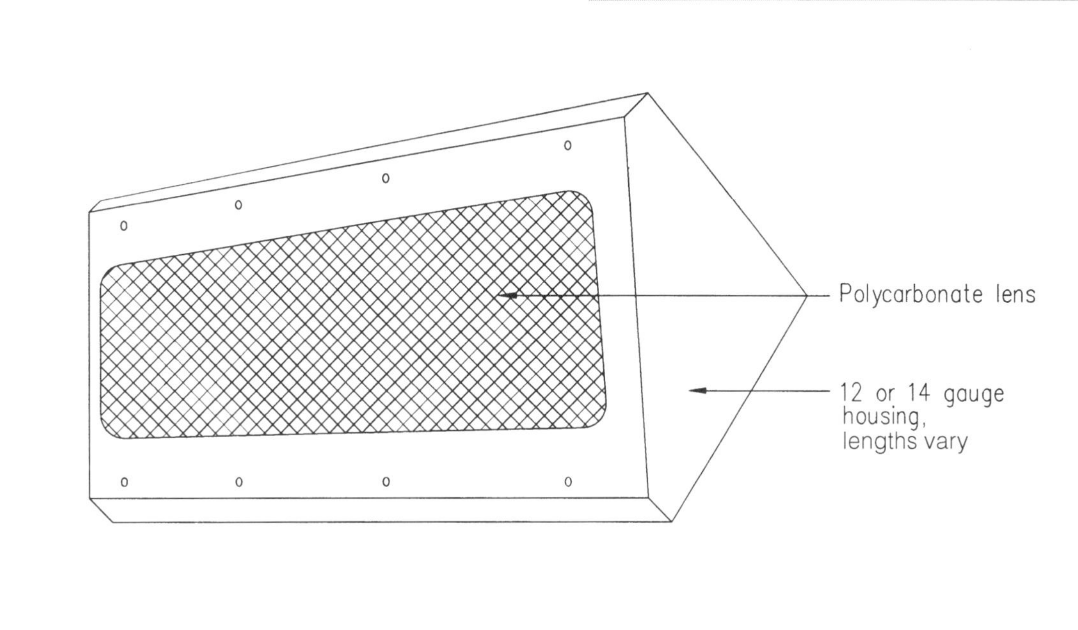

Figure 5.10.6 **Inmate cell light fixture.**

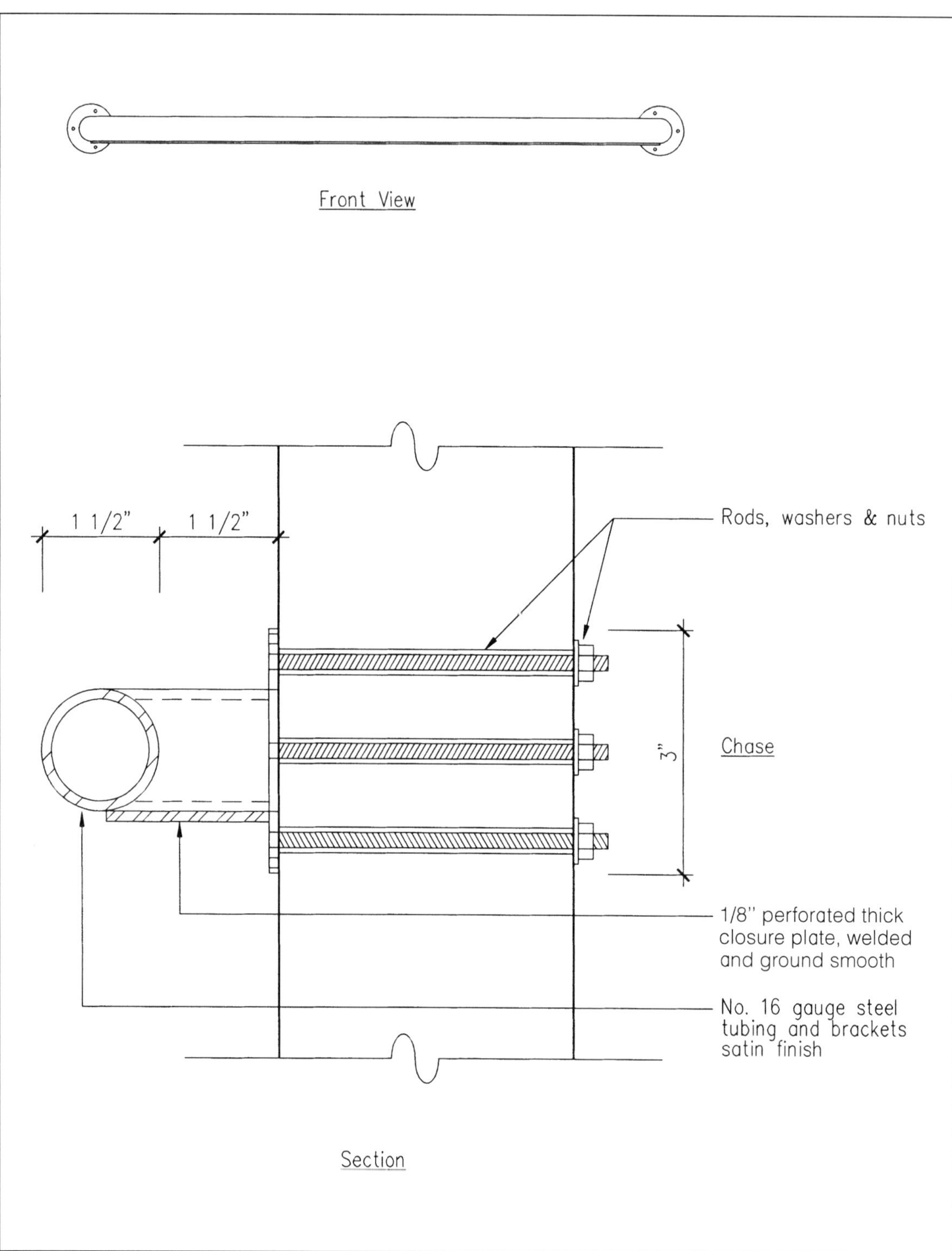

Figure 5.10.7 **Security grab bars attachment.**

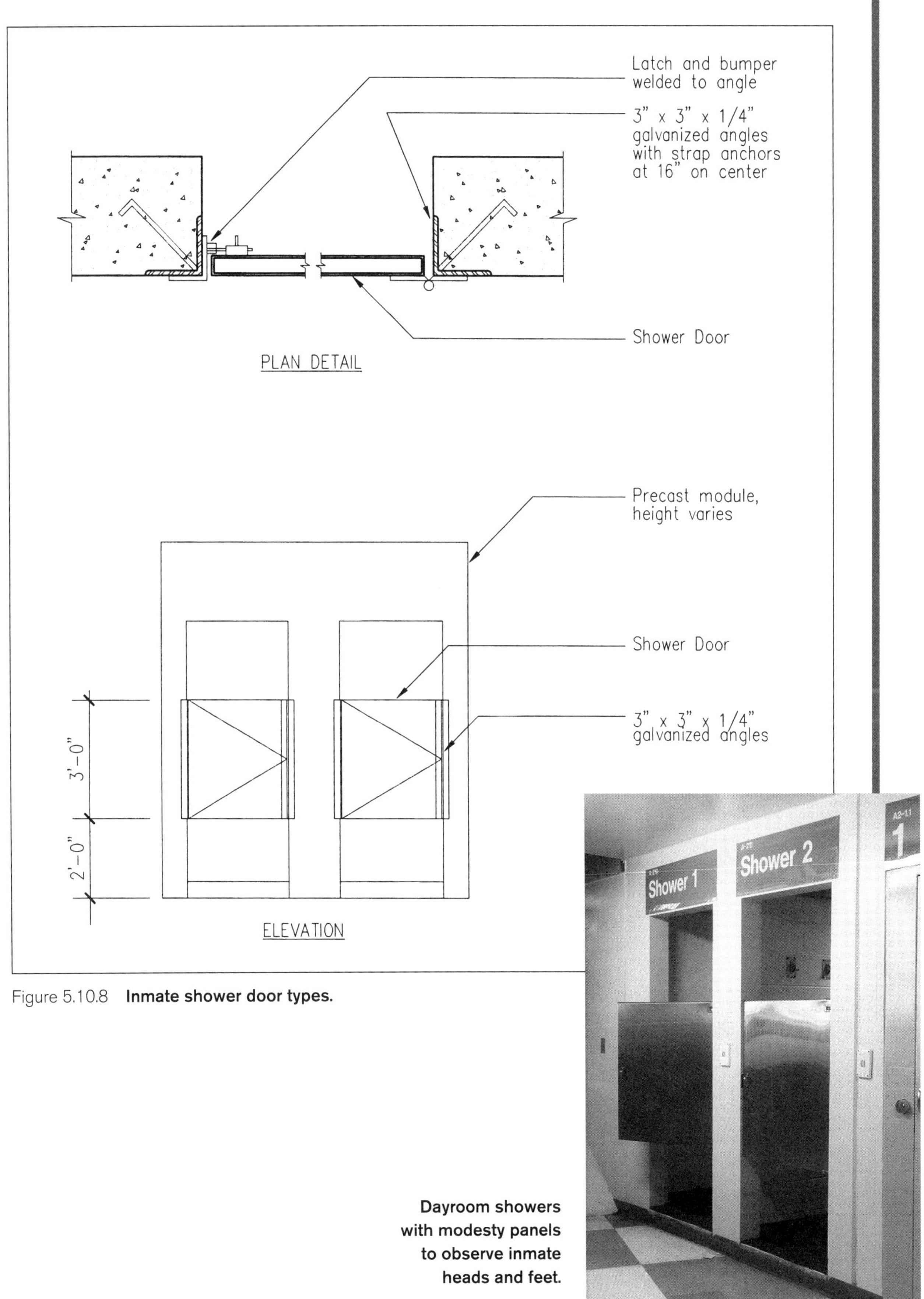

Figure 5.10.8 **Inmate shower door types.**

Dayroom showers with modesty panels to observe inmate heads and feet.

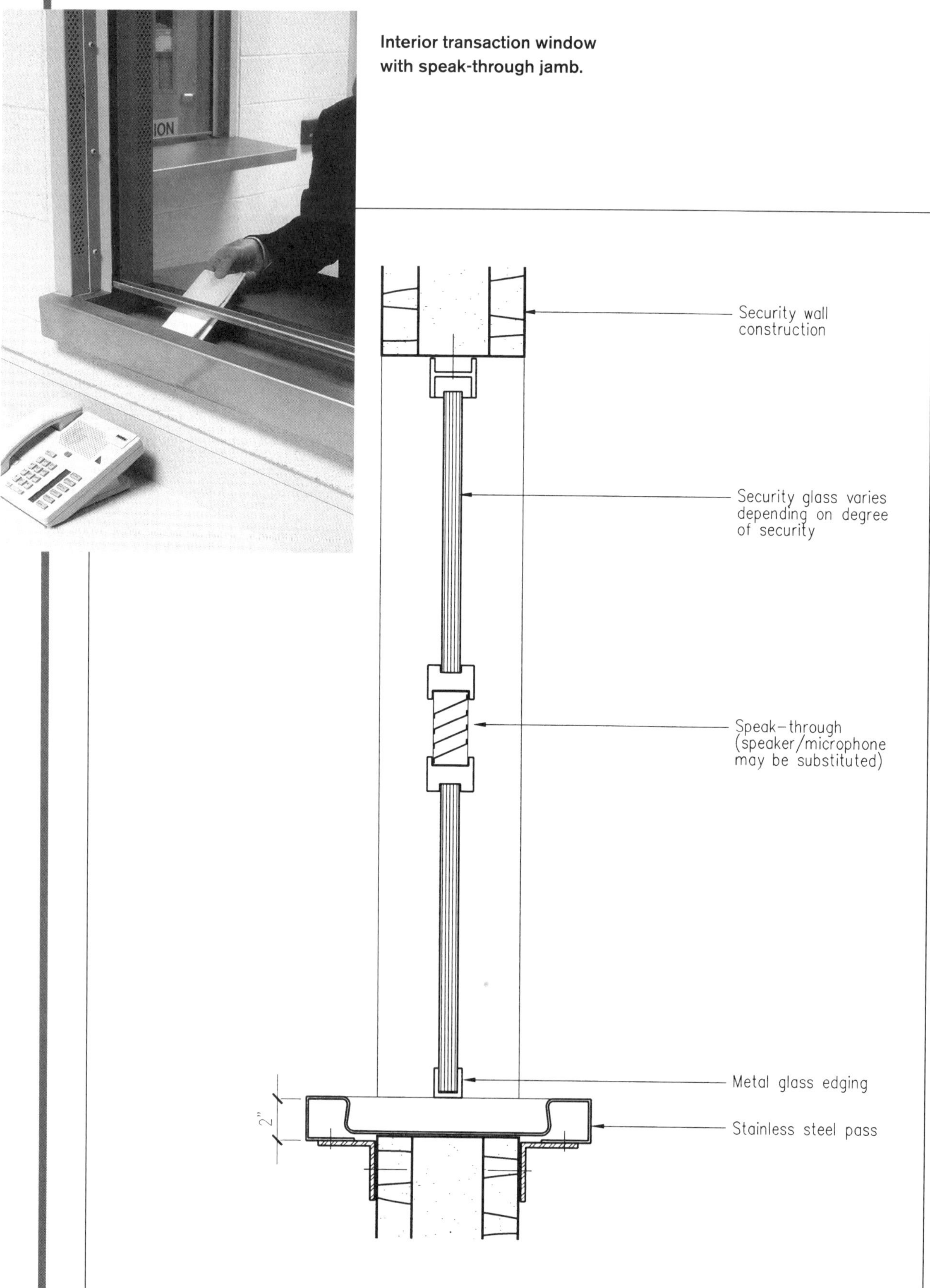

Interior transaction window with speak-through jamb.

Figure 5.10.9 **Interior transaction window and communications device.**

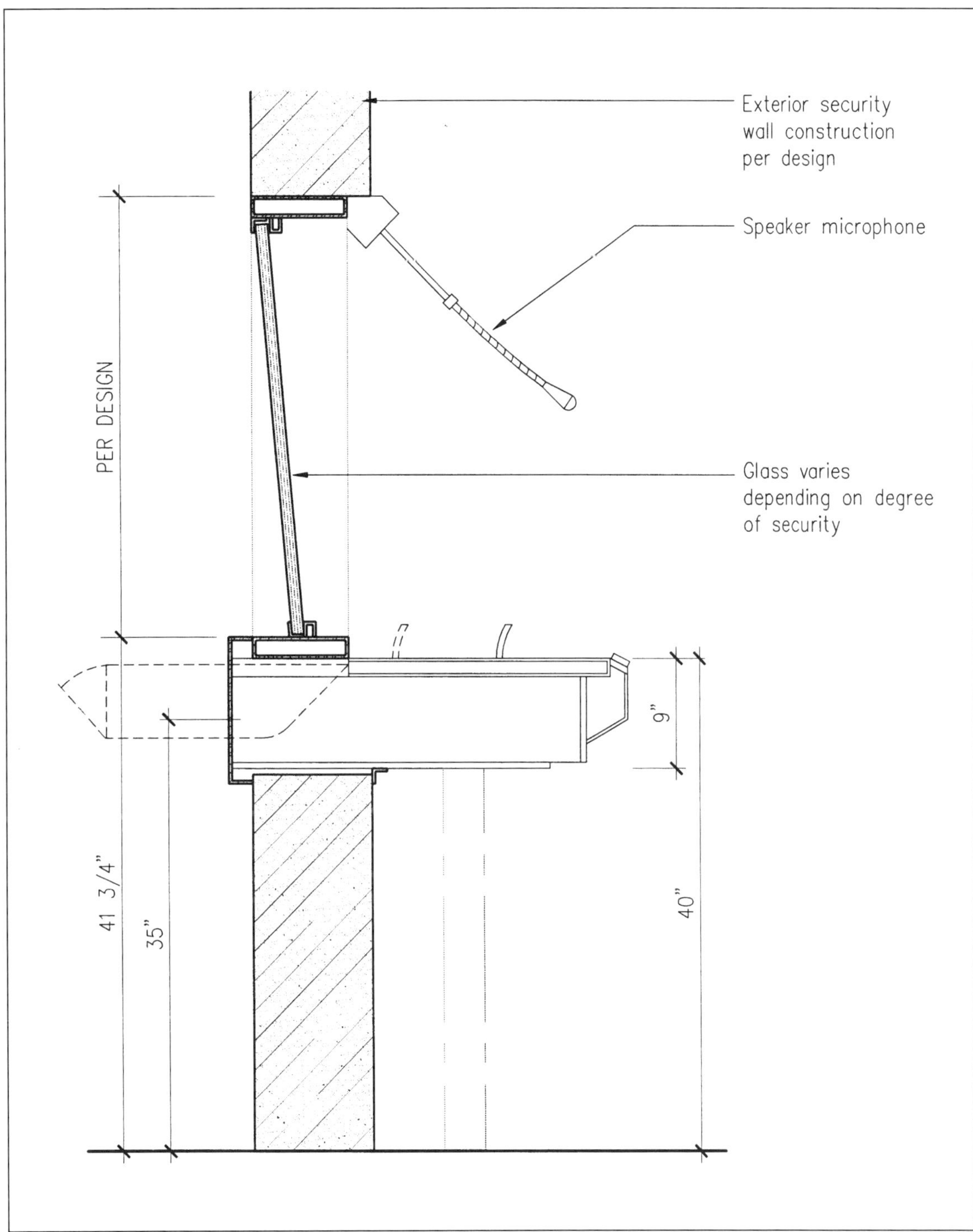

Figure 5.10.10 **Exterior transaction window and communications device.**

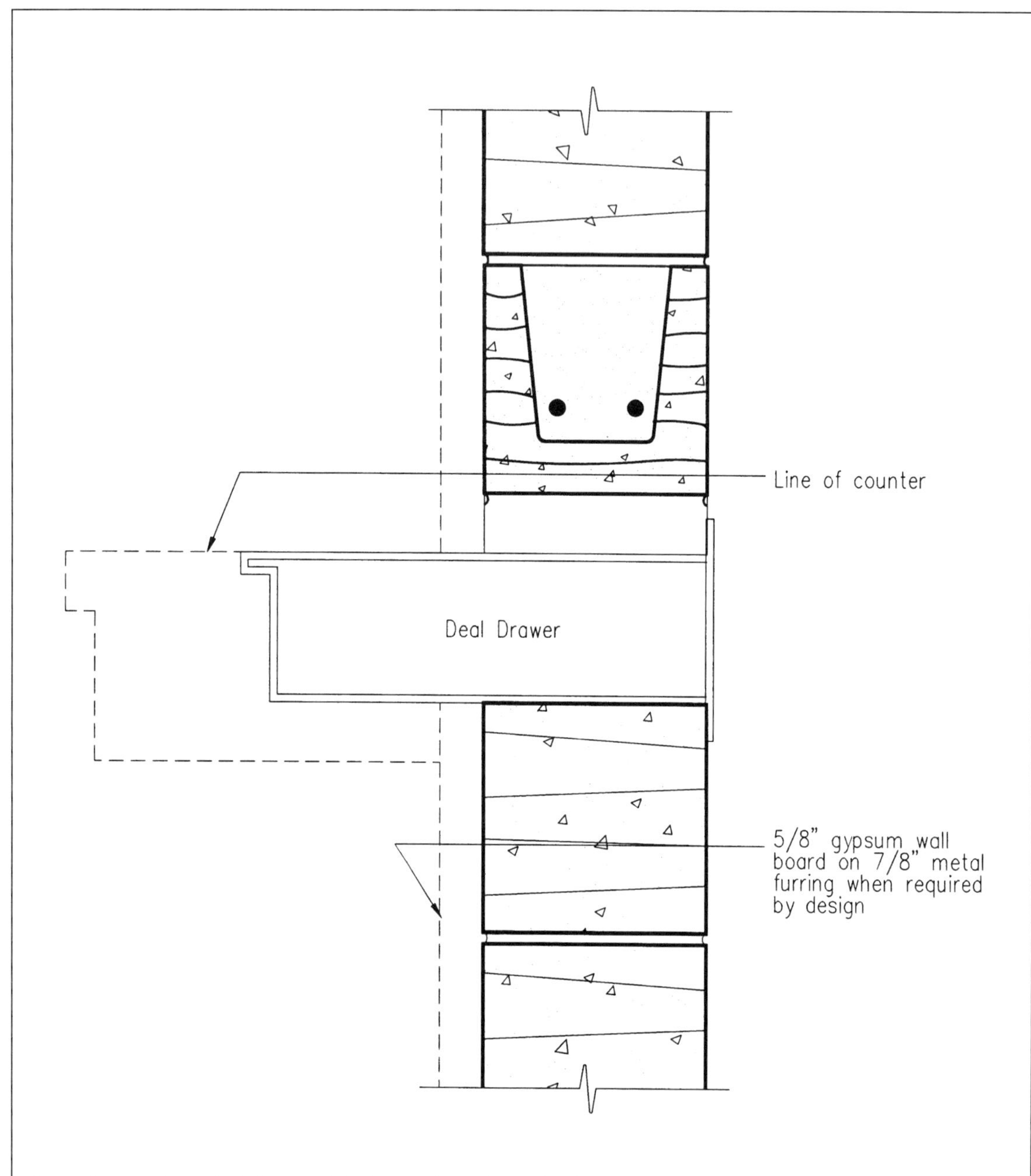

Figure 5.10.11 **Deal drawer.**

Armory and locksmith room package pass.

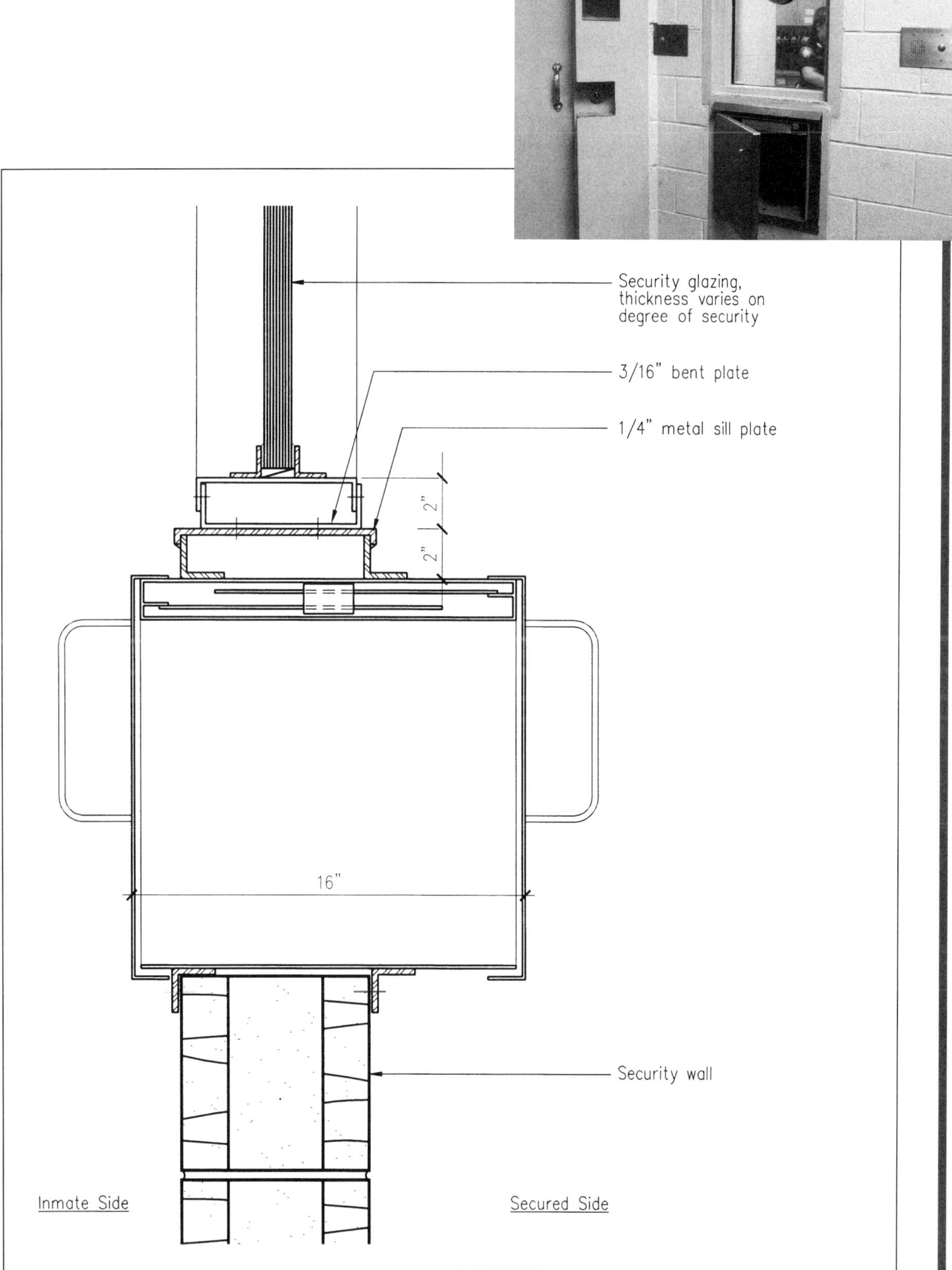

Figure 5.10.12 **Package receiver.**

Unit control station transaction hopper and intercom for inmate side access.

Transaction hopper from unit control station side.

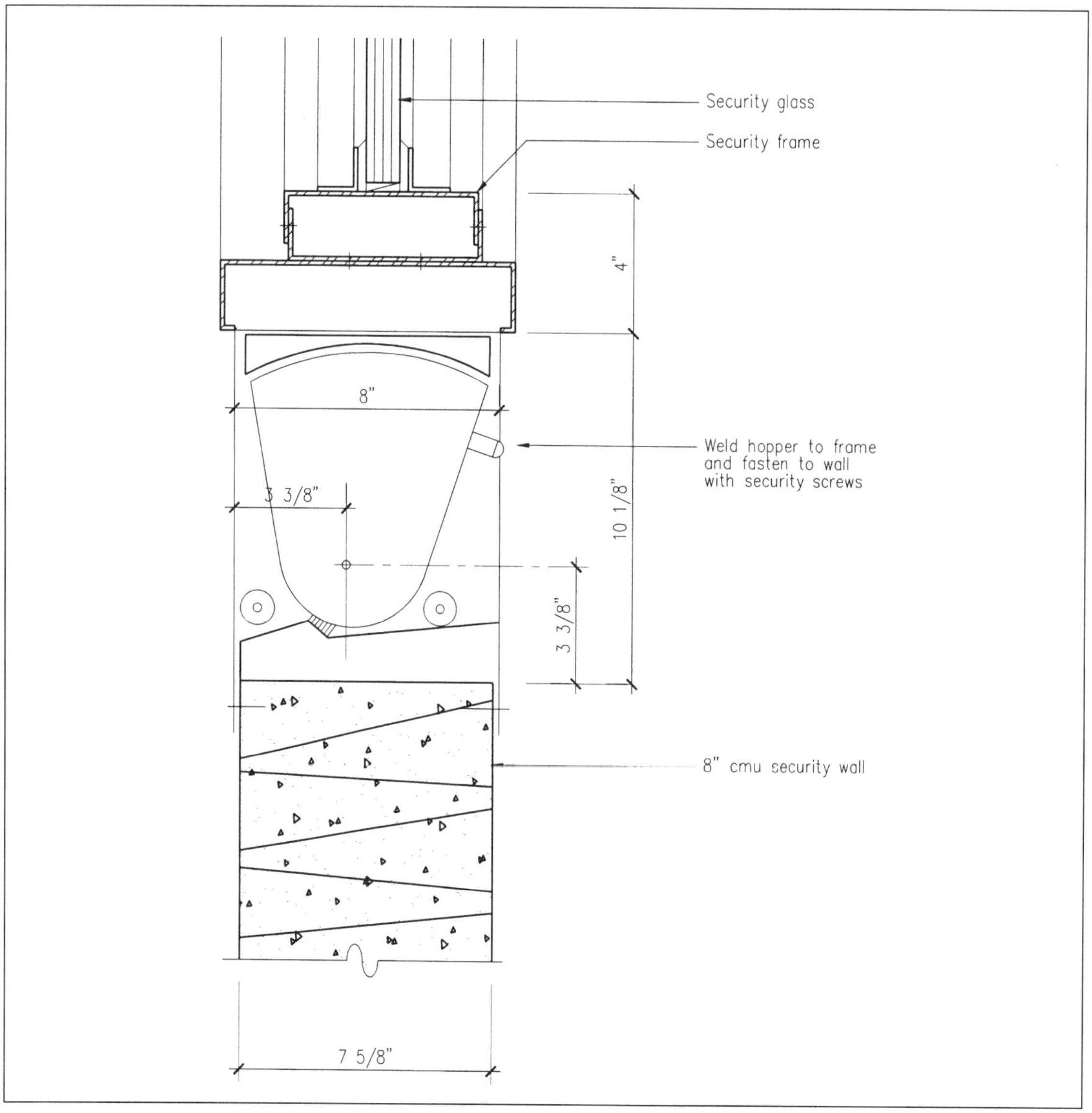

Figure 5.10.13 **Transaction hopper.**

Public lobby metal detector and exit door adjacent to officer's processing desk.

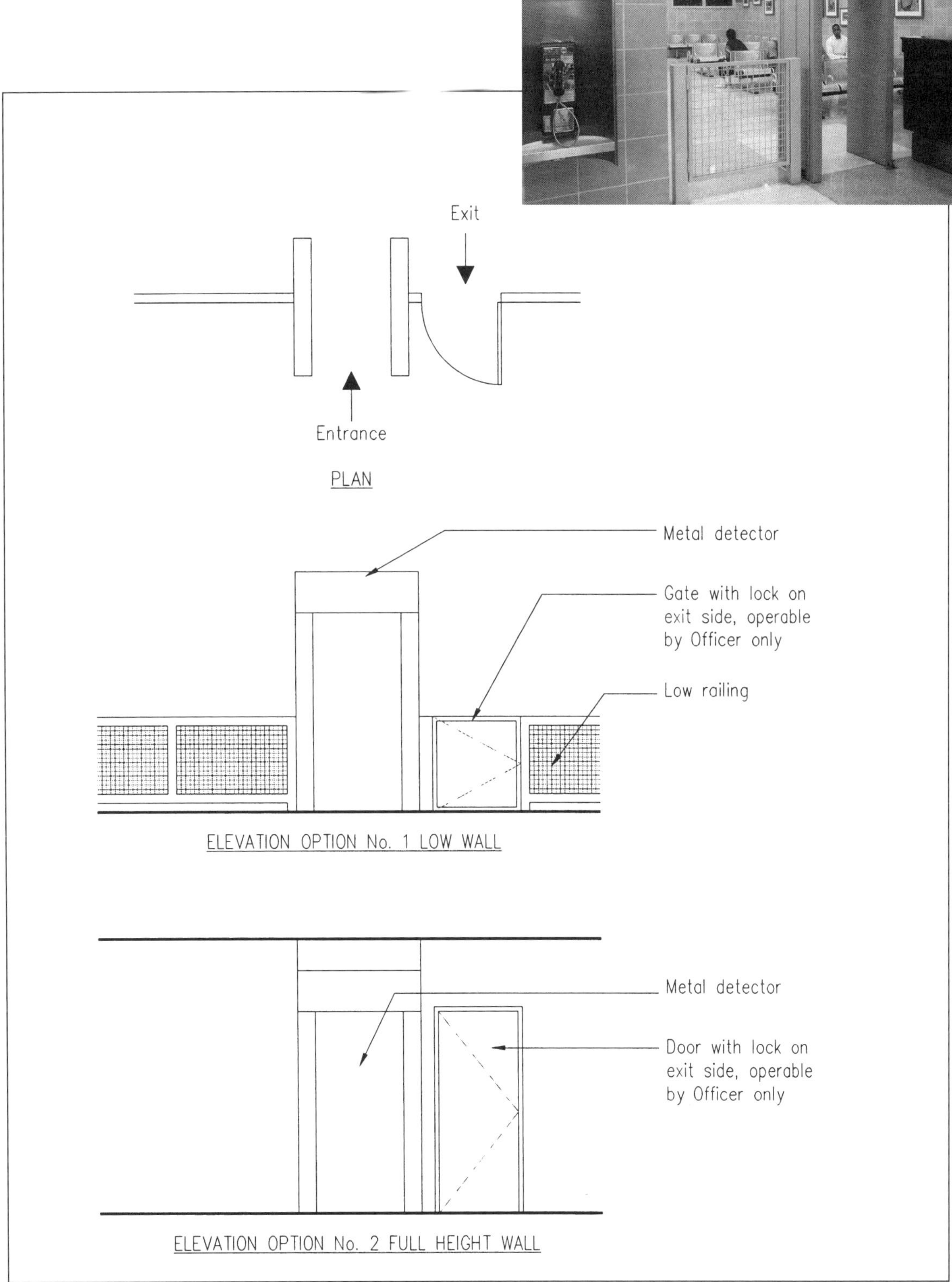

Figure 5.10.14 **Metal detector and side exit door assembly.**

Unit control station.

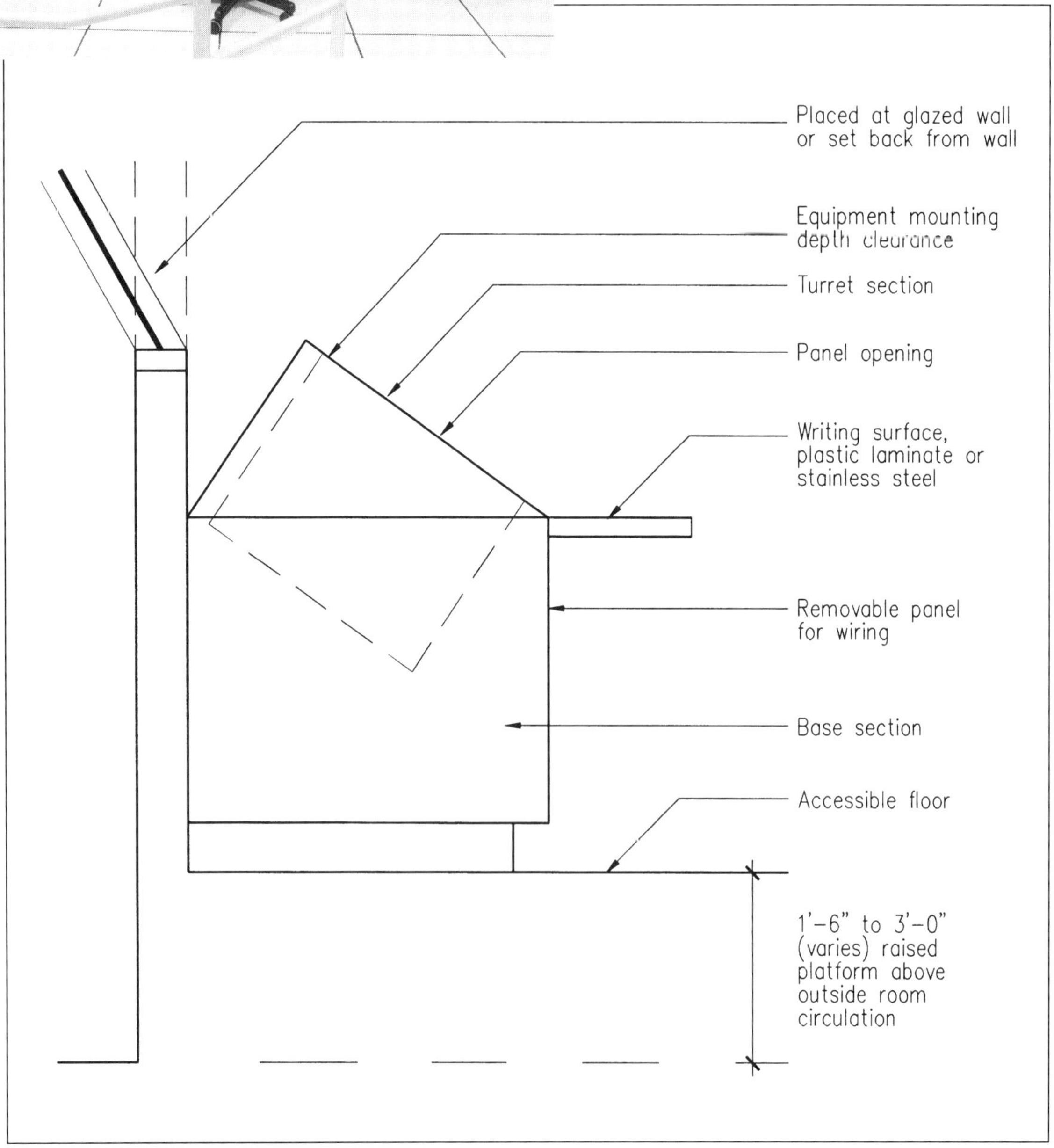

Figure 5.10.15 **Control room console millwork details.**

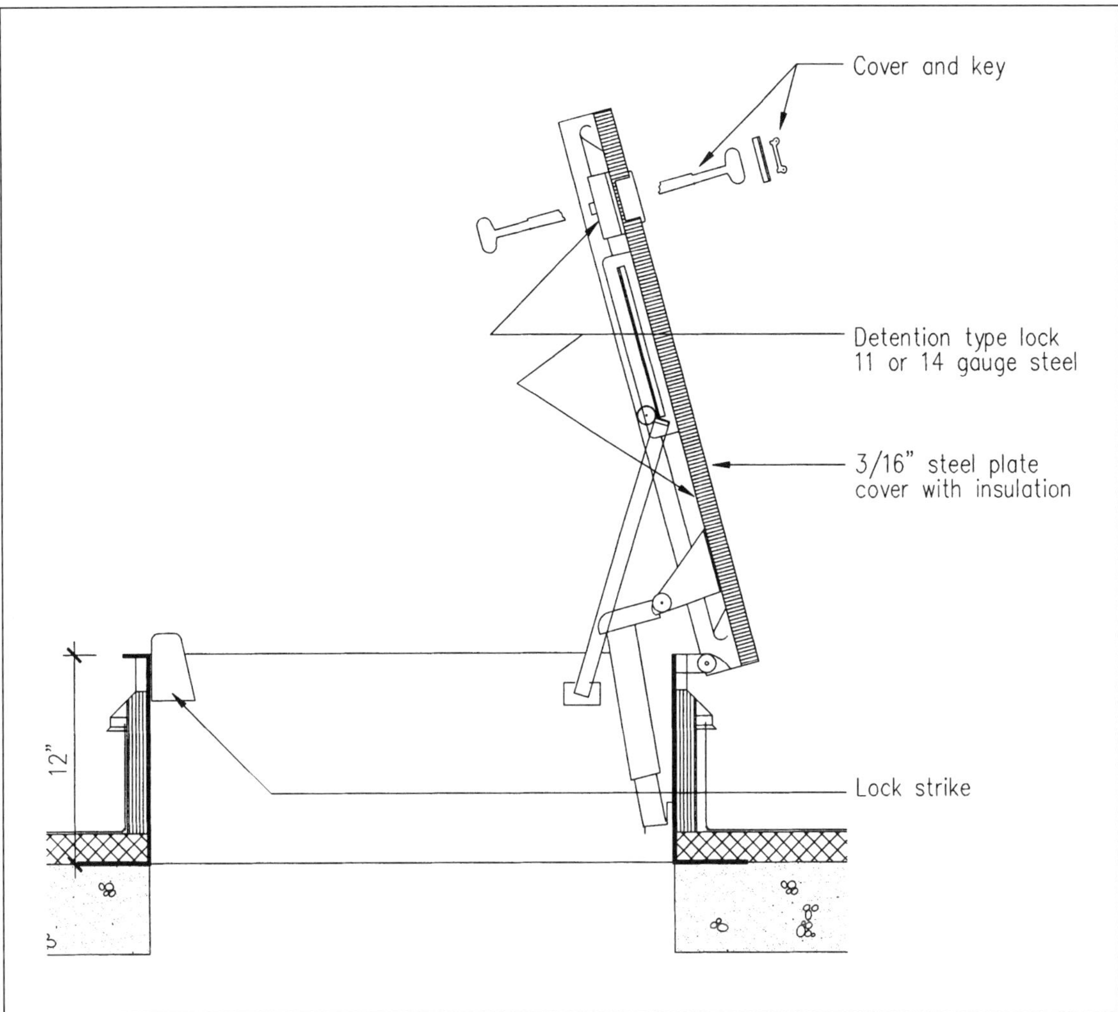

Figure 5.10.16 **Control room escape hatch access to roof.**

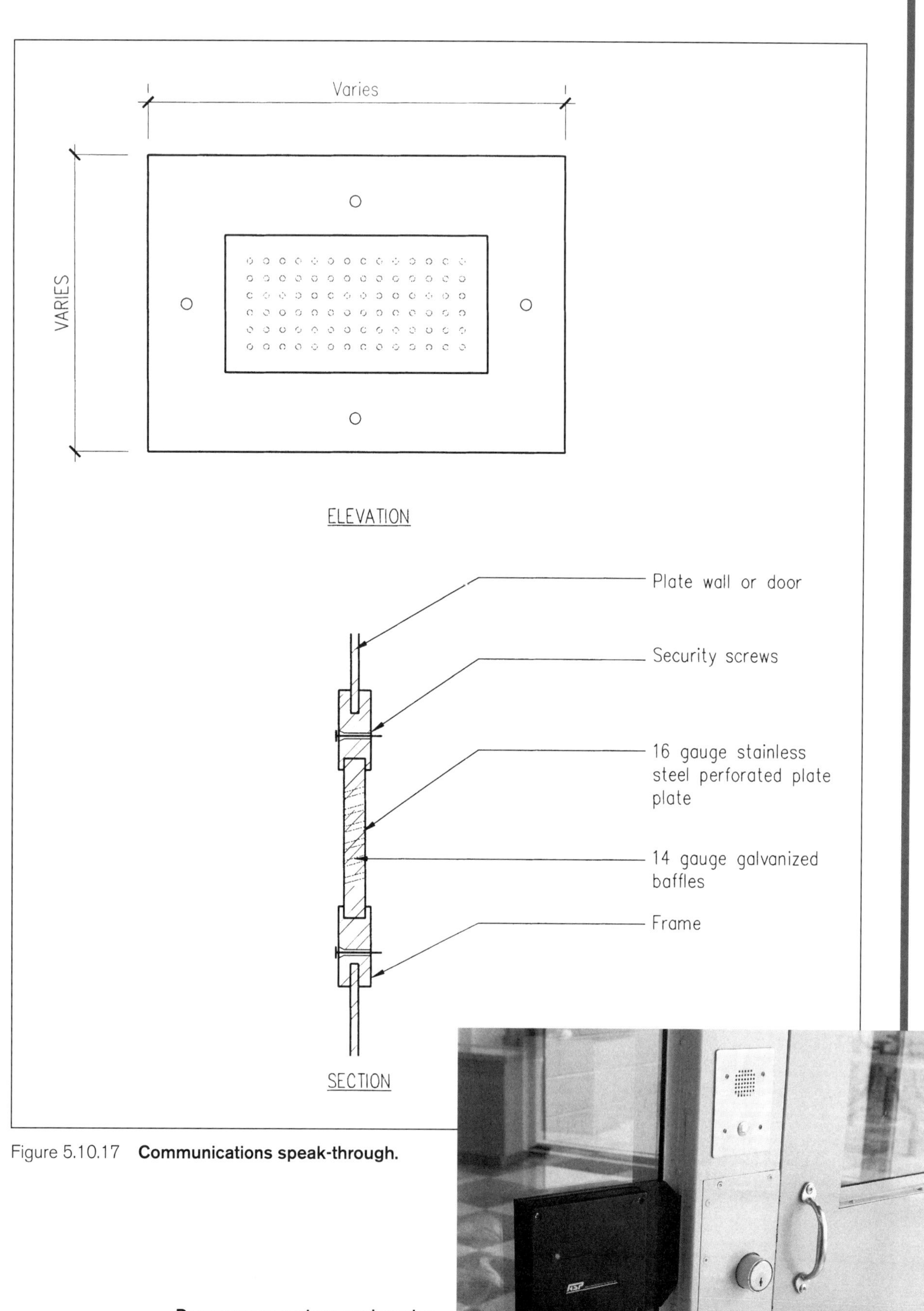

Figure 5.10.17 **Communications speak-through.**

Door access system card reader adjacent to security lock and intercom.

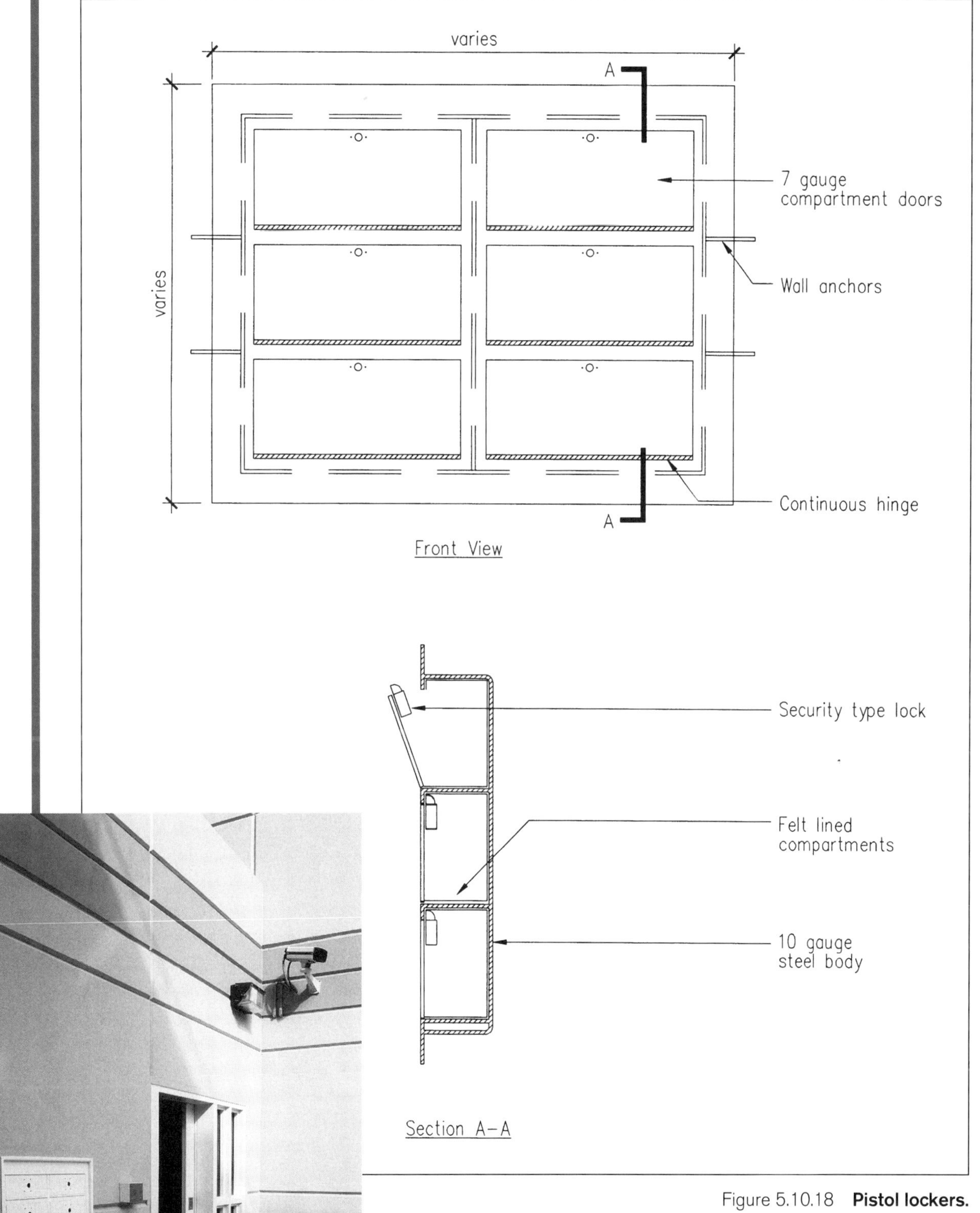

Figure 5.10.18 **Pistol lockers.**

Pistol lockers adjacent to intake sally port with CCTV and light fixture.

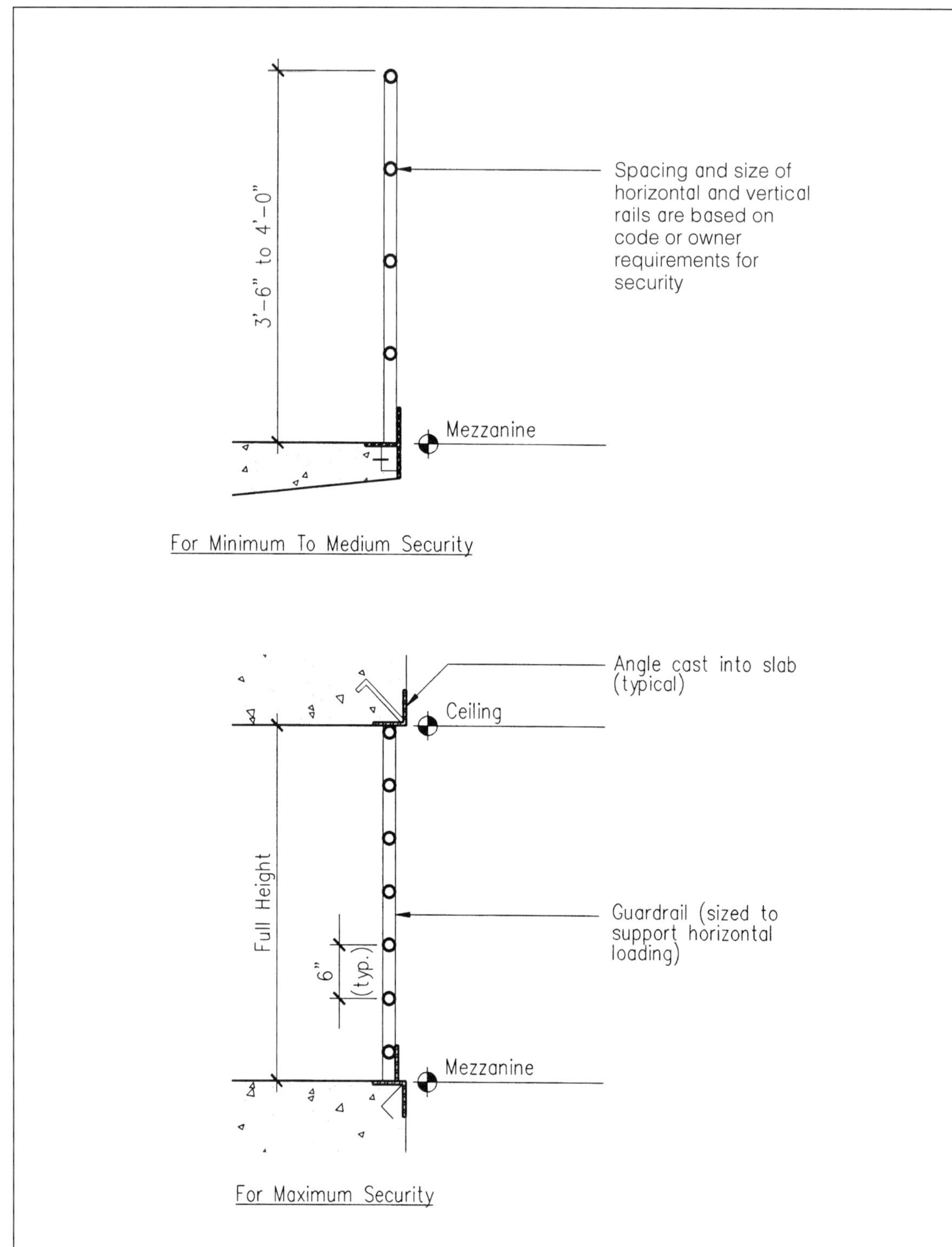

Figure 5.10.19 **Dayroom balcony guardrail options.**

Dayroom ramp with open railing design to lower level.

Dayroom lower-level passive activity area with dining platform and officer's station in the rear.

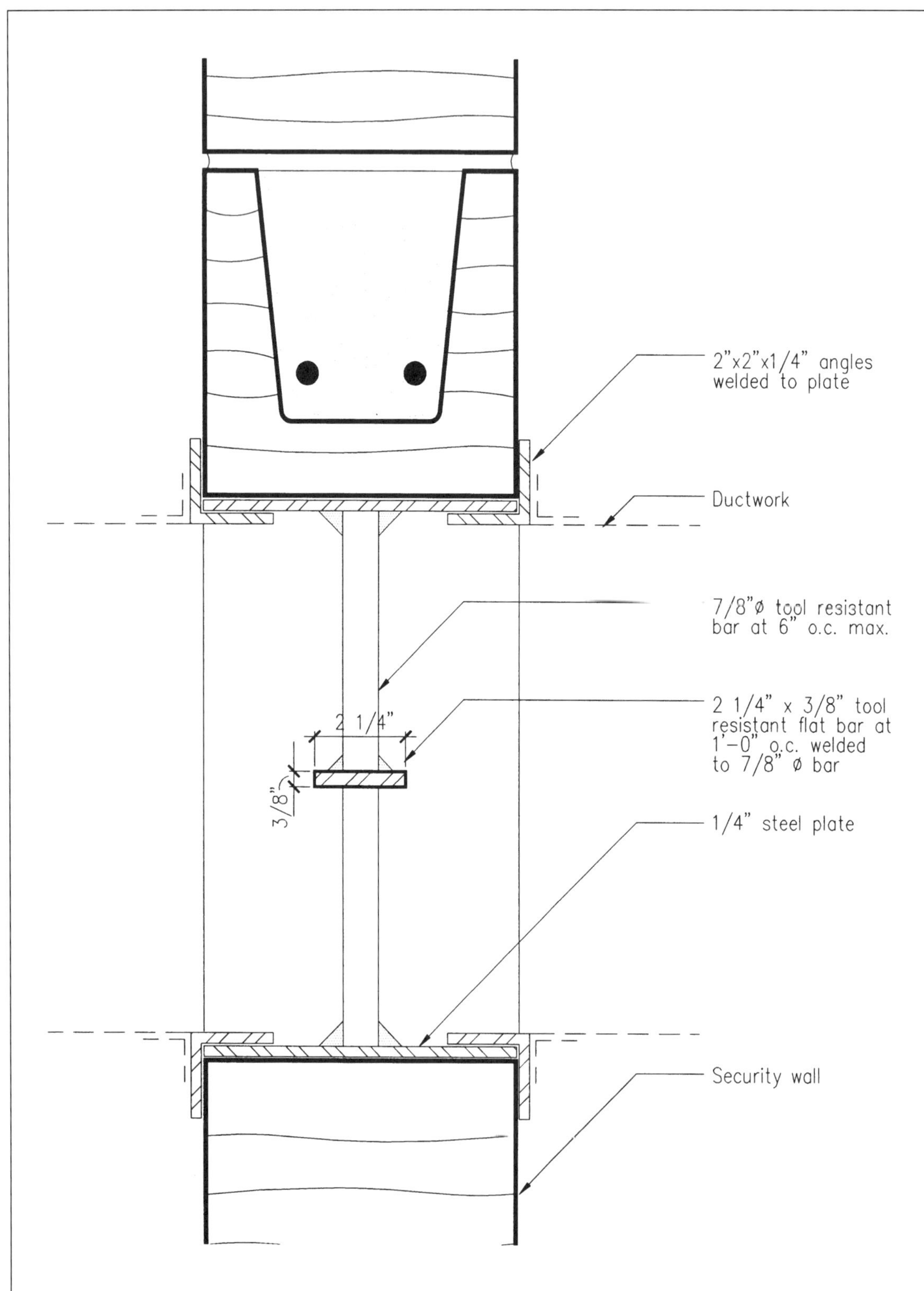

Figure 5.10.20 **Security grille in walls.**

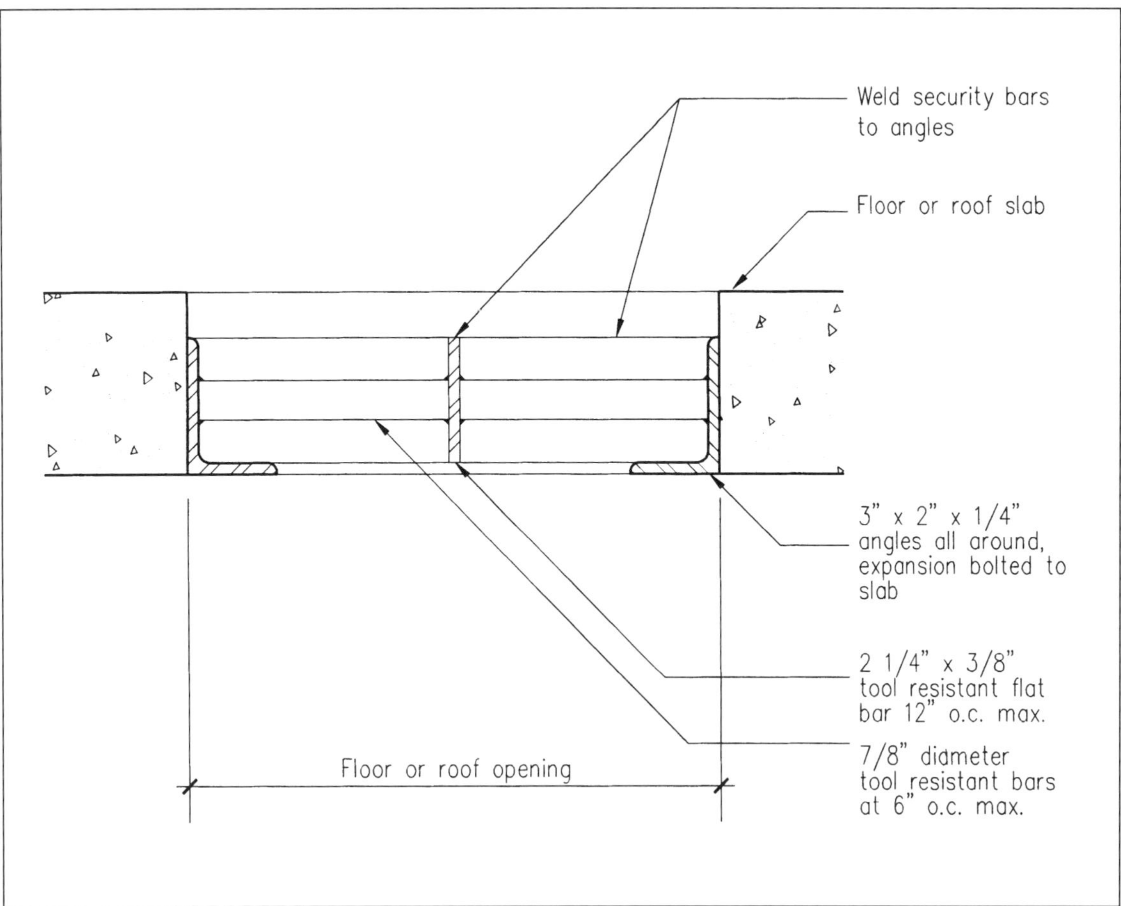

Figure 5.10.21 **Security grille in slab.**

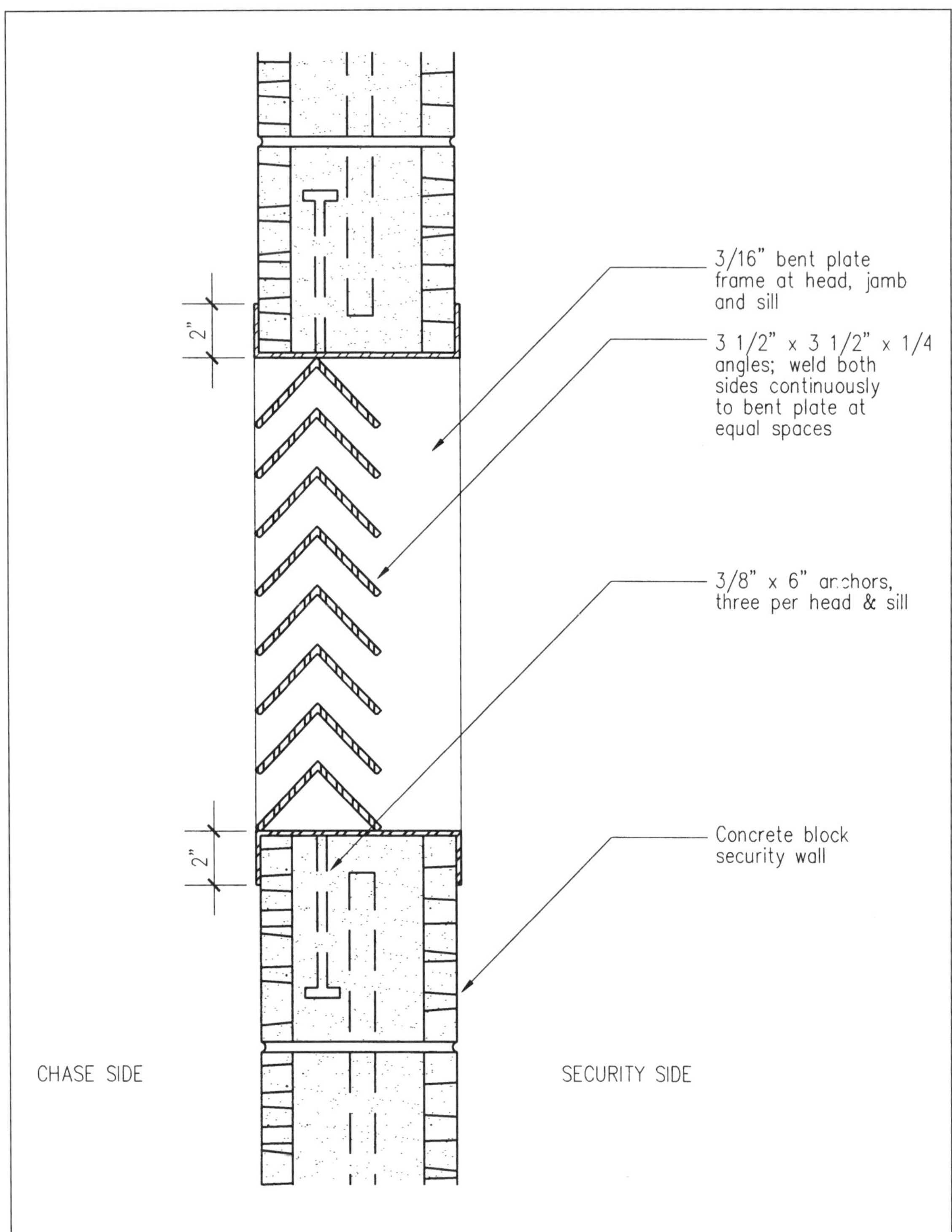

Figure 5.10.22 **Security louver.**

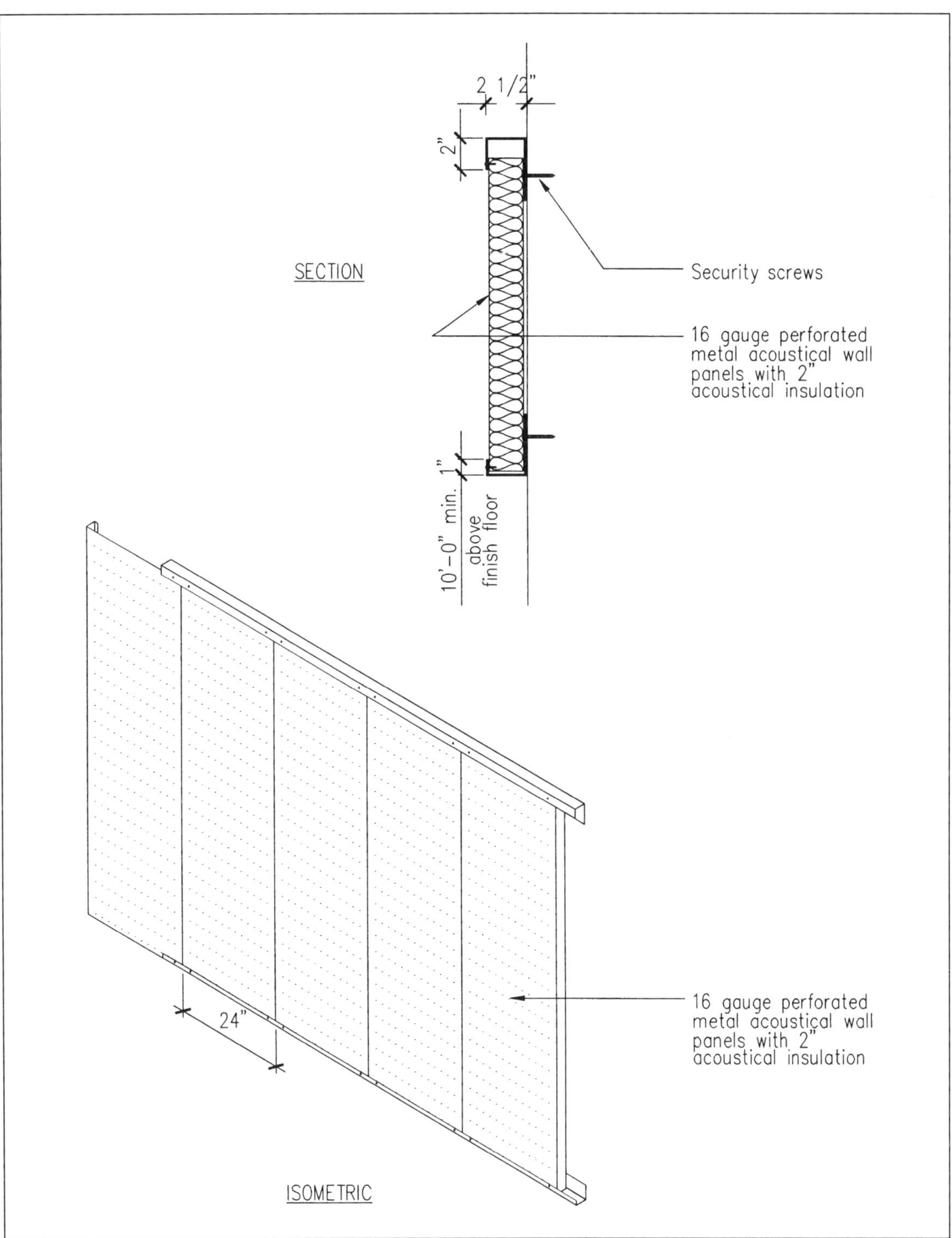

Figure 5.10.23 **Acoustical wall panels.**

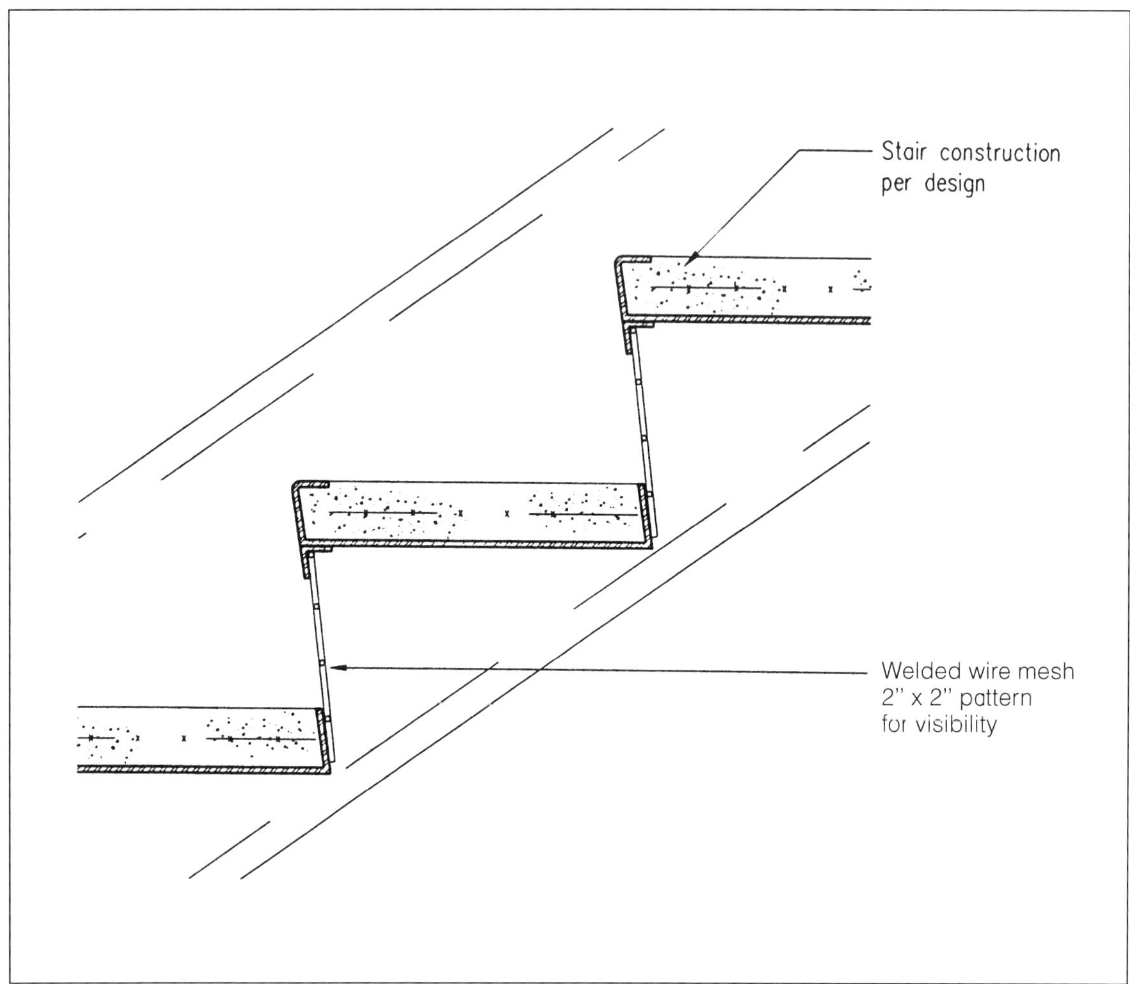

Figure 5.10.24 **Wire mesh stair riser.**

Dayroom officer's desk with touch-screen door control and observation of lower- and upper-level cell fronts.

Dayroom open stair risers with security mesh.

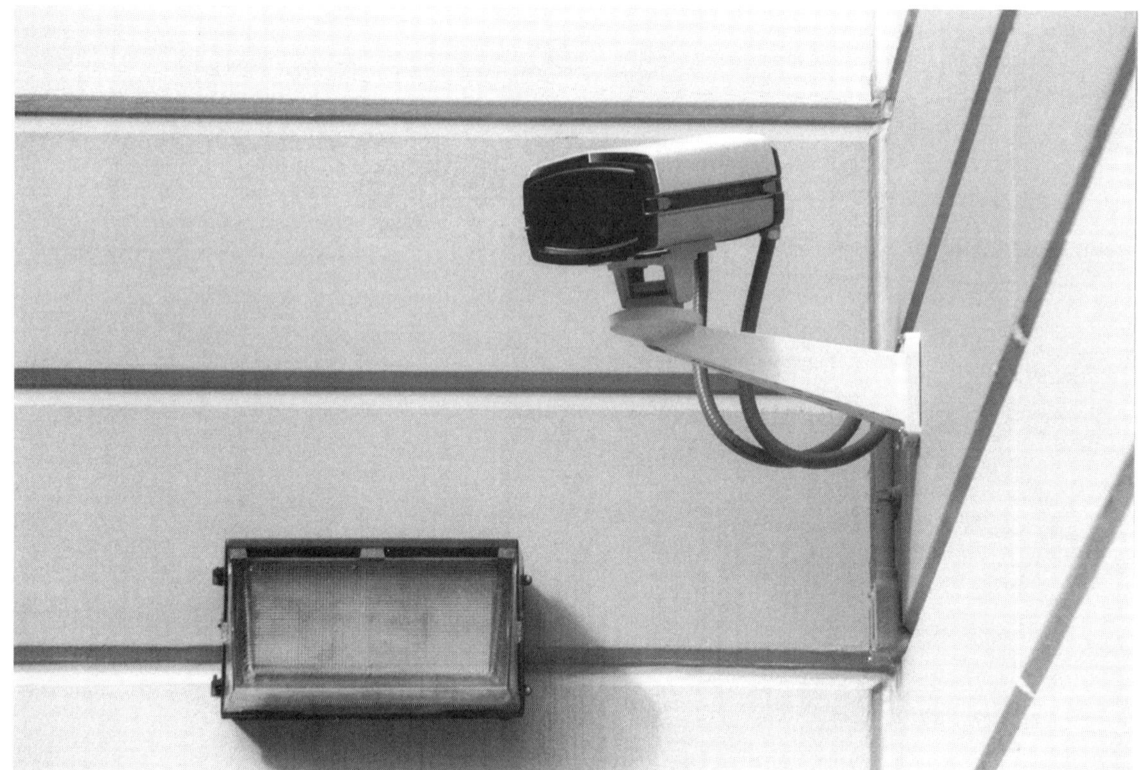

Figure 5.5 **Exterior CCTV and light fixture.**

Figure 5.6 **Dayroom skylights with security bars.**

Figure 5.7 **Inmate telephones secured to wall in dayroom.**

Figure 5.8
Shower water control panel with soap holder.

Figure 5.9 **Elevator staff access card reader, security key lock, and firefighter emergency key access.**

6
Supplemental Information: Perimeter Security Systems

GENERAL INFORMATION

The intent of this section is to provide a summary of considerations relative to the selection of primary perimeter sensor types and configurations for the employment at correctional/detention facilities.

In general, operational performance of a perimeter detection system is evaluated on the basis of the system's *Probability of detection* and its associated *false alarm rate.* Typically, the sensitivity of a system may be increased to enhance the probability of detection; however, the susceptibility to false alarms is increased. A compromise is made between probability of detection and false alarm rate when implementing a system.

In the system selection process, the specific site constraints may dictate that a system be installed with primary emphasis on low false alarm rates, while for other conditions, a higher false alarm rate is acceptable.

The systems described in this section reflect a general cross section of technologies and/or systems considered for correctional and detention facilities. Other systems and/or technologies exist which are not described in this section. The rapidly changing field of technology, the increasing computing power of the microprocessor, and the general reduction in cost of electronic systems requires constant evaluation of products and technologies which are to be considered for electronic perimeter detection systems.

Generally, the design of a perimeter system will incorporate multiple technologies or system elements. Each segment of the perimeter must be evaluated to ensure that the selected system will perform to the desired expectations when implemented.

Successful implementation of an electronic perimeter detection system requires the following:

- Selection of an appropriate technology to support the site constraints and facility objectives
- Assurance that the system is installed properly and in conformance with the system manufacturer's recommendations
- Thorough system testing to ensure system performance supports the design objectives
- Routine testing of the system to verify system performance
- A maintenance program to ensure that the system is maintained in order to perform according to initial acceptance standards

Following is a brief overview of systems and/or technologies which may be considered when selecting primary perimeter security systems.

SYSTEMS REVIEW

The following brief descriptions of sensors and/or technologies are those generally considered in the process of selecting a perimeter detection system. It is the intent of this section to provide an overview of systems and identify factors relative to specific sensors and/or technologies.

Cost estimates are made on a zone basis assuming a zone length of approximately 300 feet. Certain systems inherently can provide greater zone lengths at a minimal cost increase; however, detection resolution of approximately 300 feet is assumed. Costs do not include the central processor, map displays, or remote enunciation which are common to all systems. Since cost will vary depending on time and specific site conditions, the cost data included herein reflects a basis for cost comparison rather than absolute costs.

TAUT WIRE

Taut wire systems consist of an array of sense wires that are under tension, with each wire connected to a sensor located at the midpoint of the wire. The spacing of the wires is selected such that an intruder must displace the wires in order to pass through the array. Upon deflecting the wires greater than a predetermined amount, the sensor is activated and an alarm signal is generated. (See Fig. 6.1.)

The wire array may be either free standing or attached to an existing standard wire fabric-type fence.

Significant system use considerations

- System moderately conforms to the site topography and may be installed essentially along any path for which a fence is installed.
- Height of the sensor array is dictated by the number of wires in the array and sense wire spacing.
- System has extremely low nuisance and false alarm rate.
- Detection zones are limited to linear segments. Changes in fence-line direction generally require termination of a detection zone at the fence transition point.
- Long-term physical stability of anchor and sensor post is mandatory to support system performance.
- Cost of maintenance and testing of the system is relatively high and influenced by seasonal variations.

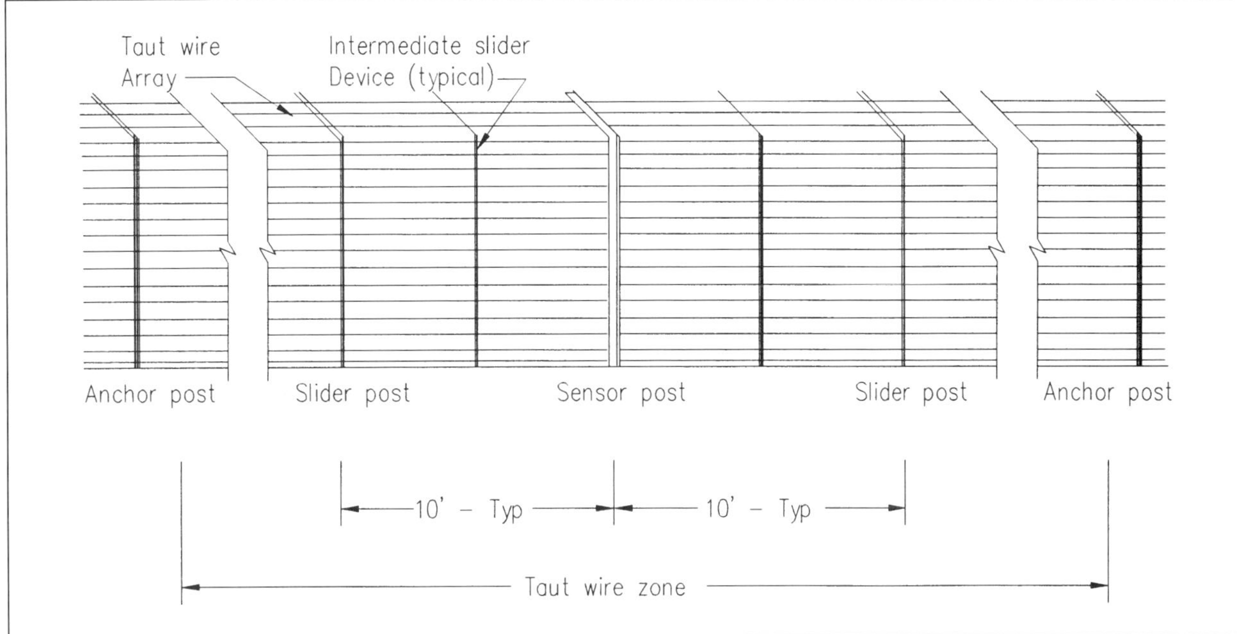

Figure 6.1 **Typical stand-alone taut wire zone configuration.**

Installed cost is approximately $180 per foot for a free-standing 8-foot-high array with an approximately 3-foot outrigger. Installed cost of a similar array mounted on an existing fence is estimated to be approximately $150 per foot.

MICROWAVE

Microwave systems provide detection by sensing changes in the received radio frequency carrier resulting from disturbances in a radio frequency (rf) field. These systems typically operate in the 10 and 24 GHz frequency ranges. (See Fig. 6.2.)

Significant system use considerations:

- Topography must be stringently controlled between the transmitter and receiver in order to insure detection reliability which can be impaired by shadow effects.
- Horizontal beam width must be controlled to limit the horizontal width of the detection zone. This consideration is significant when employing the system in the vicinity of a fence or other objects which could potentially affect the rf field. This system may require a wider "no man's land" than other types of systems.
- Vertical detection boundaries are controlled by the antenna patterns of the transmitter and receiver. To provide adequate vertical zone control, transmitters and receivers must be *set back* from the defined zone of detection. This is referred to as a *cross-over zone.* The site constraints affect the available setback distances and thus impact on the available zone of detection.
- Systems are subject to nuisance and false alarms primarily from blowing debris, high-level elec-

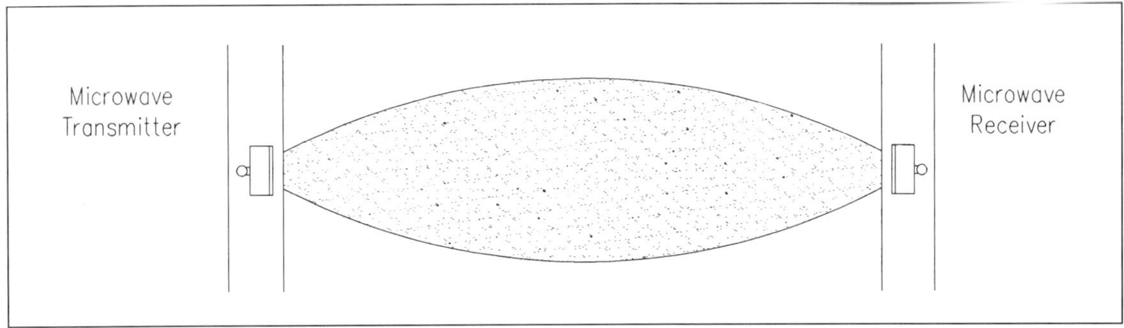

Figure 6.2 **Typical plan view—microwave system detection envelope. A typical microwave link may have a detection pattern similar to the one shown in this diagram.**

tromagnetic interference, uncontrolled vegetation, small animals, water flowing across the detection zone, and alarm sensitivity settings. The system operation is significantly affected by deep snow.

- Installation of the physical hardware is relatively simple. Special attention must be given to insure a stable mounting post.

Installed cost of a single-link microwave system is approximately $5000 per zone. A dual-stacked microwave link is estimated to have an installed cost of approximately $8000 per zone. These costs are exclusive of grading costs.

SEISMIC GEOPHONE

Seismic geophone–type systems provide detection based on processing electrical signals generated via discrete geophones. *Geophones* generate electrical signals when relative motion exists between a permanent magnet and a suspended sense coil. The geophone translates motion or vibrations of the medium to which the geophone is attached into electrical signals. Geophones translate only vibrations which exist in the plane of the axis of the sense coil. This response characteristic provides a mechanism to discriminate against certain undesirable signals or vibrations. (See Fig. 6.3.) Geophones may be fence-mounted or buried in an array.

Significant system use considerations:

- Fence-mounted arrays are dependent on the rigidity of the fence to minimize false alarms due to casual fence movement.
- Single-axis sensing of the geophone provides some isolation or suppression of undesired horizontal fence movement.
- Detectors have high immunity to alarms resulting from rain, snow, and ice.
- Fence or buried arrays conform to the fence line or site topography.
- Medium in which buried arrays are installed must be controlled to optimize sensor performance.
- System sensitivity of buried arrays is affected by freezing of the medium in which the array is buried.
- Systems are subject to nuisance and/or false alarms caused primarily by casual fence movement, high-level acoustic vibrations, ice falling from fence and impacting sensor, and fence movement caused by high winds.
- Installation of fence-mounted geophones is relatively simple and the detector array is secured to the fence using cable ties. Each array is custom-fabricated by the manufacturer to provide the detection zone as specified. Buried arrays must be placed in a medium which provides a controlled response.

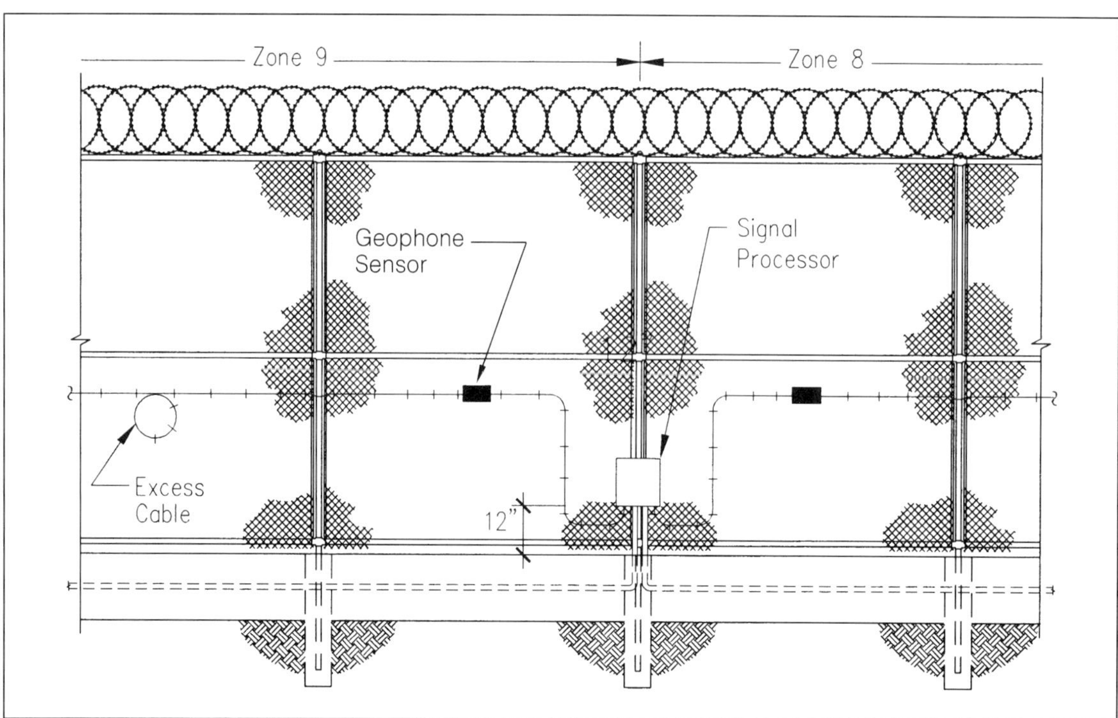

Figure 6.3 **Typical fence-mounted seismic geophone configuration zone transition.**

Installed cost of a fence-mounted detection zone is approximately $45 per foot. A buried array could approximately cost the same, excluding preparation of the array bed.

PORTED CABLE

Ported cable systems provide detection by sensing variations in electromagnetic surface waves generated in the VHF radio spectrum. Certain systems employing this dctection concept generate the surface wave via a leaky transmission line (leaky cable) excited by a signal source operating in the 40-MHz region. The signal coupled to a receiver cable has characteristics which are dictated by the dielectric constant between the cables and the conductivity of the material in which the lines are buried. Objects of a certain size and composition, such as a human body, entering the field change the effected dielectric constant and this results in perturbations in the signal sensed by the receiver cable. These perturbations are detected, processed, and alarms are generated if these disturbances characterize the presence of an intruder. (See Fig. 6.4.)

Significant system use considerations

- Buried lines follow site topography.
- Detection zone width is a function of line spacing.
- Fence, conduits, drainage lines, and other materials which would alter the uniformity of the dielectric between the transmitter and receiver lines must be removed from the detection zone.
- Ground surface in the vicinity of detection zone must be graded to prevent ponding of water.
- System is subject to radio frequency (rf) interference; however, special coding and filtering provides reasonable isolation from undesired signals.
- Rapid changes in the conductivity of the material in which the cable is buried will modify the system's performance.
- Abrupt transitions cannot occur in line placement, such as sharp corners, since rf signal reflections are caused by these impedance discontinuities.
- System is relatively immune to snow, ice, surface vegetation, and blowing debris.
- Certain systems employ transmitter and receiver lines as power and data lines thus eliminating additional conductors.
- Systems are subject to nuisance and/or false alarms primarily from water ponding, rapid changes in the ground conductivity due to rain and/or freezing conditions, and from rf interferences.
- Installation of the system is relatively simple with particular emphasis being placed on ground preparation, uniform cable spacing, controlling linearity of the cable to avoid rf discontinuities, and maintaining separation between the zone of detection and materials which modify the dielectric constant and/or the conductivity.

Installed cost of a zone of electromagnetic buried line is approximately $45 per foot. This cost

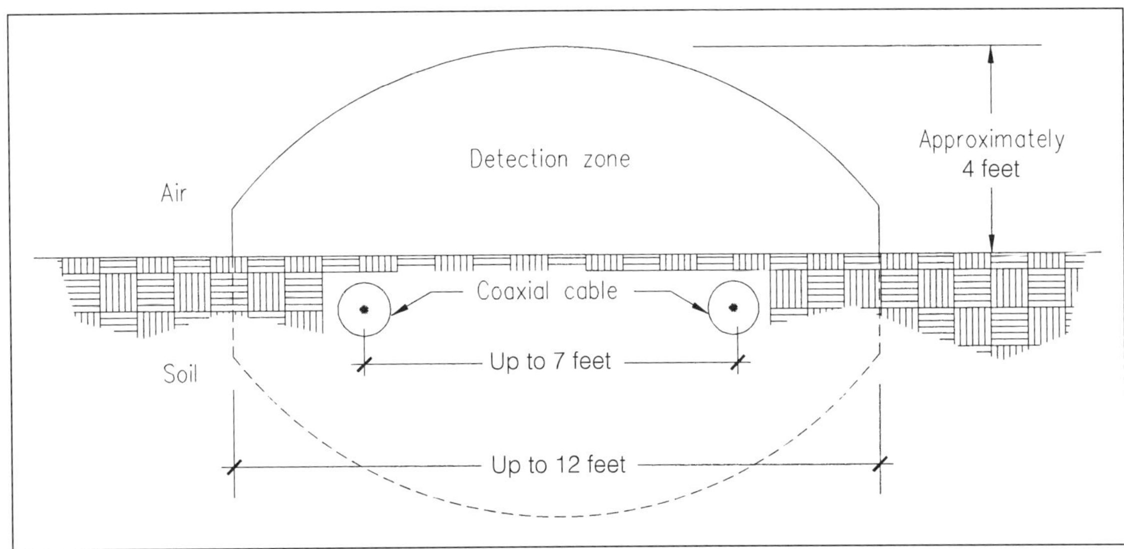

Figure 6.4 **Typical detection envelope pattern for a buried ported coaxial cable system.**

is exclusive of costs associated with preparation of the soil, if required.

ELECTRET CABLE

Electret cable systems employ the principle of a continuous microphonic cable to detect noise generated on a fence. This noise is processed by observing the signal magnitude and the number of detector threshold crossings within a selected time frame. This system consists of a sensitized cable attached to a fence using cable ties. The cable is terminated in a signal processor. (See Fig. 6.5.)

Significant system use considerations

- Fence must be taut to minimize nuisance alarms generated by fence movement.
- Cable may be installed in flexible conduit to prevent the abrasive galvanized surface of the fence from damaging the cable and to protect the cable from certain environmental factors and vandalism.
- Zone detection follows the fence line and is not constrained by topography or straight-line zone segments.
- Systems are subject to nuisance and false alarms primarily from heavy rain, sleet, hail, fence movement, and level or threshold sensitivity set on the signal processor.
- Installation of the physical cable and processors is relatively simple and inexpensive compared to buried systems or systems requiring beam alignment. Primary concern with regard to installation is to insure that the fence is designed and constructed within the rigidity limits as established by the sensor manufacturer.

Installed cost of a zone of electret cable is approximately $35 per foot.

ELECTROMAGNETIC CABLE

Certain *electromagnetic cable systems* incorporate a strain-sensitive technology within a cable configuration to affect a linear transducer. The principle of operation is similar to that of a discrete geophone. The cable system detects fence movements and possesses the cable signals to generate alarms based on signal characteristics. (See Fig. 6.6.)

Significant system use considerations:

- Fence must be taut to minimize nuisance alarms generated by fence movement.
- Cable may be installed in flexible conduit to prevent the abrasive galvanized surface of the fence from damaging the cable and to protect the cable from certain environmental factors.
- Zone detection follows the fence line and is not constrained by topography or straight-line zone segments.

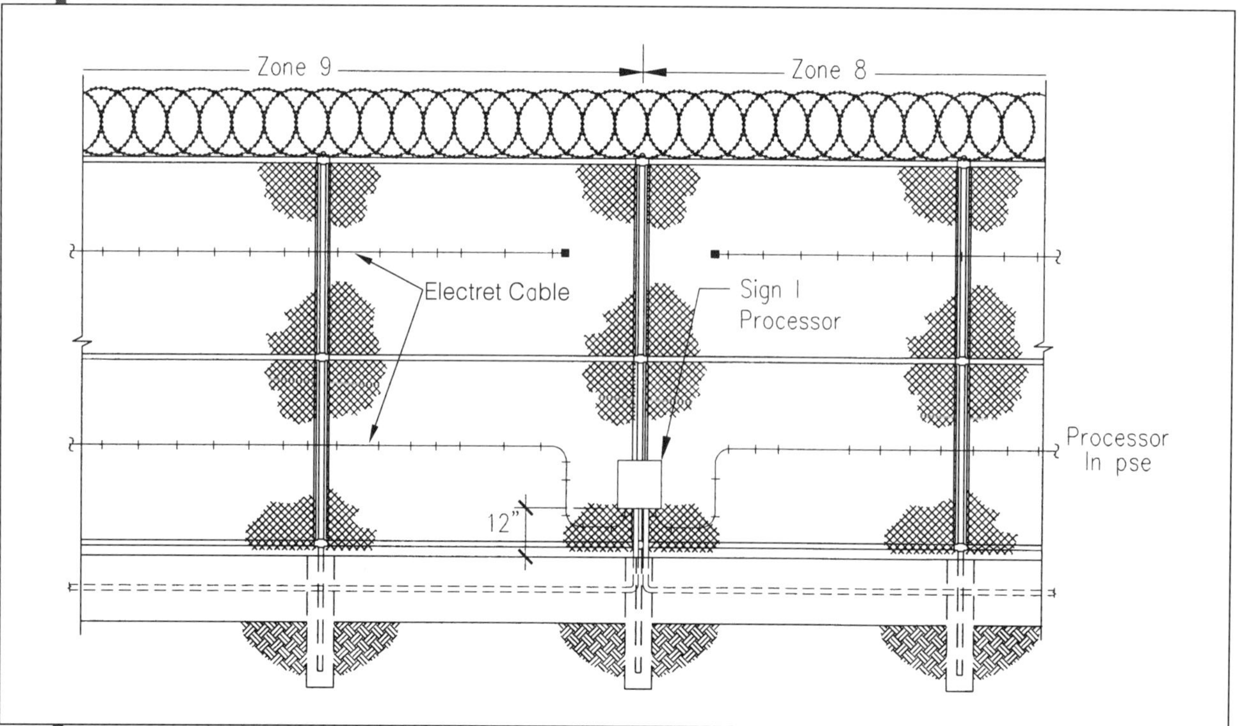

Figure 6.5 **Typical electret cable sensor configuration.**

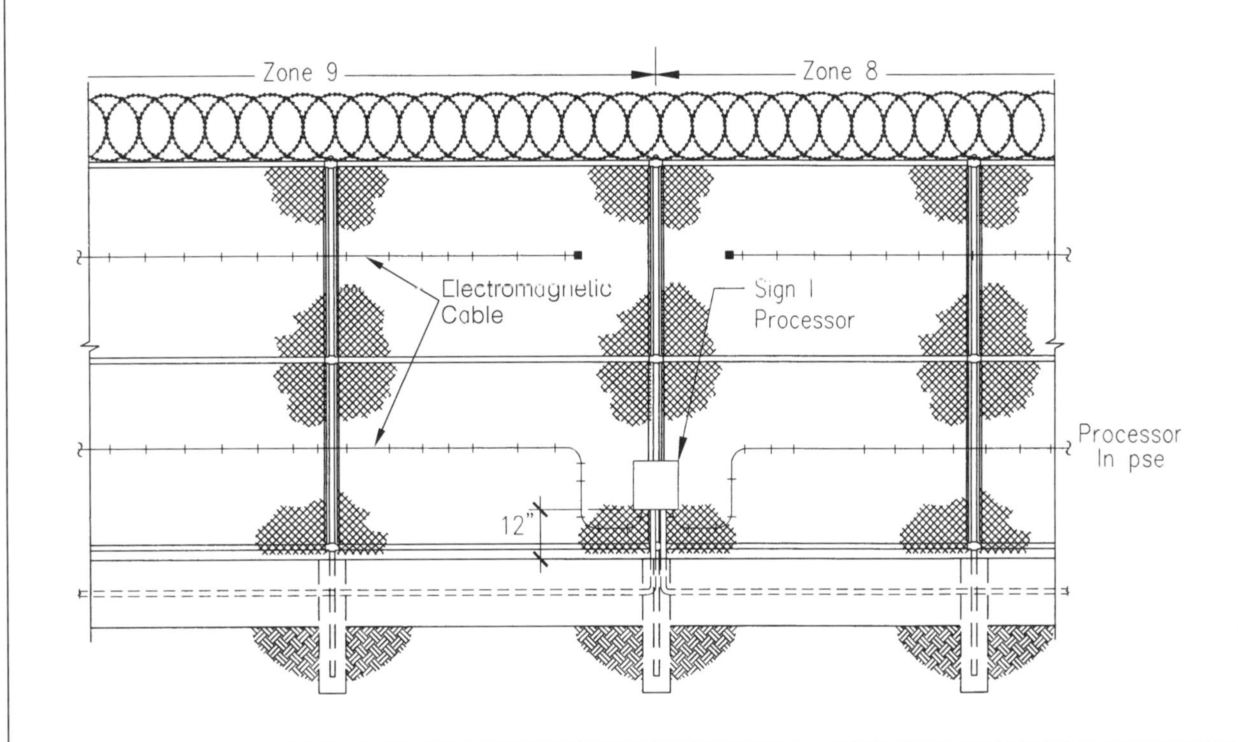

Figure 6.6 **Typical electromagnetic cable configuration.**

- Systems are subject to nuisance and false alarms primarily from heavy rain, sleet, hail, fence movement, and level of threshold sensitivity set on the signal processor.
- Installation of the physical cable and processors is relatively simple and inexpensive as compared to buried systems or systems requiring beam alignment. Primary concern with regard to installation is to insure that the fence is designed and constructed within the rigidity limits as established by the sensor manufacturer.

Installed cost of an electromagnetic cable sensor is approximately $35 per foot.

POST-MOUNTED ELECTROMAGNETIC LINE

Post-mounted electromagnetic line systems provide detection by sensing an unbalance in an electric field. The electric field is typically established by exciting a transmit line and sensing the field using one or more sense lines or by sensing current changes resulting from changes in dielectric constants. Systems of this type may be post-mounted on isolated posts or may be mounted on extensions projecting from a fence. Several systems employ this concept and each incorporates unique features for line excitation, sensing techniques, and operating frequency. (See Fig. 6.7.)

Significant system use considerations

- Systems follow site topography.
- Zones may deviate from a straight line.
- Reasonable detection is realized in the vertical plane.
- Detection zone in the horizontal plane is reasonably controlled.
- A fence or other structure may be integrated into the detection field.
- Systems are subject to nuisance and/or false alarms caused primarily by high winds, electromagnetic interference, blowing debris, uncontrolled vegetation, and sensitivity of threshold settings.
- Installation of these systems is relatively simple with primary emphasis on establishing stable mounting posts and maintaining taut lines.

Installed cost of post-mounted electromagnetic lines is approximately $35 per foot.

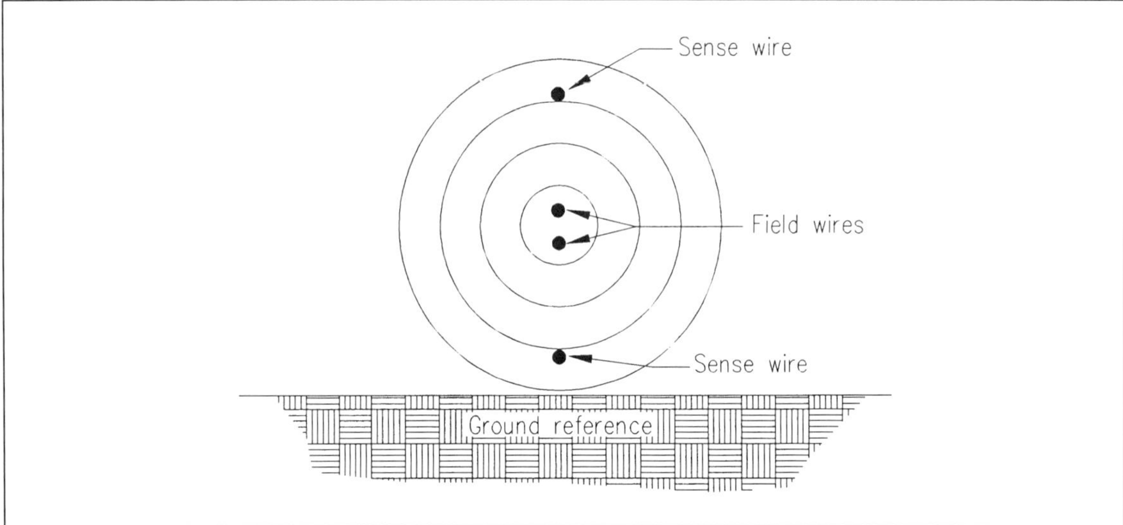

Figure 6.7 **Typical post-mounted electromagnetic line detection field envelope.**

INFRARED

Infrared systems provide detection by sensing a change in the received level of infrared energy at a receiver. The zone of detection is defined by a vertical plane between the transmitter and receiver posts. Some systems incorporate the transmitter and receiver into a common post and use a repeater post in lieu of a separate receiver post. (See Fig. 6.8.)

Significant system use considerations

- Topography must be controlled between the transmitter and receiver in order to insure detection reliability. Since the effective infrared beam is extremely narrow in cross section, spe-

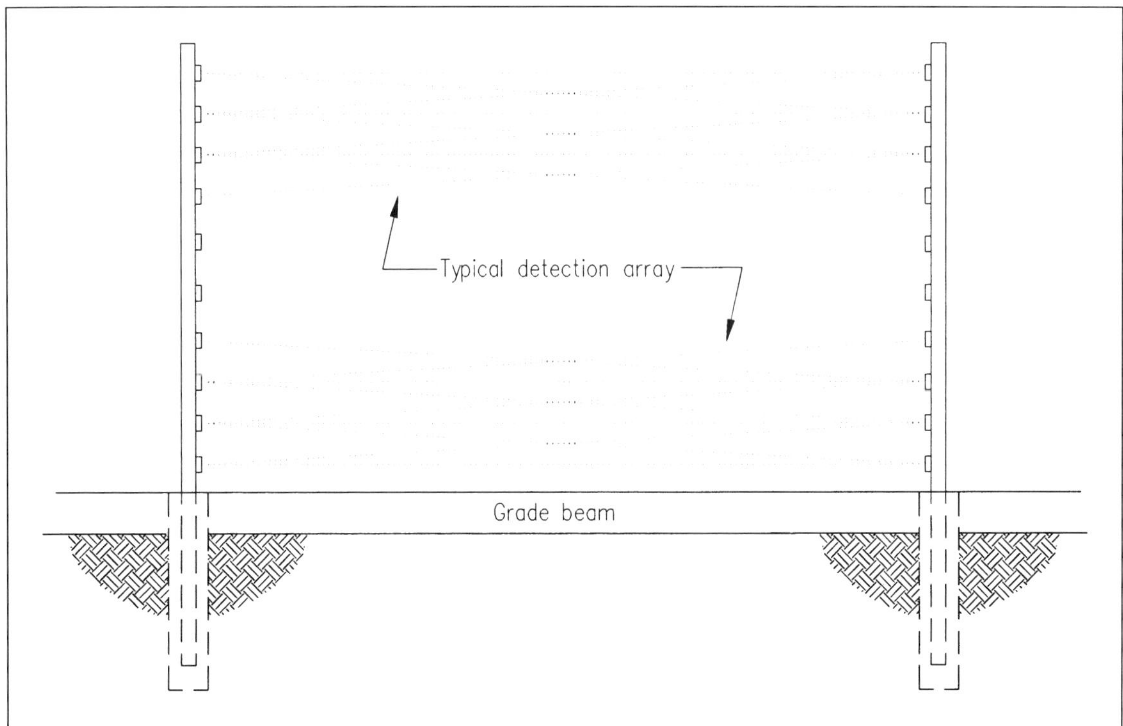

Figure 6.8 **Typical infrared zone configuration.**

cial attention must be given to controlling the distance between the ground and the lower beam.

- Horizontal width of the detection zone is extremely narrow and provides an effective system where potential disturbances may be in close proximity to the zone of detection.
- Vertical height of the detection zone is limited by the number of infrared transmitters and receivers which are stacked. Practically, an infrared zone may be 6 or 7 feet in height.
- Systems are subject to nuisance and false alarms primarily from blowing debris, uncontrolled vegetation, small animals, heavy fog, snow, dust on optical lenses, and direct sunlight.
- Installation of the system requires special attention to post foundations, alignment of adjacent posts at parallel cross-over junctions, and topography control. As a result of multiple transmitters and receivers required for each zone, the installation and system alignment is more time-consuming than for many other systems.

Installed cost of an infrared zone is approximately $60 per foot, exclusive of the cost associated with topography control. It is recommended that a concrete ribbon be used to establish the ground-level boundary.

VIDEO MOTION DETECTION

Video motion detection systems employ advanced signal processing techniques to assess the video field and define the presence of an intruder. After generating an alarm condition, the video may be automatically displayed on a monitor to provide the security staff with visual assessment of the alarm event. Design of each zone of video motion detection must overlap with adjacent zones. (See Fig. 6.9.)

Significant system use considerations

- Area of assessment must always be lighted to a level adequate to support the specified camera performance.
- Emergency power systems must be sized to accommodate lighting-system loads.
- Lighting systems should have rapid response time to full lighting levels.
- Processing algorithms should provide immunity to signals caused by shadows, bird or small animal movements, camera vibrations, leaf movements, rain, snow, and other similar signal sources normally encountered in exterior conditions.
- Camera field of view must be selected to allow control of detection area.
- Location of camera mounting poles must not compromise security practices.
- Fiber-optic video transmission systems should be considered for installation between cameras and signal processors to enhance video signal quality at the signal processor.

Cost of the installed system is influenced significantly by the number of cameras and the location of cameras relative to the signal processor and video monitors. For systems having greater than 15 cameras, it is estimated that the installed cost may be approximately $75 per foot.

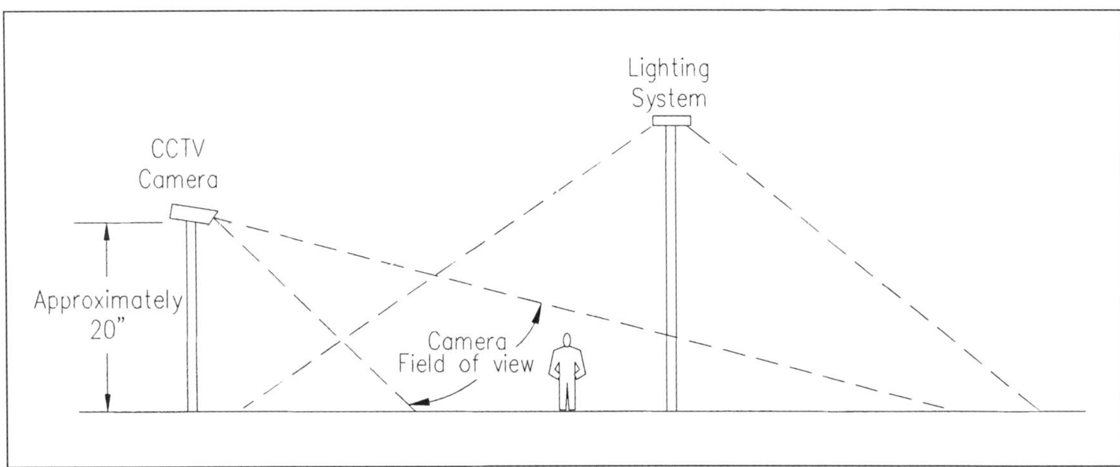

Figure 6.9 **Typical video motion detection camera-mounting configuration. This type of detection configuration uses camera and lighting systems.**

ELECTRIC FENCE

Electric fence systems typically consist of an array of electrically charged wires which are post-mounted and located between the interior and exterior perimeter fences.

The wire array perimeter typically extends from ground level to a height of approximately one foot above the fence line. Spacing of the electrically charged wires varies from the ground level to the upper level.

The system may operate in several modes. One mode is a lethal mode that provides a continuous high-voltage source to the wire array, and contact with the array is lethal. Another mode of operation is the stun mode. In this mode, the wires are charged on a pulsed or intermittent basis, and contact with the wires will stun the intruder. Systems may be designed to function in both modes with the stun mode being the normal mode of operation. Upon sensing fence contact in the stun mode, the fence controller may automatically switch to the lethal mode.

Zone lengths may extend to approximately 2500 feet with zone length primarily being dictated by economic factors. The zone control and sensing equipments are relatively expensive. (See Fig. 6.10.)

Significant system use considerations

- System conforms to site topography and may be installed essentially along any path for which a fence is installed.
- Height of the array may vary and control/sensing equipments may be configured for various heights.
- Limited data is available on actual false or nuisance alarm performance; however, the principle of operation suggests that alarms would be generated by snow accumulations, accumulation of dust on insulators, blowing debris which bridges charged lines, and small animals.
- Close proximity of charged wires in lower section of array may be lethal to birds and other wildlife.
- Due to the lethal consequences of contact with the fence, considerations must be given to the response of society to this issue and possible requirements for legislative approval of its case.
- Consider integration of conventional detection systems with zone lengths of approximately 350 feet to provide enhanced detection resolution.

Cost estimates for systems installed with approximately 2000-foot zones are approximately $200 per foot.

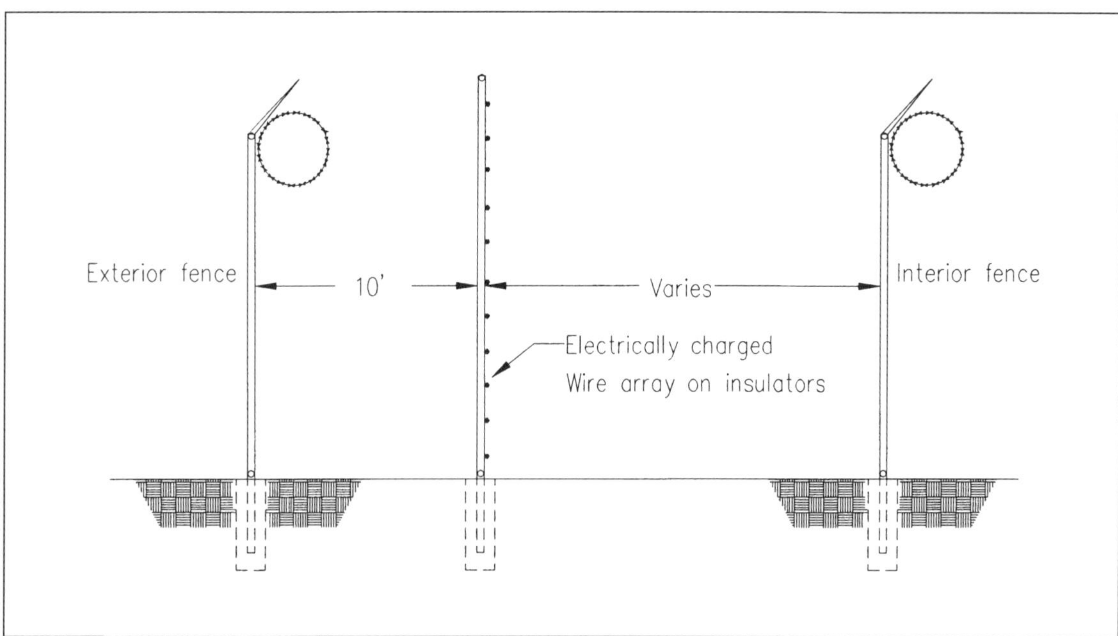

Figure 6.10 **Typical electric fence installation configuration.**

NUISANCE AND FALSE ALARM RATES

Since some facility administrators' criteria include nuisance/false alarm rates per zone, it is deemed appropriate to address general considerations related to this performance requirement.

A *nuisance/false alarm* is defined as an alarm event which occurs as a result of conditions other than those generated by an intruder. Nuisance/false alarms may be generated as a result of many factors and each sensor type has unique characteristics relative to its nuisance/false alarm sensitivity.

Factors which may affect nuisance/false alarms for one sensor type may have an entirely different effect on other sensor types. Each sensor and installation must be evaluated relative to site-specific conditions to assess potential nuisance/false alarms. Typical factors to be considered are wind, rain, snow, sleet, fog, ice, hail, blowing debris, electromagnetic interference, surface water, vegetation, sun, nearby traffic, soil conditions, and temperature variations.

Based on generally known conditions, it is estimated that the following nuisance/false alarm rates for systems may be realized. Rates are noted for several of the systems described. Many factors influence the actual system performance relative to these criteria. Each site must be evaluated and assessments made prior to system selection.

- ***Taut wire:*** Less than one (1) alarm per zone per month.
- ***Microwave:*** Less than four (4) alarms per month per zone.
- ***Fence-mounted seismic geophone:*** Less than three (3) alarms per month per zone.
- ***Fence-mounted electret/electromagnetic cable:*** Less than four (4) alarms per zone per month.

SUMMARY

Site-specific and budgetary issues are primary considerations in the selection of technologies supporting a perimeter detection system. Detailed consideration must be given to the selection of technology and the implementation of systems to ensure that the security objectives of a particular institution may be realized.

7
Supplemental Information: Security Electronics and Communications Systems

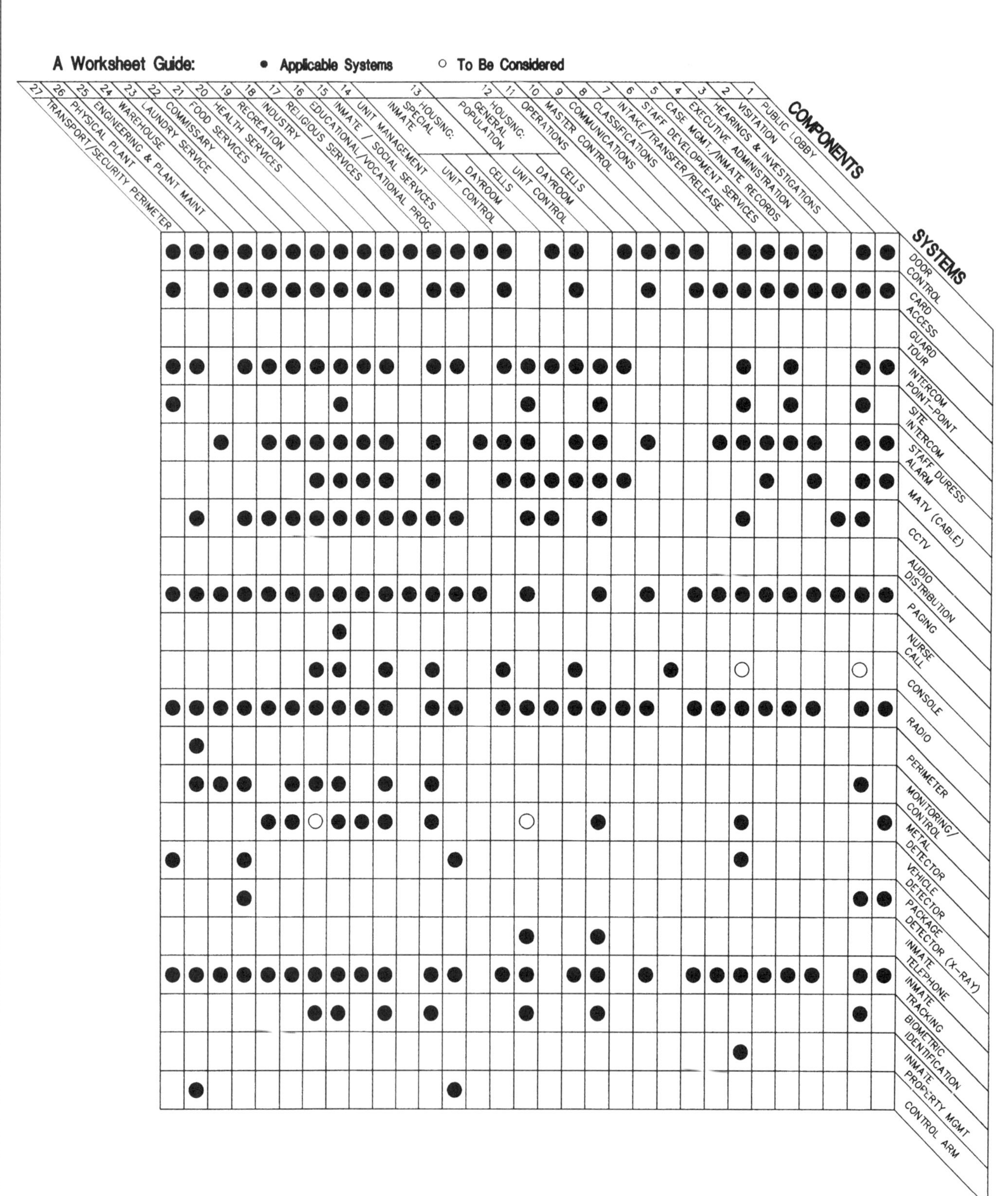

A Worksheet Guide: ● Applicable Systems ○ To Be Considered

SYSTEMS / COMPONENTS	27 Transport/Security Perimeter	26 Physical Plant	25 Engineering & Plant Maint	24 Warehouse	23 Laundry Service	22 Commissary	21 Food Services	20 Health Services	19 Recreation	18 Industry	17 Religious Services	16 Educational/Vocational Prog.	15 Inmate / Social Services	14 Unit Management	13 Housing: Special Inmate – Unit Control	13 Housing: Special Inmate – Dayroom	13 Housing: Special Inmate – Cells	12 Housing: General Population – Unit Control	12 Housing: General Population – Dayroom	12 Housing: General Population – Cells	11 Operations	10 Master Control	9 Communications	8 Classifications	7 Intake/Transfer/Release	6 Staff Development Services	5 Case Mgmt./Inmate Records	4 Executive Administration	3 Hearings & Investigations	2 Visitation	1 Public Lobby
Door Control	●	●	●	●	●	●	●	●	●	●	●	●	●	●	●		●	●		●	●	●	●		●	●	●	●		●	●
Card Access	●		●	●	●	●	●	●	●	●		●	●		●			●			●		●	●	●	●	●	●	●	●	●
Guard Tour																															
Intercom Point-Point	●	●		●	●	●	●	●	●	●		●	●		●	●	●	●	●	●					●		●			●	●
Site Intercom	●							●								●			●						●		●			●	
Staff Duress Alarm			●		●	●	●	●	●	●		●		●	●	●		●	●		●			●	●	●	●	●		●	●
MATV (Cable)							●	●	●	●		●			●	●	●	●	●	●						●		●		●	●
CCTV		●		●	●	●	●	●	●	●	●	●	●			●	●		●						●				●	●	
Audio Distribution																															
Paging	●	●	●	●	●	●	●	●	●	●	●	●	●	●		●			●		●		●	●	●	●	●	●	●	●	●
Nurse Call								●																							
Console							●	●		●		●			●			●				●			○					○	
Radio	●	●	●	●	●	●	●	●	●	●		●	●		●	●	●	●	●	●	●		●	●	●	●	●	●		●	●
Perimeter		●																													
Monitoring/Control		●	●	●		●	●	●		●		●																		●	
Metal Detector					●	●	○	●	●	●		●				○			●						●						●
Vehicle Detector	●			●									●												●						
Package Detector (X-Ray)				●																										●	●
Inmate Telephone																●			●												
Inmate Tracking	●	●	●	●	●	●	●	●	●	●		●	●		●	●		●	●		●		●	●	●	●	●	●		●	●
Biometric Identification							●	●		●						●			●											●	
Inmate Property Mgmt																									●						
Control Arm		●											●																		

Security Electronics and Communications Systems application matrix.

GENERAL INFORMATION

This chapter provides a brief description of the security electronics and communications systems which may be integrated into or considered for integration into a correctional or detention facility. These systems provide support functions for the staff to enhance both the security of the facility and its operational effectiveness and efficiency. Systems included in this section should be reviewed in concept by the project architect and facility administrative/operations staff. During the design phase, these systems should be developed in detail commensurate with the various stages of design. (See the Security Electronics and Communications Systems application matrix on preceding page.)

Systems described in this chapter represent typical system elements which may be integrated into a functional security system to support the facility security objectives. (See Fig. 7.1.)

Specific products for each system element are generally available from multiple sources thus providing the designer with product options which reflect varying performance characteristics or features and provide for competitive pricing.

The realization of an effective security electronics and communications system requires the following:

- An understanding of the mission of the facility and its security objectives
- A detailed analysis of the staffing plan and staff responsibilities
- Identification of functional areas within the facility and security issues related to each area
- An understanding of movement patterns to include staff, inmates, visitors, and service personnel
- Selection of security electronics and communications systems components to support the

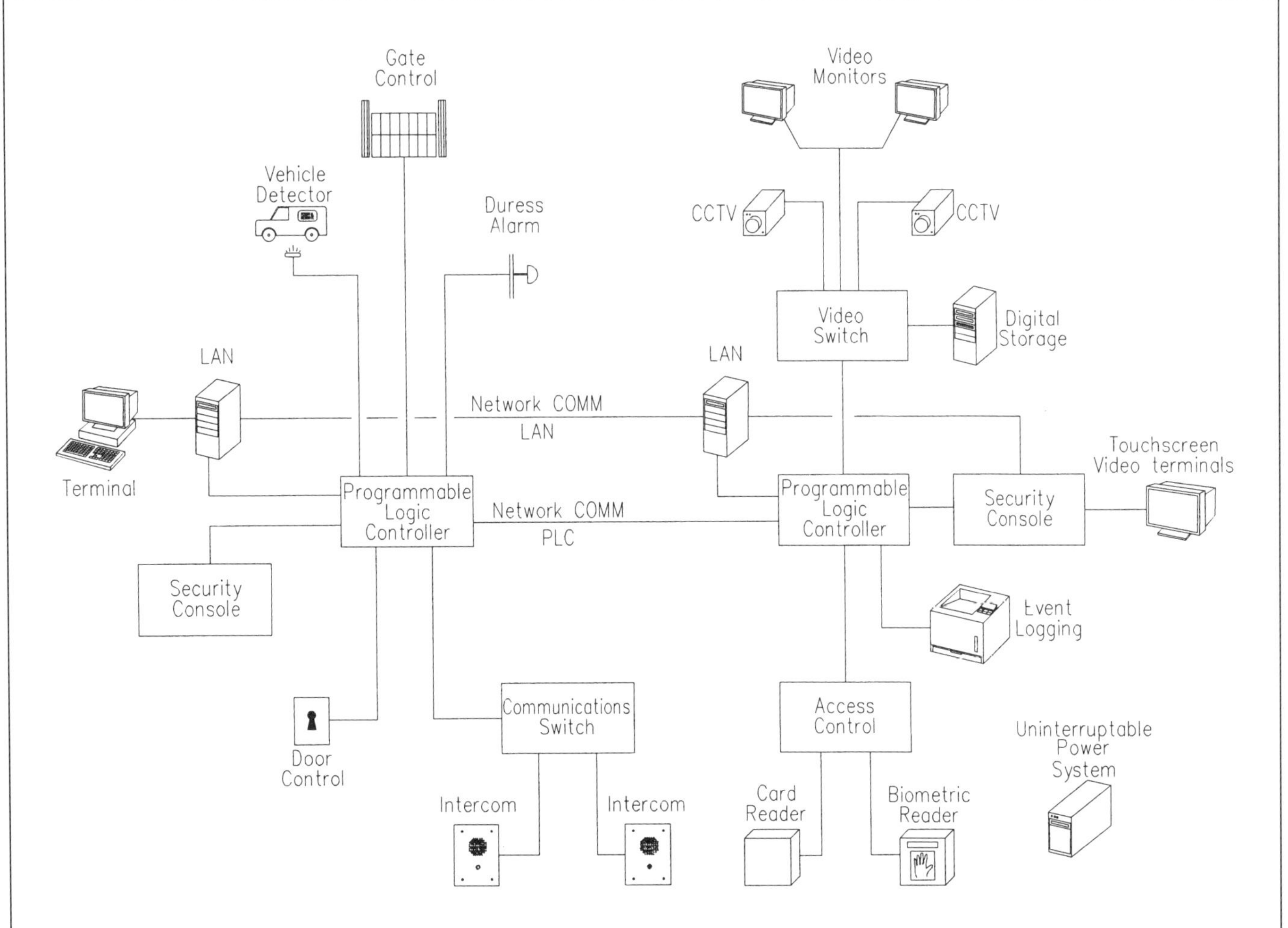

Figure 7.1 **Integrated security system functional diagram which reflects typical equipment configuration.**

operational and physical security requirements of the facility

- Development of detailed documents to clearly describe individual subsystem requirements and the process for integrating system elements into an integrated security system
- Selection of a system integration contractor experienced in the implementation of systems as developed for the specific facility
- Close coordination between the system designer and system integration contractor during implementation phase
- Thorough system testing to verify system performance prior to user acceptance
- Training of user personnel relative to operations and maintenance

Following are brief descriptions of security electronics and communications system elements or subsystems which are typically integrated into correctional or detention facilities.

SECURITY PERIMETER SYSTEMS

A perimeter security detection system should be included to affect detection at the interior perimeter security fence. A perimeter fence generally includes two fences separated by approximately 30 feet. The physical configuration of a fence is as described by architectural documents and details. A perimeter fence generally includes a single vehicular sally port and a personnel sally port which penetrates the secure perimeter.

The perimeter system would typically consist of the following:

- *Detection system* to sense when the defined security detection zone has been compromised. It is advantageous to affect the detection zone on the interior side of the inner perimeter fence or on the interior fence. Site constraints and systems sensor selection will significantly impact the specific location of the sensor system. A review of the security perimeter systems described in Chap. 6.0: Perimeter Security Systems will reflect on sensor installation options.
- *Alarm monitoring and control system* to annunciate the alarm condition at a primary security monitoring and control station. This system generally employs time division multiplex technology to reduce cables and conduit requirements as well as to simplify system installation.
- *Voice annunciation system* to transmit alarm conditions to mobile staff personnel via an rf transmitter and personnel pocket receivers. This system enhances the time response for the security staff to evaluate the alarmed event.
- *Physical barrier,* such as a double fence with razor wire or a single fence employing curvature in the vertical plane to provide adequate delay of the intruder such that security staff could physically respond to the alarmed zone prior to compromise of the perimeter boundary by the intruder.
- *CCTV cameras* may be employed at the perimeter fence to provide rapid assessment of an alarm condition. The CCTV system provides a means to record on videotape any attempted breach of the perimeter boundary. When CCTV cameras are integrated for visual assessment, an alarm condition would automatically switch the applicable camera for viewing and recording at the primary control station.
- *Physical response* is considered mandatory to accurately assess the alarm condition or conditions which caused the alarm. A trained and disciplined staff represents a vital component to the facility security plan and its operational effectiveness.
- *Lighting system* is fundamental to an effective perimeter system. A lighting system must be implemented to provide a deterrent to the intruder and provide a means to visually assess the perimeter.

MONITORING/CONTROL SYSTEMS

Within each facility, one or more locations are generally designated to provide monitoring and control functions related to the perimeter detection system and other points being monitored or assessed. A monitoring and control system provides a means to monitor alarm points distributed throughout a facility and to control activities related to the alarm points. For example, the monitoring and control system provides annunciation of an alarm event and means for the monitoring staff to acknowledge alarms, place alarm points in an access state, and place the operational mode to a secure state. Generally, recording equipment is implemented to provide a printed record of activities related to the monitoring and control system.

Typical technology for monitoring and control systems employ time division multiplex techniques which affect communications between major system components via a data circuit. Major system components include a Master Control unit located in the central monitoring area, remote terminal units distributed throughout the facility to interface with the monitored or controlled points, logging systems to provide a hard copy of system activities, and uninterruptable power system to ensure proper operation of the system during periods of power transients.

STAFF DURESS ALARM SYSTEM

A *personal alarm system* can provide emergency alarm signals generated by a staff member using a small transmitter carried by the staff member. Each area of the facility should be reviewed to determine requirements for alarm reporting within the area. The specific areas are typically identified during the design development phase of a project.

For areas requiring personal alarm support, the system will allow the officer to move freely within the facility with a personal transmitter. Upon activation of the alarm transmitter, the alarm event shall be annunciated at the designated control point. Considerations shall be given to incorporating "man-down" features into the alarm transmitter which provides automatic alarm reporting in the event a personal alarm transmitter is physically aligned in a position which would indicate a "man-down" condition.

CLOSED-CIRCUIT TELEVISION (CCTV)

CCTV cameras can be employed to provide visual information to the security staff in support of the following primary functions:

- *Movement control:* Doors which are remotely controlled from a control point require visual supervision prior to opening the door. If direct sight lines are not realized from the control point to the door being controlled, a CCTV camera can provide the required visual coverage.
- *General surveillance:* Selected areas of the facility will generally require the use of CCTV cameras to provide general surveillance of the area of interest. Specific areas are generally determined during the design development phase of a project. For administrative and public areas, the appropriateness of the camera housing and appearance should be considered.
- *Alarm:* Selected areas of the facility may be designated as sensitive areas which require remote visual observation upon initiation of an alarm event. CCTV cameras shall be located in such areas and visual information switched to the designated control points which is generally defined in the design development phase of the project.

CCTV monitors should be located at control points to provide visual information to the security staff. Monitors shall have primary and secondary functions for viewing movement control, general surveillance, or alarm activities.

CCTV cameras and monitors should preferably be colored, where feasible, to enhance security effectiveness.

Switching of CCTV cameras to specific monitors should be via the use of microprocessor-based video-matrix switching systems to provide operational flexibility.

Integration of the CCTV switching system with intercom and alarm functions enables visual information to be automatically displayed at the appropriate monitors on an as-needed basis. This approach enhances staff effectiveness and operating efficiency of the control center.

PAGING SYSTEM

A *paging system* can provide a means to distribute voice announcements throughout selected areas of the facility. During the design development phase of the project, each area requiring paging should be identified and stations identified that will have capabilities to address each specific public address or paging zone.

INTERCOM POINT-TO-POINT

Intercom systems should be integrated into the facility design to provide point-to-point communications between remote intercom stations and a master station located at a control point. Dedicated intercom systems provide a means for a remote intercom station to call a predetermined control point and establish voice communications with that control point. The dedicated intercom system provides a convenient and economical means to integrate voice and CCTV visual information at a control point.

SITE INTERCOM SYSTEM

A *site intercom system* is comprised of intercom staff stations and a microprocessor switch. Via the microprocessor switch, each staff station may selectively call any other staff station by means of a keypad integrated into the staff station. The system may be programmed to provide group calls, as may be required for certain functions. Each station can be equipped with features to effect hands-free communications between staff stations via the use of speakerphone features. Handsets are incorporated into each staff station to provide handset-to-handset communications typical to a normal telephone instrument.

INMATE TELEPHONE SYSTEM

An *inmate telephone system* is generally owner-furnished and is not included in a security electronics and communications systems design. These systems are generally provided via a contract with an equipment supplier employing revenue sharing between the user agency and the supplier.

DOOR-GATE CONTROL

Electrically operated doors and gates shall include inmate cells, sally ports, vehicle entrance gates, and other doors within the facility which are generally identified in the design development phase of the project.

Selection of doors to be controlled and locations of control is dictated by security operational issues, staffing levels, and staffing responsibilities. Selected doors will be monitored only to identify door status (secured or unsecured). These doors are also generally identified during the design development phase of the project.

Control and monitoring functions to include specific door control operational sequences should be detailed and serve as the basis for programming the logic controllers. Control and monitoring functions for each door will be executed from control panels located at designated control points. The door-gate control system will provide a means for group release of selected doors for emergency conditions.

RADIO SYSTEMS

Two-way radios are generally part of the communications systems for a facility. Most administrators/user representatives generally review the state's radio system requirements or process for integrating radio systems into the construction program of a facility. Provisions should be made in control centers to accommodate the physical placement of control equipments. Provisions should be made in equipment rooms for rf equipments.

SECURITY MANAGEMENT CARD ACCESS SYSTEM

A *security management card access system* can provide a means to affect controlled movement throughout selected areas of a facility. Individual staff can be issued access cards which define specific areas into which they are permitted. Each assignment can include doors for areas to which access is authorized and the time scheduled for each. This system provides a means to develop records which can be maintained on a computer database which reflect activities related to each card holder or activities related to a specific access point.

The card access control system provides a secure and cost-effective means to control movement without increasing staffing requirements at control points as may be required to remotely control doors from control points. Access management may be affected by computer rather than the manually rekeying of locks and key management.

Various technologies are available for card sensors and other devices such as biometric readers which, when integrated with other security system elements, provide a means to uniquely relate specific operations to an individual or access card holder.

CONSOLES

Operator consoles are typically located at each control point and other locations as determined in the design development phase of a project. Each console may be uniquely designed to integrate operator control monitoring functions into an operator position that enhances staff effectiveness and efficiency.

Each console shall integrate control panels, CCTV monitors, and annunciator panels, based on specific functions relative to the operator position. Console layout, or configuration, requires careful planning and design to ensure that the operator position provides for efficient and effective management of the tasks assigned to the operator position.

Primary considerations related to a console configuration

- Control panels provide a means for efficient monitoring and control of the desired functions.
- Closed-circuit television monitors configured to present video information as an integrated component of the monitoring and control function.

- Prioritization of operator activities to provide efficient operator access to monitoring and control panels as well as data terminals integrated into the console position.
- Ergonomic considerations.
- Shape and dimensions of the console to minimize sight-line obstructions between the operator position and functions remote from the console which require visual observation.
- Ability of the console to support multioperator positions, if required.
- Lighting systems that establish the ambient lighting conditions required for the console and panel designs.

A *control console layout* is a design layout which represents the configuration of a console to support the unique requirements of a specific facility. Consoles generally reflect various configurations that are dictated by specific requirements. (See Fig. 7.2.)

Major elements of consoles are *operator panels* which provide a means for the operator to interface with the monitoring and control functions. Various technologies may be use to affect the operator panel:

- Video terminals employing touch-screen and/or mouse/trackball cursors
- Electromechanical control switches and indicators
- Membrane switch panels with LED indicators

The specific technology employed for each panel is dictated by the density of the control/monitoring functions, panel flexibility, and economic considerations. The following is a brief narrative on each of the technologies described.

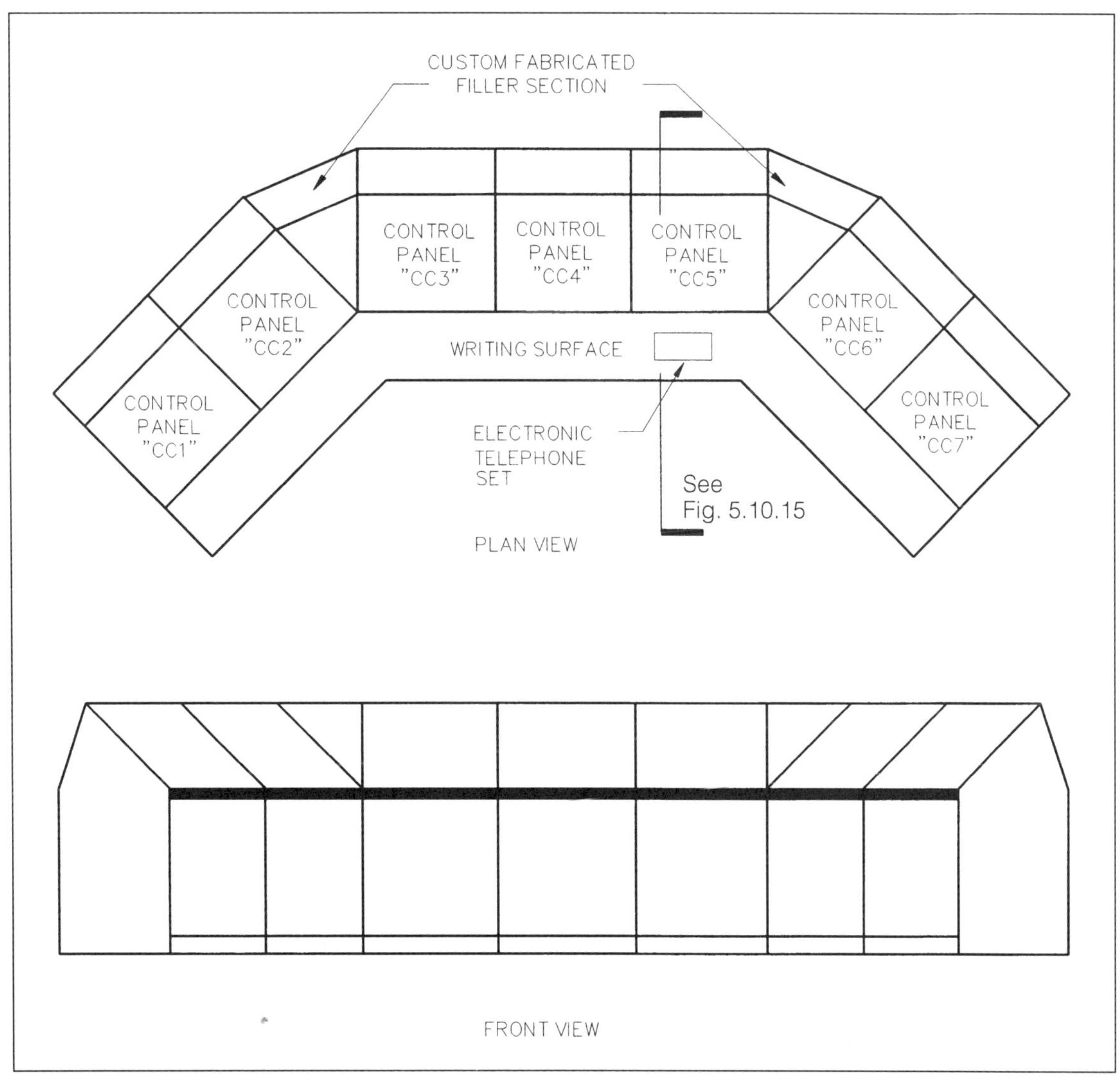

Figure 7.2 **Control console layout.**

Video terminal operator position may typically consist of a personal computer with one or two monitors. Operator interface with the terminal is normally via *touch-screen* technology and/or a mouse/trackball device. The rapidly expanding capabilities of the microprocessor, development of applications software, microprocessing speed, and integration of screen developments using auto-CAD software make the video terminal an attractive alternative when designing operator control positions. It has the capability to dynamically integrate graphics into the video presentation which provides enhanced communications between the operator and the terminal. The uniqueness of the operator position resides within the software rather than the physical construction, as is the case with traditional control panels.

A significant feature of the video terminal is that a large array of video screens may be stored within the memory of the CPU and recalled to the screen at an extremely high rate to provide a perception of instant recall. This feature when integrated with a communications network, provides the capability of a single video terminal to display control and monitoring functions for multiple or all control points within a facility. The primary significance of this feature is that staffing of a specific control position may be optimized based on operational requirements rather than being dictated by the physical constraints of the location of the traditional control panel. Staff efficiencies equate to reduced operating costs.

The power and flexibility of the microprocessor-based video terminal offers many advantages; however, they impose significant constraints when designing a system. A primary constraint is that the video terminal is limited in display area. Careful planning must be taken in the layout of screen presentations since limited information may be presented on any single screen. The flow of information from screen to screen must provide an effective means, both physically and mentally, for the operator to effect the control and monitoring functions related to the position. The design and screen presentation sequence requires detailed attention and is a task which must be included in the design phase. Special attention must be directed to the touch screen target sensitivity, size, and locations of icons configured on each screen display.

The video terminal offers the potential to integrate information management systems with security monitoring and control functions while ensuring that operational security is not compromised by the integration of these functions. Using this level of integration, selected activities or information are transported to or from the operator terminal to a database for records and development of management reports. When integrating control and monitoring functions with information management systems, careful attention must be given to the selection of information to be logged and managed on the information management system. Typically, facilities integrate management information systems (MIS) into the facilities' data systems for recording and management of selected inmate records and activities. Duplication of information is deemed to be undesirable and access to certain inmate records is not appropriate information to be accessed from security control points.

For maintenance considerations, the video terminal is a standard, commercially available computer, therefore, can be easily replaced or upgraded as technology offers enhanced terminal performance.

Figure 7.3, typical video terminal control screen is an example of a video terminal operator interface. The display employs graphic representation of selected points to be controlled. As is reflected by this screen, the graphics display restricts the effective use of the screen surface area; however, the specific application of graphics must be evaluated when developing the screen configurations. Incorporated into the display are management functions which enhance the operator position.

Electromechanical switches and membrane switches, used for many applications, as traditional control panels may be appropriate. These panels incorporate *membrane-type switches* or *electromechanical switches* with LED indicators. Each panel is configured to affect the unique control and monitoring functions of a control point. Since the surface area of a specific control panel is well defined, all monitoring and control functions must be configured within the physical constraints of the panel. For relatively simple or less-complex panels, this panel configuration offers a simple and effective method to interface the security officer with operational requirements of the specific control point.

A significant disadvantage of the traditional panel is that it is custom-fabricated, and if changes or replacements are required, a new panel must be fabricated at, generally, a considerably higher cost than the original panel cost at the time of initial implementation.

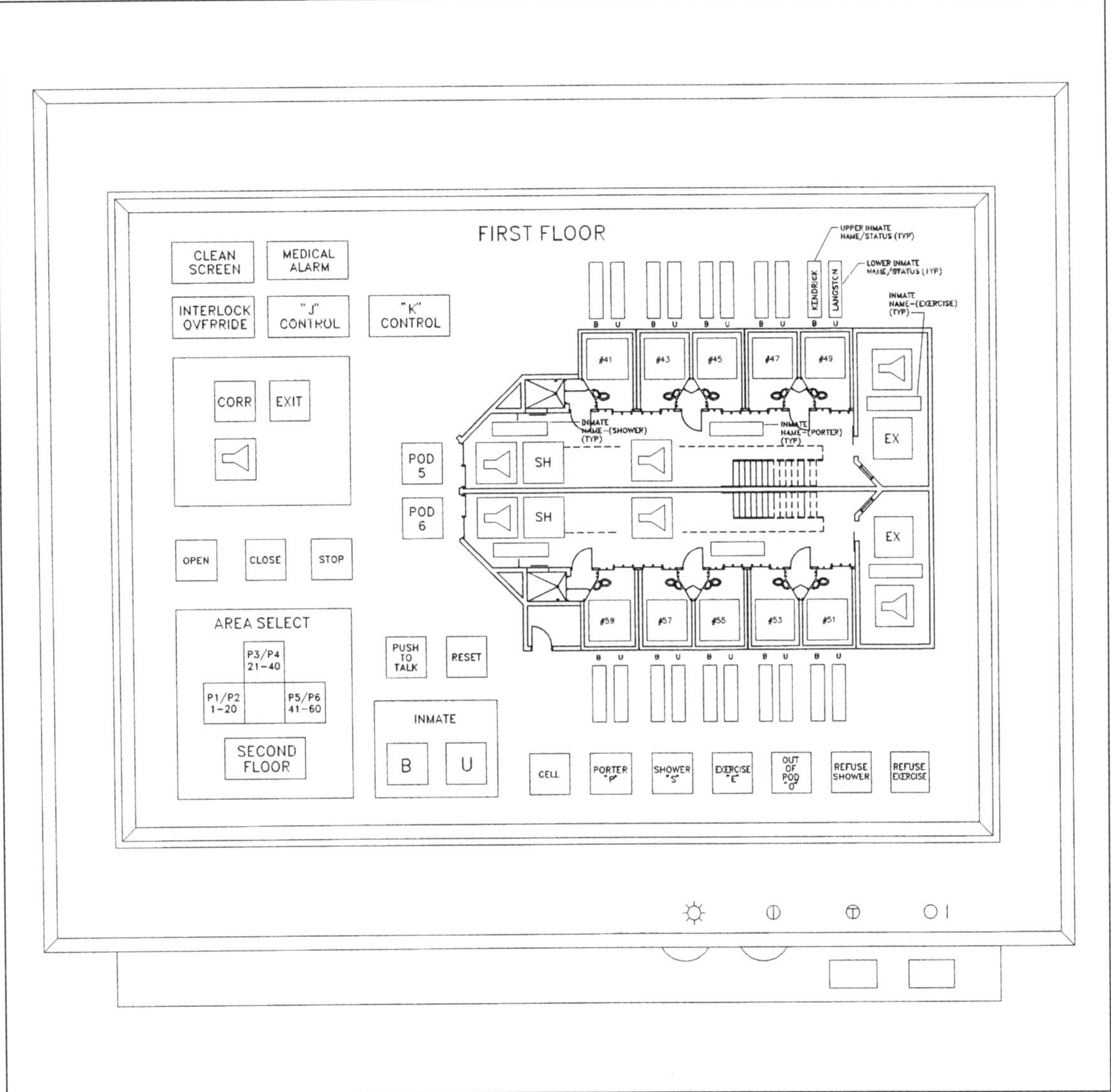

Figure 7.3 **Typical video terminal control screen.**

Figure 7.4 typical electromechanical switch control panel is a control panel employing electromechanical switches and LED indicators. This particular panel configuration employs a tabular or functional layout rather than the graphic layout. This configuration provides functional grouping of control and monitoring functions and maximizes the use of the panel space.

Figure 7.5 typical membrane switch panel—graphic configuration can use graphics to reflect a plan view of the areas or points to be monitored and controlled. As can be observed by a review of this panel configuration, the use of a graphic representation restricts the total number of monitoring and control points which may be integrated into a specific panel surface area.

Figure 7.6 typical membrane switch panel—tabular configuration can use a tabular or functional control configuration generally provided for a higher density of control and monitoring points which may be integrated into the panel. It is a panel configuration which reflects efficient use of the panel surface area and is configured into functional units.

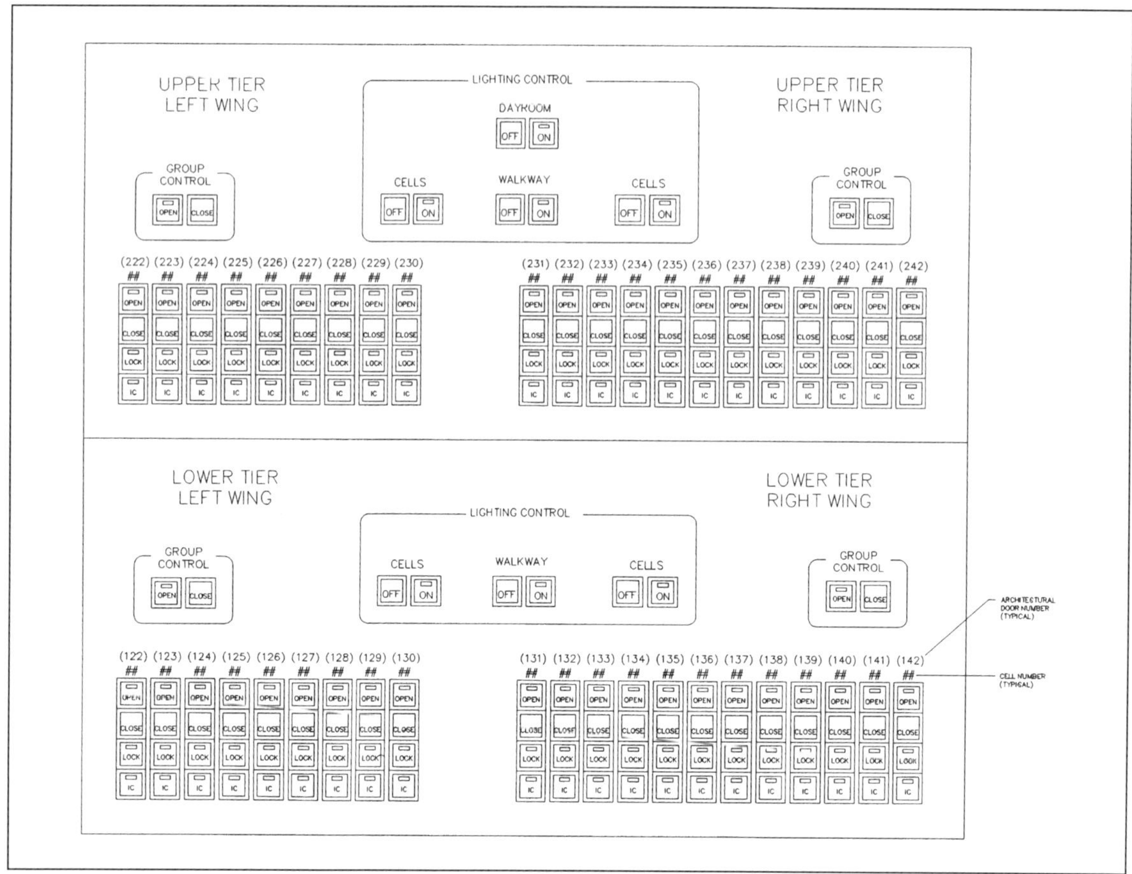

Figure 7.4 **Typical electromechanical switch control panel.**

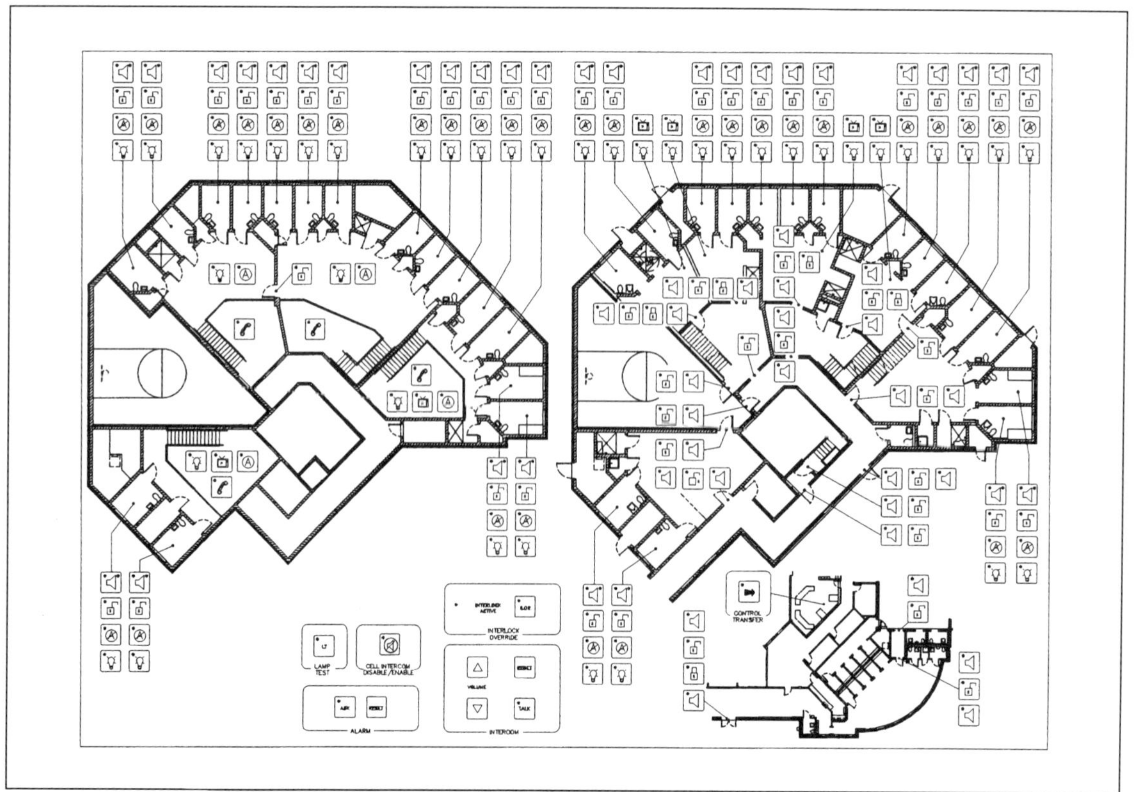

Figure 7.5 **Typical membrane switch panel graphic configuration.**

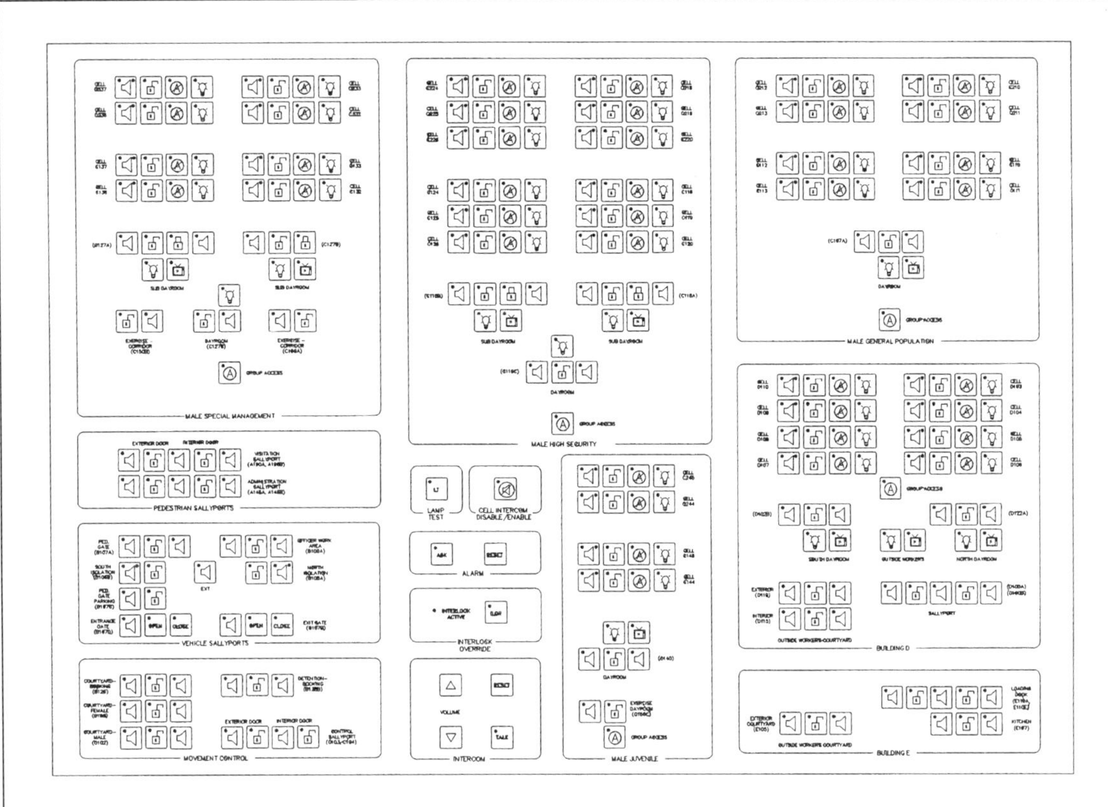

Figure 7.6 **Typical membrane switch panel tabular configuration.**

METAL DETECTION/PACKAGE DETECTOR

Equipment capable of detecting metals and other contraband is usually selected and dedicated for specific conditions or applications and located at screening points within the facility. Specific locations of the screening points and location of the detection equipment are generally identified in the design development phase of a project.

NURSE CALL SYSTEM

A nurse call system is generally utilized and incorporated into the medical unit of a facility to enhance staff effectiveness. Stations can be located in patient rooms and at designated staff positions to provide call annunciation at the nurse's station. Light annunciators shall be located in corridor spaces for each patient room which shall annunciate a call request by a patient.

MASTER ANTENNA TELEVISION SYSTEM

A television distribution system can provide distribution of network broadcast channels and facility-originated programming to designated areas within the facility.

A central antenna and signal-processing system can receive broadcast channels and process these channels for local distribution. Consideration should be given to interfacing the interior distribution system to a local cable carrier in lieu of installation of an antenna and signal-processing system. Multiple channels can be allocated for local origination. These channels can be distributed to all outlets on the system. The location of the origination injection points should be defined in the design development phase of a project or the system design should provide the flexibility to originate signals from any outlet on the distribution system.

INFORMATION MANAGEMENT SYSTEM (IMS)

An inmate information management system provides a means to identify an inmate, staff member, or visitor using various identification technologies including biometric identifiers, bar code readers, and video image storage. The following systems are part of the information management system:

- Inmate tracking
- Biometric identification
- Inmate property management

The inmate tracking function does not automatically track the location of an individual but can provide a means to identify the sensor locations which register the presence of an individual. A sensor station would typically be a bar code reader or biometric identification unit.

CONTROL ARM

Control arms can be located at roadway control points to provide management of vehicular traffic.

VEHICLE DETECTORS

Vehicle detectors can be employed at selected vehicle control points. Detectors can detect the presence of a vehicle and provide a means to annunciate this information to the control stations responsible for control of specific access points.

SUMMARY

To ensure that the security objectives of a facility are realized, detailed considerations must be given in the planning and design phases of the project, identifying security issues and system elements, which may be integrated into the security system. Facilities may in general have some common security requirements, however, the unique security and operational requirements of a facility will dictate the final system design and system architecture.

8
Supplemental Information: Acoustical Design Guidelines

One of the most important aspects of operating a correctional facility relates to observing inmate behavior. In support of visual contact, hearing is the other critical issue. The environment of any inmate occupied space must provide officers, counselors, and other staff with an environment that is acoustically clear, with minimum reverberation and a reduced level of sound (noise).

Spaces with the largest gathering of inmates are the ones which require the most attention in the reduction of noise levels and reverberation. Housing unit dayrooms, dining rooms, gymnasiums, classrooms, and visitation rooms are among the most critical. Acoustical engineers can be of great assistance in providing professional services in support of the spaces that an architect and client must address. The Committee on Acoustics in Corrections has created a helpful guide in addressing the broad subject and is listed in the bibliography.

As a member of this committee, I assisted in providing them with reprinting of a short form guide entitled "The Acoustical Design of Dayrooms." This subject was originally published in *American Jails,* issue no. 11, dated December 1994. The dayroom is perhaps the most critical of all inmate occupied spaces requiring clarity of officer's speech for instructions and the ability to hear inmate responses. For this reason, this guide should provide the reader with sufficient criteria in choosing materials in the dayroom. For more complex designs and room shapes, an acoustical engineering consultant is always recommended.

Figure 8.1 **Housing interior split-level dayroom with carpeted floor and acoustic tile ceiling.**

The Acoustical Design Of Dayrooms*

Committee On Acoustics In Corrections

One of the most important factors to consider in the design of a dayroom is the reduction of noise. If left unchecked, high noise levels can lead to extraordinary stress for a correctional facility's inmates and staff alike. Our goal is to provide the necessary background information and a simplified calculation procedure to select dayroom construction materials and furnishings that absorb sound and hence reduce dayroom noise to the lowest possible level. The procedure, when combined with material cost estimates, affords the designer the opportunity to compare the cost effectiveness of various alternative acoustical treatment scenarios.

Controlling excessive noise levels is important to effective operations.

TABLE 1
SIGNIFICANCE OF NOISE AND REVERBERATION

1. Reverberation Time Range	Significance
Over 2.0 Seconds	Extremely live. Poor speech intelligibility
Between 1.5 and 2.0 Seconds	Live. Fair speech intelligibility
Below 1.5 and 1.0 Seconds	Fairly dead. Good speech intelligibility
Below 1.0 Seconds	Dead. Excellent speech intelligibility.

2. Noise Level	Significance
Over 80 dBA	Extremely noisy. Communication nearly impossible
70 dBA	Noisy. Communication requires raised voice level
60 dBA	Moderate noise level. Communication in normal voice level.

There is a direct relationship between dayroom noise level, reverberation time, and total room sound absorption. Table 1 summarizes the significance of noise levels and reverberation; Table 2 summarizes dayroom acoustical objectives.

TABLE 2
SUMMARY OF DAYROOM ACOUSTICAL OBJECTIVES

Dayroom Scenario Objectives	Sound Level
1. Reverberation Time	
a. Recreational and dining only	1.5 seconds or less
b. Classroom or direct supervision	0.75 seconds
2. Noise Level	
During recreation	Less than 65 dBA
3. Noise Level	
HVAC only	50 dBA or less

*Reprinted with permission of the American Jail Association from "The Acoustical Design of Dayrooms," by Jerry P. Christoff, Knut A. Rostad, and Morton J. Liebowitz, *American Jails*, 11-12/94.

Figure 8.2

Committee
On Acoustics
In Corrections

General Acoustical Design Principles

① Irregularly shaped rooms are preferable to simple, rectangular spaces.

② Distribute acoustical materials between ceiling, wall, and floor surfaces.

③ For maximum effectiveness, acoustical materials should be at least an inch thick.

④ Airspace behind acoustical materials helps to absorb low frequency sound and to prevent the room from sounding "boomy."

⑤ Carpeting provides effective sound absorption and controls impact noise.

⑥ Acoustical materials located near sound sources are more effective than at a distance.

⑦ Upholstered furniture will provide incidental sound absorption.

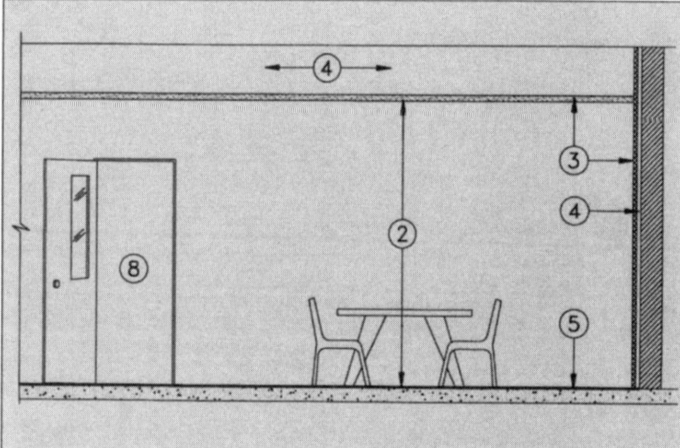

⑧ When cell doors are left open, the sound absorption provided by the bedding, etc., will actually help to reduce dayroom noise levels.

⑨ All acoustical treatment does not have to utilize conventional, manufactured products. For example, suspended banners made of porous fabric with a concealed fiberglass pad between the faces, located to avoid blocking surveillance, can provide effective sound absorption. A large, porous, cloth-faced supergraphic on a wall surface with fiberglass behind is another effective approach.

⑩ Acoustical materials within reach must be selected considering damage resistance and maintainability.

⑪ The volume of television sets should be limited, set, and maintained by the staff. If possible, television sets should have directional loudspeakers which direct sound at listeners, rather than spraying the entire room. Ceiling loudspeakers in a lowered soffit are effective.

Figure 8.2 (*Continued*)

Committee
On Acoustics
In Corrections

Table 3 provides an analysis of the acoustical and security aspects of dayroom construction materials and furnishings.

TABLE 3. ANALYSIS OF ACOUSTICAL AND SECURITY ASPECTS OF DAYROOM CONSTRUCTION MATERIALS AND FURNISHINGS

	Finish Material/ Furnishing	Sound Absorption Rating	NRC	Security/Acoustical Comments
DAYROOM WALLS	2" metal security panel	Good	0.95	Abuse-resistant
	1" metal security panel	Good	0.80	Abuse-resistant
	1" cloth or perforated vinyl acoustical panel	Good	0.80	Must be inaccessible to inmates.
	1" shredded fiber acoustical panel	Fair	0.40	Must be inaccessible to inmates.
	Wall carpet	Fair	0.20	Abuse-resistant
	Concrete	Poor	0.02	Provides optimum security, but unnecessary for most custody levels
	Masonry	Poor	0.05	Most commonly used construction type in direct supervision facilities; meets security requirements for all custody levels with appropriate reinforcing. Painting reduces sound absorption
	Drywall	Poor	0.05	Meets security needs for medium custody levels and lower with direct supervision style of management. Does provide low frequency sound absorption.
DAYROOM CEILING	1.5" acoustical metal deck	Good	0.70	Acoustical material is behind metal deck perforated flutes.
	2" security panels	Good	0.95	No major security problems associated with use.
	1" security panels	Good	0.80	No major security problems associated with use.
	2" shredded fiber panels	Good	0.60	Must be inaccessible to inmates.
	3/4"–5/8" acoustical tile	Good	0.90–0.40	Must be inaccessible to inmates; higher ratings apply to fiberglass products with an air space behind.
	1" spray-on acoustical material	Good	0.40–0.60	Must be inaccessible to inmates; may be damaged by thrown objects.
	Concrete, metal deck	Poor	0.02	Security is excessive for most deck custody level facilities.
CELL DOORS	Open bars, screen	Good	0.25	Visibility. Furnishings in cells provide sound absorption.
	Metal, etc.	Poor	0.05	Cell furnishings provide sound absorption when open.
DAYROOM FLOOR	Carpet	Fair	0.35	No major security problems in direct supervision facilities; requires regular maintenance and upkeep: compares favorably with vinyl tile in capital maintenance costs. Reduces impact noise
	Concrete	Poor	0.02	Worst material available for acoustics; unnecessary for security purposes in most custody level facilities, although as a security material concrete is one of the most effective.
	Vinyl tile	Poor	0.02	No major security problems associated with use.
TABLES	Metal/stainless steel, wood, plastic	Poor	—	Meets security requirements for direct supervision facilities.
DAYROOM SEATING	Wood/fabric	Fair	—	Same as plastic, but provides sound absorption.
	Stainless steel	Poor	—	Meets high risk security requirements.
	Plastic	Poor	—	Meets security needs for most medium and below custody level direct supervision facilities.

Figure 8.2 (*Continued*)

A summary of the calculations is shown in Table 4. Clearly, example 4 is the preferred approach. Four examples have been selected for a 56-cell, 5,500 square-foot dayroom.

TABLE 4. ANALYSIS OF ACOUSTICAL AND SECURITY ASPECTS OF DAYROOM CONSTRUCTION MATERIALS AND FURNISHINGS

	MATERIAL/FINISH	AREA (sq. ft.)	NRC	EXAMPLE 1 All Surfaces sound reflecting	EXAMPLE 2 Suspended acoustical ceiling	EXAMPLE 3 Suspended acoustical ceiling (partial) & security panels	EXAMPLE 4 Same as 3 plus carpet & acoustical wall panels
CEILING	Concrete (exposed area)	5530	0.02	110	54	—	—
	Concrete walkway soffits	1870	0.02	37	37	37	37
	5/8" suspended acoustical tile (in center of ceiling area)	2800	0.55	—	1540	1540	1540
	2" metal security panels (at perimeter of ceiling above walkway)	2730	0.95	—	—	2593	2593
WALLS	Concrete walkway facias	150	0.02	3	3	3	3
	Glass windows	100	0.10	10	10	10	10
	Painted concrete block	4200	0.05	210	210	210	210
	Steel doors (cell doors closed)	1120	0.05	56	56	56	56
	1" acoustical wall panels	250	0.80	—	—	—	—
FLOOR	Concrete main floor (exposed area)	5500	0.02	110	110	110	110
	Concrete mezzanine walkways	1860	0.02	37	37	37	37
	Carpeted main floor (excludes walkways)	3640	0.35	—	—	—	1274
OCCUPANTS	(including officers) 50 (each occupant provides 5 Sabins of sound absorption)	50	5.00	250	250	250	250
SUMMARY	**Total sound absorption, A Sabins (sq. ft.)**	**—**	**—**	**822**	**2307**	**4848**	**6234**
	Results:						
	Reverberation time = 0.05 V/A	**—**	**—**	**5.6 seconds**	**2.0 seconds**	**1.0 second**	**0.7 seconds**
	Estimated noise level	**—**	**—**	**76dBA**	**69dBA**	**66dBA**	**63 dBA**

Committee
On Acoustics
In Corrections

The Committee on Acoustics in Corrections is an organization of leading architects, corrections administrators and acoustical consultants. Its mission is to educate the corrections industry on the importance of acoustics. The Committee has published *Acoustics in Corrections*: A Practical Guide for Administrators and Planners; published articles and conducted briefings at industry trade conferences. Planners and administrators who have questions on acoustics are encouraged to call acoustical consultants and *Acoustics in Corrections* editors.

For a copy of *Acoustics in Corrections* contact Knut A. Rostad, Committee on Acoustics in Corrections, 1899 L Street NW, Suite 500, Washington DC 20036, 202/466-7001 (fax) 202/872-0896.

"The Committee on Acoustics in Corrections is appreciative of DMJM and Justice Design Principal Peter Krasnow for offering the idea and providing the professional design and printing services for this reprint. Without this support, this reprint would not have been possible. It is our hope that this checklist will provide planners and administrators a brief and useful resource for improving the acoustics environment in corrections institutions."

– *Knut A. Rostad, Managing Director*

Figure 8.2 (*Continued*)

Glossary

Current corrections terminology.

ACA American Correctional Association. An organization that provides the community with standards, guidelines, and conferences in the support of sharing information regarding operations, design, and technology.

accreditation ACA certification that any given facility may achieve for meeting minimum standards set forth in its publication. (See Bibliography for document titles.)

ADA (or **ADAG**) Americans with Disabilities Act (and Guidelines) is a federal act that provides civil rights protection in facility physical design accessibility, employment opportunities, and other services for individuals with disabilities. (See Bibliography for document title.)

adjudicate To determine judicially, as a case by a judge in a court.

adjudicatory hearing A hearing to determine whether allegations of a petition against an individual, beyond a reasonable doubt or preponderance of evidence, are supportable.

administrative segregation Special housing area in cells and housing units for inmates who potentially pose a security threat to other inmates or require separation from the general population while awaiting a due process hearing.

administrator An official who has the responsibility for managing and operating a facility. Also known as director, superintendent, and warden, depending on jurisdiction.

admissions (booking) The process used in obtaining information from inmates entering a correctional facility, including but not limited to obtaining charged or sentenced material, receiving personal property, fingerprinting, photographing, medical exam, and issuing facility clothing and bedding.

adult community residential facility See **community residential facility.**

adult correctional institution See **correctional institution.**

adult detention facility See **detention facility.**

affirmative action A policy whereby all persons, regardless of race, religion, age, sex, or ethnic origin, are ensured equal opportunities in job selection, job retention, payment for positions held, promotions, demotions, layoffs, transfers, and so forth.

agency A governing authority responsible for the operations of corrections policy and programs.

Airpack A product name for a self-contained breathing apparatus.

AJA American Jail Association. An organization that provides the community with conferences and publications, in the support of sharing information regarding operations, design, and technology. More focused on detention (jail) facilities than prisons.

armory (arsenal) A room provided in most correctional facilities for the secure storage of weapons and riot-related equipment.

avocation Instruction or opportunity for a hobby, such as music or arts and crafts, provided for inmates in addition to their general programs.

bail A guarantee given to the authorities, in money or by person, that an inmate released from custody prior to trial will appear for a scheduled court appearance.

bailiff Court officer responsible for security within the courtroom. May also be responsible for inmate transportation to and from the jail.

barrier free Areas accessible to all citizens, including those with disabilities.

body cavity search (strip search) All body cavities are examined for concealed weapons and contraband; often referred to as a *strip search procedure.* In testing inmates for substance abuse chemicals, a body content search will solicit urine, stool, and blood samples from inmates. Also referred to as *body content search.*

booking See **admissions.**

boot camp A correctional facility that administers an alternate and volunteer program to inmates, which combines the rigors and discipline of military training with correctional policies for a specific duration of time.

CAC Commission of Accreditation for Corrections.

cadre A group of inmates that performs maintenance functions within an institution; group members may be of a minimum-custody classification and be the most trusted, particularly for outside assignments. Cadre assignments typically include housekeeping, kitchen, laundry, maintenance, grounds keeping, and the like.

canteen (commissary) A room within a correctional facility that provides inmates with the sale of personal items such as grooming items, snack foods, radios, and so on.

capacity A number of beds permitted in an institution by an agency, exclusive of holding cells, medical infirmary beds, and disciplinary cells.

cell A secure room, where inmates are temporarily held or reside, constructed of materials which will prevent escape. The holding cell will generally include bench or bed and plumbing fixtures. A housing cell will generally include bed (or bunk beds), desk (or writing surface), storage unit, clothing hooks (breakaway type), plumbing fixtures, mirror, light, and stool (or chair).

cell block A group of cells forming a housing unit, generally connected to one another and surrounding a space referred to as a dayroom.

central control (master control) The main control room in an institution responsible for the emergency procedures, the security and safety of visitors, staff, and inmates, supported with security electronics and communications systems. Most often located on the line between the nonsecure and the secure side of the facility.

chase road Also known as **patrol road.** See **security patrol road.**

citation release An arresting officer can issue this citation in lieu of detention, but it requires an appearance in court.

classification The process that determines the requirements of an inmate regarding the inmate's needs, capability, security risk, and so forth. The process is used for placing inmates in appropriate housing unit levels and in determining their participation in programs.

close custody (close security) Level of security classification between medium and maximum security. Each jurisdiction and agency varies in its requirements for operations and design.

cocorrectional facility A facility that is designed and operated for both male and female (juvenile and/or adult) inmates.

combination unit (combo unit) A single high-strength stainless steel plumbing fixture in an inmate cell, incorporating a sink and toilet compartment. Generally used for close, maximum, and segregation inmates. On occasion used for medium security as a preference by some administrators.

community residential facility (halfway house) A group residence for incarcerated inmates with probation, parole, and other statuses, who the courts or system administrators have determined can serve their sentences in facilities, such as houses, work release centers, and prerelease centers.

community resources Agencies, religious and citizen groups, and volunteer groups that provide facilities with assistance in guidance services, counseling, financial support, and materials.

concertina wire (razor wire) Generally, a continuous roll of integrated razor-sharp steel tape and steel spikes, most often used in multiple rows, depending on facility classification and client preference. Commonly referred to as *Razor Ribbon,* which is trade name.

conjugal visit A room or area where certain jurisdictions provide inmates with private visits with their spouses/families.

consent decree A court order related to facility operations.

contact visit A room, area, or condition where inmates can visit with relatives, friends, and so on, without physical barriers.

contraband Illegal and/or unauthorized materials brought into a facility.

contractor An organization that provides materials and/or services to an institution for an agreed upon amount of payment. Most often referred to for construction of a facility as *general contractor.* Also provides services to operating facilities, such as outside food (and medical) service contractors.

control room A secure room occupied by a facility officer who is responsible for monitoring and controlling inmate movement and activity spaces. The space generally contains security electronics and communications equipment and systems for monitoring and controlling locking devices.

convict A person serving a sentence in a correctional institution, either in a detention (jail) or correctional (prison) facility.

correctional officer A person trained for the management and control of inmates within a correctional institution. There are sworn and unsworn correctional officers.

correctional program A mission statement and facility goals statement for the institution, including inmate programs to be provided.

counselor A nonuniformed professional who provides counseling to inmates for social and psychological issues.

custody See **security** (custody).

custody administration The group of officers responsible for administration of officer security assignments within the institution, including but not limited to shift changes and unit management at housing units.

dayroom An area or room located within a housing unit that provides for inmate activities, including but not limited to TV viewing, reading, educational programs, and often dining.

detainee An individual held in a detention (jail) facility awaiting court action, who has not been sentenced for a criminal offense.

detainer A legal certificate issued from one jurisdiction to another describing its intention to take custody of the releasing institution's inmate.

detention facility (jail) A facility designed for the holding of individuals prior to, during, and after trial proceedings. Generally referred to as *jail,* and in certain jurisdictions as *correctional facility,* too. Confinement is generally short term for jails and up to two years for sentenced inmates.

detox unit A cell or group of cells used for the holding of detainees who have been arrested on misdemeanor or criminal charges while intoxicated with drugs or alcohol.

diagnostic unit A unit for the evaluation and processing of newly received inmates, generally in a correctional (prison) facility. After a period of evaluation and testing, an inmate is placed in a specific facility based upon security level, needs, and so forth.

director See **superintendent.**

direct supervision An inmate management mode of operation whereby inmates are supervised by officers within their living environment and without secure barriers between inmates and staff. This continual direct contact and interaction between staff and inmates promotes a positive environment proven to reduce tensions and assaults by inmates on staff and other inmates.

disciplinary segregation (punitive segregation) Inmates who have committed serious violations of institutional policy as determined by a due process hearing are held in a housing area away from the general population for specified periods of time.

dormitory An inmate housing unit that generally consists of beds and/or bunk beds in an open area and used primarily for inmates with minimum classification status. Sometimes referred to as *dorms* occupied by two or more inmates, usually without individual plumbing fixtures.

dress out The exchange of civilian clothing for institutional during the intake/admissions process.

drunk tank A holding cell located in intake/admissions area for inmates who are intoxicated.

dry cell A cell without plumbing fixtures.

DUI Driving under intoxication.

DWI Driving while intoxicated.

emergency (evacuation) Any situation which causes a threat to life and property at an institution, such as fire or natural disasters, riots, or escapes. Facilities provide staff with inmate emergency containment and/or evacuation procedures for these occurrences.

escort A correctional officer's personal physical supervision (accompaniment) of inmate(s) in movement within and outside of a correctional facility.

exercise (recreation) yard An outdoor space dedicated for inmate exercise activity, secured and monitored and/or controlled by a correctional officer.

facility A place, building, or group of buildings identified for the lawful treatment and/or custody of individuals, as in detention, correctional, and/or medical facilities.

facility program A written description of the facility mission, desired operational procedures, and physical space requirements that defines user needs for a project.

fail-safe An electronic security locking function which describes the status of a lock; it is automatically placed in an open release mode when there is an electric power failure.

fail-secure An electronic security locking function which describes the status of a lock; it is automatically placed in a closed (secured) or locked position mode when there is an electric power failure.

felon Describes a person who has committed a crime that is punishable with confinement for one year or more.

fence Generally, indicates the description of fencing used for a secure perimeter or for separation of one inmate activity from another.

fence-mounted sensor An electronic security perimeter sensor device which reacts to movement (physical contact) on the fencing material which in turn triggers an alarm at a control center.

footcandle Measurement of light intensity at a distance one foot away from light source onto an illuminated surface. ACA, national, state, and local standards establish minimum light levels for occupied spaces such as cells and dayrooms.

four-point restraint A restraint used to prevent inmate movement having attachments to each arm and each leg.

FTE Full-time equivalent. This calculation is used in determining staffing requirements. To obtain a total number for operations, each staff position is evaluated for number of shifts and relief factor requirements. (See the staffing sections of Chap. 1: Planning and Design Principles.)

furlough Also referred to as *work release.* It is a program whereby inmates classified by law with less potential risk to others are permitted to work outside of their correctional institution environment; they may work and/or attend school in the community. At the end of every normal workday, they return to their institution for confinement.

gatehouse A building located at the entrance to a correctional facility for the purpose of screening and processing visitors and staff. At times, it is used for vendors (vehicles) for the same purpose.

good time A reward earned by inmates for good behavior and work initiative in the form of reduced sentence time.

group gang release A device used for the manual release of sliding cell doors simultaneously and in groups.

guard tower An elevated structure generally located at the secure fenced perimeter of an institution for the monitoring of movement toward, through, and over the perimeter. Communications with central control coordinates activity. Also known as *gun tower.*

gun locker A secure locker compartment, placed adjacent to staff entrances, for the personal storage of weapons before entering a correctional facility. They may also be located within the secured armory space of an institution, which is often located outside of the secure perimeter.

gun tower See **guard tower.**

gunwalk An elevated walkway that provides armed officers' observation of inmate activity spaces and movement within and outside of a correctional facility. Access to these areas is from the outside of the institution since weapons are not typically permitted within the secure perimeter.

halfway house See **community residential facility.**

handicapped An individual having physical or mental disabilities that impede or disadvantage that person's mobility or participation in programs and services.

hearing A proceeding whereby arguments, witnesses, or evidence are reviewed by a judicial officer or administrative body for determining guilt or innocence resulting in a specific course of action.

holding A room or area used for the containment of inmates for short duration during the admissions/booking process and for court appearance and transfer to other institutions. Other areas where holding rooms are utilized are found in medical treatment areas, TV arraignments, and visitation areas.

HONI How to Open New Institutions. The National Institute of Corrections (NIC) conducts on-site staff training programs designed for user agency groups at the completion of their new facility construction and prior to inmate occupation.

honor farm A minimum-security housing unit located outside of a facility's security perimeter used for inmates of low risk who can work within the community during a normal workday and who must return to the unit at the end of each day.

housing (unit) The area that contains inmate sleeping quarters and other support functions such as toilet, lavatories, showers, and dayroom space. In many jurisdictions, outdoor exercise, dining, medical screening, personal laundrying, and counseling functions are located in or adjacent to the housing unit.

HSU Health services unit provides general medical support to the institution in medical and dental exam and treatment, optometry, and x-ray and laboratory services. This unit also contains the infirmary for inmates with medical and mental health conditions that isolate them from the general population.

incident A circumstance of provocation/disturbance by an inmate(s) toward other inmates or staff.

indigent An individual without available funds or source of income.

indirect supervision operation The method of operation which physically separates the control officer from those inmates he or she is assigned responsibility. The monitoring and control of activity and access doors to cells (housing and other functions) is by remote electronic security and communications systems and generally requires 24-hour security staffing, either at the source or by CCTV remote observation.

industry (industries) A program run by the institution or by outside organizations where inmates can earn payment for producing useful products. In most institutions, the industry space remains flexible during the design process, with identification of industry during or after the new facility construction is complete.

information (inmate) management system Technological support of the gathering and organization of information for a facility's administrative use. Sometimes referred to as *management information system* (*MIS*), for systemwide/multiple facilities.

infrared photo-beam sensor system A security perimeter detection system utilizing a beam of light, which, when interrupted, will sound an alarm. (See Chap. 6, Perimeter Security Systems.)

inmate A person who is confined in a detention or correctional facility, including those with pretrial, convicted/unsentenced, and sentenced status.

intake An area in a detention or correctional facility used for all newly admitted inmates and those who have been transferred from other institutions. This area is also referred to the *admissions area.* In jails, it is generally a large and complex area including holding cells, open seating, medical screening, showering/clothing exchange, attorney/bondsman visiting, and processing functions such as fingerprinting and photo identification. In prisons, it is generally a smaller area including holding cells and property exchange.

intensive sanctions An alternated sentencing program for inmates of lower risk that can be electronically monitored outside of a correctional facility and/or active in a program, both of which are supervised by a parole agent.

interlock Two or more locking devices which cannot be opened or closed at the same time. Generally found in sally ports, where the secure staging and control of movement is desired.

intermittent sentence A sentence permitting a prisoner to live at home and serve a sentence during a normal work week schedule. Court-specified alternative can limit program to weekends. Also referred to as *weekenders.*

intermittent supervision Observation of inmate holding cells and housing unit areas on a noncontinuous basis without the aid of electronic security equipment.

jail (detention) A facility used for the containment of persons (male, female, and sometimes juvenile) accused of a crime awaiting trial and those convicted of a crime awaiting sentences. In many jurisdictions, a jail is used for the incarceration of inmates serving sentences of one to two years.

jail commander A detention facility officer responsible for the operations of an institution.

joint domain An electronic security detection system utilizing two separate detection devices before, on, or between the double-fenced perimeter that are desired to work in conjunction with one another. (See Chap. 6: Perimeter Security Systems.)

juvenile Depending on a particular jurisdiction but most often refers to a person who is under 21 years of age.

juvenile correction A facility designated for juveniles sentenced for crimes and serving time. Programs are designed for the treatment of juveniles for their return to society. This sentenced program can also be administered in a juvenile detention facility, depending on jurisdiction.

juvenile detention A facility designated for the holding before, during, and after trial of juveniles under the ages of 18 or 21, which are located out of sight and sound of adult detention populations. Can be used for sentenced juvenile population, depending on jurisdiction.

juvenile offender A person under the age of 18 or 21 who has been detained for an offense or who has committed a crime as would be considered under adult status.

law library A designated space or room within an institution for inmate access to legal reference materials, which is currently required by constitutional law to be provided.

Life-Safety Code Published by the National Fire Protection Association, this document provides minimum standard requirements for the life and safety of building construction with specific sections devoted to detention/correctional facility design and construction. Used in conjunction with other state and local construction codes, if any.

linear supervision See **intermittent supervision.**

lineup (room) An area or room used in detention facilities for witnesses' direct physical observation of inmates for identification.

livescan fingerprinting A fingerprinting device utilizing electronic imaging in lieu of traditional ink-pad prints.

lockdown A status whereby inmate population is confined to individual cells and/or housing units (pods) for a period of time during disturbances and other conditions.

lockup Another name for a local municipal jail facility or section of a facility used for detaining inmates.

management information system (MIS) System-wide inmate records: court, jail, prison.

management unit A separated housing unit used for inmates that cannot or are unable to function within the general population. Also referred to as *administrative segregation unit.*

master control See **central control.**

maximum security The level of security designated for inmates who pose escape risks or who could cause physical harm to other inmates and/or staff. This inmate population generally experiences restricted movement, although each jurisdiction defines the rules and regulations for maximum security. The secure perimeter is designed to prevent escapes, and, in addition to detection systems and physical barriers, guard towers or vehicle patrol roads are utilized for observation and control.

medical records Individual records for inmates recording their medical examinations and diagnoses maintained by a physician of responsibility.

medical restraints Chemicals, sedatives, and physical (straight-jacket) restraints for inmates used in order to treat medical and mental conditions.

medical screening A structured system of observation of inmates' medical status in the admissions/intake process to assess conditions that may affect their health and that of other inmates and staff.

medium security The level of security designated for inmates who pose less risk of escape or physical harm to other inmates and/or staff. Less controlled movement within the institution is generally provided and monitored. Secure perimeters vary between jurisdictions in their security electronic detection systems, although a double-fenced perimeter is typically used.

mezzanine level The upper-level location of cells contained within a typical housing unit or pod overlooking a double-height and centralized dayroom space. The mezzanine is also referred to as the second story of this unit. At times, housing units are stacked, requiring definition of terms when referring to this condition as two-story housing units with mezzanines or four-story housing units.

microwave sensor system A security electronic detection device utilizing radio transmission energy across a field which, when interrupted, will sound an alarm. (See Chap. 6: Perimeter Security Systems.)

minimum security A level of security designated for inmates who pose significantly less risk of escape or physical harm to other inmates and/or staff. Freer movement within the institution is provided, either in campus style or connected building arrangements. Fenced perimeters vary from none to double-fenced but generally do not incorporate security electronic detection system(s).

misdemeanor A legal status designation of persons charged or convicted of crimes of a less serious nature than that of felonies. Each state specifies this status, but generally a misdemeanor is punishable for up to a year, where a felony is for more than one year.

mission statement Defines and describes the goals and objectives of an institution and/or each governing agency.

mogul lock A heavy-duty locking device used in high-security areas. Its cylinder diameter is greater than 2 inches, which is twice that of a typical locking cylinder, and utilizes an oversized key.

NCCHC National Commission on Correctional Health Care.

NCJRS National Criminal Justice Resources Service.

NFPA National Fire Protection Association. See **Life Safety Code.**

NIC National Institute of Corrections.

NIJ National Institute of Justice.

no-man's-land An area or open space within the secure fenced perimeter and buildings of an institution restricted to operations and maintenance staff only and where inmates are denied access.

noncontact visitation A room or booth designated for nonphysical contact inmate visitation with relatives, friends, attorneys, clergy, social workers, and so on. Generally used for inmates who pose potential or actual physical risks to their visitors and/or other inmates and staff.

NSA National Sheriff's Association.

offender An individual accused of, detained for, or convicted of a criminal offense.

open booking An area provided for inmate waiting such as a direct supervision facility's intake (admissions) area where inmates may sit in an open, more normative environment to wait, read, and watch TV. It is used for inmates who do not pose risk to other inmates or staff and therefore can reduce the number of holding cells required and create improved observation of the entire admissions processing area. This area is generally screened from viewing holding cells.

operational capacity The inmate population level a facility is currently accommodating in the short term, often in excess of rated capacity.

outside assignment A cadre or inmate work assignment that is located outside the security perimeter of a facility (e.g., farm, road work detail).

paracentric lock A heavy-duty locking cylinder device using keys 6 inches in length. The cylinder plug has projections on the side of the keyway that extend beyond the vertical centerline of the keyway.

paramedic A facility staff person who is supervised by a licensed physician and assigned responsibility for administering limited medical services to the inmate population.

parole A conditional release of an incarcerated felon who has not completed his or her sentence to an agency responsible for administering supervision during a designated period.

penitentiary A prison or correctional facility holding persons convicted of crimes or serving court-mandated sentences. Originally stems from the term used for the place that a person did penitence for a crime.

perimeter Primary exterior barrier of a correctional facility, generally referred to as security perimeter and denoted by fences, physical barriers, and detection systems.

podular (pod) housing An architectural design describing the layout of a self-contained housing unit whereby groups of cells and other support functions (showers, pantries, etc.) are arranged in an orderly manner around a central activity space. Sometimes the term *podular housing* refers to direct supervision operations, although indirect supervision management can use the same physical arrangement.

POE Post-occupancy evaluation. A valuable service and report used in the analysis of facility operations after a period of time following completion and inmate occupation. Periodic follow-ups can provide valuable information in the adjustment of operations and in the planning of additional facilities.

policy A course of action that guides and determines specific facility decisions in operation and activities. Guidelines generally follow a facility's goals and objectives, as stated in its mission statement.

PONI Planning of New Institutions. The National Institute of Corrections (NIC) provides user agencies with training sessions in developing their mission statement, goals, and objectives for the specific institution.

population Refers to the total number of inmates detained in jails or confined in prisons at any one time, generally exclusive of medical infirmary rooms or intake/admission holding cells. Can also refer to the level of security, as in minimum, medium, close custody, maximum, and segregation populations.

ported coaxial cable sensor system A security perimeter detection system utilizing two cables that emit an electromagnetic field, which, when broken, will sound an alarm. (See Chap. 6: Perimeter Security Systems.)

post A designated position, area, or room assigned to a correctional officer. The time that a post is occupied is determined by a staffing plan and is described in Chap. 1: Planning and Design Principles.

pretrial (presentence) An individual's status as adjudicated by a court, also referred to as *presentence* or *retainee.*

pretrial release A condition whereby an individual, accused of a criminal offense, is released before or during trial.

prison An institution responsible for the holding of inmates who are convicted and sentenced for a crime, for a designated period of time (generally for one year or longer). Also referred to as a correctional facility.

probation A program for inmates released from a correctional facility supervised by a governing agency. Sometimes referred to as *parole.*

procedure A course of action for a particular situation or specific task, as identified in the guidelines of policy.

program Refers to general activities inmates are engaged in during their time spent in a detention or correctional facility. They include, but are not limited to, education, vocation, industry, training, and food service, among others. As a result of longer periods of incarceration, inmates within a correctional institution are offered a greater number of programs. Although recent trends in detention facilities are providing a greater number of activity programs for inmates.

property Inmate personal property and clothing held in jails and prisons for the inmate's period of incarceration. In jails and law enforcement facilities, *property* can refer to evidence associated with crimes being held for court proceedings.

protective custody Inmates held in separated housing units away from the general population who require protection for a variety of reasons, such as, but not limited to, those of lesser physical strength or size who may become victims of other inmates that have singled them out for a particular crime or witness status.

punitive segregation See **disciplinary segregation.**

rated capacity The specific number of cells (rooms) designated or designed for a particular institution as required and/or assigned by a governing agency's standards. Medical beds, holding cells, and segregation housing cells, among others, are generally not included in the rated capacity, as they are occupied by inmates assigned to specific housing units, and use of these facilities is on a temporary basis only.

Razor Ribbon A trade name for barbed wire tape and razor sharp steel spikes. See **concertina wire.**

recognizance An obligation of record, with the condition to do some particular act, such as appear in court.

released on bail The release of an individual accused of a criminal offense by a judicial officer with the promise of appearing in court. See **ROR.**

releasing authority A decision-making body and/or individual responsible for granting, denying, and revoking an individual's official release from an institution. See **parole.**

renovation A change in physical condition of a facility, as in structural or design renovation.

retainees See **pretrial (presentence)**.

revocation The status or condition of a person removed from probation or parole supervision.

ROR Released on own recognizance of an accused person comes with the stipulation that the releasee will appear for court on a specific scheduled date. See **released on bail.**

rover A correctional officer assigned a position requiring the officer to move about several particular areas to observe inmate activity and behavior. Rovers are required to transfer information for inmate counts.

safekeepers Inmates that are kept by one institution in safety at the request of another institution or agency.

safety vestibule Similar to sally port, but can separate inmate areas from other areas, not necessarily from secure to nonsecure sides of the facility. As an example, a safety vestibule can be a controlled entry from an inmate corridor into the maintenance shop area, both located within the secure perimeter.

sally port A controlled space, room, or area with one or more access points (in or out) which requires one access point to be in a closed status before another can be opened. Interlocking devices prevents the opening of more than one door at a time and can be used for visitors, staff, inmates, and vehicles.

scenario An outline of processes for events or movement within a particular operational area, such as the visitation scenario, booking scenario, or emergency evacuation scenario.

secure institution A facility designed and operated by the facility's staff to contain an incarcerated population by monitoring, supervising, and controlling all entrances/exits of the secure perimeter.

secure property Inmates' personal property of value (jewelry, money, etc.) requiring separate and secure provisions; these items are generally taken at intake/admissions and returned at release.

security (custody) Degree of inmate restriction and/or movement within an institution. The levels of security are described by levels 1 through 5 or by name: minimum, medium, close custody, maximum, and segregation.

security custody level Refers to classification of inmate population, as previously described by minimum, medium, and maximum custody level, and as related to movement within an institution.

security devices Physical barriers and/or products used in the containment of detainees, or prisoners, such as walls, floors, ceilings, locks, doors, bars, gates, fences and screens. To support these barriers, security electronics and communications systems are employed. See Chaps. 6 and 7: Perimeter Security Systems and Security Electronics and Communications Systems.

security patrol road Provides officer vehicle access around the outside of the entire continuous secure perimeter (fence or walls) to observe and respond to incidents involving attempted inmate escapes and others entering from the outside. Also referred to as *chase road.*

security perimeter This is the generally more often used term in describing the secure perimeter location. See **perimeter.**

security zone Division of a facility into a series of areas to offer control in maintaining security. An area defined within two defined boundaries, for example: the area between a high level of security surrounding a housing unit (or building) and the next level of security adjacent to it, such as program support. See Chap. 1: Planning and Design Principles.

seismic sensor system A security perimeter detection system that, when it detects seismic disturbances, will sound an alarm. See Chap. 6: Perimeter Security Systems.

sentenced A person convicted of a crime and serving time in a detention or correctional facility.

servery A satellite food service area or room that distributes meals to inmates and, in certain institutions, can provide for the preparation of limited menu items such as bacon and eggs for breakfast meals. The servery can be located adjacent to central dining room(s) or adjacent to or within housing units (pods).

shakedown The process of searching inmate cells (rooms) and other spaces (visitation, for example) for weapons and contraband.

sheriff The chief elected officer responsible for law enforcement within most counties in the nation.

shift relief factor See **FTE.**

shift tour commander A supervising officer responsible for the custody administration of a correctional facility for a designated period of time (shift) during a 24-hour period. See **jail commander.**

SHU Special housing unit. A designated housing unit for inmates who require special attention due to their physical or mental behavior who cannot live within the general population. See **special needs inmate.**

SIS Special issues seminar. A NIC program provided to user agencies for assistance and instruction in facility planning, design, and technical issues.

slider Refers to a horizontally sliding door used in correctional facilities which requires electrical, pneumatic, or manual operation. Currently used in sally ports, maximum-security cells, and secure holding facilities.

SMU Special management unit. See **SHU.**

special management inmate An inmate housed in a special management unit.

special needs inmate Inmates requiring special assistance and attention because of drug or alcohol habits, emotional condition, mental retardation, suspected mental illness, physical handicaps, chronic illness, physical disabilities, and/or medical illnesses.

staffing charts Describes the type and location of staff required to operate a facility during the daily three-shift period and for any continuous 365-day period. Indicates the posts to be covered for the duration of each shift.

stash Contraband.

status offender Juvenile status of conduct that under the law would not be considered a crime if committed by an adult.

strip search See **body cavity search.**

superintendent The chief administrator of a detention or correctional facility. Also referred to as *director* or *warden.*

support The spaces, buildings, and/or services associated with administration, inmate programs, food/laundry service, and others in support of the inmate housing buildings (units).

swamp A housing unit in a detention (jail) facility containing unclassified inmates.

swinger Refers to a hinged swinging door which can be operated electrically, pneumatically, or manually for control of housing cells, sally ports, and so forth.

target staffing level The staffing level set as part of facility planning for which a facility design should achieve in terms of staffing efficiency.

taut wire A security perimeter detection system that, when deflected, will sound an alarm. See Chap. 6: Perimeter Security Systems.

telephone pole A liner facility layout that aligns cells on either side of a long corridor. These units or wings are linked with a central spine thus providing the appearance, in plan, of a telephone pole.

temporary release A period of time of permitted inmate leave from an institution, with unsupervised community involvement, and which is respectful of public interest.

tiers Refers to the number of cell floors arranged vertically around a central space, used as dayrooms in direct supervision operations. Today, most housing units (pods) limit the number of cell tiers to two, however, older facilities still in operation provide for three, four, or more tiers (levels of cells) overlooking one central space.

training An organized activity designed for learning, in the enhancement of staff job performance. Training can occur on-site at a facility or away from an institution in a training academy. Programs include requirements, and activities and are recorded by officials, teachers, and/or trainers for staff recognition.

training school Associated with the juvenile population, known as juvenile development centers, juvenile corrections facilities, juvenile treatment centers, home for boys and girls, among others. These facilities provide supervised programs available to total resident population typically of 150 beds or less. They are designed and operated as secure facilities.

trustee See **cadre.**

turf Refers to an area of a housing unit (pod) that inmates have acquired or control as their own space separate from another group of inmates. Also refers to outdoor exercise yards.

unit management The operational style of separately managing a group of inmates within an institution. This concept can enhance interaction and contact between staff and inmate population in managing behavior, with more informed decisions learned by staff involvement with smaller and permanent groups. The basis for determining unit management requirements are size limits between 150 to 500: population classification; population work program; staff assignments requiring interpersonal relationship skills with inmates and decision-making authority within a unit and/or with program policies; inmate assignments to particular units based upon security (custody) levels, controls, and programs.

vehicle sally port Used for authorized vehicles entering and leaving a secured perimeter or building. See **sally port.**

video motion detection sensor system A security perimeter detection system that utilizes CCTV, and, when change is monitored, it will sound an alarm. (See Chap. 6: Perimeter Security Systems.)

vision port A small glazed opening in a door or wall, permitting observation by an officer of inmate activity.

volunteer An individual who donates time in support of an institution's social, counseling, educational, and recreational programs.

waiver A release of responsibility of an institution in complying with a standard, granted by a commissioned panel or agency.

warden See **superintendent.**

warrants A judicial writ (written authorization) or order authorizing arrest, search, seizure, and so on.

watch commander See **shift tour commander** and **jail commander.**

weekenders See **intermittent sentence.**

workers' compensation A statewide system of personal employee benefits paid for injury or disabilities occurred during workers performance of their jobs.

work release See **furlough.**

yard An open recreation space, courtyard, or field used by inmates in detention and correctional facilities. Small spaces are provided for jails with hard playing surfaces (basketball) and soft playing fields for larger group activities, such as baseball, for correctional facilities.

zone See **security zone.**

Bibliography

Sources of related corrections facility information.

American Institute of Architects (AIA)
1735 New York Avenue, NW
Washington, DC 20006-5292
202-626-7300
Justice Facilities Review Catalog, 1998 edition
Design Resource File, 5th edition, May 1993

American Correctional Association (ACA)
4380 Forbes Road
Lanham, MD 20706-4322
1-800-ACA-JOIN
Standards Supplement, June 1996, supporting the following documents:
Standards for Adult Local Detention Facilities, 3d edition, 1991
Standards for Adult Correctional Institutions, 3d edition, 1990
Standards for Adult Juvenile Community Residential Facilities, 3d edition, 1994
Standards for Juvenile Detention Facilities, 3d edition, 1991
Standards for Juvenile Training Schools, 3d edition, 1991
Standards for Small Jail facilities, 3d edition, 1989
Directory of Juvenile and Adult Correctional Departments, 1997 edition
National Jail and Adult Detention Directory, 1996–1998 edition
Corrections Today. A seven month per year publication of the American Correctional Institution featuring articles on current operational issues, facility designs, and technological advances for correctional facilities.

Americans with Disabilities Act (ADA)
Federal Register, Part II, 36 CFR Part 1191
Section 12 Retention and Correctional Facilities
June 20, 1994 edition
Accessibility Guidelines for Buildings and Facilities; state and local government; interim final rule

American Jail Association (AJA)
2053 Day Road, Suite 100
Hagerstown, MD 21740-9795
301-790-3930
American Jails. A bimonthly publication of the American Jail Association, featuring articles on current operational issues, facility designs, and technological advances for jail facilities.

National Institute of Corrections Information Center (NIC)
1860 Industrial Circle
Longmont, CO 80501
800-995-NICW
A variety of publications is available through NIC, including, but not limited to, material related to case studies and premanufactured housing for correctional facilities; small jail design guide; and direct supervision information.

National Criminal Justice Reference Service National Institute of Justice (NIJ)
P.O. Box 6000
1600 Research Boulevard
Rockville, MD 20850
801-851-3420
301-251-5063
An international clearinghouse for criminal justice–related information and the primary research agency for the Department of Justice. Service available, by appointment only, to graduate students and criminal justice professionals.

National Sheriff's Association
1450 Duke Street
Alexandria, VA 22314-3490
703-836-7827
Sheriff, a bimonthly publication, featuring articles on current, related issues.

National Commission on Correctional Health Care (NCCHC)
2105 North Southport, Suite 200
Chicago, IL 60614
312-528-0818
Related standards for correctional health care publications are available through the NCCHC.

Federal Bureau of Prisons (FBOP) Office of Facilities Development and Operations
320 First Street, NW
Washington, DC 20534
202-514-5942
Design and construction information is available upon request to criminal justice professionals.

Criminal Justice Institute, Inc.
Spring Hill West
South Salem, New York 10590
914-533-2000
An annual publication including nationwide statistics related to adult corrections, jail systems, juvenile corrections, probation profiles, institutional profiles, budgets, programs, and personnel profiles.

Committee on Acoustics in Corrections
1099 L Street NW, Suite 500
Washington, DC 20036
202-466-7001
Acoustics in Corrections is a practice guide for administrators and planners. Write for a free copy.

National Fire Protection Association (NFPA)
1 Batterymarch Park
P.O. Box 9146
Quincy, MA 02269-9959
800-344-3555
Life Safety Code Handbook (NFPA 101), 5th edition, 1991. Specific related detention and correctional facilities chapters.
National Electrical Code (NFPA 70), 1990 edition.

American Society for Standards Testing and Materials (ASTM)
100 Barr Harbor Drive
West Conshohocken, PA 19428-2959
ASTM Committee F-33 on Detention and Correctional Facilities. An independent testing agency that sets industry standards for construction materials.

Hollow Metal Manufacturers Association (HMMA, a division of National Association of Architectural Metal Manufacturers)
600 South Federal Street
Chicago, IL 60605
Sets standards for hollow metal frames and doors; a detention guide specification.

Underwriters Laboratories Inc.
333 Pfingsten Road
Northbrook, IL 60062-2096
Performance testing procedures for construction materials and products.

Contributors

The names of individuals who assisted the author.

All of my colleagues have become friends during the many years of our productive working relationships. Without these trusted and talented souls this book would not have been possible.

Justice Technology
Ruben Caro
AutoCAD Detail Drawings
Edgar Woh
AutoCAD Plan Drawings
John Gregory
Stephanie Marshall
Andrea Harris
Security Electronics and Communications
Buford Goff, Principal
Buford Goff & Associates, Columbia, South Carolina
Architectural Photography
Bo Parker
Bo Parker Photography, Wilton, Connecticut

Material review for the following categories:

Correctional Operations
Camille Camp, Principal
Criminal Justice Institute, Salem, New York
Planning/Programming
Jeff Buck, Director
DMJM Planning/Programming
Bill Garnos, Principal
CSG Consultants, Overland Park, Kansas
Food/Laundry Services
Stan Gatland, Principal
Romano Gatland, Lindenhurst, New York
Cost Estimating
Jay Schondorf, Principal
AMIS Inc., New York, New York

Core team contributors: (*from left to right*) Andrea Harris, John Gregory, Bo Parker, Peter Krasnow, Ruben Caro, Edgar Woh, Stephanie Marshall, and Buford Goff (not shown). In the background, McGraw-Hill Building original headquarters Art Deco Building, 1931, Raymond Hood, Architect.

Index

About the Author

Peter Krasnow was born in New York City in 1942, raised in Queens, architecturally educated in Brooklyn at Pratt Institute, and currently resides in Manhattan with his wife Christine and son Christopher.

His 32 years of architectural experience in planning and design have seen the past 22 years focused on justice facilities including law enforcement, courts, jails, prisons, and juvenile facilities. His fresh approach brought to each project has produced outstanding and innovative architectural designs with consistent client satisfaction.

Peter holds licenses to practice architecture in New York as well as in New Jersey, Pennsylvania, Connecticut, Massachusetts, Mississippi, and Florida, including NCARB Certification. He is a member of the AIA (American Institute of Architects) both national, New York State, and New York City chapters; the ACA (American Correctional Association); and the AJA (American Jail Association). He is an active member of the AIA/CAJ (Committee on Architecture for Justice), national and New York City chapters, and the Committee on Acoustics for Correctional Facilities.

Peter has been a moderator and speaker at many AJA and ACA conferences, including workshops focused on subjects such as "Human Warehouses, Why the Differences between Prisons and Jails?" and "A Jail Odyssey 2010."

Currently, Peter is a vice president for justice architecture with Daniel, Mann, Johnson, & Mendenhall (DMJM), a firm providing architectural, engineering, and program/construction services worldwide. For 10 years prior to joining DMJM in 1984, he was a studio design director for The Gruzen Partnership, one of the country's early leaders in justice facility design.

Peter's projects have received attention in the following publications: *Architectural Record, Progressive Architecture, CM Architecture, Engineering News Review, Architecture, Building and Construction News, Corrections Compendium, Corrections Today,* and *Correctional Construction News.*

In addition to these national magazines, 12 of his justice designs have been recognized, exhibited, and published by the AIA in its Justice Review program from 1979–1997/98. However, his most prestigious award was given by the AIA/Kentucky Chapter for its 1990 Honor Award for Design Excellence for DMJM's Eastern Kentucky Correctional Complex.

Peter Krasnow loves the challenge of providing new approaches with creative thinking for each new project undertaking. His satisfaction comes from working with clients by offering them a variety of options and opportunities for their facility designs that provide safe, humane, and aesthetically pleasing environments that operate with maximum efficiency and for reduced annual costs. He looks forward to continuing justice design opportunities incorporating cutting-edge technologies into the next century.